RAC

BED & BREAKFAST

GREAT BRITAIN & IRELAND 1995

Grey Friar Lodge, Ambleside

Published by RAC Publishing, RAC House,
PO Box 100, South Croydon, CR2 6XW

ISBN 0 86211 302 4

A CIP catalogue record for this book is available from
the British Library

Regional introductions compiled by Hilary White
Contributor: Hilary Hughes
Design by Chuck Goodwin
Database management: West One Publishing, London
Cartography by RAC Publishing
Printed and bound by Grafo, S.A. Bilbao, Spain

Cover picture: Chase Lodge, Kingston upon Thames

Advertising Managers:
West One Publishing
104 New Bond Street, London W1Y 9LG
Tel: 0171-493 4769

Contents

The British Isles

Regions used in this guide

THURSO

INVERNESS

ABERDEEN

Scotland

DUNDEE

OBAN

GLASGOW · EDINBURGH

BERWICK-UPON-TWEED

LONDONDERRY

Northern Ireland

BELFAST

ARMAGH

SLIGO

DUMFRIES

CARLISLE

NEWCASTLE UPON TYNE

North West

North East

LEEDS

ATHLONE

GALWAY

DUBLIN

Republic of Ireland

PORT LAOISE

LIVERPOOL · MANCHESTER

SHEFFIELD

LLANDUDNO

NOTTINGHAM

SHREWSBURY

NORWICH

Midlands

LIMERICK

Wales

BIRMINGHAM

East Anglia

CAMBRIDGE

WEXFORD

West Country

TRALEE

CARDIGAN

CORK

OXFORD

LONDON

CARDIFF

BRISTOL

South East

DOVER

South

South West

SOUTHAMPTON

BRIGHTON

EXETER

PLYMOUTH

PENZANCE

Introduction

We have called this guide Bed & Breakfast, because it expresses the key factor linking all the establishments in it. But many of the hotels and guest houses in this guide offer far more than just bed and breakfast. In it you will find small hotels with elegant restaurants that serve gourmet meals, popular pubs with satisfying bar meals or full-scale restaurants, and, of course, the traditional establishments where the only meals offered are those delicious full English breakfasts. Many of the establishments in the guide offer exceptional value for money, with bed and breakfast being under £20 per person in some.

There are other aspects where you may find more than bed and breakfast. At some, you can find leisure facilities, others have facilities for small conferences and almost all have comfortable lounges where guests can relax. Because of the more informal nature of these establishments, the lounges often have books to read, games to play, suggestions of places to visit. For one thing joins all the establishments in this guide; the personal service offered. These are very different from the efficient, mainly business hotels. Characteristically, the owners and managers of bed and breakfast places care for their guests as if they were friends. They want them to be not only comfortable but happy as well.

It is this caring service that draws many people to them and is the secret of their charm. We hope that within the pages of this guide you will find a place to stay that offers you what you want as you travel round Britain and Ireland.

How to use this Guide

The entries are arranged in 15 regions throughout the British Isles (see map opposite). Each region is introduced with a list of suggested places to visit and a list of some of the events which take place in that region throughout the year.

Within each region, towns are listed alphabetically, and establishments alphabetically within that town. All RAC inspected establishments are indicated by the RAC logo in their entry and those that have been awarded Highly Acclaimed or Acclaimed status are shown. Some small villages are listed under the nearest town.

The map section at the back of the guide shows all places which have a hotel or guest house listed in the guide. Use the maps to choose which town you want to stay in, and refer to the entries to choose a hotel. Remember that if none of the hotels in that town are suitable, the maps will show you nearby towns which might have what you want.

An entry explained

For details of the symbols used see p.6 and inside the front cover flap.

1 **GOLDENFORD** Surrey   Map 4 D3

2 **Cherry Tree** 36 London Rd, Goldenford
3 GO1 2AF 0453-598768 Fax 0483-34669   RAC
4 *Friendly family-run hotel close to town centre. Ideal base to explore countryside.*
5 Closed Christmas
,7 36 bedrs, 19 ➡/WC, 4 ➡; TV tcf 🐕 ✏ P40
8 sB&B £26-£36; HB weekly £224-£294; D £6; cc Ac, Amex, Vi.

1 Town, county and map reference
2 Name, address and telephone and fax number of hotel or guest house
3 RAC indicates an RAC inspected establishment
4 Short description, sometimes with a picture of the hotel or guest house
5 Dates when the hotel or guest house is open
6 Bedroom information:
10 bedrs - number of bedrooms
5 ➡/WC - number of rooms with bath/WC en suite
4 🐚/WC - number of rooms with Shower/WC en suite
1 🐚- number of rooms with shower cubicle
TV-TV in at least some bedrooms
tcf- tea/coffee making facilities in at least some bedrooms
7 Facilities in the hotel or guest house:
🐕 No dogs allowed or some restrictions on vistors dogs
✏ no smoking anywhere in the hotel or guest house or smoking is not allowed in some areas
P40 Number of parking places
Child restrictions - Some restrictions on the age of child guests. Please telephone for details
8 Details of prices and credit cards accepted.

PRICE INFORMATION
sB&B £20-£30: range of prices for one night bed and breakfast for one person
dB&B £30-£45: range of prices for one night bed and breakfast for two people in a double room
HB weekly £150-£225: cost of dinner, bed and breakfast for 7 nights for one person

B £5: price of full breakfast
L £8.50: price of table d'hôte lunch
D £10: price of table d'hôte dinner or evening meal
[10%V w/d] 10% vouchers accepted on weekdays
w/e: at weekends
cc credit cards accepted
Access: (includes Mastercharge and Eurocard)
Amex: American Express
Diners: Diners Club
JCB: Japan Card Bank
Visa/B'card: Barclaycard and Visa cards
deposit: deposit required on booking
Prices: Prices given in the Guide are forecasts by
hoteliers of what they expect to charge in 1995. As
the information is, of necessity, compiled well in
advance of publication, varying conditions may have
brought about changes in published charges. It is
always wise to check with a hotel what the relevant
charges are before booking. All prices quoted
should include VAT where applicable
The prices range from that for low season in
standard rooms to that for superior rooms in
high season.

Arrival times: Small hotels, guest houses and inns
may close for part of the afternoon. It is wise to inform
them of your expected arrival time when booking, and
courteous to telephone them if you are delayed.

New Telephone Numbers

All UK telephone codes are being changed. The
number 1 is being inserted after the first 0. For
example, 081 is changing to 0181. The new codes
were available in August 1994 and the two codes
will run in parallel until 16 April 1995, when the
new code will take over. The new codes are
given throughout the guide, as they will be in
use in November when the guide is published
The old codes can be used up to 16 April 1995.
Five cities will have a complete change of code
and an additional digit to the number.

	OLD	NEW
Bristol	0272-xxxxxx	0117-9xxxxxx
Leeds	0532-xxxxxx	0113-2xxxxxx
Leicester	0533-xxxxxx	0116-2xxxxxx
Nottingham	0602-xxxxxx	0115-9xxxxxx
Sheffield	0742-xxxxxx	0114-2xxxxxx

Symbols & Abbreviations

ENGLISH		FRANÇAIS	DEUTSCHE
RAC	RAC Inspected	Hôtel classement RAC	Hotel mit RAC – Klassifizierung
♿	Facilities for the disabled	Aménagements pour handicapés	Einrichtungen für Behinderte
➡/WC	Bath/WC en suite	Salles de bains et WC privés	Privatbad mit WC
↑/WC	Shower/WC en suite	Douche et WC privés	Privatdusche mit WC
↑	Shower cubicle	Douche privée sans WC	Privatdusche ohne WC
➡	General bathrooms	Salles de bains	Badezimmer
✕	No dogs or restrictions	Interdit aux chiens	Hundeverbot im Hotel
⊬	No smoking or restrictions	Interdiction de fumer dans l'hôtel	Rauchverbot im Hotel
tcf	Tea/coffee-making facilities	Équipement pour faire du thé/café dans les chambres	Tee-/Kaffee- Aufgußeinrichtungen
P	Parking	Parking	Parken
sB&B	Price of single room and breakfast	Prix d'une chambre d'une personne + petit déjeuner	Preis für Einzelzimmer und Frühstück
dB&B	double room and breakfast	Chambre pour deux personnes + petit dejeuner	Preis für Doppelzimmer und Frühstück
HB	Half-board weekly	Demi-pension	Teilverpflegung
B	Breakfast	Petit déjeuner	Frühstück
L	Lunch	Déjeuner	Mittagessen
D	Dinner	Dîner	Abendessen
fr	From	A partir de	von
[V]	RAC vouchers accepted	RAC tickets/bons de réduction acceptés	RAC Gutscheine werden angenommen
cc	Credit cards	Cartes de crédit	Kreditkarten

Cancellation of reservations: Should it become necessary to cancel reserved accommodation, guests are advised to telephone at once to the hotel or guest house, followed by written confirmation. If rooms which are reserved and not occupied cannot be re-let, the hotel proprietor may suffer loss, and guests may be held legally responsible for part of the cost.

Maps: Map references in the guide are to the relevant square on the maps at the end of the guide.

Disabled facilities Establishment entries shown with & are, in the opinion of their owner or manager, suitable for disabled people. We recom-

mend disabled visitors contact the hotel manager direct to discuss whether their particular requirements can be met.

Discount vouchers: Many establishments are prepared to offer readers of this guide discounts on accommodation prices. They are shown by a [V] at the end of the price section. Use the vouchers on page 15.to obtain your discount.

Shortened hotel entries: A number of hotels or guest houses failed to provide detailed information for the 1994 season. In such cases the entry may be abbreviated.

RAC Awards

The RAC recognises the very high standards reached by some of the Listed hotels we inspect by the Awards of Highly Acclaimed and Acclaimed status. To gain such recognition, a hotel or guest house must have a proportion of rooms with en suite bathrooms, have decorations and furnishings with a certain degree of elegance and above average fittings and equipment. You will find a list of Highly Acclaimed hotels, arranged by county on page 8-11.

Each year, RAC inspectors choose a hotel or guest house in each of eight regions to receive the Regional Best of the Year Award.

We congratulate the winners for 1994, described overleaf.

South-East England
Pembridge Court, London W2

South-West England
Meryan House Hotel, Taunton

The Midlands
Aylestone Court, Hereford

North of England
Grey Friars Lodge Country House, Ambleside

Scotland
Well View, Moffat

Wales
Castle Cottage, Harlech

Ireland
Merrion Hall, Dublin

Regional winners from previous years

South-East	**1993**	Hooke Hall, Uckfield
	1992	Tottington Manor, Henfield
	1991	Cockle Warren Cottage, Hayling Island
	1990	Langshott Manor, Horley
South-West	**1993**	The Long House, West Down
	1992	Victoria Court, Plymouth
	1991	Nanscawen House, St Austell
	1990	Hayne Farm, Black Torrington
East Anglia	**1993**	Sankence Lodge, Aylsham
	1992	Pipps Ford, Needham Market
	1991	Old Guildhall, Gislingham
The Midlands		
	1993	Hanchurch Manor, Stoke-on-Trent
	1992	Redland Hotel, Chester
	1991	Old Rectory, Willersey
	1990	Lypiatt House, Cheltenham
North of England		
	1993	Victorian House, Thornton Clevelys
	1992	Coniston Lodge, Coniston
	1991	Wind in the Willows, Glossop
	1990	Manor House, Beverley
Scotland	**1993**	Cavens House, Kirkbean
	1992	Coul House, Contin
	1991	Knockendarroch House, Pitlochry
	1990	Ravenscourt House, Grantown-on-Spey
Wales	**1993**	Lochmeyler Farm Guest House, Solva
	1992	Ty Mawr, Carmarthen
	1991	Borthwynog Hall, Bontddu
	1990	Three Wells Farm, Llandrindod Wells
Ireland	**1993**	Kathleen's Country House, Killarney
	1992	Rusheen Lodge, Ballyvaughan

Highly Acclaimed Hotels and Guest Houses

England

Inner London
Academy
Alexander
Byron
Diplomat
Pembridge Court
Royal Cambridge
Windermere

Outer London
Croft Court
Vanburgh

Avon

Bath
Arden
Armstrong House
Ashley Villa
Badminton Villa
Bailbrook Lodge
Tasburgh
Bloomfield House
Brompton House
Cheriton House
Dorian House
Gainsborough
Haydon House
Haute Combe House
Highways House
Laura Place
Leighton House
Meadowland
Monkshill
Monmouth Lodge
Oakleigh House
Old Courthouse
Old School House
Orchard House
Sydney Gardens
Underhill Lodge
Villa Magdala
Wheelbrook Mill

Blagdon
Aldwick Court Farm

Bristol
Westbury Park

Keynsham
Grasmere Court

Old Sodbury
Sodbury House

Weston-super-Mare
Ashcombe Court
Braeside
Milton Lodge
Wychwood

Berkshire

Windsor
Netherton

Buckinghamshire

Adstock
The Folly

Cambridgeshire

Cambridge
Brooklands
Lensfield

Cheshire

Chester
Cavendish
Green Gables
Redland

Crewe
Clayhanger Hall Farm

Cleveland

Middlesbrough
Grey House

Cornwall

Camborne
Lowenac

Fowey
Carnethic House

Launceston
Wheatley Farm

Looe
Coombe Farm
Polraen Country House

Newquay
Porth Enodoc
Windward

Padstow
Green Waves Private
Woodlands

Penryn
Prospect House

Penzance
Estoril
Tarbert

St Austell
Nanscawen Country House
Wheal Lodge

St Ives
Dean Court

Cumbria

Ambleside
Elder Grove
Gables
Grey Friar Lodge
Rowanfield Country House
Rysdale

Bassenthwaite
Lakeside
Ravenstone

Brampton
Oakwood House

Buttermere
Pickett Howe

Carlisle
Bessiestown Farm

Coniston
Coniston Lodge

Grange-over-Sands
Elton

Grasmere
Bridge House

Kendal
Lane Head House

Keswick
Abacourt House
Acorn House
Allerdale House
Applethwaite Country House
Beckside
Dalegarth House
Greystones
Lynwood
Ravensworth
Rooking House
Shemara
Silverdale
Skiddaw Grove
Stonegarth
Swiss Court
Thornleigh

Kirkby Stephen
Augill House Farm
Thrang Country
Town Head House

Sawrey
Garth Country House
West Vale Country

Windermere
Beaumont
Blenheim Lodge
Boston House
Broad Oak Country House
Cranleigh
Fairfield Country House
Fir Trees
Glencree
Glenville
Hawksmoor
Holly Park
Kirkwood
Newstead
St John's Lodge
Westlake
Woodlands

Workington
Morven

Derbyshire

Belper
Dannah Farm

Buxton
Brookfield On Longhill
Netherdale
Staden Grange
Thorn Heyes
Westminster

Glossop
Wind in the Willows

Devon

Chagford
Blackaller

Dartmouth
Ford House

Hope Cove
Hope Cove

Lifton
The Thatched Cottage

Lynton
Millslade
Victoria Lodge
Waterloo House

Plymouth
Georgian House

Salcombe
Lyndhurst

Torquay
Barn Hayes Country
Glenorleigh
Haldon Priors
Kingston House
Newton House
Robin Hill

West Down
The Long House

Woolacombe
Sunnycliffe

Dorset

Bournemouth
Boltons
Tudor Grange

Dorchester
Casterbridge

Evershot
Rectory House

Horton
Northill House

Durham

Bishop Auckland
Greenhead Country House

East Sussex

Battle
Moonshill Farm

Brighton
Adelaide
Amblecliffe
Ascott House
Kempton House Private
New Steine
Twenty One

Hartfield
Bolebroke Watermill

Hastings & St Leonards
Eagle House

Rye
Holloway House
Jeakes House
Old Vicarage

Uckfield
Hooke Hall

Essex

Chelmsford
Snows Oaklands

Southend-on-Sea
Ilfracombe House

Gloucestershire

Chipping Campden
Orchard Hill House

Blakeney
Lower Viney

Blockley
Lower Brook House

Bourton-on-the-Water
Ridge

Cheltenham
Beaumont House
Cotswold Grange
Hannaford's
Hilden Lodge
Hollington House
Lypiatt House
Milton House
Moorend Park

Regency House
Stretton Lodge

Cirencester
La Ronde
Wimborne

Gloucester
Gilberts
Rotherfield House

Nailsworth
Apple Orchard House

North Nibley
Burrows Court Private

Tetbury
Tavern House

Greater London

Kingston upon Thames
Chase Lodge

Greater Manchester

Manchester
Highbury

Altrincham
Ash Farm
Old Packet House

Hampshire

Brockenhurst
Cottage

Fordingbridge
Forest Cottage Farm

Hayling Island
Cockle Warren Cottage

Lyndhurst
Knightwood Lodge

Ringwood
Moortown Lodge

Winchester
The Wykeham Arms

Hereford & Worcester

Bredwardine
Bredwardine Hall

Broadway
Leasow House
The Old Rectory

Evesham
Church House

Hereford
Aylstone Court

Kidderminster
Cedars

Malvern
Red Gate

Symonds Yat
Saracens Head

Worcester
Loch Ryan

Hertfordshire

St Albans
Ardmore House

Humberside

Beverley
The Manor House

Isle of Wight

Freshwater Bay
Blenheim House

Sandown
Rooftree

St Catherines

Shanklin
Apse Manor Country House
Aqua
Avenue
Bay House
Bondi
Hambledon
Luccombe Chine
Orchardcroft
Osborne House
White House

Ventnor
Lake

Isles of Scilly

St Mary's
Carnwethers Country House

Kent

Ashford
Croft
Warren Cottage

Canterbury
Ebury
Old Poor House
Pilgrims
Thanington

Dover
East Lee
Number One

Tunbridge Wells
The Old Parsonage

Lancashire

Blackpool
Arosa
Brooklands
Burlees
Cliff Head
Hartshead Private
Lynstead
Lynwood
Old Coach House
Sunray
Windsor

Clayton-le-Woods
Brook House

Clitheroe
Brooklyn

Morecambe
Beach Mount
Hotel Prospect

Preston
Tulketh

Thornton Cleveleys
Victorian House

Leicestershire

Hinckley
Ambion Court
Kings

Lincolnshire

Lincoln
D'Isney Place
Minster Lodge

Norfolk

Aylsham
Sankence Lodge

Cromer
Westgate Lodge

Garboldisham
Ingleneuk Lodge

Hilgay
Crosskeys Riverside

Holt
Lawn's

Hunstanton
Sunningdale

King's Lynn
Russet House

Norwich
Belmonte
Cavalier

Sheringham
Fairlawns

Swaffham
Horse & Groom

Yarmouth, Great
Georgian House
Trotwood

North Yorkshire

Bainbridge
Riverdale House

Bedale
Elmfield Country House

Harrogate
Ruskin
Shannon Court

Ingleton
Pines Country House

Kettlewell
Langcliffe Country

Knaresborough
Newton House Private

Malton
Greenacres Country House

Reeth
Arkleside

Richmond
Hartforth Hall

Scarborough
Premier

Whitby
Dunsley Hall
Kimberley
York House

York
Arndale
Byron House
Curzon Lodge & Stables Cottages
Holmwood House

Northumberland

Alnmouth
Marine House

Nottinghamshire

Nottingham
Balmoral

Oxfordshire

Banbury
Easington House
La Madonette

Burford
Elm Farm House

Kidlington
Bowood House

Nettlebed
White Hart

Oxford
Chestnuts

Cotswold House
Gables
Marlborough House
Tilbury Lodge

Thame
Essex House

Somerset

Minehead
Gascony
Marston Lodge
Mayfair

Taunton
Meryan House

Staffordshire

Leek
Choir Cottage & Choir House

Lichfield
Oakleigh House

Stoke-on-Trent
Hanchurch Manor Country House

Suffolk

Bury St Edmunds
Twelve Angel Hill

Gislingham
Old Guildhall

Surrey

Reigate
Cranleigh

Tyne & Wear

Tynemouth
Hope House

Warwickshire

Henley-in-Arden
Ashleigh House
Lapworth Lodge

Stratford-upon-Avon
Avon View
Melita
Sequoia House
Twelfth Night
Victoria Spa Lodge

Warwick
Park Cottage

West Midlands

Birmingham
Bridge House
Chamberlain

West Sussex

Gatwick Airport
Lawns
Vulcan Lodge

Henfield
Tottington Manor

Rustington
Kenmore

Steyning
Springwells

Worthing
Moorings

West Yorkshire

Bingley
Hallbank

Wiltshire

Bradford-on-Avon
Burghope Manor
Widbrook Grange

Marlborough
Vines

Salisbury
Byways House
Grasmere House

Swindon
Fir Tree Lodge

Scotland

Central

Callander
Arden House
Arran Lodge

Denny
Highland House
Topps

Dumfries & Galloway

Gretna
Surrone House

Moffat
Well View

New Abbey
Cavens

Fife

Anstruther
Spindrift

Auchtermuchty
Ardchoille Farmhouse

Cupar
Redlands Country Lodge

Grampian

Aberdeen
Craiglynn

Cullen
Bayview

Huntly
Old Manse of Marnoch

Highland

Carrbridge
Fairwinds

Contin
Coul House

Dornoch
Highfield

Fort William
Ashburn House

Grantown-on-Spey
Culdearn House
Ravenscourt House

Inverness
Clach Mhuillin
Culduthel Lodge

Isle of Bute

Rothesay
Ardyne

Isle of Mull

Dervaig
Druimard Country

Tobermory
Strongarbh House

Lothian

Edinburgh
Ashgrove House

Brunswick
Cumberland
Dorstan
Lodge
Roselea House
Thrums

Haddington
Brown's

Strathclyde

Ayr
Brenalder Lodge
Windsor

Cardross
Kirkton House

Dunoon
Anchorage
Cedars

Oban
Foxholes

Tayside

Blairgowrie
Rosebank House

Pitlochry
Knockendarroch House

Wales

Dyfed

Carmarthen
Ty Mawr

Fishguard
Tregynon Country Farmhouse

Haverfordwest
Wilton House

New Quay
Park Hall

Solva
Lochmeyler Farm

Tenby
Harbour Heights
Kinloch Court
Waterwynch House

Tresaith
Bryn Berwyn

Gwent

Tintern
Parva Farmhouse

Gwynedd

Bontddu
Borthwnog Hall

Harlech
Castle Cottage

Aberdyfi (Aberdovy)
Brodawel

Betws-y-Coed
Tan-y-Foel Country House

Powys

Brecon
Coach

Llandrindod Wells
Three Wells Farm

Llanwrtyd Wells
Lasswade House

West Glamorgan

Swansea
St James
Tredilion House

Isle of Man

Port Erin
Regent House

Channel Islands

Guernsey

Castel
Le Galaad

L'Ancresse
Lynton Park

St Martins
La Michele

St Peter Port
Marine
Midhurst House

St Sampsons
Ann-Dawn

Jersey

St Ouen
Hotel Des Pierres

Republic of Ireland

Co. Carlow

Carlow
Barrowville Town House

Co. Clare

Ballyvaughan
Rusheen Lodge

Bunratty
Bunratty View

Ennistymon
Grovemount House

Kilkee
Halpins

Co. Cork

Macroom
Mills Inn

Co. Dublin

Dublin
Aberdeen Lodge
Ariel House
Glengora House
Merrion Hall
Raglan Lodge
Regem

Co. Galway

Clifden
Maldua

Oughterard
Currarevagh House

Co. Kerry

Caragh Lake
Caragh Lodge

Dingle
Cleevaun House
Doyle's Seafood Bar & Restaurant
Greenmount House
Milltown House

Killarney
Foley's Townhouse
Kathleens Country House
Victoria House

Sneem
Tahilla Cove Country House

Co. Laois

Port Laoise
Chez Nous

Co. Louth

Drogheda
Tullyesker House

Co.Cork

Kinsale
Moorings
Old Bank House

Co.Sligo

Riverstown
Coopershill House

Guest Houses of the Year

SOUTH-EAST ENGLAND

The Pembridge Court Hotel
34 Pembridge Gardens
London W2 4DX
Tel. 0171-229-9977

Pembridge Gardens is a quiet, tree-lined square in the Royal Borough of Kensington and Chelsea, just off the Bayswater Road, with Queensway, Bayswater and Notting Hill Gate tube stations within easy walking distance. The Pembridge Court Hotel is a privately-owned 19th century town house which has been stylishly refurbished

by Paul Capra's Danish wife Merete. The 20 well-appointed bedrooms are all individually designed and are complemented by extremely comfortable public rooms. The bistro-style restaurant is called Caps (as in sports) and is known for its warm ambience, good food and cheerful, informal service. A typical menu might include mushroom stroganoff, fillet of pork served with apple stuffing and sage sauce, followed by mango and chocolate torte. And the Cellar Bar provides a cosy place to relax and enjoy a quiet drink after your meal.

SOUTH-WEST ENGLAND

Meryan House Hotel
Bishops Hull
Taunton, Somerset
Tel. 01823-337445

Meryan House Hotel is only one mile from the centre of Taunton and yet this charming 300-year-old house, which has been upgraded and extended during the last six years, is quietly set in its own grounds and exudes peace and tranquillity. The 12 bedrooms are provided with many thoughtful extras from luxury toiletries to sweets, biscuits and paper handkerchiefs as well as the usual tea and coffee, radio and baby alarms, telephone and television. The recently refurbished restaurant is open to non-residents on Friday and Saturday evenings and for Sunday lunch, Cher

Clark does most of the cooking, making use of local and seasonal produce with as much as possible from the Hotel's own garden. Mr and Mrs Clark combine the high standards of a fine hotel with the warmth and attention normally given to a house guest.

THE MIDLANDS

Aylestone Court Hotel
Aylestone Hill
Hereford HR1 1HS
Tel. 01432-341891

Within easy walking distance of the centre of the cathedral city of Hereford, Aylestone Court is a fine listed red brick town house which dates from around 1650. Now a private, family-run hotel, the elegant proportions of the public rooms, spacious bedrooms and personal welcome, offer guests a pleasant and friendly atmosphere in which to recuperate after a day's sightseeing or business. The Louis-styled dining room can seat 26, and home cooking is the aim. Special requests such as vegetarian meals, can be encompassed as Mrs Holloway cooks to order for residents. Suggestions might include a salmon roulade, or warm smoked oyster and chicken salad, followed by an English roast of beef with a red-wine sauce. A special dessert might be Swedish marshmallow meringues or a prune and almond pie. The wine list is short but adequate with an emphasis on classic French wines.

NORTH OF ENGLAND

Grey Friar Lodge
Country House Hotel
Clappersgate, Ambleside
Cumbria LA22 9NE
Tel. 01539-43 3158

Grey Friar Lodge Country House Hotel is in a delightful Victorian former vicarage built of Lakeland stone in 1869, and lovingly converted and refurbished, first opening its doors to guests in 1984. Its secluded gardens are surrounded by woodland at the foot of Loughrigg Fell, midway between Ambleside and Skelwith Bridge, and overlooking the beautiful Brathay River valley. With only eight double bedrooms, Sheila and Tony Sutton make every effort to provide a homely but luxurious atmosphere, pampering their guests with imaginative evening menus which aim to blend traditional English home cooking with the mildly exotic. Fresh local produce and herbs from the hotel garden feature daily and they have an interesting wine selection. Home-made chocolates add a charming personal note to the end of your meal.

SCOTLAND

Well View Hotel
Ballplay Road
Moffat, Dumfriesshire
Tel. 01683 20184

This three-storey Victorian house was built for a shoemaking family in 1864 and named for the health giving waters which led to Moffat's heyday as a spa town. Moffat is in a deep valley at the heart of the magnificent Border country, and the Well View Hotel is set at the foot of the hills overlooking the town which is about half a mile away, making the hotel convenient for business visitors and holiday-makers alike. The traditional furnishings provide a relaxing and peaceful backdrop to the intended home-from-home atmosphere. Janet Schuckardt is gaining a wide reputation for her adventurous and beautifully presented cuisine, and her husband John keeps pace with an extensive and exciting wine cellar.

WALES

Castle Cottage Hotel and Restaurant

Harlech
Gwynedd LL46 2YL
Tel. 01766-780479

Just yards from the imposing 13th century castle, this family-run hotel and restaurant is to be found in one of the oldest houses in Harlech. There is plenty of car parking space by the hotel making this an ideal base for touring the magnificent Snowdonia National Park. The small but comfortable bedrooms have cottage-style furniture with co-ordinated soft furnishings beneath exposed beams and timbers. The restaurant has recently been extended and chef/proprietor Glyn Roberts is rapidly becoming known for light, healthy, attractively presented food making use of the wide range of locally produced vegetables, cheeses, smoked fish and meats. The extensive wine list concentrates on the lesser known regions of France, Italy and Spain, as well as introducing wines from the New World. The cosy bar and comfortable lounge make for a relaxing end to a busy day in the hills.

IRELAND

Merrion Hall

54–56 Merrion Road
Ballsbridge
Dublin
Eire
Tel. 01-668 1426

Merrion Hall is a large red brick Victorian house in one of Dublin's most elegant residential areas, just a mile and a half from the city centre. It is minutes from Lansdowne Road, the University and most of the city's embassies. The grounds of the hotel include an enclosed car park and there is a charming conservatory overlooking the gardens where breakfast is served. The 15 bedrooms have been carefully and tastefully renovated and decorated, and are all en suite, two with showers the rest with their own bathrooms. The public rooms, too, are elegantly furnished, comfortable and welcoming.

RAC DISCOUNT VOUCHERS

The RAC has arranged discounts with many of the hotels in this guide. These advantageous terms are limited to two 10% discounts and two 5% discounts off accommodation at these selected hotels for each guide user, with a maximum of £50 for a 10% voucher and £25 for a 5% one.

These discounts are only given on the appropriate full tariff for the room and the date. Vouchers will not be accepted for week-end breaks, rooms occupied by children at a reduced rate or against other tariffs already discounted. Hotels usually do not offer discounts over Bank Holidays, at Christmas and Easter or when there are local events in progress, for instance Gold Cup week at Cheltenham or major conferences at Harrogate. Hotels may limit the day of the week or the time of year the vouchers can be used; this may be weekdays or weekends depending on whether the hotel is mainly a business one or mainly a holiday one.

The four vouchers opposite can be used to obtain the relevant discount on your bill at any hotel showing a V at the end of the price information in its entry in the Guide. A copy of this edition of RAC Bed & Breakfast must be produced when you use the vouchers. Please inform the hotel when booking that you are planning to use an RAC voucher in part payment of your bill. Then if there is any confusion over when the discounts are offered it can be sorted out easily.

The vouchers are only available against accommodation costs NOT against bills for food and drink.

Whether it is a business trip, a short break or a holiday, remember to check whether the hotel you are booking accepts RAC Vouchers - you could save pounds!

RAC

DISCOUNT VOUCHER

10%

UP TO £50

off accommodation at hotels
Only one voucher per visit
(not valid after 31 December 1995)

RAC

DISCOUNT VOUCHER

5%

UP TO £25

off accommodation at hotels
Only one voucher per visit
(not valid after 31 December 1995)

RAC

DISCOUNT VOUCHER

10%

UP TO £50

off accommodation at hotels
Only one voucher per visit
(not valid after 31 December 1995)

RAC

DISCOUNT VOUCHER

5%

UP TO £25

off accommodation at hotels
Only one voucher per visit
(not valid after 31 December 1995)

CONDITIONS

1. Vouchers are only accepted for hotel accommodation at full tariff rates for the room and season, not against already discounted tariffs such as week-end breaks.

2. Only one voucher accepted per person or party per stay.

3. Hotels should be informed that an RAC voucher is to be used in part payment when a room is booked.

4. A copy of this 1995 RAC Guide must be produced when the voucher is used.

5. These vouchers are not valid after 31 December 1995.

CONDITIONS

1. Vouchers are only accepted for hotel accommodation at full tariff rates for the room and season, not against already discounted tariffs such as week-end breaks.

2. Only one voucher accepted per person or party per stay.

3. Hotels should be informed that an RAC voucher is to be used in part payment when a room is booked.

4. A copy of this 1995 RAC Guide must be produced when the voucher is used.

5. These vouchers are not valid after 31 December 1995.

CONDITIONS

1. Vouchers are only accepted for hotel accommodation at full tariff rates for the room and season, not against already discounted tariffs such as week-end breaks.

2. Only one voucher accepted per person or party per stay.

3. Hotels should be informed that an RAC voucher is to be used in part payment when a room is booked.

4. A copy of this 1995 RAC Guide must be produced when the voucher is used.

5. These vouchers are not valid after 31 December 1995.

CONDITIONS

1. Vouchers are only accepted for hotel accommodation at full tariff rates for the room and season, not against already discounted tariffs such as week-end breaks.

2. Only one voucher accepted per person or party per stay.

3. Hotels should be informed that an RAC voucher is to be used in part payment when a room is booked.

4. A copy of this 1995 RAC Guide must be produced when the voucher is used.

5. These vouchers are not valid after 31 December 1995.

London

A ll the world beats a path to London. The River Thames has long determined her history, character and traffic chaos threading through the kaleidoscope of architectural styles that surround her many parks. Already an internationally famous centre of aesthetics, 1995 adds a year-long Festival of Arts & Culture in London and indeed, all over Britain. It would take a lifetime to see all that this great city has to offer. The following tiny selection draws attention to new sights and some recent additions to well known places.

A SELECTION OF ATTRACTIONS:

Unless otherwise stated, all can be visited between April and October – some longer. Telephone for days/times of opening.

Age Exchange Reminiscence Centre, Blackheath, SE3: *Hands-on experience of bits and bobs from 1920's-40's.* Tel: 0181-318 9105.

Bank of England Museum, EC2: *Opportunity to penetrate the home of Britian's gold reserves. Closes end Sep.* Tel: 0171-601 5545.

British Library, WC1: *National literary treasures on display – Magna Carta, first folio Shakespeare etc.* Tel: 0171-636 1544.

British Museum, WC1: *Four new galleries added to the world's largest museum, three on Europe, one on Mexico.* Tel: 0171-636 1555.

Buckingham Palace, SW1: *Eighteen major rooms on view, including Throne Room and State Dining Room.* Tel: 0171-799 2331.

Cabinet War Rooms, SW1: *21-room labyrinth beneath Whitehall time-encapsulated World War ll.* Tel: 0171-930 6961.

Courtauld Institute Galleries, Somerset House, WC2: *Impressionist & Post-Impressionist paintings in former palace.* Tel: 0171-872 0220.

Chelsea Physic Garden, SW3: *Founded 1673, 2nd oldest in Britian. 4 acres with some 5,000 plants.* Tel: 0171-352 5646.

Design Museum, Butlers Wharf, SE1: *How mass-produced 20th-c consumer objects work.* Tel: 0171-407 6261.

Fantasy Island Playcentre, Wembley: *New multi-level soft-clad wonderland for children.* Tel: 0181-904 9044.

Geffrye Museum, E2: *Presents the changing style of domestic interiors 17th – 20th centuries.* Tel: 0171-739 9893.

George Inn, 77, Borough High St., SE1. *Mentioned in 'Little Dorrit', 18th-c galleried coaching inn still drawing pints. NT.* Tel: 0171-407 2056.

H.M.S. Belfast, The Thames, off Tooley St., SE1: *Europe's largest preserved World War ll battleship.* Tel: 0171-407 6434.

Imperial War Museum, SE1: *Devoted to war efforts since 1914. New exhibition – 'London at War'.* Tel: 0171-416 5320.

Dr. Johnson's House, Gough Sq. EC4: *Home of the lexicographer.* Tel: 0171-353 3745.

Kensington Palace, W8: *Extended by Wren as royal residence. State apartments. Royal Ceremonial dress collection.* Tel: 0171-937 9561.

Kenwood, NW3: *Attractive lakeside house on edge Hampstead Heath. Important Old Master paintings.* Tel: 0181-348 1286.

Kew Bridge Steam Museum, Brentford: *Gathering of great beam engines. Open daily but in steam w/ends only.* Tel: 0181-568 4757.

Leighton House Museum & Art Gallery, W14: *High Victorian fantasy home of artist Lord Leighton. Paintings, garden.* Tel: 0171-602 3316.

London Planetarium, NW1: *Should re-open transformed in April. New Digistar Mark 2 projector.* Tel: 0171-486 1121.

London Transport Museum, Covent Garden, WC2: *Catch that elusive bus at last!* Tel: 0171-379 6344.

London Zoo, NW1: *Occupies 36 acres. Reputedly the finest in the world. Children's Zoo newly refurbished.* Tel: 0171-722 3333.

Museum of London, EC2: *Artifacts and mementos, history and social life of London from 500,000 BC.* Tel: 0171-600 3699.

Museum of the Moving Image, South Bank SE1: *Actor guides, movie props plus history of cinema in 44 exhibit areas.* Tel: 0171-401 2636.

Natural History Museum, SW7: *Les dinosaures, dinosauri or die dinosaurier can now be found in 6 language guides.* Tel: 0171-938 9123.

Old Royal Observatory, SE10: *Est. 1675. On zero meridian of longitude. 24-hour clock shows Greenwich Mean Time. Views.* Tel: 0181-858 4422.

Science Museum, SW7: *Recently added gallery on development of 20th-c medicine. Hands-on exhibits.* Tel: 0171-938 8000.

Sir John Soane's Museum, WC2: *Architect's own design and home. Personal collection, paintings, oddities.* Tel: 0171-430 0175.

Shakespeare's Globe, Bankside, SE1: *Watch authentic, round Elizabethan theatre being built on original site. Visitor Centre.* Tel: 0171-928 6406.

Spencer House, SW1: *18th-c town house of Princess Diana's ancestors. Sundays only, closed Aug.* Tel: 0171-409 0526.

Sutton House, Hackney, E9: *Furnished early 16th-c Tudor manor, opened 1994. Chapel in cellar, craft workshop in kitchen. NT* Tel: 0181-896 2264.

Tower Bridge: *Explore the towers, examine the engines which raise the bascules, enjoy the view.* Tel: 0171-403 3761.

Tower of London, EC3: *Enlarged Jewel House with additional information enhances visits.* Tel: 0171-709 0765/488 5718.

Victoria & Albert Museum, SW7: *National Museum of applied & fine arts of all countries. Recently added glass gallery.* Tel: 0171-589 6371.

Westminster Abbey, SW1: *New 15-minute multimedia presentation enhances visit to England's premier church.* Tel: 0171-222 5152.

SOME ANNUAL EVENTS:

BOC Covent Garden Festival: *Dedicated to youth & youthful performers. 8-21 May.* Tel: 0171-240 0390.

Chelsea Flower Show, SW3: *Britian's major flower show. 23-26 May. (Members only 23 & 24).* Tel: 0171-630 7422.

City of London Festival, *various venues: Held in interesting buildings – St. Pauls, The Tower. 9-26 Jul.* Tel: 0171-377 0540.

Greenwich Festival, Various venues SE10: *Childrens' & fringe events with classical, rock, reggae. 2-18 Jun.* Tel: 0181-317 8687.

Henry Wood Promenade Concerts, Royal Albert Hall, SW7: *Centenary year. 21 Jul-16 Sep.* Tel: 0171-589 8212.

Horse of the Year Show, Wembley Arena: *Top showjumpers compete in tough indoor event. 26 Sep-1 Oct.* Tel: 0181-900 1234.

Ideal Home Exhibition, Earls Court, SW5: *16 Mar- 9 Apr.* Tel: 0171-373 8141.

International Festival of Flowers with Music, Westminster Cathedral: *Celebrating cathedral's 100th anniversary. 16-21 May.*

London Marathon, Greenwich to The Mall. *2 Apr. [provisional].* Tel: 0171-620 4117.

London Motor Show, Earls Court, SW5: *19 - 29 Oct.* Tel: 0171-373 8141.

London Thames Festival: Teddington to Barking. *Arts and sporting events on river. Early Sep.* Tel: 0171-700 6452.

Notting Hill Carnival, W11: *West Indian street carnival, steel bands, dancing, costumes. 27-28 Aug.* Tel: 0181-964 0544.

Oxford & Cambridge Boat Race, *River Thames, Putney to Mortlake. Begins 2.45 p.m. 1 Apr.*

Royal Tournament, Earls Court, SW5: *Military display of skill & pageantry. 18-29 Jul.* Tel: 0171-373 8141.

Spitalfields Festival, E1: *An exciting array of artists performing magnificent concerts. 7-28 Jun.* Tel: 0171-377 0287.

Trooping the Colour, Horseguards Parade, SW1: *H.M. The Queen takes salute in colourful official birthday pageant. Tickets by ballot but streetwatch free. 10 Jun.*

Wimbledon Lawn Tennis Championships, SW19. *26 Jun-9 Jul. Tickets by ballot Dec. '94 or at gate on day.*

Symbols

For an explanation of the symbols used in hotel entries, please see inside the front cover.

INNER LONDON 5D2

Academy *Highly Acclaimed* RAC
17-21 Gower Street, London WC1E 6HG
0171-6314115 Fax 0171-6363442
33 bedrs, 25 ➡/WC, 5 ➡;
[10%V]; cc Ac Amex DC Vi

Alexander *Highly Acclaimed* RAC
9 Sumner Place, London SW7 3EE
0171-5811591 Fax 0171-5810824
36 bedrs, 2 ➡/WC, 4 ➡/WC; TV tcf
sB&B £90 dB&B £117 Breakfast only; cc Ac
Amex DC Vi

Apollo RAC
18-22 Lexham Gdns, London W8 5JE
0171-835-1133 Fax 0171-370-4853
52 bedrs, 35 ➡/WC, 11 ➡/WC, 4 ➡; TV
sB&B £50-£55 dB&B £60-£66 Breakfast only
[10%V]; cc Ac Amex DC Vi

Ashley RAC
15 Norfolk Square, London W2 1RU
0171-7233375 Fax 0171-7230173
16 bedrs, 10 ➡/WC, 3 ➡; TV tcf
sB&B £26-£29 dB&B £48-£51 Breakfast only
[10%V]; cc Ac Vi

Averard RAC
10 Lancaster Gate, London W2 3LH
0171-7238877 Fax 0171-7060860
60 bedrs, 60 ➡/WC;
sB&B £40-£46 dB&B £60-£64 Breakfast only;
cc Ac Amex DC Vi

Barry House RAC
12 Sussex Place, London W2 2TP
0171-7237340 Fax 0171-7239775
18 bedrs, 1 ➡/WC, 13 ➡/WC, 2 ➡; TV tcf ✕
sB&B £26-£29 dB&B £48-£55 Breakfast only
[10%V]; cc Ac Amex DC Vi

Blair House RAC
34 Draycott Place, London SW3 2SA
0171-581-2323 Fax 0171-823-7752
17 bedrs, 17 ➡/WC; TV tcf
sB&B £50-£70 dB&B £90-£98 Breakfast only
[10%V]; cc Ac Amex DC Vi

Blandford *Acclaimed* RAC
80 Chiltern Street, London W1M 1PS
0171-4863103 Fax 0171-4872786

Bryanston Court *Acclaimed* RAC
50-56 Great Cumberland Place, Marble Arch,
London W1H 8DD 0171-262 -3141 Fax
0171-262-7248 ; cc Ac Amex DC Vi JCB

Byron *Highly Acclaimed* RAC
36-38 Queensborough Terrace, Bayswater,
London W2 3SH 0171-2430987 Fax
0171-7921957
42 bedrs, 42 ➡/WC;
sB&B £75.50 dB&B £89 [10%V]; cc Ac Amex
DC Vi

Camelot *Acclaimed* RAC
45-47 Norfolk Square, London W2 1RX
0171-723-9118 Fax 0171-402-3412 ♿
44 bedrs, 36 ➡/WC, 1 ➡; P3
Breakfast only [10%V]; cc Ac DC Vi

Caswell RAC
25 Gloucester Street, London SW1V 2DB
0171-834-6345
18 bedrs, 7 ➡/WC, 5 ➡; TV tcf
Child restrictions
sB&B £40-£47 dB&B £52-£60 Breakfast only

Claverley *Acclaimed*   ℞
13-14 Beaufort Gardens, Knightsbridge,
London SW3 1PS 0171-589-8541 Fax
0171-584-3410
32 bedrs, 28 ℞/WC, 7 🛁; TV ⌦
sB&B £60-£65 dB&B £85-£90 Breakfast only
[5%V]; cc Ac Amex Vi

★★★Coburg Resort   ℞
129 Bayswater Road, Hyde Park, London W2
4RJ 0171-2212217 Fax 0171-2290557
132 bedrs, 132 🛁/WC;
[10%V]

Colonnade   ℞
2 Warrington Crescent, London W9 1ER
0171-2861052 Fax 0171-2861057   ♿
48 bedrs, 48 🛁/WC; TV tcf 🐾 ⌦ P4
sB&B £66 dB&B £90 D £12.50; cc Ac Amex Vi

★★★Commodore   ℞
**50-52 Lancaster Gate, Hyde Park, London
W2 3NA 0171-4025291 Fax 0171-262-1088**

90 bedrs, 86 🛁/WC, 4 ℞/WC;

Concorde   ℞
50 Great Cumberland Place, Marble Arch,
London W1H 7FD 0171-402-6169
28 bedrs, 28 🛁/WC; P2
sB&B £55-£65 dB&B £80-£85 Breakfast only
[10%V]; cc Ac Amex DC Vi

Crescent   ℞
49/50 Cartwright Gardens, London WC1H 9EL
0171-3871515 Fax 0171-3832054
27 bedrs, 7 ℞/WC, 5 🛁; TV tcf
sB&B £34-£36 dB&B £50-£52 Breakfast only
[5%V]; cc Ac Vi

Dawson House   ℞
72 Canfield Gardens, London NW6 3ED
0171-6240079
15 bedrs, 7 🛁/WC, 3 🛁; 🐾

Child restrictions
Breakfast only [10%V]

Diplomat *Highly Acclaimed*   ℞
2 Chesham Street, Belgrave Square, London
SW1X 8DT 0171-2351544 Fax 0171-2596153
27 bedrs, 27 🛁/WC;
Breakfast only [10%V]

Dylan   ℞
14 Devonshire Terrace, Lancaster Gate,
London W2 3DW 0171-7233280 Fax
0171-4022443
Terraced hotel overlooking Queen's Gardens.
18 bedrs, 8 🛁/WC, 4 🛁; TV tcf
sB&B £30-£32 dB&B £42-£45 Breakfast only
[5%V]; cc Ac Amex Vi

THE DIPLOMAT HOTEL
*2 Chesham Street, Belgravia,
London SW1X 8DT.*

The Diplomat Hotel, a charming Victorian
building built in 1882, is situated in the heart of
London's Belgravia. A tranquil neighbourhood for
those seeking solitude from the usual hustle &
bustle of London and yet within walking distance
of Buckingham Palace, Harrods of Knightsbridge,
the famous antique markets and trendy shops of
Kings Road, Piccadilly & Hyde Park.
Singles fr. £65.00 Doubles fr. £99.00 inclus. of
VAT + Full English Breakfast. Also available
Snack Menu + English afternoon tea in lounge.

RAC Highly Acclaimed
Telephone: 0171 235 1544
Telefax: 0171-259 6153

Ecclestone
Ecclestone Square, London SW1V 1PS
0171-8348042 Fax 0171-6308942
114 bedrs, 83 🛁/WC, 31 🚿/WC, 1 🛁; TV tcf 🐕 🚭
sB&B £49.50-£64.25 dB&B £83.50-£99 D £13.50; cc Ac Amex DC Vi JCB

Edward Lear
30 Seymour Street, London W1H 5WD
0171-4025401 Fax 0171-7063766
31 bedrs, 3 🛁/WC, 1 🚿/WC, 6 🛁; TV tcf 🚭
sB&B £37.50-£44.50 dB&B £49.50-£54.50 Breakfast only [10%V]; cc Ac Vi

Elizabeth
37 Eccleston Square, London SW1V 1PB 0171-828-6812

Friendly, private hotel in an ideal, central location overlooking the magnificent gardens of a stately residential square (c 1835). On the fringe of Belgravia yet within walking distance of Victoria.
40 bedrs, 25 🛁/WC, 6 🛁; 🚭
sB&B £36-£55 dB&B £60-£80 Breakfast only [10%V]

Executive
57 Pont Street, London SW1X 0BD
0171-58124 Fax 0171-5899456
27 bedrs, 27 🛁/WC; 🚭
Breakfast only [10%V]; cc Ac Amex DC Vi

★★★Fenja
69 Cadogan Gardens, London SW3 2RB
0171-5897333

Four Seasons
173 Gloucester Place, London NW1 6DX
0171-7243461 Fax 0171-4025594
227 bedrs, 227 🛁/WC; P80
Breakfast only; cc Ac Amex DC Vi

Garden Court
30/31 Kensington Garden Square, London W2 4BG 0171-2292553 Fax 0171-7272749
35 bedrs, 12 🛁/WC, 5 🛁; TV 🐕
sB&B £27 dB&B £38 Breakfast only [5%V]; cc Ac Vi

Georgian House *Acclaimed*
87 Gloucester Place, London W1H 3PG
0171-9352211 Fax 0171-4867535
19 bedrs, 19 🛁/WC;
Child restrictions
Breakfast only [5%V]; cc Ac Amex Vi

Haddon Hall
39/40 Bedford Place, Russell Square, London WC1B 5JT 0171-6362474 Fax 0171-5804527
32 bedrs, 2 🛁/WC, 10 🚿/WC, 7 🛁;
sB&B £34-£36 dB&B £46-£50 Breakfast only [10%V]; cc Ac Vi

Hamilton House
60 Warwick Way, London SW1V 1SA
0171-8217113 Fax 0171-6300806
40 bedrs, 24 🛁/WC, 11 🚿/WC, 5 🛁; TV tcf 🚭
sB&B £35-£54 dB&B £45-£65 [10%V]; cc Ac Vi

Hart House
51 Gloucester Place, London W1H 3PE
0171-9352288 Fax 0171-9358516
16 bedrs, 11 🛁/WC, 2 🛁;
sB&B £40-£50 dB&B £55-£75 Breakfast only [5%V]; cc Ac Amex Vi

Henley House *Acclaimed* ᴿᴬᴄ
30 Barkston Gardens, Earls Court, London
SW5 OEN 0171-3704111 Fax 0171-3700026
20 bedrs, 20 ⬧/WC; TV tcf ✱
sB&B £45-£64 dB&B £60-£81 [10%V]; cc Ac
Amex DC Vi JCB

★★★Hogarth ᴿᴬᴄ
Hogarth Road, Kensington, London SW5 0QQ
0171-3706831 Fax 0171-3736179
85 bedrs, 85 ⬧/WC; ✱ P20
Breakfast only [10%V]; cc Ac Amex DC Vi

Hotel Atlas ᴿᴬᴄ
24-30 Lexham Gardens, London W8 5JE
0171-835-1155 Fax 0171-370-4853
57 bedrs, 13 ⬧/WC, 30 ⬧/WC, 5 ⬧; TV
sB&B £50-£55 dB&B £60-£66 Breakfast only
[10%V]; cc Ac Amex DC Vi

Kensington Court *Acclaimed* ᴿᴬᴄ
33 Nevern Place, London SW5 9NP
0171-3705151 Fax 0171-3703499
35 bedrs; TV tcf P10
sB&B £45-£48 dB&B £59 Breakfast only
[10%V]; cc Ac Amex Vi

Kensington Manor *Acclaimed* ᴿᴬᴄ
8 Emperor's Gate, London SW7 4HH
0171-370-7516 Fax 0171-373-3163
14 bedrs, 8 ⬧/WC;
Breakfast only [10%V]; cc Ac Amex DC Vi

Langdorf *Acclaimed* ᴿᴬᴄ
20 Frognal, Hampstead NW3 6AG
0171-7944483 Fax 0171-4359055

*An elegant Edwardian hotel with friendly,
personal service. Conveniently located near
Finchley Road Underground station and 15
minutes from Hampstead Village and Heath.*
31 bedrs, 31 ⬧/WC; TV tcf
sB&B £53-£61 dB&B £50-£75 Breakfast only
[10%V]; cc Ac Amex DC Vi

Merlyn Court   RAC
2 Barkston Gardens, London SW5 0EN
0171-3701640 Fax 0171-3704986
Grade II listed, Edwardian building set off a
quiet garden square in Kensington.
17 bedrs, 8 ➡/WC, 6 ➡; ✖
sB&B £25-£30 dB&B £40-£45 Breakfast only
[10%V]; cc Ac Vi

Mitre House *Acclaimed*   RAC
178-184 Sussex Gardens, Lancaster Gate,
London W2 1TU 0171-7238040 Fax
0171-4020990   &

A family-run hotel, established over 30 years.
Recently refurbished, renovated and
upgraded.
70 bedrs, 70 ➡/WC; TV ✖ P20
sB&B £50-£60 dB&B £65-£70 Breakfast only;
cc Ac Amex DC Vi JCB

Park Lodge   RAC
73 Queensborough Terrace, Bayswater,
London W2 3SU 0171-2296424 Fax
0171-2214772
29 bedrs, 29 ➡/WC;
sB&B £41 dB&B £51 Breakfast only [10%V];
cc Ac Amex DC Vi JCB

Using RAC discount vouchers

Please tell the hotel when booking if
you plan to use an RAC discount
voucher in part payment of your bill.
Only one voucher will be accepted per
party per stay. Discount vouchers will
only be accepted in payment for
accommodation, not for food.

Parkwood   RAC
4 Stanhope Place, London W2 2HB
0171-402-2241 Fax 0171-402-1574
18 bedrs, 12 ➡/WC, 3 ➡; TV tcf ✖
sB&B £39.75-£55 dB&B £54.50-£67.50
Breakfast only [10%V]; cc Ac Vi

Pembridge Court *Highly Acclaimed*   RAC
34 Pembridge Gdns, London W2 4DX
0171-2299977 Fax 0171-7274982
20 bedrs, 20 ➡/WC; TV ✖ P2
sB&B £115 dB&B £140 [10%V]; cc Ac Amex
DC Vi

Rosslyn House   RAC
2 Rosslyn Hill, London NW3 1PH
0171-4313873 Fax 0171-4331775
18 bedrs, 17 ➡/WC, 17 ➡/WC, 2 ➡;
TV tcf P10
sB&B £39 dB&B £49 Breakfast only [10%V];
cc Ac Vi

Royal Cambridge *Highly Acclaimed*   RAC
124 Sussex Gardens, London W2 1WB
0171-8730000 Fax 0171-8730830
31 bedrs, 31 ➡/WC; P3
Breakfast only [10%V]

Slavia   RAC
2 Pembridge Square, London W2 4EW
0171-7271316 Fax 0171-2290803
31 bedrs, 31 ➡/WC; P1
sB&B £33-£49 dB&B £42-£66 Breakfast only
[10%V]; cc Ac Amex DC Vi

Swiss House   RAC
171 Old Brompton Road, South Kensington,
London SW5 0AN 0171-3739383 Fax
0171-3734983
16 bedrs, 1 ➡/WC, 10 ➡/WC, 1 ➡; TV ✖ ✖
sB&B £34-£48 dB&B £50-£60 Breakfast only
[10%V]; cc Ac Amex DC Vi

Tregaron   RAC
17 Norfolk Square, Hyde Park, London W2
1RU 0171-7239966 Fax 0171-7230173
16 bedrs, 12 ➡/WC, 3 ➡; TV tcf
sB&B £26-£29 dB&B £48-£50 Breakfast only
[10%V]; cc Ac Vi

Westland *Acclaimed*   RAC
154 Bayswater Rd, London W2 4HP
0171-229-9191 Fax 0171-727-1054
44 bedrs, 44 ➡/WC; ✖ P9
[10%V]; cc Ac Amex DC Vi

Willett RAC
32 Sloane Gardens, Sloane Square, London
SW1W 8DJ 0171-824-8415 Fax 0171-730-4830
19 bedrs, 16 ✒/WC, 1 ✒; TV tcf ✘ ✔
sB&B £71.03 dB&B £90.42-£97.47 Breakfast
only [5%V]; cc Ac Amex DC Vi

Winchester RAC
17 Belgrave Road, London SW1 1RB
0171-8282972 Fax 0171-8285191
22 bedrs, 22 ✒/WC;
Child restrictions
Breakfast only

Windermere *Highly Acclaimed* RAC
142-144 Warwick Way, Victoria, London
SW1V 4JE 0171-834-5163 Fax 0171-630-8831
A small, friendly hotel with well equipped
bedrooms. There is a cosy lounge with
inviting Chesterfields, while English
breakfast and dinner are served in the
elegant dining room.
23 bedrs, 19 ✒/WC, 2 ✒; ✔
sB&B £49-£55 dB&B £59-£69 Breakfast only;
cc Ac Amex Vi JCB

OUTER LONDON 5D2

Granada Lodge RAC
Phoenix Way, Heston TW5 9NA 0181-5747271

Abbey Lodge RAC
51 Grange Park, Ealing, London W5 3PR
0181-5677914 Fax 0181-5795350
17 bedrs, 16 ✒/WC; ✘
sB&B £33 dB&B £39 Breakfast only [10%V];
cc Ac Vi

Aber RAC
89 Crouch Hill, Hornsey, London N8 9EG
0181-3402847 Fax 0181-3402847
9 bedrs, 2 ✒; ✔
sB&B £20-£26 dB&B £34-£38 Breakfast only
[5%V]; cc Ac Vi
(see advertisement on p.19)

Acton Park RAC
116 The Vale, Acton, London W3 7JT
0181-743-9417 Fax 0181-743-9417
21 bedrs, 20 ✒/WC; P15
Breakfast only; cc Ac Amex DC Vi

Anchor *Acclaimed* RAC
10 West Heath Drive, London NW11 7QH
0181-4588764 Fax 0181-4553204
12 bedrs, 9 ✒/WC, 1 ✒; ✘ P3
sB&B £26-£30 dB&B £45 Breakfast only
[5%V]; cc Ac Vi

Bedknobs RAC
58, Glengarry Road, East Dulwich, London
SE22 8QD 0181-2992004
3 bedrs, 2 ✒;
sB&B £23 dB&B £39 Breakfast only

Central RAC
35 Hoop Lane, London NW11 8BS
0181-4585636 Fax 0181-4554792
13 bedrs, 13 ✒/WC; TV P8
sB&B £35-£40 dB&B £50-£60 Breakfast only
[10%V]; cc Ac Amex DC Vi

Croft Court *Highly Acclaimed* RAC
44 Ravenscroft Avenue, Golders Green,
London NW11 8AY 0181-4583331 Fax
0181-4559175
20 bedrs, 20 ⇥/WC; P3
sB&B £54 dB&B £60 Breakfast only; cc Ac
Amex Vi

Crystal Palace Tower RAC
114 Church Road, Crystal Palace, London
SE19 2UB 0181-6530176
11 bedrs, 4 ⇥/WC, 4 🐾/WC, 1 ⇥; TV tcf 🦮
P10
sB&B £21-£25 dB&B £36-£39 Breakfast only
[5%V]; cc Ac DC Vi

Garth RAC
72-76 Hendon Way, Cricklewood, London
NW2 2NL 0181-20915 Fax 0181-45547
60 bedrs, 56 ⇥/WC, 6 ⇥; P50
Breakfast only

Grange Lodge RAC
50 Grange Road, London W5 5BX
0181-567-1049 Fax 0181-579-5350
14 bedrs, 9 ⇥/WC, 2 ⇥; 🦮 P8
sB&B £27-£33 dB&B £33-£39 Breakfast only
[10%V]; cc Ac Vi

Grove Hill RAC
38 Grove Hill, South Woodford, London E18
3JG 0181-989-3344 Fax 0181-530-5286 ♿
21 bedrs, 21 ⇥/WC, 3 ⇥; TV tcf 🦮
sB&B £23-£35 dB&B £35-£49 Breakfast only
[10%V]; cc Ac Amex Vi

Hazelwood House RAC
865 Finchley Road, Golders Green, London
NW11 0181-458-8884
6 bedrs, 2 ⇥; TV tcf 🦮 P7
sB&B £25-£27.50 dB&B £35-£38 Breakfast
only

Hounslow 41 Hounslow Rd, Feltham, Gtr
London, London SW14 0AU 0181-896-2358
Fax 0181-751-6103

Lakeside RAC
51 Snaresbrook Road, Wanstead, London E11
1PQ 0181-9896100
3 bedrs, 2 ⇥/WC, 1 ⇥;
Child restrictions
Breakfast only [10%V]

Lodge 52 Upper Richmond Rd, Putney,

London SW15 2RN 0181-8741598 Fax
0181-8740910

Redland RAC
418 Seven Sisters Road, London N4 2LX
0181-800-1826 Fax 0181-802-7080
22 bedrs, 6 ⇥; P9
sB&B £27 dB&B £35 Breakfast only [10%V];
cc Ac Amex DC Vi

Regal RAC
170 Golders Green Road, London NW11 9BY
0181-45570 ♿
10 bedrs, 2 ⇥; 🦮 P6
Breakfast only [5%V]; cc Ac Amex DC Vi

Sleeping Beauty Motel RAC
543 Lea Bridge Road, Leyton, London E10
7EB 0181-5568080 Fax 0181-5568080
♿ cc Ac Amex DC Vi

Trochee RAC
52 Ridgeway Place, Wimbledon, London
SW19 4SW 0181-9461579 Fax 0181-7854058
17 bedrs, 3 ⇥; TV tcf P6
Breakfast only [10%V]; cc Ac Vi

Trochee RAC
21 Malcolm Road, Wimbledon, London SW19 4AS 0181-9461579 Fax 0181-7854058
17 bedrs, 3 🛁; TV tcf 🐕 P8
sB&B £37-£48 dB&B £46-£62 Breakfast only [5%V]; cc Ac Amex Vi

Vanburgh *Highly Acclaimed* RAC
St John's Park, Blackheath, London SE3 7TD
0181-8534051 Fax 0181-8587387

White Lodge RAC
1 Church Lane, Hornsey, London N8
0181-348-9765
16 bedrs, 8 🚿/WC; TV tcf
sB&B £26 dB&B £40; HB weekly £144; D £15; cc Ac Vi

Wimbledon RAC
78 Worple Road, London SW19 4HZ
0181-9469265 Fax 0181-9469265
14 bedrs, 7 🛁/WC, 2 🛁; TV tcf
sB&B £40 Breakfast only; cc Ac Amex DC Vi

Worcester House *Acclaimed* RAC
38 Alwyne Road, London SW19 7AE
0181-9461300 Fax 0181-7854058
9 bedrs, 9 🚿/WC; TV tcf 🐕 P2
sB&B £47.50 dB&B £52.50 Breakfast only [5%V]; cc Ac Amex DC Vi

Yardley Court *Acclaimed* RAC
18 Court Yard, Eltham, London SE9 5PZ
0181-850-1850
9 bedrs, 5 🛁/WC, 2 🛁; P8
Breakfast only

LONDON AIRPORT-HEATHROW

Hounslow RAC
41 Hounslow Road, Feltham, London TW14 0AH 0181-8902358 Fax 0181-7516103
23 bedrs, 23 🛁/WC;
Breakfast only; cc Ac DC Vi

Shepiston Lodge RAC
31 Shepiston Lane, Hayes, London UB3 1LJ
0181-5730266 Fax 0181-5692536; cc Ac Amex DC Vi

New Telephone Numbers

All UK telephone codes are being changed. The number 1 is being inserted after the first 0. For example, 081 is changing to 0181. The new codes were available in August 1994 and the two codes will run in parallel until 16 April 1995, when the new code will take over. The new codes are given throughout the guide, as they will be in use in November when the guide is published The old codes can be used up to 16 April 1995. Five cities will have a complete change of code and an additional digit to the number.

	OLD	NEW
Bristol	0272-xxxxx	0117-9xxxxxx
Leeds	0532-xxxxx	0113-2xxxxxx
Leicester	0533-xxxxx	0116-2xxxxxx
Nottingham	0602-xxxxx	0115-9xxxxxx
Sheffield	0742-xxxxx	0114-2xxxxxx

South East

Kent • Sussex • Surrey • Bucks • Herts • S. Essex

S uch a profusion of historic homes and gardens cannot be matched anywhere else in Britain. Bring a healthy thirst, for there must surely be as many vineyards in Sussex and Surrey as there are oasts and hops in The Garden of England. As for museums, even the odd martello tower has been pressed into service as a Visitor Centre [Folkestone]. Theme Parks are on the increase, as are wildlife centres – even Gatwick has a zoo! Hertfordshire has Roman remains to rival those at Fishbourne near Chichester. On the varied coastline, Brighton is as brittle and sophisticated as Bosham is unspoiled.

A SELECTION OF ATTRACTIONS:

Unless otherwise stated, all can be visited between April and October – some longer. Telephone for days/times of opening.

Barkham Manor Vineyard, Piltdown, E. Sussex: *35 acre vineyard & oast. Tastings in 18th-c thatched barn.* Tel: 0182572-2103/4220.

Bentley House & Gardens, Halland, E. Sussex: *Interesting designer mix of Tudor and 20th-c plus 'Room' gardens.* Tel: 01825-840573.

Capel Manor, nr. Enfield, Herts: *30 acres of themed gardens for the compulsive gardener.* Tel: 01992-763849.

Charleston Farmhouse, Firle, Lewes, Sussex: *Country retreat of Bloomsbury Group. Unique artists decor.* Tel: 01323-811265.

Chartwell, Westerham, Kent: *Intimate, well loved home of Winston Churchill, kept unchanged.* Tel: 01732-866368.

Denbies Wine Estate, Dorking, Surrey: *18 varieties of vines in panoramic setting. Tour, taste, purchase.* Tel: 01306-876616.

Dover Castle, Kent: *Contemporary with the Tower of London. Tunnels, a Roman lighthouse plus views.* Tel: 01304-201628.

Filching Manor Motor Museum, nr. Polegate, E. Sussex: *Exciting sportscars some with celebrity connections.* Tel: 01323-487838.

Gardens of the Rose, nr. St. Albans, Herts: *Showground of the Royal National Rose Society. 10 Jun-15 Oct.* Tel: 01727-850461.

Great Comp Garden, nr. Borough Green, Kent: *A 20th-c garden of 7 acres, creating areas of varied character.* Tel: 01732-882669.

Gt. Thorpe Park, Chertsey, Surrey: *Canadian theme introduces Stampedes, Loggers Leaps plus usual crazy stuff.* Tel: 01932-562633.

Gomshall Mill, Surrey: *Working watermill on River Tillingbourne. Small shops, miller's stone.* Tel: 01483-202433.

Hatfield House, Herts: *Hatfield Palace rebuilt by Robert Cecil 1607-11. Elizabeth I spent childhood here. Closes early Oct.* Tel: 01707-262823.

Headcorn Flower Centre & Vineyard, Kent: *Vines, wildlife & flower houses – orchid lillies/chrysanths.* Tel: 01622-890250.

Hever Castle & Gardens, nr. Edenbridge, Kent: *Shades of Anne Boleyn linger in Itanianate garden and 13th-c moated castle.* Tel: 01732-865224.

Ightham Moat, Ivy Hatch, Kent: *Beautifully conserved romantic moated manor.* Tel: 01732-810378.

Knole, Sevenoaks, Kent: *365 rooms they say, in Elizabethan castellated home with 17th-c furniture.* Tel: 01732-450608.

Leeds Castle, nr. Maidstone, Kent: *Norman Castle in fairy tale setting. Grounds have every diversion/events.* Tel: 01622-765400.

Loseley House, Guildford, Surrey: *Delightful home with interesting features. Pleasing garden plus own ice cream products. Open May-early Oct.* Tel: 01483-304440.

Dovecote, Nymans Gardens

Nymans Gardens, Handcross, W. Sussex: *Rare plants in romantic garden in Sussex Weald. NT.* Tel: 01444-400321/400002.

Penshurst Place, Tunbridge Wells, Kent: *Impressive family owned baronial home & gardens. Lots for children too. Closes early Oct.* Tel: 01892-870307.

Planet Earth, Newhaven, E. Sussex: *Simulated earthquakes, motorised dinosaurs, interesting and fun.* Tel: 01273-512123.

Polesden Lacey, nr. Dorking, Surrey: *Beautiful grounds surround the Greville collection of paintings in Cubitt designed house.* Tel:01372-458203.

Polesden Lacey

Roman Theatre, St. Albans. *By entrance to Gorhambury House off A4147.*

Romney, Hythe & Dymchurch Railway: *World's only main line in miniature. Carries you over 14 miles of Romney Marsh.* Tel: 01797-362353/363256.

Rye Museum, E. Sussex: *Former castle/gaol houses topographical table of area. Views. Ancient Cinque Port town:* 01797-226728.

St. Augustine's Abbey, Canterbury, Kent: *Preceeded Canterbury Cathedral. Extensive ruins. Open daylight hours.*

Sarre Windmill, nr. Birchington, Kent: *Restored 19th-c flour grinding windmill. Bakery, farm animals.* Tel: 01843-847573.

Sheffield Park, nr. Uckfield, E. Sussex: *Year-round colour in 150 acres of garden with lakes. NT.* Tel: 01825-790655.

Sissinghurst, Kent: *Vita Sackville-West's series of gardens within romantic ruins. NT.* Tel: 01580-712850.

Thorpe Park, Chertsey, Surrey: *400 acres on Canadian theme. Recent additions: Depth Charge & Calgary Stampede.* Tel: 01932-562633.

Whitbread Hop Farm, Paddock Wood, Kent: *Oasts, Shire horses, plus flying birds of prey. Events.* Tel: 01622-872068.

Verulamium Museum, St. Albans, Herts. *Re-created Roman rooms & lifestyle, mosaics, hypocaust.* Tel: 01727-819339.

Welwyn Roman Baths, Herts: *Hiding under A1(M), a 3rd-c Roman villa preserved bath.* Tel: 01707-271362.

SOME ANNUAL EVENTS:

Antique Dealers Fair, Goodwood House, W. Sussex: *12-14 May.* Tel: 01243-774107.

Balloon & Bentley Fiesta, Leeds Castle, Kent: *Hot air balloons pursued by vintage Bentleys. 3-4 Jun.* Tel: 01622-765400.

Bexhill 100th Festival of Motoring, E. Sussex. *Fancy dress, historic cars, events, side shows. 7-8 May.* Tel: 01424-730564.

Brighton International Festival, E. Sussex: *450 events in mixed arts festival. 5-28 May.* Tel: 01273-676926.

Broadstairs Dickens Festival, Kent: *Dickensian Garden Party, a play, country fair plus. 17-24 Jun.* Tel: 01843-863453.

Canterbury Festival, Kent: *Over 200 events, some concerts in cathedral. Jazz, dance, walks. 7-21 Oct.* Tel: 01227-472820.

Chichester Festivities, W. Sussex: *Exhibitions to opera. Childrens' events. Fireworks. 2-18 Jul.* Tel: 01243-785718.

Brighton Pavilion

Eastbourne International Lawn Tennis Championship, E. Sussex: *Ladies tournament with champagne & strawberries. 19-25 Jun.* Tel:01323-415442.

Hertford Art Society Open Exhibition, Herts: *Paintings, sculpture & ceramics. 1-13 May.* Tel: 01438-723535.

Horseracing: At Glorious Goodwood: *23-25 May; 9, 16, 23, 30 Jun; 25-29 Jul; 25-27 Aug; 8, 9, 29-30 Sep.* Tel: 01243-774107.

Kent County Show, Detling, Kent: *500 trade stands, sheep dog demos, marching bands plus cattle. 13-15 Jul.* Tel: 01622-630975.

Medieval Fair, Bodiam Castle, E. Sussex: *Craft fair with medieval theme by moated castle. NT. 7-8 May.* Tel:01892-890651.

Polesden Lacy Open Air Theatre, Great Bookham, Surrey: *14 Jun-9 Jul.* Tel: 01372-453401.

Rickmansworth Canal Festival, Herts: *20-21 May.* Tel: 01923-778382.

Rochester Sweeps Festival, Kent: *Processions, craft fairs, ceilidhs throughout Rochester. 1-8 May.* Tel: 01634-843666.

ADSTOCK Buckinghamshire   8B4

(Inn) The Folly *Highly Acclaimed*   RAC
Buckingham Road, Adstock MK18 2HS
01296-712671   &
5 bedrs, 5 ☞/WC; TV tcf ✻ P40
sB&B £20-£24 dB&B £37.95 [10%V]; cc Ac
Amex Vi

AMERSHAM Buckinghamshire   4C2

(Inn) The Chequers   RAC
London Road, Amersham HP7 9DA
01494-727866
4 bedrs, 3 ☞/WC; TV tcf P27
sB&B £15 dB&B £35 [10%V]

The Old Barn Rectory Hill, Old Amersham,
Amersham HP7 0BT 01494-721990

63 Hundred Acres Lane Amersham HP7
9BX 01494-433095
3 bedrs, 1 ➡; ✻ P4
sB&B £24.50 Breakfast only

ARUNDEL West Sussex   4C4

Arundel Park Inn & Travel Lodge
Acclaimed   RAC
**The Causeway, Station Approach, Arundel
BN18 9JL 01903-882588 Fax 01903-883808**
&
*Pleasant building with outside garden at
front and patio with tables and brollies*
12 bedrs, 6 ➡/WC, 6 ☞/WC; TV tcf ⊁ P60
sB&B £32-£38 dB&B £42-£48 Breakfast only
[10%V]; cc Ac Vi

ASHFORD Kent   5E3

Croft *Highly Acclaimed*   RAC
Canterbury Road, Ashford TN25 4DU
01233-622140 Fax 01233-622140
15 bedrs, 2 ➡/WC, 13 ☞/WC, 1 ➡; ✻ P30
sB&B £31.50 dB&B £41.50 Breakfast only; cc
Ac Amex Vi

Warren Cottage *Highly Acclaimed*   RAC
136 The Street, Willesborough, Ashford TN24
0NB 01233-621905 Fax 01233-623400
4 bedrs, 4 ☞/WC, 2 ➡; TV tcf ⊁
sB&B £20-£25 dB&B £50; HB weekly £238; D
£9 [10%V]; cc Ac Vi

AYLESBURY Buckinghamshire   4C2

★★(Inn) Horse and Jockey   RAC

Buckingham Road, Aylesbury HP19 3QL
01296-23803 Fax 01296-395142
24 bedrs, 24 ➡/WC; TV tcf P60
sB&B £24-£43 dB&B £42; cc Ac Amex DC Vi

Baywood 98 Weston Road, Aylesbury HP22
5EJ 01296-630612
11 bedrs, 1 ➡/WC, 10 ☞/WC; TV tcf ✻ P11
sB&B £20 Breakfast only

Belton House 26 Chiltern Road, Aylesbury
HP22 6DB 01296-622351
3 bedrs; TV
sB&B £12 Breakfast only

East Riding Bacombe Lane, Aylesbury HP22
6EQ 01296-622654

Foxhill Kingsey, Aylesbury HP17 8LZ
01844-291650

Wallace Farm Dinton, Aylesbury HP17 8UF
01296-748660

9 Ballard Close Aylesbury HP21 9UY
01296-84465

17 Icknield Close Aylesbury HP22 6HG
01296-623859

46 Lionel Avenue Aylesbury HP22 6LP
01296-623426

BATTLE East Sussex   8E4

Little Hemingfold Farmhouse
Acclaimed   RAC
Telham, Battle TN33 0TT 01424-774338
13 bedrs, 10 ➡/WC, 2 ➡; TV tcf ✻ ⊁ P50
sB&B £30-£35 dB&B £60-£65; HB weekly
£273-£294; D £19.50 [10%V]; cc Ac Amex Vi

Moonshill Farm *Highly Acclaimed*   RAC
The Green, Moons Hill, Ninefield, Battle
TN33 9JL 01424-892645
3 bedrs, 1 ➡;
Breakfast only

Netherfield Hall   RAC
Netherfield, Battle TN33 9PQ 01424-774450 &
3 bedrs, 1 ☞/WC, 1 ➡; tcf ⊁ P9
sB&B £20-£25 dB&B £30-£35 Breakfast only
[5%V]

BEXHILL-ON-SEA East Sussex 5E4

Park Lodge *Acclaimed* 🏰RAC
16 Egerton Road, Bexhill-on-Sea TN39 3HH
01424-216547

Tastefully furnished family run hotel in central position adjacent to the seafront.
10 bedrs, 4 🛏/WC, 2 🛁/WC, 1 🛏; ✗; cc Ac Vi

BICKLEY Kent 5D2

Glendevon House 🏰RAC
80 Southborough Road, Bickley BR1 2EN
0181-467-2183
11 bedrs, 1 🛏/WC, 2 🛁/WC, 1 🛏; TV tcf ✗ P6
sB&B £23.50 dB&B £37 Breakfast only [5%V]; cc Ac Vi

BISHOP'S STORTFORD Hertfordshire 5D1

(Inn) George 🏰RAC
North Street, Bishop's Stortford HP4 2DF
01279-504128 Fax 01279-655135
20 bedrs, 4 🛏; TV tcf ✗
sB&B £20.30 dB&B £40.10 D £11; cc Ac Vi

The Cottage *Acclaimed* 🏰RAC
71 Birchanger Lane, Birchanger, Bishop's Stortford CM23 5QA 01279-812349
15 bedrs, 2 🛏/WC, 11 🛁/WC; TV tcf P20
sB&B £34 dB&B £44 D £10; cc Ac Vi

BLETCHINGLEY Surrey 5D3

★★★(Inn) Whyte Hart 🏰RAC
11-21 High Street, Bletchingley RH1 4PB
01883-743231 Fax 01883-743231
12 bedrs, 9 🛏/WC, 1 🛏; P14

BRIGHTON East Sussex 5D4

Adelaide *Highly Acclaimed* 🏰RAC
51 Regency Square, Brighton BN1 2FF
01273-205286 Fax 01273-220904

12 bedrs, 3 🛏/WC, 9 🛁/WC, 1 🛏; TV tcf ✗
sB&B £38 dB&B £65 D £12.50 [10%V]; cc Ac Amex DC Vi

Allendale *Acclaimed* 🏰RAC
3 New Steine, Brighton BN2 1PB
01273-675436 Fax 01273-602603

Ambassador 🏰RAC
22 New Steine, Marine Parade, Brighton BN2 1PD 01273-676869 Fax 01273-689988

10 bedrs, 2 🛏/WC, 8 🛁/WC; TV tcf ✗
Breakfast only [10%V]; cc Ac Amex DC Vi JCB

Amblecliffe *Highly Acclaimed* 🏰RAC
35 Upper Rock Gardens, Brighton BN2 1QF
01273-681161 Fax 01273-676945
8 bedrs, 2 🛏/WC, 6 🛁/WC, 1 🛏; TV tcf ✗ P2
Child restrictions
dB&B £39-£56 Breakfast only [10%V]; cc Ac Amex Vi

Arlanda *Acclaimed* 🏰RAC
20 New Steine, Brighton BN2 1PD
01273-699300 Fax 01273-600930
12 bedrs, 2 🛏/WC, 10 🛁/WC; TV tcf
sB&B £22-£36 dB&B £38-£70 Breakfast only [10%V]; cc Ac Amex DC Vi JCB

Ascott House *Highly Acclaimed* 🏰RAC
21 New Steine, Marine Parade, Brighton BN2 1PD 01273-688085 Fax 01273-623733
12 bedrs, 9 🛁/WC, 2 🛏; TV tcf ✗
Child restrictions
dB&B £42 D £15; cc Ac Amex DC Vi

Cavalaire House *Acclaimed* 🏰RAC
34 Upper Rock Gardens, Brighton BN2 1QF
01273-696899
9 bedrs, 3 🛁/WC, 1 🛏; TV tcf ✗ ✗
sB&B £16-£18 dB&B £38-£44 Breakfast only; cc Ac Vi

Dudley House   RAC
10 Madeira Place, Brighton BN2 1TN
01273-676794
6 bedrs, 3 ↾/WC, 2 ➹;
HB weekly £95-£160;

Fyfield House   RAC
26 New Steine, Brighton BN2 1PP
01273-602770
9 bedrs, 5 ↾/WC, 1 ➹; TV tcf ✂
sB&B £15-£26 dB&B £32-£52; HB weekly
£150-£180; [10%V]; cc Ac Amex DC Vi JCB

Gullivers *Acclaimed*   RAC
10 New Steine, Brighton BN2 1PB
01273-695415
9 bedrs, 5 ↾/WC, 1 ➹; TV tcf 🐾 ✂
sB&B £18 dB&B £20-£30 Breakfast only
[5%V]; cc Ac Amex DC Vi

Kempton House Private
Highly Acclaimed   RAC
33-34 Marine Parade, Brighton BN2 1TR
01273-570248 Fax 01273-570248
12 bedrs, 12 ↾/WC; TV tcf 🐾
sB&B £30 dB&B £40; HB weekly £211;
[10%V]; cc Ac Amex DC Vi

Kimberley   RAC
17, Atlingworth Street, Brighton BN2 1PL
01273-603504 Fax 01273-603504

Regency style terraced family run hotel.
15 bedrs, 2 ➹/WC, 2 ↾/WC, 1 ➹; TV tcf
sB&B £14-£18 dB&B £32-£34 Breakfast only;
cc Ac Amex DC Vi JCB

Malvern *Acclaimed*   RAC
33 Regency Square, Brighton BN1 2GG
01273-324302 Fax 01273-324302
12 bedrs, 12 ↾/WC, 1 ➹; TV tcf ✂
Child restrictions
sB&B £30-£35 dB&B £45-£60 Breakfast only
[5%V]; cc Ac Amex DC Vi JCB

Manor Farm Poynings, Brighton BN45 7AG
01273-857371

Marina House *Acclaimed*   RAC
8 Charlotte Street, Marine Parade, Brighton
BN2 1AG 01273-605349 Fax 01273-605349

*A white, Victorian building, in the heart of
popular Kemp Town, once a fashionable part
of Regency Brighton. Set among Regency
Grade II listed buildings, one minute away
from the seaside.*
10 bedrs, 7 ↾/WC, 1 ➹; TV tcf
sB&B £13.50-£23 dB&B £29-£45; HB weekly
£177-£210; D £11 [10%V]; cc Ac Amex DC Vi
JCB

Melford Hall *Acclaimed*   RAC
41 Marine Parade, Brighton BN2 1PE
01273-681435 Fax 01273-624186
25 bedrs, 1 ➹/WC, 22 ↾/WC, 2 ➹; TV tcf P12
Child restrictions
sB&B £28-£32 dB&B £42-£50 Breakfast only
[10%V]; cc Ac Amex DC Vi

New Steine *Highly Acclaimed*   RAC
12a New Steine, Marine Parade, Brighton BN2
1PB 01273-681546
11 bedrs, 7 ↾/WC, 2 ➹; TV tcf ✂
Child restrictions
sB&B £16 dB&B £35 Breakfast only [5%V]

Child Restrictions

Most hotels and guest houses are happy
to welcome children. A few prefer to
welcome only adults and older children;
these are shown by 'Child restrictions' in
the entry. If you are travelling with children,
please telephone the establishment to check
the age limit set by the management.

Paskins RAC
19 Charlotte Street, Brighton BN2 1AG
01273-601203 Fax 01273-621973
20 bedrs, 1 ➥/WC, 15 🐾/WC, 1 ➥; TV tcf ✕
Child restrictions
sB&B £15-£17 dB&B £25-£30 Breakfast only
[10%V]; cc Ac Vi

Pier View RAC
28 New Steine, Marine Parade, Brighton BN2
1PB 01273-605310 Fax 01273-688604
11 bedrs, 1 ➥;
Breakfast only

Regency *Acclaimed* RAC
28 Regency Square, Brighton BN1 2FH
01273-202690 Fax 01273-220438

Rowland House RAC
21 St George Terrace, Marine Parade,
Brighton BN2 1JJ 01273-603639

★★Topps RAC
17 Regency Sq, Brighton BN1 2FG
01273-729334 Fax 01273-203679

Trouville *Acclaimed* RAC
11 New Steine, Marine Parade, Brighton BN2
1PB 01273-697384
9 bedrs, 4 🐾/WC, 2 ➥; TV tcf
sB&B £18 dB&B £42 Breakfast only [5%V];
cc Ac Amex Vi

Twenty One *Highly Acclaimed* RAC
21 Charlotte Street, Marine Parade, Brighton
BN2 1AG 01273-686450
6 bedrs, 1 ➥/WC, 5 🐾/WC; TV tcf
Child restrictions
sB&B £35-£50 dB&B £46-£68 Breakfast only
[10%V]; cc Ac Amex Vi JCB

York Lodge RAC
22-23 Atlingworth Street, Marine Parade,
Brighton BN2 1PL 01273-605140
20 bedrs, 6 🐾/WC, 4 ➥; TV tcf ✕
sB&B £13-£16 dB&B £28-£32 Breakfast only
[10%V]; cc Ac Vi

BROADSTAIRS Kent   5F2

Bay Tree *Acclaimed* RAC
**12 Eastern Esplanade, Broadstairs CT10
1DR 01843-862502**
11 bedrs, 3 ➥/WC, 8 🐾/WC; TV tcf ✕
Child restrictions

sB&B £18-£20 dB&B £36-£40; HB weekly
£165; [10%V]; cc Ac Vi

Devonhurst *Acclaimed* RAC
13 Eastern Esplanade, Broadstairs CT10 1DR
01843-863010 Fax 01843-868940
9 bedrs, 9 🐾/WC, 1 ➥; TV tcf
Child restrictions
sB&B £18-£24 dB&B £40-£46; HB weekly
£165-£179; [5%V]; cc Ac Amex DC Vi

East Horndon RAC
4 Eastern Esplanade, Broadstairs CT10 1DP
01843-868306

A large, Victorian house on the sea front.
10 bedrs, 4 🐾/WC, 2 ➥; TV tcf ✕
sB&B £18 dB&B £40; HB weekly £150; D
£7.50; cc Ac Vi

Gull Cottage *Acclaimed* RAC
5 Eastern Esplanade, Broadstairs CT10 1DP
01843-861936

*A character Victorian property situated on
cliff top overlooking sea and sandy beaches
close to harbour town and shops.*
8 bedrs, 6 🐾/WC; TV tcf P6
Child restrictions
sB&B £20 dB&B £40 Breakfast only; cc Ac
Amex DC Vi

BUCKINGHAM Buckinghamshire   4B1

Folly Farm Padbury, Buckingham MK18 2HS
01296-712413

The Old Manor Thornborough, Buckingham
MK18 2DF 01280-812345

BURNHAM-ON-CROUCH Essex   5E2

(Inn) Anchor   RAC
The Quay, Burnham-on-Crouch CM0 8AT
01621-782117
4 bedrs, 4 ☞/WC; TV tcf ✘ P30
sB&B £16.95 dB&B £35 D £9.50; cc Ac DC Vi

CAMBERLEY Surrey   4C3

Camberley   RAC
116 London Road, Camberley GU15 3TJ
01276-24410

CANTERBURY Kent   5E3

Castle Court   RAC
8 Castle Street, Canterbury CT1 2QF
01227-463441
11 bedrs, 2 ➤/WC, 1 ☞/WC, 2 ➤; TV tcf ✘ P4
sB&B £16-£22 dB&B £28-£40 Breakfast only
[10%V]; cc Ac Vi

Ebury *Highly Acclaimed*   RAC
65/67 New Dover Road, Canterbury CT1 3DX
01227-768433 Fax 01227-459187
15 bedrs, 12 ➤/WC, 3 ☞/WC; TV tcf ✖ P25
sB&B £41-£48 dB&B £59.50-£62; HB weekly
£235-£250; [10%V]; cc Ac Amex Vi

Ersham Lodge *Acclaimed*   RAC
12 New Dover Road, Canterbury CT1 3AP
01227-463174 Fax 01227-455482
14 bedrs, 2 ➤/WC, 9 ☞/WC, 1 ➤;
TV ✘ ✖ P12
sB&B £28-£36 dB&B £44 Breakfast only; cc
Ac Amex Vi

Highfield   RAC
Summer Hill, Harbledown, Canterbury CT2
8NH 01227-462772
8 bedrs, 3 ☞/WC, 2 ➤; tcf ✖ P12
Child restrictions
sB&B £27-£29 dB&B £38-£52 Breakfast only;
cc Ac Vi

Old Poor House *Highly Acclaimed*   RAC
Kake Street, Petham, Canterbury CT4 5RY
0122-770-413 Fax 0171-247-1478

Oriel Lodge *Acclaimed*   RAC
3 Queens Avenue, Canterbury CT2 8AY
01228-462845

*An Edwardian family house, with period
character, in a residential road near the city
centre. Comfortable bedrooms and a lounge
area with a log fire.*
6 bedrs, 2 ☞/WC, 2 ➤; TV tcf ✖ P6
Child restrictions
sB&B £19-£23 dB&B £33-£39 Breakfast only

(Inn) Pilgrims *Highly Acclaimed*   RAC
18 The Friars, Canterbury CT1 2AS
01227-464531 Fax 01227-762514
15 bedrs, 15 ➤/WC; TV tcf
sB&B £45 dB&B £55 Breakfast only [10%V];
cc Ac Vi

Pointers   RAC
1 London Road, Canterbury CT2 8LR
01227-456846 Fax 01227-831131
14 bedrs, 4 ➤/WC, 4 ☞/WC, 2 ➤; TV tcf ✘
P8
sB&B £35-£38 dB&B £42-£55 D £12.95; cc Ac
Amex DC Vi JCB

Thanington *Highly Acclaimed*   RAC
140 Wincheap, Canterbury CT1 3RY
01227-453227
10 bedrs, 10 ➤/WC, 2 ➤; TV tcf ✘ ✖ P12
sB&B £39-£48 dB&B £55-£62 Breakfast only;
cc Ac Amex DC Vi JCB

CHALFONT ST GILES Buckinghamshire   4C2

Gorelands Corner Gorelands Lane, Chalfont
St Giles HP8 4HQ 01494-872689

The Shieling 81 Bottrells Lane, Chalfont St
Giles HP8 4EH 01494-872147 Fax
01494-871431
3 bedrs, 1 ➤/WC, 2 ☞/WC; TV tcf P5
sB&B £25 Breakfast only

CHELMSFORD Essex   5E2

Beechcroft   RAC
211 New London Road, Chelmsford CM2 0AJ
01245-352462 Fax 01245-347833
20 bedrs, 9 ♠/WC, 4 ➡; TV tcf ✖ P15
sB&B £28 dB&B £42.50 Breakfast only;
cc Ac Vi

Boswell House *Acclaimed*   RAC
118/120 Springfield Road, Chelmsford CM2
6LF 01245-287587 Fax 01245-287587
13 bedrs, 9 ➡/WC, 4 ♠/WC; TV tcf ✂ P13
sB&B £42-£45 dB&B £60 D £10 [5%V]; cc Ac
Amex DC Vi

Snows Oaklands *Highly Acclaimed*   RAC
240 Springfield Road, Chelmsford CM2 6BP
01245-352004   🔾
16 bedrs, 14 ➡/WC, 1 ➡; ✂
sB&B £30.36 dB&B £41.46 Breakfast only
[5%V]

Tanunda   RAC
217-219 New London Road, Chelmsford CM2
0AJ 01245-354295 Fax 01245-345503
20 bedrs, 11 ➡/WC, 3 ➡; P20
sB&B £28 dB&B £42.50 Breakfast only; cc Ac
Amex DC Vi

CHICHESTER West Sussex   4C4

(Inn) The Globe   RAC
1 Southgate, Chichester PO19 20H
01243-782035
11 bedrs, 2 ➡/WC, 3 ♠/WC, 2 ➡; TV tcf P22
Child restrictions
sB&B £17-£21 dB&B £42
[10%V]; cc Ac Amex Vi

(Inn) The Woolpack   RAC
Main Road, Fishbourne, Chichester PO19 3JJ
01243-782792
4 bedrs, 2 ➡; TV tcf ✖ P20
sB&B £15-£20 dB&B £30-£40 D £10.95
[10%V]; cc Ac Amex Vi

CLIFTONVILLE Kent   5F2

Falcon Holiday *Acclaimed*   RAC
4 Ethelbert Road, Cliftonville CT9 1RY
01843-223846
30 bedrs, 22 ➡/WC, 3 ➡; P6
sB&B £21-£25 dB&B £42-£50; HB weekly
£130-£150; [5%V]

The Greswolde *Acclaimed*   RAC
20 Surrey Road, Cliftonville CT9 2LA
01843-223956
6 bedrs, 1 ➡/WC, 5 ♠/WC, 1 ➡; TV tcf ✖
sB&B £21 dB&B £36 Breakfast only [10%V];
cc Ac Vi

COLCHESTER Essex

Highfields Farm Kelvedon, Colchester CO5
9BJ 01376-570334 Fax 01376-570334
6 bedrs, 2 ➡/WC, 1 ♠/WC; ✖
sB&B £16 Breakfast only

CROYDON Surrey   5D3

Alpine   RAC
16-18 Moreton Road, Croydon CR2 7DL
0181-6886116 Fax 0181-6671822
35 bedrs, 29 ➡/WC, 2 ➡; P30
Breakfast only [10%V]

Kirkdale *Acclaimed*   RAC
22 St Peters Road, Croydon CR0 1HD
0181-6885898 Fax 0181-6806001
19 bedrs, 19 ♠/WC; TV tcf ✂ P12
sB&B £35 dB&B £40 [5%V]; cc Ac Amex Vi

Markington *Acclaimed*   RAC
9 Haling Park Road, Croydon CR2 6NG
0181-6816494 Fax 0181-6886530
22 bedrs, 5 ➡/WC, 17 ♠/WC, 3 ➡; TV tcf ✂ P17
sB&B £45 dB&B £45-£50 D £6.50 [10%V]; cc
Ac Amex Vi

DODDINGTON Kent   5E3

Palace Farmhouse Doddington ME9 0AU
01795-886820   🔾
6 bedrs, 2 ➡/WC, 1 ♠/WC, 1 ➡; ✖ P4
sB&B £14; HB weekly £144-£165;

DORKING Surrey   4C3

(Inn) The Pilgrim   RAC
Station Road, Dorking RH4 1HF 01306-889951
   🔾
6 bedrs, 3 ➡; TV tcf ✖ P14
sB&B £18-£22 dB&B £39 D £3.95; cc Ac Vi

DOVER Kent   5F3

Ardmore *Acclaimed*   RAC
18 Castle Hill Road, Dover CT16 1QW
01304-205895 Fax 01304-208229
4 bedrs, 4 ♠/WC; TV tcf
dB&B £30-£45 Breakfast only

Beaufort House *Acclaimed*
18 Eastcliff Marine Parade, Dover CT16 1LU
01304-216444 Fax 01304-211100
28 bedrs, 28 🛁/WC, 3 🛁; P26
Breakfast only

Beulah House
94 Crabble Hill, Dover CT17 0SA
01304-824615
8 bedrs, 2 🛁; 🚭 P10
sB&B £18 dB&B £36 Breakfast only [10%V]

East Lee *Highly Acclaimed*
108 Maison Dieu Road, Dover CT16 1RT
01304-210176 Fax 01304-210176
4 bedrs, 4 🛁/WC; TV tcf P4
dB&B £36 Breakfast only [5%V]; cc Ac Vi

Elmo
120 Folkestone Road, Dover CT17 9SP
01304-206236
6 bedrs, 2 🛁; TV tcf 🚭 P6
sB&B £12-£16 dB&B £28-£32 Breakfast only [5%V]

Fleur de Lis 9-10 Effingham Cres, Dover CT17 9RH 01304-240224

Gateway Hovertel *Acclaimed*
Snargate Street, Dover CT17 9BZ
01304-205479 Fax 01304-211504
27 bedrs, 27 🛁/WC; P27
Breakfast only [10%V]

Hubert House *Acclaimed*
9 Castle Hill Road, Dover CT16 1QW
01304-202253
8 bedrs, 3 🛁/WC, 2 🛁; 🐕 P7
Breakfast only; cc Ac Vi

Number One *Highly Acclaimed*
1 Castle Street, Dover CT16 1QH
01304-202007
6 bedrs, 4 🛁/WC; P6
dB&B £36-£40 Breakfast only [10%V]

Pennyfarthing *Acclaimed*
109 Maison Dieu Road, Dover CT16 1RT
01304-205563
6 bedrs, 4 🚿/WC; TV tcf 🚭 P6
sB&B £20-£24 dB&B £34-£38 Breakfast only

Peverell House *Acclaimed*
28 Park Avenue, Dover CT16 1HD
01304-202573
6 bedrs, 2 🛁/WC, 2 🛁; P6
Breakfast only

St Brelade's
82 Buckland Avenue, Dover CT16 2NW
01304-206126 Fax 01304-211486
8 bedrs, 4 🚿/WC, 2 🛁; TV tcf 🚭 P7
sB&B £18-£24 dB&B £32-£42 Breakfast only [5%V]; cc Ac Vi

St Martins
17 Castle Hill Road, Dover CT16 1QW
01304-205938 Fax 01304-208229
6 bedrs, 6 🚿/WC; TV tcf 🚭
dB&B £30-£40 Breakfast only

Tower *Acclaimed*
98 Priory Hill, Dover CT17 0AD 01304-208212
5 bedrs, 3 🛁/WC, 1 🛁; TV tcf P3
Breakfast only [10%V]

Westbank
239 Folkestone Road, Dover CT17 9LL
01304-201061
6 bedrs, 1 🛁/WC, 5 🚿/WC, 1 🛁; TV tcf 🐕 P6
sB&B £17 dB&B £34; HB weekly £168; D £7

Whitmore
261 Folkestone Road, Dover CT17 9LL
01304-203080
4 bedrs, 1 🚿/WC, 1 🛁; TV tcf 🐕 P4
sB&B £12-£18 dB&B £24-£32 Breakfast only [5%V]

DYMCHURCH Kent 5E3

Chantry
Sycamore Gardens, Dymchurch TN29 0LA
01303-873137
6 bedrs, 5 🛁/WC, 1 🛁; TV tcf 🐕 P10
sB&B £19.95-£22.50 dB&B £39.90-£45; HB weekly £150-£190; D £9.95 [10%V]; cc Ac Amex Vi

EASTBOURNE East Sussex 5D4

Alfriston
16 Lushington Road, Eastbourne BN21 4LL
01323-725640
13 bedrs, 9 🛁/WC, 2 🛁; 🚭 P2
Child restrictions
Breakfast only

Symbols
For an explanation of the symbols used in hotel entries, please see inside the front cover.

Bay Lodge *Acclaimed*   RAC
61-62 Royal Parade, Eastbourne BN22 7AQ
01323-732515 Fax 01323-735009
Small, centrally situated family-run seafront
hotel with a large sun lounge, overlooking the
Redoubt Gardens. Take the A22 to the
seafront, turn right towards the pier and hotel
is 200 yards on the right.
12 bedrs, 5 ➡/WC, 4 ➡/WC, 2 ➡; TV tcf
Child restrictions
sB&B £18-£22 dB&B £37-£45; HB weekly
£163-£189; D £8.50 [5%V]; cc Ac Vi

Beachy Rise *Acclaimed*   RAC
20 Beachy Head Road, Eastbourne BN20 7QN
01323-639171
6 bedrs, 6 ➡/WC; ✂
dB&B £40-£44 Breakfast only; cc Ac Vi

Chack Farm Coopers's Hill, Willingdon,
Eastbourne BN20 9JD 01323-503800
9 bedrs, 1 ➡/WC, 2 ➡;
Breakfast only

Chalk Farm Cooper's Hill, Willingdon,
Eastbourne BN20 9JT 01323-503800

Courtlands   RAC
68 Royal Parade, Eastbourne BN22 7AQ
01323-726915
12 bedrs, 1 ➡/WC, 4 ➡; P1
Breakfast only [10%V]; cc Ac Amex Vi

Flamingo *Acclaimed*   RAC
20 Enys Road, Eastbourne BN21 2DN
01323-721654   &
11 bedrs, 11 ➡/WC; ✂
Child restrictions
sB&B £21-£22.50 dB&B £42-£45 [5%V]; cc Ac
Amex Vi

Meridale   RAC
91 Royal Parade, Eastbourne BN22 7AE
01323-729686
8 bedrs, 2 ➡;
Breakfast only

Sherwood   RAC
7 Lascelles Terrace, Eastbourne BN21 4BJ
01323-724002
12 bedrs, 2 ➡/WC, 9 ➡/WC, 2 ➡;
TV tcf ✖ ✂
sB&B £10-£24 dB&B £27-£48; HB weekly
£110-£150;

★★★The Mansion   RAC
Grand Parade, Eastbourne BN21 3YS
01323-27411 Fax 01323-20665
90 bedrs, 90 ➡/WC, 1 ➡;

EPSOM Surrey   4C3

Epsom Downs *Acclaimed*   RAC
9 Longdown Road, Epsom KT17 3PT
01372-740643 Fax 01372-723259
14 bedrs, 12 ➡/WC; TV tcf ✖ ✂ P10
sB&B £58.75 dB&B £39.50 D £15 [10%V]; cc
Ac Amex DC Vi

ESHER Surrey   4C3

Lakewood House *Acclaimed*   RAC
Portsmouth Road, Esher KT10 9JH
01932-867142 Fax 01923-867142   &
12 bedrs, 6 ➡/WC, 3 ➡; TV tcf ✖ ✂ P50
sB&B £30-£35.25 dB&B £82.25 D £12 [10%V]

FARTHING CORNER Kent   5E3

Pavilion Lodge   RAC
M2, Gillingham, Farthing Corner ME8 8PW
01634-377337

FAVERSHAM Kent   5E3

Granary *Acclaimed*   RAC
Plumford Lane, Brogdale Road, Faversham
ME13 0DS 01795-538416
3 bedrs, 3 ➡/WC; P8

FELTHAM Middlesex   4C2

Crompton 49 Lampton Rd, Feltham TW3
1JG 0181-570-7090

FOLKESTONE Kent   5F3

Westward Ho   RAC
13 Clifton Crescent, Folkestone CT20 2EL
01303-252663
12 bedrs, 11 ➡/WC, 1 ➡;
[10%V]; cc Ac Vi

GATWICK AIRPORT West Sussex   5D3

Barnwood *Acclaimed*   RAC
Balcombe Road, Pound Hill, Crawley RH10
7RU 01293-882709 Fax 01293-886041
35 bedrs, 4 ➡/WC, 33 ➡/WC; TV tcf ✂ P55
sB&B £28-£36 dB&B £41 D £9; cc Ac Amex
DC Vi JCB

Chalet *Acclaimed*   RAC
77 Massetts Road, Horley RH6 7EB
01293-821666 Fax 01293-821619
6 bedrs, 5 ⇥/WC, 1 ⇥; ⚹ P14
sB&B £24 dB&B £42 Breakfast only [10%V];
cc Ac Vi

Gainsborough Lodge *Acclaimed*   RAC
39 Massetts Road, Horley RH6 7DT
01293-783982
12 bedrs, 12 ⇥/WC;
Breakfast only [10%V]

Lawns *Highly Acclaimed*   RAC
30 Massetts Road, Horley RH6 7DE
01293-775751 Fax 01293-821803
7 bedrs, 3 🕭/WC, 2 ⇥; TV tcf 🐾 ⚹ P9
Child restrictions
sB&B £24 dB&B £35 Breakfast only [5%V]; cc
Ac Amex DC Vi JCB

Manor House *Acclaimed*   RAC
Bonnetts Lane, Crawley RH11 ONY
01293-510000
5 bedrs, 2 ⇥/WC, 1 ⇥; TV tcf ⚹ P15
sB&B £25 dB&B £35 Breakfast only; cc Ac Vi

Massetts Lodge *Acclaimed* 28 Massetts Rd,
Horley RH6 7DE 01293-782738 Fax
01293-782738

Melville Lodge   RAC
15 Brighton Road, Horley RH6 7HH
01293-784951 Fax 01293-784957
6 bedrs, 3 🕭/WC, 2 ⇥; TV tcf 🐾 P15
sB&B £17.50 dB&B £35-£40 Breakfast only; cc
Ac Amex DC Vi JCB

Prinsted   RAC
Oldfield Road, Horley RH6 7EP 01293-785233
6 bedrs, 3 ⇥; TV tcf 🐾
sB&B £25 dB&B £35 Breakfast only; cc Amex

Stone Court   RAC
64, Smallfield Road, Horley RH6 9AT
01293-774482
3 bedrs, 1 ⇥; tcf ⚹ P10
Child restrictions
sB&B £20-£25 dB&B £35 Breakfast only

Location Maps

Hotel locations are shown on the maps at
the back of the guide. All towns and
villages containing an hotel listed in the
guide are shown in black.

Vulcan Lodge *Highly Acclaimed*   RAC
27 Massetts Road, Horley RH6 7DQ
01293-771522
4 bedrs, 3 🕭/WC, 1 ⇥; TV tcf P10
sB&B £24-£31 dB&B £40-£44 Breakfast only;
cc Ac Vi

Woodlands   RAC
42 Massetts Road, Horley RH6 7DS
01293-782994 Fax 01293-776358
*Family-run guest house in an attractive,
double-fronted, detached property. 1/4 mile
from Gatwick Airport, ideal early and late
flights. All rooms en-suite with colour TV and
tea/ coffee making facilities.*
5 bedrs, 5 🕭/WC, 1 ⇥; TV tcf ⚹ P22
sB&B £25-£27.50 dB&B £35-£38 Breakfast
only [10%V]

Mill Lodge   RAC
25 Brighton Road, Salfords RH1 6PP
01293-771170
10 bedrs, 2 ⇥/WC, 2 ⇥; P34
Breakfast only

GERRARDS CROSS Buckinghamshire   4C2

Tree Tops Main Drive, Bulstrode Path,
Gerrards Cross SL9 7PR 01753-887083

Tudor Acre South Park Crescent, Gerrards
Cross SL9 8AJ 01753-885874

GODALMING Surrey   4C3

Meads   RAC
65 Meadow, Godalming GU7 3HS
01483-421800 Fax 01483-429313
15 bedrs, 1 ⇥/WC, 5 🕭/WC, 2 ⇥; TV tcf 🐾
P14
sB&B £23-£38 dB&B £35-£45 Breakfast only;
cc Ac Amex Vi

GRAVESEND Kent   5D2

Sunnyside 3 Sunnyside, off Windmill St,
Gravesend DA12 1LG 01474-365445

GUILDFORD Surrey   4C3

Blanes Court   RAC
Albury Road, Guildford GU1 2BT
01483-573171
19 bedrs, 13 ⇥/WC, 1 ⇥; 🐾 P20
Breakfast only

Carlton   RAC
36 London Road, Guildford GU1 2AF
01483-575158 Fax 01483-34669
*Family run hotel, very comfortable, 5 minutes
walk from town centre. Picturesque town.*
33 bedrs, 7 🛏/WC, 6 🛁/WC, 5 🛏; TV tcf 🕇 P40
sB&B £36 dB&B £46; HB weekly £203; D £6;
cc Ac Amex Vi

HARROW Greater London   4C2

Central   RAC
6 Hindes Road, Harrow HA1 1SJ
0181-4270893
13 bedrs, 3 🛏/WC, 5 🛏;
sB&B £25-£28 dB&B £32 Breakfast only; cc Ac Vi

Crescent Lodge *Acclaimed*   RAC
58-62 Welldon Crescent, Harrow HA1 1QR
0181-8635491 Fax 0181-4275965
21 bedrs, 13 🛏/WC, 3 🛏; 🕇
Breakfast only [10%V]; cc Ac Amex Vi

Hindes *Acclaimed*   RAC
Hindes Road, Harrow HA1 1SJ 0181-427-7468
Fax 0181-424-0673
14 bedrs, 7 🛁/WC, 2 🛏; TV tcf P25
sB&B £29 dB&B £39 Breakfast only [10%V];
cc Ac Amex Vi

HARTFIELD East Sussex   5D3

Bolebroke Watermill *Highly Acclaimed*   RAC
Perry Hill, Edenbridge Road (B2026),
Hartfield TN7 4JP 01892-770425 Fax
01892-770872
4 bedrs, 4 🛏/WC; TV tcf ⚡ P8
Child restrictions
sB&B £45 dB&B £50 Breakfast only; cc Ac
Amex Vi

HASTINGS & ST LEONARDS East Sussex 5E4

Argyle   RAC
32 Cambridge Gardens, Hastings & St
Leonards TN34 1EN 01424-421294
8 bedrs, 3 🛁/WC, 2 🛏; TV tcf
Child restrictions
sB&B £15-£20 dB&B £30-£35 Breakfast only

Beechwood   RAC
59 Baldslow Road, Hastings & St Leonards
TN34 2EY 01424-420078
10 bedrs, 4 🛁/WC, 1 🛏; 🕇 ⚡ P6
sB&B £12-£14 dB&B £26; HB weekly £140; D
£8 [5%V]

Eagle House *Highly Acclaimed*   RAC

12 Pevensey Road, Hastings & St Leonards
TN38 0JZ 01424-430535
19 bedrs, 19 🛏/WC, 2 🛏; P12
sB&B £31.60 dB&B £49 D £18.95 [10%V]; cc
Ac Amex DC Vi

French's Inn   RAC
24 Robertson Street, Hastings TN34 1HL
01424-421195
4 bedrs, 4 🛏/WC; 🕇
Child restrictions

Gainsborough   RAC
5 Carlisle Parade, Hastings TN34 1JG
01424-434010
8 bedrs, 8 🛏/WC, 1 🛏; 🕇
sB&B £17-£20 dB&B £34-£40; HB weekly
£169-£190; [5%V]; cc Vi

Highlands Inn 1 Boscobel road, St Leonards
On Sea, Hastings & St Leonards TN38 0LU
01424-420299 Fax 01424-465065
9 bedrs;
Child restrictions under 1
Breakfast only

Waldorf   RAC
4 Carlisle Parade, Hastings TN34 1JG
01424-422185
12 bedrs, 5 🛏/WC, 2 🛏;
Breakfast only

HEMEL HEMPSTEAD Herts   4C2

Southville   RAC
9 Charles Street, Hemel Hempstead HP1 1JH
01442-251387
19 bedrs, 6 🛏; 🕇 P10
sB&B £23.50 dB&B £33 Breakfast only
[10%V]; cc Ac Vi

HENFIELD West Sussex   4C4

Sparright Farm Rackam, Pulborough, Henfield RH20 2EY 01798-872132

This 17th century farmhouse, complete with inglenook fireplace, makes an ideal base for touring. Tea/coffee facilities. Surrounded by peaceful woods, it is located west of the A283 between Pulborough and Storrington.
2 bedrs, 1 ➡; ✖
sB&B £15 Breakfast only

Tottington Manor *Highly Acclaimed*   RẢC
Edburton, Henfield BN5 9LJ 01903-815757
Fax 01903-879331   ᴪ
6 bedrs, 3 ➡/WC, 3 ➡/WC; TV tcf P100
sB&B £35-£50 dB&B £60-£85 Breakfast only
[10%V]; cc Ac Amex DC Vi

HIGH WYCOMBE Buckinghamshire   4C2

Belmont 9-11 Priory Avenue, High Wycombe HP13 6SQ 01494-527046 Fax 01494-473596
Town house hotel located within easy walking distance of the museum, rail & bus stations.
18 bedrs, 10 ➡/WC, 4 ➡; TV tcf P20
sB&B £25 D £5-£10; cc Ac Amex DC Vi

Drake Court   RẢC
141 London Road, High Wycombe HP11 1BT
01494-523639 Fax 01494-472696
20 bedrs, 3 ➡/WC, 4 ➡; P30
Breakfast only [10%V]

Harfa House Station Road, High Wycombe
HP13 6AD 01494-529671

Wayside House 2 Hampden Road, High
Wycombe HP13 6SX 01494-465746

2 Grays Lane Downley, High Wycombe
HP13 5TZ 01494-523014

HITCHIN Hertfordshire   4C1

Ashford 24 York Road, Hitchin SG5 1XA
01462-454183

HORSHAM West Sussex   4C3

Blatchford House *Acclaimed*   RẢC
52 Kings Road, Horsham RH13 5PR
01403-265317 Fax 01403-211592
12 bedrs, 2 ➡/WC, 7 ➡/WC; TV tcf P12
sB&B £17.50-£25 dB&B £35-£40 Breakfast
only [10%V]; cc Ac Vi

Horsham Wimblehurst 6 Wimblehurst Rd,
Horsham RH12 2ED 01403-272723
Fax 01403-211212

HOUNSLOW Greater London (Middx)   4C2

Crompton   RẢC
49 Lampton Road, Hounslow TW3 1JG
0181-5707090 Fax 0181-5771975   ᴪ
10 bedrs, 10 ➡/WC, 2 ➡; TV tcf P10
sB&B £27-£30 dB&B £40 Breakfast only
[10%V]; cc Ac Amex DC Vi

Heathrow *Acclaimed*   RẢC
17-19 Haslemere Avenue, Hounslow TW5
9UT 0181-3843333 Fax 0181-3843321   ᴪ
11 bedrs, 9 ➡/WC, 1 ➡; ✖ P10
sB&B £20-£30 dB&B £30-£35
Breakfast only [5%V]

ILFORD Greater London (Essex)   5D2

Cranbrook *Acclaimed*   RẢC
24 Coventry Road, Ilford IG1 4QR
0181-554-6544 Fax 0181-518-1463   ᴪ
30 bedrs, 26 ➡/WC, 1 ➡; ✖ P24
sB&B £23-£25.02 dB&B £35.76 D £7.50 [5%V];
cc Ac Amex DC Vi

Park *Acclaimed*   RẢC
327 Cranbrook Road, Ilford IG1 4UE
0181-5549616 Fax 0181-5182700
20 bedrs, 5 ➡/WC, 12 ➡/WC, 1 ➡; TV tcf ✖ P20
sB&B £26.50 dB&B £36.50 D £12 [10%V];
cc Ac Vi

ISLEWORTH Greater London   4C2

Kingswood   RẢC
33 Woodlands Road, Isleworth TW7 6NR
0181-560-5614
14 bedrs, 10 ➡/WC, 4 ➡; P5
Breakfast only; cc Ac Amex DC Vi

KINGSDOWN Kent 5F3

Blencathra ⚜RAC
Kingsdown Hill, Kingsdown CT14 8EA
01304-373725
5 bedrs, 4 ☛/WC, 2 ➽; **TV tcf** P7
sB&B £17 dB&B £36 Breakfast only

KINGSTON UPON THAMES
Greater London 4C2

Chase Lodge *Highly Acclaimed* ⚜RAC
10 Park Road, Hampton Wick, Kingston-upon-Thames KT1 4AS 0181-9431862 Fax 0181-9431863

9 bedrs, 7 ➽/WC, 1 ➽; ✗ P20
sB&B £48 Breakfast only; cc Ac Amex Vi

LENHAM Kent 5E3

The Harrow Inn *Acclaimed* ⚜RAC
Warren Street, Lenham ME17 2ED
01622-858727 Fax 01622-850026 ♿
15 bedrs, 15 ➽/WC; **TV tcf** P75
sB&B £45 dB&B £58 Breakfast only; cc Ac Amex Vi

LITTLEHAMPTON West Sussex 4C4

Colbern *Acclaimed* ⚜RAC
South Terrace, Sea Front, Littlehampton BN17 5LQ 01903-714270 Fax 01903-730955
9 bedrs, 9 ☛/WC, 1 ➽; **TV tcf** ✂
sB&B £22.50-£24 dB&B £45-£48; HB weekly £175; D £10 [10%V]; cc Ac Amex DC Vi

(Inn) Dolphin ⚜RAC
34 High Street, Littlehampton BN17 5ED
01903-715789

Regency ⚜RAC
85 South Terrace, Littlehampton BN17 5LJ
01903-717707
8 bedrs, 1 ➽/WC; **TV tcf**

sB&B £21-£22 dB&B £38-£40 Breakfast only;
cc Ac Amex DC Vi JCB

(Inn) The Lamb Inn ⚜RAC
The Square, Angmering, Littlehampton BN16 4EQ 01903-784499 Fax 01903-784499
5 bedrs, 2 ➽; **TV tcf** ✗ P30
sB&B £16-£18 dB&B £30 D £4.50 [10%V]

LUDGERSHALL Buckinghamshire 4B2

The Briars High Street, Ludgershall HP18 9PF 01844-237721

MAIDSTONE Kent 5E3

Court Farm Village High Street, Aylesford, Maidstone ME20 7AZ 01622-717293
3 bedrs, 1 ➽; **TV tcf** P6
sB&B £14 Breakfast only

Court Lodge Court Lodge Farm, The Street, Teston, Maidstone ME18 5AQ 01622-812570 Fax 01622-814200
3 bedrs, 2 ☛/WC;
Child restrictions under 10
sB&B £34 Breakfast only; cc Vi

MALDON Essex 5E2

(Inn) Swan ⚜RAC
73 High Street, Maldon CM9 7EP
01621-853170 Fax 01621-854490
6 bedrs, 4 ➽/WC, 4 ☛/WC, 1 ➽;
TV tcf ✂ P25
sB&B £35 dB&B £48; HB weekly £300; D £6.50; cc Ac Amex DC Vi

MARGATE Kent 5F2

Beachcomber ⚜RAC
3-4 Royal Esplanade, Westbrook, Margate CT9 5DL 01843-221616
15 bedrs, 3 ➽; **TV tcf**
sB&B £16.50-£17.50 dB&B £33-£35; HB weekly £152-£155; D £9.50

MERSHAM Kent 5E3

(Inn) Farriers Arms ⚜RAC
Nr Ashford, Mersham TN25 6NN 01720-444
3 bedrs, 1 ➽; **TV tcf** ✗ P22
sB&B £20 dB&B £40 Breakfast only [10%V];
cc Ac Vi

MILTON KEYNES Buckinghamshire 4C1

(Inn) The Swan Inn RAC
36 Watling Street, Fenny Stratford MK2 2BL
01908-370100 Fax 01908-270096
10 bedrs, 3 🛁; TV tcf P30
sB&B £27-£32 dB&B £45; HB weekly £210; D £4 [10%V]; cc Ac Vi

Balney Grounds Hanslope Road, Castlethorpe, Milton Keynes MK19 7HD 01908-510208

Chantry Farm Pindon End, Hanslope, Milton Keynes MK19 7HL 01908-510269

Fegans View 119 High Street, Stony Stratford, Milton Keynes MK11 1AT 01908-562128

Giffard House 10 Broadway Avenue, Giffard Park, Milton Keynes MK13 0QP 01908-311820

Grange Barn Haversham, Milton Keynes MK19 7DX 01908-313613

Green Farm Little Horwood, Milton Keynes MK17 0PB 01296-712421

Haversham Grange Haversham, Milton Keynes MK19 7DX 01908-312389 Fax 01908-221554

A most attractive, 14th century grange, set in 10 acres of gardens and fields in an unspoilt village near Milton Keynes.
3 bedrs, 2 🛁/WC, 1 🚿/WC; TV tcf P6
Child restrictions under 5
sB&B £20 Breakfast only

Leamington Farm Castlethorpe, Milton Keynes MK19 7ET 01908-510235

Michelville House Newton Road, Bletchley, Milton Keynes MK3 5BS 01908-371578

Milford Leys Farm Castlethorpe, Milton Keynes MK19 7HH 01908-510153
3 bedrs, 3 🛁; 🐕 P5
sB&B £15 Breakfast only

Serendib 15 Market Place, Woburn, Milton Keynes MK17 9PZ 01525-290464

Woad Farm Tathall End, Hanslope, Milton Keynes MK19 7NE 01908-510985

11 George Street Woburn, Milton Keynes MK17 9PX 01525-290405

45 High Street Great Linford, Milton Keynes MK14 5AX 01908-666139

MINSTER Kent 5F3

Durlock Lodge RAC
Durlock, Minster CT12 4HD 01843-821219
3 bedrs, 3 🛁/WC; P4
Breakfast only

NEWHAVEN East Sussex 5D4

Old Volunteer RAC
1 South Road, Newhaven BN9 9QL
01273-515204
17 bedrs, 4 🛁/WC, 3 🚿/WC, 3 🛁; TV tcf 🐕 P3
sB&B £18-£19 dB&B £32-£46 Breakfast only; cc Ac Amex Vi

NEWPORT PAGNELL Buckinghamshire 4C1

Thurston RAC
90 High Street, Newport Pagnell MK16 8EH
01908-611377
8 bedrs, 8 🛁/WC; P12
Breakfast only

PRINCES RISBOROUGH Buckinghamshire 4C2

(Inn) George & Dragon RAC
74 High Street, Princes Risborough HP17 0AX
01844-343087 Fax 01844-343087 ♿
8 bedrs, 1 🛁/WC, 2 🛁; TV tcf P40
sB&B £25 dB&B £38 Breakfast only [10%V]; cc Ac Vi

RAMSGATE Kent 5F3

Goodwin View RAC
19 Wellington Crescent, Ramsgate CT11 8JD
01843-591419
13 bedrs, 4 🛁/WC, 3 🛁; TV tcf
sB&B £18-£21 dB&B £32-£35 D £9.50; cc Ac Amex DC Vi

St Hilary
21 Crescent Road, Ramsgate CT11 9QU
01843-591427
7 bedrs, 1 ⇥; tcf ✂
Child restrictions
sB&B £16-£18 dB&B £28-£32; cc Ac Amex Vi

REDHILL Surrey 5D3

Ashleigh House *Acclaimed*
39 Redstone Hill, Redhill RH1 4BG
01737-764763 Fax 01737-780308

A family-run Edwardian hotel, situated on A25 about 600 yards from Redhill station.
8 bedrs, 1 ⇥/WC, 5 ⌗/WC, 1 ⇥; TV tcf P9
sB&B £25-£40 dB&B £45-£50 Breakfast only;
cc Ac Vi

REIGATE Surrey 5D3

Cranleigh *Highly Acclaimed*
41 West Street, Reigate RH2 9BL
01737-223417 Fax 01737-223734
10 bedrs, 8 ⇥/WC, 2 ⇥; TV tcf P6
sB&B £52 dB&B £52 D £15 [10%V];
cc Ac Amex DC Vi JCB

RICKMANSWORTH Hertfordshire 4C4

Croxley Green 30 Hazelwood Road,
Rickmansworth WD3 3EB 01923-226666
3 bedrs, 2 ⇥; TV tcf ✗ P2
sB&B £15 Breakfast only

The Millwards 30 Hazelwood Road, Croxley
Green, Rickmansworth WD3 3EB
01923-233751
3 bedrs, 2 ⇥; ✗ P2
sB&B £17 Breakfast only

ROTTINGDEAN East Sussex 5D4

Braemar House
Steyning Road, Rottingdean BN2 7GA
01273-304263

15 bedrs, 3 ⇥; ✗
sB&B £15 dB&B £30 Breakfast only [5%V]

RUSTINGTON West Sussex 4C4

Kenmore *Highly Acclaimed*
Claigmar Road, Rustington BN16 2NL
01903-784634
7 bedrs, 1 ⇥/WC, 6 ⌗/WC, 1 ⇥; TV tcf ✗
✂ P7
sB&B £16.50-£25 dB&B £45-£50 [10%V];
cc Ac Amex Vi

RYE East Sussex 5E3

Aviemore
28 Fishmarket Road, Rye TN31 7LP
01797-223052
A charming Tudor style house, c. 1870.
8 bedrs, 4 ⌗/WC, 2 ⇥;
sB&B £20-£28 dB&B £30 D £8 [10%V]; cc Ac
Amex DC Vi

Cliff Farm
Iden Lock, Rye TN31 7QE 01797-280331
3 bedrs, 1 ⇥;
Breakfast only

Holloway House *Highly Acclaimed*
High Street, Rye TN31 7JF 01797-224748
6 bedrs, 6 ⇥/WC, 1 ⇥; TV tcf
sB&B £39 dB&B £50-£70 Breakfast only;
cc Ac Vi

Jeakes House *Highly Acclaimed* RAC
Mermaid Street, Rye TN31 7ET 01797-222828
Fax 01797-222623
12 bedrs, 10 ➡/WC, 2 ➡; ✖
cc Ac Amex Vi

(Inn) Old Borough Arms RAC
The Strand, Rye TN31 7DB 01797-222128 Fax
01797-222128
*18th century weatherboarded property, Grade II
listed. Situated at the foot of the famous Mermaid
Street adjacent to riverside walks and local shops.*
9 bedrs, 9 ➡/WC; TV tcf ✖ P2
sB&B £20-£25 dB&B £40-£60 Breakfast only
[5%V]; cc Ac Vi

Old Vicarage *Highly Acclaimed* RAC
15 East Street, Rye TN31 7JY
01797-225131 Fax 01797-225131

*Queen Anne town house hotel in centre of
Rye with panoramic views over Romney Marsh.*
4 bedrs, 4 ➡/WC; TV tcf ✖ ✂
Breakfast only; cc Ac Amex DC Vi JCB

SEAFORD East Sussex

Abbot's Motor Lodge RAC
Marine Parade, Seaford BN25 2RB
01323-891055 Fax 01323-892266
63 bedrs, 63 ➡/WC; ✖ P63
Breakfast only; cc Ac Amex DC Vi

SEDLESCOMBE East Sussex 5E3

Platnix Farm Oast Harts Green,
Sedlescombe, Nr Battle TN33 0RT 01870-214

*A delightful oast house with heavily beamed
interior, on a working 100 acre sheep farm.*
3 bedrs, 3 ➡;
Breakfast only

SEVENOAKS Kent 5D3

Moorings *Acclaimed* RAC
**97 Hitchen Hatch Lane, Sevenoaks TN13
3BE 01732-452589 Fax 01732-456462** ♿
13 bedrs, 10 ➡/WC, 1 ➡; TV tcf ✂ P22
sB&B £32 dB&B £44; HB weekly £260; D £12
[10%V]; cc Ac Amex Vi

SHEERNESS Kent 5E2

(Inn) Victoriana RAC
103-109 Alma Road, Sheerness ME12 2PD
01795-665555 Fax 01795-580633
20 bedrs, 9 ➡/WC, 3 ➡; TV tcf ✖ P8
sB&B £16 dB&B £32 D £8.50; cc Ac Amex Vi

SMALLFIELD Surrey 5D3

Chithurst Farm Chithurst Lane, Horne,
Smallfield RH6 9JU 01342-842487
3 bedrs, 1 ➡;
sB&B £14 Breakfast only

SOUTHEND-ON-SEA Essex 5E2

Argyle RAC
12 Cliff Town Parade, Southend-on-Sea SS1
1DP 01702-339483
11 bedrs, 3 ➡; TV tcf ✖
Child restrictions
sB&B £17-£18 dB&B £35

Ilfracombe House *Highly Acclaimed*
11-13 Wilson Road, Southend-on-Sea SS1
1HG 01702-351000 &
14 bedrs, 14 ➥/WC;
[10%V]

Mayflower RAC
6 Royal Terrace, Southend-on-Sea SS1 1DY
01702-340489
24 bedrs, 4 ➥/WC, 5 ➥;

Terrace RAC
8 Royal Terrace, Southend-on-Sea SS1 1DY
01702-348143
9 bedrs, 3 ➥/WC, 2 ➥; TV tcf ✗
sB&B £20 dB&B £30 [5%V]

ST ALBANS Herts   4C2

Ardmore House *Highly Acclaimed* RAC
54 Lemsford Road, St Albans AL1 3PR
01727-859313 Fax 01727-859313
24 bedrs, 3 ➥/WC, 20 ➥/WC, 1 ➥;
TV tcf ✗ P30
sB&B £47; cc Ac Amex Vi

Avalon RAC
260 London Road, St Albans AL1 1TJ
01727-856757 Fax 01727-856757
10 bedrs, 4 ➥/WC, 6 ➥/WC; TV tcf P14
sB&B £39-£49 dB&B £45 D £10.50 [10%V]; cc
Ac Vi

Melford RAC
**24 Woodstock Road North, St Albans AL1
4QQ 01727-53642 Fax 01727-53642**
11 bedrs, 1 ➥/WC, 4 ➥/WC, 2 ➥; ✗ P12
sB&B £24-£38 dB&B £38-£45 Breakfast only

STAINES Surrey   4C2

(Inn) Swan *Acclaimed* RAC
The Hythe, Staines TW18 3JB 01784-452494
Fax 01784-461593
11 bedrs, 5 ➥/WC, 2 ➥; ⅙
sB&B £38 dB&B £54.50 [10%V];
cc Ac Amex DC Vi

Location Maps
Hotel locations are shown on the maps at
the back of the guide. All towns and
villages containing an hotel listed in the
guide are shown in black.

STEYNING West Sussex   4C4

Nash Country *Acclaimed* RAC
Horsham Road, Steyning BN4 3AA
01903-814988

*Edwardian house with parts dating from 16th
century and some modern additions.
Beautifully situated overlooking South Downs,
quiet with lovely views.*
4 bedrs, 1 ➥/WC, 3 ➥; ✗ P50
sB&B £30 dB&B £48; HB weekly £36; [5%V]

Springwells *Highly Acclaimed* RAC
High Street, Steyning BN4 3GG
01903-812446
10 bedrs, 8 ➥/WC, 1 ➥;
Breakfast only

STONY STRATFORD Buckinghamshire   4C1

(Inn) Bull RAC
64 High Street, Stony Stratford MK11 1AQ
01908-567104 Fax 01908-563765
14 bedrs, 11 ➥/WC, 3 ➥/WC; TV tcf ✗ P24
sB&B £29 dB&B £39 Breakfast only [10%V];
cc Ac Amex DC Vi

SURBITON Greater London   4C3

Amber Lodge RAC
54 The Avenue, Surbiton KT5 8JL
0181-399-3058 Fax 0181-399-7639
10 bedrs, 10 ➥/WC;
Breakfast only; cc Ac Vi

Pembroke Lodge RAC
35 Cranes Park, Surbiton KT5 8AB
0181-390-0731
10 bedrs, 2 ➥/WC, 2 ➥; P10
sB&B £25.85 dB&B £60
Breakfast only [10%V]

SUTTON Greater London	5D3

Ashling Tara *Acclaimed*   RAC
50 Rosehill, Sutton SM1 3EU 0181-641-6142
Fax 0181-644-7872
6 bedrs, 6 ➡/WC, 3 ➡; TV tcf ⅍
Child restrictions
sB&B £35-£50 dB&B £45-£50; HB weekly
£300-£350; D £10.50 [10%V]; cc Ac Amex Vi

Athelstone Lodge 25 Trusthorpe Rd, Sutton
LN12 2LR 01507-441521

Dene   RAC
39 Cheam Road, Sutton SM1 2AT
0181-6423170 Fax 0181-6423170   ♿
28 bedrs, 8 ➡/WC, 4 ☞/WC, 4 ➡;
TV tcf ✖ P18
sB&B £21-£40 dB&B £40 [5%V]

Eaton Court   RAC
49 Eaton Road, Sutton SM2 5ED
0181-643-6766
21 bedrs, 9 ➡/WC, 2 ➡; TV tcf ✖ P10
[10%V]; cc Ac Amex Vi

Thatched House *Acclaimed*   RAC
135 Cheam Road, Sutton SM1 2BN
0181-6423131 Fax 0181-7700684
28 bedrs, 19 ➡/WC, 4 ➡; P20
[5%V]; cc Ac Vi

TENTERDEN Kent	5E3

★★(Inn) White Lion   RAC
High Street, Tenterden TN30 6BD
01580-765077 Fax 01580-764157
15 bedrs, 15 ➡/WC; ✖ P35
[10%V]; cc Ac Amex DC Vi

THAXTED Essex	5D1

★★★(Inn) Swan Inn   RAC
Bull Ring, Watling Street, Thaxted CM6 2PL
01371-830321 Fax 01371-831186
20 bedrs, 20 ➡/WC; ✖ P30
[5%V]; cc Ac Amex DC Vi

TONBRIDGE Kent	5D3

Chimneys Motor Inn   RAC
Pembury Road, Tonbridge TN11 ONA
01732-773111   ♿
38 bedrs, 38 ➡/WC; TV tcf ⅍ P120
sB&B £36-£41 dB&B £46 D £10.75; cc Ac Vi

TRING Hertfordshire	4C2

**Royal Station Road, Tring HP23 5QR
01442-827616 Fax 01442-890383**
20 bedrs, 18 ➡/WC, 1 ➡; TV tcf ✖ P40
sB&B £18; HB weekly £200-£300; D £5-£20;
cc Ac Amex DC Vi

TUNBRIDGE WELLS Kent	5B3

The Old Parsonage *Highly Acclaimed* RAC
Church Lane, Frant, Tunbridge Wells TN3
9DX 01892-750773
3 bedrs, 2 ➡/WC, 1 ☞/WC; TV tcf ✖ ⅍ P12
sB&B £32-£39 dB&B £52-£59 [10%V]

UCKFIELD East Sussex	5D3

Hooke Hall *Highly Acclaimed*   RAC
250 High Street, Uckfield TN22 1EN
01825-761578 Fax 01825-768025
9 bedrs, 8 ➡/WC; TV tcf P8
Child restrictions
sB&B £37.50-£46.50 dB&B £70 D £17;
cc Ac Amex Vi

WATFORD Hertfordshire	4C2

YMCA Charter House, Charter Place, Watford
WD1 2RT 01923-233034 Fax 01923-226299
177 bedrs, 177 ☞/WC, 91 ➡;
sB&B £20; HB weekly £97-£120; D £4; cc Ac
Vi

WEMBLEY Greater London	4C2

Adelphi *Acclaimed*   RAC
4 Forty Lane, Wembley HA9 9EB
0181-9045629 Fax 0181-9085314   ♿
11 bedrs, 7 ☞/WC, 4 ➡; TV tcf P10
sB&B £22-£35 dB&B £35-£45; HB weekly
£160-£175; [10%V]; cc Ac Amex Vi

Arena *Acclaimed*   RAC
6 Forty Lane, Wembley HA9 9EB
0181-9040019 Fax 0181-9082007   ♿
10 bedrs, 7 ➡/WC, 2 ➡; TV tcf P15
sB&B £25-£28 dB&B £40-£45; HB weekly
£150-£170; cc Ac Amex Vi

Brookside   RAC
32 Brook Avenue, Wembley HA9 8PH
0181-9040252 Fax 0181-3850800   ♿
13 bedrs, 7 ☞/WC; P6
sB&B £20-£25 dB&B £35 Breakfast only [5%V]

Elm Elm Rd, Wembley HA9 7JA
0181-9021764 Fax 0181-9038365

Wembley Park *Acclaimed* ♦RAC
8 Forty Lane, Wembley HA9 9EB
0181-9046329 Fax 0181-3850472 &
7 bedrs, 5 ♠/WC, 2 ➤; TV tcf ✗ P15
sB&B £25-£32 dB&B £38-£45 Breakfast only
[10%V]; cc Ac Amex DC Vi

WEST MALLING Kent 5D3

Scott House *Acclaimed* ♦RAC
37 High Street, West Malling ME19 6QH
01732-841380 Fax 01732-870025
3 bedrs, 3 ♠/WC; TV tcf
Child restrictions
sB&B £39 dB&B £49; cc Ac Vi JCB

WESTCLIFF-ON-SEA Essex 5E2

Cobham Lodge *Acclaimed* ♦RAC
2 Cobham Road, Westcliff-on-Sea SS0 8EA
01702-346438
29 bedrs, 10 ➤/WC, 13 ♠/WC, 3 ➤; TV tcf
sB&B £27.50-£29.50 dB&B £38-£40; HB
weekly £150-£175; D £8.95; cc Ac Vi

Rose House ♦RAC
21 Manor Road, Westcliff-on-Sea SS0 7SR
01702-341959

WOKING Surrey 4C3

(Inn) Star ♦RAC
Wyck Hill, Hook Heath, Woking GU22 OEU
01483-760526
3 bedrs, 2 ➤; TV tcf
sB&B £25 dB&B £45 [5%V]; cc Ac Amex Vi

WOMENSWOLD Kent 5F3

Woodpeckers Country ♦RAC
Womenswold CT4 6HB 01227-831319 Fax
01227-831319 &
11 bedrs, 11 ➤/WC, 11 ♠/WC, 2 ➤; TV tcf
✗ ⅀ P42
sB&B £26 dB&B £52; HB weekly £210; D
£14.50 [10%V]; cc Ac Vi

WORTHING West Sussex 4C4

★★★Berkeley ♦RAC
86-95 Marine Parade, Worthing BN11 3QD
01903-820000

Bonchurch House *Acclaimed* RAC
1 Winchester Road, Worthing BN11 4DJ
01903-202492
6 bedrs, 2 ⇥/WC, 3 ⬀/WC; TV tcf P4
Child restrictions
sB&B £18-£20 dB&B £36-£40; HB weekly
£180-£200; [5%V]

★★★**Chatsworth** RAC
Steyne, Worthing BN11 3DU 01903-236103
Fax 01903-823726 ⟁
107 bedrs, 107 ⇥/WC; ✖ P150
sB&B £49.90-£59.90 dB&B £77 D £14.95
[10%V]; cc Ac Amex DC Vi

Delmar *Acclaimed* RAC
1-2 New Parade, Worthing BN11 2BQ
01903-211834 Fax 01903-850249 ⟁
14 bedrs, 2 ⇥/WC, 11 ⬀/WC; TV tcf ✖ ✂ P5

sB&B £26 dB&B £48; HB weekly £258; D £15
[10%V]; cc Ac Amex DC Vi JCB

Moorings *Highly Acclaimed* RAC
4 Selden Road, Worthing BN11 2L
01903-208882
8 bedrs, 2 ⇥/WC, 6 ⬀/WC; P3
sB&B £18.50-£22 dB&B £33-£42 D £10.50
[10%V]; cc Ac Amex Vi

Osborne RAC
175 Brighton Road, Worthing BN11 2EX
01903-235771
7 bedrs, 2 ⇥/WC, 2 ⇥; TV tcf ✖
Child restrictions
sB&B £12-£15.50 dB&B £24-£31 Breakfast
only; cc Ac Amex DC Vi

Penshurst

South of England

Hants • Isle of Wight • Dorset • Wilts • Oxfordshire • Berks

Although few miles separate them, no two counties of southern England look alike. Dorset appeals to those who appreciate Thomas Hardy but prefer to avoid his 'madding crowds'. Off that coast, the Isle of Wight could be Britain in miniature. Neolithic man clearly opted for the plains of Wiltshire as the more sophisticated might perhaps be drawn to Oxford with its vital combination of old buildings and young blood. Near by, the picturesque Cotswolds rival the beech-covered Chilterns – both totally different. The choice is yours. Each county is a delight.

Beaulieu

A SELECTION OF ATTRACTIONS:

Unless otherwise stated, all can be visited between April and October – some longer. Telephone for days/times of opening.

Abbotsbury Swannery, Dorset: *Curious Chesil Bank shelters swans in 600-year-old managed colony.* Tel: 01305-871852.

Avebury Museum, Wilts: *Easy-to-understand explanation of surrounding Stonehenge, Avebury Stone Circle, Silbury Hill & West Kennet Long Barrow.* Tel: 01672-539250.

Beaulieu, Buckler's Hard, Hants: *Ancestral home of Montagu family, park and renowned Motor Museum, events.* Tel: 01590-612123.

Blenheim Palace, Woodstock, Oxon: *Important Vanbrugh building with Churchill connections. Family activities, events.* Tel: 01993-811325.

The Bournemouth Bears, ExpoCentre, Dorset: *Teddy-bear personalities, limited edition bears, old and new.* Tel: 01202-293544.

Broadlands, Romsey, Hants: *Home of the Mountbatten family with romantic associations. Closes end Sep.* Tel: 01794-516878.

Brownsea Island, via Poole Harbour, Dorset. *A 500-acre island wildlife reserve. Also Naturalists Trust. NT.* Tel: 01202-707744.

Chiltern Open Air Museum, Chalfont St. Giles, Bucks: *Explore an Iron Age House, an Edwardian loo or a Prefab.* Tel: 01494-872163.

Cholderton Rare Breeds Farm Park, nr. Andover, Hants: *Touch/feed rare-breed farm animals.* Tel: 0198064-438.

Claydon House, nr. Buckingham, Bucks: *Associated with Florence Nightingale – memorabilia. NT.* Tel: 01296-730349/730693.

Compton Acres, nr. Poole, Dorset: *Renowned separate themed gardens including one authentic Japanese* Tel: 01202-700778.

D-Day Museum, Portsmouth, Hants: *Home of 272ft 'Overlord Embroidery' of D-Day. Audio visual show.* Tel: 01705-827261

Forde Abbey & Gardens, nr. Chard, Dorset: *Outstanding ceilings and Mortlake tapestries designed by Raphael.* Tel: 01460-20231.

Greys Court, Henley-on-Thames, Oxon: *17th-c house amidst 14th-c courtyard. Maze, ice house, lovely gardens. Closes end Sep. NT.* Tel: 01491-628529.

Lacock Abbey, Wilts: *Unusual 13th-c abbey home of early photographer Fox-Talbot. Museum by gate.* Tel: 01249-730227.

Littlecote House, nr. Hungerford, Berks: *Fairy Glen, crafts, events round stately home. Closes early Oct.* Tel: 01488 684000.

Longleat House, nr. Warminster, Wilts: *Safari Park surrounds magnificent, haunted Elizabethan house. Many activities/attractions/events in park.* Tel: 01985-844885.

Montisfont Abbey, nr. Romsey, Hants: *House with garden of old fashioned roses by the River Test.* Tel: 01794-340757/341220.

Nuffield Place, Nettlebed, Oxon: *Home of founder of Morris Minor cars in Thameside village. Restricted opening.* Tel: 01491-641224.

Osbourne House, East Cowes, I o W: *Italianate holiday home of Queen Victoria.* Tel: 01983-200022.

Parnham House, nr. Beaminster, Dorset; *Golden Ham Hill stone home of individual furniture designer John Makepeace. House and workshop.* Tel: 01308-862204.

Poole Pottery, Dorset: *Quayside factory shop and new pretty restaurant. Have a go and throw a pot.* Tel: 01202-666200.

The Rapids, Romsey, Hants: *Flume ride, storm shower, under-water bubble seats. Latest water high tech.* Tel: 01794-830333.

Royal Naval Museum, Portsmouth: *Large dockside complex housing historic ships, Mary Rose, etc.* Tel: 01705-733060

Savill Garden, Windsor Great Park, Berks: *35 acres of extensive garden. Plant Centre.* Tel: 01753-860222.

Sherborne Castle, Dorset: *Fully furnished historic home built by Sir Walter Raleigh. Closes end Sep.* Tel: 01935-813182.

Stratfield Saye, nr. Basingstoke, Hants: *Historic home of Dukes of Wellington. Open 1 May-end Sep.* Tel: 01256-882882.

Stourhead, Stourton, Wilts: *Magnificent landscaped estate & finely furnished 18th-c house. NT.* Tel:01747-840348.

The Tank Museum, Bovington Camp, Dorset: *Over 260 different tanks, sometimes mobilised.* Tel: 01929-403329.

University of Oxford Botanic Gardens: *Oldest in Britain, set peacefully on banks of Cherwell, 8,000 species.* Tel: 01865-276920.

Waddesdon Manor, Bucks: *Rothschild collection of Sevres, Meissen, furnishings, in 19th-c chateau-style house.* Tel: 01296-651211.

Waterperry Gardens, nr. Wheatley, Oxon: *A garden lovers delight. Plant centre too.* Tel: 01844-339226/339254.

Wellington Country Park, Heckfield, Hants: *Three miles from Stratfield Saye. All family activities.* Tel: 01734-326444.

Wilton House, nr. Salisbury, Wilts: *Impressive paintings, furniture and architecture. Adventure playground.* Tel: 01722-743115.

Windsor Castle, Berks: *Closed when in Royal use. State Apartments contain world treasures of art/furniture. Famous Queen Mary's Doll's House. Changing of Guard:* Tel: 01753-831118.

Blenheim Palace

SOME ANNUAL EVENTS:

Blenheim International Horse Trials, Woodstock, Oxon: *Lavish annual equestrian occasion. mid-Sep.* Tel: 01993-813335.

Bournemouth International Festival, Hants: *Concerts, dance, drama. Various venues. 13-28 May.* Tel: 01202-297327.

Cowes Week, Isle of Wight: *Yachting festival and racing, all classes. 29 Jul-5 Aug.* Tel: 01983-293303.

Henley Royal Regatta, Henley-on-Thames, Oxon: *International rowing and social event. 28 Jun-2 Jul.* Tel: 01491-572153/4.

Lyme Regis Lifeboat Week, Dorset: *Red Arrows & RAF Falcons display, air-sea rescue, sports, disco, fireworks. 22-30 Jul.* Tel: 01297-443724.

Newbury Spring Festival, Berks: *Music including jazz and visual arts. 6-20 May.* Tel: 01635-32421.

Open Air Theatre, Hazelbury Manor Gardens, Box, Wilts: *Will be Shakespeare. 10-5 Jul.* Tel: 01249-714317.

Royal Ascot, Ascot Racecourse, Berks: *Delightful fashion event attended by Royal Family and top racehorses. 20-23 Jun.* Tel: 01344-22211

Royal Ballet [Birmingham], Mayflower Theatre, Southampton, Hants: *5-10 Jun.* Tel: 01703-229771.

Royal Windsor Horse Show, Home Park, Berks: *Major showjumping event. 10 -14 May.* Tel: 01753-860633.

St. George's Spring Festival, Salisbury, Wilts: *Variety of events at various venues. 16-23 Apr.* Tel: 01722-334956.

The Sarcen Trail, Avebury to Stonehenge across Salisbury Plain: *Sponsored walk , wonderful country. 7 May. Pre-register.* Tel: 01380-725670.

Tolpuddle Rally, Dorset: *Marks birthplace of Trade Union movement. Parades, speeches. 16 Jul.* Tel: 01202-294333.

Welsh National Opera, Mayflower Theatre, Southampton, Hants: *19-24 Jun.* Tel: 01703-229771.

Wimborne Folk Festival, Wimborne Minster, Dorset: *9-11 Jun.* Tel: 01202-740792.

ALDERSHOT Hampshire   4C3

(Inn) George   RAC
Wellington Street, Aldershot GU11 1DX
01252-330800
9 bedrs, 1 ⇥/WC;
sB&B £18 dB&B £36 [5%V]; cc Ac Amex Vi

Potters International   RAC
Leet Road, Aldershot GTU11 2ET
01252-344000
102 bedrs, 102 ⇥/WC;
Awaiting inspection

ASCOT Berkshire   4C2

Ennis Lodge *Acclaimed*   RAC
Winkfield Road, Ascot SL5 7EX 01344-21009

★★Highclere   RAC
Kings Road, Sunninghill, Ascot SL5 9AD
01344-25220 Fax 01344-872528; cc Ac Amex Vi

Tanglewood Birch Lane, Off Longhill Road,
Chavey Down, Ascot SL5 8RF 01344-882528
3 bedrs, 2 ⇥/WC, 2 ⋒/WC, 1 ⇥; tcf P6
sB&B £17.50 D £10

54 King Edwards Road Ascot SL5 8NY
01344-882313

BAMPTON Oxfordshire   4B2

The Farmhouse *Highly Acclaimed*   RAC
University Farm, Lew, Bampton OX18 2AU
01993-850297 Fax 01993-850965   ⅃
6 bedrs, 3 ⇥/WC, 3 ⋒/WC; TV tcf ✂ P30
Child restrictions
sB&B £39 dB&B £50 D £14.50; cc Ac Vi

BANBURY Oxfordshire   4B1

Easington House *Highly Acclaimed*   RAC
50 Oxford Road, Banbury OX16 9AN
01295-270181 Fax 01295-269527
12 bedrs, 12 ⇥/WC, 1 ⇥; TV tcf ✄ P27
sB&B £40-£45 dB&B £59.70; cc Ac Amex DC Vi

La Madonette *Highly Acclaimed*   RAC
North Newington, Banbury OX15 6AA
01295-730212 Fax 01295-730363
5 bedrs, 2 ⇥/WC, 3 ⋒/WC; TV tcf ✄
sB&B £32 dB&B £42; cc Ac Vi

New House Farm Brailes, Banbury OX15
5BD 0160875-239
4 bedrs, 1 ⇥; ⋔
sB&B £14

BASINGSTOKE Hampshire   4B3

Lamb High Street, Hartley Wintney,
Basingstoke RG27 8NW 01252-842006   ⅃
15 bedrs, 4 ⋒/WC, 5 ⇥; ✄ P50
sB&B £25 Breakfast only

BOURNEMOUTH Dorset   3F3

Amitie   RAC
1247 Christchurch Road, Bournemouth BH7
6BP 01202-427255
8 bedrs, 3 ⇥/WC, 2 ⋒/WC, 2 ⇥; TV tcf P8
sB&B £12-£16 dB&B £26-£32 Breakfast only
[10%V]

Avonwood   RAC
20 Owls Road, Boscombe, Bournemouth BH5
1AF 01202-394704

Boltons *Highly Acclaimed*   RAC
**9 Durley Chine Road South, Westcliff,
Bournemouth BH2 5JT 01202-751517 Fax
01202-751629**   ⅃

*Victorian, country house style hotel, set in its
own grounds on the West Cliff. Now elegantly
refurbished with every modern comfort.*

12 bedrs, 8 ⇥/WC, 4 ❧/WC; TV tcf P12
Child restrictions
sB&B £24-£26 dB&B £48-£52; HB weekly
£155-£190; cc Ac Vi

Borodale *Acclaimed*   RAC
10 St Johns Road, Boscombe, Bournemouth
BH5 1EL 01202-395285
15 bedrs, 3 ⇥/WC, 4 ❧/WC, 1 ⇥; TV tcf P12
sB&B £13-£15 dB&B £26-£30; HB weekly
£120-£140; [10%V]; cc Ac Vi

Carisbrook *Acclaimed*   RAC
42 Tregonwell Road, Bournemouth BH2 5NT
01202-290432 Fax 01202-310499

Cherry View *Acclaimed*   RAC
66 Alum Chine Road, Bournemouth BH4 8DZ
01202-760910
11 bedrs, 1 ⇥/WC, 10 ❧/WC; TV tcf ⚹ P12
Child restrictions
sB&B £22.50-£33 dB&B £36-£46; HB weekly
£150-£180; D £7 [10%V]; cc Ac Amex DC Vi

Chinebeach   RAC
14 Studland Road, Alum Chine, Bournemouth
BH4 8JA 01202-767015

Cransley *Acclaimed*   RAC
11 Knyveton Road, East Cliff, Bournemouth
BH1 3QG 01202-290067
12 bedrs, 6 ⇥/WC, 6 ❧/WC; TV tcf P10
sB&B £15-£20 dB&B £32-£40; HB weekly
£135-£175; [10%V]

Croham Hurst *Acclaimed*   RAC
9 Durley Road, West Cliff, Bournemouth BH2
5JH 01202-552353

Dene Court *Acclaimed*   RAC
19 Boscombe Spa Road, Bournemouth BH5
1AR 01202-394874
18 bedrs, 17 ⇥/WC, 1 ⇥; P12
Breakfast only

Dorset Westbury   RAC
62 Lansdowne Road North, Bournemouth
BH1 1RS 01202-551811 ; cc Ac Vi

★★Durley Chine   RAC
Chine Crescent, Westcliff, Bournemouth BH2
5LR 01202-551926 Fax 01202-310671
23 bedrs, 15 ⇥/WC, 8 ❧/WC; TV tcf ✕ ⚹ P50
sB&B £25-£40 dB&B £50-£80; HB weekly
£165-£239; D £15; cc Ac Amex DC Vi

Durley Court   RAC
5 Durley Road, West Cliff, Bournemouth BH2
5JR 01202-556857
17 bedrs, 5 ⇥/WC, 7 ❧/WC, 1 ⇥; TV tcf P16
sB&B £16-£24 dB&B £32-£48 [10%V]

East Cliff Cottage *Acclaimed*   RAC
57 Grove Road, Bournemouth BH1 3AT
01202-552788 Fax 01202-556400
70 bedrs, 70 ⇥/WC; ✕ P6
sB&B £16-£20 dB&B £36-£45; HB weekly
£118-£154; D £7.95 [10%V]; cc Ac Amex Vi

Gervis Court   RAC
38 Gervis Road, Bournemouth BH1 3DH
01202-556871 ; cc Ac Vi

Golden Sands *Acclaimed*   RAC
83 Alumhurst Road, Alum Chine,
Bournemouth BH4 8HR 01202-763832
10 bedrs, 5 ⇥/WC, 5 ❧/WC; TV tcf P10
Child restrictions
sB&B £18.50-£24 dB&B £37-£46; HB weekly
£147-£189;

Highclere *Acclaimed*   RAC
15 Burnaby Road, Alum Chine, Bournemouth
BH4 8JF 01202-761350
9 bedrs, 4 ⇥/WC, 5 ❧/WC; TV tcf ✕ P6
sB&B £18-£22 dB&B £40-£48; HB weekly
£140-£155; [5%V]; cc Ac Amex DC Vi JCB

Holmcroft *Acclaimed*   RAC
5 Earle Road, Alum Chine Westbourne,
Bournemouth BH4 8JQ 01202-761289
19 bedrs, 6 ⇥/WC, 13 ❧/WC; TV tcf ✕ ⚹
P12
Child restrictions
sB&B £14-£24 dB&B £36-£48; HB weekly
£167-£189; [10%V]; cc Ac Vi

Hotel Cavendish *Acclaimed*   RAC
20 Durley Chine Road, West Cliff,
Bournemouth BH2 5LF 01202-290489
17 bedrs, 7 ⇥/WC, 7 ❧/WC, 2 ⇥; TV tcf P14
sB&B £18-£24 dB&B £36-£48; HB weekly
£138-£180; [5%V]

Hotel Sorrento   RAC
16 Owls Road, Boscombe, Bournemouth BH5
1AG 01202-394019
19 bedrs, 6 ⇥/WC, 9 ❧/WC, 1 ⇥;
TV tcf ✕ P19
sB&B £16-£20 dB&B £32-£40; HB weekly
£130-£175; [10%V]; cc Ac Vi

Ingledene 🏠ʀᴀᴄ
20 Derby Road, Bournemouth BH1 3QA
01202-555433
8 bedrs, 2 ➡/WC, 4 🛏/WC, 1 ➡; TV tcf P3
Child restrictions
sB&B £14-£18 dB&B £28-£40; HB weekly
£102-£152; [10%V]

Linwood House *Acclaimed* 🏠ʀᴀᴄ
11 Wilfred Road, Boscombe, Bournemouth
BH5 1ND 01202-397818
10 bedrs, 1 ➡/WC, 7 🛏/WC, 1 ➡; TV tcf ✂ P7
Child restrictions
sB&B £16-£20 dB&B £32-£40; HB weekly
£129-£160

Mae Mar 🏠ʀᴀᴄ
91-95 West Hill Road, Bournemouth BH2 5PQ
01202-553167 Fax 01202-311919 ♿
39 bedrs, 6 ➡/WC, 27 🛏/WC, 2 ➡; TV tcf ✗
sB&B £16-£22.50 dB&B £32-£45; HB weekly
£130-£180; [10%V]; cc Ac Vi

Northover 🏠ʀᴀᴄ
10 Earle Road, Alum Chine, Bournemouth
BH4 8JQ 01202-767349
10 bedrs, 1 ➡/WC, 6 🛏/WC, 2 ➡;
TV tcf ✗ ✂ P10
sB&B £19-£25 dB&B £38-£50; HB weekly
£150-£200; [5%V]

Oak Hall 🏠ʀᴀᴄ
9 Wilfred Road, Boscombe, Bournemouth
BH5 1ND 01202-395062 ♿

13 bedrs, 9 🛏/WC, 1 ➡; TV tcf ✗ ✂ P80
HB weekly £179; D £7.50 [10%V]; cc Ac Amex Vi

Ocean Wave 🏠ʀᴀᴄ
30 St Catherines Road, Southbourne,
Bournemouth BH6 4AB 01202-423636

Ravenstone *Acclaimed* 🏠ʀᴀᴄ
36 Burnaby Road, Alum Chine Westbourne,

Bournemouth BH4 8JG 01202-761047
9 bedrs, 5 ➡/WC, 4 🛏/WC; TV tcf P5
sB&B £15-£22 dB&B £32-£44; HB weekly
£121.50-£170; D £5 [5%V]; cc Ac Vi

Sea View Court 🏠ʀᴀᴄ
14 Boscombe Spa Road, Bournemouth BH5
1AZ 01202-397197

Silver Trees Touring *Acclaimed* 🏠ʀᴄ
57 Wimborne Road, Bournemouth BH3 7AL
01202-556040 Fax 01202-556040
5 bedrs, 5 🛏/WC, 2 ➡; TV tcf P10
Child restrictions
sB&B £24 dB&B £38-£40 Breakfast only;
cc Ac Amex Vi

★Taurus Park 🏠ʀᴀᴄ
16 Knyveton Rd, Bournemouth BH1 3QN
01202-557374

Thanet *Acclaimed* 🏠ʀᴀᴄ
2, Drury Road, Alum Chine, Bournemouth
BH4 8HA 01202-761135
8 bedrs, 5 🛏/WC, 2 ➡; TV tcf P6
Child restrictions
sB&B £14.50-£18 dB&B £29-£36; HB weekly
£126.50-£148; [5%V]

Tudor Grange *Highly Acclaimed* 🏠ʀᴀᴄ
31 Gervis Road, Bournemouth BH1 3EE
01202-291472
12 bedrs, 9 ➡/WC, 2 🛏/WC, 1 ➡; TV tcf ✗
P11
sB&B £15-£20 dB&B £30-£60; HB weekly
£130-£240; [5%V]; cc Ac Vi

Valberg 🏠ʀᴀᴄ
1a Wollenstonecraft Road, Boscombe,
Bournemouth BH5 1JQ 01202-394644
10 bedrs, 10 🛏/WC; TV tcf ✂ P7
Child restrictions
dB&B £30-£40; HB weekly £139-£163;

Washington 🏠ʀᴀᴄ
3 Durley Road, West Cliff, Bournemouth BH2
5JQ 01202-557023

West Dene *Acclaimed* 🏠ʀᴀᴄ
117 Alumhurst Road, Alum Chine,
Bournemouth BH4 8HS 01202-764843
17 bedrs, 5 ➡/WC, 7 🛏/WC, 3 ➡; TV tcf P17
Child restrictions
sB&B £22-£29 dB&B £44-£50 D £15;
cc Ac Amex DC Vi

Wood Lodge *Acclaimed* 🚗 RAC
10 Manor Road, East Cliff, Bournemouth BH1
3EY 01202-290891

Wychcote *Acclaimed* 🚗 RAC
2 Somerville Road, Bournemouth BH2 5LH
01202-557898
12 bedrs, 2 ➡/WC, 9 ☏/WC, 1 ➡; TV tcf P15
Child restrictions
sB&B £20-£29.50 dB&B £40-£59; HB weekly
£140-£213; D £7 [10%V]; **cc** Ac Vi

BRACKNELL Berkshire 4C2

Deepfold Farm London Road, Bracknell
RG12 6QR 01344-428367 Fax 01344-428367

An old farm coach house standing in 5 acres
of grounds and gardens. Set back from the
main road.
7 bedrs, 1 ➡/WC, 3 ➡; TV tcf P12
sB&B £17.50 Breakfast only

Fern Cottage Chavey Down Road, Winkfield,
Bracknell RG12 6PB 01344-886923

Market Inn 🚗 RAC
Station Road, Bracknell RG12 1HY
01344-851734
5 bedrs, 5 ➡/WC; P28

BRADFORD-ON-AVON Wiltshire 3F1

Barge Inn 🚗 RAC
17 Frome Road, Bradford-on-Avon BA15 2EA
01225-863403

Burghope Manor *Highly Acclaimed* 🚗 RAC
Winsley, Bradford-on-Avon BA15 2LA
01225-723557 Fax 01225-723113
5 bedrs, 5 ➡/WC; ✈ P24
Child restrictions
sB&B £45-£55 dB&B £65 D £25;
cc Ac Amex Vi JCB

Widbrook Grange *Highly Acclaimed* 🚗 RAC
Trowbridge Road, Bradford-on-Avon BA15
1UH 01225-863173 Fax 01225-862890

BRIDPORT Dorset 3E3

Britmead House *Acclaimed* 🚗 RAC
West Bay Road, Bridport DT6 4EG
01308-422941 &
7 bedrs, 6 ➡/WC, 1 ☏/WC; TV tcf 🐾 ✈ P8
sB&B £24-£33 dB&B £38-£52; HB weekly
£189-£224; [10%V]; **cc** Ac Amex DC Vi

BROCKENHURST Hampshire 4B4

Cottage *Highly Acclaimed* 🚗 RAC
Sway Road, Brockenhurst SO4 7SH
01590-622296
7 bedrs, 4 ➡/WC, 2 ☏/WC; TV tcf ✈ P11
Child restrictions
sB&B £36-£40 dB&B £50-£64 Breakfast only;
cc Ac Vi

BURFORD Oxfordshire 4A2

Elm Farm House *Highly Acclaimed* 🚗 RAC
Meadow Lane, Fulbrook, Burford OX18 4BW
01993-823611 Fax 01993-823-937
7 bedrs, 2 ➡/WC, 2 ☏/WC, 1 ➡; TV tcf ✈ P12
Child restrictions
sB&B £29.50 dB&B £55; HB weekly £451.50;
cc Ac Amex Vi

CADNAM Hampshire 4B4

The Old Well RAC
Romsey Road, Copythorne, Cadnam SO4 2PE
01703-812321 Fax 01703-812700
6 bedrs, 3 ➡/WC, 2 ➡; TV tcf P10
sB&B £21 dB&B £32 D £10.50; cc Ac Vi

CHARMOUTH Dorset 3E3

★★Hensleigh RAC
Lower Spa Lane, Charmouth DT6 6LW
01297-560830
11 bedrs, 5 ➡/WC, 6 ☞/WC; TV tcf ✖ ✗ P30
Child restrictions
sB&B £21.50-£24 dB&B £43-£48; HB weekly
£210-£227; D £10.50; cc Ac Vi

Newlands House *Acclaimed* RAC
Stonebarrow Lane, Charmouth DT6 6RA
01297-560212
12 bedrs, 7 ➡/WC, 4 ☞/WC, 1 ➡; TV tcf ✖
✗ P15
Child restrictions
sB&B £22.50-£25 dB&B £45-£50; HB weekly
£228.70-£244.60

CHIPPENHAM Wiltshire 3F1

Knowle Hill Farm Beeks Lane, Marshfield,
Chippenham SN14 8AA 01225-891503

Old Brewery House Langley Burell,
Chippenham SN15 4LQ 01249-652694

Oxford RAC
32-36 Langley Road, Chippenham SN15 1BX
01249-652542
13 bedrs, 7 ➡/WC, 1 ➡; ✖ P9
Breakfast only

CHIPPING NORTON Oxfordshire 4B1

Southcombe Lodge RAC
Southcombe, Chipping Norton OX7 5JF
01608-643063
6 bedrs, 3 ➡/WC, 2 ➡; P10
Breakfast only [5%V]

CHOLDERTON Wiltshire 4A3

Fayre Deal Motel RAC
Parkhouse Corner, Cholderton SP4 0EG
01980-629542 Fax 01980-629542 ♿
35 bedrs; TV tcf ✖
sB&B £31.75 dB&B £31.75 D £10 [5%V]

CHRISTCHURCH Dorset 3F3

Pines 39 Mudeford, Christchurch BH23 3NQ
01202-475121

DEVIZES Wiltshire 4A3

Corners Cottage The Street, All Cannings,
Devizes SN10 3PA 01380-860626

The Woodbridge Inn *Acclaimed* RAC
North Newnton SN9 6JZ 01980-630266
Fax 01980-630266
3 bedrs, 1 ➡/WC, 1 ☞/WC, 1 ➡; TV tcf P60
sB&B £25-£30 dB&B £30-£35; HB weekly
£170-£270; D £9.25 [10%V];
cc Ac Amex DC Vi

DORCHESTER Dorset 3E3

Casterbridge *Highly Acclaimed* RAC
49, High East Street, Dorchester DT1 1HU
01305-264043 Fax 01305-260884 ♿
9 bedrs, 7 ➡/WC, 2 ☞/WC; TV tcf
sB&B £30-£36 dB&B £48-£60 Breakfast only
[10%V]; cc Ac Amex DC Vi

Lamperts Farmhouse Sydling St Nicholas,
Nr Dorchester, Dorchester DT2 8QR
01300-341790
*17th century, thatched, listed farmhouse
offering both traditional ensuite farmhouse or
self-catering accommodation.*
2 bedrs, 2 ➡/WC; ✖
sB&B £20; HB weekly £196; D £10-£12

DOWNTON Wiltshire   3F2

The Warren *Acclaimed*   RAC
**15 High Street, Salisbury, Downton SP5
3PG 01725-510263**

*A Grade II listed village house with parts
dating back to Elizabethan times set in a
large walled garden.*
6 bedrs, 2 ➥/WC, 2 ➥; ✕ ✉ P8
Child restrictions
sB&B £25-£30 dB&B £40-£42 Breakfast only
[5%V]

DROXFORD Hampshire   4B4

Coach House Motel Brockbridge, Droxford
SO3 1QT 01489-877812

EMSWORTH Hampshire   4C4

Jingles *Acclaimed*   RAC
77 Horndean Road, Emsworth PO10 7PU
01243-373755
130 bedrs, 1 ➥/WC, 6 ✿/WC, 1 ➥;
TV tcf ✕ P130
sB&B £23 dB&B £38 D £8.50 [5%V]; cc Ac Vi

Merry Hall *Acclaimed*   RAC
73 Horndean Road, Emsworth PO10 7PU
01243-372424
10 bedrs, 7 ➥/WC; P12
Breakfast only [10%V]; cc Ac Vi

EVERSHOT Dorset   3E3

Rectory House *Highly Acclaimed*   RAC
Fore Street, Evershot DT22 0JW 01935-832273
Fax 01935-83273
2 bedrs, 2 ➥/WC; TV tcf ✉ P6
Child restrictions
sB&B £30-£50 dB&B £50-£60; HB weekly
£245-£270; D £16 [10%V]; cc Ac Vi

FAREHAM Hampshire   4B4

Avenue House *Acclaimed*   RAC
22 The Avenue, Fareham PO14 1NS
01329-232175 Fax 01329-232196   &
13 bedrs, 13 ➥/WC; ✕ P13
sB&B £29.50-£45 Breakfast only [10%V]

FARINGDON Oxfordshire   4B2

Faringdon   RAC
Market Place, Faringdon SN7 7HL
01367-240536 Fax 01367-243250
15 bedrs, 9 ➥/WC, 6 ✿/WC; TV tcf P5
sB&B £46.50 dB&B £56.50 D £7.95 [10%V]; cc
Ac Amex DC Vi

FORDINGBRIDGE Hampshire   4A4

Forest Cottage Farm *Highly Acclaimed*   RAC
Godshill, Fordingbridge SP76 2LH
01425-652106

FRESHWATER BAY Isle of Wight

Blenheim House *Highly Acclaimed*   RAC
Gate Lane, Freshwater Bay PO40 9QD
01983-752858
8 bedrs, 8 ➥/WC, 1 ➥; TV tcf P5
Child restrictions
sB&B £21 dB&B £42; HB weekly £203

GOSPORT Hampshire   4B4

Manor *Acclaimed*   RAC
**Brewers Lane, Bridgemary, Gosport PO13
0JY 01329-232946 Fax 01329-220392**
*A completely modernised, two-storey building
with parts dating back over 200 years.*
9 bedrs, 4 ➥/WC, 9 ✿/WC; TV tcf ✉ P45
sB&B £40 dB&B £60 D £6.50 [10%V]; cc Ac
Amex Vi

HAVANT Hampshire   4B4

Old Mill Mill Lane, Bedhampton, Havant PO9
3JH 01705-454948

Location Maps
Hotel locations are shown on the maps at
the back of the guide. All towns and
villages containing an hotel listed in the
guide are shown in black.

HAYLING ISLAND Hampshire 4B4

Cockle Warren Cottage *Highly Acclaimed* RAC
36 Seafront, Hayling Island PO11 9HL 01705-464961

An attractive seafront hotel set in a large garden with a swimming pool. Four poster beds.

HENLEY-ON-THAMES Oxfordshire 4B2

Flohr's *Acclaimed* RAC
Northfield End, Henley-on-Thames RG9 2JG 01491-573412 Fax 01491-579721
9 bedrs, 1 bath/WC, 2 shower/WC, 2 bath; TV tcf P4
sB&B £54 dB&B £69 Breakfast only; cc Ac Amex Vi

The Two Brewers Wargrave Road, Remenham, Henley-on-Thames RG9 01491-574375

HIGH WYCOMBE Buckinghamshire 4C2

Clifton Lodge *Acclaimed* RAC
210-212 West Wycombe Road, High Wycombe HP12 3AR 01494-440095 Fax 01494-536322
32 bedrs, 12 bath/WC, 6 shower/WC, 4 bath; TV tcf dogs no-smoking P35
sB&B £36-£47 dB&B £54 D £14 [10%V]; cc Ac Amex DC Vi

HOOK Hampshire 4B3

Cedar Court RAC
Reading Road, Hook RG27 9DB 01256-762178

A hotel with ground floor accommodation set in secluded grounds.
6 bedrs, 3 shower/WC, 1 bath; TV tcf P6
sB&B £19-£25 dB&B £32-£35 Breakfast only [10%V]; cc Ac Amex DC Vi

Cherry Lodge RAC
Reading Road, Hook RG27 9DB 01256-762532 Fax 01256-762532
6 bedrs, 2 bath/WC, 1 bath; P6
Breakfast only [10%V]

★★(Inn) The White Hart RAC
London Road, Hook RG27 9DZ 01256-762462 Fax 01256-768351
22 bedrs, 22 bath/WC; TV tcf dogs P60
sB&B £38-£57 dB&B £45 Breakfast only; cc Ac Amex Vi

HORTON Dorset 3F2

Northill House *Highly Acclaimed* RAC
Wimborne, Horton BH21 7HL 01258-840407 ♿
9 bedrs, 9 bath/WC; no-smoking P12
Child restrictions
sB&B £37 dB&B £65; HB weekly £286.65; D £13 [10%V]; cc Ac Amex Vi

Discount vouchers
Hotels with a (V) at the end of the price information will accept RAC discount vouchers in part payment for accommodation bills on the full, standard rate, not against bargain breaks or any other special offer.

HUNGERFORD Berkshire 4B3

Marshgate Cottage *Acclaimed* RAC
Marsh Lane, Hungerford RG17 0QX
01488-682307 Fax 01488-685475 &

Small, friendly, family-run hotel in superb countryside, adjoining the Kennet & Avon Canal. Close to Hungerford for antiques enthusiasts.
9 bedrs, 1 ⇥/WC, 6 ♜/WC, 2 ⇥; TV tcf ⅍ P9
Child restrictions
sB&B £35.50 dB&B £48.50 Breakfast only
[5%V]; cc Ac Amex Vi

KIDLINGTON Oxfordshire 4B2

Bowood House *Highly Acclaimed* RAC
238 Oxford Road, Kidlington OX5 1EB
01865-842288 Fax 01865-841858 &
22 bedrs, 20 ⇥/WC, 2 ⇥; ⅍ P25
sB&B £35-£43 dB&B £50-£55 D £12.50; cc Ac Vi

KINGHAM Oxfordshire 4A1

Conygree Gate *Acclaimed* RAC
Church Street, Kingham OX7 6YA
01608-658389 &
9 bedrs, 8 ⇥/WC, 2 ⇥; ♉ ⅍ P12
Breakfast only [5%V]; cc Ac Amex Vi

LYME REGIS Dorset 3E3

The White House *Acclaimed* RAC
47 Silver Street, Lyme Regis DT7 3HR
01297-44342
7 bedrs, 7 ⇥/WC; ♉ P7

LYMINGTON Hampshire 4B4

Durlston House *Acclaimed* RAC
Gosport Street, Lymington SO41 9EG
01590-676908
4 bedrs, 4 ♜/WC, 1 ⇥; TV P6
sB&B £15-£20 dB&B £30-£35 Breakfast only
[10%V]

Efford Cottage *Acclaimed*   RAC
Everton, Lymington SO41 0JD 01590-642315

Friendly, spacious, part Georgian, family home. Four course (five choice) breakfast, homemade bread and preserves. Traditional country cooking by a qualified chef using home grown produce when available. Angling, bird watching, sports within easy reach.
3 bedrs, 2 ⚑/WC, 1 ⚑; TV tcf 🐾 P3
Child restrictions
sB&B £18-£25 dB&B £30-£32; HB weekly £145.50-£164

Our Bench *Acclaimed*   RAC
9 Lodge Road, Pennington, Lymington SO41 8HH 01590-673141 Fax 01590-673141
3 bedrs, 2 ⚑/WC, 1 ⚑; ✄ P5
Child restrictions
sB&B £17-£19 dB&B £37-£39 [5%V]

Wheatsheaf House 25 Gosport Street, Lymington SO41 9RR 01590-679208

LYNDHURST Hampshire   4B4

Fritham Farm Fritham, Lyndhurst SO43 7HH 01703-812333 Fax 01703-812333
3 bedrs, 1 ⚑/WC, 2 🐾/WC; tcf 🐾 P6
Child restrictions under 10
sB&B £16.50 Breakfast only

Knightwood Lodge *Highly Acclaimed*   RAC
Southampton Road, Lyndhurst SO43 7BU 01703-282502 Fax 01703-283730
15 bedrs, 15 ⚑/WC, 1 ⚑; ✄
Breakfast only [10%V]; cc Ac Amex DC Vi

Ormonde House *Private*   RAC
Southampton Road, Lyndhurst SO43 7BT 01703-282806 Fax 01703-283775

Penny Farthing ⚜RAC
Romsey Road, Lyndhurst SO43 7AA
01703-284422 Fax 01703-284488
11 bedrs, 10 ⇥/WC, 1 ⇥; ✘
Breakfast only [10%V]; cc Ac Vi

MAIDENHEAD Berkshire   4C2

Bridge Cottage Bath Road, Taplow,
Maidenhead SL6 0AR 01628-26805

Clifton ⚜RAC
21 Crauford Rise, Maidenhead SL6 7LR
01628-23572   ♿
12 bedrs, 12 ⇥/WC, 3 ⇥;
Breakfast only [10%V]; cc Ac Amex Vi

Copperfields 54 Bath Road, Maidenhead SL6
4JY 01628-74941

Hope Cottage 74 Bath Road, Maidenhead
SL6 4JZ 01628-789799

Laburnham 31 Laburnham Road,
Maidenhead SL6 4DB 01628-76748 Fax
01682-76748
4 bedrs, 4 ☏/WC; P4
sB&B £25 Breakfast only

Moor Farm Holyport, Maidenhead SL6 2HY
01628-33761 Fax 01628-33761

770 year old Manor on working farm Suffolk
sheep, horses.
5 bedrs, 1 ⇥/WC, 1 ☏/WC;
sB&B £30 Breakfast only

Sheephouse Manor Sheephouse Road,
Maidenhead SL6 8HJ 01628-776902 Fax
01628-25138
5 bedrs, 2 ⇥/WC, 3 ☏/WC; TV tcf ✘ P8
sB&B £28 Breakfast only; cc Ac Vi

(Inn) The Bell ⚜RAC
King Street, Maidenhead SL6 1DP
01628-24409
7 bedrs, 2 ⇥; P8
Breakfast only

MALMESBURY Wiltshire   4A2

★★★Knoll House ⚜RAC
Swindon Road, Malmesbury SN16 9LU
01666-823114 Fax 01666-823897   ♿
12 bedrs, 8 ⇥/WC, 4 ☏/WC; TV tcf ✘ P40
sB&B £55.50 dB&B £72.50 D £15 [10%V]; cc
Ac Amex Vi

MARLBOROUGH Wiltshire   4A2

Merlin ⚜RAC
High Street, Marlborough SN8 1LW
01672-52151
16 bedrs, 14 ⇥/WC, 1 ⇥; ✘
Breakfast only [10%V]

Vines *Highly Acclaimed* ⚜RAC
High Street, Marlborough SN4 1HJG
01672-516583 Fax 01672-516583
6 bedrs, 6 ⇥/WC; ✘ P6
Child restrictions
sB&B £25 dB&B £40 Breakfast only; cc Ac
Amex DC Vi

MARLOW Bucks   4C2

Acha Pani Bovingdon Green, Marlow SL7 2JL
01628-483435
3 bedrs, 1 ⇥/WC, 1 ⇥; TV tcf P3
Child restrictions under 10
D £5

MELKSHAM Wiltshire   4A3

Regency ⚜RAC
10-12 Spa Road, Melksham SN12 7NS
01225-702971
11 bedrs, 6 ⇥/WC, 2 ⇥; ✘
Breakfast only

MILTON COMMON Oxfordshire   4B2

Three Pigeons Inn ⚜RAC
Milton Common OX9 2NS 01844-279247 Fax
01865-726845; cc Ac Amex DC Vi

NETTLEBED Oxfordshire 4B2

White Hart *Highly Acclaimed* RAC
nr Henley on Thames, Nettlebed RG9 5DD
01491-641245 Fax 01491-641423

NEWBURY Berkshire 4B3

Adbury Holt House RAC
Burghclere, Newbury RG15 9BW 01635-46061
Fax 01635-35777
5 bedrs, 1 ⇥/WC, 2 ⇥; ✖ ⊁ P20
[10%V]

Laurels Goose Hill, Headley, Newbury RG15
8AT 01635-268448

Manor House Crux Easton, Newbury RG15
9QF 01635-254314
3 bedrs, 2 ⇥; P6
sB&B £16.50 D £9.50

Mousefield Farm Long Lane, Shaw,
Newbury RG16 9LG 01635-40333

Paddock House 17 Derby Road, Newbury
RG14 6DA 01635-47444

Starwood 1 Rectory Close, Newbury RG14
6DF 01635-49125

The Old Farmhouse Downend Lane,
Chieveley, Newbury RG16 8TN 01635-248361

The Swan East Ilsley, Newbury RG16 0LF
01635-281238

Thurston House 9 Stanley Road, Newbury
RG14 7PB 01635-38271
3 bedrs, 1 ⇥; TV tcf P3
Child restrictions under 5
sB&B £17 Breakfast only

Tonayne House Oxford Road, Donnington,
Newbury RG13 2JD 01635-523138

Westridge Open Centre Andover Road,
Highclere, Newbury RG15 9PJ 01635-253322

19 Fieldridge Stoney Lane, Newbury RG13
2NG 01635-524059

NORTH WARNBOROUGH Hampshire 4B3

(Inn) Jolly Miller *Acclaimed* RAC
Nr. Odiham, North Warnborough RG25 1ET

01256-704030 Fax 01256-704030 ♿
8 bedrs, 4 ⇥/WC, 2 ⇥; TV tcf ✖ P60
sB&B £30 dB&B £39; cc Ac Amex Vi

OXFORD Oxfordshire 4B2

Acorn RAC
260 Iffley Road, Oxford OX4 1SE
01865-247998
6 bedr 2 ⇥; P5
Breakfast only [5%V]; cc Ac Vi

Ascot RAC
283 Iffley Road, Oxford OX4 4AQ
01865-240259
6 bedrs, 2 ⌀/WC, 1 ⇥; P2
sB&B £18-£28 dB&B £36-£45 Breakfast only
[10%V]; cc Ac Amex Vi JCB

Bravalla RAC
242 Iffley Road, Oxford OX4 1SE
01865-241326
5 bedrs, 4 ⇥/WC, 2 ⇥; TV tcf ✖ P4
sB&B £18-£22 dB&B £36-£44 Breakfast only
[10%V]; cc Ac DC Vi

Brown's RAC
281 Iffley Road, Oxford OX4 4AQ
01865-246822
7 bedrs, 2 ⇥/WC, 3 ⇥; P4
Breakfast only [10%V]; cc Ac DC Vi

Chestnuts *Highly Acclaimed* RAC
45 Davenant Road, Off Woodstock Road,
Oxford OX2 8BU 01865-53375
4 bedrs, 4 ⌀/WC; TV tcf ⊁ P4
Child restrictions
sB&B £30-£33 dB&B £46-£50 Breakfast only

COURTFIELD
PRIVATE HOTEL
RAC Acclaimed

CATHERINE TONG
367 IFFLEY ROAD, OXFORD, OX4 4DP
Telephone: OXFORD (01865) 242991 Telex no. same as Telephone.
An individually designed house situated in tree-lined road; with
modern spacious bedrooms, majority of **En Suite**. Close to
picturesque Iffley Village and River Thames yet easily accessible to
Oxford's historic city centre and Colleges. **Private car park.**

Conifer   RAC
116 The Glade, Headington, Oxford OX3
7DX 01865-63055 Fax 01865-63055
8 bedrs, 3 ➥/WC, 1 ➥; TV tcf P8
sB&B £21 dB&B £42 Breakfast only; cc Ac Vi

Cotswold House *Highly Acclaimed*   RAC
363 Banbury Road, Oxford OX2 7PL
01865-310558
7 bedrs, 7 ➥/WC; P7
Child restrictions
sB&B £34-£36 Breakfast only

Courtfield *Acclaimed*   RAC
367 Iffley Road, Oxford OX4 4DP
01865-242991 Fax 01865-242991
6 bedrs, 4 ➥/WC, 1 ➥; P6
Child restrictions
sB&B £27-£35 dB&B £42-£45 Breakfast only
[10%V]; cc Ac Amex DC Vi JCB

Eltham Villa *Acclaimed*   RAC
148 Woodstock Road, Yarnton, Oxford OX5
1PW 01865-376037 Fax 01865-376037
73 bedrs, 2 ➥/WC, 5 ➥/WC; TV tcf P7
sB&B £20 dB&B £30 D £10 [5%V]

Gables *Highly Acclaimed*   RAC
6 Cumnor Hill, Oxford OX2 9HA
01865-862153

*An attractive detached house in a quiet
residential area of the city. All rooms are
comfortably furnished and tastefully
decorated.*
6 bedrs, 1 ➥/WC, 4 ➥/WC, 1 ➥; TV tcf ⅍ P6
sB&B £20 dB&B £38 Breakfast only; cc Ac Vi

Galaxie *Acclaimed*   RAC
180 Banbury Road, Oxford OX2 7BT
01865-515688 Fax 01865-515688
31 bedrs, 15 ➥/WC, 10 ➥/WC, 6 ➥; TV tcf ✻ P31
sB&B £30-£45 dB&B £46-£60 Breakfast only;
cc Ac Vi

Marlborough House *Highly Acclaimed* RAC
321 Woodstock Road, Oxford OX2 7NY
01865-311321 Fax 01865-515329

Mead Close Mead Close, Forest Hill, Oxford
OX33 1DY 01865-872248
3 bedrs, 1 ➥; tcf P5
sB&B £16; HB weekly £161-£220; D £7-£12

Melcombe House   RAC
227 Iffley Road, Oxford OX4 1SQ
01865-249520
9 bedrs, 1 ➥/WC, 2 ➥; TV tcf ✻ P6
sB&B £20-£22 dB&B £34 Breakfast only

Pickwicks *Acclaimed*   RAC
17 London Road, Headington, Oxford OX3
7SP 01865-750487 Fax 01865-742208
15 bedrs, 9 ➥/WC, 4 ➥; P17
Breakfast only; cc Ac Amex DC Vi

Pine Castle   RAC
290 Iffley Road, Oxford OX4 4AE
01865-241497
6 bedrs, 1 ➥; P3
Breakfast only [15%V]; cc Ac Vi

River   RAC
17 Botley Road, Oxford OX2 0AA
01865-243475 Fax 01865-724306
16 bedrs, 5 ➥/WC, 7 ➥/WC; TV tcf ✂ P25
sB&B £39-£57 dB&B £52-£70 D £6.50; cc Ac Vi

Tilbury Lodge *Highly Acclaimed*   RAC
5 Tilbury Lane, Botley, Oxford OX2 9NB
01865-862138
9 bedrs, 9 ➥/WC; P8
Breakfast only; cc Ac Vi

Willow Reaches 1 Wytham Street, Oxford
OX1 4SU 01865-721545 Fax 01865-251139

Windrush   RAC
11 Iffley Road, Oxford OX4 1EA
01865-247933
8 bedrs, 2 ➥;
Breakfast only; cc Ac Vi

Location Maps
Hotel locations are shown on the maps at
the back of the guide. All towns and
villages containing an hotel listed in the
guide are shown in black.

POOLE Dorset   3F3

Avoncourt   RAC
245 Bournemouth Road, Parkstone, Poole
BH14 9HX 01202-732025 Fax 01202-732025

Hotel of smart appearance, situated on the A35. Lawns to front and rear, with pleasant rear view over a residential area.
6 bedrs, 1 ⇥/WC, 1 ⇥; TV tcf P6
sB&B £16-£19 dB&B £32-£44; HB weekly £133-£154; [10%V]; cc Ac Amex DC Vi

Bays   RAC
82 Bournemouth Road, Parkstone, Poole
BH14 0HA 01202-740110
6 bedrs, 2 ⇥/WC, 1 ⇥; TV tcf ✻ P8
Child restrictions
sB&B £18-£20 dB&B £36-£40 Breakfast only
[10%V]

Fairlight *Acclaimed*   RAC
1 Golf Links Road, Broadstone, Poole BH18 8BE 01202-694316 Fax 01202-694316

Comfortable Edwardian hotel standing in its own grounds in a peaceful setting yet close to all amenities.
9 bedrs, 5 ⇥/WC, 2 ⇡/WC, 1 ⇥; TV tcf ✻ ⅟
P10
sB&B £20-£30 dB&B £34-£46; HB weekly £144-£228; D £10 [5%V]; cc Ac Amex DC Vi

Sheldon Lodge *Acclaimed*   RAC
22 Forest Road, Branksome Park, Poole BH13
6DA 01202-761186   よ
14 bedrs, 14 ⇥/WC; ✻
sB&B £21-£26 dB&B £42-£46; HB weekly £185-£195; D £10 [10%V]; cc Ac

PORTESHAM Dorset   3E3

★★Millmead Country   RAC
Goose Hill, Portesham DT3 4HE
01305-871432   よ
6 bedrs, 6 ⇥/WC; ✻ P20
sB&B £27-£37 dB&B £56-£64; HB weekly £210-£228; D £13.95 [10%V]; cc Ac Amex DC Vi

PORTLAND Dorset   3E3

Alessandria Hotel & Italian Restaurant   RAC
71 Wakeham, Easton, Portland DT5 1HW
01305-822270

PORTSMOUTH & SOUTHSEA Hampshire 4B4

Abbeville   RAC
26 Nettlecombe Avenue, Portsmouth & Southsea PO4 0QW 01705-826209
11 bedrs, 2 ⇡/WC, 2 ⇥; TV tcf ✻ P5
sB&B £15 dB&B £30 Breakfast only

Aquarius Court   RAC
34 St Ronan's Road, Portsmouth & Southsea PO4 0PT 01705-822872
12 bedrs, 3 ⇡/WC, 2 ⇥; TV tcf ⅟ P6
sB&B £15.50-£31 dB&B £31-£64; HB weekly £138.50-£148; D £7.50 [10%V]; cc Ac DC Vi

Bembell Court   RAC
69 Festing Road, Southsea, Portsmouth & Southsea PO4 0NQ 01705-735915 Fax 01705-756497
14 bedrs, 2 ⇥/WC, 6 ⇡/WC, 3 ⇥; TV tcf ⅟ P10
sB&B £18-£24 dB&B £42-£44; HB weekly £195-£210; [10%V]; cc Ac Amex DC Vi

Birchwood   RAC
44 Waverley Road, Portsmouth & Southsea PO5 2PP 01705-811337
6 bedrs, 3 ⇥/WC, 1 ⇥;
Breakfast only [10%V]; cc Ac Amex DC Vi

Bristol   RAC
55 Clarence Parade, Portsmouth & Southsea, PO5 2HX 01705-821815
13 bedrs, 11 ⇥/WC, 2 ⇥; P7
Breakfast only [10%V]; cc Ac Amex Vi

Britannia 8 Outram Road, Portsmouth & Southsea PO5 1QU 705814234

Collingham ᴿᴬᶜ
89 St Ronans Road, Portsmouth & Southsea PO4 0PR 01705-821549
6 bedrs, 2 🛁;
Breakfast only

Dolphins ᴿᴬᶜ
10-11 Western Parade, Portsmouth & Southsea PO5 3JF 01705-823823 Fax 01705-820833
32 bedrs, 19 🛁/WC, 5 🛁;
Breakfast only; cc Ac Amex DC Vi

Gainsborough House ᴿᴬᶜ
9 Malvern Road, Portsmouth & Southsea PO5 2LZ 01705-822604
7 bedrs, 2 🛁; TV tcf
Child restrictions
sB&B £14-£15 dB&B £28-£30 Breakfast only

Goodwood House 1 Taswell Rd, Portsmouth & Southsea PO5 2RG 01705-824734

Hamilton House *Acclaimed* ᴿᴬᶜ
95 Victoria Road North, Portsmouth & Southsea PO5 1PS 01705-823502 Fax 01705-823502

Delightful, family-run guest house with bright, modern rooms, centrally located five minutes from the Ferryport and Portsmouth/Southsea tourist attractions.
8 bedrs, 3 🐾/WC, 2 🛁; TV tcf ✄
sB&B £16-£18 dB&B £32-£36; HB weekly £144-£158

Saville *Acclaimed* ᴿᴬᶜ
38-39 Clarence Parade, Portsmouth & Southsea PO5 2EU 01705-822491 Fax 01705-291709
45 bedrs, 14 🛁/WC, 13 🐾/WC, 8 🛁; TV tcf P4
sB&B £16-£20 dB&B £34-£40; HB weekly £140-£160; cc Ac Amex DC Vi

Turret *Acclaimed* ᴿᴬᶜ
Clarence Parade, Portsmouth & Southsea PO5 2HZ 01705-291810
13 bedrs, 7 🛁/WC, 3 🛁;
Child restrictions
Breakfast only; cc Ac Amex DC Vi

Upper Mount House *Acclaimed* ᴿᴬᶜ
The Vale, Clarendon Road, Portsmouth & Southsea PO5 2EQ 01705-820456
11 bedrs, 11 🛁/WC, 1 🛁;
Breakfast only [10%V]; cc Ac Vi

READING Berkshire 4B2

Abadair House 46 Redlands Road, Reading RG1 5HE

Abbey House ᴿᴬᶜ
118 Connaught Road, Reading 01734-590549
Fax 01734-56929 ♿
22 bedrs, 13 🛁/WC, 3 🛁; ✄
sB&B £29-£45.50 Breakfast only [10%V]

Aeron RAC
191 Kentwood Hill, Tilehurst, Reading RG3
6JE 01734-424119 Fax 01734-451953
15 bedrs, 7 ✆/WC, 3 🛏; TV tcf ✖ ⅍ P30
sB&B £26-£41 dB&B £31-£54 Breakfast only
[5%V]; cc Ac Amex Vi

Boot Farm Southend Road, Reading RG7 6ES
01734-744298

**Crescent 35 Coley Avenue, Reading RG1
6LL 01734-507980 Fax 01734-507980**
*From town centre Castle Hill lights turn left
into Coley Park Ave. Hotel situated 200 yards
to Junction 12, M4.*
16 bedrs, 4 🛏; TV tcf ✖ P25
sB&B £20 D £4-£7; cc Ac Amex Vi

Kennet House Burghfield Bridge, Reading
RG3 3RA 01734-571060

Wetherby 35 The Avenue, Mortimer, Reading
RG7 3QU 01734-33316

Windy Brow 204 Victoria Road, Wargrave-
On-Thames, Reading RG10 8AJ 01734-403336
*Detached Victorian house overlooking fields
in 1/3 acre. Colour TV & tea/coffee facilities
in all rooms. Good pub food locally
overlooking Thames.*
4 bedrs, 1 ✆/WC, 2 🛏; TV tcf ✖ P6
Child restrictions under 8
sB&B £18.50 Breakfast only

10 Greystoke Road Caversham, Reading
RG4 0EL 01734-475784

35 The Avenue Mortimer, Reading RG7 3QU
01734-333166

RINGWOOD Hampshire 4A4

Greenacres Farmhouse Christchurch Road,
Lower Kingston, Ringwood BH24 3BJ
01425-480945

Discount vouchers

Hotels with a (V) at the end of the price
information will accept RAC discount
vouchers in part payment for
accommodation bills on the full,
standard rate, not against bargain breaks
or any other special offer.

Moortown Lodge *Highly Acclaimed* RAC
244 Christchurch Road, Ringwood BH24 3AS
01425-471404 Fax 01425-476052

*Georgian hotel situated on the edge of the
New Forest. Once part of the Gladstone estate.
1 mile from Ringwood town centre on B3347.*
6 bedrs, 2 🛏/WC, 3 ✆/WC, 1 🛏; TV tcf ⅍ P8
sB&B £29-£42 dB&B £50-£80; HB weekly
£228-£260; D £14.95; cc Ac Amex Vi

ROMSEY Hampshire 4B3

**Wykeham House 88 The Hundred,
Romsey SO51 8BX 01794-511905 Fax
01794-511478**

*Beautifully restored Queen Anne House built
1715. Luxury suite with 7' waterbed & petal
shaped Jaccuzi, Queen Ann suite etc..*
5 bedrs, 2 🛏/WC, 1 ✆/WC, 2 🛏; TV tcf ✖ P5
Child restrictions
sB&B £25; HB weekly £35-£45; D £12.99

SALISBURY Wiltshire 3F2

Byways House *Highly Acclaimed* RAC
31 Fowler's Road, Salisbury SP1 2QP
01722-328364 Fax 01722-322146 &
23 bedrs, 4 🛏/WC, 16 ✆/WC, 1 🛏; TV tcf ✖ P15
sB&B £22-£24 dB&B £39-£44 Breakfast only
[10%V]; cc Vi

Glen Lyn *Acclaimed* 🏅RAC
6 Bellamy Lane, Milford Hill, Salisbury SP1
2SP 01722-327880
9 bedrs, 2 ➡/WC, 2 ♟/WC, 2 ➡; TV tcf P7
Child restrictions
sB&B £19-£21 dB&B £34-£40 Breakfast only
[10%V]

Grasmere House *Highly Acclaimed* 🏅RAC
70 Harnham Road, Salisbury SP2 8JN
01722-338388 Fax 01722-333710
5 bedrs, 3 ➡/WC, 2 ♟/WC; P12
sB&B £45-£50 dB&B £55-£75 D £14.50
[10%V]; cc Amex Vi

Hayburn Wyke 🏅RAC
72 Castle Road, Salisbury SP1 3RL
01722-412627
6 bedrs, 2 ♟/WC, 2 ➡; TV tcf P6
sB&B £22 dB&B £33 Breakfast only [5%V]

Holmhurst 🏅RAC
Downton Rd, Salisbury SP2 8AR
01722-323164

Leena's 🏅RAC
50 Castle Road, Salisbury SP1 3RL
01722-335419
6 bedrs, 3 ➡/WC, 4 ♟/WC, 1 ➡; TV tcf ⅍ P7
sB&B £17 dB&B £29-£37 Breakfast only [5%V]

**Newton Farmhouse Southampton Road
(A 36), Whiteparish, Salisbury SP5 2QL
01794-884416**

*Grade 2 listed 16th century farmhouse,
formerly part of Trafalgar Estate. All rooms
en-suite, one with 4 poster. Flagstone floor
and oak beamed dining room. Large gardens
with swimming pool*
8 bedrs, 2 ➡/WC, 6 ♟/WC; TV tcf P10
sB&B £17.50 D £14 Breakfast only

Richburn 🏅RAC
23-25 Estcourt Road, Salisbury SP1 3AP
01722-325189
10 bedrs, 1 ➡/WC, 1 ♟/WC, 2 ➡; tcf 🐕 ⅍ P10
sB&B £16.50 dB&B £28-£36 Breakfast only

Rokeby 3 Wain-A-Long Road, Salisbury SP1
1LJ 01722-329800

Templeman Old Farmhouse Redlynch,
Salisbury SP5 2JS 01725-20331
3 bedrs, 1 ➡;
Child restrictions under 5
sB&B £17 Breakfast only

SANDOWN Isle of Wight 4B4

Belmore 🏅RAC
101 Station Avenue, Sandown PO36 8HD
01983-404189
9 bedrs, 5 ➡/WC, 1 ➡; 🐕 ⅍
[10%V]; cc Ac Vi

Bertram Lodge 🏅RAC
3 Leed Street, Sandown PO36 9DA
01983-402551
9 bedrs, 9 ♟/WC; TV tcf ⅍ P5
Child restrictions
sB&B £17-£18.50 dB&B £34-£37 [5%V]

Chester Lodge *Acclaimed* 🏅RAC
7 Beachfield Road, Sandown PO36 8NA
01983-402773 ♿
18 bedrs, 14 ➡/WC, 3 ➡; 🐕 P15
cc Vi

Cygnet *Acclaimed* 🏅RAC
58 Carter Street, Sandown PO36 8DQ
01983-402930 Fax 01983-405112 ♿
50 bedrs, 27 ➡/WC, 13 ♟/WC, 4 ➡; TV tcf P30
sB&B £21-£26 dB&B £42-£52 [10%V]; cc Ac
Amex Vi

Denewood *Acclaimed* 🏅RAC
7 Victoria Road, Sandown PO36 8AL
01983-402980 Fax 01983-40298
16 bedrs, 11 ➡/WC, 1 ➡; P10
Breakfast only; cc Ac Vi

Norton Lodge 🏅RAC
22 Victoria Road, Sandown PO36 8AL
01983-402423 ♿
9 bedrs, 5 ♟/WC, 1 ➡; TV tcf P8
Child restrictions
sB&B £13.50-£17 dB&B £27-£34 [5%V]

Rooftree *Highly Acclaimed* RAC
26 Broadway, Sandown PO36 9BY
01983-403175 Fax 01983-407354
9 bedrs, 7 ♠/WC, 2 ➡; TV tcf P10
sB&B £10-£19.50 dB&B £28-£38 [5%V];
cc Ac Vi

Rose Bank High St, Sandown PO36 8DA
01983-403854

St Catherines *Highly Acclaimed* RAC
1 Winchester Park Road, Sandown PO36 8HJ
01983-402392
20 bedrs, 20 ➡/WC; ⚲ P8
sB&B £14.50-£21.45 dB&B £37-£42.90; HB
weekly £159.25-£194.65; D £9 [5%V];
cc Ac Vi

SHAFTESBURY Dorset   3F2

★★★Royal Chase RAC
Royal Chase Roundabout, Shaftesbury SP7
8DB 01747-853355 Fax 01747-851969
35 bedrs, 35 ➡/WC; TV tcf ✖ P100
sB&B £66 dB&B £83; HB weekly £372; D
£9.15; cc Ac Amex DC Vi

The Benett Arms Semley, Shaftesbury SP7
9AS 01747-830221 Fax 01747-830152
5 bedrs, 1 ➡/WC, 5 ♠/WC; TV tcf ✖ P40
sB&B £22 D £8-£18; cc Ac Amex DC Vi

Whitebridge Farm Semley, Shaftesbury SP7
9JT 01747-830462

SHANKLIN Isle of Wight   4B4

Apse Manor Country House *Highly*
Acclaimed RAC
Apse Manor Road, Shanklin PO37 7NP
01983-866651
7 bedrs, 7 ➡/WC; ✖ P10
Child restrictions
Breakfast only; cc Ac Vi

Aqua *Highly Acclaimed* RAC
The Esplanade, Shanklin PO37 6BN
01983-863024 Fax 01983-864841
22 bedrs, 5 ➡/WC, 17 ♠/WC; TV tcf P2
sB&B £18-£24 dB&B £36; HB weekly £160-
£210; D £7.50; cc Ac Amex DC Vi

Avenue *Highly Acclaimed* RAC
Avenue Road, Shanklin PO37 7BG
01983-862746
10 bedrs, 9 ➡/WC, 1 ➡; ⚲ P8

Child restrictions
dB&B £50 Breakfast only [10%V]

Bay House *Highly Acclaimed* RAC
8 Chine Avenue Keats Green, Shanklin PO36
6AG 01983-863180 Fax 01983-866604
21 bedrs, 21 ➡/WC, 3 ➡; ✖
Breakfast only

Bondi *Highly Acclaimed* RAC
Clarence Road, Shanklin PO37 7BH
01983-862507 Fax 01983-862326
9 bedrs, 9 ➡/WC, 1 ➡; TV tcf ✖ P3
sB&B £18-£24 dB&B £24-£36 [10%V]; cc Ac
Amex DC Vi

Braemar 1 Grange Rd, Shanklin PO37 6NN
01983-863172

Burlington RAC
6 Chine Avenue, Shanklin PO37 6AG
01983-86209
13 bedrs, 5 ➡/WC, 3 ➡; P7
Breakfast only [10%V]

Carlton Eastcliffe Prom, Shanklin PO37 6AY
01983-862517

Cranleigh Court *Acclaimed* RAC
15 Clarence Road, Shanklin PO37 7BH
01983-862393
9 bedrs, 4 ♠/WC, 2 ➡; TV tcf P5
sB&B £14.50-£17.25 dB&B £29-£34.50
Breakfast only [10%V]; cc Ac Amex Vi

Culver Lodge Culver Rd, Shanklin PO37 6ER
01983-863515

Delphi Cliff *Acclaimed* RAC
St Boniface Cliff Road, Shanklin PO37 6ET
01983-862179
10 bedrs, 8 ➡/WC, 2 ♠/WC, 1 ➡; TV tcf P7
Child restrictions
sB&B £17-£19 dB&B £34-£38 [10%V]; cc Ac Vi

Ferriby RAC
10 Park Road, Shanklin PO37 6AY
01983-862879

Glen *Acclaimed* RAC
4 Avenue Road, Shanklin PO37 7BG
01983-862154
6 bedrs, 2 ➡/WC, 1 ➡; P3
Child restrictions
Breakfast only [10%V]; cc Ac Vi

Glendene   RAC
7 Carter Avenue, Shanklin PO37 7LQ
01983-862924
6 bedrs, 4 ➡/WC, 2 ➡; P6
sB&B £18.15-£20.60 dB&B £36.30-£41.20
[10%V]

Hambledon *Highly Acclaimed*   RAC
11 Queens Road, Shanklin PO37 6AW
01983-862403 Fax 01983-867894
11 bedrs, 11 ➡/WC, 1 ➡; ⊬
sB&B £17-£22 dB&B £34-£44; HB weekly
£145-£190; [10%V]; cc Ac Vi

Hazelwood *Acclaimed*   RAC
14 Clarence Road, Shanklin PO37 7BH
01983-862824
10 bedrs, 8 ➡/WC, 1 ➡; TV ✗ P4
sB&B £16-£19.50 dB&B £32-£39 [10%V]; cc Ac
Amex DC Vi

Heatherleigh *Acclaimed*   RAC
17 Queens Road, Shanklin PO37 6AW
01983-862503 Fax 01983-862503
9 bedrs, 1 ➡/WC, 6 ☞/WC, 1 ➡; TV tcf P4
sB&B £12-£19 dB&B £32-£38 Breakfast only
[10%V]; cc Ac Vi

Lindens *Acclaimed*   RAC
6 Clarence Road, Shanklin, Shanklin PO37
7BH 01983-862172
12 bedrs, 8 ➡/WC, 1 ➡; ⊬
Breakfast only [5%V]; cc Ac Vi

Luccombe Chine Country House *Highly*
Acclaimed   RAC
Luccombe Chine Bonchurch, Shanklin PO37
6RH 01983-862719 Fax 01983-863082
8 bedrs, 8 ➡/WC; P20
Child restrictions
sB&B £61; cc Ac Vi

Mount House *Acclaimed*   RAC
20 Arthurs Hill, Shanklin PO37 6EE
01983-862556 Fax 01983-867551
10 bedrs, 10 ➡/WC; P8
Breakfast only; cc Ac Vi

Orchardcroft *Highly Acclaimed*   RAC
53 Victoria Avenue, Shanklin PO37 6LT
01983-862133
16 bedrs, 7 ➡/WC, 9 ☞/WC; TV tcf ✗ ⊬ P12
Child restrictions
sB&B £15-£25 dB&B £40-£50; HB weekly
£198-£229; D £9.90 [10%V]; cc Ac Vi

Osborne House *Highly Acclaimed*   RAC
Esplanade, Shanklin PO37 6BN 01983-862501
Fax 01983-862501
12 bedrs, 4 ➡/WC, 8 ☞/WC, 2 ➡; TV tcf ⊬
P2
Child restrictions
sB&B £30 dB&B £60 D £13.75 [5%V]; cc Ac Vi

Overstrand Howard Rd, Shanklin PO37 6HD
01983-862100

Pulboro 6 Park Rd, Shanklin PO37 6AZ
01983-862740

Richmond *Acclaimed*   RAC
23 Palmerston Road, Shanklin PO37 6AS
01983-862874
12 bedrs, 11 ➡/WC, 1 ➡; ✗ ⊬
Breakfast only [5%V]; cc Vi

Roseglen *Acclaimed*   RAC
12 Palmerston Road, Shanklin PO37 6AS
01983-863164   ♿

*In an excellent position, the hotel offers
specialised advice on walking trips, with
guidance if necessary. Vegetarian and special
diets are catered for.*
17 bedrs, 8 ➡/WC, 4 ➡; ✗
Breakfast only [10%V]; cc Ac Amex Vi

No Smoking/Dogs

⊬ Indicates a hotel which either bans
smoking throughout the establishment or
does not allow smoking in some areas.

✗ Indicates a hotel which either does not
welcome dogs or restricts dogs to certain
areas of the hotel.
Please telephone the hotel
for further details.

Rowborough *Acclaimed* RAC
32 Arthurs Hill, Shanklin PO37 6EX
01983-866072 Fax 01983-864000

A detached hotel standing in attractive garden setting.
8 bedrs, 7 🛁/WC, 1 🛁; P5
Child restrictions
sB&B £17-£21 dB&B £34-£42; HB weekly £156-£177; D £8 [10%V]; cc Ac DC Vi

Scotsgrove RAC
4 Sandy Lane, Shanklin PO37 7DT
01983-862565
9 bedrs, 2 🛁/WC, 2 🛁; tcf 🐕 P9
sB&B £14-£16 dB&B £28-£32 [5%V]; cc Ac Vi

Soraba *Acclaimed* RAC
2 Paddock Road, Shanklin PO37 6NZ
01983-862367

A double fronted, two storey Victorian house occupying a corner position in quiet residential area near Shanklin Old Village.
7 bedrs, 4 🚿/WC, 1 🛁; TV 🐕 🚭 P4
Child restrictions
sB&B £14.50-£17 dB&B £29-£34; HB weekly £120-£136; D £7 [10%V]; cc Ac Vi

St Leonards RAC
22 Queens Road, Shanklin PO37 6AW
01983-862121
7 bedrs, 2 🛁/WC, 5 🚿/WC, 1 🛁; TV tcf P6
sB&B £17-£20 dB&B £34-£40 Breakfast only [10%V]; cc Ac Vi

Suncliffe *Acclaimed* RAC
8 Hope Road, Shanklin PO37 6EA
01983-863009 Fax 01983-864868

Small family run hotel centrally located just minutes from both beach and town centre.
11 bedrs, 1 🛁/WC, 8 🚿/WC, 1 🛁; TV tcf 🚭 P7
sB&B £15.99-£21.50 dB&B £31.98-£43; HB weekly £135-£175; [10%V]; cc Ac Vi

Victoria Lodge RAC
Alexandra Road, Shanklin PO37 6AF
01983-862361
23 bedrs, 8 🛁/WC, 8 🚿/WC, 1 🛁; TV tcf 🚭 P20
sB&B £16-£23 dB&B £32-£46; HB weekly £145-£180; cc Ac Vi

White House *Highly Acclaimed* RAC
7 Park Road, Shanklin PO37 6AY
01983-862776 Fax 01983-865980
11 bedrs, 2 🛁/WC, 9 🚿/WC; P11
sB&B £16-£26 dB&B £44-£52 Breakfast only [10%V]; cc Ac Amex DC Vi

SHERBORNE Dorset 3E2

Ashclose Farm Charlton-Horethorn, Sherborne DT9 4PG 01963-220360

SLOUGH Berkshire 4C2

Oaklands Bangors, Road South, Iver, Slough SL0 0BB 01753-653003

The Old Vicarage 18 Thorney Lane North, Iver, Slough SL0 9JY 01753-653924

55 London Road Datchet, Slough SL3 9JY 01753-580401

SOUTHAMPTON Hampshire — 4B4

Banister House ⚓RAC
**11 Brighton Road, Banister Park,
Southampton SO15 2JJ 01703-221279 Fax
01703-221279**
23 bedrs, 1 🛁/WC, 13 🛁/WC, 5 🛁; TV tcf
P14
sB&B £21.50 dB&B £29.50 Breakfast only
[10%V]; cc Ac Amex Vi

Beacon 49 Archers Road, Southampton SO1
2NF 01703-225910

Darwin Lodge 164 Hill Lane, Southampton
SO1 5DB 01703-334961

Dormy House *Acclaimed* ⚓RAC
21 Barnes Lane, Southampton, SO31 7DA
01489-572626
12 bedrs, 12 🛁/WC; TV tcf ✖ P18
sB&B £36.50 dB&B £45 D £9.95 [10%V]; cc Ac
Amex Vi

Four Seasons Hamilton Road, Hythe,
Southampton SO4 6PD 01703-845151

Hunters Lodge *Acclaimed* ⚓RAC
25 Landguard Road, Shirley, Southampton
SO1 5DL 01703-227919 Fax 01703-230913
16 bedrs, 9 🛁/WC, 2 🛁; ✖ P18
sB&B £23.50 dB&B £40-£44.50 Breakfast
only; cc Ac Amex Vi

Landguard Lodge ⚓RAC
21 Landguard Road, Southampton SO1 5DL
01703-636904 Fax 01703-636904
13 bedrs, 4 🛁/WC, 3 🛁; TV tcf P3
Child restrictions
sB&B £16-£19 dB&B £32-£35 [10%V]; cc Ac
Amex DC Vi

Linden ⚓RAC
51 The Polygon, Southampton SO1 2BP
01703-225653
13 bedrs, 3 🛁;
sB&B £13-£15 dB&B £26-£30 Breakfast only
[5%V]

Nirvana ⚓RAC
386 Winchester Road, Bassett, Southampton
SO1 7DH 01703-790087
18 bedrs, 9 🛁/WC, 3 🛁; ✖ P18
[5%V]

**Ophir Villa 7-9 Roberts Road, Hill Lane,
Southampton SO1 5DF 01703-226876**
16 bedrs, 13 🛁/WC, 2 🛁; TV tcf P16
sB&B £22 Breakfast only; cc Ac Vi

(Inn) Villa Capri *Acclaimed* ⚓RAC
50/52 Archers Road, Southampton SO1 2LU
01703-632800
15 bedrs, 11 🛁/WC, 1 🛁; TV tcf ✖ P140
sB&B £19 dB&B £36 [5%V]; cc Ac Vi

STEEPLE ASTON Oxfordshire — 4B1

Westfield Farm Motel *Acclaimed* ⚓RAC
**The Fenway, Steeple Aston OX5 3SS
01869-40591** ♿
7 bedrs, 7 🛁/WC; ✖ P18
sB&B £32-£36 dB&B £40 Breakfast only
[5%V]; cc Ac Vi

STOCKBRIDGE Hampshire — 4B3

Carbery *Acclaimed* ⚓RAC
Salisbury Hill, Stockbridge SO20 6EZ
01264-810771 Fax 01264-811022

*A fine old Georgian house situated in one
acre of landscaped gardens and lawns
overlooking the River Test.*
11 bedrs, 1 🛁/WC, 6 🛁/WC, 1 🛁; TV tcf P14
sB&B £22-£29.50 dB&B £44-£48

Old Three Cups *Acclaimed* ⚓RAC
High Street, Stockbridge SO20 6HB
01264-810527
8 bedrs, 3 🛁/WC, 1 🛁; P8
[5%V]; cc Ac Vi

SWANAGE Dorset   3F3

Chines   RAC
9 Burlington Road, Swanage BH19 1LR
01929-422457
12 bedrs, 8 ♠/WC, 2 ➡; TV tcf ✂ P10
sB&B £15 dB&B £30-£35 [5%V]

Eversden   RAC
5 Victoria Road, Swanage BH19 1LY
01929-423276

Firswood   RAC
29 Kings Road, Swanage BH19 9HF
01929-422306
6 bedrs, 2 ➡/WC, 2 ♠/WC, 1 ➡; TV tcf ✂ P7
Child restrictions
sB&B £14-£16 dB&B £30

Glenlee   RAC
6 Cauldon Avenue, Swanage BH19 1PQ
01929-425794
7 bedrs, 5 ➡/WC, 2 ♠/WC; TV tcf ✈ P8
Child restrictions
dB&B £36-£43; HB weekly £175-£198; cc Ac Vi

Havenhurst *Acclaimed*   RAC
3 Cranborne Road, Swanage BH19 1EA
01929-424424
17 bedrs, 7 ➡/WC, 10 ♠/WC; tcf P20
sB&B £17.50-£29 dB&B £35 D £10

Sandringham *Acclaimed*   RAC
20 Durlston Road, Swanage BH19 2HX
01929-423076
11 bedrs, 9 ♠/WC, 1 ➡; tcf P8
sB&B £22-£26 dB&B £44-£52; HB weekly
£192-£216; cc Ac Vi

Seashells *Acclaimed*   RAC
7 Burlington Road, Swanage BH19 1LR
01920-4227949
8 bedrs, 2 ➡/WC, 6 ♠/WC, 1 ➡; TV tcf P10
sB&B £22.50; HB weekly £162-£186; [10%V]

St Michaels   RAC
31 Kings Road, Swanage BH19 1HF
01920-422064
5 bedrs, 3 ♠/WC, 1 ➡; TV tcf ✈ P5
Child restrictions
dB&B £30-£32; HB weekly £151-£176;
D £7.50

SWINDON Wiltshire   4A2

Fir Tree Lodge *Highly Acclaimed*   RAC

17 Highworth Road, Stratton St Margaret,
Swindon SN3 4QL 01793-822372   &
11 bedrs, 11 ➡/WC; ✈
Breakfast only [10%V]

Grove Lodge 108 Swindon Rd, Stratton St
Margaret, Swindon SN3 4PT 01793-825343

Kingsbridge House Coate Water, Swindon
SN3 6AA 01793-522861

★★★Stanton House   RAC
The Avenue, Stanton Fitzwarren, Swindon
SW6 7SD 01793-861777 Fax 01793-861857 &
86 bedrs, 86 ➡/WC; TV tcf ✂ P100
sB&B £65-£90 dB&B £58-£75; cc Amex DC Vi
JCB

Treetops 8 Marshield Way, Stratton St
Margaret, Swindon SN3 4PS 01793-822954

THAME Oxfordshire   4B2

Essex House *Highly Acclaimed*   RAC
Chinnor Road, Thame OX9 3LS 01844-217567
Fax 01844-216420
7 bedrs, 5 ♠/WC, 1 ➡; TV tcf ✂ P20
sB&B £43 dB&B £45; cc Ac Amex DC Vi

TOTLAND BAY Isle of Wight   4B4

Littledene Lodge *Acclaimed*   RAC
Granville Road, Totland Bay PO39 0AX
01983-752411

Nodes Country   RAC
Alum Bay Road, Totland Bay PO39 0HZ
01983-752859 Fax 01705-20162
11 bedrs, 4 ➡/WC, 6 ♠/WC, 1 ➡; TV tcf ✈
✂ P15
sB&B £20.50-£24 dB&B £41-£58; HB weekly
£185-£238.50; D £7.50; cc Ac Vi

TROWBRIDGE Wiltshire   4A3

Gordons   RAC
65 Wingfield Road, Trowbridge BA14 9EG
01225-752072 Fax 01225-755902
13 bedrs, 2 ➡; TV tcf ✂ P20
sB&B £22 dB&B £38; HB weekly £154; cc Ac Vi

Old Manor   RAC
Trowle, Trowbridge BA14 9BL 01225-777393
Fax 01225-765443   &
14 bedrs, 14 ➡/WC, TV tcf P20
sB&B £45-£50 dB&B £58-£75 Breakfast only
[10%V]; cc Ac Amex DC Vi JCB

VENTNOR Isle of Wight   4B4

Channel View   ☆RAC
Hambrough Road, Ventnor PO38 1SQ
01983-852230

★★Highfield   ☆RAC
Leeson Road, Ventnor PO38 1PU
01983-852800
12 bedrs, 12 ➥/WC; TV tcf 🐾 ⊬ P12
Child restrictions
dB&B £66-£74; HB weekly £229-£255; D
£11.95 [10%V]; cc Ac Vi

Hillside Private *Acclaimed*   ☆RAC
Mitchell Avenue, Ventnor PO38 1DR
01983-852271
11 bedrs, 4 ➥/WC, 7 ☏/WC; TV tcf 🐾 ⊬ P12
Child restrictions
D £6.50 [10%V]; cc Ac Amex Vi

Hotel Picardie   ☆RAC
Esplanade, Ventnor PO38 1JX 01983-852647
10 bedrs, 3 ➥/WC, 7 ☏/WC; TV tcf 🐾
sB&B £17.25 dB&B £34.50; HB weekly £175;
cc Ac Vi

Lake *Highly Acclaimed*   ☆RAC
Shore Road, Ventnor PO38 1RF 01983-852613
11 bedrs, 1 ➥/WC, 9 ☏/WC, 2 ➥; tcf 🐾 ⊬ P20
Child restrictions
sB&B £23.25-£28.25 dB&B £37-£53; HB
weekly £169.75-£185.50; D £7 [5%V]

Llynfi   ☆RAC
23 Spring Hill, Ventnor PO38 1PF
01983-852202
10 bedrs, 7 ➥/WC, 2 ➥; P6
sB&B £16-£21 dB&B £32-£42; HB weekly
£145-£180; [10%V]; cc Ac Vi

Madeira Hall *Highly Acclaimed*   ☆RAC
Trinity Road, Bonchurch, Ventnor PO38 1NS
01983-852624
8 bedrs, 5 ➥/WC, 3 ☏/WC; TV tcf ⊬ P10
Child restrictions
sB&B £35 dB&B £70 [10%V]; cc Ac Vi

Richmond Private *Acclaimed*   ☆RAC
Esplanade, Ventnor PO38 1JX 01983-852496
12 bedrs, 9 ➥/WC, 3 ➥; 🐾 P4
[5%V]; cc Ac DC Vi

St Martins *Acclaimed*   ☆RAC
The Esplanade, Ventnor PO38 1JX

01983-852345
6 bedrs, 4 ➥/WC;
Child restrictions
Breakfast only; cc Ac Amex DC Vi

St Maur   ☆RAC
Castle Road, Ventnor PO38 1LG 01983-852570
Fax 01983-852306
14 bedrs, 13 ➥/WC, 2 ➥; ⊬ P12
Child restrictions
sB&B £18-£24 dB&B £48; HB weekly £210;
[10%V]; cc Ac Amex DC Vi

Under Rock Shore Road, Ventnor PO38 1RF
01983-852714

WAREHAM Dorset   4A4

Cromwell House   ☆RAC
Lulworth Cove, Wareham 01929-400253 Fax
01929-400566
14 bedrs, 11 ➥/WC, 3 ☏/WC; TV tcf 🐾 P15
sB&B £23.50-£32.60 dB&B £47-£75; HB
weekly £203-£225; D £10 [10%V];
cc Ac Amex Vi

★★Worgret Manor   ☆RAC
Worgret, Wareham BH20 6AB 01929-553339
Fax 01929-552846

WARMINISTER Wiltshire   3F2

Granada Lodge   ☆RAC
A36 Bath Road, Warminster BA12 7RU
01985-219539

Lane End Cottage   ☆RAC
**72 Lane End, Corsley, Warminster BA12
7PG 01373-83239**
3 bedrs, 1 ➥/WC, 1 ➥;
Child restrictions
Breakfast only

WEYMOUTH Dorset   3E3

Birchfields   ☆RAC
22 Abbotsbury Road, Weymouth DT4 0AE
01305-773255
9 bedrs, 3 ☏/WC, 2 ➥; TV tcf 🐾 P3
sB&B £13-£18 dB&B £30-£36; HB weekly
£113-£131; [10%V]

Ferndown 47 Walpole Street, Weymouth
DT4 7HQ 01305-775228
8 bedrs, 2 ➥;
Breakfast only

Greenhill   RAC
8 Greenhill, Weymouth DT4 7SQ
01305-786026
17 bedrs, 12 ⬧/WC, 2 ⬌; TV tcf P14
sB&B £15-£17.50 dB&B £20-£22.50; HB
weekly £170-£180; cc Ac Vi

Hazeldene   RAC
16 Abbotsbury Road, Weymouth DT4 OAE
01305-782579
6 bedrs, 3 ⬌; TV tcf P8
sB&B £10-£17 dB&B £28-£34; HB weekly
£90-£100

Hotel Concorde   RAC
131 The Esplanade, Weymouth DT4 7RY
01305-776900
15 bedrs, 1 ⬌/WC, 11 ⬧/WC, 1 ⬌; TV tcf ✕
P4
Breakfast only

Kenora *Acclaimed*   RAC
5 Stavordale Road, Westham, Weymouth DT4
0AD 01305-771215
15 bedrs, 4 ⬌/WC, 9 ⬧/WC, 1 ⬌; TV tcf P15
sB&B £22-£30 dB&B £44-£50; HB weekly
£165-£194; D £10; cc Ac Vi

Kings Acre   RAC
140 The Esplanade, Weymouth DT4 7NH
01305-782534
12 bedrs, 8 ⬧/WC, 1 ⬌; TV tcf P9
sB&B £23-£29 dB&B £38-£40; HB weekly
£148-£182; cc Ac Vi

Redcliff   RAC
18-19 Brunswick Terrace, Weymouth DT4 7SE
01305-784682

Sou West Lodge   RAC
Rodwell Road, Weymouth DT4 8QT
01305-783749   ♿
8 bedrs, 4 ⬌/WC, 4 ⬧/WC; TV tcf ✕ P10
sB&B £20.25-£21.90 dB&B £40.50-£43.80;
[5%V]

Sunningdale   RAC
52 Preston Road, Weymouth DT3 6QD
01305-832179
18 bedrs, 8 ⬌/WC, 4 ⬧/WC, 3 ⬌; TV tcf ✕ P18
sB&B £19-£24.50 dB&B £38-£49; HB weekly
£154-£194; D £6.50 [5%V]; cc Ac DC Vi

Tamarisk *Acclaimed*   RAC
12 Stavordale Road, Weymouth DT4 0AB

01305-786514
16 bedrs, 4 ⬌/WC, 8 ⬧/WC, 3 ⬌; TV tcf P19
sB&B £18-£21 dB&B £36-£42; HB weekly
£130-£159

Trelawney   RAC
1 Old Castle Road, Weymouth DT4 8QB
01305-783188
10 bedrs, 5 ⬌/WC, 5 ⬧/WC, 1 ⬌; TV tcf ✕
sB&B £22 dB&B £39-£47 Breakfast only; cc Vi

Westwey *Acclaimed*   RAC
62 Abbotsbury Road, Weymouth DT4 0BJ
01305-784564

WIMBORNE MINSTER Dorset   3F3

Riversdale   RAC
33 Poole Road, Wimborne Minster BH21 1QB
01202-884528
8 bedrs, 1 ⬌/WC, 2 ⬌; TV tcf ✕ P3
Child restrictions
sB&B £15-£22 dB&B £33-£40 Breakfast only

WINCHESTER Hampshire   4B3

Shawlands *Acclaimed*   RAC
46 Kilham Lane, Winchester SO22 5QD
01962-861166 Fax 01962-861166   ♿
4 bedrs, 1 ⬌/WC, 1 ⬧/WC, 1 ⬌; TV tcf ✕ ⤙
P4
sB&B £20 dB&B £34-£38 Breakfast only

(Inn) The Wykeham Arms *Highly Acclaimed*   RAC
75, Kingsgate Street, Winchester SO23 9PE
01962-853834 Fax 01962-854411
7 bedrs, 7 ⬌/WC; TV tcf ✕ ⤙
Child restrictions
sB&B £65 dB&B £75; cc Ac Amex Vi

WINDSOR Berkshire   4C2

Allbrown House 15 Princess Avenue,
Windsor SL4 3LU 01753-862704

Clarence   RAC
9 Clarence Road, Windsor SL4 5AE
01753-864436 Fax 01753-857060
20 bedrs, 4 ⬌/WC, 16 ⬧/WC, 1 ⬌; TV tcf ✕
P4
sB&B £30-£36 dB&B £46-£52 Breakfast only
[10%V]; cc Ac Amex DC Vi JCB

Elansey 65 Clifton Rise, Windsor SL4 5SX
01753-3864438

Halcyon House 131 Clarence Road, Windsor SL4 5AR 01753-863262
4 bedrs, 1 🛏/WC, 2 ℝ/WC, 1 🛏; TV tcf P6
sB&B £26 Breakfast only

Melrose House *Acclaimed*　　　　　　🏅RAC
53 Frances Road, Windsor SL4 3AQ
01753-865328
9 bedrs, 2 🛏/WC, 7 ℝ/WC; ✖ ⅙ P9
sB&B £25-£28 dB&B £42 Breakfast only
[10%V]; cc Ac Vi

Netherton *Highly Acclaimed*　　　　🏅RAC
96-98 St Leonards Road, Windsor SL4 3NU　　🚻
01753-855508　　　　　　　　　　　　　　　&
11 bedrs, 7 🛏/WC, 4 ℝ/WC; TV tcf P14
sB&B £30 dB&B £40 Breakfast only [5%V];
cc Ac Vi

Oxford Blue Inn Crimp Hill Road,
Old Windsor, Windsor SL4 2DY
01753-620419

77 Whitehorse Road Windsor SL4 4PG
01753-866803

88 St Leonards Road Windsor SL4 3DA
01753-853984

169 Oxford Road Windsor SL4 5DX
01753-854489

WOODSTOCK Oxfordshire　　　　　　　4B1

Gorseland　　　　　　　　　　　　　　🏅RAC
Gorseland, Boddington Lane, Woodstock OX8
6PU 01993-881895 Fax 01993-882799
5 bedrs, 1 🛏/WC, 4 ℝ/WC; TV tcf ✖ ⅙ P8
sB&B £19-£24 dB&B £28-£38; HB weekly
£175-£225; [10%V]; cc Ac Amex Vi

Laurels *Acclaimed*　　　　　　　　　　🏅RAC
40 Hensington Road, Woodstock OX20 1JL
01993-812583

(Inn) The Star　　　　　　　　　　　　🏅RAC
22 Market Place, Woodstock OX2O 1TA
01993-811373 Fax 01993-811373
4 bedrs, 4 🛏/WC; TV tcf ✖ ⅙
sB&B £35-£45 dB&B £45 D £10.85 [10%V]; cc
Ac Amex Vi

Stonehenge

South West

Somerset • Devon • Cornwall

Peninsulas, like islands entice the escapist in us. The converging coasts of Devon and Cornwall are no exception. As if poles apart, wild cliffs of granite and slate brave the Atlantic surf while the southern aspect enjoys gentle creeks with picturesque coves and fishing harbours. Between lie awesome moors which fade into the time-encapsulated flat 'wet-lands' of Somerset.

A SELECTION OF ATTRACTIONS:

Unless otherwise stated, all can be visited between April and October – some longer. Telephone for days/times of opening.

Barbara Hepworth Museum, St. Ives, Cornwall: *Hepworth sculptures set in the artist's former home. Admin. by Tate Gallery.* Tel: 01736-796226.

Buckfast Abbey, Buckfastleigh, Devon. *A living 20th-c Benedictine monastry selling own produce of wine, honey & cream teas.* Tel: 01364-42519.

Buckland Abbey

Buckland Abbey, Yelverton, Devon: *Former 13th-c Cistercian monastery became home of Sir Francis Drake. NT.* Tel: 01822-853607.

Castle Drogo, Drewsteignton, Devon: *Lutyens designed granite castle. Terraced garden and superb views at 900 ft. NT.* Tel: 0164 743-3306.

Chard & Dist. Museum, Somerset: *Varied interests here, costume, forge, carpenter's & plumber's workshops plus early artificial limbs! May-early Oct.* Tel: 01460-65091.

Chysauster Iron-Age Village: *remains nr. Penzance, Cornwall. All year.*

Compton Castle, nr. Torquay, Devon: *Fortified medieval manor with great hall, solar, kitchen, chapel & fine rose garden. NT.* Tel: 01803-872112.

Cothele, Calstock, Cornwall: *Splendid medieval house, fine tapestries & armour. Terraced garden above Taymar. Water Mill and Quay Museum. NT.* Tel: 01579-50434.

Dartington Cider Press Centre, Skinners Bridge, nr. Totnes, Devon. *Visitor centre containing leading local craftwork and cider.* Tel: 01803-864171.

Exeter Cathedral, Devon: *dates from 12th-c.*

Glastonbury Abbey, Somerset: *ruins dating from 12th-c, associations with King Arthur & Joseph of Arimathea.* Tel: 01458-832267

Abbey Gardens & Valhalla Figurehead Collection, Tresco. Isles of Scilly: *Tropical garden paradise and display of ship-wrecked figureheads.*

Kents Cavern, Torquay, Devon. *Temperature controlled cave home of early Brits & pre-historic animals. Guided tours.* Tel: 01803-294059.

Killerton House, nr. Exeter, Devon. *18th-c home with costume collection, colourful garden and viewpoint from Iron Age hill fort. NT.* Tel: 01392-881345.

Knightshayes Court, nr. Tiverton, Devon: *Victorian house plus garden lovers' paradise –*

bulbs, borders, rare shrubs and specimen trees. *NT.* Tel: 01884-254665.

Lanhydrock, nr. Bodmin, Cornwall: *42 superb rooms and fun servants' quarters. Formal & woodland gardens. NT.* Tel: 01208-73320.

Montacute House, nr. Yeovil, Somerset: *Golden Elizabethan house of Ham Hill stone. Notable heraldic glass, tapestries & panelling. NT.* Tel: 01935-823289.

Morwellham Quay, nr. Tavistock, Devon: *Former copper port peopled and restored to Victorian life.* Tel: 0822-832766

Okehampton, Museum of Dartmoor Life: *Life of moorland folk through the ages plus varied geological, archeological displays in pretty watermill.* Tel: 01837-52295.

Old Post Office, Tintagel, Cornwall: *14th-c miniature manor, still operates as village P.O. NT.* Tel: 01840-770024.

Poldark Mine, Helston, Cornwall. *18th-c tin mine & museums.* Tel: 01326-573173.

Potters Museum of Curiosity at Jamaica Inn, Bolventor, Cornwall. *Wonderworld of small stuffed animals by Victorian taxedermist plus Daphne du Maurier study at Jamaica Inn.* Tel: 01566-86838.

Powderham Castle

Powderham Castle, Kenton, nr. Exeter, Devon: *Dates from 1390. Private aristocratic medieval castle home and deer park. Easter-Oct.* Tel: 01626-890243.

Prideaux Place, Padstow, Cornwall: *Castellated 16th-c private home plus 60 acres grounds with deer park. Open: Easter-Sep.* Tel: 01841-532411.

River Dart Country Park, nr. Ashburton, Devon. *Something for everyone – Anaconda Run, pony riding, adventure playgrounds, bathing, fishing, riverside walks, picnic areas.* Tel: 01364- 52511.

St. Austell Brewery, Cornwall. *Tours & tastings of the Duchy's main brewhouse.* Tel: 01726-66022.

St. Michael's Mount, Marazion, Cornwall. *Spectactular 14th-c castle set on island. NT.* Tel: 01736-710507.

Saltram*: nr. Plymouth, Devon: *Georgian mansion with some fine Adam rooms and beautiful gardens. NT.* Tel: 01752-336546.

Shaldon Wildlife Trust, Shaldon, Devon. *Breeding centre for endangered small mamals, exotic birds, reptiles. Mid-Apr-Sep.* Tel: 01626-872234.

Shire Horse Centre, Yealmpton, nr. Plymouth, Devon. *Arena events, falconry centre, adventure playground, butterflies, petting paddocks.* Tel: 01752-880268 & 880806.

Somerset Rural Life Museum, Glastonbury: *Award winning exhibitions plus regular summer events, 14th-c barn.* Tel: 01458-831197.

Tate Gallery, St. Ives, Cornwall: *Recently opened important venue for work of local artists.* Tel: 01736-796226.

Torre Abbey, Torquay: *Mementoes of Agatha Christie gives added interest to displays of art, silver. Attractive garden setting.* Tel: 01803-293593.

Ugbrooke, Chudleigh, Devon: *Private home re-vamped from 12th-c by Robert Adam, landscaped by Capability Brown. Mid-Jul-Sep.* Tel: 01626-852179.

Wells Cathedral & 13th-c Bishops Palace, Somerset. Tel: 01749-678691.

Yeovilton Fleet Air Arm Museum, nr. Ilchester, Somerset. *Interior of Concorde plus over 40 historic naval aircraft,* Tel: 01935-840565.

SOME ANNUAL EVENTS:

Britannia Royal Naval College Open Day,
Dartmouth: *mid-Jun.*
Tel: 01803-834224.

Bude Folk Arts & Cider Festival, Cornwall:
*Best international folk artists plus 80 ciders to
taste! 2-4 Jun.* Tel: 01288-356888.

Bude Jazz Festival: *100 live sessions, New
Orleans, Trad. 26 Aug-2 Sept.*
Tel: 01684-566956.

Cornwall Gardens Festival: *Over 70
gardens open on different days. 1 Apr-
31 May.* Tel: 01872- 74057.

Cornwall Folk Festival, Wadebridge: *100
events, all under cover, Town Hall and pubs.
25-28 Aug.* Tel: 01208- 813100.

Devon County Show, Clyst St. Mary, Exeter:
*Livestock, Ideal Home & Leisure, the 100th
Show. 18-20 May.*Tel: 01392-444777.

Exeter Festival, Exeter & Nat. Trust
properties in Devon: *Celebrating the arts &
500 years of GB enterprise. 30 Jun-16 Jul.*
Tel: 01392-265265.

**Golf – Benson & Hedges International
Open**, St, Mellion, Cornwall: *The first event of
the PGA European Tour. 10-14 May.*
Tel: 01932-859777.

Great Cornwall Balloon Festival, Newquay:
*Hot air balloon event on seafront. 28 Apr-
1 May.* Tel: 01637-872211.

Helston Furry Dance, Cornwall: *Whole town
en fete in Celtic spring festival of flowers and
dancing. May 6.* Tel: 01326-572082.

Minack Theatre Summer Festival,
Porthcurno, Cornwall: *Plays and musicals in
unique open air cliff-top setting. 29 May-
16 Sep.* Tel: 01736-810694.

Mystery of the English Riviera Festival,
Torbay, Devon: *A celebration of mystery &
crime fiction. 22-27 May* Tel: 01803-296296.

Padstow 'Obby 'Oss, Cornwall: *Celtic street
dance festival, dawn to dusk, led by raunchy
'oss and teaser. 1 May.* Tel: 01872-74057.

Paignton, Festival of Arts & Culture,
Devon: *Special events to mark 700th
anniversary of the town. 18-21 May*
Tel: 01803-296296.

Port of Dartmouth Royal Regatta: *Plus lots
of fun events like barrel rolling, Red Arrows
display. 24-26Aug.* Tel: 01803- 832435.

Royal Bath & West of England Show,
Shepton Mallet, Somerset: *The region's top
livestock plus ring extravaganzas, 4 miles of
trade stands. 31 May-3 Jun.*
Tel: 01749-823211.

Royal Cornwall Show, Wadebridge,
Cornwall: *Showpiece of Cornish agriculture,
flower display, rare breeds, crafts, show
jumping. 8-10 Jun.* Tel: 01208-812183.

Three Spires Festival, Truro Cathedral,
Cornwall: *23 Jun-8 Jul.* Tel: 01872-863346.

Victory in Europe Extravaganza, Plymouth,
Devon: *Dance on Plymouth Hoe to American
bands in massive street party. Fireworks,
wartime vehicle rally, and more. May.*
Tel: 01752-261125.

Widecombe Fair, Devon: *Yes, really!* 12 Sept
Tel: 013643-368.

*'Uncle Tom Cobleigh and All' village sign at
Widecombe*

ASHBURTON Devon   3D3

Gages Mill *Acclaimed*   RAC
Buckfastleigh Road, Ashburton TQ13 7JW
01364-652391

*Carefully converted former 14th Century wool
mill, set in 1.25 acres on edge of Dartmoor
National Park. 8 delightful en-suite rooms -
all with country views - home cooked food to
a very high standard, licensed, ample parking*
8 bedrs, 7 ➡/WC; TV tcf ✗ P8
Child restrictions
sB&B £21.50-£22.50 dB&B £43-£45; HB
weekly £192-£203; D £9.50

AXBRIDGE Somerset   3E4

Webbington   RAC
Loxton, Axbridge BS26 2XA 01934-750100
Fax 01934-750100
Awaiting Inspection

AXMINSTER Devon   3E3

(Inn) Tuckers Arms   RAC
Dalwood, Axminster EX13 7EG 01404-881342
5 bedrs, 5 ☎/WC; TV tcf P8
sB&B £25 dB&B £40 Breakfast only [10%V];
cc Ac Vi

BARNSTAPLE Devon   2C2

Broomhill Country Muddiford, Barnstaple
EX31 4EX 01271-850262

Cedars Lodge Inn   RAC
Bickington Road, Barnstaple EX31 2HP
01271-71784   &
23 bedrs, 9 ➡/WC, 14 ☎/WC; TV tcf ✗ P120
sB&B £32-£37 dB&B £53 D £7;
cc Ac Amex Vi

Highland Farm Long Lane, Kentisbury,
Barnstaple EX31 4NU 01271-883701

Yeo Dale *Acclaimed*   RAC
Pilton Bridge, Barnstaple EX31 1PG
01271-42954
10 bedrs, 1 ➡/WC, 5 ☎/WC, 2 ➡; TV tcf ✗
sB&B £18-£24 dB&B £35-£44; HB weekly
£189-£231; [10%V]; cc Ac Amex DC Vi

BEAFORD Devon   2C2

Beaford House   RAC
Winkleigh, Beaford EX19 8AB 0180-53-305

BIDEFORD Devon   2C2

Goutilsland Farm Buckland Brewer,
Bideford EX39 5NG 01237-4511665
5 bedrs, 1 ➡; TV tcf ✗ P10
sB&B £8 Breakfast only

Pines *Acclaimed*   RAC
Eastleigh, Bideford EX39 4PA 01271-860561
Fax 01271-860561   &
2 bedrs, 1 ➡/WC, 2 ➡; TV tcf P20
sB&B £20-£25 dB&B £34-£40; HB weekly
£90-£99; D £9.95 [10%V]

Sunset   RAC
Landcross, Bideford EX39 5JA 01237-472962

BOSCASTLE Cornwall   2B3

Old Coach House   RAC
Tintagel Road, Boscastle PL35 OAS
01840-250398   &
6 bedrs, 1 ➡/WC, 5 ☎/WC; TV tcf ✗ P9
Child restrictions
sB&B £15-£24 dB&B £30-£48 Breakfast only;
cc Ac Amex Vi

Tolcarne Tintagel Road, Boscastle PL35 0AS
01840-250654

BOVEY TRACEY Devon   3D3

★★(Inn) Riverside Inn   RAC
Fore Street, Bovey Tracey TQ13 9AF
01626-832293

BRAUNTON Devon   2C2

Denham Farm *Acclaimed*   RAC
North Buckland, Braunton EX33 1HY
01271-890297

BRIDGWATER Somerset 3E2

Castle of Comfort *Acclaimed* RAC
Dodington, Nether Stowey, Bridgwater TA5 1LE 01278-741264
5 bedrs, 1 🛁/WC, 3 🚿/WC, 1 🛁; TV tcf 🐕 🚭 P14
sB&B £32 dB&B £42 D £10; cc Ac Amex Vi

Quantock View House Taunton Road, Bridgwater TA6 6PR 01278-663309 Fax 01278-663309 ♿

Comfortable, family-run, guest house in central Somerset, close to the hills and coast.
4 bedrs, 3 🚿/WC; TV tcf 🐕 P5
sB&B £16; HB weekly £135-£155; D £7; cc Ac Vi

The Grange Stawell, Bridgwater TA7 9AF 01278-722452

BRIXHAM Devon 3D4

Raddicombe Lodge RAC
Kingswear Road, Brixham TQ5 0EX 01803-882125
8 bedrs, 3 🚿/WC, 2 🛁; TV tcf P8
sB&B £16.60-£18.20 dB&B £33-£36.40 Breakfast only [5%V]; cc Ac DC Vi

Richmond House Higher Manor Road, Brixham TQ5 8HA 01803-882391

Sampford House RAC
57-59 King Street, Brixham TQ5 9TH 01803-857761
6 bedrs, 1 🛁/WC, 3 🚿/WC, 1 🛁; TV tcf 🐕 P2
sB&B £15-£19 dB&B £30-£35 Breakfast only [10%V]

BUCKFASTLEIGH Devon 2C3

Dartbridge Manor RAC
Dartbridge Road, Buckfastleigh TQ11 0SZ 01364-43575

BUDE Cornwall   2B3

★★Camelot   RAC
Downs View, Bude EX23 8RE 01288-352361
Fax 01288-355470
21 bedrs, 21 ⇒/WC; ✘ P21
sB&B £20-£25 dB&B £40-£50; HB weekly
£199-£230; D £44 [10%V]; cc Ac Vi

Court Farm Marhamchurch, Bude EX23 0EN
01288-361494

Mornish 20 Summerleaze Crescent, Bude
EX23 8HJ 01288-352972

Pencarrol   RAC
21 Downs View, Bude EX23 8RF
01288-352478
8 bedrs, 2 ☞/WC, 2 ⇒; TV tcf
sB&B £11-£15.50 dB&B £28-£31; HB weekly
£140.50-£150.50; [10%V]

The Bay View Inn Widemouth Bay, Bude
EX23 0AW 01288-361273

Trevelyan St Gennys, Bude EX23 0NP
01840-230459

Trevigue Crackington Haven, Bude EX23
0LQ 01840-230418

BUDLEIGH SALTERTON Devon   3D3

Long Range *Acclaimed*   RAC
Vales Road, Budleigh Salterton EX9 6HS
013954-43321
7 bedrs, 2 ⇒/WC, 4 ☞/WC; TV tcf ✘ P6
sB&B £21.50 dB&B £43; HB weekly £212; D
£12.50 [10%V]

Tidwell House   RAC
Knowle, Budleigh Salterton EX9 7AG
01395-442444

Discount vouchers
Hotels with a (V) at the end of the price
information will accept RAC discount
vouchers in part payment for
accommodation bills on the full,
standard rate, not against bargain breaks
or any other special offer.

BURNHAM-ON-SEA Somerset   3E1

The Old Rectory Church Road, Brean,
Burnham-on-Sea TA8 2SF 01751-447

CAMBORNE Cornwall   2A4

Lowenac *Highly Acclaimed*   RAC
Bassett Road, Camborne TR14 8SL
01209-719295

CARBIS BAY Cornwall   2A4

White House   RAC
The Valley, Carbis Bay TR26 2QY
01736-797405

CHAGFORD Devon   2C3

Blackaller *Highly Acclaimed*   RAC
North Bovey, Chagford TQ13 8QY
01647-40322
5 bedrs, 5 ⇒/WC; TV tcf ✘ P7
Child restrictions
sB&B £27-£30 dB&B £60-£64 D £20 [10%V]

Glendarah House *Acclaimed*   RAC
Newton Abbot, Chagford TQ13 8BZ
01647-433270

CHARD Somerset   3E2

Ammonite Lodge 43 High Street, Chard
TA20 1QL 01460-63839

The Cotley Inn Wambrook, Chard TA20 3DF
01460-62348

Watermead *Acclaimed*   RAC
83 High Street, Chard TA20 1QT 01460-62834

CHEDDAR Somerset   3E1

Market Cross *Acclaimed*   RAC
Church Street, The Cross, Cheddar BS27 3RA
01934-742264
6 bedrs, 3 ☞/WC, 1 ➟; TV tcf ✂ P6
sB&B £19-£29 dB&B £37-£40 Breakfast only;
cc Ac Vi

**South Barn The Hayles, Cheddar TA20
1QL 01934-743146**

COLYTON Devon   3D3

Old Bakehouse   RAC
Lower Church Street, Colyton EX13 6ND
01297-552518
6 bedrs, 6 ➟/WC; Breakfast only

The Grove South Street, Colyton EX13 6ER
01297-552438

COMBE MARTIN Devon   2C2

Blair Lodge *Acclaimed*   RAC
Moory Meadow, Seaside, Combe Martin EX34
0DG 01271-882294

Channel Vista *Acclaimed*   RAC
Woodlands, Combe Martin EX34 0AT

01271-883514
7 bedrs, 1 ➟/WC, 6 ☞/WC; TV tcf ✂ P7
Child restrictions
dB&B £34-£40; cc Ac Vi

Saffron House *Acclaimed*   RAC
King Street, Combe Martin EX34 0BX
01271-883521
10 bedrs, 2 ➟/WC, 6 ☞/WC, 1 ➟;
TV tcf ✂ P10
sB&B £20-£23 dB&B £34-£40; HB weekly
£144-£179;; cc Ac Vi

Woodlands   RAC
2 The Woodlands, Combe Martin EX34 0AT
01271-882769
8 bedrs, 1 ➟; P8
Child restrictions
Breakfast only

CRACKINGTON HAVEN Cornwall   2B3

Crackington Manor Crackington Haven,
Bude EX23 0JG 01840-230397

(Inn) Coombe Barton Inn   RAC
Crackington Haven EX23 0JG 01840-230345
Fax 01840-230788
5 bedrs, 3 ➟/WC, 2 ➟; ✂ P40
sB&B £17.50-£19.50 dB&B £38-£50 Breakfast
only [10%V]; cc Ac Amex Vi

Manor Farm Crackington Haven EX23 0JW
01840-230304

CROYDE Devon   2C2

West Winds Moor Lane, Croyde Bay, Croyde,
Braunton EX33 1PA 01271-890489 Fax
01271-890489

*A hotel in a picturesque water's edge location
with private access to Croyde Beach. A
comfortable and relaxed atmosphere with
well-equipped rooms.*

---

5 bedrs, 1 ➥/WC, 2 ☞/WC, 1 ➥; TV tcf ✖ P7
sB&B £19; HB weekly £187-£201; D £27.50-
£29.50; cc Ac Vi

Moorsands House Moor La, Croyde EX33
1NP 01271-890781

DARTMOUTH Devon   3D4

Ford House *Highly Acclaimed*   RAC
44 Victoria Road, Dartmouth TQ6 9DX
01803-834047
3 bedrs, 3 ➥/WC; TV tcf ✖ P5
Child restrictions
sB&B £40 dB&B £46-£60; HB weekly £318.50;
D £22.50 [10%V]; cc Ac Amex Vi

Gitcombe House Cornworthy, Totnes,
Dartmouth TQ6 7HH 01804-21678

**The Captain's House 18 Clarence St,
Dartmouth TQ6 9NW 01803-832133**

Victoria Cote 105 Victoria Road, Dartmouth
TQ6 9DY 01803-832997
3 bedrs, 1 ➥/WC, 2 ☞/WC; TV tcf ✖ P6
sB&B £18; HB weekly £196-£224; D £11

DAWLISH Devon   3D3

Mimosa   RAC
11 Barton Terrace, Dawlish EX7 9QH
01626-863283
9 bedrs, 1 ☞/WC, 2 ➥; tcf ✂ P4
sB&B £13-£14 dB&B £26-£28; HB weekly
£127-£134;

West Hatch *Acclaimed*   RAC
34 West Cliff, Dawlish EX7 9DN
01626-864211   ♿
11 bedrs, 10 ☞/WC, 1 ➥; TV tcf ✂ P11
sB&B £28-£38 dB&B £42-£50; HB weekly
£150-£210; D £6.95 [5%V]

DULVERTON Somerset   3D2

Exton House Exton, Dulverton TA22 9TJ
01643-85365   ♿
6 bedrs, 4 ➥/WC, 2 ☞/WC; TV tcf ✖ P6
sB&B £24; HB weekly £248.50-£276.50; D
£12.50; cc Ac Vi

**Town Mills Dulverton TA22 9HB
01398-323124**

*An 18th century mill house in a secluded
position in the centre of Dulverton. Some
rooms with log fires.*
5 bedrs, 1 ➥; TV tcf P5
sB&B £15 Breakfast only

DUNSTER Somerset   3D2

Bilbrook Lawns   RAC
Bilbrook, Dunster TA24 6HE 01984-40331
7 bedrs, 4 ➥/WC, 1 ➥; TV tcf ✖ ✂ P8
sB&B £26.50 dB&B £40; HB weekly £160; D
£11.50 [10%V]; cc Amex

★★Exmoor House   RAC
West Street, Dunster TA24 6SN
01643-821268   ♿
7 bedrs, 7 ➥/WC; ✖
Child restrictions
dB&B £52; HB weekly £252-£262.50; D
£14.50 [10%V]; cc Ac Amex DC Vi

EXETER Devon   3D3

Braeside   RAC
21 New North Road, Exeter EX4 4HF
01392-56875
7 bedrs, 2 ➥; ✖
Breakfast only

Croft Cockwood Harbour, Cockwood Bridge,
Starcross, Exeter EX6 8QY 01626-890282
9 bedrs, 3 ➥/WC, 2 ➥; ✖ P14
sB&B £17 Breakfast only

Dunmore 22 Blackall Road, Exeter EX4 4HE
01392-431643

Gledhills *Acclaimed*
32 Alphington Road, Exeter EX2 8HN
01392-430469 Fax 01392-430469
11 bedrs, 10 🛁/WC, 1 🛁;
sB&B £22 dB&B £39 Breakfast only; cc Ac Vi

New Park Farm Silverton, Exeter EX5 4DH
01392-861182 ♿
4 bedrs, 1 🛁;
sB&B £15 Breakfast only

Park View *Acclaimed*
8 Howell Road, Exeter EX4 4LG 01392-71772
Fax 01392-53047
15 bedrs, 9 🛁/WC, 4 🛁; TV tcf 🐕 🚭 P6
sB&B £20 dB&B £35 Breakfast only [5%V]; cc Ac Vi

Regent's Park
Polsloe Road, Exeter EX1 2NU 01392-59749
11 bedrs, 3 🛁; P16
sB&B £17 dB&B £33 Breakfast only

Telstar
77 St David's Hill, Exeter EX4 4DW
01392-72466
17 bedrs, 2 🛁/WC, 2 🚿/WC, 2 🛁; tcf P7
sB&B £12-£15 dB&B £26-£28 Breakfast only [5%V]

The Old Thatch Inn Cheriton Bishop, Exeter
EX16 6HS 01647-24204

Trees Mini
2 Queens Crescent, York Road, Exeter EX4
6AY 01392-59531

EXMOUTH Devon 3D3

Aslema 61 St Andrews Road, Exmouth EX18
1AS 01395-270737

FALMOUTH Cornwall 2A4

Bosanneth *Acclaimed*
Gyllyngvase Hill, Falmouth TR11 4DW
01326-314649
8 bedrs, 2 🛁/WC, 6 🚿/WC; TV tcf 🚭 P8
Child restrictions
sB&B £18-£20 dB&B £36-£40; HB weekly £143-£170; D £8 [5%V]; cc Ac Vi

Chellowdene *Acclaimed*
Gyllyngvase Hill, Falmouth TR11 4DN
01326-314950
6 bedrs, 2 🛁/WC, 4 🚿/WC; TV tcf 🚭 P6
Child restrictions
dB&B £32-£36; HB weekly £130-£160; [10%V]

Cotswold House *Acclaimed*
49 Melvill Road, Falmouth TR11 4DF
01326-312077
10 bedrs, 4 🛁/WC, 5 🚿/WC; TV tcf
Child restrictions
sB&B £17-£18 dB&B £34-£36; HB weekly £145-£165

Four Seasons *Acclaimed*
43 Melvill Road, Falmouth TR11 4DG
01326-311465 Fax 01326-311465
9 bedrs, 1 🛁/WC, 5 🚿/WC, 1 🛁; TV tcf 🚭 P7
Child restrictions
sB&B £14-£17 dB&B £28-£34; HB weekly £135-£160; [10%V]

Grove Grove Place, Falmouth TR11 4AU
01326-319577

Gyllngvase House *Acclaimed*
Gyllngvase Road, Falmouth TR11 4DJ
01326-312978
15 bedrs, 4 🛁/WC, 8 🚿/WC, 2 🛁; TV tcf 🐕 🚭 P15
sB&B £17-£19 dB&B £38-£42; HB weekly £175-£189;

Hawthorne Dene *Acclaimed*
12 Pennance Road, Falmouth TR11 4EA
01326-311427
9 bedrs, 9 🚿/WC; TV tcf P9
sB&B £17-£22 dB&B £34-£44; HB weekly £135-£168;

★★★Hotel St Michaels
Gyllyngvase Beach, Seafront, Falmouth TR11
4NB 01326-312707 Fax 01326-211772
66 bedrs; 66 🛁/WC
sB&B £55 dB&B £86

Ivanhoe
7 Melvill Road, Falmouth TR11 4AS
01326-319083
7 bedrs, 5 🛁/WC, 2 🛁; P2
sB&B £16 Breakfast only [10%V]; cc Ac Amex DC Vi

Melvill House 52 Melvill Road, Falmouth
TR11 4DQ 01326-316645

Rathgowry *Acclaimed*   RAC
Gyllyngvase Hill, Falmouth TR11 4DN
01326-313482
10 bedrs, 2 ➡/WC, 8 🛆/WC; TV tcf ✈ ✗ P10
sB&B £15-£22 dB&B £30-£44; HB weekly
£140-£173

Trelawney   RAC
6 Melvill Road, Falmouth TR11 4AS
01326-311858
7 bedrs, 3 🛆/WC; TV tcf ✈
sB&B £12-£16 dB&B £30-£32 Breakfast only
[5%V]; cc Ac Vi

Trevaylor 8 Pennance Rd, Falmouth TR11
4EA 01326-313041

Tudor Court   RAC
55 Melvill Road, Falmouth TR11 4DF
01326-312807
11 bedrs, 9 ➡/WC, 1 ➡; ✗
Child restrictions
sB&B £17.50-£18.50; cc Ac Amex DC Vi

FOWEY Cornwall   2B4

Ashley House   RAC
14 The Esplanade, Fowey PL23 1HY
01726-832310 Fax 0181-6654010
6 bedrs, 4 ➡/WC, 1 ➡; ✗
Breakfast only; cc Vi

Carnethic House *Highly Acclaimed*   RAC
Lambs Barn, Fowey PL23 1HQ
01726-833336   &
8 bedrs, 5 ➡/WC, 2 ➡; TV tcf ✈ ✗ P20
sB&B £30-£40 dB&B £44-£60 Breakfast only
[10%V]; cc Ac Amex DC Vi

Fowey Hall Fowey PL23 1ET 01726-833104

Holly House 18 Fore Street, Polruan, Fowey
PL23 01726-870478

GLASTONBURY Somerset   3E2

Cradlebridge Farm   RAC
Glastonbury BA16 9SD 01458-831827   &
2 bedrs, 2 ➡/WC; ✈ P10
sB&B £25 dB&B £35 Breakfast only

★★★(Inn) George & Pilgrims   RAC
High Street, Glastonbury BA5 9DP
01458-831146 Fax 01458-832252   &
13 bedrs, 13 ➡/WC; ✈ P4
[5%V]; cc Ac Amex DC Vi

Shambhala Healing Centre Coursing
Batch, Glastonbury BA6 8BH
01458-833081 Fax 01458-834757   &
A sunny and spacious hotel with beautiful
balconied rooms with fabulous views of the
"Vale of Avalon". Set in beautiful gardens, with
ponds and waterfall. Own sauna and jacuzzi.
4 bedrs, 1 🛆/WC, 3 ➡; P4
sB&B £15; D £7.50; cc Ac Amex DC Vi

GUNNISLAKE Cornwall   2C3

Hingston House Country *Acclaimed*   RAC
St Ann's Chapel, Gunnislake PL18 9HB
01822-832468
10 bedrs, 8 ➡/WC, 8 🛆/WC, 1 ➡; TV tcf ✈
✗ P12
sB&B £26 dB&B £44; HB weekly £138; D
£14; cc Ac Vi

Sandhill House Tavistock Road, Gunnislake
PL18 9DR 01822-832442

HAYLE Cornwall   2A4

Sandsifter 1 Godrevy Beach, St Ives Bay,
Hayle TR27 5ED 01736-753314

HELSTON Cornwall   2A4

Alma House Hotel & Restaurant Mullion,
Helston TR12 7BZ 01326-2240509
A centrally situated, well-appointed hotel close
to beaches, shops and golf course, with sea
views across Mounts Bay. Candlelit restaurant.
3 bedrs, 1 ➡/WC, 1 🛆/WC, 2 ➡; TV tcf ✈ P12
sB&B £15.50; HB weekly £166-£185; D £8.85-
£15; cc Ac Amex DC Vi

Boak House Coverack, Helston TR12 6SH
01326-280608

Higher Trevurvas Farm Ashton, Helston
TR13 9TZ 01736-763613
4 bedrs, 1 ➡/WC, 3 🛆/WC;
Child restrictions
sB&B £16.50; HB weekly £185.50-£213;
D £10-£12

Strathallan Monument Road, Helston TR13
8EH 01326-573683

Trenance Farmhouse Mullion, Helston
TR12 7HB 01326-240639

HOLSWORTHY Devon   2C3

Leworthy Farm   RAC
Holsworthy EX22 6SJ 01409-253488 Fax
01409-254671
*A Georgian-style farmhouse set in pretty
wooded countryside with lawns, lake and
river.*
10 bedrs, 3 ⇥/WC, 2 ⇥; tcf ✂ P20
sB&B £14.50-£19 dB&B £35-£38; HB weekly
£144-£186; D £10 [5%V]; cc Ac Vi

HOPE COVE Devon   2C4

Hope Cove *Highly Acclaimed*   RAC
Hope Cove TQ7 3HH 01548-561233
7 bedrs, 5 ⇥/WC, 2 ↑/WC; P19
Child restrictions
sB&B £32.50 dB&B £45; HB weekly £208; D
£10.50 [10%V]; cc Ac Vi

HORRABRIDGE Devon   2C4

Overcombe *Acclaimed*   RAC
Yelverton, Horrabridge PL20 7RN
01822-853501   &
11 bedrs, 10 ⇥/WC, 1 ⇥;
Breakfast only; cc Ac Vi

ILFRACOMBE Devon   2C2

Avalon *Acclaimed*   RAC
6 Capstone Crescent, Ilfracombe EX34 9BT
01271-863325
11 bedrs, 6 ↑/WC, 2 ⇥; TV tcf ✂ P10
sB&B £15.50-£17.50 dB&B £31-£35; HB
weekly £140; D £7 [10%V]; cc Ac Vi

Avenue   RAC
Greenclose Road, Ilfracombe EX34 8BT
01271-863767
22 bedrs, 9 ⇥/WC, 4 ⇥;
Breakfast only

Cairn House 43 St Brannocks Road,
Ilfracombe EX34 8EH 01271-863911

Capstone   RAC
15-16 St James' Place, Ilfracombe EX34 9BJ
01271-863540 Fax 01271-862277
12 bedrs, 10 ⇥/WC, 1 ↑/WC, 1 ⇥; TV tcf ✂
sB&B £14-£17 dB&B £28-£34; HB weekly
£145-£165; D £6; cc Ac Amex Vi

Carlton Mount Coronation Terrace,
Hillsborough Road, Ilfracombe EX34 9NN
01271-864456

Collingdale *Acclaimed*   RAC
Larkstone Terrace, Ilfracombe EX34 9NU
01271-863770

Cresta *Acclaimed*   RAC
Torrs Park, Ilfracombe EX34 8AY
01271-863742

Floyde Brookdale Avenue, Ilfracombe EX34
8DB 01271-862594

Hillview Woodlands, Ilfracombe EX34 0AT
01271-882331

Lympstone   RAC
14 Cross Park, Ilfracombe EX34 8BJ
01271-863038
14 bedrs, 9 ↑/WC, 2 ⇥; TV tcf ✗ P5
sB&B £13-£15 dB&B £26-£32 Breakfast only

Lyncott   RAC
56 St Brannocks Road, Ilfracombe EX34 8EQ
01271-862425
9 bedrs, 3 ↑/WC, 3 ⇥; tcf ✗ P8
sB&B £12-£14.50 dB&B £26-£29; HB weekly
£110-£128; [10%V]

Merlin Court *Acclaimed*   RAC
Torrs Park, Ilfracombe EX34 8AY
01271-862697

Miramar Ilfracombe EX34 0JS
01271-883558
10 bedrs, 6 ➥/WC, 2 ➥; ✕ P12
sB&B £16; HB weekly £161;

Southcliffe *Acclaimed*   RAC
Torrs Park, Ilfracombe EX34 8AZ
01271-862958
14 bedrs, 13 ☞/WC, 1 ➥; tcf ✗ P12
sB&B £15 dB&B £30-£34 Breakfast only
[10%V]

St Brannocks House   RAC
61 St Brannocks Road, Ilfracombe EX34
8EQ 01271-863873

A detached, Victorian hotel set in its own
grounds within walking distance of the town
centre and seafront.
16 bedrs, 4 ➥/WC, 5 ☞/WC, 2 ➥; TV tcf ✗
✗ P20
sB&B £16-£19.50 dB&B £32-£39; HB weekly
£140-£174; D £7.95 [10%V]; cc Ac Amex Vi

Strathmore *Acclaimed*   RAC
57 St Brannocks Road, Ilfracombe EX34 8EQ
01271-862248
9 bedrs, 2 ➥/WC, 6 ☞/WC, 1 ➥; TV tcf ✗ P7
sB&B £18-£20 dB&B £36-£40; HB weekly
£140-£164; [10%V]; cc Ac Amex DC Vi

Trafalgar *Acclaimed*   RAC
Larkstone Terrace, Ilfracombe EX34 9NU
01271-862145
25 bedrs, 24 ➥/WC; TV tcf P7
sB&B £24 dB&B £46; HB weekly £157; D £10
[10%V]

Westwell Hall *Acclaimed*   RAC
Torrs Park, Ilfracombe EX34 8AZ
01271-862792
9 bedrs, 4 ➥/WC, 5 ☞/WC; TV tcf ✗ P10
sB&B £23 dB&B £46; HB weekly £210; D
£10.50 [10%V]; cc Ac Vi

Wildercombe House *Acclaimed*   RAC
St Brannocks Road, Ilfracombe EX34 8EP
01271-862240 ; cc Ac Vi

INSTOW Devon   2C2

Anchorage *Acclaimed*   RAC
The Quay, Bideford, Instow EX39 4HX
01271-860655   &
17 bedrs, 2 ➥/WC, 15 ☞/WC, 1 ➥; ✗ P24
sB&B £21-£23 dB&B £42-£46; HB weekly
£200-£220; D £12.50; cc Ac Vi

KINGSBRIDGE Devon   2C4

Coombe Farm Kingsbridge TQ7 4AB
01548-852038
3 bedrs, 3 ➥/WC; ✗ P4
sB&B £18.50 Breakfast only

Crabshell Motor Lodge   RAC
Embankment Road, Kingsbridge TQ7 1JZ
01548-853301
24 bedrs, 24 ➥/WC; ✗ P31
Breakfast only; cc Ac Vi

La Mer Thurlestone Sands, Kingsbridge TQ7
3JY 01548-561207
8 bedrs, 5 ➥/WC, 1 ➥; ✗ P9
sB&B £16 Breakfast only

Lodge Malborough, Kingsbridge TQ7 3RN
01548-561405

Rockwood Embankment Road,
Kingsbridge TQ7 1JZ 01548-852480

The Atlantic Marine Drive, Bigbury On Sea,
Kingsbridge TQ7 4AS 01548-810682
3 bedrs, 3 ➥/WC; TV tcf P3
Child restrictions under 5
sB&B £16 D £10-£20

KINGSTON Devon   2C4

Trebles Cottage *Acclaimed*   RAC
Kingsbridge, Kingston TQ7 4PT 01548-810268
5 bedrs, 5 ➥/WC; TV tcf ✗ ✗ P10
Child restrictions
sB&B £30 dB&B £45; HB weekly £230; D £14
[5%V]; cc Ac Amex Vi

LANGPORT Somerset   3E2

Gothic House Mulchelney, Langport TA10
0DW 01250-626
3 bedrs, 2 ☞/WC, 1 ➥; TV tcf ✗ P6
sB&B £14; HB weekly £145-£170; D £9

LAUNCESTON Cornwall   2C3

Hurdon Farm   🔛
Launceston PL15 9LS 01566-772955
6 bedrs, 4 ➥/WC; tcf P6
sB&B £14.50-£17.50 dB&B £29-£35; HB
weekly £138-£159

Trethorne Leisure Farm Kennards House,
Launceston PL15 8QE 01566-86324

Wheatley Farm *Highly Acclaimed*   🔛
Maxworthy, Launceston PL15 8LY
01566-781232 Fax 01566-781232
4 bedrs, 4 ➥/WC; P4
Breakfast only

LIFTON Devon   2C3

The Thatched Cottage *Highly Acclaimed* 🔛
Sprytown, Lifton PL16 0AY 01566-784224 Fax
01566-784334

*16th century thatched cottage housing the
Restaurant, the accommodation is in a
converted Coachouse all set in 2 and a half
acres of garden.*
5 bedrs, 1 ➥/WC, 4 ☞/WC; TV tcf P14
Child restrictions
sB&B £35 dB&B £70 Breakfast only; cc Ac
Amex DC Vi

Location Maps

Hotel locations are shown on the maps at
the back of the guide. All towns and
villages containing an hotel listed in the
guide are shown in black.

LISKEARD Cornwall   2B3

Hyvue House   🔛
Barras Cross, Liskeard PL14 6BN
01579-348175
3 bedrs, 2 ➥/WC; P6
Breakfast only

Manor House Inn   🔛
Rilla Mill, Nr Callington, Liskeard PL17 7NT
01579-62354

Trewint Farm   🔛
Menheniot, Liskeard PL14 3RE 01579-347155

*A 200 acre working farm with a 300 year old
farmhouse. Set in peaceful, rural
surroundings. Good facilities for families
including pony rides and play area.*
3 bedrs, 3 ☞/WC; TV tcf P4
sB&B £18-£20 dB&B £28-£32 Breakfast only

LIZARD Cornwall   2A4

Landewednack House   🔛
Church Cove, Lizard TR12 7PQ 01326-290909
Fax 01326-290909
3 bedrs, 1 ➥/WC, 1 ➥; ✁ P6
Breakfast only; cc Ac Vi

Parc Brawse House *Acclaimed*   🔛
Penmenner Road, Lizard TR12 7NR
01326-290466
6 bedrs, 2 ☞/WC, 2 ➥; TV tcf ✁ P6
sB&B £13-£16 dB&B £25-£29; HB weekly
£150.50-£168; D £9 [5%V]; cc Ac Vi

Penmenner House   🔛
Penmenner Road, Lizard TR12 7NR
01326-290370

LOOE Cornwall 2B4

Bodrigan RAC
Hannafore Road, Looe PL13 2DD
01503-262065
21 bedrs, 11 ➥/WC, 3 ➥;
Breakfast only

Bucklawren Farm RAC
St Martin, Looe PL13 1NZ 01503-240738
Fax 01503-240481

A delightful farmhouse of character offering excellent accommodation, a relaxed atmosphere and delicious home cooking. Awaiting Inspection

5 bedrs, 5 ☏/WC, 1 ➥; TV tcf P6
sB&B £16 D £9; cc Ac Vi

Colwells House Pelynt, Looe PL13 2JX
01503-220201

Coombe Farm *Highly Acclaimed* RAC
Widegates, Looe PL13 1QN 01503-240223 ♿
6 bedrs, 6 ☏/WC; tcf ✻ P20
Child restrictions
sB&B £18-£24 dB&B £36-£48; HB weekly
£200-£240; D £12

Deganwy RAC
Station Road, Looe PL13 1HL 01503-262984
A small, friendly hotel in a three-storey building with a white and blue facade. Situated opposite the river overlooking the Looe Valley five minutes from the Beach, harbour and town centre.
10 bedrs, 3 ☏/WC, 2 ➥; TV tcf P6
sB&B £12-£15 Breakfast only [5%V]

Harecombe Lodge 🏰RAC
Watergate, Looe PL13 2N8 01503-263158
3 bedrs, 2 ➼/WC, 1 ♟/WC; tcf P10
Child restrictions
dB&B £34-£38 Breakfast only [5%V]

Hillingdon 🏰RAC
Portuan Road, Hannafore, Looe PL13 2DW
01503-262906
7 bedrs, 4 ➼/WC, 1 ➼; ✔
sB&B £13 [10%V]; cc Ac Vi

Kantara 7 Trelawney Terrace, Looe PL13
2AG 01503-252093
6 bedrs, 2 ➼; TV tcf 🐾 P1
sB&B £12.50 Breakfast only; cc Ac Amex Vi

Panorama 🏰RAC
Hannafore Road, Looe PL13 2DE
01503-262123 Fax 01503-265654
10 bedrs, 10 ➼/WC, 1 ➼; TV tcf ✔ P7
sB&B £22 dB&B £44; HB weekly £195; D
£10.50 [5%V]; cc Ac Amex DC Vi

Pixies Holt 🏰RAC
Shutta, Looe PL13 1JD 01503-262726
7 bedrs, 4 ➼/WC, 1 ➼; P8
Child restrictions
Breakfast only; cc Ac Amex Vi

Polraen Country House
Highly Acclaimed 🏰RAC
Sandplace, Looe PL13 1PJ 01503-263956
5 bedrs, 1 ➼/WC, 4 ♟/WC, 1 ➼;
TV tcf 🐾 ✔ P28
sB&B £25-£27.50 dB&B £50-£55; HB weekly
£234.50-£248.50; D £15 [10%V]; cc Ac Vi

Sea Breeze Lower Chapel Street, Looe
PL13 1AT 01503-263131
*A comfortable and friendly hotel situated in
the centre of eastern Looe, close to the beach,
harbour and shops.*
5 bedrs, 3 ♟/WC, 1 ➼; TV tcf 🐾 P2
sB&B £14; HB weekly £130-£160; D £7-£8;
cc Ac Vi

The Duchy Top of West Looe Hill, Portlooe
Barton, Looe PL13 2HY 01503-262664

Location Maps

Hotel locations are shown on the maps at
the back of the guide. All towns and
villages containing an hotel listed in the
guide are shown in black.

Trenderway Farm Pelynt, Polperro, Looe
PL13 2LY 01503-72214

Treveria Farm Widegates, Looe PL13 1QR
01503-4237

Westcliff Hannafore Road, Looe PL13 2DE
01503-262500

LYDFORD Devon   2C3

Moor View *Acclaimed* 🏰RAC
Vale Down, Lydford EX20 4BB 01822-82220
5 bedrs, 4 ➼/WC, 1 ➼; 🐾 ✔ P15
sB&B £35 dB&B £90 Breakfast only [10%V];
cc Ac DC Vi

LYNMOUTH Devon   2C2

Beacon *Acclaimed* 🏰RAC
Countisbury Hill, Lynmouth EX35 6ND
01598-753268
*An Edwardian building with spacious rooms
and splendid views, situated on the cliff top
overlooking Lynmouth Bay.*
7 bedrs, 2 ➼/WC, 3 ♟/WC, 2 ➼; TV tcf P10
Child restrictions under 12
sB&B £20 Breakfast only

Bonnicott House *Acclaimed* 🏰RAC
Watersmeet Rooad, Lynmouth EX35 6EP
01598-753346

East Lyn House *Acclaimed* 🏰RAC
17 Watersmeet Road, Lynmouth EX35 6EP
01598-752540
8 bedrs, 3 ➼/WC, 3 ♟/WC; TV tcf P12
Child restrictions
dB&B £48; HB weekly £224; D £12 [10%V];
cc Ac Vi

Heatherville *Acclaimed* 🏰RAC
Tors Park, Lynmouth EX35 6NB 01598-752327
9 bedrs, 1 ➼/WC, 4 ♟/WC, 2 ➼; TV tcf 🐾 P9

Child restrictions
sB&B £22 dB&B £44; HB weekly £228

LYNTON Devon 2C2

Alford House *Acclaimed*   RAC
3 Alford Terrace, Lynton EX35 6AT
01598-752359
8 bedrs, 8 ➡/WC, 1 ➡;
Child restrictions
[5%V]; cc Ac Vi

Denes Longmead, Lynton EX15 6DQ
01598-753573

Hazeldene *Acclaimed*   RAC
27 Lee Road, Lynton EX35 6BP 01598-752364
9 bedrs, 9 ➡/WC; ✗ P8
Child restrictions
Breakfast only [5%V]

Ingleside *Acclaimed*   RAC
Lee Road, Lynton EX35 6HW 01598-752223

Mayfair *Acclaimed*   RAC
The Lynway, Lynton EX35 6AY 01598-753227
9 bedrs, 6 ➡/WC; ✗ P6
[5%V]; cc Ac Vi

Millslade *Highly Acclaimed*   RAC
Brendon, Lynton EX35 6PS 01598-77322
6 bedrs, 6 ➡/WC, 1 ➡; ✗
cc Ac Amex DC Vi

St Vincent *Acclaimed*   RAC
Castle Hill, Lynton EX35 6JA 01598-752244

6 bedrs, 1 ➡/WC, 2 ➡/WC, 1 ➡; TV tcf P3
Child restrictions
sB&B £14-£17 dB&B £32-£34; HB weekly
£170-£177; D £11 [10%V]

Sylvia House Lydiate Lane, Lynton EX35 6HE
01598-52391

8 bedrs, 6 ➡/WC, 1 ➡; ✗
sB&B £15; HB weekly £165

Victoria Lodge *Highly Acclaimed*   RAC
31 Lee Road, Lynton EX35 6BP 01598-753203
10 bedrs, 10 ➡/WC, 1 ➡; ✗
sB&B £21-£40 Breakfast only; cc Ac Vi

Waterloo House *Highly Acclaimed*   RAC
Lydiate Lane, Lynton EX35 6AJ 01598-53391
10 bedrs, 8 ➡/WC, 1 ➡; ✗ ✗ P3
sB&B £17.50 dB&B £51; HB weekly £180;
[10%V]

MARAZION Cornwall 2A4

Chymorvah *Highly Acclaimed*   RAC
Marazion TR17 0DQ 01736-710497   ♿
9 bedrs, 9 ➡/WC, 1 ➡; ✗ ✗ P12
[5%V]; cc Ac Amex Vi

MAWGAN PORTH Cornwall 2B3

White Lodge   RAC
Mawgan Porth TR8 4BN 01637-860512
18 bedrs, 12 ➡/WC, 2 ➡; ✗ P18
sB&B £18.50-£22 dB&B £37-£44; HB weekly
£165-£195; D £8 [10%V]; cc Ac Amex Vi

MEVAGISSEY Cornwall 2B4

Headlands   RAC
Polkirt Hill, Mevagissey PL26 6UX
01726-843453
14 bedrs, 9 ➡/WC, 2 ➡; ✗ P11
[10%V]

Location Maps
Hotel locations are shown on the maps at
the back of the guide. All towns and
villages containing an hotel listed in the
guide are shown in black.

Mevagissey House *Acclaimed* RÁC
Vicarage Hill, Mevagissey PL26 6SZ
01726-842427

An elegant, Georgian country house, set in 4 acres of ground with panoramic views of the harbour and sea beyond.
6 bedrs, 4 ➡/WC, 1 ➡; P12
Child restrictions
sB&B £16-£23 dB&B £36-£48; HB weekly
£210-£252;; cc Ac Vi

Sharksfin *Acclaimed* RÁC
The Quay, Mevagissey PL26 6OU
01726-843241 Fax 01726-842552
11 bedrs, 4 ➡/WC, 1 ➡; TV tcf
sB&B £23 dB&B £56 D £13.95 [10%V]; cc Ac
Amex DC Vi

(Inn) Ship Inn RÁC
Fore Street, Mevagissey PL26 6TU
01726-843324

Treleaven Farm House RÁC
Mevagissey PL26 6RZ 01726-842413
6 bedrs, 6 ➡/WC, 1 ➡;
Breakfast only

MINEHEAD Somerset 3D2

Avill House *Acclaimed* RÁC
Townsend Road, Minehead TA24 5RG
01643-704370
9 bedrs, 2 ➡/WC, 2 ➡; P9
Child restrictions
Breakfast only

Culborne Inn Porlock, Minehead TA24 8JW
01643-862259
3 bedrs, 1 ➡/WC, 2 ➡; ✝
sB&B £16.50 Breakfast only

Exmoor House Wheddon Cross,
Minehead TA24 7DU 01841-432

Fern Cottage Allerford, Minehead TA24
8HN 01862-892150

Gascony *Highly Acclaimed* RÁC
50 The Avenue, Minehead TA24 5BB
01643-705939
13 bedrs, 13 ➡/WC, 1 ➡; ✝ P14
Child restrictions
sB&B £23-£24 dB&B £44-£46; HB weekly
£175-£185;; cc Vi

Marshfield RÁC
Tregonwell Road, Minehead TA24 5DU
01643-702517 &
12 bedrs, 8 ➡/WC, 3 ➡; P7
Breakfast only

Marston Lodge *Highly Acclaimed* RÁC
St Michael's Road, North Hill, Minehead TA24
5JP 01643-702510
12 bedrs, 5 ➡/WC, 7 ➡/WC; TV tcf P10
Child restrictions
sB&B £20-£27 dB&B £50-£54 D £12 [10%V]

Mayfair *Highly Acclaimed* RÁC
The Avenue, Minehead TA24 5AY
01643-702719
16 bedrs, 3 ➡/WC, 13 ➡/WC; TV tcf ✂ P20
sB&B £24-£25 dB&B £46-£50; HB weekly
£157-£170; D £9; cc Ac Vi

Mentone The Parks, Minehead TA24 8BS
01705-229

Woodbridge 12 The Parks, Minehead TA24
8BS 01643-704860

MORETONHAMPSTEAD Devon 3D3

Cookshayes *Acclaimed* RÁC
33 Court Street, Moretonhampstead TQ13 8LG
01647-40374
8 bedrs, 6 ➡/WC, 2 ➡; TV tcf ✝ ✂ P15
Child restrictions
sB&B £21; HB weekly £210; D £14 [5%V]; cc
Ac Amex Vi

Gatehouse North Bovey, Moretonhampstead
TQ13 8RB 01647-40479

Wray Barton Manor Moretonhampstead
TQ13 8SE 01647-40467

MORTEHOE Devon — 2C2

Baycliffe Chapel Hill, Mortehoe EX34 7DZ 01271-870393

MOUSEHOLE Cornwall — 2A4

Carn Du Mousehole TR9 6SS 01736-731233

MULLION Cornwall — 2A4

Henscath House RAC
Mullion TR12 7EP 01326-240537
5 bedrs, 3 🛁/WC, 2 🚿/WC, 1 🛁; tcf P8
dB&B £44-£50; HB weekly £194-£217

NEWQUAY Cornwall — 2A3

Arundel RAC
Mount Wise, Newquay TR7 2BS 01637-872481
Fax 01637-850001
35 bedrs, 35 🛁/WC, 3 🛁; TV tcf ✂ P32
sB&B £15-£25 dB&B £30-£50; HB weekly £143-£199; D £6 [10%V]; cc Ac Amex DC Vi

Brakespear RAC
44-46 Edgcumbe Avenue, Newquay TR7 2NJ
01637-874771
10 bedrs, 7 🛁/WC, 2 🛁; P8
Breakfast only [10%V]

Copper Beach *Acclaimed* RAC
70 Edgcumbe Avenue, Newquay TR7 2NN
01637-873376 ♿
15 bedrs, 15 🛁/WC; ✂ P16
Breakfast only

Degembris Farm *Acclaimed* RAC
St Newlyn East, Newquay TR8 5HY
01872-510230

Hotel Trevalsa RAC
Watergate Road, Porth, Newquay TR7 3LX
01637-873336 ♿
24 bedrs, 20 🛁/WC;
[10%V]; cc Ac Amex Vi

Kellsboro RAC
12 Henver Road, Newquay TR7 3BJ
01637-874620 ♿
16 bedrs, 14 🛁/WC, 1 🛁; P20
[5%V]; cc Vi

Links RAC
Headland Road, Newquay TR7 1HN
01637-873211
15 bedrs, 10 🛁/WC;
Breakfast only

Minerva The Crescent, Newquay TR7 1PB 01637-872984

Pendeen RAC
7 Alexandra Road, Porth, Newquay TR7 3ND
01637-873521
15 bedrs, 15 🛁/WC; P15
Breakfast only [10%V]; cc Ac Amex Vi

Philema RAC
Esplanade Road, Pentire, Newquay TR7 1PY
01637-872571 Fax 01637-873188
39 bedrs, 34 🛁/WC, 5 🛁; 🐕 P37
sB&B £15-£26 dB&B £36-£52; HB weekly £140-£210; D £7.50 [10%V]; cc Ac Vi

Porth Enodoc *Highly Acclaimed* RAC
4 Esplanade Road, Pentire, Newquay TR7 1PY 01637-872372
15 bedrs, 15 🚿/WC, 1 🛁; TV tcf 🐕 ✂ P16
sB&B £19.50-£23.50 dB&B £39-£47; HB weekly £146-£186

Priory Lodge *Acclaimed* RAC
30 Mount Wise, Newquay TR7 2BH
01637-874111 ♿
22 bedrs, 7 🛁/WC, 13 🚿/WC, 1 🛁;
TV tcf ✂ P27
sB&B £25-£28 dB&B £50-£56; HB weekly £150-£200; D £9 [5%V]; cc Ac Vi

Quies RAC
84 Mount Wise, Newquay TR7 2BS
01637-872924
10 bedrs, 1 🛁/WC, 7 🚿/WC, 1 🛁;
TV tcf ✂ P10
Child restrictions
sB&B £14-£20 dB&B £28-£40 Breakfast only [10%V]; cc Ac Vi

Rolling Waves RAC
Alexandra Road, Porth, Newquay TR7 3NB
01637-873236

Surf Riders Tredragon Road, Mawgan Porth, Newquay TR8 4BW 01637-860383

Wheal Treasure *Acclaimed* RAC
72 Edgcumbe Avenue, Newquay TR7 2NN
01637-874136
12 bedrs, 11 🛁/WC, 2 🛁;
Child restrictions
Breakfast only [10%V]

Windward *Highly Acclaimed* RAC
Alexandra Road, Porth, Newquay TR7 3NB
01637-873185
14 bedrs, 12 🛁/WC, 2 🚿/WC; TV tcf 🚭 P14
sB&B £15-£23 dB&B £30-£46; HB weekly £105-£195; [5%V]; cc Ac Amex Vi

NEWTON ABBOT Devon 3D3

Lamorna RAC
Ideford Coombe, Newton Abbot TQ13 0AR
01626-65627
8 bedrs, 7 🛁/WC; P15
Breakfast only

★★★Passage House RAC
Hackney Lane, Kingsteignton, Newton Abbot TQ12 3QH 01626-55515 Fax 01626-63336

A modern purpose built hotel with a swiss chalet appearance standing on the beautiful Teign Estuary
39 bedrs, 39 🛁/WC; TV tcf 🐕 🚭 P150
sB&B £59 dB&B £75 D £16.95 [10%V]; cc Ac Amex DC Vi

OTTERY ST MARY Devon 3D3

Venn Ottery Barton RAC
Ottery St Mary EX11 1RZ 01404-812733
16 bedrs, 11 🛁/WC, 3 🛁; P20
Breakfast only [5%V]; cc Ac Vi

PADSTOW Cornwall 2B3

Bay House RAC
Porthcothan Bay, Padstow PL28 8LW
01841-520472
16 bedrs, 4 🛁; P14
Breakfast only

Green Waves Private *Highly Acclaimed* RAC
Trevone Bay, Padstow PL28 8RD
01841-520114
19 bedrs, 2 🛁/WC, 15 🚿/WC, 2 🛁;
TV tcf 🐕 P18
Child restrictions
sB&B £20; HB weekly £175-£210; D £10; cc Ac Vi

Old Mill Country House *Acclaimed* RAC
Little Petherick, Padstow PL27 7QT
01841-540388

16th century corn mill.
6 bedrs, 5 🛁/WC; tcf 🐕 🚭 P8
Child restrictions
dB&B £46-£48; HB weekly £220-£235; D £11.25

Tregea 16 High St, Padstow PL28 8BB
01841-532455

Woodlands *Highly Acclaimed* RAC
Treator, Padstow PL28 8RU 01841-532426
9 bedrs, 9 🚿/WC; TV tcf 🐕 🚭 P20
Child restrictions
sB&B £25-£30 dB&B £40-£48; HB weekly £177.50-£205.50

PAIGNTON Devon 3D4

Arden House 10 Youngs Park Road, Paignton TQ4 6BU 01803-558443

Beresford RAC
Adelphi Road, Paignton TQ4 6AW
01803-551560
8 bedrs, 6 🚿/WC, 2 🛁; TV tcf 🚭 P3
sB&B £27 dB&B £44; HB weekly £160

Bredon 5 Warefield Road, Paignton TQ3 2BH
01803-556911

Channel View *Acclaimed* RAC
8 Marine Parade, Sea Front, Paignton TQ3
2NU 01803-522432 Fax 01803-52243
13 bedrs, 13 ➡/WC; P10
[5%V]; cc Ac Vi

Commodore 14 Esplanade Road, Paignton
TQ4 6EB 01803-553107

Lyncourt 14 Elmsleigh Park, Paignton TQ4
5AT 01803-557124

Palm Sands RAC
21 Morin Road, Preston, Paignton TQ3 2PL
01803-523226
7 bedrs, 2 ☎/WC, 2 ➡; TV tcf P7
dB&B £23-£28; HB weekly £99-£114

Redcliff Lodge *Acclaimed* RAC
1 Marine Drive, Paignton TQ3 2NJ
01803-551394 ♿
17 bedrs, 17 ➡/WC; P17
cc Ac Vi

Sattva RAC
29 Esplanade, Paignton TQ4 6BL
01803-557820 ♿
20 bedrs, 3 ➡/WC, 17 ☎/WC, 2 ➡;
TV tcf ⚹ P10
sB&B £18-£26 dB&B £36-£52; HB weekly
£170-£199; cc Ac Vi

Sea Verge *Acclaimed* RAC
Marine Drive, Preston, Paignton TQ3 2NJ
01803-557795
12 bedrs, 5 ➡/WC, 2 ➡; P14
Breakfast only

Sealawn *Acclaimed* RAC
20 Esplanade Road, Paignton TQ4 6BE
01803-559031
12 bedrs, 5 ➡/WC, 7 ☎/WC; TV tcf ⚹ P12
sB&B £14-£29 dB&B £36-£48; HB weekly
£161-£189; D £10 [10%V]

Silversea 14 Norman Road, Paignton TQ3
2BE 01803-556331

St Weonards *Acclaimed* RAC
12 Kernou Road, Paignton TQ4 6BA
01803-558842
8 bedrs, 5 ➡/WC, 2 ➡; ⚹ P2

sB&B £13-£15 dB&B £26-£60; HB weekly
£135-£149; cc Ac

Summerhill Braeside Road, Paignton TQ4
6BX 01803-558101

Sunnybank RAC
2 Cleveland Road, Paignton TQ4 6EN
01803-525540
12 bedrs, 2 ☎/WC, 2 ➡; TV tcf ⚹ P8
sB&B £10-£16 dB&B £25-£32; HB weekly
£110-£140; [5%V]; cc Vi

The Barbican 5 Beach Road, Paignton TQ4
6AY 01803-551332

Torbay Sands RAC
16 Marine Parade, Preston, Paignton TQ3
2NU 01803-525568
13 bedrs, 11 ➡/WC, 2 ➡; P6
Breakfast only; cc Ac Vi

PAR Cornwall   2B4

Elmswood House *Acclaimed* RAC
73 Tehidy Road, Tywardreath, Par PL24 2QD
01726-814221
7 bedrs, 1 ➡/WC, 4 ☎/WC, 1 ➡; TV tcf P8
sB&B £18 dB&B £40; HB weekly £140; D £8

PENRYN Cornwall   2A4

Prospect House *Highly Acclaimed* RAC
1 Church Road, Penryn TR10 8DA
01326-373198 Fax 01326-373198

*A late Georgian "Gentleman's Residence"
appropriately decorated and furnished with
antiques, set in a small typically Cornish
garden and with a walled rose garden.*
3 bedrs, 1 ➡/WC, 2 ☎/WC, 1 ➡; tcf ⚹ ⚹ P3
Child restrictions
sB&B £25-£30 dB&B £45-£50; HB weekly
£395-£425; D £18 [5%V]

PENZANCE Cornwall   2A4

Alexandra   ⚓RAC
Alexandra Terrace, Penzance TR18 4NX
01736-62644

Carlton   ⚓RAC
Promenade, Penzance TR18 4NW
01736-62081
10 bedrs, 8 ☞/WC, 2 ➡; TV tcf
Child restrictions
sB&B £16.50 dB&B £36 Breakfast only [5%V]

Carnson House   ⚓RAC
East Terrace, Penzance TR18 2TD
01736-65589

*An 18th century, granite built, small private
hotel close to the harbour with a friendly
atmosphere.*
8 bedrs, 2 ☞/WC, 1 ➡; ✂
Child restrictions
sB&B £15-£17 dB&B £30-£34; HB weekly
£150-£175; D £9 [10%V]; cc Ac Amex DC Vi

Dunedin   ⚓RAC
Alexandra Road, Penzance TR18 4LZ
01736-62652
9 bedrs, 1 ➡/WC, 7 ☞/WC; TV tcf ✖
Child restrictions
sB&B £13-£15 dB&B £26-£30

Estoril *Highly Acclaimed*   ⚓RAC
46 Morrab Road, Penzance TR18 4EX
01736-62468

*An elegant Victorian granite house with
garden, retaining its period charm.*
10 bedrs, 10 ➡/WC; ✂ P4
sB&B £22-£25 dB&B £44-£50; HB weekly
£231-£245; [10%V]; cc Ac Vi

Glencree Private 2 Menraye Road, Penzance
TR18 4NG 01736-62026

Keigwin   ⚓RAC
Alexandra Road, Penzance TR18 4LZ
01736-63930
8 bedrs, 5 ☞/WC, 1 ➡; TV tcf
sB&B £12-£16 dB&B £24-£32; HB weekly
£143-£169; cc Ac Vi

Kimberley House   ⚓RAC
10 Morrab Road, Penzance TR18 4EZ
01736-62727
9 bedrs, 3 ➡; P4
Child restrictions
sB&B £13-£15 dB&B £26-£30; HB weekly
£140-£150; cc Ac Vi

Lynwood   ⚓RAC
41 Morrab Road, Penzance TR18 4EX
01736-65871
6 bedrs, 3 ➡; ✖
Breakfast only; cc Ac Amex DC Vi

Mount Royal   ⚓RAC
Chyandour Cliff, Penzance TR18 3LQ
01736-62233
7 bedrs, 4 ➡/WC, 2 ➡; TV tcf ✖ P10
sB&B £17-£19 dB&B £34-£38 Breakfast only
[10%V]

Panorama ᴿᴬᶜ
Chywoone Hill, Newlyn, Penzance TR18 5AR
01736-68498
7 bedrs, 5 🛁/WC, 1 🛁; P10
Child restrictions
Breakfast only; cc Ac Amex DC Vi

Pendennis Alexandra Road, Penzance TR18
01736-63823

Penmorvah ᴿᴬᶜ
Alexandra Road, Penzance TR18 4LZ
01736-63711

Sea & Horses *Acclaimed* ᴿᴬᶜ
6 Alexandra Terrace, Penzance TR18 4NX
01736-61961 Fax 01736-330499
11 bedrs, 2 🛁/WC, 6 🛁/WC; TV tcf P11
sB&B £22-£26 dB&B £44-£52; HB weekly
£210-£235; D £10; cc Ac Amex Vi

Tarbert *Highly Acclaimed* ᴿᴬᶜ
11 Clarence Street, Penzance TR18 2NU
01736-63758
12 bedrs, 1 🛁/WC, 11 🛁/WC, 1 🛁;
TV tcf ✂ P5
Child restrictions
sB&B £25-£27.50 dB&B £45-£50; HB weekly
£201-£216; D £12.50 [10%V]; cc Ac Amex Vi

Trevelyan ᴿᴬᶜ
16 Chapel Street, Penzance TR18 4AW
01736-62494
9 bedrs, 1 🛁/WC, 4 🛁/WC, 2 🛁; TV tcf ✂ P6
sB&B £13-£14 dB&B £26-£28 Breakfast only

Woodstock ᴿᴬᶜ
29 Morrab Road, Penzance TR18 4EL
01736-69049
5 bedrs, 1 🛁/WC, 2 🛁; TV tcf
sB&B £10-£15 dB&B £20-£30 Breakfast only
[5%V]; cc Ac Amex DC Vi

PERRANPORTH Cornwall 2A4

Beach Dunes *Acclaimed* ᴿᴬᶜ
Ramoth Way, Reen Sands, Perranporth TR6
0BY 01872-572263 Fax 01872-573824
6 bedrs, 2 🛁/WC, 2 🛁/WC; TV tcf ✂ ✂ P15
Child restrictions
sB&B £23.50-£27.50 dB&B £47-£55; HB
weekly £190-£235; D £12.50 [10%V];
cc Ac Amex Vi

PLYMOUTH Devon 2C4

Alexander ᴿᴬᶜ
**20 Woodland Terrace, Greenbank,
Plymouth PL4 8NL 01752-663247 Fax
01752-225536**
*Converted Victorian merchants house with
large spacious rooms, double glazed and
centrally heated*
8 bedrs, 2 🛁/WC, 2 🛁; TV tcf P6
sB&B £15 dB&B £30; HB weekly £165; [5%V];
cc Ac Amex Vi

Ashgrove 218 Citadel Road, The Hoe,
Plymouth PL1 3BB 01752-664046

Benvenuto ᴿᴬᶜ
69 Hermitage Road, Mannamead, Plymouth
PL3 4RZ 01752-667030
8 bedrs, 2 🛁/WC, 2 🛁; TV tcf ✂
sB&B £13.50-£15 dB&B £28-£35 Breakfast only

Bowling Green ᴿᴬᶜ
9-10 Osborne Place, Lockyer Street, Plymouth
PL1 2PU 01752-667485
12 bedrs, 8 🛁/WC; P4
Breakfast only; cc Ac Amex DC Vi

Chester ᴿᴬᶜ
54 Stuart Road, Pennycomequick, Plymouth
PL3 4EE 01752-663706

Crescent House 18 Garden Crescent, West
Hoe, Plymouth PL1 3DA 01752-266424

Denver 112a North Road East, Plymouth PL4
6AW 01752-660687

Devonia ⚜️RAC
27 Grand Parade, West Hoe, Plymouth PL1
3DQ 01752-665026

Victorian hotel on the waterfront overlooking Plymouth sound. Pleasant patio and lawned garden.
6 bedrs, 3 🐾/WC, 1 🛁; TV tcf 🐕
Breakfast only; cc Vi

Drakes View *Acclaimed* ⚜️RAC
33 Grand Parade, West Hoe, Plymouth PL1
3DQ 01752-221500

Dudley ⚜️RAC
42 Sutherland Road, Mutley, Plymouth PL4
6BN 01752-668322
7 bedrs, 5 🐾/WC; tcf 🐕 ✂️ P2
[10%V]; cc Ac Vi

First
13 Pier Street, West Hoe, Plymouth PL1
3BS 01752-26870

Georgian House *Highly Acclaimed* ⚜️RAC
**51 Citadel Road, The Hoe, Plymouth PL1
3AU 01752-663237 Fax 01752-253953**

Victorian building with a small garden
12 bedrs, 4 🛁/WC, 8 🐾/WC, 1 🛁;
TV tcf 🐕 P2
sB&B £31-£32 dB&B £36-£41 Breakfast only;
cc Ac Amex DC Vi

Headland ⚜️RAC
1a Radford Road, West Hoe, Plymouth PL1
3BY 01752-660866
3 bedrs, 1 🛁/WC, 2 🐾/WC, 4 🛁; TV tcf 🐕
sB&B £16 dB&B £28 D £7.50; cc Ac Vi

Hotel Campanile · ⚜️RAC
Longbridge Road, Marsh Hills, Plymouth PL6
8LD 01752-601087

Kildare
82 North Road East, Plymouth PL4
6AN 01752-229375

Merville ⚜️RAC
73 Citadel Road, The Hoe, Plymouth PL1 3AX
01752-66759
10 bedrs, 2 🛁; 🐕 P4
Breakfast only

Mon Abri
52 Pentyre Terrace, Lipson,
Plymouth PL4 8RP 01752-269032

Oliver's ⚜️RAC
33 Sutherland Road, Mutley, Plymouth PL4
6BN 01752-663923
6 bedrs, 4 🛁/WC, 4 🐾/WC, 1 🛁; TV tcf ✂️ P3
Child restrictions
sB&B £28 dB&B £42 D £10.95 [10%V]; cc Ac
Amex DC Vi

Phantele ⚜️RAC
176 Devonport Road, Stoke, Plymouth PL1
5RD 01752-561506
6 bedrs, 2 🛁/WC, 2 🛁; ✂️
sB&B £14.50-£20.50 dB&B £27-£34; HB
weekly £117-£159;

Sea Breezes
28 Grand Parade, West Hoe,
Plymouth PL1 3DJ 01752-667205

St James ⚜️RAC
49 Citadel Road, The Hoe, Plymouth PL1 3AU
01752-661950
10 bedrs, 10 🛁/WC;
Child restrictions
Breakfast only

Teviot
20 North Road East, Plymouth PL4
6AS 01752-262656

Location Maps
Hotel locations are shown on the maps at the back of the guide. All towns and villages containing an hotel listed in the guide are shown in black.

Victoria Court *Acclaimed*　　RAC
64 North Road East, Plymouth PL4 6AL
01752-668133 Fax 01752-668133
13 bedrs, 9 ☇/WC, 2 ➡; TV tcf P6
sB&B £37.50 dB&B £45; HB weekly £245; D
£12.50 [10%V]; cc Ac Amex DC Vi

POLBATHIC Cornwall　　2C4

Old Mill House Private　　RAC
Polbathic, Torpoint, Polbathic PL11 3HA
01503-30596
10 bedrs, 3 ➡; tcf ✚ ⅄ P14
sB&B £10-£15 dB&B £25-£30; HB weekly
£120-£150; D £7 [10%V]; cc Ac DC Vi

POLPERRO Cornwall　　2B4

Penryn House　　RAC
The Coombes, Polperro PL13 2RG
01503-72157

PORLOCK Somerset　　3D2

Lorna Doone *Acclaimed*　　RAC
High Street, Porlock TA24 8PS 01643-862404
11 bedrs, 4 ➡/WC, 7 ☇/WC, 1 ➡;
TV tcf ✚ P6
sB&B £20.50 dB&B £39-£42 D £9.50 [10%V];
cc Ac Vi

PORT ISAAC Cornwall　　2B3

Bay　　RAC
1 The Terrace, Port Isaac PL29 3SC
01208-880380
10 bedrs, 4 ➡/WC, 2 ➡; tcf ✚ P10
sB&B £17-£21 dB&B £34-£42; HB weekly
£164-£185; D £10

(Inn) Shipwright Inn　　RAC
The Terrace, Port Isaac PL29 3SG
01208-880305 Fax 01208-814405
4 bedrs, 4 ☇/WC; TV tcf
sB&B £16.50-£28.50 dB&B £37; HB weekly
£170; D £9.25 [10%V]; cc Ac Vi

REDRUTH Cornwall　　2A4

Lyndhurst　　RAC
80 Agar Road, Redruth TR15 3NB
01209-215146
8 bedrs, 4 ➡/WC; P8
Breakfast only

SALCOMBE Devon　　2C4

Devon Tor *Acclaimed*　　RAC
Devon Road, Salcombe TQ8 8HJ
01548-841306
7 bedrs, 1 ➡/WC, 5 ☇/WC, 1 ➡; TV tcf P5
Child restrictions
sB&B £20-£25 dB&B £40-£52; HB weekly
£140-£169; [10%V]

Lyndhurst *Highly Acclaimed*　　RAC
Bonaventure Road, Salcombe TQ8 8BG
01548-842481
8 bedrs, 8 ☇/WC; TV tcf P4
Child restrictions
sB&B £20-£27 dB&B £40-£54; HB weekly
£210-£255;

Old Porch House　　RAC
Shadycombe Road, Salcombe TQ8 8DJ
01548-842157 Fax 01548-843750
8 bedrs, 6 ➡/WC, 1 ➡; ✚ ⅄ P9
sB&B £18.50 dB&B £45-£53 Breakfast only
[5%V]; cc Ac Amex Vi

Penn Torr　　RAC
Herbert Road, Salcombe TQ8 8HN
01548-842234
7 bedrs, 5 ➡/WC; P9
Child restrictions
dB&B £16.50-£21 Breakfast only

Terrapins　　RAC
Buckley Street, Salcombe TQ8 8DD
01548-842861 Fax 01548-842265
7 bedrs, 6 ➡/WC, 1 ➡; ✚
Breakfast only

The Lodge Devon Road, Salcombe TQ8 8HL
01548-844008

Torre View　　RAC
Devon Road, Salcombe TQ8 8HJ
01548-842633
*Cosy detached Victorian residence with every
modern convenience.*
8 bedrs, 2 ➡/WC, 3 ☇/WC, 3 ➡; TV tcf P4
Child restrictions
sB&B £23-£26 dB&B £44-£52; HB weekly
£218-£242; D £11.50 [5%V]; cc Ac Vi

SALTASH Cornwall　　2C4

Granada Lodge　　RAC
Callington Road, Carkeel, Saltash PL12 6LF
01752-848414

SEATON Devon   2C4

Mariners *Acclaimed*   ᴿᴬC
The Esplanade, Seaton EX12 2NP
01297-20560
10 bedrs, 10 ➡/WC; TV tcf ✖ P10
sB&B £23-£27.50 dB&B £38-£41.50; HB
weekly £118-£131.75; cc Ac Amex Vi

SENNEN Cornwall   2A4

Sunny Bank   ᴿᴬC
Seaview Hill, Sennen TR19 7AR 01736-871278
11 bedrs, 2 ➡; tcf P20
sB&B £13-£15 dB&B £26-£30; HB weekly
£120-£130; D £6

SHEPTON MALLET Somerset   3E2

Batcombe Vale Shepton Mallet BA4 6BW
01749-830246
3 bedrs, 1 ➡; TV tcf ✖ P3
sB&B £15 Breakfast only

Belfield *Acclaimed*   ᴿᴬC
34 Charlton Road, Shepton Mallet BA4 5PA
01749-344353
6 bedrs, 2 ☏/WC, 2 ➡; TV tcf P6
sB&B £18-£25 dB&B £34-£40 Breakfast only

SIDMOUTH Devon   3D3

Bramley Lodge Vicariage Road, Sidmouth
EX10 8UQ 01395-515710
8 bedrs, 1 ➡/WC, 1 ☏/WC, 2 ➡; ✖ P7
sB&B £14; HB weekly £91-£231;

Canterbury House   ᴿᴬC
Salcombe Road, Sidmouth EX10 8DR
01395-513373   &
8 bedrs, 2 ➡/WC, 5 ☏/WC, 1 ➡; TV tcf P6
sB&B £16-£18 dB&B £32-£36 [10%V]; cc Ac Vi

Groveside *Acclaimed*   ᴿᴬC
Vicarage Road, Sidmouth EX10 8UQ
01395-513406
6 bedrs, 5 ➡/WC, 1 ➡; P7
Child restrictions
Breakfast only

★★Hotel Elizabeth   ᴿᴬC
Esplanade, Sidmouth EX10 8AT 01395-513503
28 bedrs, 28 ➡/WC, 1 ➡; P10
[10%V]; cc Ac Vi

Southcombe *Acclaimed*   ᴿᴬC
Vicarage Road, Sidmouth EX10 8UQ
01395-513861

Torbay   ᴿᴬC
Station Road, Sidmouth EX10 8NW
01395-513456
32 bedrs, 28 ➡/WC, 3 ➡; ✖ P10
Breakfast only; cc Ac Vi

Willow Bridge *Acclaimed*   ᴿᴬC
1 Mill Ford Road, Sidmouth EX10 8DR
01395-513599

SOUTH MOLTON Devon   2C2

Heasley House *Acclaimed*   ᴿᴬC
Heasley Mill, South Molton EX36 3LE
01598-740213
8 bedrs, 5 ➡/WC, 2 ➡; ✖ ⚹ P11
sB&B £22.50 dB&B £45; HB weekly £240; D
£12.50 [10%V]; cc Ac DC Vi

ST AGNES Cornwall   2A4

Penkerris   ᴿᴬC
Penwinnick Road (B3277), St Agnes TR5 0PA
01872-552262
6 bedrs, 2 ☏/WC, 3 ➡; TV tcf ✖ P8
sB&B £15-£20 dB&B £30-£35; HB weekly
£130-£155; D £7.50 [10%V]; cc Ac Amex Vi

Porthvean *Acclaimed*   ᴿᴬC
Churchtown, St Agnes TR5 0QP 01872-552581
Fax 01872-552581
7 bedrs, 7 ☏/WC, 1 ➡; TV tcf ⚹ P8
sB&B £35-£40 dB&B £50-£57.50 Breakfast
only [10%V]; cc Ac Vi

ST AUSTELL Cornwall   2B4

Alexandra   ᴿᴬC
52-54 Alexandra Road, St Austell PL25 4QN
01726-74242   &
14 bedrs, 4 ☏/WC, 3 ➡; TV tcf ✖ P20
sB&B £26 dB&B £42 D £9 [10%V]; cc Ac
Amex DC Vi

Lynton House   ᴿᴬC
48 Bodmin Road, St Austell PL25 5AF
01726-73787
5 bedrs, 1 ➡; ⚹ P6
sB&B £14 dB&B £28-£30; HB weekly £84

Nanscawen Country House *Highly Acclaimed* RAC
Prideaux Road, St Blazey, Par, St Austell PL24 2SR 01726-814488 Fax 01726-814488
3 bedrs, 3 ⇥/WC; P5
Child restrictions under 12

Selwood House RAC
60 Alexandra Road, St Austell PL25 4QN
01726-65707 Fax 01726-68951 &
11 bedrs, 11 ⇥/WC; ✖ P14
Child restrictions
sB&B £34 dB&B £63; HB weekly £305;
[10%V]; cc Ac Amex DC Vi

Steep House Portmellon Cove, Mevagissey, St Austell PL26 6PH 01726-843732

Tregorran Cliff Street, Mevagissey, St Austell PL26 6QW 01726-842319

Wheal Lodge *Highly Acclaimed* RAC
91 Sea Road, Carlyon Bay, St Austell PL25 3SH 01726-815543
6 bedrs, 5 ⇥/WC, 1 ⬥/WC; P20
Child restrictions
sB&B £30-£40 dB&B £60-£70; HB weekly £239-£259; D £12.50 [10%V]; cc Ac Vi

ST EVAL Cornwall   2B3

Bedruthan House RAC
Bedruthan Steps, St Eval PL27 7UW
01637-860346
5 bedrs, 4 ⇥/WC, 1 ⬥/WC; P12
Child restrictions
sB&B £16-£17 dB&B £32-£34; HB weekly £145-£150;

ST IVES Cornwall   2A4

Blue Mist RAC
6 The Warren, St Ives TR26 2EA
01736-795209
8 bedrs, 8 ⇥/WC, 1 ⇥; TV tcf P4
Child restrictions
sB&B £20.75-£23.75 dB&B £20.75-£23.75
Breakfast only; cc Ac Amex Vi

Borthalan Boskerris Road, Carbis Bay, St Ives, Cornwall TR26 2NQ 01736-795946

Dean Court *Highly Acclaimed* RAC
Trelyon Avenue, St Ives TR26 2AD
01736-796023
12 bedrs, 6 ⇥/WC, 6 ⬥/WC; TV tcf P12

Child restrictions
sB&B £29-£33 dB&B £54-£62; HB weekly £205-£235; cc Ac Vi

Dunmar RAC
1-3 Pednolver Terrace, St Ives TR26 2EL
01736-796117 Fax 01736-796117
17 bedrs, 13 ⇥/WC, 2 ⇥; TV tcf ✖ ✂ P22
sB&B £16-£26 dB&B £32-£52; HB weekly £145-£220; cc Ac Amex Vi

Hollies RAC
Talland Road, St Ives TR26 2DF 01736-796605
10 bedrs, 2 ⇥/WC, 8 ⬥/WC; TV tcf ✂ P12
sB&B £17.50-£24 dB&B £35-£48; HB weekly £140-£200; [10%V]

Longships RAC
2 Talland Road, St Ives, Cornwall TR26 2DF 01736-798180 Fax 01736-798180

A granite-built hotel with a warm and friendly atmosphere. Situated on the main route through St. Ives, overlooking the harbour and town with beautiful views across the bay and of the North Cornish Coast.
25 bedrs, 25 ⇥/WC; ✖ P20
sB&B £17-£25 dB&B £34-£50 D £8

Lyonesse *Acclaimed* RAC
Talland Road, St Ives TR26 2DF
01736-796315
150 bedrs, 15 ⬥/WC; TV tcf ✂ P10
sB&B £17-£23 dB&B £34-£46; HB weekly £160-£217; [5%V]; cc Vi

Penclawdd 1 Seaview Place, Old Quay, St Ives, Cornwall TR26 1PS 01736-796869

Primrose Valley RAC
Primrose Valley, St Ives TR26 2ED
01736-794939
11 bedrs, 6 ⇥/WC, 2 ⇥; P12
Breakfast only

St Margarets   RAC
3 Park Avenue, St Ives, Cornwall TR26 2DN
01736-795785

St Merryn   RAC
Trelyon, St Ives TR26 2PF 01736-795767

ST JUST-IN-ROSELAND Cornwall   2B4

Rose-da-Mar *Acclaimed*   RAC
Truro, St Just-in-Roseland TR2 5JB
01326-270450
8 bedrs, 4 ➽/WC, 1 ➽/WC, 2 ➽; tcf ✂ P9
Child restrictions
sB&B £27 dB&B £50.50-£61; HB weekly
£278.25-£318.50; D £15.50 [10%V]

ST MARY'S Isles of Scilly   2A3

Brantwood   RAC
Rocky Hill, St Mary's TR21 0NW 01720-22531
Fax 01720-22301
4 bedrs, 4 ➽/WC;
Child restrictions
Breakfast only [10%V]; cc Ac Amex Vi

Carnwethers Country House *Highly*
Acclaimed   RAC
Pelistry Bay, St Mary's TR21 0NX
01720-422415
10 bedrs, 10 ➽/WC, 1 ➽; ✂ ✕ P20
Child restrictions
sB&B £42 Breakfast only

TAUNTON Somerset   3D2

Blorenge 57 Staplegrove Road, Taunton TA1
1DL 01823-283005   &
20 bedrs, 11 ➽/WC, 3 ➽; TV tcf P20
sB&B £18; HB weekly £165-£210; D £5-£8

Brookfield   RAC
16 Wellington Road, Taunton TA1 4EQ
01823-27278
8 bedrs, 2 ➽; ✂ P7
Breakfast only [5%V]

**Foresters Arms 55 Long Street, Williton,
Taunton TA4 4QY 01984-632508**
9 bedrs, 6 ➽/WC, 1 ➽; ✂ P19
sB&B £17.50 Breakfast only

Meryan House *Highly Acclaimed*   RAC
Bishops Hull, Taunton TA1 5EG 01823-337445
Fax 01823-322355   &
12 bedrs, 12 ➽/WC, 1 ➽; TV tcf ✂ ✕ P17
sB&B £36 dB&B £42 D £12 [5%V]; cc Ac Vi

Old Manor Farmhouse *Acclaimed*   RAC
Norton Fitzwarren, Taunton TA2 6RZ
01823-28980 Fax 01823-28980
7 bedrs, 7 ➽/WC, 1 ➽; P12
Breakfast only [10%V]; cc Ac Amex DC Vi

Roadchef Lodge   RAC
Taunton Dene Motorway, M5 Southbound,
Taunton TA1 4BA 01823-332228 Fax
01823-338131   &
39 bedrs, 39 ➽/WC; TV tcf ✕
sB&B £32; cc Ac Amex DC Vi

TEIGNMOUTH Devon   3D3

Beachley 3 Brunswick Street, Teignmouth
TQ14 8AE 01626-774249
6 bedrs, 2 ➽;
sB&B £14

Cotteswold   RAC
Second Drive, Landscore Road, Teignmouth
TQ14 9JS 01626-774662

Sea View House Brunswick Street,
Teignmouth TQ14 8AE 01626-773029

TEMPLECOMBE Somerset   3E2

Fountain Inn Motel Henstridge, Templecombe BA8 0RA 01963-36722

TINTAGEL Cornwall   2B3

The Wharncliffe Arms Fore Street, Tintagel PL34 0DA 01840-770393

Trethin Manor Advent, Tintagel PL23 9QW 01840-213522

Old Cornish manor house, circa 1337, listed for architectural and historical interest. Birthplace of Captain Samuel Wallis, (1728) circumnavigator and discoverer of Tahiti.
3 bedrs, 3 ➡/WC, 3 🛁/WC; TV tcf P20
Child restrictions under 14
sB&B £16 Breakfast only

TIVERTON Devon   3D2

Bridge *Acclaimed*   RAC
23 Angel Hill, Tiverton EX16 6PE
01884-252804
9 bedrs, 5 ➡/WC, 2 ➡; 🐾 P6
sB&B £17.50-£18 dB&B £34-£42; HB weekly £170-£192; D £9 [10%V]

★★Fisherman's Cot   RAC
Bickleigh, Tiverton EX16 8RN 01884-855289
Fax 01884-855241

Lodge Hill Farm   RAC
Ashley, Tiverton EX16 5PA 01884-252907 Fax
01884-242090
9 bedrs, 7 🛁/WC, 2 ➡; TV tcf 🐾 P12
sB&B £16 dB&B £32; HB weekly £155;
[10%V]

Symbols
For an explanation of the symbols used in hotel entries, please see inside the front cover.

TORPOINT Cornwall   2C4

Friary Manor Maker Heights, Mount Edgcumbe, Millbrook, Torpoint PL10 1JB
01752-822112   ♿
7 bedrs, 7 ➡/WC, 7 🛁/WC; 🐾 P25
sB&B £21 Breakfast only

Whitsand Bay *Acclaimed*   RAC
Portwinkle, Crafthole, Torpoint PL11 3BU
01503-30276 Fax 01503-30329   ♿
36 bedrs, 31 ➡/WC, 32 🛁/WC, 2 ➡; TV tcf
🐾 ✂ P50
sB&B £20-£25 dB&B £40-£55; HB weekly £210-£240; D £13.50 [5%V]; cc Ac Vi

---

TORQUAY Devon   3D3

Ascot House 7 Tor Church Rd, Torquay TQ2 5UR 01803-295142

Ashurst Lodge Ashfield Road, Torquay TQ2 5SG 01803-292132

Avron   RAC
70 Windsor Road, Torquay TQ1 1SZ
01803-294182
14 bedrs, 6 ➡/WC, 2 ➡; 🐾 P8
sB&B £15-£25 dB&B £30-£50; HB weekly £115-£160; [5%V]

Barn Hayes Country *Highly Acclaimed*   RAC
Brim Hill, Maidencombe, Torquay TQ1 4TR
01803-327980

Warm, friendly and comfortable Country House style hotel set in an area of outstanding natural beauty.
10 bedrs, 8 🛁/WC, 1 ➡; TV tcf 🐾 P14
sB&B £24-£27 dB&B £48-£54 [10%V]; cc Ac Vi

Beau Vista 14 Ash Hill Road, Torquay TQ1 3HZ 01803-297202

Belmont *Acclaimed* RAC
66 Belgrave Road, Torquay TQ2 5HY
01803-295028
13 bedrs, 9 ➡/WC, 1 ➡;
Breakfast only; **cc** Ac Amex DC Vi

Blue Haze *Acclaimed* RAC
Seaway Lane, Torquay TQ2 6PS
01803-607186
10 bedrs, 10 ➡/WC; P20
Breakfast only [10%V]; **cc** Ac Amex Vi

Brandize 19 Avenue Road, Torquay TQ2 5LB
01803-297798

Briarfields RAC
84-86 Avenue Road, Torquay TQ2 5LF
01803-297844
12 bedrs, 8 ➡/WC, 1 ➡; ✖ P10
Breakfast only [10%V]; **cc** Ac Amex Vi

Carieden 104 Avenue Road, Torquay TQ2
5LF 01803-211382

Cavendish RAC
Belgrave Road, Torquay TQ2 5HN
01803-293682

Chesterfield *Acclaimed* RAC
62 Belgrave Road, Torquay TQ2 5HY
01803-292318
11 bedrs, 11 ⛧/WC, 1 ➡; ✖ P3
sB&B £17-£24 dB&B £28-£38; HB weekly
£128-£168; [10%V]; **cc** Ac Vi

Clevedon RAC
Meadfoot Sea Road, Torquay TQ1 2LQ
01803-294260
12 bedrs, 4 ➡/WC, 8 ⛧/WC, 1 ➡;
TV tcf ✖ P9
sB&B £14-£22.50 dB&B £37-£45; HB weekly
£156-£192; [10%V]; **cc** Ac Vi

Colindale *Acclaimed* RAC
20 Rathmore Road, Torquay TQ2 6NY
01803-293947
8 bedrs, 2 ⛧/WC, 2 ➡; tcf P5
Child restrictions
sB&B £14-£15 dB&B £26-£34; HB weekly
£135-£142; [5%V]; **cc** Ac Vi

Concorde 26 Newton Rd, Torquay TQ2 5BZ
01803-292330

Courtlands Rawlyn Road, Cockington,
Chelston, Torquay TQ2 6PL 01803-605506 Fax
01803-605970

Craig Court *Acclaimed* RAC
10 Ash Hill Road, Torquay TQ1 3HZ
01803-294400 ♿
10 bedrs, 5 ➡/WC, 3 ➡; tcf ✖ P7
sB&B £16.50-£22.50 dB&B £33-£45; HB
weekly £154-£196; D £8.50 [10%V]

Cranborne *Acclaimed* RAC
58 Belgrave Road, Torquay TQ2 5HY
01803-298046
12 bedrs, 6 ➡/WC, 5 ⛧/WC, 1 ➡; TV tcf P3
sB&B £12-£23 dB&B £30-£46; HB weekly
£126-£172; [10%V]; **cc** Ac Vi

Cranmore *Acclaimed* RAC
89 Avenue Road, Torquay TQ2 5LH
01803-298488
8 bedrs, 3 ➡/WC, 5 ⛧/WC, 1 ➡; TV tcf P4
sB&B £14-£17 dB&B £28-£34; HB weekly
£143.50-£164.50; D £6.50; **cc** Ac Amex DC Vi

Daphne Court Lower Warberry Rd, Torquay
TQ1 1QS 01803-212011

Devon Court RAC
Croft Road, Torquay TQ2 5UE 01803-293603
13 bedrs, 8 ⛧/WC, 3 ➡; TV tcf P13
sB&B £13.50-£19 dB&B £27-£38; HB weekly
£112-£154; **cc** Ac Vi

Elmdene *Acclaimed* RAC
Rathmore Road, Torquay TQ2 6NZ
01803-294940
11 bedrs, 7 ➡/WC, 1 ➡; TV tcf ✖ ✂ P10
Child restrictions
sB&B £16-£17 dB&B £32-£34; HB weekly
£150-£180; D £8.50; **cc** Ac Vi

Exmouth View *Acclaimed* RAC
St Albans Road, Babbacombe, Torquay
TQ1 3LG 01803-327307 Fax 01803-329967 &
A modern hotel, with friendly atmosphere
and good food. Close to shops and beach.
Own entertainment every evening.
32 bedrs, 25 ➹/WC, 2 ➹; P16
[5%V]; cc Ac DC Vi

Fairways *Acclaimed* RAC
72 Avenue Road, Torquay TQ2 5LF
01803-298471
6 bedrs, 4 ➹/WC, 1 ➹; ✣ P7
[5%V]; cc Ac DC Vi

Ferns No1 The Ferns, St Lukes Road,
Torquay TQ2 5NX 01803-212703

Fontenay 19 Cleveland Road, Torquay TQ2
5BD 01803-295555

Glenorleigh *Highly Acclaimed* RAC
26 Cleveland Road, Torquay TQ2 5BE
01803-292135
16 bedrs, 9 ➹/WC, 3 ➹; P10
cc Ac Vi

Glenwood *Acclaimed* RAC
Rowdens Road, Torquay TQ2 5AZ
01803-296318
11 bedrs, 2 ➹/WC, 7 ➹/WC, 1 ➹;
TV tcf ✣ P10
Child restrictions
sB&B £16-£22 dB&B £34-£44; HB weekly
£175-£196; D £8 [10%V]; cc Ac Vi JCB

Haldon Priors *Highly Acclaimed* RAC
Meadfoot Sea Road, Torquay TQ1 2LQ
01803-213365
8 bedrs, 4 ➹/WC, 3 ➹/WC; tcf ✦ P7
sB&B £22 [10%V]

Hantwell 487 Babbacombe Road, Torquay
TQ1 1HL 01803-293990

Hotel Blue Conifer Higher Downs Road,
Babbacombe, Torquay TQ1 3LD
01803-327637

Hotel Concorde *Acclaimed* RAC
26 Newton Road, Torquay TQ2 5BZ
01803-292330

Hotel Fiesta St Marychurch Road, Torquay
TQ1 3JE 01803-292388

Ingoldsby *Acclaimed* RAC
1 Chelston Road, Torquay TQ2 6PT
01803-607497 &
15 bedrs, 12 ➹/WC, 1 ➹; P12
[5%V]; cc Ac Vi

Kingston House *Highly Acclaimed* RAC
75, Avenue Road, Torquay TQ2 5LL
01803-212760
6 bedrs, 1 ➹/WC, 5 ➹/WC; TV tcf P6
Child restrictions
sB&B £19-£22.50 dB&B £27-£35; cc Ac DC Vi

Lindens *Acclaimed* RAC
31 Bampfylde Road, Torquay TQ2 5AY
01803-212281 &
7 bedrs, 2 ➹/WC, 5 ➹/WC; TV tcf ✦ ✄ P7
Child restrictions
sB&B £12-£18 dB&B £30-£36; HB weekly
£150-£169; D £7 [10%V]

Lindum RAC
Abbey Road, Torquay TQ2 5ND
01803-292795 &
20 bedrs, 1 ➹/WC, 13 ➹/WC, 3 ➹;
TV tcf ✦ P14
sB&B £12-£20 dB&B £24-£40; HB weekly
£125; [5%V]; cc DC

Newton House *Highly Acclaimed* RAC
31 Newton Road, Torre, Torquay TQ2 5DB
01803-297520

Norbeck 35 New Street, Paignton, Torquay
TQ3 3HL 01803-558033

Norwood *Acclaimed* RAC
60 Belgrave Road, Torquay TQ2 5HY
01803-294236
12 bedrs, 10 ➹/WC, 1 ➹;
Breakfast only [10%V]; cc Ac Vi

Patricia *Acclaimed* RAC
Belgrave Road, Torquay TQ2 5HY
01803-293339
9 bedrs, 9 ➹/WC, 2 ➹; P9
Child restrictions
Breakfast only [10%V]; cc Ac Vi

Ravenhurst Ruckamore Road, Torquay TQ2
6HF 01803-607165
10 bedrs, 1 ➹/WC, 2 ➹; tcf ✦ P5
sB&B £15; HB weekly £145-£155; D £22-£24

Rawlyn House *Acclaimed* ♔RAC
Rawlyn Road, Chelston, Torquay TQ2 6PL
01803-605208
17 bedrs, 4 ➡/WC, 10 🐾/WC, 1 ➡;
TV tcf ✗ P17
sB&B £21-£25 dB&B £42-£50; HB weekly
£190-£222; D £7 [10%V]

Red Squirrel Lodge *Acclaimed* ♔RAC
Chelston Road, Torquay TQ2 6PU
01803-605496 Fax 01803-690170
14 bedrs, 3 ➡/WC, 6 🐾/WC, 1 ➡;
TV tcf ✗ P10
Child restrictions
sB&B £16.50-£23 dB&B £37-£46; HB weekly
£155-£182;; cc Ac Amex Vi

Richwood *Acclaimed* ♔RAC
20 Newton Road, Torquay TQ2 5BZ
01803-293729 Fax 01803-213632
21 bedrs, 5 ➡/WC, 13 🐾/WC, 1 ➡; P14
sB&B £12-£22 dB&B £24-£44; HB weekly
£112-£185; D £7 [5%V]; cc Ac Amex Vi

Robin Hill *Highly Acclaimed* ♔RAC
Braddons Hill Road East, Torquay TQ1 1HF
01803-214518 Fax 01803-291410
18 bedrs, 18 🐾/WC; TV tcf ✗ P12
Child restrictions
sB&B £18-£26 dB&B £36-£52; HB weekly
£190-£246; D £10 [10%V]; cc Ac Vi

Sandpiper Rowdens Rd, Torquay TQ2 5AZ
01803-292779

Seaway *Acclaimed* ♔RAC
Chelston Road, Torquay TQ2 6PU
01803-605320 Fax 01803-605320

Sherwood ♔RAC
Belgrave Road, Torquay TQ2 5HP
01803-294534
55 bedrs, 46 ➡/WC, 6 ➡; P25
Breakfast only

No Smoking/Dogs

✗ Indicates a hotel which either bans
smoking throughout the establishment or
does not allow smoking in some areas.

✗ Indicates a hotel which either does not
welcome dogs or restricts dogs to certain
areas of the hotel.
Please telephone the hotel
for further details.

Shirley *Acclaimed* ♔RAC
Braddons Hill Road East, Torquay TQ1 1HF
01803-293016

*Elegant Victorian villa situated in a quiet
area. Close to harbour and amenities.*
14 bedrs, 1 ➡/WC, 10 🐾/WC, 1 ➡; TV tcf ✗ P4
Child restrictions
sB&B £15-£20 dB&B £34-£44; HB weekly
£155-£190; D £6.50 [10%V]; cc Ac Vi

Silver Palms 14 Bampfylde Road, Torquay
TQ2 5AR 01803-299764

Silverlands ♔RAC
27 Newton Road, Torquay TQ2 5DB
01803-292013
11 bedrs, 6 ➡/WC, 2 ➡; ✗ P13
sB&B £12-£14 dB&B £17.50-£24 Breakfast only

Skerries ♔RAC
25 Morgan Avenue, Torquay TQ2 5RR
01803-293618
12 bedrs, 3 ➡/WC, 2 ➡; ✗
[5%V]; cc DC

St Kilda ♔RAC
49 Babbacombe Road, Torquay TQ1 3SJ
01803-327238 Fax 01803-327238
25 bedrs, 3 ➡/WC, 15 🐾/WC, 3 ➡;
TV tcf ✗ P30
sB&B £16.50-£17.25 dB&B £33-£34.50; HB
weekly £147-£150;

Sunnymead 501 Babbacombe Road, Torquay
TQ1 1HL 01803-296938

The Parkside 164 Avenue Road, Torquay
TQ2 5LQ 01803-294068

The Pines *Acclaimed* ♔RAC
19 Newton Road, Torre, Torquay TQ2 5DB
01803-292882
3 bedrs, 2 ➡/WC, 2 ➡; ✗ P4

Torbay Rise 🛏️RAC
Old Mill Road, Chelston, Torquay TQ2 6HL
01803-605541
15 bedrs, 10 ➤/WC, 5 ➤/WC, 1 ➤; TV tcf ✹ P10
Child restrictions
sB&B £19-£24 dB&B £38-£48; HB weekly
£150-£198; cc Ac Vi

Trafalgar House 🛏️RAC
30 Bridge Road, Torquay TQ2 5BA
01803-292486
12 bedrs, 7 ➤/WC, 3 ➤; P10
Child restrictions

Trelawney *Acclaimed* 🛏️RAC
48 Belgrave Road, Torquay TQ2 5HS
01803-296049
15 bedrs, 15 ➤/WC, 1 ➤; TV tcf ✹ P2
dB&B £34-£44 Breakfast only; cc Ac Vi

Walnut Lodge 48 Bampfylde Road, Torquay
TQ2 5AY 01803-297402

Westwood 111 Abbey Road, Torquay TQ2
5NP 01803-293818

TORRINGTON Devon 2C2

Smytham Manor *Acclaimed* 🛏️RAC
Little Torrington EX38 8PU 01805-22110
7 bedrs, 5 ➤/WC, 1 ➤; tcf ✹ P14
D £10; cc Ac Vi

TOTNES Devon 3D3

(Inn) Old Church House Inn 🛏️RAC
Torbryan, Ipplepen, Totnes TQ12 5UR
01803-812372
7 bedrs, 7 ➤/WC; P30
sB&B £30-£35 dB&B £45-£55 D £12.50
[10%V]; cc Ac Vi

Old Forge At Totnes Seymour Place, Totnes
TQ9 5AY 01803-862174 ♿
Recently restored 600-year-old stone building
with coach and through to walled garden.
Still a working forge too. All modern comforts
in luxuriously appointed cosy bedrooms.
Licensed parking.
10 bedrs, 3 ➤/WC, 8 ➤/WC, 2 ➤; TV tcf P11
sB&B £20 Breakfast only; cc Ac Vi

Wadstray House Blackawton, Totnes TQ9
7DE 01803-712539 ♿
5 bedrs, 5 ➤/WC, 5 ➤/WC; ✹ P7
sB&B £25; HB weekly £290

TRURO Cornwall 2B4

Carvean Farm 🛏️RAC
Probus, Truro TR2 4HY 01872-520243
3 bedrs, 1 ➤/WC, 2 ➤/WC; tcf ✹ P10
Child restrictions
sB&B £19.50 dB&B £37; HB weekly £192.50;
D £12; cc Ac Vi

Marcorrie 🛏️RAC
20 Falmouth Road, Truro TR1 2HX
01872-77374 Fax 01872-41666
12 bedrs, 12 ➤/WC, 1 ➤;
Breakfast only [10%V]; cc Ac Amex Vi

Penhale Farm Grampound Road, Truro TR2
4ER 01872-74555
A spacious farmhouse with a pleasant garden
on a 240 acre working farm with cereal, beef
cattle and sheep.
3 bedrs, 1 ➤; ✹
sB&B £13 Breakfast only

New Telephone Numbers

All UK telephone codes are being changed. The number 1 is being inserted after the first 0. For example, 081 is changing to 0181. The new codes were available in August 1994 and the two codes will run in parallel until 16 April 1995, when the new code will take over. The new codes are given throughout the guide, as they will be in use in November when the guide is published The old codes can be used up to 16 April 1995.

Five cities will have a complete change of code and an additional digit to the number.

	old	new
Bristol	0272-xxxxx	0117-9xxxxxx
Leeds	0532-xxxxx	0113-2xxxxxx
Leicester	0533-xxxxx	0116-2xxxxxx
Nottingham	0602-xxxxx	0115-9xxxxxx
Sheffield	0742-xxxxx	0114-2xxxxxx

Rock Cottage *Acclaimed* ⛯RAC
Blackwater, Truro TR4 8EU 01872-560252
3 bedrs, 3 ☏/WC; tcf ✂ P3
Child restrictions
dB&B £37 Breakfast only

Trevispan-Vean Farm ⛯RAC
St Erme, Truro TR4 9BL 01872-79514

4 Upper Lemon Villas Lemon Street, Truro
TR1 2PD 01872-777000

TWO BRIDGES Devon 2C3

Cherrybrook ⛯RAC
Two Bridges PL20 6SP 01822-88260
7 bedrs, 7 ➹/WC, 1 ➹; ✂ P12

WADEBRIDGE Cornwall 2B3

Hendra Country *Acclaimed* ⛯RAC
St Kew Highway, Wadebridge PL30 3EQ
0120884-343
5 bedrs, 1 ➹/WC, 3 ☏/WC, 1 ➹; TV tcf ✂ P8
sB&B £18-£23.50 dB&B £36-£47 Breakfast
only [5%V]; cc Ac Vi

Lundy House Rock Road, St Minver,
Wadebridge PL27 6PP 01208-862401

Tregellist Farm *Acclaimed* ⛯RAC
Tregellist, St Kew, Bodmin, Wadebridge PL30
3HG 01208-880537
3 bedrs, 3 ☏/WC, 1 ➹; TV tcf P10
sB&B £18 dB&B £34; HB weekly £182

Trevanion House Trevanion Road,
Wadebridge PL27 7JY 01208-814903

WATCHET Somerset 3D2

Langtry Country House Washford, Watchet
TA23 0NT 01984-40303

(Inn) West Somerset ⛯RAC
Swain Street, Watchet TA23 0AB 01984-34434
Fax 01984-34434
9 bedrs, 3 ➹/WC, 2 ☏/WC, 2 ➹; TV tcf ✂
sB&B £17.50 dB&B £35 Breakfast only;
cc Ac Vi

WELLINGTON Shropshire 7E2

Blue Mantle 2 Mantle St, Wellington TA21
8AW 01823-662000

WELLS Somerset 3E2

Bekynton *Acclaimed* ⛯RAC
7 St Thomas Street, Wells BA5 2UU
01749-672222

Old stone-built house with converted barn at back.
8 bedrs, 6 ➹/WC, 2 ➹; P6
Child restrictions
sB&B £22-£24 dB&B £38-£46 Breakfast only
[5%V]; cc Ac Vi

Tor *Acclaimed* ⛯RAC
20 Tor Street, Wells BA5 2US 01749-672322
Fax 01749-672322
8 bedrs, 5 ➹/WC, 3 ☏/WC, 2 ➹; P12
Child restrictions
Breakfast only [10%V]; cc Ac Vi

17 Priory Road Wells BA5 1SU 01749-677300

WEST DOWN Devon 2C2

The Long House *Highly Acclaimed* The
Square, West Down EX34 8NF 01271-863242

WESTWARD HO! Devon 2C2

Buckleigh Lodge *Acclaimed* ⛯RAC
Bay View Road, Westward Ho! EX39 1BJ
01237-475988
6 bedrs, 1 ➹/WC, 2 ☏/WC, 2 ➹; TV tcf ✂ P6
sB&B £16 dB&B £32; HB weekly £158; [10%V]

WHEDDON CROSS Somerset   3D2

(Inn) The Rest & Be Thankful Inn
Acclaimed   RAC
Nr Minehead, Wheddon Cross TA24 7DR
01643-841222 Fax 01643-841222
4 bedrs, 4 ↑/WC, 1 ➡; TV tcf ✂ P60
Child restrictions
sB&B £24.50 dB&B £49; HB weekly £220; D
£10 [5%V]; cc Ac Vi

WILLITON Somerset   3D2

Fairfield House *Acclaimed*   RAC
51 Long Street, Williton TA4 4RY
01984-632636
5 bedrs, 1 ➡/WC, 4 ↑/WC; tcf P10
Child restrictions
sB&B £23 dB&B £40; HB weekly £210; D £11
[5%V]; cc Ac Vi

WOOLACOMBE Devon   2C2

Caertref *Acclaimed*   RAC
Beach Road, Woolacombe EX34 7BT
01271-870361
14 bedrs, 10 ➡/WC, 2 ➡; ✈ P14
Breakfast only; cc Ac Vi

Holmesdale Bay View Road, Woolacombe
EX34 7DQ 01271-870335

**Lundy House Chapel Hill, Mortehoe,
Woolacombe EX34 7RZ 01271-870372**

★★Narracott Grand   RAC
Beach Road, Woolacombe EX34 7BS
01271-870418 Fax 01271-870600

Pebbles Combesgate Beach, Woolacombe
EX34 7EA 01271-870426

Sunnycliffe *Highly Acclaimed*   RAC
Mortehoe, Woolacombe EX34 7EB
01271-870597
8 bedrs, 4 ➡/WC, 4 ↑/WC, 2 ➡; TV tcf ✂
Child restrictions
sB&B £25-£32 dB&B £50-£64; HB weekly
£235-£270; [10%V]

YELVERTON Devon   2C3

Harrabeer Country House *Acclaimed*   RAC
Harrowbeer Lane, Yelverton PL20 6EA
01822-853302
7 bedrs, 2 ➡/WC, 3 ↑/WC, 1 ➡; TV tcf P7
sB&B £22 dB&B £48 [5%V]; cc Ac Amex DC Vi

The Rosemont Greenbank Terrace,
Yelverton PL20 6DR 01822-852175

YEOVIL Somerset   3E2

Gallery 69 West Coker Road, Yeovil BA20
2JD 01935-21930

**Greystones 152 Hendford Hill, Yeovil
BA20 2RG 01935-26124**

*Historic house set amongst trees on Hendford
Hill, close to Ninesprings beauty spot. Close to
Yeovil showground and dry ski slope. Walking
distance to town is 10 minutes.*
6 bedrs, 1 ➹/WC, 2 ➹; TV tcf ✖ P7
sB&B £18 Breakfast only; cc Ac Vi

Wyndham 🅁🅐🅒
142 Sherborne Rd, Yeovil BA21 4HQ
01935-21468
6 bedrs, 1 ➹; TV tcf ✖ P8
sB&B £15-£17 dB&B £30-£34 Breakfast only

ZELAH Cornwall 2A4

Nanteague Farm *Acclaimed* 🅁🅐🅒
Marazanvose, Truro, Zelah TR4 9DH
01872-540351
4 bedrs, 4 ➹/WC, 1 ➹; ✖ P8
Breakfast only [5%V]; cc Ac Amex Vi

ZENNOR Cornwall 2A4

Boswednack Manor Zennor TR26 3DD
01736-794183

East Anglia

Norfolk • Suffolk • Cambridgeshire • Beds. • N. Essex

Long before European Union, East Anglia was physically joined to it and the River Ouse was a tributary of the Rhine. Low horizons account for the awesome size of the sun at dusk. In Suffolk, it sets behind pink-washed thatched cottages which cluster round churches, impressive in their size and flush work. On the Norfolk coast, silk-soft sands give way to salt flats and bird-filled marshes. Inland, the Broads network the land and life is leisurely at four mph. Cambridgeshire spreads out in the flat, flat Fens, and in the south there's the ancient University. Essex boasts Constable country and East Anglia has the lowest rainfall in Britain.

Anglesey Abbey

A SELECTION OF ATTRACTIONS:

Unless otherwise stated, all can be visited between April and October – some longer. Telephone for days/times of opening.

Anglesey Abbey & Gardens, Lode, Cambs: *12th-c abbey/Tudor manor. Art treasures, garden, water mill. NT.* Tel: 01223-811200.

Audley End House, Saffron Walden, Essex: *Formal Jacobean mansion in fine park. Closes end Sep.* Tel: 01799-522399.

Blickling Hall, Norfolk: *Imposing 17th-c house with Dutch gables. Formal gardens.* Tel: 01263-733084.

Bruisyard Vineyard & Herb Centre, Suffolk: *10 acre vineyard, winery, herb & water garden. Play area.* Tel: 01728-75281.

Cecil Higgins Art Gallery & Museum, Bedford: *Bedroom designed by Wm. Burgess in Victorian mansion:* Tel: 01234-211222.

Duxford Airfield, Cambridge: *Ride simulator & adventure playground. Fine display of aircraft.* Tel: 01223-835000.

Ely Cathedral, Cambs: *12th-c cathedral with landmark octagonal tower houses Stained Glass Museum.* Tel: 01353-778645.

Framlingham Castle, Suffolk: *Massive medieval ruins with 13 towers and splendid curtain wall, Tudor chimneys:* Tel: 01728-724189.

Gainsborough's House, Sudbury, Suffolk: *Birthplace with pleasant garden. Many of the artist's works.* Tel: 01787-372958.

Grimes Graves, nr. Brandon, Norfolk: *Neolithic flint mines – two excavated shafts open:* Tel: 01842-810656.

Guildhall, Lavenham, Suffolk: *16th-c Tudor building. Garden with Lock-Up and old Mortuary in idyllic village.* Tel: 01787-247646.

Holkham Hall, nr. Wells, Norfolk: *Palladian mansion. State apartments, deer park, pottery, lake & beach. Jun-Sep.* Tel: 01328-710227.

Kentwell Hall, Long Melford: *Family restores romantic moated Tudor House as home. Rare breeds, events.* Tel: 01787-310207.

Kingdom of the Sea, Hunstanton, Norfolk: *Seals and pups awaiting re-habilitation plus all marine life.* Tel: 01485-533576.

Layer Marney Tower, nr. Colchester, Essex: *Views of Essex from England's tallest Tudor gatehouse. Closes Sep.* Tel: 01206-330784.

Luton Hoo, Beds: *Fabergé jewelled flowers feature among mementoes of Russian Imperial life. Closes mid-Oct.* Tel:01582-22955.

Melford Hall, Long Melford, Suffolk: *16th-c. Fine pictures, furnishings, Beatrix Potter display. NT.* Tel: 01787-880286.

Museum of East Anglian Life, Stowmarket, Suffolk: *Varied displays in reconstructed buildings.* Tel: 01449-612229.

National Horseracing Museum, Newmarket, Suffolk: *Super half-day tours. Gallops, equine baths & stud in a.m. plus museum.* Tel: 01638-667333.

Norwich Castle Museum: *Impressive 11th-c castle now principal East Anglian museum: Norwich School paintings.* Tel: 01603-223624.

Old Warden, nr. Biggleswade, Beds: *Old aeroplanes and cars in working order. Flying days.* Tel: 01767-627288.

Oxburgh Hall, nr. Swaffham, Norfolk: *15th-c moated manor. Mary Queen of Scots needlework, parterre garden. NT.* Tel: 0136 621-258.

Peckover House & Garden, North Brink, Cambs: *18th-c domestic architecture. Victorian garden. NT.* Tel: 01945-583463.

Pettit's Animal Adventure Park, Reedham, Norfolk: *Live shows, tame animals, rides, mazes & more.* Tel: 01493-700094.

Pleasurewood Hills American Theme Park, nr. Gt. Yarmouth, Suffolk: *Pay once and all attractions are free.* Tel: 01502-508200.

Priory Vineyards, Little Dunmow, Essex: *10-acre vineyard on site of medieval priory & fishpond.* Tel: 01371-820577.

Sandringham House & Museum, Norfolk: *H.M.The Queen's country retreat. All main rooms open. Royal Daimlers, family pictures. Closed mid-Jul-early Aug.* Tel: 01553-772675.

Saxtead Mill, Suffolk: *White clapboarded mill of 1776. Climb to 'buck', see machinery. Closes end Sep.* Tel: 01728-685789.

Somerleyton Hall, nr. Lowestoft, Suffolk: *Superb family furnishings, tapestries & carving. Garden maze, miniature railway. Closes end Sep.* Tel:01502-730224.

Stockwood Craft Museum & Gardens, Luton, Beds: *Rural trades and large collection horse drawn vehicles.* Tel: 01582-38714.

The Thursford Collection, Fakenham, Norfolk: *Wurlitzer and many mechanical organs plus traction engines.* Tel: 01328-878477.

Wimpole Hall, Arrington, Cambs: *Capability Brown, Thornhill & Soane all contributed to this 18th-c mansion. NT.* Tel: 01223-207257.

Woburn Abbey, Beds: *Something for everyone in house or grounds. Antique Centre, Safari Park, events.* Tel: 01525-290666.

Woodbridge Tide Mill, Suffolk: *On superb coastal setting below picturesque hilltop town. Closes end Sep.* Tel: 01728-685789.

Ormesby Broad

SOME ANNUAL EVENTS:
= dates provisional.

Aldeburgh Festival, Snape Maltings, Suffolk: *Britten inspired up-market music event. 9-25 Jun.* Tel: 01728-452935.

Blickling Country Skills & Working Craft Fair, Blickling Hall, Norfolk. *15-17 Apr*.*

Bury St. Edmunds Festival, Suffolk: *Classical music, dance, drama, jazz, shows. 11-27 May.* Tel: 01284-757080.

Cambridge Summer Music, *Various venues, orchestral music. 11-16 Jul** Tel: 01223-300795.

Wren's Chapel, Emmanuel College, Cambridge

Chelmsford Spectacular, Essex: *Jousting, circus, civil war battles, fireworks, falcons, etc. 24-28 Aug*.* Tel: 01245-490490

Clacton Jazz Festival, Essex. *Traditional jazz bands at various venues. 25-28 Aug.** Tel: 01255-425501.

Ely Folk Weekend, Cambs: *30 events, international performers. Major dance displays: 7-9 Jul*.* Tel: 01353-740999.

Felbrigg Coast & Country Craft Fair, Norfolk: *Coast & country skills. 27-29 May.* Tel: 01263-734711.

Felixstowe Folk Festival, Suffolk: *Clog & garland dancing among varied events for all family. 13-16 May.* Tel: 01394-276770.

Horseracing: Newmarket – Tel: 01638-663482 Gt. Yarmouth – 01493-842527. Huntingdon – 01480-453373.

Ickworth Craft Festival, Ickworth House, Suffolk: *High quality craftware for sale. Demonstrations. 26-28 Aug.*

King's Lynn Festival, Norfolk: *Theatre, comedy, film cabaret themed to 'Carnival Colours'. 15-29 July.* Tel: 01553-774725.

Snape Proms, Snape Maltings, Suffolk: *Riverside Centre shops, galleries in old maltings. Proms 1-31 Aug.* Tel: 01728-452935.

South Suffolk Show, Ampton Park, Ingham, Suffolk: *120 trade stands, showjumping, farm animals. Childrens' area. 14 May.* Tel: 01638-750879.

Wings & Wheels Model Spectacular, North Weald Airfield, Essex: *Radio controlled displays. Trade stands, childrens fun. 8-9 Jul.* Tel: 01684-594505.

ALDEBURGH Suffolk 9F4

Margarets 50 Victoria Road, Aldeburgh IP15 5EJ 01728-453269

AYLSHAM Norfolk 9E2

Sankence Lodge *Highly Acclaimed* RAC
Cawston Road, Aylesham NR11 6NW
01263-734120

BEDFORD Bedfordshire 4C1

A & J 3 St Michaels Road, Bedford MK40 2LY
01234-344217

Bedford Oak House 33 Shakespear Road, Bedford MK40 2DX 01234-266972 Fax 01234-266972

Mock-Tudor style house near the town centre and railway station. Offering motel style accommodation with a large private car park.
15 bedrs, 10 ⬧/WC, 2 ⬧; TV tcf P17
sB&B £29 Breakfast only; cc Ac Amex DC Vi

Firs Farm Stagsden, Bedford MK43 8TB
01234-822344

Pond Farm 7 High Street, Pulloxhill, Bedford MK45 5HA 01525-712316

★★★**(Inn) Queens Head** RAC
2 Rushden Road, Milton Ernest, Bedford
MK44 1RU 01234-272822
12 bedrs, 12 ⬧/WC; P30
cc Ac Amex Vi

Rifle Range Farm Yielden, Bedford MK44
1AW 01933-53151
2 bedrs, 1 ⬧; tcf ⚭ P10
sB&B £15 D £7-£10

★★★**(Inn) The Wayfarer** RAC
403 Goldington Road, Bedford MK41 0DS

01234-272707 Fax 01234-272707 ♿
29 bedrs, 29 ⬧/WC; TV tcf P100
sB&B £40-£55 dB&B £45 D £10; cc Ac Amex
DC Vi

Victoria House 17 Shakespeare Road,
Bedford MK40 2DZ 01234-214135

71 Chaucer Road Bedford MK40 2LY
01234-355634

BIGGLESWADE Bedfordshire 4C1

The New Hill Market Square, Biggleswade,
Biggleswade SG18 8AS 01767-313198

BLAKENEY Norfolk 9E2

Flintstones *Acclaimed* RAC
**Wiveton, Blakeney NR25 7TL
01263-740337**
Guest house situated in a picturesque rural surroundings near the village green. Located one mile from Blakeney on the B1156.
5 bedrs, 5 ⬧/WC; TV tcf ⚭ P5
sB&B £24.50 dB&B £32-£37; HB weekly £182;

BRAINTREE Essex 5E1

Nags Head RAC
Market Place, Braintree CM7 6HG
01376-323348
3 bedrs, 1 ⬧; TV
sB&B £16 dB&B £32 Breakfast only

Spicers Farm Rotten End, Wethersfield,
Braintree CM7 4AL 01371-851021
5 bedrs, 1 ⬧/WC, 2 ⬧/WC; ⚭
sB&B £15 Breakfast only

BURY ST EDMUNDS Suffolk 9E4

Chantry *Acclaimed* RAC
8 Sparhawk Street, Bury St Edmunds IP33

1RY 01284-767427 Fax 01284-760946
14 bedrs, 5 ➥/WC, 9 ⬧/WC, 1 ➥; TV tcf ✕ ✕ P17
sB&B £32.50-£36.50 dB&B £49.50 D £15
[10%V]; cc Ac DC Vi

Dunston 8 Springfield Road, Bury St
Edmunds IP33 3AN 01284-767981

The Olde White Hart *Acclaimed*   RAC
35 Southgate Street, Bury St Edmunds IP33
2AZ 01284-755547
10 bedrs, 5 ➥/WC, 7 ⬧/WC, 1 ➥; TV tcf ✕ P100
sB&B £39.50-£42.50 dB&B £49.50-£54.50
Breakfast only; cc Ac Amex DC Vi

Twelve Angel Hill *Highly Acclaimed*   RAC
12 Angel Hill, Bury St Edmunds 1P33 1UZ
01284-704088 Fax 01284-725549
6 bedrs, 2 ➥/WC, 4 ⬧/WC; TV tcf P3
Child restrictions
sB&B £45 dB&B £65 Breakfast only [10%V];
cc Ac Amex DC Vi

CAMBRIDGE Cambridgeshire   9D4

Ashtrees   RAC
128 Perne Road, Cambridge CB1 3RR
01223-411233
6 bedrs, 1 ⬧/WC, 1 ➥; TV tcf P6
sB&B £18 dB&B £38 Breakfast only [10%V];
cc Ac Vi

Assisi Guest House

193 Cherry Hinton Road, Cambridge CB1 4BX
Tel: 01223 246648 or 211466 Fax: 01223 412900

Fine detached Victorian house ideally situated
for the city centre and the famous
Addenbrookes Hospital. Family run guest house
offering personal service. Spacious rooms with
all modern facilities including showers & colour
TV in all rooms. Full English breakfast, ample
garden with large car park.
Single £25-29; Double £35-39; Family £49 for three

Assisi   RAC
187 Cherry Hinton Road, Cambridge CB1 4BX
01223-211466 Fax 01223-412900

Avimore   RAC
310 Cherry Hinton Road, Cambridge CB1
4AU 01223-410956

Bon Accord House *Acclaimed*   RAC
20 St Margarets Square, (off Cherry Hinton
Road), Cambridge CB1 4AP 01223-411188
9 bedrs, 1 ⬧/WC, 2 ➥; TV tcf P9
sB&B £21-£22 dB&B £35-£37 Breakfast only;
cc Ac Vi

(Inn) Bridge   RAC
Clayhythe, Waterbeach, Cambridge CB5 9ND
01223-860252 Fax 01223-440448
30 bedrs, 20 ➥/WC; TV tcf ✕ P70
sB&B £30 dB&B £45 D £14.95 [10%V]; cc Ac
Amex Vi

Brooklands *Highly Acclaimed*   RAC
95 Cherry Hinton Road, Cambridge CB1 4BS
01223-242035 Fax 01223-242035
5 bedrs, 1 ➥/WC, 4 ⬧/WC; TV tcf ✕ P5
sB&B £27 dB&B £36.40 [10%V]; cc Ac Amex
DC Vi

Cambridge Lodge *Acclaimed*   RAC
139 Huntingdon Road, Cambridge CB3 0DQ
01223-352833 Fax 01223-355166

Cristinas   RAC
47 St Andrews Road, Cambridge CB4 1DL
01223-327700

*Small family-run business in quiet location, a
short walk from city Centre and colleges.*
6 bedrs, 5 ⬧/WC; TV tcf ✕
sB&B £24-£25 dB&B £35-£43 Breakfast only

De Freville House *Acclaimed* ♣RAC
166 Chesterton Road, Cambridge CB4 1DA
01223-354993 Fax 01223-321890
9 bedrs, 5 ♠/WC, 2 ➥; TV tcf P2
Child restrictions
sB&B £18-£22 dB&B £34-£46 Breakfast only
[5%V]

Hamden ♣RAC
89 High Street, Cherryhinton, Cambridge CB1
4LU 01223-413263

Lensfield *Highly Acclaimed* ♣RAC
53 Lensfield Road, Cambridge CR2 1GH
01223-355017 Fax 01223-312022
32 bedrs, 9 ➥/WC, 18 ♠/WC, 2 ➥; TV tcf ✹ P5
sB&B £42-£45 D £7 [5%V]; cc Ac Amex DC Vi

Suffolk House *Acclaimed* ♣RAC
69 Milton Road, Cambridge CB4 1XA
01223-352016 Fax 01223-566816
10 bedrs, 1 ➥/WC, 9 ♠/WC; TV tcf P9
Child restrictions
sB&B £35 dB&B £45; cc Ac Vi

Tenison Tower 148 Tenison Road,
Cambridge CB1 2DP 01223-566511

The Manor House High Street, Oakington,
Cambridge CB4 5AG 01223-232450 Fax
01223-411276
4 bedrs, 2 ➥; tcf ✗ P6
sB&B £19 Breakfast only; cc Ac Vi

CRANFIELD Bedfordshire 4C1

14 Redlion Close Cranfield MK43 0JA
01234-750738

CAWSTON Norfolk 9E2

Grey Gables *Acclaimed* ♣RAC
Norwich Road, Eastgate, Cawston NR10 4EY
01603-871259
8 bedrs, 5 ➥/WC, 1 ♠/WC, 1 ➥; TV tcf ✗ ✹ P15
sB&B £19-£20 dB&B £54-£56; HB weekly
£219-£226; D £16 [10%V]; cc Ac Vi

CLACTON-ON-SEA Essex 5E1

Chudleigh *Acclaimed* ♣RAC
Agate Road, Marine Parade West, Clacton-on-
Sea CO15 1RA 01255-425407 Fax
01255-425407 ⚓
*Attractive, Victorian, red-brick, detached house
with unique architectural features. Conveniently
situated by the seafront a short distance from the*
pier and main shopping centre.
12 bedrs, 12 ➥/WC, ✗ P7
Breakfast only [10%V]; cc Ac Amex DC Vi

CROMER Norfolk 9F2

Birch House ♣RAC
34 Cabbell Road, Cromer NR27 9HX
01263-512521

Chellow Dene *Acclaimed* ♣RAC
23 Macdonald Road, Cromer NR27 9AP
01263-513251
7 bedrs, 2 ➥; P6
Breakfast only

Sandcliff ♣RAC
Runton Road, Cromer NR27 0HJ
01263-512888
23 bedrs, 15 ➥/WC, 2 ➥; ✗ P14
Breakfast only

Westgate Lodge *Highly Acclaimed* ♣RAC
Macdonald Road, Cromer NR27 9AP
01263-512840 Fax 01263-512840
11 bedrs, 11 ♠/WC, 1 ➥; TV tcf ✹ P11
Child restrictions
dB&B £47; HB weekly £197.40;

DEDHAM Essex 9E4

(Inn) Marlborough Head ♣RAC
Mill Lane, Dedham CM7 6HG 01376-23348
3 bedrs, 1 ➥/WC, 2 ♠/WC; TV tcf ✗ P25
sB&B £32.50-£36 dB&B £57 D £13; cc Ac Vi

DEREHAM Norfolk 9E3

Peacock House Peacock Lane, Old Beetley,
Dereham NR20 4DG

DERSINGHAM Norfolk 9D2

Westdene House *Acclaimed* ♣RAC
60 Hunstanton Road, Dersingham PE31 6HQ
01485-540395
5 bedrs, 1 ➥/WC, 1 ➥; ✗ P10
sB&B £15 dB&B £27; HB weekly £142.50;
£7.50 [5%V]; cc Ac Vi

DUNSTABLE Bedfordshire 4C1

Northway 126 High Street North, Dunstable
LU6 1NL 01582-662236

Regent House 79a High Street North,
Dunstable LU6 1JF 01582-660196

Ridgeway End 5 Ivinghoe Way, Edlesborough, Dunstable LU6 2EL
01525-220405 &
3 bedrs, 1 ➡/WC, 1 ⬥/WC, 1 ➡; P3
sB&B £15 Breakfast only

5 Brightwell Avenue Totternhoe, Dunstable LU6 1QT 01582-601287

10 St Peters Road Dunstable LU5 4HY 01582-699470

23 Priory Road Dunstable LU5 4HR 01582-667396

ELY Cambridgeshire 9D3

The Three Pickerels 19 The Bridge, Mepal, Ely CB6 2AT 01353-777777

FELIXSTOWE Suffolk 9E4

(Inn) Dolphin ᴿᴬᶜ
41 Beach Station Road, Felixstowe IP11 8EY
01394-282261
8 bedrs, 2 ⬥/WC, 2 ➡; TV tcf P35
sB&B £18 dB&B £28 D £6; cc Ac Amex Vi

GARBOLDISHAM Norfolk 9E3

Ingleneuk Lodge *Highly Acclaimed* ᴿᴬᶜ
Hopton Road, Diss, Garboldisham IP22
2RQ 0195-381-541 &

A large modern bungalow set in 10 acres of part-wooded grounds with a stream. Single level accommodation suitable for the disabled. South-facing patio.
9 bedrs, 2 ➡/WC, 6 ⬥/WC, 1 ➡; TV tcf ✕ ⤙ P20
sB&B £31.50 dB&B £49; HB weekly £252;
[10%V]; cc Ac Amex Vi

GISLINGHAM Suffolk 9E4

Old Guildhall *Highly Acclaimed* ᴿᴬᶜ
Mill Street, Eye, Gislingham IP23 8JT
01379-783361
4 bedrs, 4 ➡/WC; TV tcf ✕ P5
dB&B £50; HB weekly £200; [5%V]

GORLESTON-ON-SEA Norfolk 9F3

Balmoral ᴿᴬᶜ
65 Avondale Road, Gorleston-on-Sea NR31
6DJ 01493-6625318
7 bedrs, 2 ➡/WC, 2 ➡; ✕
Breakfast only [5%V]

Squirrel's Nest *Acclaimed* ᴿᴬᶜ
71 Avondale Road, Gorleston-on-Sea NR31
6DJ 01493-662746 &
9 bedrs, 9 ➡/WC, 1 ➡; ✕ ⤙ P5
sB&B £15-£27 dB&B £30-£54; HB weekly
£130-£220; D £7.50 [10%V]; cc Ac Amex DC Vi

HEACHAM Norfolk 9D2

St Annes ᴿᴬᶜ
53 Neville Road, Heacham PE31 7HB
01485-70021
8 bedrs, 3 ➡/WC, 2 ➡; P3
Child restrictions
Breakfast only

HILGAY Norfolk 9D3

Crosskeys Riverside *Highly Acclaimed* ᴿᴬᶜ
Downham Market, Hilgay PE38 0LN
01366-387777
A small hotel in a converted 17th century building besides the River Wissey.
3 bedrs, 3 ➡/WC; TV tcf ✕ ⤙ P10
Breakfast only [10%V]; cc Ac Vi

HOLT Norfolk   9E2

★★Feathers   RAC
6 Market Place, Holt NR25 6BW 01263-712318

Lawn's *Highly Acclaimed*   RAC
26 Station Road, Holt NR25 6BS 01263-713390
11 bedrs, 11 ➡/WC; ✕
Breakfast only [5%V]; cc Ac Amex DC Vi

HUNSTANTON Norfolk   9D2

Sunningdale *Highly Acclaimed*   RAC
3 Avenue Road, Hunstanton PE36 5BW
01485-532562
11 bedrs, 11 ➡/WC, 1 ➡; ✕
Child restrictions
sB&B £25 dB&B £42-£46; HB weekly £215-
£240; D £11.50

IPSWICH Suffolk   5E1

Anglesea *Acclaimed*   RAC
Oban Street, Ipswich IP1 3PH 01473-255630
7 bedrs, 3 ➡/WC, 4 ☏/WC; TV tcf ✕ P9
sB&B £39 dB&B £42 Breakfast only; cc Ac
Amex DC Vi

Bridge 4 Ancaster Road, Ipswich IP1 9AA
01473-601760

Highfield Harkstead Road, Holbrook,
Ipswich IP9 2RA 01473-328250

Highview House *Acclaimed*   RAC
56 Belstead Road, Ipswich IP2 8BE
01473-688659
11 bedrs, 3 ➡/WC, 6 ☏/WC, 3 ➡; TV tcf ✕ P12
sB&B £33-£38.50 dB&B £43.65-£48.50
Breakfast only [10%V]; cc Ac Vi

Lions Head Cauldwell Hall Road, Ipswich
IP4 5AS 01473-727418

KING'S LYNN Norfolk   9D2

Beeches *Acclaimed*   RAC
2 Guannock Terrace, King's Lynn PE30 5QT
01553-766577 Fax 01553-776664
7 bedrs, 4 ➡/WC, 1 ➡; TV tcf P2
D £8; cc Ac Vi

Guanock   RAC
South Gates, King's Lynn PE30 5JG
01553-772959 Fax 01553-772959
17 bedrs, 5 ➡;
[5%V]; cc Ac Amex DC Vi

Havana *Acclaimed*   RAC
117 Gaywood Road, King's Lynn PE30 2PU
01553-772331
7 bedrs, 3 ☏/WC, 1 ➡; TV tcf ✕ P7
sB&B £16 dB&B £28 Breakfast only

Maranatha   RAC
115 Gaywood Road, King's Lynn PE30 2PU
01553-774596
6 bedrs, 1 ☏/WC, 1 ➡; TV tcf ✕ P6
sB&B £15 dB&B £26 Breakfast only

Oakwood House *Acclaimed*   RAC
Tottenhill, King's Lynn PE33 0RH
01553-810256   &
7 bedrs, 4 ➡/WC, 1 ☏/WC, 1 ➡; TV tcf ✕
P20
sB&B £30 dB&B £40 D £11 [10%V]; cc Ac Vi

Russet House *Highly Acclaimed*   RAC
Goodwins Road, Vancouver Avenue, King's
Lynn PE30 5PE 01553-773098 Fax
01553-773098
12 bedrs, 8 ➡/WC, 4 ☏/WC; TV tcf ✕ ✕ P14
sB&B £29.50 dB&B £46.50 D £12.50; cc Ac
Amex DC Vi

LEIGHTON BUZZARD Bedfordshire   4C1

Grovebury Farm Grovebury Road, Leighton
Buzzard LU7 8TF 01525-373363

The Peacock 1-3 Lake Street, Leighton
Buzzard LU7 8RS 01525-371174 Fax
01525-371174
2 bedrs, 1 ➡/WC, 1 ☏/WC, 2 ➡; TV tcf P8
sB&B £16 Breakfast only

The Red Lion Watling Street, Hockliffe,
Leighton Buzzard LU7 9LR 01525-210240

LEISTON Suffolk   9F4

White Horse Station Road, Leiston IP16 4HD
01728-830694
13 bedrs, 1 ➡/WC, 2 ➡;
Breakfast only

LOWESTOFT Suffolk   9F3

Aarland House 36 Lyndhurst Road,
Lowestoft NR32 4PD 01502-585148

Albany *Acclaimed* RAC
400 London Road South, Lowestoft NR33
0BQ 01502-574394
7 bedrs, 3 ➥/WC;
sB&B £16 dB&B £32; HB weekly £142;
[10%V]; cc Ac Vi

Hotel Katherine RAC
49 Kirkley Cliff Road, Lowestoft NR33 0DF
01502-567858
10 bedrs, 10 ➥/WC; ✗ P3
Breakfast only [10%V]; cc Amex

Rockville House *Acclaimed* RAC
6 Pakefield Road, Lowestoft NR33 0HS
01502-581011
7 bedrs, 2 ➥/WC, 1 ❀/WC, 2 ➥; TV tcf ✄
Child restrictions
sB&B £22 dB&B £37.50; HB weekly £185;
[5%V]; cc Ac Vi

Somerton Kirkley Cliff, Lowestoft NR33 0BY
01502-565665

18 Kirkley Cliff Lowestoft NR33 0BY
01502-515839

LUTON Bedfordshire 4C1

**Belzayne 70 Lalleford Road, Luton LU2
9JH 01582-36591**

*A modern, semi-detached hotel with friendly,
personal service.*
3 bedrs, 1 ➥; tcf P5
Child restrictions
sB&B £22 Breakfast only

Stockwood 41-43 Stockwood Crescent, Luton
LU1 3SS 01582-21000
18 bedrs, 4 ❀/WC, 3 ➥; P14
sB&B £20 Breakfast only

1 Bracklesham Gardens Stopsley, Luton
LU2 8QJ 01582-33122

MANNINGTREE Essex 5E1

(Inn) Thorn Inn RAC
High Street, Mistley, Manningtree CO11 1HG
0106-392821
4 bedrs, 4 ❀/WC; TV tcf P10
Child restrictions
sB&B £30 dB&B £45 D £13.50; cc Ac Vi

MARCH Cambridgeshire 9D3

★★(Inn) Olde Griffin RAC
High Street, March PE15 9EJ 01354-52517 Fax
01354-50086 ♿
20 bedrs, 17 ➥/WC, 3 ❀/WC, 1 ➥; TV tcf P30
sB&B £35 dB&B £47.50 D £9.50 [10%V]; cc Ac
Amex Vi

MOLESWORTH Cambridgeshire 8C3

(Inn) Cross Keys RAC
nr Huntingdon, Molesworth PE11 0QF
01832-710283 ♿
10 bedrs, 3 ➥/WC, 7 ❀/WC; TV tcf ✗ P40
sB&B £20-£23.25 dB&B £36.50; cc Ac Vi

MUNDESLEY-ON-SEA Norfolk 9F2

Manor *Acclaimed* RAC
Mundesley-on-Sea NR11 8BG 01263-720309
Fax 01263-721731
26 bedrs, 9 ➥/WC, 17 ❀/WC, 2 ➥; tcf ✗ P50
sB&B £24.75-£29.50 dB&B £43.50-£49.50

NEEDHAM MARKET Suffolk 9E4

Pipps Ford *Acclaimed* RAC
Needham Market IP6 8LJ 0144-208 Fax
0144-561 ♿
6 bedrs, 6 ➥/WC; P20
Child restrictions

NORTHWOLD Norfolk 9E3

Woodland Lodge RAC
Thetford Road, Northwold IP26 5LQ
01366-728888 Fax 01366-727121 ♿
34 bedrs, 34 ➥/WC; TV tcf ✗ ✄ P250
sB&B £31.95 D £7.95; cc Ac Amex DC Vi

NORWICH Norfolk 9F3

Belmonte *Highly Acclaimed* ᴿᴬ̊C
60-62 Prince Of Wales Road, Norwich NR1
1LT 01603-622533 Fax 01603-760805
9 bedrs, 9 🛏/WC;
sB&B £29.95 D £10 [10%V]; cc Ac Amex DC Vi

Cavalier *Highly Acclaimed* ᴿᴬ̊C
244 Thorpe Road, Norwich NR1 1TP
01603-34291 Fax 01603-31744
20 bedrs, 3 🛏/WC, 17 📻/WC, 1 🛏; TV tcf 🐕
⤢ P30
D £12.50 [10%V]; cc Ac Vi

Old Corner Shop ᴿᴬ̊C
26 Cromer Rd, Hellesdon, Norwich NR6 6LZ
01603-419000

Wedgewood *Acclaimed* ᴿᴬ̊C
42 St Stephens Road, Norwich NR1 3RE
01603-625730
11 bedrs, 3 🛏/WC, 5 📻/WC, 1 🛏; tcf ⤢ P11
sB&B £18-£22 dB&B £34-£40; HB weekly
£203-£224; D £12 [5%V]; cc Ac Amex Vi

PAPWORTH EVERARD Cambridgeshire 9D4

★★Papworth ᴿᴬ̊C
Ermine Street South, Papworth Everard CB3
8PB 01954-718851 Fax 01954-718069
20 bedrs, 20 🛏/WC; P50
sB&B £25-£30 dB&B £40 [10%V]; cc Ac Amex
DC Vi

PETERBOROUGH Cambridgeshire 8C3

Aaron Park ᴿᴬ̊C
109-112 Park Road, Peterborough PE1 2TR
01733-64849 Fax 01733-64849
8 bedrs, 1 🛏/WC, 7 📻/WC; TV tcf 🐕 P11
sB&B £31-£36 dB&B £36 D £12 [10%V]; cc Ac
Amex Vi

Dalwhinnie Lodge *Acclaimed* ᴿᴬ̊C
31-33 Burghley Road, Peterborough PE1 2QA
01733-65968 Fax 01733-890838
18 bedrs, 3 🛏/WC, 3 🛏; 🐕 P14
sB&B £15-£25 dB&B £30-£35 Breakfast only
[5%V]; cc Ac Amex DC Vi

Formule 1 ᴿᴬ̊C
Boongate, Eastern Industry, Peterborough
PE1 5QT 01733-894400

Hawthorn House *Acclaimed* ᴿᴬ̊C
89 Thorpe Road, Peterborough PE3 6JQ
01733-40608
8 bedrs, 8 🛏/WC; 🐕 P7
Breakfast only; cc Ac Vi

Lodge *Acclaimed* ᴿᴬ̊C
130 Lincoln Road, Peterborough PE1 2NR
01733-341489 Fax 01733-52072
9 bedrs, 9 📻/WC; TV tcf 🐕 ⤢ P6
Child restrictions
sB&B £35-£45 dB&B £40-£55; HB weekly
£200; D £13 [5%V]; cc Ac Amex Vi

Thorpe Lodge *Acclaimed* ᴿᴬ̊C
83 Thorpe Road, Peterborough PE3 6JQ
01733-348759 Fax 01733-891598
18 bedrs, 3 🛏/WC, 15 📻/WC, 2 🛏; TV tcf 🐕
P20
sB&B £36 dB&B £48-£50 Breakfast only
[10%V]; cc Ac Amex Vi

SAFFRON WALDEN Essex 5D1

(Inn) Cross Keys ᴿᴬ̊C
32 High Street, Saffron Walden CB10 1AX
01799-522207 Fax 01799-526550
5 bedrs, 2 🛏/WC, 1 📻/WC, 1 🛏; TV tcf 🐕 ⤢ P14
sB&B £30 dB&B £39 D £9.50; cc Ac Amex Vi

Wigmores Farm Debden Green, Saffron
Walden CB11 3ST 01371-830050 ♿

3 bedrs, 2 🛏; 🐕 P30
sB&B £18; HB weekly £198;

Location Maps
Hotel locations are shown on the maps at
the back of the guide. All towns and
villages containing a hotel listed in the
guide are shown in black.

SANDY Bedfordshire   4C1

Elms Farm 52 Main Road, Little Gransden,
Sandy SG19 3DL 01767-677459
*A fully-renovated farmhouse offering a
friendly atmosphere. Set in a lovely garden in
a peaceful location overlooking farmland.*
3 bedrs, 1 🐾/WC, 1 ➡; TV tcf P10
sB&B £16 Breakfast only

Highfield Farm Tempsford Road, Sandy
SG19 2AQ 01767-682332 Fax 01767-682332
16 bedrs, 4 ➡/WC, 6 🐾/WC, 1 ➡; 🐕
sB&B £16 Breakfast only

Old Warden Old Warden, Biggleswade,
Sandy SG18 9HQ 01767-627201

SAXMUNDHAM Suffolk   9F4

Sibton White House Halesworth Road,
Sibton, Saxmundham IP17 2JJ 01728-79337

SHERINGHAM Norfolk   9E2

Beacon *Acclaimed*   RAC
1 Nelson Road, Sheringham NR26 8BT
01263-822019
6 bedrs, 3 🐾/WC, 2 ➡; tcf P5
Child restrictions
sB&B £22 dB&B £44; HB weekly £196; cc Ac Vi

Child Restrictions

Most hotels and guest houses are happy
to welcome children. A few prefer to
welcome only adults and older children;
these are shown by 'Child restrictions' in
the entry. If you are travelling with children,
please telephone the establishment to check
the age limit set by the management.

Fairlawns *Highly Acclaimed*   RAC
26 Hooks Hill Road, Sheringham NR26 8NL
01263-824717
*Large Victorian house set in attractive lawned
setting, close to town centre. Turn into Holt
Rd opposite the police station and take second
left into Vicarage Rd. At T junction turn
immediately right into cul-de-sac.*
5 bedrs, 5 ➡/WC; TV tcf P6
Child restrictions
dB&B £39-£42 [5%V]

Melrose   RAC
9 Holeway Road, Sheringham NR26 8HN
01263-823299

STILTON Cambridgeshire   8C3

Bell Inn   RAC
Great North Road, Stilton PE7 3RA
01733-241066 Fax 01733-245173
19 bedrs, 18 ➡/WC, 1 🐾/WC; TV tcf P30
sB&B £30-£54 dB&B £50 D £15.50 [10%V]; cc
Ac Amex DC Vi

SUDBURY Suffolk   9E4

Old Bull & Trivets   RAC
Church Street, Sudbury CO10 6BL
01787-374120
9 bedrs, 3 ➡/WC; 🐕 P16
sB&B £23-£30 dB&B £38-£52 D £10 [10%V];
cc Ac Amex DC Vi

SWAFFHAM Norfolk   9E3

Horse & Groom *Highly Acclaimed*   RAC
40 Lynn Street, Swaffham PE37 7AX
01760-721567   ♿
14 bedrs, 11 ➡/WC, 1 ➡;

THORPENESS Suffolk   9F4

Dolphin   RAC
Peace Place, Thorpeness IP16 4NB
01728-45268 Fax 01728-45424
18 bedrs, 6 ⇥/WC, 5 ⇥; 🐕 🎯
Breakfast only [10%V]

THURROCK Essex   5D2

Granada Lodge   RAC
Thurrock RM16 3BG 01708-891111

TODDINGTON Bedfordshire   4C1

Granada Lodge   RAC
Toddington LU5 6HR 01525-875150

WELLS-NEXT-THE-SEA Norfolk   9E2

Scarborough House *Acclaimed*   RAC
Clubbs Lane, Wells-next-the-Sea NR23 1DP
01328-710309   ♿
14 bedrs, 5 ⇥/WC, 9 🐾/WC; TV tcf 🎯 P14
sB&B £29-£34 dB&B £48-£58 Breakfast only
[10%V]; cc Ac Amex DC Vi

WEST MERSEA Essex   5E2

(Inn) Victory   RAC
92 Coast Road, West Mersea CO5 0LS
01206-382907
3 bedrs, 1 ⇥/WC, 2 🐾/WC; TV tcf P25
sB&B £19.50 dB&B £35.50 D £10; cc Ac
Amex Vi

WITHAM Essex   5E1

★(Inn) Spread Eagle   RAC
Newland Street, Witham CM8 2BD
01376-511097 Fax 01376-521033
10 bedrs, 1 ⇥/WC, 3 ⇥; TV tcf P40
sB&B £15-£25 dB&B £30 Breakfast only
[10%V]; cc Ac Amex Vi

WOODBRIDGE Suffolk   9F4

★★★★Seckford Hall   RAC
Great Bealings, Woodbridge IP13 6NU
01394-385678 Fax 01394-380610
22 bedrs, 22 ⇥/WC; 🎯 P100
sB&B £79 dB&B £99; cc Ac Amex DC Vi

YARMOUTH, GREAT Norfolk   9F3

Georgian House *Highly Acclaimed*   RAC
17 North Drive, Great Yarmouth, NR30 4EW
01493-842623
19 bedrs, 11 ⇥/WC, 6 🐾/WC, 2 ⇥; TV tcf
P19
Child restrictions
dB&B £30-£50 Breakfast only

Midland *Acclaimed*   RAC
7/9 Wellesley Road, Great Yarmouth, NR30
2AP 01493-330046
35 bedrs, 4 ⇥/WC, 22 🐾/WC, 3 ⇥; TV tcf 🎯
⅟ P25
sB&B £30 dB&B £40; HB weekly £150; D
£7.50; cc Ac Vi

Trotwood *Highly Acclaimed*   RAC
2 North Drive, Great Yarmouth, NR30 1ED
01493-843971
9 bedrs, 8 🐾/WC, 1 ⇥; TV tcf 🎯 ⅟ P11
sB&B £26 dB&B £40-£54 Breakfast only

★★Two Bears   RAC
South Town Road, Great Yarmouth, NR31
0HV 01493-603198 Fax 01493-330156
11 bedrs, 11 ⇥/WC; P50

New Telephone Numbers
All UK telephone codes are being
changed. The number 1 is being inserted
after the first 0. For example, 081 is
changing to 0181. The new codes were
available in August 1994 and the two
codes will run in parallel until 16 April
1995, when the new code will take over.
The new codes are given throughout the
guide, as they will be in use in November
when the guide is published The old codes
can be used up to 16 April 1995.
Five cities will have a complete change of
code and an additional digit to the number.

	old	new
Bristol	0272-xxxxx	0117-9xxxxxx
Leeds	0532-xxxxx	0113-2xxxxxx
Leicester	0533-xxxxx	0116-2xxxxxx
Nottingham	0602-xxxxx	0115-9xxxxxx
Sheffield	0742-xxxxx	0114-2xxxxxx

Midlands

Warwicks • W. Midlands • Staffs • Derbys • Northants • Leics • Notts • Lincs

Few areas hold so much of the past. Our industrial heritage is well represented in lively reconstruction. Some of today's industries produce beautiful end products like Staffordshire china and Nottingham lace. By contrast, the beauty of the peaks and dales of Derbyshire are wild and solitary. Linconshire's coastal resorts offer wide sandy beaches and the best of traditional seaside entertainment, while Warwickshire is home to Shakespeare and the world famous theatre company at Stratford-upon-Avon.

A SELECTION OF ATTRACTIONS:

Unless otherwise stated, all can be visited between April and October – some longer. Telephone for days/times of opening.

Alton Towers, Staffs: *Winner of best theme park award, 1993. It's got the lot. Pay once only.* Tel: 01538-702200

American Adventure, Ilkeston, Derby: *200 acres, over 100 rides, shows, attractions. Scream for more!* Tel: 01773-531521.

Ayscoughfee Hall, Spalding, Lincs: *Displays in 15th-s merchant's house on bulb industry. Bird collection.* Tel: 01775-725468.

Belton House, nr. Grantham, Lincs: *Superbly appointed 17th-c house. Gardens, park, adventure playground. NT.* Tel: 01476-66116.

Belgrave Hall, Leics: *Small Q. Anne house. Period rooms. Agricultural bygones, botanic gardens.* Tel: 01533-666590.

Bass Museum & Shire Horse Stables, Burton upon Trent, Staffs: *Museum of brewing industry. Brewery visit. Book a Shire horse drawn tour of town.* Tel: 01283-542031.

Belvoir Castle, nr. Grantham, Lincs: *Fabulous view over Vale of Belvoir. Fabulous interior. Events. Closes Sept.* Tel: 01476-870262.

Blue John Caves & Mine, Casleton, Derbys: *Source of rare Blue John stone. Tour water-worn caverns.* Tel: 01433-620638/620642.

Brandy Wharf Cider Centre, Waddingham, Lincs: *200 years of cider making history with choice of 60.* Tel: 01652-678364.

Bromham Mill, Beds: *Restored water mill in working order. Art gallery, craft sales, picnic site.* Tel: 01234-228330.

Burghley House, Stamford, Lincs: *England's finest Elizabethan house. State Rooms, paintings, porcelain.* Tel: 01780-52451.

Burghley House

Cadbury World, Selly Oak, W. Mid: *Book for Visitor Centre. Light-hearted chocolate demos. Tastings!* Tel:0121-451 4159.

Chatsworth, Bakewell, Derbys: *One of the grandest homes in England. Adventure playgrond, farmyard.* Tel: 01246-582204.

Doddington Hall, Lincs: *Delightful E shaped Tudor family home. Gatehouse, walled rose garden. May-Sept.* Tel: 01522-694308.

Drayton Manor Park & Zoo, nr. Tamworth, Staffs: *Family theme park with stand-up roller coaster!* Tel: 01827-287979.

Eyam Hall, nr. Sheffield: *17th-c manor family home. Clocks, costumes, toys, lovely old kitchen.* Tel: 01433-631976.

Haddon Hall, Bakewell, Derbys: *Medieval manor in heart of Peak District. Closes end Sept.* Tel: 01629-812855.

Heights of Abraham, Matlock Bath, Derbys: *Cable car across Derwent Valley to Alpine Centre, caves, dinosaurs.* Tel: 01629-582365.

Heritage Motor Centre, Gaydon, Warks: *More than museum. Land Rover circuit rides, racing prototypes.* Tel: 01926-641188.

Keddleston Hall, Derbys: *Outstanding Robert Adam House, marble hall, state rooms. NT.* Tel: 01332-842191.

The Lace Centre, Nottingham: *In 15th-c building, shows all types of Nottingham lace. Demonstrations.* Tel: 01602-413539.

D.H. Lawrence Birthplace Museum, Eastwood, Notts: *Insight into author's childhood.* Tel: 01773-763312.

Lincoln Castle, Lincs: *Parapet walks and Victorian prison chapel in Wm the Conqueror's castle.* Tel: 01522-511068.

Mablethorpe's Animal Gardens, Lincs: *Wildlife sanctuary in gardens and dunes. Seal hospital.* Tel: 01507-473346.

Museum of Costume & Textiles, Nottingham: *Collection of 17th-c costume, embroideries, hand-made lace.* Tel: 01602-483504.

National Tramway Museum, Crich, Derbys: *Working museum dedicated to restoring vintage trams.* Tel: 01773-852565.

Nene Valley Railway, Stibbington, Northants: *7½ mile track. Over 28 steam and diesel locos.* Tel: 01780-782854/782921.

Newstead Abbey, Notts: *Period rooms, lovely gardens, Adv. playground at Byron's ancestral home.* Tel: 01623-793557.

Ragley Hall, Alcester, Warks: *Ancestral home, built 1680. Superb interior plus gardens, maze. Closes early Oct.* Tel: 01789-762090.

Snibston Discovery Park, Coalville, Liecs: *Walk through a tornado, cycle with a skeleton, plus.* Tel: 01530-510851/813608.

The Snowdome, Tamworth, Staffs: *Recreational skiing at indoor snow slope or lessons all levels.* Tel: 01827-67905.

Springfields Show Gardens, Spalding, Lincs: *Massed bulbs, flower displays, events. Closes Sept.* Tel: 01775-724843.

Stamford Steam Brewery Museum, Lincs: *Complete Victorian Steam Brewery in timber-frame medieval building.* Tel: 01780-52186.

Tales of Robin Hood, Marian Way, Nottingham: *Audio visual show. Archery range, medieval market.* Tel: 01602-414414/483284.

Robin Hood Statue, Nottingham Castle

Twycross Zoo, Atherstone, Warks: *Pets Corner, Adventure Playground, donkey rides plus zoo.* Tel: 01827-880250.

Woolsthorpe Manor, nr. Grantham, Lincs: *17th-c farm & birthplace of Isaac Newton. NT.* Tel: 01476-860338.

SOME ANNUAL EVENTS
* = *provisional date.*

Alford Oyez '95, Lincs: *Town Crier Championship. Morris Men, Silver Band, open museum, pottery.* Tel: 01507-466063.

Brackenfield Well Dressings, Derbys: *Five wells decorated. Side shows, competitions, arts/crafts. 27-30 May.* Tel: 01629-534767.

British Grand Prix '95, Silverstone: *FIA Formula 1. 7-9 Jul*.* Tel: 01327-857271.

British Int'l Antiques Fair, Birmingham, W. Mid: *Major exhibition in 12th year. 25-30 Apl.* Tel: 0121-780 4141 x 2760.

Burghley Horse Trials, Stamford, Lincs: *Clothes, furnishings & crafts round famous event. 31 Aug-3 Sept.* Tel: 01780-52131.

Casleton Ancient Garland Ceremony, Derbys: *Pagan fertility procession. Don't miss this one! 29 May.* Tel: 01433-620560.

Civil War Commemoration – *Battle of Naseby, Sieges of Leicester. Various venues. 1 May – 1 July.* Tel: 01533-657313.

Crufts Dog Show, Nat. Exhibition Centre, Birmingham, W. Mid: *16-19 Mar.* Tel: 0121-780 4141.

Dronfield Festival of Flowers & Well Dressing, Derbys: *Costume town market, floats, drama, opera. 22-30 Jun.* Tel: 01246-412367.

International Cricket, Trent Bridge, Notts: *Eng. v W. Indes Test. 10-14 Aug.* Tel: 01602-821525.

Lamport Hall Craft Festival, Northants: *High quality crafts and garden show. Childrens' fun fair. 7 – 8 May.* Tel: 01664-840363.

Lichfield Festival, Staffs: *Various venues. Recitals, chamber, orchestral music. 7-16 Jul.* Tel: 01543-257298.

Nottingham Goose Fair: *700th anniversary year of traditional fair with modern amusements too. 5 -7 Oct.* Tel: 01602-417324.

Rushden Festival, Northants: *Widely varied imaginative entertainments. 17Jun – 3Jul.* Tel: 01832-742000.

Shots in the Dark, Nottingham: *International Mystery & Thriller Festival. 30Sept – 9 Oct*.* Tel: 01602-526600.

Spalding Flower Parade & Festival, Springfields Show Gardens: *20 flower floats, marching bands, entertainment. 6 – 8 May.* Tel: 01775-724843.

Stratford on Avon Festival, Warks: *Various venues. Music, theatre, art & dance. 8-22 Jul.* Tel:01789-267969.

Tallington Beer Festival, Lincs: *Real ale and live music. Keep Dad happy!. 17 – 21- May.* Tel: 01780-480560.

World Figure Skating Championships, Nat. Exhibition Centre, Birmingham, W. Mid: *7 – 12Mar.* Tel: 0121-767 4848.

ABTHORPE Nottinghamshire   8B4

Stone Cottage   RAC
Main Street, Abthorpe NN12 8QN
01327-857544
3 bedrs, 2 ➥; ✗ ⅌ P4
sB&B £17.50 dB&B £30 Breakfast only

ALFRETON Derbyshire   8B2

Oaktree Farm Matlock Road, Oakerthorpe,
Alfreton DE55 7NA 01773-832957

ASHBOURNE Derbyshire   8A2

Hurtswood Sandybrook, Ashbourne DE6
2AQ 01335-342031

St Leonards Cottage Thorpe Cloud,
Ashbourne DE6 2AW 01335-29224

ASHOVER Derbyshire   7F1

Old School Farm   RAC
Uppertown, Ashover S45 0JF 01246-590813
4 bedrs, 2 ☞/WC, 1 ➥; TV P10
Breakfast only

ATHERSTONE Warwickshire   8A3

★★(Inn) Old Red Lion   RAC
Long Street, Atherstone CV9 1BB
01827-713156 Fax 01827-711404
22 bedrs, 22 ➥/WC; ✗ P22
cc Ac Amex DC Vi

BAKEWELL Derbyshire   8A2

Sheldon House Chapel Street, Monyash,
Bakewell DE45 1JJ 01629-813067

3 bedrs, 3 ☞/WC; TV tcf P4
Child restrictions under 7
sB&B £17.50 Breakfast only

BELPER Derbyshire   8B2

Dannah Farm *Highly Acclaimed*   RAC
Bowmans Lane, Shottle, Belper DE5 2DR
0177-389273 Fax 0177-389590
7 bedrs, 6 ➥/WC, 1 ➥; P30
cc Ac Vi

Shottle Hall   RAC
Shot · Belper DE5 2EB 01773-550203   ♿
8 bedrs, 2 ➥/WC, 2 ☞/WC, 2 ➥; TV tcf P30
sB&B £23-£27 dB&B £42-£50 D £12

Ye Olde Bear Inn Alderwasley, Belper DE4
4GD 01629-822585

BIRMINGHAM West Midlands   8A3

Alexander *Acclaimed*   RAC
44 Bunbury Road, Northfield, Birmingham
B31 2DW 0121-475-4341
cc Ac Vi

Beech House *Acclaimed*   RAC
21 Gravelly Hill North, Erdington,
Birmingham B23 6BT 0121-373-0620
9 bedrs, 2 ➥/WC, 2 ☞/WC, 1 ➥; TV tcf ✗ ⅌
P10
Child restrictions
sB&B £26 dB&B £40; cc Ac Vi

Bridge House *Highly Acclaimed* RAC
49 Sherbourne Road, Acocks Green,
Birmingham B27 6DX 0121-706-5900

Bristol Court RAC
250 Bristol Road, Edgbaston, Birmingham B5
7SL 0121-4720-078

Chamberlain *Highly Acclaimed* RAC
Alcester Road, Birmingham B12 0TJ
0121-6270627 Fax 0121-6270628
250 bedrs, 20 ⇥/WC, 230 ⬧/WC; TV tcf ✗
P200
sB&B £35 dB&B £35 D £7.50 [10%V]; cc Ac
Amex DC Vi

Fairview B & B RAC
1639 Coventry Road, South Yardley,
Birmingham B26 1DD 0121-708-2712

Granada Lodge RAC
Illey Lane, Frankley, Birmingham B32 4AR
0121-550-3131

Greswolde Park *Acclaimed* RAC
980 Warwick Road, Acocks Green,
Birmingham B27 6QG 0121-7064068 Fax
0121-7064068

Heath Lodge *Acclaimed* RAC
117 Coleshill Road, Marston Green,
Birmingham B37 7HT 0121-779-2218 Fax
0121-779-5673

Highfield House RAC
Holly Road, Rowley Regis, Birmingham B65
0BH 0121-5591066

Homestead 215 Barrows Lane, Sheldon,
Birmingham B26 1QS 0121-6284103 Fax
0121-6284103
6 bedrs, 1 ⬧/WC, 2 ⇥; TV tcf ✗ P6
sB&B £18 Breakfast only

Hurstwood RAC
775 Chester Road, Erdington, Birmingham
B24 0BY 0121-3828212

Lyndhurst *Acclaimed* RAC
135 Kingsbury Road, Erdington, Birmingham
B24 8QT 0121-3735695 Fax 0121-3735695
14 bedrs, 1 ⇥/WC, 12 ⬧/WC, 1 ⇥; TV tcf ✗ P15
sB&B £36.50-£39.50 dB&B £39.50-£49.50; HB
weekly £275-£285; D £11.50 [10%V]; cc Ac
Amex DC Vi

Remwick House RAC
13 Bournbrook Road, Selly Oak, Birmingham
B29 7BL 0121-4724640

Rollason Wood RAC
Wood End Road, Erdington, Birmingham B24
8BJ 0121-373-1230 Fax 0121-382-2578
35 bedrs, 1 ⇥/WC, 10 ⬧/WC, 6 ⇥;
TV tcf ✗ P40
sB&B £20-£34.50 dB&B £28.50-£49.50 D £7.50
[10%V]; cc Ac Amex DC Vi

Tri-Star *Acclaimed* RAC
Coventry Road, Elmdon, Birmingham B26
3QR 0121-7821010

Wentworth *Acclaimed* RAC
103 Wentworth Road, Harborne, Birmingham
B17 9SU 0121-4272839

Willow Tree RAC
759 Chester Road, Erdington, Birmingham
B24 0BY 0121-373-6388

Woodlands Farm Lilley Green Lane,
Alvechurch, Birmingham B48 7EX
01564-823130

BOSTON Lincolnshire 9D2
Admiral Nelson RAC
Bennington, Boston PE22 0BT 01205-760460

Castle Inn RAC
Haltoft End, Freiston, Boston PE22 0MY
01205-760393

BRERETON Staffordshire 7F2
★★**Cedar Tree** RAC
Main Road, Rugeley, Brereton WS15 1DY
01889-584241
28 bedrs, 21 ⇥/WC, 4 ⇥; P80
sB&B £23-£29 dB&B £40-£50 D £10.50; cc Ac
Amex DC Vi

BURTON-UPON-TRENT Staffordshire 7F2
Delter *Acclaimed* RAC
5 Derby Road, Burton-upon-Trent DE14 1RU
01283-535115
5 bedrs, 1 ⇥/WC, 4 ⬧/WC; TV tcf P8
sB&B £27 dB&B £38 Breakfast only [10%V];
cc Ac Vi

Edgecote 179 Ashby Road, Burton-upon-Trent DE15 0LB 01283-568966

A family-run, Victorian hotel with a friendly atmosphere, 5 minutes from the town centre.
12 bedrs, 3 🚿/WC, 2 🛁; TV tcf 🐕 P8
sB&B £17 D £6.50-£12; cc Ac Amex Vi

Westlake 204 Ashby Road, Burton-upon-Trent DE15 0LB 01283-46717

BUXTON Derbyshire 8A1

Brookfield On Longhill *Highly Acclaimed* RAC
Brookfield Hall, Longhill, Buxton SK17 6SU 01298-24151

Hawthorn Farm RAC
Fairfield Road, Buxton SK17 7ED 01298-23230
6 bedrs, 1 🚿/WC, 1 🛁; tcf 🐕 P12
sB&B £19-£20 dB&B £38-£44 Breakfast only [10%V]

Lakenham 11 Burlington Road, Buxton SK17 9AL 01298-79209 ♿

Victorian elegance in Derbyshire's most famous Spa town, offering all modern facilities yet successfully retaining its Victorian character. Tastefully furnished with period furniture and antiquities. Cleanliness and comfort assured by resident owners.
6 bedrs, 1 🛁/WC, 5 🚿/WC; TV tcf 🐕 P9
sB&B £17.50; HB weekly £176.75-£376.50; D £9-£12; cc Ac Vi

Mossley House Farm Maynestone Road, Chinley, Buxton SK12 6AH 01663-750240
2 bedrs, 1 🛁; TV tcf P5
sB&B £14 Breakfast only

Netherdale *Highly Acclaimed* RAC
16 Green Lane, Buxton SK17 9DP 01298-23896
10 bedrs, 1 🛁/WC, 7 🚿/WC, 1 🛁; TV tcf 🚭 P13
sB&B £20 dB&B £40; HB weekly £207; D £11 [10%V]

Old Hall *Acclaimed* RAC
The Square, Buxton SK17 6BD 01298-22841 Fax 01298-72437

Roseleigh RAC
19 Broad Walk, Buxton SK17 6JR 01298-24904
13 bedrs, 2 🛁/WC, 7 🚿/WC, 3 🛁; TV tcf 🐕 P12
sB&B £20 dB&B £40-£42; HB weekly £185;; cc Ac Vi

Sandringham Broad Walk, Buxton SK17 6JT 01298-72257
34 bedrs, 15 🛁/WC, 3 🛁; 🐕 P7
cc Ac Vi

September Cottage Biggin-by-Hartington, Buxton SK17 0DH 01298-84764

Staden Grange *Highly Acclaimed* RAC
Staden, Buxton SK17 9RZ 01298-24965
14 bedrs, 14 🛁/WC
cc Vi

Thorn Heyes *Highly Acclaimed* RAC
137 London Road, Buxton SK17 9NW 01298-23539

Westminster *Highly Acclaimed* RAC
21 Broad Walk, Buxton SK17 6JR 01298-23929

CASTLE DONINGTON Leicestershire 8B2

★★★Donington Manor RAC
Castle Donington DE7 2PP 01332-810253 Fax 01332-850330

Park Farmhouse *Acclaimed* RAC
Melbourne Road, Isley Walton, Castle Donington DE7 2RN 01332-862409 Fax

01332-862364 ♿
9 bedrs, 5 🛁/WC, 4 🚿/WC; TV tcf 🐕 P15
sB&B £36-£39.50 dB&B £50-£62 D £15
[10%V]; cc Ac Amex DC Vi JCB

The Four Poster RAC
73 Clapgun Street, Castle Donington DE7 2LF
01332-810335

CHAPEL-EN-LE-FRITH Derbyshire 8A1

(Inn) Squirrels RAC
1 Green Lane, Chinley, Chapel-en-le-Frith
SK12 6AA 01663-751200
6 bedrs, 6 🛁/WC; TV tcf 🐕 🚭 P20
sB&B £28 dB&B £35 D £12.50; cc Ac Vi

CHEADLE Staffordshire 7E2

Royal Oak RAC
69 High Street, Cheadle ST10 1AN
01538-753116
10 bedrs, 10 🛁/WC, 1 🛁; 🐕 P50
Breakfast only

The Manor Guest House & Restaurant Watt Place, Cheadle ST10 1NZ 01538-753450
9 bedrs;
Breakfast only

CHESTERFIELD Derbyshire 8B1

★★Abbeydale RAC
Cross Street, Chesterfield S40 4TD
01246-277849 Fax 01246-558223

The cream coloured walls enhance this corner sited Victorian building. Access is from Cross Street which is a one way road.
11 bedrs, 9 🚿/WC, 1 🛁; TV tcf P15
sB&B £16-£37 dB&B £45; HB weekly £250; D £12 [10%V]; cc Ac Amex DC Vi JCB

COALVILLE Leicestershire 8B3

★★★Hermitage Park RAC
Whitwick Road, Coalville LE67 3FA
01530-814814 Fax 01530-814202 ♿
25 bedrs, 25 🛁/WC; TV tcf P40
sB&B £59.50 D £9.95 [10%V]; cc Ac Amex Vi

CODSALL West Midlands 8A3

Moors Farm *Acclaimed* RAC
Chillington Lane, Codsall WV8 1QF
01902-842330 Fax 01902-842330
6 bedrs, 3 🚿/WC, 2 🛁; TV tcf 🚭 P20
Child restrictions
sB&B £24-£29 dB&B £40-£48 D £10.50

COVENTRY West Midlands 8B3

Croft House RAC
23 Stoke Green, Coventry CV3 1FP
01203-457846
12 bedrs, 4 🛁/WC, 2 🛁; 🐕 P15
Breakfast only

Falcon RAC
13-19, Manor Road, Coventry CV1 2LH
01203-258615 Fax 01203-520680 ♿
33 bedrs, 33 🛁/WC; P30
sB&B £28.50-£35 dB&B £35-£40 Breakfast only [10%V]; cc Ac Amex DC Vi

Fir Trees 11 Eastern Green Road, Coventry CV5 7LG 01203-465746

Forte Posthouse RAC
Rye Hill, Allesley, Coventry CV5 9PH
01203-402151 Fax 01203-402235
184 bedrs, 184 🛁/WC; 🐕 P200
sB&B £60.45 dB&B £67.40; cc Ac Amex DC Vi

Hearsall Lodge RAC
1 Broad Lane, Coventry CV5 7AA
01203-674543
18 bedrs, 1 🛁/WC, 4 🛁; P19
Breakfast only

DARLASTON West Midlands 8A3

Hotel Petite Stafford Rd, Darlaston WS10 8UA 0121-526-5482 Fax 0121-526-2921

DERBY Derbyshire 8B2

European Inn RAC
Midland Road, Derby DE1 2SL 01332-292000
Fax 01332-293940 ♿

88 bedrs, 88 ➡/WC; TV tcf ✗ ✗ P80
Breakfast only; cc Ac Amex DC Vi

★★★International RAC
Burton Rd, Derby DE3 6AD 01332-369321
Fax 01332-29443

**Ivy House Farm Stanton-by -Bridge,
Derby DE73 1HT 01332-863152**
*18th century farmhouse on a working farm
in a quiet picturesque village overlooking the
Trent Valley.*
5 bedrs, 1 ➡/WC, 2 ➡; TV tcf ✗ P10
sB&B £15 Breakfast only

Mickleover Court RAC
Etwall Road, Derby, Derby DE3 5XX
01332-521234
80 bedrs, 80 ➡/WC;
Awaiting Inspection

Rangemoor Park *Acclaimed* RAC
67 Macklin Street, Derby DE1 1LF
01332-47252
20 bedrs, 6 ➡; P18
Breakfast only

Rollz RAC
684-688 Osmaston Road, Derby DE2 8GT
01332-41026
14 bedrs, 3 ➡; P3
Child restrictions
Breakfast only

DORSINGTON Warwickshire 7F3

Church Farm Dorsington CV37 8AX
01789-720471

ECCLESHALL Staffordshire 7E2

Round House *Acclaimed* RAC
Butters Bank, Croxton, Eccleshall ST21 6NN
0163-082631
3 bedrs, 3 ➡/WC; ✗ P4
Child restrictions
Breakfast only [10%V]

ETWALL Derbyshire 8A2

Blenheim House *Acclaimed* RAC
56 Main Street, Etwall DE6 6LP 01283-732254
11 bedrs, 10 ➡/WC; ✗
Breakfast only

GLOSSOP Derbyshire 10C4

George RAC
34 Norfolk Street, Glossop SK13 9QU
01457-855449 Fax 01457-857033 ♿
9 bedrs, 6 ➡/WC, 1 ➡;
sB&B £25 dB&B £40 D £11 [5%V]; cc Ac
Amex DC Vi

(Inn) Snake Pass Inn RAC
nr Ashopton Woodlands, Glossop S30 2BJ
01433-651480 Fax 01433-651480
7 bedrs, 1 ➡/WC, 6 ➡/WC; TV tcf ✗ ✗ P38
sB&B £25 dB&B £45 D £11 [10%V]; cc Ac
Amex Vi

Wind in the Willows *Highly Acclaimed* RAC
Derbyshire Level, Off Sheffield Road (A57),
Glossop SK13 9PT 01457-868001 Fax
01457-853354
8 bedrs, 8 ➡/WC; P20
Child restrictions
sB&B £55-£75 dB&B £66-£95; cc Ac Amex Vi

GRANTHAM Lincolnshire 8C2

Garden RAC
86 Barrowby Road, Grantham NG31 9AF
01476-62040
11 bedrs, 7 ➡/WC, 2 ➡;
sB&B £23-£32 dB&B £36-£42 Breakfast only

Grantham RAC
Colsterworth, Grantham NG35 5JR
01476-861077

Hawthornes RAC
51 Cambridge Street, Grantham NG31 6EZ
01476-73644
3 bedrs, 1 ➡; ✗
Breakfast only [5%V]

Sycamore Farm *Acclaimed* RAC
Bassingthorpe, Grantham NG33 4ED
01476-585274
3 bedrs, 2 ➡/WC, 1 ➡; ✗ P6
Child restrictions
Breakfast only

The Lanchester *Acclaimed* RAC
84 Harrowby Road, Grantham NG31 9DS
01476-74169
3 bedrs, 1 ➡/WC, 1 ➡; TV tcf ✗ P3
sB&B £15 dB&B £30 Breakfast only [10%V]

HAMPTON IN ARDEN West Midlands 7F3

The Cottage RAC
Kenilworth Road, Balsall Common, Hampton
In Arden B92 0LW 01675-442323 Fax
01675-443323
10 bedrs, 5 ⁿ/WC, 2 ➡; TV tcf ✗ ✗ P15
sB&B £20-£25 dB&B £34-£39 Breakfast only
[5%V]

The Hollies RAC
Kenilworth Road, Balsall Common, Hampton
In Arden B92 0LW 01675-442941 Fax
01675-442941
8 bedrs, 5 ➡/WC, 6 ⁿ/WC, 1 ➡; TV tcf ✗
P12
sB&B £20 dB&B £38 Breakfast only; cc Ac
Amex DC Vi JCB

HENLEY-IN-ARDEN Warwicks 7F3

Ashleigh House *Highly Acclaimed* RAC
Whitley Hill, Henley-in-Arden B95 5DL
01564-792315 Fax 01564-794133
10 bedrs, 10 ➡/WC;
Child restrictions
Breakfast only; cc Ac Vi

Irelands Farm RAC
Irelands Lane, Henley-in-Arden B95 5SA
01564-792476
3 bedrs, 3 ➡/WC; ✗ ✗ P6
Child restrictions
Breakfast only

Lapworth Lodge *Highly Acclaimed* RAC
Bushwood Lane, Lapworth, Henley-in-Arden
B94 5PJ 01564-783038 Fax 01564-783635
7 bedrs, 7 ⁿ/WC; TV tcf ✗ P16
sB&B £35 dB&B £45 Breakfast only; cc Ac Vi

HIMLEY Staffordshire 7E3

★★★Himley Country Club RAC
School Road, Himley DY3 4LG 01902-896716
Fax 01902-896668
76 bedrs, 76 ➡/WC;
sB&B £55 dB&B £70

HINCKLEY Leicestershire 8B3

Ambion Court *Highly Acclaimed* RAC
The Green, Dadlington, Hinckley CV13 6JB
01455-212292 Fax 01455-213141
7 bedrs, 1 ➡/WC, 6 ⁿ/WC; TV tcf ✗ P8
sB&B £40-£45 dB&B £45-£50 Breakfast only
[10%V]; cc Ac Vi

Kings *Highly Acclaimed* RAC
13-19 Mount Road, Hinckley LE10 1AD
01455-637193 Fax 01455-636201
7 bedrs, 7 ➡/WC; P16
sB&B £35-£49.50 dB&B £50-£55; HB weekly
£350-£450; D £12.90 [10%V]; cc Ac Amex DC Vi

HUSBANDS BOSWORTH Leicestershire 8B3

★★★Fernie Lodge RAC
Berridges Lane, nr Lutterworth, Husbands
Bosworth LE17 6LE 01858-432315 Fax
01858-880014

KEGWORTH Leicestershire (Derbyshire) 8B2

Kegworth RAC
Packington Hill, Kegworth DE7 2DF
01509-672427 Fax 01509-674664 &
52 bedrs, 52 ➡/WC; TV tcf ✗ ✗ P200
sB&B £30-£46.95 dB&B £43.90 D £9.45
[10%V]; cc Ac Amex Vi

KETTERING Northamptonshire 8C3

Headlands RAC
49-51 Headlands, Kettering NN15 7ET
01536-524624 Fax 01536-83367
13 bedrs, 5 ➡/WC, 3 ➡; ✗ ✗
Breakfast only [10%V]; cc Ac Vi

★★★★Kettering Park RAC
Kettering Parkway, Kettering NN15 6XT
01536-416666 Fax 01536-416171 &
88 bedrs, 88 ➡/WC; TV tcf ✗ ✗ P250
sB&B £90 dB&B £98 D £20 [10%V]; cc Ac
Amex DC Vi

LEAMINGTON SPA Warwickshire 8B4

Charnwood House RAC
47 Avenue Road, Leamington Spa CV31 3PF
01926-831074
6 bedrs, 1 ➡/WC, 1 ⁿ/WC, 2 ➡; TV tcf ✗ P5
Breakfast only; cc Ac Vi

**Courtyard Olympus Avenue, Tachbrook
Park, Leamington Spa CV34 6RJ
01926-425522 Fax 01926-881322** &
94 bedrs, 94 ➡/WC; ✗ P100
[10%V]; cc Ac Amex DC Vi

Eaton Court 1-7 St Marks Road, Leamington
Spa CV32 6DL 01926-885848

Hedley Villa 31 Russel Terrace, Leamington
Spa CV31 1EZ 01926-424504

Milverton House   RAC
1 Milverton Terrace, Leamington Spa CV32
5BE 01926-428335 Fax 01926-428335
10 bedrs, 3 ➹/WC, 4 🛁/WC, 2 ➹; TV tcf 🗶 P5
sB&B £17-£26 dB&B £32-£66; HB weekly
£168-£220; D £10; cc Ac Vi

LEEK Staffordshire   7E1

Choir Cottage & Choir House *Highly*
Acclaimed   RAC
Osters Lane, Cheddleton, Leek ST13 7HS
01538-360561

*A 17th century, stone-built cottage, quietly
situated at the edge of the village with fields to
the rear. Individually decorated, cottage style
bedrooms.*
3 bedrs, 3 ➹/WC; P5
Child restrictions
sB&B £35-£39 dB&B £48-£52 Breakfast only

Country Cottage Back Lane Farm, Winkhill,
Leek ST13 7PJ 01538-308273 Fax
01538-308098
4 bedrs, 1 ➹/WC, 3 🛁/WC, 1 ➹;
sB&B £17 D £11-£11.50

The Abbey Inn Abbey Green Road, Leek
ST13 8SA 01538-382865

LEICESTER Leicestershire   8B3

Burlington   RAC
Elmfield Avenue, Leicester LE2 1RB
0116-2705112 Fax 0116-2704207
16 bedrs, 11 ➹/WC, 1 ➹; 🗶 P18
sB&B £34 dB&B £38 D £10 [10%V]; cc Ac
Amex Vi

Scotia 10 Westcotes Dr, Leicester LE3 0QR
0116-2549200

Stoneycroft   RAC
5-7 Elmfield Avenue, Leicester LE2 1RB
0116-2707605 Fax 0116-2706067
44 bedrs, 25 ➹/WC, 5 ➹; 🗶 P20
[10%V]; cc Ac Vi

The Old Tudor Rectory   RAC
Main Street, Glenfield, Leicester LE3 8DG
0116-2320220 Fax 0116-2876002
16 bedrs, 8 ➹/WC, 15 🛁/WC; TV tcf 🗶 P37
sB&B £34-£41 dB&B £42-£52; HB weekly
£105-£245; D £9.50 [10%V]; cc Ac Amex DC
Vi

LICHFIELD Staffordshire   8A3

Coppers End   RAC
Walsall Road, Muckley Corner, Lichfield WS14
0BG 01543-372910   ♿

*Quiet, friendly, guest house in a former 1930s
police station. Set in its own grounds in a
rural setting.*
6 bedrs, 1 🛁/WC, 1 ➹; TV tcf 🗶 ⅙ P10
sB&B £21 dB&B £34-£40 [5%V]; cc Ac Amex
DC Vi

Oakleigh House *Highly Acclaimed*   RAC
25 St Clad's Road, Lichfield WS13 7LZ
01543-262688
10 bedrs, 8 ➹/WC, 1 ➹; 🗶 P20
Breakfast only

Woodmuir 4 Nether Beacon, Lichfield WS13
7AT 01543-251269

LINCOLN Lincolnshire   8C1

Brierley House *Acclaimed*   RAC
54 South Park, Lincoln LN5 8ER 01522-526945
7 bedrs, 2 ➹/WC, 4 🛁/WC, 1 ➹; TV tcf
sB&B £25 dB&B £39.50 Breakfast only [5%V]

Carline *Acclaimed* RAC
3 Carline Road, Lincoln LN1 1HN
01522-530422
9 bedrs, 9 ⇥/WC; TV tcf P10
Child restrictions
sB&B £18 dB&B £38 Breakfast only [5%V]

D'Isney Place *Highly Acclaimed* RAC
Eastgate, Lincoln LN2 4AA 01522-528881 Fax
01522-511321 &
17 bedrs, 17 ⇥/WC; P10
sB&B £49 dB&B £54 Breakfast only; cc Ac
Amex DC Vi

Halfway Farm *Acclaimed* RAC A46
Swinderby, Lincoln LN6 9HN 01522-868749
Fax 01522-868082

Hollies RAC
65 Carholme Road, Lincoln LN1 1RT
01522-522419 Fax 01522-522419 &
10 bedrs, 5 ⇥/WC, 5 ☏/WC, 3 ⇥;
TV tcf ✂ P7
Child restrictions
sB&B £25 dB&B £50 Breakfast only; cc Ac
Amex DC Vi

Minster Lodge *Highly Acclaimed* RAC
3 Church Lane, Lincoln LN2 1QJ
01522-513220 Fax 01522-513220
6 bedrs, 6 ⇥/WC; ✖ P6
sB&B £35-£42 dB&B £48-£55 Breakfast only;
cc Ac Amex DC Vi

★Tennyson RAC
7 South Park Avenue, Lincoln LN5 8EN
01522-521624 Fax 01522-521624
8 bedrs, 2 ⇥/WC, 6 ☏/WC; TV tcf ✂ P8
sB&B £28 dB&B £38-£40 [10%V];
cc Ac Amex DC Vi

LONG EATON Derbyshire 8B2

Sleep Inn RAC
Bostock Lane, Long Eaton NG10 5NL
0115-9460000 Fax 0115-9460726 &
101 bedrs, 4 ⇥/WC, 97 ☏/WC; TV tcf ✖ ✂ P150
sB&B £29.95-£44.45 dB&B £44.85 D £7.95
[10%V]; cc Ac Amex DC Vi

LOUGHBOROUGH Leicestershire 8B3

De Montfort ᴿᴬC
88 Leicester Road, Loughborough LE11 2AQ 01509-216061 Fax 01509-233667

Family-run, comfortable hotel, on the Leicester side of the town centre.
9 bedrs, 1 ➧/WC, 4 ➧/WC, 1 ➧; TV tcf ✗
sB&B £21.50-£25 dB&B £30-£38 [5%V]; cc Ac Amex Vi

Garendon Park *Acclaimed* ᴿᴬC
92 Leicester Road, Loughborough LE11 2AQ
01509-236557 Fax 01509-265559
9 bedrs, 1 ➧/WC, 4 ➧/WC, 2 ➧; TV tcf ✗✗ ✲
sB&B £21.50-£25 dB&B £35-£40 Breakfast only [10%V]; cc Ac Amex Vi

LOUTH Lincolnshire 11F4

Priory *Acclaimed* ᴿᴬC
Eastgate, Louth LN11 9AJ 01507-602930
12 bedrs, 9 ➧/WC, 1 ➧; P20

(Inn) The Boars Head ᴿᴬC
12 New Market, Louth LN11 9HH
01507-603561
4 bedrs, 2 ➧; P6

LUTTERWORTH Leicestershire

★★★(Inn) Greyhound ᴿᴬC
9 Market Street, Lutterworth LE17 4EJ
01455-553307
21 bedrs, 21 ➧/WC;
cc Ac Amex DC Vi

Location Maps

Hotel locations are shown on the maps at the back of the guide. All towns and villages containing an hotel listed in the guide are shown in black.

MARKFIELD Leicestershire 8B3

Granada Lodge ᴿᴬC
Leicester North S/a, A50, Markfield LE6 OPP
01530-244237

MATLOCK Derbyshire 8A2

Henmore Grange Hopton, Wirksworth,
Matlock DE4 4DF 01629-540420 ᴖ
14 bedrs, 12 ➧/WC, 1 ➧; ✗ P50
sB&B £31; HB weekly £217-£385;

Jackson Tor House ᴿᴬC
76 Jackson Road, Matlock DE4 3JQ
01629-582348
26 bedrs, 7 ➧;
Breakfast only

Lane End House Green Lane, Tansley, Matlock DE4 5FJ 01629-583981

Georgian farmhouse in quiet rural location with spectacular views. Beautifully furnished throughout offering excellent food accompanied by good wine selections. Christmas, Winter and 'Bargain' breaks available.
3 bedrs, 3 ➧/WC, 1 ➧; TV tcf ✗ P6
sB&B £29; HB weekly £168-£239; D £13.50-£14.50; cc Ac Vi

Packhorse Farm ᴿᴬC
Tansley, Matlock DE4 5LF 01629-582781
4 bedrs, 2 ➧; P20
Child restrictions
sB&B £17-£18 dB&B £28-£30 Breakfast only

Sheriff Lodge 51 Dimple Road, Matlock DE4 3JX 01629-582973
A family-run hotel in the Peak District with a high standard of cuisine.
12 bedrs, 1 ➧/WC, 9 ➧/WC, 1 ➧; TV tcf ✗ P20
sB&B £18 D £4-£13; cc Ac Vi

MELTON MOWBRAY Leics 8B3

Elms Farm Long Clawson, Melton Mowbray
LE14 4NG 01664-822395 Fax 01664-822395
3 bedrs, 1 📷/WC, 1 🛏;
sB&B £15; HB weekly £130-£175; D £7-£12

NORTHAMPTON Northamptonshire 8B4

Poplars *Acclaimed* RAC
Cross Street, Moulton, Northampton NN3 1RZ
01604-643983 Fax 01604-790223
21 bedrs, 15 📷/WC, 2 🛏; TV tcf P21
sB&B £34 dB&B £38; D £10 [5%V]; cc Ac
Amex Vi

Simpson's RAC
13 Leicester Parade, Barrack Road,
Northampton NN2 6AA 01604-32127 Fax
01604-233012
10 bedrs, 7 🛏/WC, 2 🛏;
Breakfast only; cc Ac Amex DC Vi

NOTTINGHAM Nottinghamshire 8B2

Balmoral *Highly Acclaimed* RAC
55-57 Loughborough Road, West Bridgford,
Nottingham NG2 7LA 0115-9455020 Fax
0115-9455683
31 bedrs, 31 🛏/WC; P35
Breakfast only [5%V]; cc Ac DC Vi

Crantock RAC
480 Mansfield Road, Sherwood, Nottingham
NG5 2EL 0115-9623294 ♿
25 bedrs, 9 🛏/WC, 2 🛏; 🐾
Breakfast only [10%V]; cc Ac Vi

Fairhaven *Acclaimed* RAC
19 Meadow Road, Beeston Rylands,
Nottingham NG9 1JP 0115-9227509
10 bedrs, 4 📷/WC, 3 🛏; TV tcf ✂ P12
sB&B £16.50-£28 dB&B £28-£38 D £6 [10%V]

P & J RAC
277-279 Derby Road, Lenton, Nottingham
NG7 2DP 0115-978399 Fax 0115-9783998
Large, family-run, Victorian hotel. Situated
near the city centre.
20 bedrs, 9 🛏/WC, 4 🛏;
Breakfast only; cc Ac Amex Vi

Royston RAC
326 Mansfield Road, Nottingham NG5 2EF
0115-9622947
14 bedrs, 9 🛏/WC, 2 🛏;
Breakfast only

St Andrews RAC
310 Queens Road, Beeston, Nottingham NG9
1JA 0115-9254902
10 bedrs, 4 📷/WC, 3 🛏; TV tcf ✈ P6
Child restrictions
sB&B £17-£18.50 dB&B £30 D £6.95 [5%V]

NUNEATON Warwickshire 7F3

La Tavola Calda RAC
68 & 70 Midland Road, Nuneaton CV11 5DY
01203-383195 Fax 01203-381816
8 bedrs, 1 🛏/WC, 8 📷/WC; TV tcf P50
sB&B £18 dB&B £32 D £7.50; cc Amex DC Vi

OAKAMOOR Staffordshire 7F1

Ribden Farm *Acclaimed* RAC
Oakamoor ST10 3BW 01538-702830
3 bedrs, 1 🛏/WC, 2 📷/WC; TV tcf ✂ P4
dB&B £32-£36; HB weekly £210

OLLERTON Nottinghamshire 8B2

The Old Rectory RAC
Main Street, Kirton, Ollerton NG22 9LP
01623-860083 Fax 01623-860751
10 bedrs, 5 🛏/WC, 3 🛏; P15
Breakfast only; cc Ac Vi

OUNDLE Northamptonshire 8C3

The Maltings ⚓RAC
Main Street, Aldwincle, Oundle NN14 3EP
3 bedrs, 3 ➡/WC; tcf ⊁ P10
Child restrictions
sB&B £26-£30 dB&B £42 Breakfast only
[5%V]; cc Ac Vi

OXHILL Warwickshire 8A4

Nolands Farm & Country Restaurant
Oxhill CV35 0RJ 01926-640309 Fax
01926-640309 ⚓RAC

REDMILE Leicestershire (Notts) 8C2

Peacock Farm *Acclaimed* ⚓RAC
(In the Vale of Belvoir), Redmile NG13 0GQ
01949-842475 Fax 01949-843127 ♿
10 bedrs, 6 ➡/WC, 2 ➡; ✈ ⊁ P30
sB&B £19.50 dB&B £36; cc Ac Amex Vi

RIPLEY Derbyshire 8B2

Britannia 243 Church St, Waingroves, Ripley
DE5 9TF 01773-43708

RUGBY Warwickshire 8B3

Avondale ⚓RAC
16 Elsee Road, Rugby CV21 3BA
01788-578639
4 bedrs, 1 ✶/WC, 2 ➡; TV tcf P5
sB&B £19 dB&B £38 Breakfast only [10%V]

SHIPSTON-ON-STOUR Warwickshire 7F4

The Halford Bridge Inn Fosseway, Halford,
Shipston-on-Stour CV36 5BN 01789-740382
6 bedrs, 2 ➡;

SKEGNESS Lincolnshire 9D2

Abbey ⚓RAC
North Parade, Skegness PE25 2UB
01754-763677
25 bedrs, 21 ➡/WC, 2 ➡; ✈ P8
Breakfast only [10%V]

Red Lion ⚓RAC
33 High Street, Wainfleet, Skegness PE24 4BN
01754-880301

Royal Oak ⚓RAC
73 High Street, Wainfleet, Skegness PE24 4BZ
01754-880328

South Lodge *Acclaimed* ⚓RAC
147 Drummond Road, Skegness PE25 3BT
01754-765057
7 bedrs, 7 ➡/WC; ✈ P6
[10%V]

Woolpack ⚓RAC
39 High Street, Wainfleet, Skegness PE24 4BJ
01754-880353

SLEAFORD Lincolnshire 8C2

Black Bull Inn ⚓RAC
10 Rectory Road, Ruskington, Sleaford NG34
9AB 01526-832270

SOLIHULL West Midlands 8A3

Cedarwood House *Acclaimed* ⚓RAC
347 Lyndon Road, Sheldon, Solihull B92 7QT
0121-7435844
5 bedrs, 5 ➡/WC; P5
Child restrictions
sB&B £20-£30 dB&B £35 Breakfast only [5%V]

Flemings 141 Warwick Road, Olton, Solihull
B92 7HW 0121-7060371 Fax 0121-7064494
78 bedrs, 78 ➡/WC; ✈ P80
sB&B £24.50-£45 dB&B £40; cc Ac Amex DC
Vi

Richmond House ⚓RAC
47 Richmond Road, Olton, Solihull B92 7RP
0121-707-9746 Fax 0121-707-9746
16 bedrs, 16 ➡/WC; P50
Breakfast only [10%V]; cc Ac Amex Vi

STAFFORD Staffordshire 8A2

Leonards Croft ⚓RAC
80 Lichfield Road, Stafford ST17 4LP

01785-22367   &
12 bedrs, 4 ⇥; ⋕ P12
Breakfast only

STAMFORD Lincolnshire   8C3

Candlesticks   RAC
1 Church Lane, Stamford PE9 2JU
01780-64033 Fax 01780-56071
8 bedrs, 8 ⇥/WC; tcf ⋕ P6
sB&B £27.50 dB&B £40 [5%V]; cc Ac Vi

STOKE-ON-TRENT Staffordshire   7E1

Central Park   RAC
Wellesley Street, Shelton, Sroke-on-Trent ST1
4NW 01872-272380
Awaiting inspection

Hanchurch Manor Country House *Highly Acclaimed*   RAC
Hanchurch, Stoke-on-Trent ST4 8SD
01782-643030 Fax 01782-643035   &
40 bedrs, 4 ⇥/WC; TV tcf ⋌
Child restrictions
sB&B £65 dB&B £75 [10%V]; cc Ac Amex Vi

Tollgate   RAC
Ripon Road, Blurton, Stoke-on-Trent ST3 3BS
01782-313029 Fax 01782-593959

STOURBRIDGE West Midlands   7E3

Limes   RAC
260 Hagley Road, Pedmore, Stourbridge DY9
0RW 01562-882689
10 bedrs, 3 ⇥/WC, 3 ⌑/WC, 3 ⇥; TV tcf ⋕
⋌ P10
sB&B £25 dB&B £30 [10%V]; cc Ac Amex DC Vi

STRATFORD-UPON-AVON Warwickshire 4A1

Allors   RAC
62, Evesham Road, Stratford-upon-Avon CV37
9BA 01789-26998
2 bedrs, 2 ⇥/WC; P4
Child restrictions
Breakfast only

Ambleside *Acclaimed*   RAC
41 Grove Road, Stratford-upon-Avon CV37
6PB 01789-297239 Fax 01789-295670
6 bedrs, 3 ⇥/WC, 1 ⇥; P20
Breakfast only; cc Ac Vi

Avon View *Highly Acclaimed*   RAC
121 Shipston Road, Stratford-upon-Avon CV37
9LQ 01789-297542

Chadwyns   RAC
6 Broad Walk, Stratford-upon-Avon CV37 6HS
01789-269077

Compton House 22 Shipston Road, Stratford-upon-Avon CV37 7LP 01789-205646

Small family run guest house extending a warm homely welcome to all our guests.
5 bedrs, 1 ⇥; TV tcf P6
sB&B £14 Breakfast only

Cymbeline House   RAC
24 Evesham Place, Stratford-upon-Avon CV37
6HT 01789-292958
5 bedrs, 3 ⇥/WC, 1 ⇥; ⋕ P2
Breakfast only

Dylan   RAC
10 Evesham Place, Stratford-upon-Avon CV37
6HT 01789-204819
5 bedrs, 5 ⇥/WC; ⋕ P3
Child restrictions
sB&B £18-£22 dB&B £34-£40 Breakfast only

Child Restrictions

Most hotels and guest houses are happy to welcome children. A few prefer to welcome only adults and older children; these are shown by 'Child restrictions' in the entry. If you are travelling with children, please telephone the establishment to check the age limit set by the management.

Hardwick House *Acclaimed* RAC
1 Avenue Road, Stratford-upon-Avon CV37 6UY 01789-204307 Fax 01789-296760

A large Victorian house set in a quiet, mature, tree-lined avenue a few minutes walk from the town centre.

Marlyn RAC
3 Chestnut Walk, Stratford-upon-Avon CV37 6HG 01789-293752
8 bedrs, 2 🛏;
sB&B £18 dB&B £34 Breakfast only

Melita *Highly Acclaimed* RAC
37 Shipston Road, Stratford-upon-Avon CV37 7LN 01789-292432 Fax 01789-204867
12 bedrs, 6 🛏/WC, 6 🛁/WC; TV tcf 🐾 ✂ P12
sB&B £29-£39 dB&B £45-£57 Breakfast only [5%V]; cc Ac Amex Vi

Midway 182 Evesham Road, Stratford-upon-Avon CV37 9BS 01789-204154

Minola RAC
25 Evesham Place, Stratford-upon-Avon CV37 6HT 01789-293573
5 bedrs, 4 🛏/WC, 1 🛏; P1
Breakfast only [5%V]

Nando's *Acclaimed* RAC
18 & 19 Evesham Place, Stratford-upon-Avon CV37 6HT 01789-204907 Fax 01789-204907 ♿
21 bedrs, 9 🛏/WC, 3 🛏; 🐾 P8
sB&B £17 D £7 [5%V]; cc Ac Amex DC Vi JCB

Parkfield RAC
3 Broad Walk, Stratford-upon-Avon CV37 6HS 01789-293313
7 bedrs, 5 🛏/WC, 1 🛏; 🐾 P6
Child restrictions
sB&B £17-£18 dB&B £38-£40 Breakfast only [5%V]; cc Ac Amex DC Vi JCB

Penryn ⛫RAC
126 Alcester Road, Stratford-upon-Avon CV37
9DP 01789-293718
7 bedrs, 5 ➥/WC, 1 ➥; TV tcf ✖ ✠ P8
sB&B £15-£35 dB&B £30-£46 Breakfast only
[5%V]; cc Ac Amex DC Vi JCB

Penshurst 34 Evesham Place, Stratford-upon-
Avon CV37 6HT 01789-205259 Fax
01789-295322 ♿

Prettily refurbished Victorian town house.
Centrally located, delicious choice of
breakfast, excellent value for money.
8 bedrs, 2 ✖/WC, 2 ➥; TV tcf
sB&B £13.50; HB weekly £120-£173; D £6-£7.50

HARDWICK GUEST HOUSE

A delightful Victorian Building dating from 1887. Situated at
the bottom of Avenue Road, in a quiet mature area. Only a
few minutes walk to the Shakespearian properties and Royal
Shakespeare Theatre. Ideal position for Warwick Castle,
Birmingham Arena and the National Exhibition Centre.

Large comfortable rooms. En/Suite and standard available.
All with colour T.V., Tea/Coffee making facilities, hot &
cold water, full central heating, ample car parking.

RESIDENT PROPRIETORS
DRENAGH AND SIMON WOOTTON
Hardwick House, 1, Avenue Road,
Stratford-upon-Avon, Warwickshire. CV37 6UY

⛫RAC   English Tourist Board
                        APPROVED
                        ♔♔♔
TELEPHONE
RESERVATIONS   GUESTS
01789 204307   **01789 296174**
FAX: 01789 296760   Credit Cards accepted

Quilt & Croissants 33 Evesham Place,
Stratford-upon-Avon CV37 6HT 01789-267629

Sequoia House *Highly Acclaimed* ⛫RAC
51-53, Shipston Road, Stratford-upon-Avon
CV57 7LN 01789-268852 Fax 01789-414559 ♿
24 bedrs, 20 ➥/WC, 2 ➥; ✠
sB&B £29-£49 dB&B £39-£72 Breakfast only

Twelfth Night *Highly Acclaimed* ⛫RAC
Evesham Place, Stratford-upon-Avon CV37
6HT 01789-414595
7 bedrs, 7 ➥/WC; P7
Child restrictions
sB&B £22-£26 dB&B £42-£58 Breakfast only;
cc Ac Vi

Victoria Spa Lodge *Highly Acclaimed* ⛫RAC
Bishopton Lane, Bishopton, Stratford-upon-
Avon CV37 9QY 01789-267985 Fax
01789-204728
7 bedrs, 7 ➥/WC; ✖ P12
sB&B £35-£38 dB&B £45-£50 Breakfast only;
cc Ac Vi

Virginia Lodge *Acclaimed* ⛫RAC
12 Evesham Place, Stratford-upon-Avon CV37
6HT 01789-292157
7 bedrs, 7 ✖/WC; TV tcf ✖ ✠ P8
sB&B £18-£20 dB&B £38-£46 Breakfast only

35 Evesham Place Stratford-upon-Avon
CV37 6HT 01789-29879

STRETTON Leicestershire 8C3

★★★(Inn) Ram Jam Inn ⛫RAC
Great North Road, nr Oakham, Stretton LE15
7QX 01780-410776 Fax 01780-410361
7 bedrs, 7 ➥/WC; ✖ P50
Breakfast only [10%V]; cc Ac Amex DC Vi

SUTTON IN THE ELMS Leicestershire 8B3

★★(Inn) Mill On The Soar ⛫RAC
B4114 Coventry Road, Sutton In The Elms
LE9 6QD 01455-282419 Fax 01455-285937
20 bedrs, 20 ➥/WC; P200
cc Ac Vi

SUTTON-ON-SEA Lincolnshire 9D1

Athelstone Lodge *Acclaimed* ⛫RAC
25 Trusthorpe Road, Sutton-on-Sea LN12 2LR
01507-441521
6 bedrs, 1 ➥/WC, 4 ✖/WC, 1 ➥; TV tcf ✖ P6
sB&B £18 dB&B £36; HB weekly £144-£150; D £8

TAMWORTH Staffordshire 7F2

Granada Lodge RAC
Green Lane, Wilnecote, Tamworth B77 1PS
01827-260123

Shrubberies 42 Victoria Road, Tamworth
B79 7HU 01827-64698

TOTON Nottinghamshire

Manor Nottingham Rd, Toton NG9 6EF
0115-9733487

UPPINGHAM Leicestershire 8C3

Old Rectory RAC
Belton-in-Rutland, Uppingham LE15 9LE
01572-86279 Fax 01572-86343
7 bedrs, 6 ➥/WC, 1 ➥; ✖ ✄ P10
sB&B £25 dB&B £36 [10%V]; cc Ac Vi

UTTOXETER Staffordshire 7F2

Hillcrest RAC
3 Leighton Road, Uttoxeter ST14 8BL
01889-564627
7 bedrs, 7 ➥/WC, 1 ➥; P12
Breakfast only; cc Ac Vi

WALSALL West Midlands 8A3

Forte Posthouse RAC
Birmingham Road, Walsall WS5 3AB
01922-33555 Fax 01922-612034

WALTHAM-ON-THE-WOLDS
Leicestershire 8B3

Royal Horseshoes Inn Waltham-on-the-
Wolds LE14 4AJ 01664-72289

WARWICK Warwickshire 8B4

Avon 7 Emscote Rd, Warwick CV34 4PH
01926-491367

Globe RAC
Theatre Street, Warwick CV34 4PP
01926-492044
Awaiting inspection

Northleigh Five Ways Rd, Hatton, Warwick
CV35 7HZ 01926-484203

Old Rectory Stratford Road, Sherbourne,
Warwick CV35 8AB 01926-624562

Park Cottage *Highly Acclaimed* RAC
113 West Street, Warwick CV34 6AH
01926-41031 Fax 01926-41031
5 bedrs, 5 ➥/WC; P8
Child restrictions
Breakfast only

The Croft Guesthouse *Acclaimed* RAC
Haseley Knob, Warwick CV35 7NL
01926-484447 Fax 01926-484447
5 bedrs, 5 ➥/WC, 2 ➥; TV tcf ✖ P8
sB&B £19-£30 dB&B £39-£42 Breakfast only
[5%V]

Westham RAC
76 Emscote Road, Warwick CV34 5QG
01926-491756
7 bedrs, 1 ➥/WC, 1 ➥/WC, 2 ➥; TV tcf ✖ P4
sB&B £15-£16 dB&B £30-£34 Breakfast only

WELLINGBOROUGH Northamptonshire 8C4

Oak House RAC
9 Broad Green, Wellingborough NN8 4LE
01933-271133
16 bedrs, 15 ➥/WC; TV tcf ✖ P12
sB&B £28-£32 dB&B £38 Breakfast only
[5%V]; cc Ac Amex Vi

Shepherds View 4 Hinwick Road,
Podington, Wellingborough NN9 7HU
01933-315111

WOLVERHAMPTON West Midlands 8A3

Pavilion Lodge RAC
M6 Motorway (btw jn 10-11), Wolverhampton
WV11 2DR 01922-414100 Fax 01922-418762

The Wheatsheaf Market Street,
Wolverhampton WV1 3AE 01902-24446

WOODHALL SPA Lincolnshire 8C2

★★Eagle Lodge RAC
The Broadway, Woodhall Spa LN10 6ST
01526-353231

WORKSOP Nottinghamshire 8B1

★★★(Inn) Lion RAC
112 Bridge Street, Worksop S80 1HT
01909-477925 Fax 01909-479038

West Country

Avon • Gloucester • Hereford & Worcester • Shropshire

Baths are the order of the day here – Roman ones, brine ones and an elegant Regency spa punctuate an area in which the cradle of the Industrial Revolution lies only marginally north of the mellow apple growing areas round Worcester.

A SELECTION OF ATTRACTIONS.

Unless otherwise stated, all can be visited between April and October – some longer. Telephone for days/times of opening.

Acton Scott Historic Working Farm, nr. Church Stretton,Salop. *Heavy horses and 19th-c machinery.* Tel: 01694-781306/7.

The American Museum at Claverton Manor, Bath: *18 furnished rooms illustrate life of 17-19th centuries.* Information Tel: 01225-462831.

Attingham Park, nr. Shrewsbury, Salop: *Nash Picture Gallery and Regency silver enhance stately furnishings. Park by Repton. NT. Apr-Sept.* Tel: 01743-709203.

Avoncroft Museum of Buildings, nr. Bromsgrove, H & W: *Open air museum featuring constructions from pre-fab to cock-pit theatre.* Tel: 01527-831886/831363.

Beckford's Tower, Bath, Avon: *Great view of Bath and surrounds from Belvedere of rich man's folly.* Tel: 01225-338727.

Berkeley Castle, Glos: *Inhabited 12th-c castle. Exciting history,and dungeon. Terraced gardens, tropical butterflies.* Tel: 01453-810332.

Mr. Bowler's Business Centre, Bath: *Workshop, machinery and stock of Victorian brass founder.* Tel: 01225-318348.

Bristol City Museum, Bristol: *Excellent varied collection plus regular comntemporary exhibitions.* Tel: 0117-9223571.

Burford House Gardens, Tenbury Wells, H&W: *John Treasure's world famous plant centre attached to his garden.* Tel: 01584- 810777.

Bristol

Chedworth Roman Villa, Yanworth, Glos: *4th-c excavated mosaics and artifacts of Roman domestic life. NT.* Tel: 01242-890256.

Claverton Manor, nr. Bath: *Tea and American cookies refresh after delightful experience of domestic life in U.S.* Tel: 01225-460503.

Droitwich Heritage & Information Centre, H&W: *History of this salt town depicted in former brine baths. Brass rubbing.* Tel: 01905-774312.

Droitwich Private Hospital: *Brine baths from natural spring, salt as the Red Sea! Towel, tea and sauna supplied.* Tel: 01905-794894.

Dudmaston, Quatt, Bridgenorth, Salop: *Dutch flower and botanical paintings plus modern art add interest to 17th-c house and garden. NT. Closes Sep.* Tel: 01746-780866.

Hanbury Hall, nr. Droitwich, H&W: *Fine porcelain collection, 18th-c formal garden, ceiling and staircase by Thornhill. NT.* Tel: 01527-821214.

Harveys Wine Museum, Bristol: *Guided tour of vaults, film on history of sherry, tastings.* Tel: 0117-9277661.

Hellen's, Much Marcle, H&W: *Fascinating manorial home, built 1292, has remained in same family. Easter-Sep.* Tel: 01531-84668.

Hereford Museums & Art Gallery: *Varied exhibits, history, archaeology, observation beehive, early English watercolours, etc.* Tel: 01432-268121 ext 207.

Hergest Croft Gardens, Kington, H&W: *Important 50-acre year round garden. Exotic trees and shrubs, rare species.* Tel: 01544-230160.

Hidcote Manor Garden, nr Chipping Campden, Glos: *Superb 20th-c garden planned as series of enclosed themed spaces. NT.* Tel: 01386-438333.

Holburne Museum & Crafts Study Centre, Bath: *Top modern crafts – textiles, pottery, calligraphy – and decorative/fine arts of 18th-c collector.* Tel: 01225-466669.

Ironbridge Gorge Museum, Telford, Salop: *World Industrial Heritage Site, offers Coalport China Museum and Blists Hill Open Air*

Coalport China Museum, Ironbridge

Museum – a re-construction of live working Victorian community, plus much more. Several days' enjoyment. Tel: 01952-433522/432166.

Ludlow Castle, Ludlow, Salop: *Imposing medieval castle with Norman remains. Events in outer bailey.* Tel: 015840-873947.

National Waterways Museum, Gloucester Docks: *Splendid Victorian warehouses accommodate museum, antiques, food, events.* Tel: 01452-307009.

Painswick Rococo Garden, Painswick, Glos: *Unique surviving garden of this period. More vistas and vegetables than flowers.* Tel: 01452-813204.

Roman Baths Museum, Bath, Avon: *Well-preserved Roman Baths. Pump Room.* Tel: 01225-461111 ext 2785.

No. 1, Royal Crescent, Bath, Avon: *18th-c replica of interior of Bath's fabulous crescent houses.* Tel: 01225-428126.

Sally Lunn's House, Bath: *Oldest house in Bath shows excavated remains of earlier buildings – Roman, Saxon and medieval.* Tel: 01225-461634.

Shambles Museum, Newent, Glos: *Re-creation of fascinating Victorian house and town.* Tel: 01531-822144.

Broadgate, Ludlow

Snowshill Manor, nr. Broadway, Glos: *21 rooms of eccentric collections in Tudor manor. Great fun for all. NT.* Tel: 01386-852410.

Sudeley Castle, Winchcombe, Glos: *Former palace of Katherine Parr, it has everything from royal formality to adventure playground.* Tel: 01242-602308.

The Weir, nr. Hereford, H&W: *Enjoy fine views of river Wye and Black Mountains from this riverside garden. Wed-Sun, 11-6.*

Weston Park, nr. Shifnal, Salop: *17th-c house contains superb antiques and paintings. Capability Brown Park hosts adventure playground, miniature railway, pets corner. Summer events too. Easter-Sep.* Tel: 0195276-207.

SOME ANNUAL EVENTS:

Bath International Festival, Avon: *19 May-4 Jun:* Tel: 01225-462231.

Badminton Horse Trials, Avon: *Famous international horse event: 4-7 May.* Tel: 01454-218272.

Bristol – Bournemouth Vintage Car Run: Ashton Court, Bristol. *11 Jun, 7-11am.*

Bristol Harbour Regatta, Avon: *Maritime festival, parachuting, pyrotechnics, entertainments. 5-6 Aug.* Tel: 0117-929 7704.

Cheltenham Int'l Festival of Music, Glos: *Best of British comtemporary music, chamber to jazz. 1-16 Jul.* Tel: 01242-521621.

Cheltenham Festival of Literature, Glos: *Readings, book exhibitions, lectures by literary figures. 6-14 Oct.* Tel: 01242-521621.

Harveys Wine Museum, Bristol: *200th anniversary of this famous imported in Bristol. 14Apr-24Dec.* Tel: 0117-9275001.

Hay Festival, Hay-on-Wye, H&W: *An established festival of literature and related events. 26 May-4 Jun.* Tel: 01497-821299.

International Air Tattoo, Fairford, Glos: *World's largest air display. End Jul.* Tel: 01285-713300.

International Bristol Balloon Fiesta, Ashton Court: *150 hot-air balloons launched daily – weather permitting. 12-14 Aug.* Tel: 0117-953 5884.

International Kite Festival, Ashton Court, Bristol: *Fantastic shapes, kite battles, kite making for kids. 2-3 Sep.* Tel: 0117-946 6852.

Ludlow Festival, Salop. *Various venues centred round Norman castle. 24 Jun-9 Jul.* Tel: 01584-875070.

North Somerset Show, Ashton Court, Bristol: *29 May.* Tel: 0117-964 3498.

Shrewsbury Flower Show, Salop: *Flower displays, special events. 11-12 Aug.* Tel: 01743-364051.

Shrewsbury Int'l. Music Festival, Salop: *Non-competitive music & dance. 23 Jun-3 Jul.* Tel: 0171-401 9941.

South West Festival of Retirement, Ashton Court, Bristol: *Activities and entertainment for senior citizens. 25 Jun.* Tel: 0771-929 7704.

Three Choirs Festival, Gloucester: *Choirs of Worcester, Hereford & Gloucester cathedrals. 19-26 Aug.* Tel: 01452-529819.

ANDOVERSFORD Gloucestershire   7F4

The Pegglesworth Hotel & Restaurant
Dowdeswell, Andoversford GL54 4LR
01242-820349

AUST Avon   3E1

Pavilion Lodge   RAC
Aust Services (M4), Aust BS12 3BJ
014545-3789

BADMINTON, GREAT Avon   3F1

Chestnut Farm Tolmarton, Badminton GL9
1HS 01454-218563
5 bedrs, 5 ☊/WC; TV tcf ✇ P8
sB&B £18.50; HB weekly £162; D £8.50

Ivy Cottage Inglestone Common,
Hawkesbury, Badminton GL9 1BX 454294237

BATH Avon   3F1

Arden *Highly Acclaimed*   RAC
73 Great Pulteney Street, Bath BA2 4DL
01225-466601 Fax 01225-465548
10 bedrs, 10 ➼/WC; P2
Breakfast only

Armstrong House *Highly Acclaimed* ⚓RAC
41 Crescent Gardens, Upper Bristol Road, Bath
BA1 2NB 01225-442211 Fax 01225-334769
4 bedrs, 4 ♠/WC, 1 ➡; TV tcf ✗ P6
Child restrictions
dB&B £46-£54 Breakfast only [5%V]; cc Ac Vi

Arosa 124 Lower Oldfield Park, Bath BA2
3HS 01225-422992

Ashley House 8 Pultney Gardens, Bath BA2
4HG 01225-425027

Ashley Villa *Highly Acclaimed* ⚓RAC
26 Newbridge Road, Bath BA1 3TZ
01225-421683
14 bedrs, 3 ➡/WC, 11 ♠/WC; TV tcf ✗ P10
sB&B £39-£45 dB&B £49-£59 Breakfast only;
cc Ac Vi

Astor House ⚓RAC
14 Oldfield Road, Oldfield Park, Bath BA2
3ND 01225-429134 Fax 01225-429134
8 bedrs, 5 ♠/WC, 1 ➡; TV tcf P5
Child restrictions
sB&B £20-£25 dB&B £32-£46 Breakfast only
[10%V]; cc Ac Vi

Badminton Villa *Highly Acclaimed* ⚓RAC
10 Upper Oldfield Park, Bath BA2 3JZ
01225-426347 Fax 01225-420393
4 bedrs, 2 ➡/WC, 2 ♠/WC, 1 ➡; TV tcf ✗ P5
Child restrictions
sB&B £35 dB&B £48-£50 Breakfast only
[10%V]; cc Ac Vi

Bailbrook Lodge *Highly Acclaimed* ⚓RAC
35-37 London Road West, Bath BA1 7HZ
01225-859090 Fax 01225-859090
12 bedrs, 4 ➡/WC, 8 ♠/WC; TV tcf P14
sB&B £32.40 dB&B £50 D £12.50 [10%V]; cc
Ac Amex Vi

Brompton House

St Johns Road, Bath BA2 6PT
Tel: (01225) 420972 – 3 lines
Resident Proprietors: David & Susan Selby

HERITAGE CITY OF BATH
Elegant Georgian rectory set in beautiful
gardens, creating Country House
atmosphere. Car Park. Minutes level walk
to City Centre. Residential license. Choice
of Traditional English breakfast or
Wholefood Breakfast.

LEIGHTON HOUSE

Enjoy a haven of friendliness at this highly
recommended guest house which is the home of Dave
and Kath Slape. Their elegant detached Victorian
house is set in beautiful gardens with views over the
city. It has been tastefully decorated and furnished
throughout with many period pieces having been
used. The highest standards of comfort and service
are provided. Excellent choice of breakfasts including
fresh fruit salad and scrambled eggs with smoked
salmon. Ample private car parking and 10 minute
walk to the city centre. Special Breaks Available.

English Tourist Board Highly Commended
AA 5Qs Premier Selected
RAC Highly Acclaimed
Les Routiers Highly Recommended

Leighton House
139 Wells Road, Bath, Avon BA2 3AL
Telephone: Bath (01225) 314769 (Reservations)
Bath (01225) 420210 (Guest phone)

Bannerdown View Farm Cottages
Bannerdown View Farm, Ashley Road, Bathford, Bath BA1 7TS 01225-859363
A beautiful, converted, stone barn set in a small village on a working dairy farm. Within easy reach of many tourist attractions and a good choise of eating places, 5 minutes to bus and shops.

Bath Tasburgh *Highly Acclaimed* RAC
Warminster Road, Bath BA2 6SH
01225-425096 Fax 01225-463842

Spacious Victorian mansion built for Royal Photographer in 1890.Set in seven acres of grounds with beautiful gardens, canal frontage and views of the city. Situated one mile east of centre on A36.
13 bedrs, 11 🛁/WC, 11 🚿/WC, 3 🛁;
TV tcf P15
Child restrictions
Breakfast only; cc Ac Amex DC Vi

Bloomfield House *Highly Acclaimed* RAC
146 Bloomfield Road, Bath BA2 2AS
01225-420105 Fax 01225-481958
6 bedrs, 5 🛁/WC, 1 🚿/WC; TV tcf P10
Child restrictions
sB&B £35-£40 dB&B £45-£85 Breakfast only; cc Ac Vi

Bridge Cottage Northfield End, Ashley Road, Bathford, Bath BA1 7TT 01225-852399

Brompton House *Highly Acclaimed* RAC
St Johns Road, Bath BA2 6PT 01225-420972
Fax 01225-420505
18 bedrs, 3 🛁/WC, 15 🚿/WC; TV tcf P18
Child restrictions
sB&B £32-£40 dB&B £56-£74 Breakfast only [5%V]; cc Ac Vi

Cheriton House *Highly Acclaimed* RAC
9 Upper Oldfield Park, Bath BA2 3JX
01225-429862 Fax 01225-428403
9 bedrs, 2 🛁/WC, 7 🚿/WC; TV tcf 🚭 P9
Child restrictions
sB&B £35-£38 dB&B £50-£60 Breakfast only [10%V]; cc Ac Vi

Chesterfield *Acclaimed*
11 Great Pulteney Street, Bath BA2 4BR
01225-460953 Fax 01225-448770
18 bedrs, 8 🛁/WC, 10 🚿/WC; TV tcf 🚭 P8
sB&B £30 dB&B £45 Breakfast only; cc Ac Amex Vi

Claremont House 9 Grosvenor Villas, Claremont Road, Larkhall, Bath BA1 5JE
01225-428859

County
18/19 Pulteney Road, Bath BA2 4EZ
01225-425003
22 bedrs, 1 🛁/WC, 11 🚿/WC, 3 🛁; TV tcf P50
sB&B £37.50-£42.50 dB&B £55-£65 Breakfast only; cc Ac Vi

Cranleigh *Acclaimed*
159 Newbridge Hill, Bath BA1 3PX
01225-310197

Della Rosa Guesthouse 59 North Road, Combe Down, Monkton, Bath BA2 5DF
01225-837193

Dene Villa 5 Newbridge Hill, Bath BA1 3PW
01225-427676

Dorian House *Highly Acclaimed*
1 Upper Oldfield Park, Bath BA2 3JX
01225-426336 Fax 01225-444699

A well-appointed gracious Victorian house on southern slopes overlooking the historic city centre of Bath. Only a ten minute stroll to the city attractions.
8 bedrs, 5 🛁/WC, 3 🚿/WC; TV tcf 🚭 P11
sB&B £35-£42 dB&B £49-£57 Breakfast only [5%V]; cc Ac Amex DC Vi

Dorset Villa *Acclaimed*
14 Newbridge Road, Bath BA1 3JX
01225-425975

Dundas Lock Cottage Monkton Combe, Bath BA2 7BN 01225-723890

Eastfield Farm & Guesthouse Dunkerton Hill, Peasedown St John, Bath BA2 8PF
01761-432161

Edgar
64 Great Pulteney Street, Bath BA2 4DN
01225-420619

Ellesworth Fosseway, Midsomer Norton, Bath BA3 4AU 01761-412305

Flaxley Villa 9 Newbridge Hill, Bath BA1 3LE 01255-313237
3 bedrs, 2 🚿/WC, 1 🛁; TV tcf P4
sB&B £18 Breakfast only

Fyfield Ralph Allen Drive, Combe Down, Bath BA2 5AE 01225-833561

Gainsborough *Highly Acclaimed*
Weston Lane, Bath BA1 4AB 01225-311380
Fax 01225-447411
16 bedrs, 12 🛁/WC, 4 🚿/WC; TV tcf P16
sB&B £35-£42 dB&B £55-£65 Breakfast only [5%V]; cc Ac Amex Vi

Gardens 7 Pulteney Gardens, Bath BA2 4HJ 01225-337642

Glen View 162 Newbridge Road, Bath BA1 3LE

Green Lane House *Acclaimed* 🔒RAC
Green Lane, Hinton Charterhouse, Bath BA3 6BL 01225-723631
4 bedrs, 2 ➡/WC, 2 🔦/WC, 1 ➡; P6
Breakfast only

Grove Lodge 🔒RAC
11 Lambridge, Bath BA1 6BJ 01225-310860
8 bedrs, 2 ➡; TV tcf
sB&B £20-£25 dB&B £40-£45 Breakfast only
[10%V]

Haute Combe House *Highly Acclaimed* 🔒RAC
176 Newbridge Road, Bath BA1 3LE
01225-420061 Fax 01225-420061
11 bedrs, 2 ➡/WC, 9 🔦/WC; TV tcf 🐾 ✂ P11
sB&B £30-£38 dB&B £40-£52 Breakfast only
[10%V]; cc Ac Vi JCB

Haydon House *Highly Acclaimed* 🔒RAC
9 Bloomfield Park, Bath BA2 2BY
01225-444919 Fax 01225-469020

Highways House *Highly Acclaimed* 🔒RAC
143 Wells Road, Bath BA2 3AL 01225-421238
7 bedrs, 2 ➡/WC, 4 🔦/WC; TV tcf ✂ P8
Child restrictions
sB&B £32-£34 dB&B £48-£56 Breakfast only;
cc Ac Vi

Hotel St Clair 🔒RAC
1 Crescent Gardens, Upper Bristol Road, Bath
BA1 2NA 01225-425543

Kennard *Acclaimed* 🔒RAC
11 Henrietta Street, Bath BA2 6LL
01225-310472 Fax 01225-460054
13 bedrs, 11 🔦/WC, 1 ➡; TV tcf
Child restrictions
sB&B £30-£34 dB&B £48-£58 Breakfast only
[10%V]; cc Ac Amex DC Vi

Lamp Post Villa *Acclaimed* 🔒RAC
3 Crescent Gardens, Bath BA1 2NA
01225-426783 Fax 01225-331221

Laura Place *Highly Acclaimed* 🔒RAC
3 Laura Place, Great Pulteney Street, Bath
BA2 4BH 01225-463815 Fax 01225-310222
8 bedrs, 2 ➡/WC, 5 🔦/WC; TV tcf ✂ P8
Child restrictions
sB&B £50 dB&B £65.85 Breakfast only
[10%V]; cc Ac Amex Vi

Leighton House *Highly Acclaimed*
139 Wells Road, Bath BA2 3AL 01225-314769

Spacious, detached Victorian house, tastefully furnished and decorated. Offering high standards of comfort and service and a warm, friendly atmosphere.
8 bedrs, 8 ➡/WC; TV tcf P8
sB&B £29 Breakfast only; cc Ac Vi

Lynwood 6 Pulteney Avenue, Bath BA2 4HG
01225-426410

Mardon 1 Pulteney Terrace, Bath BA2 4HJ
01225-311624

Meadowland *Highly Acclaimed* RAC
36 Bloomfield Park, Bath BA2 2BX
01225-311079
30 bedrs, 30 ➡/WC;
Breakfast only; cc Ac Vi

Membland 7 Pulteney Terrace, Pulteney
Road, Bath BA2 4HJ 01225-336712

Centrally located, late Victorian guest house with private parking. Homely atmosphere, generous breakfast.
3 bedrs, 1 ➡; TV tcf ✗ P3
sB&B £27 Breakfast only

Millers RAC
69 Great Pulteney Street, Bath BA2 4DL
01225-465798 Fax 01225-832305
14 bedrs, 5 ➡/WC, 1 ➡/WC, 3 ➡; TV
sB&B £25-£27 dB&B £38-£55 Breakfast only;
cc Ac Vi

Monkshill *Highly Acclaimed* RAC
Shaft Road, Monkton Combe, Bath BA2 7HL
01225-833028

3 bedrs, 2 ➡/WC, 1 ➡; P6
Child restrictions
Breakfast only

Monmouth Lodge *Highly Acclaimed* RAC
Norton St. Philip, Bath BA3 6LH
01373-834367

No 2 Crescent Gardens Upper Bristol Road,
Bath BA1 2NA 01225-331186

Oakleigh House *Highly Acclaimed* RAC
19 Upper Oldfield Park, Bath BA2 3JX
01225-315698 Fax 01225-448223
4 bedrs, 1 ➡/WC, 3 ➡/WC; TV tcf ✗ P4
Child restrictions
sB&B £33-£45 dB&B £45-£60 Breakfast only
[10%V]; cc Ac Vi

Old Courthouse *Highly Acclaimed* RAC
Colston, Bath BA2 9AP
01225-874228

Old School House *Highly Acclaimed* RAC
Church Street, Bathford, Bath BA1 7RR
01225-859593 Fax 01225-859590 &
4 bedrs, 4 ➡/WC, 1 ➡; TV tcf P6
sB&B £40-£45 dB&B £58-£64 Breakfast only;
cc Ac Vi

Oldfields *Acclaimed* RAC
102 Wells Road, Bath BA2 3AL 01225-317984
Fax 01225-444471
14 bedrs, 1 ➡/WC, 7 🛏/WC, 3 ➡; TV tcf P10
sB&B £25-£30 dB&B £48-£60 Breakfast only;
cc Ac Vi

Orchard House *Highly Acclaimed* RAC
Warminster Road, Bathampton, Bath BA2
6XG 01225-466115
14 bedrs, 14 ➡/WC; TV tcf ✖ ⅍ P19
sB&B £39-£45 dB&B £49-£55 Breakfast only
[10%V]; cc Ac Amex DC Vi

Poplar Farm Stanton Prior, Bath BA2 9HX
01761-470382

Sydney Gardens *Highly Acclaimed* RAC
Sydney Road, Bath BA2 6NT 01225-464818
6 bedrs, 6 ➡/WC; TV tcf ✖ P6
Child restrictions
sB&B £49-£59 dB&B £59-£69 Breakfast only;
cc Ac Amex Vi

Highly Acclaimed

One Upper Oldfield Park,
Bath, Avon BA2 3JX
Tel: 01225 426336 Fax: 01225 444699

The Albany Guest house 24 Crescent
Gardens, Bath BA1 2NB 01225-313339
4 bedrs, 1 ➡; P3
sB&B £17; HB weekly £108.10-£214.20;

**The Rookery Wells Road, Radstock, Bath
BA3 3RS 01761-432626**
10 bedrs, 10 ➡/WC, 10 🛏/WC, 1 ➡; ✖ P20
sB&B £28; HB weekly £175;

Underhill Lodge *Highly Acclaimed* RAC
Warminster Road, Bathampton, Bath BA2
6XQ 01225-464992 Fax 01225-444185

Villa Magdala *Highly Acclaimed* RAC
Henrietta Road, Bath BA2 6LX 01225-466329
Fax 01225-483207
17 bedrs, 13 ➡/WC, 4 🛏/WC; TV tcf ⅍ P17
Child restrictions
sB&B £40-£49 dB&B £50-£60 Breakfast only
[10%V]; cc Ac Vi

Waltons RAC
17 Crescent Gardens, Upper Bristol Road,
Bath BA1 2NA 01225-426528
15 bedrs, 3 ➡; TV tcf
sB&B £20-£25 dB&B £35-£38 Breakfast only

Wansdyke Cottage Crosspost Lane,
Marksbury, Bath BA2 9HE 01225-873674

Wellsway 51 Wellsway, Bath BA2 4RS
01225-423434

Wentworth House *Acclaimed* RAC
106 Bloomfield Road, Bath BA2 2AP
01225-339193 Fax 01225-310460
19 bedrs, 7 ➡/WC, 9 🛏/WC, 1 ➡; TV tcf ✖
P19
Child restrictions
sB&B £36 dB&B £45 [10%V]; cc Ac Vi

Wheelbrook Mill *Highly Acclaimed* RAC
Laverton, Bath BA3 6QY 01373-830263

21 Newbridge Road Bath BA1 3HE
01225-314694

BLAGDON Avon   3E1

Aldwick Court Farm *Highly Acclaimed* RAC
nr Bristol, Blagdon BS18 7RF 01934-862305

BLAKENEY Gloucestershire   7E4

Lower Viney *Highly Acclaimed*   RAC
Viney Hill, Blakeney GL15 4LT 01594-516000
Fax 01594-516018
6 bedrs, 1 ➡/WC, 5 ▐▚/WC; TV tcf P8
sB&B £28 dB&B £38 D £11 [10%V]; cc Ac Vi

BLOCKLEY Gloucestershire   7F4

Lower Brook House *Highly Acclaimed* RAC
Moreton in Marsh, Blockley GL56 9DS
01386-700286
4 bedrs, 3 ➡/WC, 1 ▐▚/WC; TV tcf ✘ P10
Child restrictions
Breakfast only

BOURTON-ON-THE-WATER
Gloucestershire   4A1

Ridge *Highly Acclaimed* RAC
Whiteshoots, Bourton-on-the-Water GL54 2LE
01451-820660
5 bedrs, 3 ➡/WC, 2 ▐▚/WC, 1 ➡; TV tcf
Child restrictions
sB&B £20 dB&B £38 Breakfast only

Upper Farm Clapton-on-the-Hill, Bourton-
on-the-Water GL54 2LG 01451-820453

BREDWARDINE Hereford & Worcester   7D4

Bredwardine Hall *Highly Acclaimed* RAC
Bredwardine HR3 6DB 01981-500596 Fax
01981-500596
4 bedrs, 3 ➡/WC, 1 ▐▚/WC, 1 ➡; TV tcf P7
Child restrictions
sB&B £33 dB&B £46-£50; HB weekly £240-£254

BRIDGNORTH Shropshire   7E3

Haven Pasture *Acclaimed* RAC
Underton, Bridgnorth WV16 6TY 0174635-632

No Smoking/Dogs
✗ Indicates a hotel which either bans
smoking throughout the establishment or
does not allow smoking in some areas.

✘ Indicates a hotel which either does not
welcome dogs or restricts dogs to certain
areas of the hotel.
Please telephone the hotel
for further details.

Middleton Lodge *Acclaimed* RAC
Middleton Priors, Bridgnorth WV16 6UR
0174-634228
3 bedrs, 2 ➡/WC, 1 ▐▚/WC; TV tcf P4
Child restrictions
sB&B £25 dB&B £40 Breakfast only

BRISTOL Avon   3E1

Alandale *Acclaimed* RAC
4 Tyndalls Park Road, Clifton, Bristol BS8
1PG 0117-9735407

Alcove RAC
**508-510 Fishponds Road, Fishponds,
Bristol BS16 3DT 0179-652436 Fax
0179-653886**
*Late Victorian double fronted with bay
windows, car park at rear*
9 bedrs, 3 ▐▚/WC, 4 ➡; TV tcf ✘ P8
sB&B £20-£25 dB&B £34-£36 Breakfast only

Auden House Stanton Drew, Bristol BS18
4DS 01275-332232

Basca House 19 Broadway Road,
Bishopston, Bristol BS7 8ES 0117-9422182

Birkdale *Acclaimed* RAC
10 & 11 Ashgrove Road, Redland, Bristol BS6
6LY 0117-9733635

Cavendish House RAC
18 Cavendish Road, Henleaze, Bristol BS9
4DZ 0117-9621017
7 bedrs, 1 ▐▚/WC, 1 ➡; TV tcf ✘ ✗ P4
sB&B £22 dB&B £36 Breakfast only [5%V]

Downlands *Acclaimed* RAC
33 Henleaze Gardens, Henleaze, Bristol BS9
4HH 0117-9621639
9 bedrs, 3 ▐▚/WC, 2 ➡; TV tcf ✘
sB&B £23 dB&B £40 Breakfast only [10%V];
cc Ac Vi

Downs View RAC
38 Upper Belgrave Road, Clifton, Bristol BS8
2XN 0117-9737046
9 bedrs, 1 ➡/WC, 3 ▐▚/WC, 2 ➡; TV tcf ✘
sB&B £25 dB&B £35 Breakfast only [10%V];
cc Ac Vi

Kingsley RAC
93 Gloucester Road North, Filton, Bristol
BS12 7PT 0117-9699947
10 bedrs, 3 ⇌; TV tcf P9
sB&B £18 dB&B £32 Breakfast only

Mayfair 5 Henleaze Road, Westbury-on-
Trym, Bristol BS9 4EX 01272-622008
9 bedrs, 3 ↑/WC, 2 ⇌; TV tcf ✗ P9
sB&B £20 Breakfast only; cc Ac Vi

Oakdene Private RAC
45 Oakfield Road, Clifton, Bristol BS8 2BA
0117-9735900
13 bedrs, 7 ↑/WC, 3 ⇌; TV tcf P8
sB&B £32 dB&B £40 Breakfast only

Oakfield RAC
52/54 Oakfield Road, Bristol BS8 2BG
0117-9735556
27 bedrs, 8 ⇌; TV tcf ✗
sB&B £25-£27 dB&B £35-£37; HB weekly
£220.50; D £6.50; cc Ac Vi

Orchard House Bristol Road, Chew Stoke,
Bristol BS18 8UB 01275-333143

Vicarage Lawn West Harptree, Bristol BS18
6EA 01761-221668

Washington *Acclaimed* RAC
11-15 St Paul's Road, Bristol BS8 1LX
0117-9733980 Fax 0117-9741082
46 bedrs, 28 ⇌/WC, 9 ↑/WC, 5 ⇌; TV tcf ✗
✂ P20
sB&B £39.50 dB&B £46 Breakfast only
[10%V]; cc Ac Amex DC Vi

Westbury Park *Highly Acclaimed* RAC
37 Westbury Road, Bristol BS9 3AU
0117-962-0465 Fax 0117-962-8607
8 bedrs, 2 ⇌/WC, 6 ↑/WC, 1 ⇌; TV tcf P5
sB&B £36 dB&B £43 [10%V]; cc Ac Amex DC Vi

Whitegates Guesthouse Stockwood Hill,
Keynsham, Bristol BS18 2AM 0117-9862653

BROADWAY Hereford & Worcester 7F4

**Crown & Trumpet Inn Church Street,
Broadway WR12 7AE 01386-853202**

*A 17th century Cotswold inn, set in a
picturesque village, with local and seasonal
dishes homemade on the premises.*
4 bedrs, 1 ⇌/WC, 3 ↑/WC; TV tcf ✗ P6
sB&B £20 D £4.50-£10

Leasow House *Highly Acclaimed* RAC
Laverton Meadows, Broadway WR12 7NA
01386-584526 Fax 01386-584526 ♿
5 bedrs, 2 ⇌/WC, 3 ↑/WC; TV tcf ✗ ✂ P14
sB&B £30-£40 dB&B £48-£58 Breakfast only
[5%V]; cc Ac Amex Vi

Southwold House Station Road, Broadway
WR12 7DE 01386-853681

The Old Rectory *Highly Acclaimed* RAC
Church Street, Willersey, Broadway WR12
7PN 01386-853729
6 bedrs, 6 ⇌/WC, 2 ↑/WC; TV tcf ✂ P10
Child restrictions
dB&B £60-£80 Breakfast only; cc Ac Vi

The Olive Branch 🦮
78/80 High Street, Broadway WR12 7AJ
01386-853440 Fax 01386-853440
7 bedrs, 3 ⇻/WC, 2 ♟/WC, 1 ⇻; TV tcf ✳
P10
sB&B £17-£18 dB&B £40 Breakfast only
[10%V]; cc Amex

BROMSGROVE Hereford & Worcester   8A4

**Home Farm Mill Lane, Wildmoor,
Bromsgrove B61 0BX 01527-874964**
5 bedrs, 3 ⇻; P10

BROSELEY Shropshire   7E2

Cumberland 🦮
Jackson Avenue, Broseley TF12 5NB
01952-882301 Fax 01952-884438
9 bedrs, 1 ⇻/WC, 3 ⇻; TV tcf ✳ ✂ P30
sB&B £30 dB&B £40 D £11; cc DC Vi

CHELTENHAM Gloucestershire   7E4

Abbey 16 Bath Parade, Cheltenham GL53
7HN 01242-516053 Fax 01242-513034

*Elegance and taste characterise this charming
town centre hotel in a peaceful street close to
shopping arcades, town hall, bus station and
the theatres. Sky sport and Sky news. All cards
accepted. French spoken.*
11 bedrs, 1 ⇻/WC, 10 ♟/WC, 3 ⇻; ✳ P2
sB&B £28; HB weekly £315

Beaumont House *Highly Acclaimed* 🦮
**Shurdington Road, Cheltenham GL53 0JE
01242-245986 Fax 01242-520044**

*An elegant detached Grade I listed Victorian
building, with many original features. Set in
its own peaceful, picturesque gardens.*
18 bedrs, 16 ⇻/WC, 1 ⇻; TV tcf P20
sB&B £32 dB&B £45 Breakfast only [10%V];
cc Ac Vi

Broomhill 🦮
218 London Road, Cheltenham GL52 6HW
01242-513086
3 bedrs, 2 ⇻/WC, 2 ⇻; P4
sB&B £15-£19 dB&B £32-£35 Breakfast only
[10%V]; cc Ac Amex DC Vi

Cotswold Grange *Highly Acclaimed* RAC
Pittville Circus Road, Cheltenham GL52 2QH
01242-515119 Fax 01242-241537
25 bedrs, 25 ⇥/WC; ⅓ P20
sB&B £25-£45 dB&B £50 D £7.50 [10%V]; cc
Ac Amex DC Vi

Hallery House *Acclaimed* RAC
48 Shurdington Road, Cheltenham GL53 0JE
01242-578450 Fax 01242-529730
16 bedrs, 1 ⇥/WC, 9 ↰/WC, 2 ⇥; TV tcf ✻
⅓ P20
D £15 [10%V]; cc Ac Amex DC Vi

Hannaford's *Highly Acclaimed* RAC
20 Evesham Road, Cheltenham GL52 2AB
01242-515181
10 bedrs, 9 ⇥/WC, 1 ⇥;
Breakfast only [10%V]; cc Ac Amex Vi

Hilden Lodge *Highly Acclaimed* RAC
271 London Road, Charlton Kings,
Cheltenham GL52 6YL 01242-583242 Fax
01242-263511 &
10 bedrs, 10 ⇥/WC, 1 ⇥; ✻ ⅓ P12
sB&B £25-£30 dB&B £40; HB weekly £220; D
£10 [10%V]; cc Ac Amex DC Vi JCB

Hollington House *Highly Acclaimed* RAC
115 Hales Road, Cheltenham GL52 6ST
01242-256652 Fax 01242-570280

*A spacious, well-equipped Victorian House,
where excellent standards are maintained by
the resident proprietors. Conveniently situated
near the town centre and not far from the
London Road (A40).*
9 bedrs, 8 ↰/WC, 1 ⇥; TV tcf ⅓ P16
Child restrictions
sB&B £26-£40 dB&B £40-£60; HB weekly
£245-£315; [5%V]; cc Ac Amex Vi

Ivy Dene RAC
145 Hewlett Road, Cheltenham GL52 6TS
01242-521726
9 bedrs, 2 ⇥; ⅓ P7
Breakfast only [5%V]

Leeswood RAC
14 Montpellier Drive, Cheltenham GL50 1TX
01242-524813
8 bedrs, 2 ⇥/WC, 2 ⇥; TV tcf ✻ P6
sB&B £16.50-£17.50 dB&B £33-£35 Breakfast
only

Lypiatt House *Highly Acclaimed* RAC
Lypiatt Road, Cheltenham GL50 2QW
01242-224994 Fax 01242-224996
10 bedrs, 10 ⇥/WC; P14
Child restrictions
Breakfast only

Milton House *Highly Acclaimed* RAC
12 Royal Parade, Bayshill Road, Cheltenham
GL50 3AY 01242-582601 Fax 01242-222326
8 bedrs, 2 ⇥/WC, 6 ↰/WC; TV tcf ⅓ P4
sB&B £35 dB&B £50-£64 Breakfast only; cc
Ac Amex Vi

Montpellier RAC
33 Montpellier Terrace, Cheltenham GL50
1UX 01242-526009
10 bedrs, 4 ⇥/WC, 2 ⇥; ✻
sB&B £15-£26 dB&B £36-£42 Breakfast only
[5%V]; cc Amex Vi

Moorend Park *Highly Acclaimed* RAC
Moor End Park Road, Cheltenham GL53 0LA
01242-224441 Fax 01242-572413
10 bedrs, 4 ⇥/WC, 6 ↰/WC; TV tcf ✻ ⅓ P30
sB&B £39 dB&B £40; HB weekly £230;
[10%V]; cc Ac Amex Vi

North Hall RAC
Pittville Circus Road, Cheltenham GL52 2PZ
01242-520589 Fax 01242-261953
20 bedrs, 18 ⇥/WC, 2 ↰/WC, 4 ⇥; TV tcf ✻
P20
sB&B £27.50 dB&B £48 D £10.50 [10%V]; cc
Ac Vi

Parkview RAC
4 Pittville Crescent, Cheltenham GL52 2QZ
01242-575567
3 bedrs, 1 ⇥; ✻
sB&B £15.50-£16.50 dB&B £31-£33
Breakfast only

Regency House *Highly Acclaimed* RAC
50 Clarence Square, Cheltenham GL50 4JR
01242-582718 Fax 01242-262697
8 bedrs, 8 ➡/WC; TV tcf ✗ ✗ P5
sB&B £29.50-£36 dB&B £40-£48; HB weekly
£127-£146; D £12.95 [5%V]; cc Ac Amex Vi

Stretton Lodge *Highly Acclaimed* RAC
Western Road, Cheltenham GL50 3RN
01242-528724 Fax 01242-570771
9 bedrs, 9 ➡/WC; P6
Breakfast only [5%V]; cc Ac Amex Vi

Willoughby *Acclaimed* RAC
1 Suffolk Square, Cheltenham GL50 2DR
01242-522798

CHIPPING CAMPDEN Gloucester 7F4

Campden Country Pine High St, Chipping
Campden GL55 6HN 01386-840315

Orchard Hill House *Highly Acclaimed* RAC
**Broad Campden, Chipping Campden
GL55 6UU 01386-841473**

*A restored 17th century Cotswold stone
farmhouse, with open fires, oak beams and
flagstone floors.*
2 bedrs, 1 ➡/WC, 1 ✗/WC; TV tcf P6
dB&B £40; HB weekly £140;

CHURCH STRETTON Shropshire 7D3

Belvedere *Acclaimed* RAC
**Burway Road, Church Stretton SY6 6DP
01694-722232 Fax 01694-722232**

*Pleasant Edwardian house set in its own
attractive gardens and fish ponds on the edge
of the Long Mynd, yet still convenient for the
town's facilities.*
12 bedrs, 6 ✗/WC, 3 ➡; tcf ✗ P9
sB&B £20-£23 dB&B £40-£46; HB weekly
£195; [10%V]; cc Ac Vi

Brookfields *Acclaimed* RAC
Watling Street North, Church Stretton SY6
7AR 01694-722314
4 bedrs, 1 ➡/WC, 3 ✗/WC; TV tcf ✗ P8
sB&B £27 dB&B £45 Breakfast only [10%V]

Court Farm *Acclaimed* RAC
Gretton, Church Stretton SY6 7HU
01694-771219
3 bedrs, 2 ➡/WC, 2 ✗/WC;
sB&B £40-£44; HB weekly £140-£220; D £12
[5%V]; cc Amex

★★Mynd House RAC
Little Stretton, Church Stretton SY6 6RB
01694-722212 Fax 01694-724180
8 bedrs, 8 ➡/WC; TV tcf ✗ ✗ P16
sB&B £35-£42 dB&B £55-£65 [10%V]; cc Ac
Amex Vi

Strefford Hall RAC
Strefford, Cravens Arms, Church Stretton SY7
8DE 01588-672383

(Inn) Travellers Rest Inn RAC
Upper Affcot, Church Stretton SY6 6RL
01694-781275
10 bedrs, 4 ➡/WC, 1 ➡; ✗ ✗
sB&B £20-£27 dB&B £40-£45 [10%V]

CIRENCESTER Gloucestershire 7F4

Arkenside
44 46 Lewis Lane, Cirencester GL7 1EB
01285-653072
17 bedrs, 3 🛁/WC, 4 🛁;
Breakfast only [10%V]

La Ronde *Highly Acclaimed*
52/54 Ashcroft Road, Cirencester GL7 1QX
01285-654611
10 bedrs, 10 🛁/WC; 🐕
Breakfast only; cc Ac Vi

Wimborne *Highly Acclaimed*
91 Victoria Road, Cirencester GL7 1ES
01285-653890
5 bedrs, 5 🛁/WC; P6
Child restrictions
sB&B £20-£28 dB&B £30-£35 Breakfast only

CLEARWELL Gloucestershire 7E4

★★★Wyndham Arms
Coleford, Clearwell GL16 8JT 01594-833666
Fax 01594-836450
5 bedrs, 5 🛁/WC; 🐕 P52
sB&B £35-£50 dB&B £60 D £15.25 [10%V]; cc Ac Amex DC Vi

CLEEVE HILL Gloucestershire 7F4

Cleeve Hill
Cleeve Hill GL52 3PR 01242-672052

CLEVEDON Avon 3E1

Maybank 4 Jesmond Road, Victoria Road, Clevedon BS21 7SA 01275-876387
14 bedrs, 4 🚿/WC, 3 🛁; TV tcf 🐕 P8
sB&B £15 Breakfast only

Salthouse Inn Salthouse Rd, Clevedon BS21 7TY 01275-871482

COLESBOURNE Gloucestershire 7E4

(Inn) Colesbourne Inn
Colesbourne GL53 9NP 01242-870376 Fax 01242-870397
10 bedrs, 10 🛁/WC; 🐕 P50
Breakfast only [10%V]; cc Ac Amex DC Vi

DIDDLEBURY Shropshire 7D3

Glebe Farm *Acclaimed*
Craven Arms, Diddlebury SY7 9DH
01584-841221
3 bedrs, 1 🛁/WC, 2 🚿/WC; TV tcf 🐕 🚭 P10
Child restrictions under 8
dB&B £45-£52 Breakfast only

DROITWICH Hereford & Worcester 7E3

Phepson Farm Himbleton, Droitwich
01905-391205 ♿
4 bedrs, 2 🛁/WC, 2 🚿/WC; 🐕 P6
sB&B £20 Breakfast only

DYMOCK Hereford & Worcester 7E4

Lower House Farm Kempley, Dymock
01531-890301

EVESHAM Hereford & Worcester 7F4

Church House *Highly Acclaimed*
Greenhill Park Road, Evesham WR11 4NL
01386-40498
3 bedrs, 3 🛁/WC; 🐕 🚭 P3
Breakfast only [5%V]

Croft *Acclaimed*
54 Greenhill, Evesham WR11 4NF
01386-446035
3 bedrs, 2 🛁/WC, 1 🛁; 🐕 P6
sB&B £20-£28 dB&B £36-£42 Breakfast only [5%V]

Park View
Waterside, Evesham WR11 6BS 01386-442639

Child Restrictions

Most hotels and guest houses are happy to welcome children. A few prefer to welcome only adults and older children; these are shown by 'Child restrictions' in the entry. If you are travelling with children, please telephone the establishment to check the age limit set by the management.

FALFIELD Gloucestershire 3E1

Green Farm Falfield GL12 8DL 01454-260319

A tastefully converted, 16th century, stone-built farmhouse with beams, ingelnook fireplaces and flagstone floors.
8 bedrs, 1 ➟/WC, 1 ➟; TV tcf ✖ P10
sB&B £16 D £10-£17

GLOUCESTER Gloucestershire 7E4

Gilberts *Highly Acclaimed* 🔚
Gilberts Lane, Brookthorpe, Gloucester GL4 0UH 01452-812364 Fax 01452-812364

A Grade II listed, 400 year old, Jacobean manor house, sympathetically restored and modernised.
4 bedrs, 4 ➟/WC, 4 ➟/WC; P6
sB&B £21 dB&B £42 Breakfast only [10%V]

Lulworth *Acclaimed* 🔚
12 Midland Road, Gloucester GL1 4UF
01452-521881
8 bedrs, 3 ➟/WC, 2 ➟; ✖ P14
Breakfast only

Pembury *Acclaimed* 🔚
9 Pembury Road, St Barnabas, Gloucester GL2 6NA 01452-521856 Fax 01452-303418
11 bedrs, 5 ➟/WC, 1 ➟; TV tcf P10
sB&B £16 dB&B £30 Breakfast only [5%V]; cc Ac Vi

Rotherfield House *Highly Acclaimed* 🔚
5 Horton Road, Gloucester GL1 3PX
01452-410500 Fax 01452-381922
13 bedrs, 8 ➟/WC, 2 ➟; ✖ ✄
sB&B £29.50 dB&B £43.50; HB weekly £200-£230; D £9.25 [5%V]; cc Ac Amex DC Vi

Westville 🔚
255 Stroud Road, Gloucester GL1 5JZ
01452-301228

Large, red-brick guest house in a residential area less than 2 miles from the city centre.
6 bedrs, 2 ➟/WC, 2 ➟; ✖ P6
Breakfast only

HEREFORD Hereford & Worcester 7D4

Aylestone Court *Highly Acclaimed* 🔚
Aylestone Hill, Hereford HR1 1HS
01432-341891 Fax 01432-267691
10 bedrs, 10 ➟/WC; ✖ P25
Breakfast only [5%V]

Cedar 123 Whitecross Road, Whitecross, Hereford HR4 0LS 01432-267235

Hedley Lodge Belmont Abbey, Hereford HR2 9RZ 01432-277475

Hopbine 🔚
Roman Road, Hereford HR1 1LE .
01432-268722
15 bedrs, 15 ➟/WC, 2 ➟; TV tcf ✖ ✄
sB&B £20 dB&B £35 Breakfast only [10%V]

La Fosse Oxford Road, Hay on Wye,
Hereford HR3 5AJ 01497-820613
*A three storey, 18th century cottage, with a
rendered and stucco facade. Surrounded by
a walled floral garden.*
5 bedrs, 1 ⇋/WC, 4 ⋔/WC; TV tcf ⋔ P5
sB&B £16 Breakfast only; cc Vi

Webton Court Farmhouse Kingstone,
Hereford HR2 9NF 01981-250220   ⅏

*The hotel is a Georgian Farmhouse on a 220
acre working farm. Situated 7 miles west of
Hereford in the "Golden Valley".*
8 bedrs, 2 ⋔/WC, 8 ⇋; TV tcf ⋔ P12
sB&B £12; HB weekly £124-£52.50; D £7.50

Ye Olde Salutation Inn Market Pitch,
Weobley, Hereford HR4 8SJ 01544-318443
4 bedrs, 1 ⇋/WC, 3 ⋔/WC, 1 ⇋; ⋔ P20
sB&B £32 Breakfast only; cc Ac Amex DC Vi

KEYNSHAM Avon   3E1

Grasmere Court *Highly Acclaimed*   🏅
22 Bath Road, Keynsham BS18 1SN
0117-9862662 Fax 0117-9862762
17 bedrs, 17 ⇋/WC, 1 ⇋; ⅄ P18
sB&B £43 dB&B £46 Breakfast only [5%V]; cc
Ac Amex Vi

KIDDERMINSTER Hereford & Worcester 7E3

Cedars *Highly Acclaimed*   🏅
Mason Road, Kidderminster DY11 6AL
01562-515595 Fax 01562-753110   ⅏
20 bedrs, 20 ⇋/WC; ⋔ ⅄ P22
sB&B £49.80 Breakfast only [10%V]; cc Ac
Amex DC Vi

KINGTON Hereford & Worcester   7D3

★★**Burton** Mill Street, Kington HR5 3BQ   🏅
01544-230323

LEDBURY Hereford & Worcester   7E4

★★**(Inn) Royal Oak**   🏅
5 The Southend, Ledbury HR8 2EY
01531-632110 Fax 01531-634761
9 bedrs, 6 ⇋/WC, 1 ⇋; P16
Breakfast only; cc Ac Vi

LEOMINSTER Hereford & Worcester   7D3

Wharton Bank *Acclaimed*   🏅
Wharton Bank, Leominster HR6 0NX
01568-612575
4 bedrs, 1 ⇋/WC, 1 ⇋; P6
Child restrictions
Breakfast only

LUDLOW Shropshire   7D3

Brooklyn Marlbrook Hall, Elton, Ludlow SY8
2HR 01568-86230
3 bedrs, 1 ⇋; ⋔ P2

Cecil *Acclaimed*   🏅
Sheet Road, Ludlow SY8 1LR 01584-872442

(Inn) Church Inn *Acclaimed*   🏅
Church Street, Butterworth, Ludlow SY8 1AW
01584-872174
8 bedrs, 8 ⇋/WC; ⅄
sB&B £28 dB&B £40 Breakfast only; cc Ac Vi

MALVERN Hereford & Worcester   7E4

Red Gate *Highly Acclaimed*   🏅
32 Avenue Road, Malvern WR14 3BJ
01684-565013 Fax 01684-565013

*A small, friendly Victorian hotel. We are well
known for food and decor. All rooms are non-
smoking. Vegetarian meals available.*
7 bedrs, 3 ⇋/WC, 4 ⋔/WC; TV tcf P7
Child restrictions
sB&B £27-£32 dB&B £48-£52; HB weekly
£164; D £13 [5%V]; cc Ac Amex Vi

MALVERN, GREAT Hereford & Worcester 7E3

Sidney House *Acclaimed*
40 Worcester Road, Great Malvern WR14 4AA
01684-574994
8 bedrs, 5 [bath]/WC, 1 [bath]; [dog] P9
cc Ac Amex Vi

MALVERN WELLS Hereford & Worcester 7E4

Mellbreak
177 Wells Road, Malvern Wells WR14 4HE
01684-561287
4 bedrs, 1 [bath]; [dog] P4
Breakfast only

MARKET DRAYTON Shropshire 7E2

Mickley House Faulsgreen Terne Hill, Market Drayton TS9 3QW 01630-638505

MORETON-IN-MARSH Gloucestershire 7F4

Moreton House *Acclaimed*
High Street, Moreton-in-Marsh GL56 0LQ
01608-650747
A family owned and managed hotel.
12 bedrs, 1 [bath]/WC, 4 [shower]/WC, 3 [bath]; TV tcf [dog] P5
sB&B £20.50 dB&B £37-£47 [5%V]; cc Ac Vi

NAILSWORTH Gloucestershire 3F1

Apple Orchard House *Highly Acclaimed*
Orchard Close, Springhill, Nailsworth GL6 0LX 01453-832503 Fax 01453-836213 [wheelchair]
3 bedrs, 2 [bath]/WC, 1 [shower]/WC; TV tcf [dog] P3
sB&B £18-£24 dB&B £32 D £11 [10%V]; cc Ac Amex Vi

Blackberry Hill
Blackberry Hill, Rockness, Nailsworth GL6 0PJ 01453-833652
3 bedrs, 1 [bath]/WC; P12
Breakfast only

NEWENT Gloucestershire 7E4

New House Farm Aston Ingham Lane, Longhope, Newent GL17 0LS 0145-830484

NORTH NIBLEY Gloucestershire 3F1

Burrows Court Private *Highly Acclaimed*
Nibley Green, North Nibley GL11 6AZ
01453-546230
10 bedrs, 6 [bath]/WC, 4 [shower]/WC; TV tcf [no smoking] P20
sB&B £26.50-£28 dB&B £43; HB weekly £168-£175; D £11.50; cc Ac Amex Vi

OLD SODBURY Avon 3F1

Sodbury House *Highly Acclaimed* RAC
Badminton Road, Old Sodbury BS17 6LU
01454-312847 Fax 01454-273105
6 bedrs, 3 ➡/WC, 3 👢/WC; TV tcf 🐾 P30
sB&B £39.45 dB&B £55.70 Breakfast only
[10%V]; cc Ac Amex Vi

PAINSWICK Gloucestershire 7E4

Hambutts Mynd *Acclaimed* RAC
Edge Rd, Painswick GL6 6UP 01452-812352
3 bedrs, 1 ➡/WC, 1 ➡; 🐾 P4
Breakfast only; cc Vi

REDDITCH Hereford & Worcester 7E3

Hotel Campanile RAC
Far Moor Lane, Winyates Green, Redditch
B98 OSD 01527-510710 Fax 01527-517269 ♿
47 bedrs, 47 ➡/WC; TV tcf ⅍ P60
sB&B £29.50-£40 dB&B £38 D £9.85; cc Ac
Amex DC Vi

Mandeville RAC
101 Mount Pleasant, Redditch BN7 4JE
01527-544411

THE ARCHES

Small family run hotel set in ½ acre of lawns, ideally situated only ten minutes walk from town centre and with easy access to many interesting places in the beautiful Wye Valley.
All rooms are furnished and decorated to a high standard and have views of the lawned garden.
Tea/coffee making facilities are available in bedrooms, also colour television. Some rooms en-suite. Also one ground floor en-suite available.
There is a delightful Victorian style conservatory to relax in and the garden to enjoy in the summer months.
Licensed. Ample parking. A warm and friendly atmosphere with personal service.
Bed and breakfast, reduced weekly terms.
RAC Acclaimed Les Routiers

For Brochure and Reservations, please write or phone:
**Jean & James Jones, The Arches Country House,
Walford Road, Ross-on-Wye, Herefordshire HR9 5PT.**
Telephone: (01989) 563348.

ROSS-ON-WYE Hereford & Worcester 7E4

Arches Country House *Acclaimed* RAC
Walford Road, Ross-on-Wye HR9 7PT
01989-563348
7 bedrs, 4 ➡/WC, 2 ➡; TV tcf 🐾 ⅍ P10
dB&B £32; HB weekly £178; [5%V]; cc Ac Vi

Brookfield House RAC
Overross, Ross-on-Wye HR9 7AT
01989-562188
8 bedrs, 3 ➡/WC, 3 ➡; 🐾 P15
Child restrictions
sB&B £17-£19 dB&B £34-£40 Breakfast only;
cc Ac Amex Vi

Edde Cross House *Acclaimed* RAC
Edde Cross Street, Ross-on-Wye HR9 7BZ
01989-565088
4 bedrs, 2 ➡/WC, 2 👢/WC; TV tcf
Child restrictions
dB&B £42-£46 Breakfast only

Prospect Place Llangrove, Ross-on-Wye HR9
6ET 01989-770596 ♿

*Large, recently renovated, stone house and
cottages surrounding a pretty courtyard with
cider mill feature.*
6 bedrs, 4 👢/WC, 1 ➡; TV tcf P8
sB&B £14.50 Breakfast only

Radcliffe RAC
Wye Street, Ross-on-Wye HR9 7BS
01989-563024
6 bedrs, 1 ➡/WC, 2 ➡;
Breakfast only

Ryefield House *Acclaimed* RAC
Gloucester Road, Ross-on-Wye HR9 5NA
01989-563030
8 bedrs, 5 ➡/WC, 1 ➡; P10
Breakfast only

Sunnymount *Acclaimed* RAC
Ryefield Road, Ross-on-Wye HR9 5LU
01989-563880
9 bedrs, 2 ➔/WC, 5 ↑/WC, 1 ➔; tcf ✕ P7
sB&B £26-£29 dB&B £46-£50; HB weekly
£215-£250; [10%V]; cc Ac Amex Vi

The Skates Glewstone, Ross-on-Wye HR9
6AZ 01989-770456

Vaga House RAC
Wye Street, Ross-on-Wye HR9 7BS
01989-563024

*Vaga House is a late 18th century period
building with river views, licensed residences
lounge, delightful dining room, tea/coffee
making facilities and TV in all bedrooms.*
7 bedrs, 2 ➔; TV tcf ✈ ✕ P3
sB&B £18-£22 dB&B £32; HB weekly £180;
[10%V]

Ye Olde Ferrie Inne Symonds Yat West,
Ross-on-Wye HR9 6BL 01600-890232

ST BRIAVEL'S Gloucestershire 7E4

(Inn) The George Inn *Acclaimed* RAC
High Street, St Briavel's GL15 6TA
01594-530228
3 bedrs, 3 ➔/WC; P12
Child restrictions
sB&B £25 dB&B £45 [10%V]

STOW-ON-THE-WOLD Gloucestershire 4A1

Royalist Inn Digbeth St, Stow-on-the-Wold
GL54 1BN 01451-830670

The Limes RAC
Tewkesbury Road, Stow-on-the-Wold GL54
1EN 01451-830034
3 bedrs, 2 ➔/WC, 2 ➔; P4
Breakfast only

STROUD Gloucestershire 7E4

Downfield *Acclaimed* RAC
134 Cainscross Road, Stroud GL5 4HN
01453-764496 Fax 01453-753150

*An imposing Georgian house in a quiet
location offering a comfortable atmosphere.*
21 bedrs, 15 ➔/WC, 6 ↑/WC, 3 ➔;
TV tcf ✈ P21
sB&B £29 dB&B £35 D £7.50; cc Ac Vi

(Inn) Rose & Crown   RAC
Nympsfield, Stonehouse, Stroud GL10 3TU
01453-860240

Characteristic 300 year old Cotswold stone Inn situated in a peaceful village near the Cotswold edge, within easy reach of the M4 & M5.
4 bedrs, 2 ➥/WC, 1 ☞/WC, 1 ➥; TV tcf P30
sB&B £28-£48 dB&B £48 D £8.65 [10%V]; cc Ac Amex Vi

SYMONDS YAT Hereford & Worcester   7E4

Cedars Llangrove Road, Whitchurch, Symonds Yat HR9 6DQ 01600-890351
7 bedrs, 3 ☞/WC, 1 ➥; TV tcf P7
sB&B £16; HB weekly £192.50-£217; D £11.50

Garth Cottage *Acclaimed*   RAC
Symonds Yat HR9 6JL 01600-89036
4 bedrs, 4 ➥/WC, 1 ➥; P9
Child restrictions
dB&B £44; HB weekly £251.50;

(Inn) Saracens Head *Highly Acclaimed*   RAC
Symonds Yat HR9 6JL 01600-890435 Fax 01600-890034
10 bedrs, 7 ➥/WC, 1 ➥; tcf ✕ P30
sB&B £23-£28 dB&B £50; HB weekly £170; D £15 [10%V]; cc Ac Amex DC Vi

Woodlea *Acclaimed*   RAC
Symonds Yat HR9 6BL 01600-890206
9 bedrs, 1 ➥/WC, 5 ☞/WC, 2 ➥; tcf ✗ P9
sB&B £22 dB&B £44; HB weekly £210; D £13.25 [10%V]; cc Ac Vi

TAVERN HOUSE

**Willesley,
Nr.Tetbury Gloucs
GL8 9QU
Tel: (01666) 880444
Fax: (01666) 880444**

Delightfully situated 17th century former coaching inn, only 1 mile from Westonbirt Arboretum. Superb luxury bed & breakfast. All rooms with private bath and shower en-suite. D D phone. TV. Tea maker, hairdryer etc. Charming secluded walled garden. Convenient for visiting Bath, Bristol, Gloucester and Cheltenham. An excellent base from which to explore the Cotswolds. A combination of the standards of an excellent hotel with the warmth of a country house.
**RAC Highly Commended. ETB 2 Crown De Luxe Award
English Tourist Board Silver Award - Bed And Breakfast Of The Year - 1993.**

TETBURY Gloucestershire   4A2

Tavern House *Highly Acclaimed*   RAC
Willesley, Tetbury GL8 8QU 01666-880444

A 17th century, Cotswold stone, grade II listed, former staging post, with leaded windows. Charming secluded walled gardens.
4 bedrs, 4 ⇥/WC; TV tcf ⊁ P6
Child restrictions
sB&B £45-£47.50 dB&B £53-£63 Breakfast only; cc Ac Vi

TIMSBURY Avon   3E1

Old Malt House   RAC
Radstock, Timsbury BA3 1QF 01761-470106
Fax 01761-472616
10 bedrs, 10 ⇥/WC;
Breakfast only [10%V]; cc Ac Amex DC Vi

VOWCHURCH Hereford & Worcester   7D4

Croft House Country G/h   RAC
Vowchurch, Hereford HR2 0QE 01981-55022
8 bedrs, 8 ⇥/WC; P15
Child restrictions
Breakfast only; cc Ac Vi

WEM Shropshire   7D2

Lowe Hall Farm Wem SY4 5UE
01939-232236
3 bedrs, 1 ⇥/WC, 1 ⬧/WC, 1 ⇥; TV tcf P10
sB&B £16; HB weekly £161-£168; D £8

WEOBLEY Hereford & Worcester   7D3

Unicorn House High St, Weobley HR4 8SL
01544-318230

WESTON-SUPER-MARE Avon   3E1

Ashcombe Court *Highly Acclaimed*   RAC
17 Milton Road, Weston-Super-Mare BS23 2SJ
01934-625104
6 bedrs, 1 ⇥/WC, 5 ⬧/WC; TV tcf P6
HB weekly £145.50-£155.50; cc Amex

Baymead   RAC
19-23 Longton Grove Road, Weston-Super-
Mare BS23 1LS 01934-622951
32 bedrs, 9 ⇥/WC, 17 ⬧/WC, 2 ⇥; TV tcf ✕
P6
sB&B £18-£22.50 dB&B £35-£40; HB weekly
£140-£185; D £6.50

Blakeney 52 Locking Road, Weston-Super-
Mare BS23 3DN 01934-624772

Braeside *Highly Acclaimed*   RAC
**2 Victoria Park, Weston-Super-Mare BS23
2HZ 01934-626642**

A delightful, family run hotel close to the sea front. All bedrooms ensuite with colour TV and tea/coffee making facilities.
9 bedrs, 2 ⇥/WC, 7 ⬧/WC; TV tcf
sB&B £22.50 dB&B £45; HB weekly £186; D
£9.50

L'arrivee *Acclaimed*   RAC
75 Locking Road, Weston-Super-Mare BS23
3DW 01934-625328   ♿
12 bedrs, 2 ⇥/WC, 7 ⬧/WC, 1 ⇥; TV tcf ✕
P12
sB&B £15-£16 dB&B £37-£40; HB weekly
£182.50-£192.50; [10%V]; cc Ac Amex DC Vi

Milton Lodge *Highly Acclaimed* 🏵
15 Milton Road, Weston-Super-Mare BS23 2SH
01934-623161
6 bedrs, 3 ➡/WC, 3 🐾/WC; TV tcf ✂ P6
Child restrictions
sB&B £20 dB&B £34; HB weekly £140-£150;
[5%V]

Norton Court Farm Lower Norton Lane,
Keystoke, Weston-Super-Mare BS22 9YR
01934-417874

Sandringham 🏵
1 Victoria Square, Weston-Super-Mare BS23
1LS 01934-624891

Saxonia *Acclaimed* 🏵
95 Locking Road, Weston-Super-Mare BS23
3EW 01934-633856 ♿
9 bedrs, 2 ➡/WC, 7 🐾/WC; TV tcf ✂ P4
sB&B £18-£23 dB&B £30-£37 Breakfast only
[10%V]; cc Ac Amex DC Vi

The Weston Rose 2 Osborne Road, Weston-
Super-Mare BS23 3EL 01934-412690

Vaynor 🏵
346 Locking Road, Weston-Super-Mare
BS22 8PD 01934-632332

Wychwood *Highly Acclaimed* 🏵
148 Milton Road, Weston-Super-Mare BS23
2UZ 01934-627793

WORCESTER Hereford & Worcester   7E3

Hill Farm Wynniatts Way, Abberley,
Worcester WR6 6BZ 01299-896415

Loch Ryan *Highly Acclaimed* 🏵
119 Sidbury, Worcester WR5 2DH
01905-351143 ; cc Ac Amex DC Vi

Wyatt 40 Barbourne Road, Worcester WR1
1HU 01905-26311 ♿
8 bedrs, 5 🐾/WC, 1 ➡; 🗡 P10
sB&B £16 Breakfast only

North East

Yorkshire • Humberside • Cleveland • Tyne & Wear • Northumberland

Pele towers, castles and Hadrian's Wall remind us that border counties retain the excitement of past turbulence. Drama lingers too on the wild moors of Brontë country softened by Yorkshire's incomparable Dales. Some of Britain's loveliest abbey ruins are here and two National Parks. A bracing coast invigorates the robust. Those less intrepid might do well to take the Settle to Carlisle train through mind-blowing landscapes. Visit York with its Viking heritage; the solid Victorian centre of Leeds, built with the brass of industry and now excellently preserved and put to modern use. And Newcastle, with its six bridges over the Tyne, where commerce combines successfully with culture.

A SELECTION OF ATTRACTIONS:

Unless otherwise stated, all can be visited between April and October – some longer. Telephone for days/times of opening.

Allerton Park, nr. Knaresborough, N. Yorks: *Astounding Gothic building. Private collections. Closes end Sept.* Tel: 01423-330927.

Alnwick Castle, Northumberland: *Rugged border castle conceals palatial interior. Home of Percys since 1309.* Tel: 01665-510777.

Amble Quayside Market, Bedlington, Northumberland: *Cruises to Croquet Light-house, marina, market.* Tel: 01670-825895.

Beningbrough Hall, nr. York: *Fine Georgian house & garden with wilderness play area. NT.* Tel: 01904-470666.

Burton Agnes Hall, nr. Bridlington, Humberside: *Magnificent Elizabethan family home. Impressionist paintings. Garden with maze, jungle & 'giant games'* Tel: 01262-490324.

Castle Howard, nr. York: *Designed by Vanbrugh. Vast treasure-house. Equally grand gardens. A must!* Tel: 01653-648333.

Corbridge Roman Site, Northumberland: *Substantial remains of excavated settlement plus museum.* Tel: 01434-632349.

Duncombe Park, Helmsley, N. Yorks: *Restored to domesticity. 18th-c house, garden, playground, walks.* Tel: 01439-70213.

Eden Camp, Malton, N. Yorks: *Civilian life during World War II. 27 huts of varying experience.* Tel: 01653-697777.

Elsham Hall Wildlife Park, Brigg, Humberside: *Lake, miniature zoo, falcony centre, animal farm, plus.* Tel: 01652-688698.

Flamingo Land, *Family Fun Park on A169 Malton/Pickering road.* Tel: 01653-668585.

'Furever Feline', Windhill Manor, Shipley, W. Yorks: *New three dimensional animation of humanised cats!.* Tel: 01274-592955.

Fountains Abbey & Studley Royal, Ripon. *Famous monastry ruins, a Jacobean mansion and rare Green Water Garden. NT.* Tel: 01765-608888.

Fountains Abbey

Harewood House & Bird Garden, nr. Harrogate, W. Yorks: *Vast private 18th-c home has everything. Events too.* Tel: 0113 2886225.

Harlow Carr Museum of Gardening, Harrogate, N. Yorks: *Small part of famous gardens of N. Horticultural Society.* Tel: 01423-565418.

Richmond

Hexham Herbs, Chollerford, Northumberland: *900 varieties of herbs, old roses, and a Roman garden.* Tel: 01434-681483.

Housesteads Roman Fort, nr. Hexham, Northumberland: *Well defined remains of 5 acre fort on Hadrian's Wall.* Tel: 01434-344363.

Jorvic Viking Centre, York: *A market, houses & wharf re-created on uncovered 10th-c Viking city.* Tel: 01904-643211.

Lightwater Valley Theme Park, North Stainley, Ripon, N. Yorks: *Action, thrills, family adventure.* Tel: 01-765 635368.

Lindisfarne Priory, Holy Island, nr. Berwick-on-Tweed, Northumberland: *Famous ruins of 11th-c Benedictine church. Access by causeway at low tide!* Tel: 0128989-200.

Millennium, Scarborough, Yorks: *State of the Art epic adventure in time.* Tel: 01723-501000.

Nostell Priory, Wakefield, W. Yorks: *State rooms of superb Chippendale made for the house. NT.* Tel: 01924-863892.

The Old Rectory, Epworth, Humberside: *Childhood home of John & Charles Wesley.* Tel: 01427-872268.

Preston Hall Museum, Stockton-on-Tees, Cleveland: *Walk the Stockton-Darlington track. Re-created Victorian High Street. Gardens, play & picnic areas.* Tel: 01642-781184.

Rievaulx Abbey & Terrace, nr. Helmsley. N. Yorks: *Outstandingly fine ruins seen well from the Terrace.* Tel: 014396-228 & 340.

Richmond Georgian Theatre, N. Yorks: *Live shows evenings but daytime tours of our oldest original theatre.* Tel: 01748-823710.

Ripley Castle & Gardens, Ripley, N. Yorks. *Family home for 650 years.* Tel: 01423-770152.

St. Mary's Lighthouse, St. Mary's Island, Whitley Bay, T & W: *Views from top of lighthouse. Nature reserve.* Tel: 0191-2520853.

Sewerby Hall, Bridlington, Humberside: *Overlooks Bridlington Bay. Small zoo & aviary in 50 acre garden. Open all year.*

Shibden Hall, Halifax, W. Yorks: *Half-timbered house, mainly 15th-c. Craft workshops, agricultural implements.* Tel: 01422-348440.

Tynemouth Sea Life Centre, T & W: *Underwater tunnel provides close encounters with sharks, stingrays etc.* Tel: 0191-257 6100.

Wensleydale Cheese Visitor Centre, nr. Hawes, N. Yorks: *Viewing gallery – see/taste hand made local cheese. Farm animals, play area.* Tel: 01969-667664.

Worsborough Mill Museum, nr. Barnsley, S. Yorks: *17th & 19th-c corn mills at work in 200 acre country park with an open farm.* Tel: 01266-774527.

York Castle Museum: *Entire streets re-created in Victorian mode. Great fun.* Tel: 01904-653611.

Yorkshire Mining Museum, nr. Wakefield: *Pit ponies and a genuine miner to guide you 450 ft. below!* Tel: 01924-848806.

SOME ANNUAL EVENTS

Alnwick Fair, Northumberland: *Re-enactment of medieval fair. Courts, duckings, processions. 25June – 1July.*
Tel: 01665-605004.

Centenary of Cinema Festival, Nat. Museum of Photography, Bradford, Yorks: *Jun-Dec. '95.*

Durham County Show, Chester-le-Street: *Agricultural show with dog/flower shows, trade stands. 15-16 July.* Tel: 0191-388 5459.

Durham Regatta: *50 competitive events for all on River Wear. 10-11 June.*
Tel: 0191-386 8752.

Filey Edwardian Festival, N. Yorks: *Has everything from treasure hunt to talent contest. Great fun. 24 Jun – 2 July.*

Great Yorkshire Show, nr. Harrogate, N. Yorks: *11 – 13 July.* Tel: 01423-561536.

Harrogate Spring Flower Show, Yorks. *20 – 23 Apl.* Tel: 01423-561049.

Morpeth Northumbrian Gathering, Northumberland: *Festival of traditional Northumbrian music, crafts & dialect. 21 – 23 Apl.* Tel: 01670-513308.

Newcastle Hoppings, T & W: *Largest travelling fair in Britain. 16 – 24 June.*
Tel: 0191-261 0691.

North Shields Fishquay Festival, T & W: *Stalls, live entertainment for adults/children, fireworks. 28 – 29 May.* Tel: 0191-266 7421.

Ovingham Goose Fair, Northumberland: *Village green fair – Northumbrian pipes, morris dancing etc. 17 June.*
Tel: 01661-832711.

Saltburn Victorian Festival, Cleveland: *Period street theatre, music hall. Wear Victorian gear! 6 – 13 Aug.* Tel: 01642-231212.

Stockton Riverside Int'l. Festival, Cleveland: *Street theatre & world music event: 3 – 6 Aug.* Tel: 01642-670067.

Sunderland Air Show, T & W: *Biggest in the North of England. 5 – 6 Aug [provisional]*
Tel: 0191-510 9317.

Thomas the Tank Engine at Embsay Station N. Yorks:. *Themed steam rides, various weekends.* Tel: 01756-794727.

Durham Cathedral

ALNMOUTH Northumberland   13F3

Marine House *Highly Acclaimed*   RAC
1 Marine Road, Alnmouth NE66 2RW
01665-830349
10 bedrs, 4 ➤/WC, 6 ☞/WC, 1 ➤; TV tcf ✖ ✄
sB&B £46-£52; HB weekly £230-£250;
cc Ac Vi

ALNWICK Northumberland   13F3

Bondgate House *Acclaimed*   RAC
20 Bondgate Without, Alnwick NE66 1PN
01665-602025 Fax 01665-602554
8 bedrs, 5 ☞/WC, 1 ➤; TV tcf ✄
sB&B £20-£30 dB&B £33-£36; HB weekly
£231-£252; D £11 [10%V]; cc Ac Vi

AMPLEFORTH North Yorkshire   11D2

Carr House Farm Ampleforth YO6 4ED
01347-868526
3 bedrs;
Child restrictions under 7
Breakfast only

BAINBRIDGE North Yorkshire   10C2

Riverdale House *Highly Acclaimed*   RAC
Bainbridge DL8 3EW 01969-650311
12 bedrs, 11 ➤/WC, 4 ➤; P4
dB&B £53 D £15 [5%V]

BARNARD CASTLE Durham   10C2

**East Mellwaters Farm Bowes, Barnard
Castle DL12 9RH 01833-628269**

*Stone-built, Dales farmhouse in beautiful
surroundings near the River Greta. Oak
beams, open fire and good home cooking.
Comfortable en-suite rooms with tv. Situated
five miles from Barnard Castle.*
5 bedrs, 2 ➤/WC, 3 ☞/WC, 1 ➤; ✖ P20
Breakfast only; cc Ac Vi

West Roods Farm   RAC
Boldron, Barnard Castle DL12 9SW
01833-690116
3 bedrs, 2 ☞/WC, 1 ➤; P6
sB&B £16 dB&B £32; HB weekly £100;
cc Ac Amex

BARNSLEY South Yorkshire   8B1

Park View 2 Beech Grove, Kingstone,
Barnsley S70 6NG 01226-297268

BATLEY West Yorkshire   11D4

Lymans 470 Bradford Road, Batley WF17
5LW 01924-477911

BEDALE North Yorkshire   11D2

Elmfield Country House *Highly Acclaimed*   RAC
Arrathorne, Bedale DL8 1NE 01677-450558
Fax 01677-450557   ⅋

*Country house, situated in a lovely garden
and grounds with ponds of Koi Carp.*
9 bedrs, 4 ➤/WC, 5 ☞/WC; TV tcf ✄ P14
sB&B £27-£29.50 dB&B £39-£44; HB weekly
£210-£227; [5%V]; cc Vi

The Old Vicarage Crakehall, Bedale DL8
1HE 01677-422967

BELFORD Northumberland   13F3

Purdy Lodge   RAC
Adderstone Services, Belford NE70 7JU
01668-213000 Fax 01668-213111   ⅋
20 bedrs, 20 ➤/WC, 20 ☞/WC; TV tcf ✖ P40
sB&B £36-£40.95 D £10 [10%V];
cc Ac Amex Vi

BELLINGHAM Northumberland 13E3

Lyndale *Acclaimed* 🏚️RAC
Bellingham NE48 2AW 01434-220361

Guest house in an attractive bungalow with panoramic views. Follow signs for Bellingham from A68, A69 or B6318 Hadrian's Wall road.

BERWICK-UPON-TWEED Northumberland 13F2

Harvone *Acclaimed* 🏚️RAC
18, Main Street, Spittall, Berwick-upon-Ttweed TD15 1QY 01289-302580 ♿
3 bedrs, 3 ➥/WC; TV tcf ⊁
Child restrictions
dB&B £40-£48; HB weekly £200-£230; [5%V]

The Old School Paxton, Berwick-upon-Tweed TD15 1TE 01289-386449

BEVERLEY Humberside 11E3

Eastgate 🏚️RAC
7 Eastgate, Beverley HU17 0DR
01482-3868464 Fax 01482-3871899
Family run Victorian Town House between the Minster and the pedestrianised town centre.
18 bedrs, 7 ☜/WC, 3 ➥; 🐾 ⊁
sB&B £15-£19.50 dB&B £26-£32 Breakfast only [10%V]

The Manor House *Highly Acclaimed* 🏚️RAC
Northlands, Walkington, Beverley HU17 8RT
01482-3881645 Fax 01482-3866501
6 bedrs, 6 ➥/WC; TV tcf
Child restrictions
sB&B £65-£71.50 dB&B £93 D £15 [10%V]; cc
Ac Amex DC Vi JCB

BINGLEY West Yorkshire 10C3

Hallbank *Highly Acclaimed* 🏚️RAC
Beck Lane, Bingley BD16 4DD 01274-565296

9 bedrs, 4 ➥/WC, 5 ☜/WC; TV tcf ⊁
Child restrictions
sB&B £40 dB&B £40; HB weekly £250; D £10 [10%V]; cc Amex

March Cote Farm Cottingley, Bingley BD16
1UB 01274-487433 Fax 01274-488153
3 bedrs, 1 ➥;
sB&B £16; HB weekly £161-£189; D £7-£9

BIRTLEY Durham 13F4

Granada 🏚️RAC
Portobello, Birtley DH3 2ST 0191-4100076

BISHOP AUCKLAND Durham 10C1

Greenhead Country House *Highly Acclaimed* 🏚️RAC
Fir Tree, Bishop Auckland DL15 8BL
01388-763143
7 bedrs, 6 ➥/WC, 1 ☜/WC, 1 ➥; TV tcf P12
Child restrictions
sB&B £35 dB&B £45 Breakfast only; cc Ac Vi

BRADFORD West Yorkshire 10C3

New Beehive Inn Wesgate, Bradford BD1
3AA 01274-543586

Park Grove *Acclaimed* 🏚️RAC
28, Park Grove, Frizinghall, Bradford BD9 4JY
01274-543444 Fax 01274-495619 ; cc Ac Amex Vi

Westleigh 30 Eastbey Road, Bradford BD7
1QX 01274-727089

BRAMHOPE West Yorkshire 11D3

The Cottages Moor Road, Bramhope LS16
9HH 0113-2842754

BRETTON West Yorkshire

Granada Lodge 🏚️RAC
Woolley Edge S/a (M1), Btw Junc 38/39,
Bramley Lane, Bretton WF4 4LQ
01924-830569

BRIDLINGTON Humberside 11F3

Bay Ridge *Acclaimed* 🏚️RAC
Summerfield Road, Bridlington YO15 3LF
01262-673425
14 bedrs, 6 ➥/WC, 6 ☜/WC, 1 ➥; TV tcf 🐾 ⊁ P8
sB&B £19-£19.50 dB&B £38-£39; HB weekly
£148-£153; D £5.95 [10%V]; cc Ac Vi

Glen Alan 21 Flamborough Road, Bridlington YO15 2HU 01262-674650

Glencoe　　　　　　　　　　　　RAC
43-45 Marshall Avenue, Bridlington YO15 2DT 01262-676818

Heatherlands 50 South Marine Drive, Bridlington YO15 3JJ 01262-400495

Mon Fort 1 Tennyson Avenue, Bridlington YO15 2EU 01262-675984

Oaklea 26 Marshall Avenue, Bridlington YO15 2DS 01262-675186

Park View　　　　　　　　　　　RAC
9-11 Tennyson Avenue, Bridlington YO15 2EH 01262-672140

South Bay 11 Roudhay Road, Bridlington YO15 3LA 01262-674944

Spinnaker House 19 Pembroke Terrace, Bridlington YO15 3BX 01262-678440

BURNT YATES North Yorkshire　　　4D3

★★(Inn) Bay Horse　　　　　　RAC
Burnt Yates HG3 3EJ 01423-770230　　ċ
6 bedrs, 6 ➍/WC; P70
Breakfast only [10%V]; cc Ac Vi

CARLTON-IN-COVERDALE
North Yorkshire　　　　　　　　　10C2

Foresters Arms *Acclaimed*　　　RAC
Carlton-in-Coverdale DL8 2BB 01969-40272
3 bedrs, 1 ➍/WC, 2 ➐/WC; TV tcf ✖ ✂ P10
sB&B £30 dB&B £55 D £12.50; cc Ac Vi

CLEETHORPES Humberside

Mallow View　　　　　　　　　　RAC
9/11 Albert Road, Cleethorpes DN35 8LX
01472-691297
20 bedrs, 3 ➍/WC, 3 ➍;
Breakfast only

St Ives 22 Isaacs Hill, Cleethorpes DN35 8JS
01472-691852

CORBRIDGE ON TYNE Northumberland 10C1

Morningside　　　　　　　　　　RAC
Main Road, Riding Mill, Corbridge On Tyne
NE44 6HL 01434-682350

5 bedrs, 1 ➍/WC, 1 ➍;
sB&B £16-£18 dB&B £30 Breakfast only [5%V]

Tynedale *Acclaimed*　　　　　　RAC
Market Place, Corbridge On Tyne NE45 5AW
01434-632149
7 bedrs, 7 ➍/WC;
Child restrictions
Breakfast only

DONCASTER South Yorkshire　　　8B1

Almel *Acclaimed*　　　　　　　RAC
20/24 Christchurch Road, Doncaster DN1 2QL
01302-365230 Fax 01302-341434
30 bedrs, 14 ➍/WC, 3 ➍; TV tcf ✖ P8
Breakfast only; cc Ac Amex DC Vi

Formule 1　　　　　　　　　　RAC
Ten Pound Walk, Doncaster DN4 5HX
01302-761050

The Towhouse 27 Bennetthorpe, Doncaster
DN2 6AA 01302-349753

DRIFFIELD, GREAT Humberside　　11E3

Kings Mill House Kings Mill, Driffield, Great
YO25 7TT 01377-253204

EASINGWOLD North Yorkshire　　11D3

Tudor House 4 Uppleby, Easingwold YO6
3BB 01347-821912　　　　　　　　ċ

Period cottage situated in the picturesque town of Easingwold, with its cobbled, market square.
3 bedrs, 1 ➐/WC, 1 ➍; TV tcf P3
sB&B £12.50 Breakfast only

Symbols
For an explanation of the symbols used in hotel entries, please see inside the front cover.

EBBERSTON North Yorkshire   11E2

Foxholm *Acclaimed*   RAC
Ebberston YO13 9NJ 01723-859550
7 bedrs, 2 ⇨/WC, 5 ☞/WC, 2 ⇨;
TV tcf ✗ P24
sB&B £25.50-£30.50 dB&B £47-£53 D £7.75

FERRYBRIDGE West Yorkshire   11D4

Granada Lodge   RAC
Junc A1/M62, Ferrybridge NF11 OAF
0800-555300

FILEY North Yorkshire   11E2

Seafield 9-11 Rutland Street, Filey YO14 9JA
01723-513715

GOATHLAND North Yorkshire   11E2

Heatherdene *Acclaimed*   RAC
Goathland YO22 5AN 01947-86334   ♿
8 bedrs, 3 ⇨/WC, 4 ☞/WC, 1 ⇨; TV tcf ✗ P10
sB&B £28 dB&B £56 D £10

GOOLE Humberside   11E4

Norden Alpine Nursery Hirst Road, Carlton,
Goole DN14 9PX 01405-861348

GUISBOROUGH Cleveland   11D2

★★(Inn) Fox & Hounds   RAC
Slapewith, Guisborough TS14 6PX
01287-632964 Fax 01287-610778
15 bedrs, 15 ⇨/WC; ✗ P50
Breakfast only [10%V]; cc Ac Amex DC Vi

HALIFAX West Yorkshire   10C4

★★Jenny Dee's Motel   RAC
Salterhebble Hill, Huddersfield, Halifax HX3
0QT 01422-347700
31 bedrs, 31 ⇨/WC;

The Fleece Inn *Acclaimed*   RAC
Elland Road, Bankisland, Halifax HX4 0DJ
01422-822598 Fax 01422-824460
4 bedrs, 4 ⇨/WC; P60

Victoria 33-35 Horton Street, Halifax HX1
1QE 01422-351209

Ye Olde Golden Country House Hotel
Ogden, Halifax HX2 8YB 01422-244941

HARROGATE North Yorkshire   11D3

Abbey Lodge *Acclaimed*   RAC
31 Ripon Road, Harrogate HG1 2JL
01423-569712 Fax 01423-530570
19 bedrs, 5 ⇨/WC, 9 ☞/WC, 2 ⇨; TV tcf ✗
sB&B £26.50-£39.75 dB&B £47.50-£59 D
£13.25 [10%V]; cc Ac Amex Vi

Alexa House *Acclaimed*   RAC
26 Ripon Road, Harrogate HG2 2JJ
01423-501988 Fax 01423-504086   ♿
13 bedrs, 3 ⇨/WC, 10 ☞/WC; TV tcf ✗ P10
sB&B £30-£35 dB&B £50-£55; HB weekly
£220-£240; [5%V]; cc Ac DC Vi

Alexandra Court 8 Alexandra Road,
Harrogate HG1 5JS 01423-502764

Anro   RAC
90 Kings Road, Harrogate HG1 5JX
01423-503087

*An Edwardian House set in a tree-lined road
near the town centre and rail and bus
stations. 2 minutes from the Conference
Centre.*
7 bedrs, 3 ☞/WC, 1 ⇨; TV tcf
Child restrictions
sB&B £18 dB&B £38 Breakfast only [5%V]

Arden House *Acclaimed*   RAC
69/71 Franklin Road, Harrogate HG1 5EH
01423-509224
14 bedrs, 14 ⇨/WC; ✗
[10%V]; cc Ac Vi

Ashley House *Acclaimed*   RAC
36-40 Franklin Road, Harrogate HG1 5EE
01423-507474 Fax 01423-560858
16 bedrs, 3 ⇨/WC, 10 ☞/WC, 2 ⇨;
TV tcf ✗ ✄ P4
sB&B £27.50-£30 dB&B £50-£54; HB weekly
£250-£270; [10%V]; cc Ac Amex Vi

Brimham Silverdale Close, Darley, Harrogate HG3 2PQ 01423-780948

Cavendish *Acclaimed*   RAC
3 Valley Drive, Harrogate HG2 0JJ
01423-509637 Fax 01423-504429

Delaine *Acclaimed*   RAC
17 Ripon Road, Harrogate HG1 2JL
01423-567974 Fax 01423-561723
8 bedrs, 8 ➡/WC, 1 ➡; TV tcf ✂ P12
sB&B £30-£35 dB&B £50 Breakfast only; cc
Ac Amex Vi

Gillmore   RAC
98 King's Road, Harrogate HG1 5HH
01423-503699 Fax 01423-503699
Small, family-run hotel, recently extended.
Located close to the Conference Centre.
22 bedrs, 6 ➡/WC, 6 ➡; ✖ P10
sB&B £20 dB&B £36; [5%V]

Glenayr *Acclaimed*   RAC
19 Franklin Mount, Harrogate HG1 5EJ
01423-504259
6 bedrs, 5 ☚/WC, 1 ➡; TV tcf P4
sB&B £18-£19 dB&B £40-£45 Breakfast only
[5%V]; cc Ac Amex Vi

Hadleigh 33 Ripon Rd, Harrogate HG1 2JL
01423-522994

Lamont House 12 St Mary's Walk, Harrogate
HG2 0LW 01423-567143

Mrs Murray's *Acclaimed*   RAC
67 Franklin Road, Harrogate HG1 5EH
01423-505857
10 bedrs, 5 ➡/WC; ✖ P5
Breakfast only [10%V]; cc Ac Vi

Number Twenty-Six 26 Harlow Moor Drive,
Harrogate HE2 0JY 01423-524729

Oaklands 75 Valley Drive, Harrogate HG2
0JP 01423-562696

Parnas 98 Franklin Road, Harrogate HG1
5EN 01423-564493

Princes 7 Granby Rd, Harrogate HG1 4ST
01423-883469

Rosedale *Acclaimed*   RAC
86 Kings Road, Harrogate HG1 5JX
01423-566630
8 bedrs, 1 ➡/WC, 6 ☚/WC; TV tcf P8
Child restrictions
sB&B £25-£28.50 dB&B £45-£47; HB weekly
£192.50;

Rosegarth 44 Ripon Road, Killinghall,
Harrogate HG3 2DF 01423-506469

Ruskin *Highly Acclaimed*   RAC
1 Swan Road, Harrogate HG1 2SS
01423-502045 Fax 01423-506131
6 bedrs, 6 ➡/WC; TV tcf P9
Child restrictions
sB&B £38 dB&B £48-£54 D £14.95 [5%V]; cc
Ac DC Vi

★Scotia House   RAC
66 Kings Road, Harrogate HG1 5JR
01423-504361 Fax 01423-526578
14 bedrs, 1 ➡/WC, 10 ☚/WC, 2 ➡;
TV tcf ✖ ✂ P7
Child restrictions
sB&B £27 dB&B £52; HB weekly £230; D £11
[5%V]; cc Ac Vi

Shannon Court *Highly Acclaimed*   RAC
65 Dragon Avenue, Harrogate HG1 5DS
01423-509858 Fax 01423-530606
8 bedrs, 1 ➡/WC, 7 ☚/WC; TV tcf
sB&B £17-£27.50 dB&B £34-£55; HB weekly
£185.50-£199.50; [10%V]

Talbot High Street, Pateley Bridge, Harrogate
HG3 5AL 01423-711597

The Richmond 56 Dragon View, Skipton
Road, Harrogate HG1 4DG 01423-530612
6 bedrs, 6 ☚/WC; P5
sB&B £20 Breakfast only

Treetops 24 Falmount Lane, Bringham,
Darley, Harrogate HG3 2PQ 01423-70948

Wharfedale House *Acclaimed* RAC
28 Harlow Moor Drive, Harrogate HG2 0JY
01423-522233
8 bedrs, 8 ⇔/WC; ✗ P3
Breakfast only [10%V]

Youngs 15 York Road, off Duchy Road,
Harrogate HG1 2QL 01423-567336 Fax
01423-500042

HARTLEPOOL Cleveland   11D1

Durham House 38 The Front, Seaton Carew,
Hartlepool TS25 1DA 01429-236502

York 185-187 York Road, Hartlepool TS26
9EE 01429-867373

HAWES North Yorkshire   10C4

Brandymires Muker Road, Hawes DL8 9PR
01969-667482

Cocketts Hotel & Restaurant Market Place,
Hawes DL8 3RD 01969-667312

HAWORTH West Yorkshire   10C3

Ferncliffe *Acclaimed* RAC
Hebden Road, Keighley, Haworth BD22 8RS
01535-643405
6 bedrs, 6 ⬧/WC; TV tcf ✗ ⊁ P12
Child restrictions
sB&B £19.50-£22 dB&B £39; HB weekly £203;
D £9.75; cc Ac Vi

Moorfield 80 West La, Haworth BD22 8EN
01535-643689

Woodlands Grange RAC
Belle Isle, Haworth BD22 8AH 01535-646814
5 bedrs, 5 ⇔/WC; P10
Breakfast only

HEXHAM Northumberland   13E4

Westbrooke RAC
Allendale Road, Hexham NE46 2DE
01434-603818
11 bedrs, 3 ⇔/WC, 2 ⇔;
Breakfast only

HOLMFIRTH West Yorkshire   10C4

White Horse Inn RAC
Jackson Bridge, Holmfirth HD7 7HF
01484-683940   ♿
*A typical Yorkshire village pub which featured
in "The Last of the Summer Wine".*
5 bedrs, 1 ⇔/WC, 4 ⬧/WC, 2 ⇔; TV tcf P12
sB&B £24 dB&B £36 D £5.70

HORNSEA Humberside   11F3

Merlstead
59 Eastgate, Hornsea HU18 1NB
01964-533068 Fax 01964-536975

*Large, detached hotel offering spacious and
comfortable accommodation.*
6 bedrs, 6 ⇔/WC; ✗ P4
sB&B £25-£33 dB&B £45-£50; HB weekly
£175-£290; D £12.50; cc Ac Vi

Seaforth Esplanade, Hornsea HU18 1NQ
01964-532616

Location Maps
Hotel locations are shown on the maps at
the back of the guide. All towns and
villages containing an hotel listed in the
guide are shown in black.

HORTON-IN-RIBBLESDALE
North Yorkshire   10C3

(Inn) Crown   RAC
Settle, Horton-in-Ribblesdale BD24 0HF
01729-860209 Fax 01729-860209
9 bedrs, 2 ♠/WC, 2 ➡; tcf ✗ P20
sB&B £16.70 dB&B £33.40-£37.60; HB weekly
£111.50; D £8.50

HULL Humberside   11E4

Earlsmere *Acclaimed*   RAC
76-78 Sunnybank, Off Spring Bank West, Hull
HU3 1LQ 01482-341977 Fax 01482-347371
15 bedrs, 7 ♠/WC, 2 ➡; TV tcf
sB&B £15-£18.80 dB&B £35.25-£41.12; HB
weekly £190-£210; D £10 [10%V]; cc Ac Vi

HUTTON-LE-HOLE North Yorkshire   11E2

Hammer & Hand *Acclaimed*   RAC
nr York, Hutton-le-Hole YO6 6UA
01751-417300

INGLETON North Yorkshire   10B3

Ferncliffe *Acclaimed*   RAC
55 Main Street, Ingleton LA6 3HJ
015242-42405
*Late Victorian family-run guest house
situated in the Three Peaks area of the Dales,
on the A65 between Skipton and Kendal and
a few minutes' walk from Ingleton village.*
4 bedrs, 4 ➡/WC; ✗ P5
sB&B £22 dB&B £38 Breakfast only [10%V]

Langber   RAC
Tatterthorne Road, Via Carnforth, Ingleton
LA6 3DT 01524-241587
7 bedrs, 2 ➡/WC, 2 ♠/WC, 1 ➡; tcf ✗ P8
sB&B £15.50-£17.50 dB&B £29.90-£34; HB
weekly £128-£140; [5%V]

Pines Country House *Highly Acclaimed*   RAC
Via Carnforth, Ingleton LA6 3HN
015242-41252
5 bedrs, 2 ➡/WC, 2 ♠/WC, 1 ➡; TV tcf ✗ ✂ P14
sB&B £24 dB&B £38; HB weekly £125; cc Ac Vi

Springfield *Acclaimed*   RAC
Main Street, Via Carnforth, Ingleton LA6
3HJ 015242-41280
5 bedrs, 5 ♠/WC, 1 ➡; TV tcf ✗ ✂ P12
sB&B £20 dB&B £36; HB weekly £175; D
£8.50 [10%V]

KEIGHLEY West Yorkshire   10C3

Hoyle Farm Cottages Dimples Lane,
Haworth, Keighley BD22 8QT 01535-646809

Railway Cottage 59 Station Road, Oakworth,
Keighley BD22 0DZ 01535-642693

KETTLEWELL North Yorkshire   10C3

Langcliffe Country *Highly Acclaimed*   RAC
Kettlewell BD23 5RJ 01756-760243   ♿

*A detached, stone-built, country guest house
set in a beautiful garden with uninterupted
views of the Dales. Conservatory and
restaurant.*
6 bedrs, 3 ➡/WC, 3 ♠/WC; TV tcf ✂ P7
sB&B £30-£35 dB&B £46-£50; HB weekly
£223-£243; D £15 [5%V]; cc Ac Vi

> ### No Smoking/Dogs
> ✂ Indicates a hotel which either bans
> smoking throughout the establishment or
> does not allow smoking in some areas.
>
> ✗ Indicates a hotel which either does not
> welcome dogs or restricts dogs to certain
> areas of the hotel.
> Please telephone the hotel
> for further details.

KEXBY North Yorkshire   11E3

Ivy House Farm RAC
Hull Road, Kexby YO4 5LQ 01904-489368

KNARESBOROUGH North Yorkshire   11D3

Ebor Mount RAC
18 York Place, Knaresborough HG5 0AA
01423-863315
8 bedrs, 8 ⇥/WC, 1 ⇥; ✖ P8
sB&B £17.50-£19 dB&B £35-£38 Breakfast
only [10%V]; **cc** Ac Vi

Newton House Private *Highly Acclaimed* RAC
5-7 York Place, Knaresborough HG5 0AD
01423-863539 Fax 01423-869614
12 bedrs, 12 ⇥/WC;

Villa *Acclaimed* RAC
47 Kirkgate, Knaresborough HG5 8BZ
01423-865370 Fax 01423-867740
6 bedrs, 4 ⬧/WC, 1 ⇥; TV tcf ✖ P1
sB&B £25-£30 dB&B £40 Breakfast only [5%V]

LEEDS West Yorkshire   11D3

Aragon *Acclaimed* RAC
250 Stainbeck Lane, Leeds LS7 2PS
0113-275-9306 Fax 0113-275-7166
13 bedrs, 11 ⇥/WC, 2 ⇥; ✖ P24
sB&B £25.08-£39.36 dB&B £38-£46.88 D £9.80
[10%V]; **cc** Ac Amex DC Vi

**Beechwood Private 34 Street Lane, Leeds
LS8 2ET 0113-2662578**

*Detached hotel standing in its own grounds,
near Roundhay Park, 3.5 miles north east of
Leeds.*
19 bedrs, 7 ⬧/WC, 4 ⇥; TV tcf ✖ P12
sB&B £24 D £9; **cc** Ac Vi

Broomhurst *Acclaimed* RAC
12 Chapel Lane, Off Cardigan Road, Leeds
LS6 3BW 0113-2786836 Fax 0113-2786836
10 bedrs, 4 ⬧/WC, 2 ⇥; TV tcf P5
sB&B £21.50 dB&B £35; HB weekly £152.50;
D £9; **cc** Ac Vi

Newtonsman 35 New Briggate, Leeds LS2
8JD 0113-2445164

Oak Villa 57 Cardigan Rd, Headingley, Leeds
LS6 1DW 0113-2758439

Pinewood *Acclaimed* ⚓
78 Potternewton Lane, Leeds LS7 3LW
0113-2622561 Fax 0113-2622561
10 bedrs, 8 ➵/WC; TV tcf ✂
sB&B £34 dB&B £40 Breakfast only [5%V]; cc
Ac Amex Vi

LEYBURN North Yorkshire 10C2

Grayford Private Carperby, Leyburn DL8
4DW 01969-663517

Low Green House Leyburn DL8 3SZ
01969-663623

MALTON North Yorkshire 11E3

★★★(Inn) Green Man ⚓
15 Market Street, Malton YO17 0LY
01653-600370 Fax 01653-696006
26 bedrs, 21 ➵/WC, 5 ↾/WC;
TV tcf ✖ ✂ P40
sB&B £35-£49.50 dB&B £70-£99; HB weekly
£300; [10%V]; cc Ac Amex DC Vi

Greenacres Country House
Highly Acclaimed ⚓
Amotherby, Malton YO17 0TG 01653-693623
Fax 01653-693623
9 bedrs, 9 ➵/WC; P15
sB&B £26.50 dB&B £53; cc Ac Vi

MASHAM North Yorkshire 11D2

Bank Villa ⚓
Ripon, Masham HG4 4DB 01765-89605
*Stone-built, Georgian house, about 200 years
old.*
7 bedrs, 1 ➵; ✖ ✂ P7
Child restrictions
sB&B £26 dB&B £36; HB weekly £115; [5%V]

MIDDLESBROUGH Cleveland 11D2

Grey House *Highly Acclaimed* ⚓
79 Cambridge Road, Linthorpe,
Middlesbrough TS5 5NL 01642-817485
9 bedrs, 9 ➵/WC; ✖ P10
sB&B £30 dB&B £42 D £7; cc Ac Vi

Royal Oak High Green, Great Ayton,
Middlesbrough TS9 6BW 01642-722361 ♿
5 bedrs, 1 ➵/WC, 1 ➵; ✖
sB&B £25 Breakfast only

MORPETH Northumberland 13F3

North Cottage Birling, Warkworth, Morpeth
NE65 0XS 01665-711263

MURTON North Yorkshire 11D3

Dray Lodge ⚓
Moor Lane, Murton YO1 3UH 01904-489591
Fax 01904-488587
9 bedrs, 9 ➵/WC; P15
Breakfast only; cc Ac Amex Vi

NEWCASTLE UPON TYNE Tyne & Wear 11D1

Chirton House *Acclaimed* ⚓
46 Clifton Road, Newcastle Upon Tyne NE4
6XH 0191-273-0407
11 bedrs, 2 ➵/WC, 3 ↾/WC, 2 ➵;
TV tcf ✖ ✂
sB&B £23-£33 dB&B £30-£44; HB weekly
£150; [10%V]; cc Ac Vi

George *Acclaimed* ⚓
88 Osborne Road, Newcastle Upon Tyne NE2
2AP 0191-2814442 Fax 0191-2818300
14 bedrs, 7 ➵/WC, 3 ↾/WC, 1 ➵; TV tcf P4
sB&B £22-£27 dB&B £32-£39 Breakfast only
[10%V]; cc Amex DC Vi JCB

NORTHALLERTON North Yorkshire 11D2

Alverton *Acclaimed* ⚓
26 South Parade, Northallerton DL7 8SG
01609-776207
5 bedrs, 1 ➵; ✖ ✂ P3
sB&B £16.50-£18 dB&B £38 [5%V]

Otterington Shorthorn Inn South
Otterington, Northallerton DL7 9HP
01609-773816

(Inn) Station 🏛RAC
2 Boroughbridge Road, Northallerton DL7
8AN 01609-772053
10 bedrs, 3 🛏; P20
sB&B £15-£18 dB&B £25-£28 Breakfast only

Windsor 🏛RAC
56 South Parade, Northallerton DL7 8SL
01609-774100
6 bedrs, 2 🏠/WC, 2 🛏; TV tcf ✻
sB&B £16-£20 dB&B £30-£36; HB weekly
£161-£182; D £8 [10%V]; cc Ac Vi

PATELEY BRIDGE North Yorkshire   10C3

Bewerley Hall Farm Bewerley, Nr
Harrogate, Pateley Bridge HG3 5JA
01423-711636
6 bedrs, 1 🛏/WC, 2 🏠/WC, 1 🛏; 🐕 ✻
sB&B £18 Breakfast only

Roslyn *Acclaimed* 🏛RAC
King Street, Pateley Bridge HG3 5AT
01423-711374
6 bedrs, 1 🛏/WC, 5 🏠/WC; TV tcf ✻ P4
sB&B £23-£28.50 dB&B £38-£42; HB weekly
£155-£179; D £8.50 [10%V]

PICKERING North Yorkshire   11E2

Rawcliffe House Farm *Acclaimed* 🏛RAC
Newton-upon-Rawcliffe, Stape, Pickering
YO18 8JA 01751-473292

*Converted farm buildings situated in the
beautiful Yorkshire Moors.*
3 bedrs, 3 🛏/WC; P10
sB&B £18.50-£21.50 dB&B £33-£39; HB
weekly £171.50-£122.50;

POCKLINGTON Humberside   11E3

Youngwoods Farm Whitehouse Road,
Porchfield, Newport PO30 4LJ 01983-522170

Meltonby Hall Farm Meltonby, Nr
Pocklington, YO4 2PW 01759-303214
2 bedrs, 1 🛏;
sB&B £14 Breakfast only

PONTEFRACT West Yorkshire   11D4

Vissett Cottage Barnsley Road, Hemsworth,
Pontefract WF9 4PQ 01977-610765

REDCAR Cleveland   11D1

Royal The Esplanade, Redcar TS10 3AH
01642-484116

REETH North Yorkshire   10C2

Arkleside *Highly Acclaimed* 🏛RAC
Reeth DL11 6SG 01748-884200 Fax
01748-884619
9 bedrs, 8 🛏/WC, 1 🛏; 🐕 ✻ P8
dB&B £53-£57 Breakfast only [5%V]; cc Ac Vi

RICHMOND North Yorkshire   10C2

Hartforth Hall *Highly Acclaimed* 🏛RAC
Gilling West, Richmond DL10 5JU
01748-825715 Fax 01748-825781
8 bedrs, 8 🛏/WC; 🐕 P45
Breakfast only [10%V]; cc Ac Amex DC Vi

Oxnop Hall Low Oxnop, Gunnerside,
Richmond DL11 6JJ 01748-886253

Punch Bowl Inn Low Row, Richmond DL11
6PF 01748-862331

RIPON North Yorkshire   11D3

Crescent Lodge 42 North Street, Ripon HG4
1EN 01765-602331

ROBIN HOOD'S BAY North Yorkshire   11E2

Victoria Robin Hood's Bay YO22 4RL
01947-880205

ROTHERHAM South Yorkshire   11D4

Hotel Campanile 🏛RAC
Lowton Way/off Denby Way, Hellaby
Industrial Estate, Rotherham S66 8RY
01709-700255

Regis Court 🏛RAC
1 Hall Rd, Rotherham S60 2BP 01709-376666
Fax 01709-820213

Stonecroft Main Street, Bramley, Rotherham
01709-540922

SCARBOROUGH North Yorkshire   11E2

Anatolia *Acclaimed*   RAC
21 West Street, South Cliff, Scarborough YO11
2QR 01723-36086
8 bedrs, 6 ➡/WC, 2 ➡;
sB&B £12-£14 dB&B £16; HB weekly £135;

Ashcroft *Acclaimed*   RAC
102 Columbus Ravine, Scarborough YO12
7QZ 01723-375092
7 bedrs, 3 ➡/WC, 2 ➡; TV tcf ✂ P7
sB&B £15-£17 dB&B £30-£34 D £5 [5%V];
cc Ac Vi

Ashlea *Acclaimed*   RAC
119 Columbus Ravine, Scarborough YO12
7QU 01723-361874
8 bedrs, 8 ➡/WC; TV tcf ✂
sB&B £17 dB&B £34 D £6; cc Ac DC Vi

Bay 67 Esplanade, South Cliff, Scarborough
YO11 2UZ 01723-501038

Boundary 124-126 North Marine Road,
Scarborough YO12 7HZ 01723-376737

Burghcliffe 28 Esplanade, Scarborough
YO12 7NJ 01723-370234

Derwent House 6 Rutland Terrace, Queens
Parade, Scarborough YO12 7JB 01723-373880

Duke Of York 1-2 Merchants Row,
Eastborough, Scarborough YO11 1NQ
01723-373875

Gainsborough 23 Prince Of Wales Terrace,
Scarborough YO11 2AN 01723-373692

Geldenhuis   RAC
143-147 Queen's Parade, Scarborough YO12
7HU 01723-361677
30 bedrs, 9 ➡/WC, 7 ➡; P25
Breakfast only

Girvan 61 Northsead Manor Drive,
Scarborough YO12 6AF 01723-364518

Glywin   RAC
153 Columbus Ravine, Scarborough YO12
7QZ 01723-371311
7 bedrs, 3 ➡; TV tcf ✂

sB&B £13-£15 dB&B £26-£30 D £5.50 [5%V];
cc Ac Vi

Granby   RAC
Queen Street, Scarborough YO11 1HL
01723-373031 Fax 01723-373031
25 bedrs, 15 ➡/WC; tcf
sB&B £16-£18.50 dB&B £32-£38; HB weekly
£147-£168; D £6

Hazelwood 72 Columbus Ravine,
Scarborough YO12 7QU 01723-371208

Interludes 32 Princess Street, Scarborough
YO11 1QR 01723-360513

Manor Health 67 Northsead Manor Drive,
Scarborough YO12 6AF 01723-365720

Martyns 24 Esplanade Gardens, South Cliff,
Scarborough YO11 2AP 01723-360728

Mount House 33 Trinity Road, Scarborough
YO11 2TD 01273-362967
7 bedrs, 1 ➡/WC, 1 ➡;

Northcote 114 Columbus Ravine,
Scarborough YO12 7QZ 01723-367758

Parade *Acclaimed*   RAC
29 Esplanade, Scarborough YO11 2AQ
01723-361285
17 bedrs, 1 ➡/WC, 16 ➡/WC, 1 ➡; TV tcf
Child restrictions
sB&B £21-£23 dB&B £42-£46; HB weekly
£189-£203; [5%V]; cc Ac Vi

Paragon   RAC
123 Queens Parade, Scarborough YO12 7HU
01723-372676
14 bedrs, 3 ➡/WC, 11 ➡/WC, 1 ➡;
TV tcf ✖ ✂ P6
Child restrictions
sB&B £21-£22 dB&B £42-£44; HB weekly
£186-£196; D £8.50; cc Ac Vi

Parmella *Acclaimed*   RAC
17 West Street, South Cliff, Scarborough YO11
2QN 01723-361914
15 bedrs, 12 ➡/WC, 2 ➡; TV tcf
[5%V]

Pickwick Inn *Acclaimed*   RAC
Huntriss Row, Scarborough YO11 2ED
01723-375787 Fax 01723-374284

10 bedrs, 10 ➹/WC;
Child restrictions
sB&B £22.50-£27 dB&B £35-£44 [10%V]; cc Ac
Amex DC Vi

Plane Tree Cottage Farm Staintondale,
Scarborough YO13 0EY 01723-870796
3 bedrs, 1 ➹;
sB&B £15; HB weekly £150; D £9

Premier *Highly Acclaimed*　　　RAC
66 Esplanade, South Cliff, Scarborough YO11
2UZ 01723-501062
19 bedrs, 16 ➹/WC, 3 ﾒ/WC; TV tcf ✖ ✂ P6
sB&B £32 dB&B £54; HB weekly £250; D
£12; cc Ac Vi

Ramleh　　　RAC
135 Queen's Parade, Scarborough YO12 7HY
01723-365745
9 bedrs, 1 ➹/WC, 6 ﾒ/WC, 2 ➹; TV tcf P5
sB&B £18-£19 dB&B £36-£38; HB weekly
£119-£126; D £5 [5%V]; cc Ac Amex Vi

Rose Dene 106 Columbus Ravine,
Scarborough YO12 7QZ 01723-374252

Sefton　　　RAC
18 Prince Of Wales Terrace, South Cliff,
Scarborough YO11 2AL 01723-372310
14 bedrs, 7 ➹/WC, 8 ➹; ✖ ✂
sB&B £15-£19 dB&B £40-£42; HB weekly
£146-£150; [10%V]

Valley Lodge 51 Valley Rd, Scarborough
YO11 2LX 01723-375311

New Telephone Numbers

All UK telephone codes are being
changed. The number 1 is being inserted
after the first 0. For example, 081 is
changing to 0181. The new codes were
available in August 1994 and the two
codes will run in parallel until 16 April
1995, when the new code will take over.
The new codes are given throughout the
guide, as they will be in use in November
when the guide is published The old codes
can be used up to 16 April 1995.
Five cities will have a complete change of
code and an additional digit to the number.

	old	new
Bristol	0272-xxxxx	0117-9xxxxxx
Leeds	0532-xxxxx	0113-2xxxxxx
Leicester	0533-xxxxx	0116-2xxxxxx
Nottingham	0602-xxxxx	0115-9xxxxxx
Sheffield	0742-xxxxx	0114-2xxxxxx

**Villa Marina 59 Northsead Manor Drive,
Scarborough YO12 6AF 01723-361088**

*Detached three crown non-smoking hotel
overlooking Peasholm Park & Lake, close to all
northside attractions.*
12 bedrs, 11 ﾒ/WC, 1 ➹; TV tcf ✂ P9
Child restrictions under 3
sB&B £18; HB weekly £155-£175; D £24-£27;
cc Ac Vi

**West Lodge 38 West St, Scarborough YO11
2QP 01723-500754**

Weydale　　　RAC
Weydale Avenue, Scarborough YO12 6BA
01723-373393
26 bedrs, 14 ➹/WC, 3 ➹; TV tcf ✂ P12
Child restrictions
sB&B £17-£20 dB&B £36-£40; HB weekly
£155-£165; [5%V]

Wharncliffe 26 Blenheim Terrace,
Scarborough YO12 7HD 01723-347635

Wheatcroft Motel　　　RAC
156 Filey Road, Scarborough YO1 3AA
01723-374613
7 bedrs, 7 ﾒ/WC; ✂ P11
sB&B £19.50 dB&B £31.50-£49 Breakfast only

SCOTCH CORNER North Yorkshire   10C2

Pavilion Lodge   ⚕RAC
Scotch Corner Services, Scotch Corner
01325-377177 Fax 01325-377890   &
50 bedrs, 50 ⇦/WC; TV tcf ✕ ✕ P100
sB&B £34.95 D £10.50 [10%V];
cc Ac Amex DC Vi

SEAHOUSES Northumberland   13D3

★★Bamburgh Castle   ⚕RAC
Seahouses NE68 7SQ 01665-720283 Fax
01665-720283
20 bedrs, 20 ⇦/WC; TV tcf ✕ ✕ P25
sB&B £29.95-£33.95 dB&B £57.90-£66.90; HB
weekly £252-£289; D £16.95 [10%V]

SELBY North Yorkshire   11D3

The Olympia Barlby Road, Barlby, Selby
YO8 7AB 01757-702459

SETTLE North Yorkshire   10C3

★★★Falcon Manor   ⚕RAC
Skipton Road, Settle BD24 9BD 01729-823814
Fax 01729-822087   &
15 bedrs, 14 ⇦/WC, 1 ☈/WC; TV tcf ✕ ✕
P80
sB&B £55 dB&B £74 D £18.50 [10%V];
cc Ac DC Vi

(Inn) Golden Lion   ⚕RAC
5 Duke Street, Settle BD24 9DU 01729-822203
11 bedrs, 1 ☈/WC, 2 ⇦; TV tcf ✕ P12

SHEFFIELD South Yorkshire   8A1

Comfort Inn   ⚕RAC
George Street, Sheffield S1 2PF 0114-2739939
Fax 0114-2768333
50 bedrs, 30 ⇦/WC, 20 ☈/WC; TV tcf ✕ ✕
P50
sB&B £29.95-£45.90 dB&B £46.85 D £5.95
[10%V]; cc Ac Amex DC Vi

Crown Inn 21 Meadowhall Road, Sheffield
S9 1BS 0114-2431319

Etruria House   ⚕RAC
91 Crookes Road, Broomhill, Sheffield S10
5BD 0114-2662241 Fax 0114-2670853
11 bedrs, 8 ⇦/WC, 2 ⇦; ✕
Breakfast only [10%V]; cc Ac Vi

Hunter House *Acclaimed*   ⚕RAC
Eccleshall Road, Sheffield S11 8TG
0114-2686370   &
23 bedrs, 2 ⇦/WC, 9 ☈/WC, 4 ⇦;
TV tcf ✕ P9
D £8.95 [5%V]; cc Ac Vi

Lindrick House *Acclaimed*   ⚕RAC
226 Chippinghouse Road, Sheffield S7 1DR
0114-2585041 Fax 0114-2554758
23 bedrs, 15 ☈/WC, 2 ⇦; TV tcf ✕ ✕ P15
sB&B £25 dB&B £38 Breakfast only [10%V];
cc Ac Amex Vi

Lindum   ⚕RAC
91 Montgomery Road, Nether Edge, Sheffield
S7 1LP 0114-2552356
11 bedrs, 4 ⇦/WC, 2 ⇦; ✕
Breakfast only

Millingtons   ⚕RAC
70 Broomsgrove Road, Sheffield S10 2NA
0114-2669549
6 bedrs, 2 ⇦/WC, 2 ⇦; TV tcf P4
Child restrictions
sB&B £23 dB&B £42-£49 Breakfast only
[10%V]

Moorgate Edale Road, Hope, Sheffield S30
2RF 01433-621219

Westbourne House *Acclaimed*   ⚕RAC
25 Westbourne Road, Broomhill, Sheffield S10
2QQ 0114-2660109

SHIPLEY West Yorkshire   10C3

**Southgate House 145 Bradford Road,
Shipley BD18 3TH 01274-585549**
3 bedrs, 1 ⇦/WC, 1 ☈/WC, 1 ⇦; TV tcf ✕ P3
sB&B £15 D £3.50-£4

SKIPTON North Yorkshire   10C3

The Buck Inn Malham, Nr Skipton BD23
4DA 01729-830317
10 bedrs, 6 ⇦/WC;
Breakfast only

┌─────────────────────────────────────┐
│   **Location Maps**   │
│ Hotel locations are shown on the maps at │
│   the back of the guide. All towns and │
│ villages containing an hotel listed in the │
│   guide are shown in black.   │
└─────────────────────────────────────┘

Highfield *Acclaimed*
58 Keighley Road, Skipton BD23 2NB
01756-79318

*A Victorian double fronted ivy clad town
hotel on the main Keighley/Bradford Road.*
10 bedrs, 3 ➥/WC, 6 ☞/WC, 1 ➥; TV tcf
sB&B £16.50-£19.50 dB&B £37-£39 Breakfast
only; cc Ac Amex Vi

Penmar Court Duke Street, Settle, Skipton
BD23 9AS 01729-823258

Skipton Park Guest'otel *Acclaimed*
2 Salisbury Street, Skipton BD23 1NQ
01756-700640
7 bedrs, 7 ➥/WC; ✖ P2
Breakfast only

Child Restrictions
Most hotels and guest houses are happy
to welcome children. A few prefer to
welcome only adults and older children;
these are shown by 'Child restrictions' in
the entry. If you are travelling with children,
please telephone the establishment to check
the age limit set by the management.

STAMFORD BRIDGE North Yorkshire 11E3

High Catton Grange Stamford Bridge, York
01759-371374
*This 300-acre mixed working farm offers
accommodation of a high standard in a
peaceful rural setting. Ample parking.*
3 bedrs, 2 ➥/WC, 1 ➥; ✖ P6
sB&B £25 Breakfast only

STARBOTTON North Yorkshire 10C3

Hilltop nr Skipton, Starbotton BD23 5HY
01756-760321

STOCKTON-ON-TEES Cleveland 11D2

Edwardian *Acclaimed*
72 Yarm Road, Stockton-on-Tees TS18 3PQ
01642-615655
6 bedrs, 6 ➥/WC; P8
sB&B £25-£30 dB&B £42 Breakfast only; cc Ac Vi

Formule 1
Teesway, North Tees Industrial Estate,
Stockton-on-Tees TS18 2RT 01642-606560

Stonyroyd 187 Oxbridge Lane, Stockton-on-
Tees TS18 4BJ 01642-607734

STOKESLEY Cleveland 11D2

The Buck Inn Bilsdale, Chopgate, Stokesley
TS9 7JL 01642-778334
5 bedrs, 5 ☞/WC; TV tcf P44
sB&B £21; HB weekly £178.50-£197.75; D
£2.95-£9.25; cc Ac Vi

THIRSK North Yorkshire 11D2

★(Inn) Old Red House
Station Road, Carlton Miniott, Thirsk YO7 4LT
01845-524383 ♿
6 bedrs, 6 ➥/WC; ✖ P30
cc Amex Vi

Three Tuns Market Place, Thirsk YO7 1LH
01845-523124

TODMORDEN West Yorkshire   10C4

Birks Clough Hollingworth Lane, Walsden,
Todmorden OL14 6QX 01706-814438

★★★**Scaitcliffe Hall**   RAC
Burnley Road, Todmorden OL14 7DQ
01706-818888 Fax 01706-818825

TYNEMOUTH Tyne & Wear   13F4

Hope House *Highly Acclaimed*   RAC
47 Percy Gardens, Tynemouth NE30 4HH
0191-2571989 Fax 0191-2571989   &
*Elegantly furnished and decorated double
fronted Victorian house with superb coastal
views.*
3 bedrs, 2 ➔/WC, 1 ➔; P3
sB&B £30-£35 dB&B £37.50 D £13.50 [5%V];
cc Ac Amex DC Vi

WAKEFIELD West Yorkshire   11D4

Hotel Campanile   RAC
Monkton Road, Wakefield WF2 7AL
01924-201054

WASHINGTON Tyne & Wear

Campanile   RAC
Emerson Road, Washington NE37 1LE
0191-416-5010
79 bedrs, 79 ➔/WC;
Breakfast only

WHARRAM LE STREET North Yorkshire 11E3

Red House *Acclaimed*   RAC
Wharram Le Street YO17 9TL
01944-768455
3 bedrs, 3 ➔/WC; TV tcf ✸ P8
sB&B £23 dB&B £46 D £12

WHITBY North Yorkshire   11E2

Abbey House East Cliffe, Whitby YO22 4TJ
01947-600557

Banchory   RAC
3 Crescent Terrace, West Cliff, Whitby YO21
3EL 01947-821888

Corra Lynn *Acclaimed*   RAC
28 Crescent Avenue, Whitby YO21 3EW
01947-602214
6 bedrs, 4 ➔/WC, 2 ➔/WC; TV tcf ✸ ⅍ P4
Child restrictions
sB&B £20 dB&B £40-£44; HB weekly £217-
£231; [5%V]

Dale End Farm Green End, Goathland,
Whitby 01947-895371

Dunsley Hall *Highly Acclaimed*   RAC
Dunsley, Whitby YO21 3TL 01947-893437 Fax
01947-893505   &
7 bedrs, 4 ➔/WC, 3 ➔/WC; TV tcf ✸ ⅍ P10
sB&B £36.50-£45 dB&B £73; HB weekly
£325-£340;; cc Ac Vi

Estbek House Sandsend, Whitby YO21 3SU
01947-83424

Glendale   RAC
16 Crescent Avenue, Whitby YO21 3ED
01947-604242
6 bedrs, 5 ➔/WC, 2 ➔; TV tcf ✸ P6
sB&B £18-£20 dB&B £36-£40 Breakfast only

Kimberley *Highly Acclaimed*   RAC
7 Havelock Place, Whitby YO21 3ER
01947-604125

Leeway 1 Havelock Place, Whitby YO21 3ER
01947-602604

Sandbeck *Acclaimed*   RAC
2 Crescent Terrace, West Cliff, Whitby YO21
3EL 01947-604012

Seacliffe *Acclaimed*   RAC
North Promenade, Whitby YO21 3JX
01947-603139 Fax 01947-603139
20 bedrs, 3 ➔/WC, 17 ➔/WC, 1 ➔; TV tcf ✸ P6
sB&B £27.50-£37.50 dB&B £53-£57; HB
weekly £210-£230; D £15 [10%V];
cc Ac Amex DC Vi

Waverley *Acclaimed*   RAC
17 Crescent Avenue, Whitby YO21 3ED
01947-604389
6 bedrs, 5 ➔/WC, 2 ➔; TV tcf ⅍
Child restrictions
sB&B £17 dB&B £40 Breakfast only

York House *Highly Acclaimed* 🏵
High Hawsker, Whitby YO22 4LW
01947-880354
4 bedrs, 4 👣/WC, 1 ➡; TV tcf ✂ P6
Child restrictions
sB&B £22-£23 dB&B £44-£46; HB weekly
£217-£224;

WHITLEY BAY Tyne & Wear   13F4

White Surf 🏵
8 South Parade, Whitley Bay NE26 2RG
0191-253-0103

York House *Acclaimed* 🏵
30 Park Parade, Whitley Bay NE26 1DX
0191-252-8313 Fax 0191-252-8313   ♿
8 bedrs, 1 ➡/WC, 6 👣/WC; TV tcf ✂ P2
sB&B £26.50 dB&B £38 [10%V];
cc Ac Amex Vi

WIGGLESWORTH North Yorkshire   10C3

★★★(Inn) Plough Inn 🏵
Wigglesworth BD23 4RJ 01729-840243   ♿
12 bedrs, 8 ➡/WC, 4 👣/WC; ✂ P50
sB&B £28.85-£32.45 dB&B £46.40-£53; HB
weekly £126-£146.20; D £14.95 [10%V];
cc Ac Amex DC Vi

YORK North Yorkshire   11D3

Church Cottage 🏵
Escrick YO4 6EX 01904-728462

Abbeyfields 19 Bootham Terrace, York YO3
7DH 01904-636471

Acer *Acclaimed* 🏵
52 Scarcroft Hill, The Mount, York YO2 1DE
01904-653839 Fax 01904-640421

Acorn 🏵
1 Southlands Road, York YO2 1NP
01904-620081
6 bedrs, 3 👣/WC, 1 ➡; TV tcf ✂
sB&B £13-£17.50 dB&B £24-£33 Breakfast
only [5%V]; cc Ac Amex Vi

Acres Dene 🏵
87 Fulford Road, York YO1 4BD
01904-637330

Alemar 19 Queen Annes Road, Bootham,
York YO3 7AA 01904-652367

Arndale *Highly Acclaimed* 🏵
290 Tadcaster Road, York YO2 2ET
01904-702424
10 bedrs, 9 ➡/WC, 1 👣/WC; TV tcf P20
Child restrictions
sB&B £29-£39 dB&B £39-£55 Breakfast only
[5%V]

Ascot House 🏵
80 East Parade, York YO3 7YH 01904-426826
Fax 01904-431077
15 bedrs, 5 ➡/WC, 7 👣/WC, 2 ➡; TV tcf ✖ P12
sB&B £17-£20 dB&B £34-£40 Breakfast only
[10%V]; cc Ac Vi

Ashbourne House *Acclaimed* 🏵
139, Fulford Road, York YO1 4HG
01904-639912 Fax 01904-631332
6 bedrs, 1 ➡/WC, 5 👣/WC; TV tcf ✂ P6
sB&B £32-£36 dB&B £42-£48 Breakfast only;
cc Ac Amex DC Vi

Avimore House *Acclaimed* 🏵
78 Stockton Lane, York YO3 0BS
01904-425556
6 bedrs, 6 👣/WC; TV tcf ✂ P6
sB&B £18-£25 dB&B £32-£44 Breakfast only
[10%V]

Barclay Lodge 19-21 Gillygate, York YO3
7EA 01904-633274

Beckett   RAC
58 Bootham Crescent, York YO3 7AH
01904-644728

Bedford *Acclaimed*   RAC
108 Bootham, York YO3 7DG 01904-624412
14 bedrs, 4 ➥/WC, 10 ✆/WC; TV tcf P14
sB&B £28-£34 dB&B £46-£50 D £9 [10%V]; cc
Ac Vi

Beech House *Acclaimed*   RAC
6-7 Longfield Terrace, York YO3 7DJ
01904-634581
8 bedrs, 8 ✆/WC; TV tcf ✄ P3
Child restrictions
sB&B £23-£25 dB&B £34-£46 Breakfast only

Bloomsbury   RAC
127 Clifton, York YO3 6BL 01904-634031   ♿

Bootham Bar   RAC
4 High Petergate, York YO1 2EH
01904-658516
9 bedrs, 1 ➥/WC, 8 ✆/WC, 1 ➥; TV tcf P4
dB&B £52-£65 D £8; cc Ac Vi

**Burton Villa 22 Haxby Road, York YO3
7JX 01904-626364**
*High quality comfort and friendly family run
guest house. Good value for money. Our
guests recommend us.*
11 bedrs, 1 ➥/WC, 7 ✆/WC, 1 ➥;
TV tcf ✄ P7
sB&B £15 Breakfast only

Byron House *Highly Acclaimed*   RAC
7 Driffield Terrace, The Mount, York YO2
2DD 01904-632525 Fax 01904-639424
10 bedrs, 1 ➥/WC, 6 ✆/WC, 1 ➥;
TV tcf ✄ ✄ P6
sB&B £20-£22 dB&B £45 D £17 [10%V]; cc Ac
Amex DC Vi

Carlton House   RAC
134 The Mount, York YO2 2AS 01904-622265
14 bedrs, 11 ✆/WC, 1 ➥; TV tcf P7
sB&B £20 dB&B £44 Breakfast only

Cavalier   RAC
39 Monkgate, York YO3 7PB 01904-636615

**City Centre 54 Walmgate, York YO1 2TJ
01904-624048 Fax 01904-612494**

MAXWELLS HOTEL

*Typical guest house, quietly located in York
city centre at sensible prices. Evening meals
deliciously prepared by our French chef in the
bistro.*
15 bedrs, 6 ✆/WC, 4 ➥; TV tcf ✄ P12
sB&B £12.50; HB weekly £21-£23; D £8.50;
cc Vi

City House   RAC
68 Monkgate, York YO3 7PF 01904-622483
6 bedrs, 1 ➥/WC, 4 ✆/WC; TV tcf P5
Child restrictions
sB&B £14-£20 dB&B £30-£38 Breakfast only;
cc Ac Vi

Coppers Lodge 15 Alma Terrace, Fulford Road, York YO1 4DQ 01904-639871
Family run guest house, situated close to the river and only 5 minutes walk from city centre. All rooms with H+C, central heating, TV and tea/coffee making facilities. Private car parking.
8 bedrs, 1 ➡/WC, 3 ➡; TV tcf ✗ P7
sB&B £14; HB weekly £22-£24; D £7-£9

Crescent ⚙RAC
77 Bootham, York YO3 7DQ 01904-623216
Fax 01904-623216
10 bedrs, 2 ➡/WC, 8 ☖/WC, 1 ➡;
TV tcf ✗ P4
sB&B £14.50-£23 dB&B £18.50-£31; HB weekly £192.15-£251; D £10 [5%V]; cc Ac Amex DC Vi JCB

Curzon Lodge & Stables Cottages *Highly Acclaimed* ⚙RAC
23 Tadcaster Road, Dringhouses, York YO2 2QG 01904-703157
5 bedrs, 3 ➡/WC, 2 ☖/WC; TV tcf ✗ P16
Child restrictions
sB&B £29.50-£38 dB&B £45-£56 Breakfast only [5%V]; cc Ac Vi

Derwent Lodge *Acclaimed* ⚙RAC
Low Catton, Stamford Bridge, York YO4 1EA 01759-371468 ♿

5 bedrs, 1 ➡/WC, 4 ☖/WC; TV tcf ✗ P8
Child restrictions
sB&B £30.50 dB&B £45; HB weekly £213.50;

Eastons *Acclaimed* ⚙RAC
90 Bishopthorpe Road, York YO2 1JS 01904-626646
13 bedrs, 8 ☖/WC, 1 ➡; TV tcf ✗ P8
Child restrictions
sB&B £17-£20 dB&B £34-£45 Breakfast only; cc Ac Vi

Fairmount *Acclaimed* ⚙RAC
230 Tadcaster Road, York YO2 2ES 01904-638298 Fax 01904-624626

Field House *Acclaimed* ⚙RAC
2 St George's Place, York YO2 2DR 01904-639572

Fourposter Lodge *Acclaimed*　RAC
68-70 Heslington Road, off Barbican Road,
York YO1 5AU 01904-651170
10 bedrs, 1 ⇔/WC, 9 ℝ/WC; TV tcf ✈ ⊬ P7.
sB&B £35-£38 dB&B £50 Breakfast only
[5%V]; cc Ac Amex Vi

Georgian 35 Bootham, York YO3 7BT
01904-622874

Grasmead House *Acclaimed*　RAC
1 Scarcroft Hill, York YO2 1DF 01904-629996
6 bedrs, 6 ⇔/WC; TV tcf ⊬
dB&B £58 Breakfast only; cc Ac Vi

Greenside　RAC ⅁
124 Clifton, York YO3 6BQ 01904-623631
8 bedrs, 3 ⇔/WC, 2 ⇔; TV tcf ✈ ⊬ P7
sB&B £15-£16 dB&B £24 D £9.50 [10%V]

Hazlewood *Acclaimed*　RAC
24-25 Portland Street, York YO3 7EH
01904-628032 Fax 01904-628032
16 bedrs, 5 ⇔/WC, 10 ℝ/WC, 3 ⇔; ✈ P9
sB&B £19-£22 dB&B £32 Breakfast only;
cc Ac Vi

Holgate Bridge *Acclaimed*　RAC
106-108 Holgate Road, York YO2 4BB
01904-635971 Fax 01904-670049
14 bedrs, 6 ⇔/WC, 5 ℝ/WC, 1 ⇔;
TV tcf ✈ P14
sB&B £22-£38 dB&B £38-£56 D £10.75;
cc Ac Amex Vi

Holmwood House *Highly Acclaimed*　RAC
114 Holgate Road, York YO2 4BB
01904-626183 Fax 01904-670899
12 bedrs, 9 ⇔/WC, 3 ℝ/WC; TV tcf ✈ ⊬ P10
Child restrictions
sB&B £40-£45 dB&B £50-£58 Breakfast only
[10%V]; cc Ac Amex Vi

Inglewood　RAC
7 Clifton Green, Clifton, York YO3 6LH
01904-653523

Linden Lodge　RAC
6 Nunthorpe Avenue, Scarcroft Road, York
YO2 1PF 01904-620107

*A small, owner-run hotel in a converted
Victorian town house recently refurbished to
a high standard. Within walking distance of
the town centre.*
12 bedrs, 9 ℝ/WC, 1 ⇔; TV tcf
sB&B £16-£18 dB&B £32-£42 Breakfast only
[10%V]; cc Ac Amex Vi

No Smoking/Dogs
⊬ Indicates a hotel which either bans
smoking throughout the establishment or
does not allow smoking in some areas.

✈ Indicates a hotel which either does not
welcome dogs or restricts dogs to certain
areas of the hotel.
Please telephone the hotel
for further details.

Marina   RAC
Naburn, York YO1 4RW 01904-627365
A converted village railway station. Just off the A19 south of York.
8 bedrs, 3 ⇥/WC; TV tcf ✂ P12
Child restrictions
sB&B £16-£27 dB&B £36-£38 Breakfast only [5%V]

Midway House *Acclaimed*   RAC
145 Fulford Road, York YO1 4HG
01904-659272
12 bedrs, 11 ☞/WC, 1 ⇥; TV tcf P14
sB&B £30-£42 dB&B £36-£50 D £11 [5%V]; cc Ac Amex Vi

Parsonage Country House   RAC
Main Street, Escrick, York Y04 6LF
01904-728111 Fax 01904-728151
13 bedrs, 11 ⇥/WC, 2 ☞/WC; TV tcf ✂ P120
sB&B £60 dB&B £90 D £18.50 [10%V];
cc Ac Amex DC Vi

Priory *Acclaimed*   RAC
126 Fulford Road, York YO1 4BE
01904-625280

Queen Annes 24 Queen Annes Road, Bootham, York YO3 7AA 01904-629389
7 bedrs, 1 ⇥/WC, 2 ☞/WC, 1 ⇥; P4
sB&B £13 Breakfast only

St Denys   RAC
St Denys Road, York YO1 1QD 01904-622207
Fax 01904-624800
10 bedrs, 7 ⇥/WC, 3 ☞/WC, 1 ⇥;
TV tcf 🐕 ✂ P9
sB&B £25-£30 dB&B £40-£50 Breakfast only;
cc Ac Vi

St Georges House *Acclaimed*   RAC
6 St Georges Place, York YO2 2DR
01904-625056   &
10 bedrs, 2 ⇥/WC, 8 ☞/WC; TV tcf 🐕 P7
sB&B £25-£30 dB&B £40 D £11 [5%V]; cc Ac Amex DC Vi

St Raphael's   RAC
44 Queen Annes Road, Bootham, York YO3 7AF 01904-645028
8 bedrs, 3 ☞/WC, 2 ⇥; TV tcf 🐕 ✂
sB&B £14-£18 dB&B £28-£32 Breakfast only;
cc Ac Vi

Sunley Court Nunnington, York YO6 5XQ
01439-748233

The Hollies 141 Fulford Road, York YO1
4HG 01904-634279

The Limes *Acclaimed*   RAC
135 Fulford Road, York YO1 4HE
01904-624548   &
10 bedrs, 10 ☞/WC; P14
HB weekly £240

Treble Sykes Farm Helperby, York YO6 2SB
01423-360667
3 bedrs, 2 ⇥; 🐕
Breakfast only

Valley View Farm Old Byland, Helmsley, York YO6 5LG 01439-798221 ♿

Stylish farmhouse accommodation between moors and dales. Tranquil setting, warm en-suite rooms. Generous portions of good traditional home- cooked food.
4 bedrs, 2 🛁/WC, 4 🚿/WC; TV tcf 🐕̸
sB&B £22; HB weekly £224-£492; D £10-£12; cc Ac Vi

North West

Cheshire • Greater Manchester • Lancashire • Cumbria • Merseyside

When the whistle blows, the Mancunian is spoilt for choice. Most of his nearest coast is sandy and enlivened by the famed resorts of Southport, Morecambe and Blackpool. Further diversions tempt at Liverpool's Albert Dock complex while the medieval, walled city of Chester and tranquil plains of Cheshire compete for his holiday brass against all the scenic glory of the Lake District.

Elterwater

A SELECTION OF ATTRACTIONS

Unless otherwise stated, all can be visited between April and October – some longer. Telephone for days/times of opening.

Astley Hall, Chorley, Lancs: *Tudor/Stuart house furnished to display glassware, paintings & pottery.* Tel: 01257-262166.

Beatles Story, Liverpool: *Newish swinging 60s walk-through experience.* Tel: 0151-709 1963.

Beatrix Potter Gallery, Hawkshead, Cumbria: *Exhibits original B.P. drawings in related building. NT.* Tel: 015394-36355.

The Boat Museum, Ellesmere Port, Cheshire: *Working museum at junction of Shropshire Union & Manchester Ship canals.* Tel: 0151-355 5017.

British Commercial Vehicle Museum, Leyland, Lancs: *Largest collection of its kind in Europe.* Tel: 01772-451011.

Cars of the Stars Motor Museum, Keswick, Cumbria: *Del Boys' Reliant van, Chitty Chitty Bang Bang & Jas. Bond collection feature.* Tel: 017687-73757.

Cartmel Priory, Cumbria: *The sweet hilltop town 'Cathedral of the Lakes'.*

Cumberland Toy & Model Museum, Cockermouth, Cumbria: *British toys from 1900 to date.* Tel: 01900-827606.

Dove Cottage & Wordsworth Museum, Grasmere, Cumbria: *Poets home, garden & memorabilia.* Tel: 015394-35544/35003.

Experience Catalyst, Widnes, Cheshire: *A feast of hands-on exhibits.* Tel: 0151-420 1121

Lowther Leisure Park

Gawthrope Hall, nr. Burnley, Lancs: *Early 17th-s home of Shuttleworth family. Textile collection. NT.* Tel: 01282-778511.

Gawsworth Hall, Macclesfield, Cheshire: *Tudor half-timbered house plus open air summer theatre.* Tel: 01260-223456.

Hadrian's Wall, Bowness to Wallsend. *Built AD125-130. Remarkable periodic remains. Free access. Scenic walking.*

Hardknott Roman Fort, Eskdale: *2" acre site overlooks Hardknott Pass. Free Access.*

King Charles Tower, Chester, Cheshire: *Fine city views from medieval tower on city walls. W/ends only.* Tel: 01244-318780.

Lake Dist. Nat. Park Visitor Centre, Brockhole, Windermere: *Ideal introduction to the area.* Tel: 015394-46601.

Lakeland Motor Museum, Holker Hall, Cark-in-Cartmell: *Over 100 vintage & classic vehicles.* Tel: 015395-58509.

Lakeland Wildlife Oasis, Hale, Cumbria: *Live animals, 'hands-on' exhibits, aquarium, butterfly house.* Tel: 015395-63027.

Laurel & Hardy Museum, Ulverston, Cumbria: *Fun for all in town where Stan Was born.* Tel: 01229-582292.

Leighton Hall, Carnforth, Lancs: *Displays of famous Gillow furniture. Also eagle/falcon displays. Closes end Sept.* Tel: 01524-734474.

Levens Hall, nr. Kendall, Cumbria: *Rare Jacobean furniture plus magnificent topiary garden. Closes end Sept.* Tel: 015395-60321.
Lowther Leisure Park, Hackthorpe, nr. Penrith, Cumbria: *Family fun with over 40 attractions. Closes early Sept.* Tel: 019312-523.

Lyme Park, Disley, Stockport, Cheshire: *Largest house in the county. Four centuries of period interiors. NT* Tel: 01663-762023/766492.

Merseyside Maritime Museum, Albert Dock, Liverpool. *Floating exhibits, craft demonstrations.* Tel: 0151-207 0001.

Muncaster Castle, Rave ﹍ass, Cumbria: *Superb family home since 13th-c. 16th & 17th-c furniture. Views of Eskdale. Owl Centre.* Tel: 01229-717614.

Museum of Childhood, Ribchester, Lancs: *Toys galore, Punch & Judy, period dolls.* Tel: 01254-878520.

Pilkington Glass Museum, St. Helens, Merseyside: *4000 years of glassmaking.* Tel: 01744-692014.

Port Sunlight Heritage Centre, Wirral, Cheshire: *19th-c model village built to house soap factory workers.* Tel: 0151-644 6466.

Quarry Bank Mill, Styal, Cheshire: *Working museum of cotton industry housed in working, water powered mill.* Tel: 01625-527468.

Rydal Mount, Ambleside, Cumbria: *Wordsworth's home 1813-50. Family portraits, furniture. Garden.* Tel: 015394-33002.

Sellafield Visitors Centre, Seascale, Cumbria: *Take an under cover look into the nuclear age.* Tel: 019467-27027.

Sizergh Castle & Garden, nr. Kendal, Cumbria: *14th-c pele tower with castle. Worthy contents and garden. NT.* Tel: 015395-60070.

South Lakes Wild Animal Park, Dalton-in-Furness, Cumbria: *Some free roaming wallabies and racoons in new 16 acre park.* Tel: 01229-466086.

World of Beatrix Potter, Bowness-on-Windermere: *All the favourite animals re-live their adventures.* Tel: 015394-88444.

SOME ANNUAL EVENTS

Appleby Horse Fair, Cumbria: *Largest gypsy gathering in the world. Selling on final day. 8 – 14 June.* Tel: 017683-51177.

Beatles Festival, Liverpool, Merseyside: *Various venues. 25 – 29 Aug.* Tel: 0151-236 9091.

Blackpool Illuminations, Lancs: *Six miles of light-bulb art, free. Early Sept – beg. Nov.*

Bolton Festival, Gtr. Manchester: *Arts & community participation event. 25Aug.- 3Sept.* Tel: 01204-22311.

British Open Ballroom & Latin American Dance Championships, Blackpool, Lancs: *26May – 2June.* Tel: 01253-25252.

Cheshire County Show, Tabley, Cheshire: *Shire horses, rare breeds, flowers, cheeses, stands etc. 20 – 21 June.* Tel: 01270-73245.

Chorley Canal Festival, Adlington, Lancs: *Canal boat rally, cruises, folk, dancing, jazz. 19 – 21 May.* Tel: 01257-481778.

Cumberland Show, Carlisle: *Agricultural show plus all aspects of rural life. 15 July.* Tel: 01228-560364.

Dinosaurs Alive, Liverpool Museum, Merseyside: *13 roaring, moving, life-size monsters. Extinct by June 4.* Tel: 0151-207 0001.

Diving Displays in Shark Tank!, Blackpool Sealife Centre, Lancs: *Communicate directly with immersed divers.* Tel: 01253-22445.

Egremont Crab Fair, Cumbria: *Held since 1267. Apples thrown to public. Greasy pole event. 'Gurning' Championship. 17 Sept.* Tel: 01946-820376.

Grand National, Aintree Racecourse, Merseyside: *Tip-top National Hunt racing. 6 – 8 Apl.* Tel: 0151-523 2600.

Liverpool Cathedral Festival, Merseyside: *Musical event, mainly classical. 30Jun – 16July.* Tel: 0151-709 6271.

Royal Lancashire Show, Astley Park, Chorley, Lancs: *21 – 23 July.* Tel: 01254-813769.

Tatton Country Fair & Horse Driving Trials, Tatton Park, Cheshire: *Plus dog agility, rabbits, crafts, marathon. 17 – 18 June.* Tel: 01625-425556.

Westmoreland County Show, Kendal, Cumbria: *Best in the county – features Westmoreland Wrestling. 14Sept.* Tel: 015395-67804.

Wigan Int'l Jazz Festival, Wigan Pier. Gtr. Manchester: *10th year. Additional street events. 8 – 16 July.* Tel: 01942-324547.

Wigan Pier Steam Fair & Boat Rally, Gtr. Manchester: *Hundreds of canal boats, music & entertainment. 5 & 6 Aug.* Tel: 01942-828525

Ashness Bridge

ALTRINCHAM Gtr Manchester (Cheshire) 10C4

Beech Mount RAC
46 Barrington Road, Altrincham WA14 1HN
0161-928-4523 Fax 0161-928-1055
23 bedrs, 2 ⬥/WC, 21 ⬥/WC, 1 ⬥; TV tcf ✕ P34
sB&B £28 dB&B £38 D £12 [10%V]; cc Ac Vi

Old Packet House *Highly Acclaimed* RAC
Navigation Road, Broadheath, Altrincham
WA14 1LW 0161-929-1331

Ash Farm *Highly Acclaimed* RAC
Park Lane, Little Bollington, Altringham WA14
4JJ 0161-9299290

AMBLESIDE Cumbria 10B2

Anchorage *Acclaimed* RAC
Rydal Road, Ambleside LA22 9AY
01539-432046
5 bedrs, 3 ⬥/WC; TV tcf P8
Child restrictions
dB&B £34-£46 Breakfast only

Beechmount Near Sawrey, Hawkshead,
Ambleside LA22 0JZ 015394-36356
3 bedrs, 2 ⬥/WC, 1 ⬥; TV tcf ✕ P5
sB&B £18.50 Breakfast only

★★Borrans Park RAC
Borrans Road, Ambleside LA22 0EN
0153-94-33454

Elder Grove *Highly Acclaimed* RAC
Lake Road, Ambleside LA22 0DB
015394-32504
12 bedrs, 11 ⬥/WC, 1 ⬥/WC; TV tcf ✕ ✕ P12
sB&B £20-£28 dB&B £40-£56; HB weekly
£224-£286; D £15.50; cc Ac Amex Vi

Gables *Highly Acclaimed* RAC
Church Walk, Ambleside LA22 9DJ
01539-433272

Grey Friar Lodge *Highly Acclaimed* RAC
Brathay, Ambleside LA22 9NE 015394-33158
8 bedrs, 6 ⬥/WC, 2 ⬥/WC; TV tcf ✕ P12
Child restrictions
sB&B £29-£30 dB&B £40-£45; HB weekly
£215-£235;

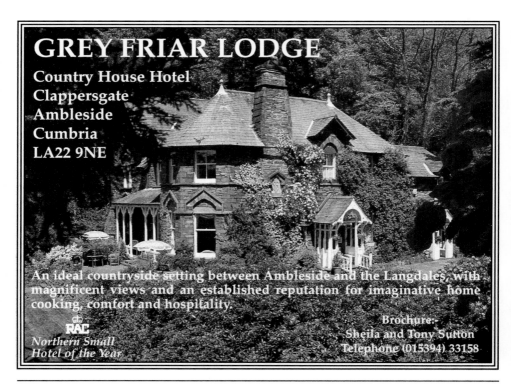

Lake View Country House Lake View Drive, Grasmere, Ambleside LA22 9TD 01539-435384

Loughrigg Brow Ambleside LA22 9SA 01539-432229

Lyndhurst *Acclaimed* RAC
Wansfell Road, Ambleside LA22 0EG
0153-94-32421 Fax 0153-94-32421
6 bedrs, 6 🚿/WC; TV tcf 🚭 P8
sB&B £39-£40 dB&B £39-£45; HB weekly £210-£245; [10%V]

Rowanfield Country House *Highly Acclaimed* RAC
Kirkstone Road, Ambleside LA22 9ET
0153-94-33686 ♿
7 bedrs, 1 🛁/WC, 6 🚿/WC; TV tcf 🐕 P7
Child restrictions
sB&B £48-£52 D £15; cc Ac Vi

Smallwood House *Acclaimed* RAC
Compston Road, Ambleside LA22 9DJ
0153-94-32330
13 bedrs, 5 🛁/WC, 6 🚿/WC, 2 🛁; TV tcf 🐕 🚭 P14
sB&B £15-£17 Breakfast only [5%V]

APPLEBY-IN-WESTMORLAND Cumbria 10B2

Ghyll View Dufton, Appleby-in-Westmoreland CA16 6DF 01768-351855

ARNSIDE Cumbria

Willowfield RAC
The Promenade, Arnside LA5 0AD
01524-761354
10 bedrs, 3 🚿/WC, 2 🛁; TV tcf 🐕 P10
sB&B £17-£18 dB&B £34-£40; HB weekly £175-£195; [10%V]; cc Ac Vi

ASHTON-UNDER-LYNE Gtr Manchester 10C4

Welbeck House *Acclaimed* RAC
324 Katharine Street, Ashton-under-Lyne 0L6 7BD 0161-344-0751 ♿
8 bedrs, 8 🚿/WC; TV tcf P20
sB&B £25-£29.50 dB&B £40 Breakfast only [5%V]; cc Ac Amex DC Vi

BARROW IN FURNESS Cumbria 10A3

Infield 276 Abbey Road, Barrow In Furness LA13 9JJ 01229-831381 Fax 01229-831381
10 bedrs, 2 🚿/WC, 2 🛁; TV tcf 🐕 P9
sB&B £18; HB weekly £21-£49; D £3-£7; cc Ac Vi

BASSENTHWAITE Cumbria 10B1

Lakeside *Highly Acclaimed* RAC
Bassenthwaite CA13 9YD 017687-76358
8 bedrs, 1 🛁/WC, 5 🚿/WC, 1 🛁; TV tcf P8
sB&B £17 dB&B £40 D £10.50 [10%V]

Ravenstone *Highly Acclaimed* RAC
Bassenthwaite CA12 4QG 0176-87-76240
20 bedrs, 1 🛁/WC, 9 🚿/WC; TV tcf 🐕 P24
sB&B £27-£29 dB&B £54-£58; HB weekly £245-£259;

BIRCH(MANCHESTER) Gtr Manchester 10C4

Granada Lodge RAC
M62 Birch, Birch(Manchester) OL10 2QH
0161-6553403

BLACKPOOL Lancashire 10B3

Arosa *Highly Acclaimed* RAC
18/20 Empress Drive, Blackpool FY2 9SD
01253-52555

Beaucliffe *Acclaimed* RAC
20-22 Holmfield Road, North Shore, Blackpool FY2 9TB 01253-51663

Brooklands *Highly Acclaimed* RAC
28-30 King Edward Avenue, North Shore, Blackpool FY2 9TA 01253-51479 ♿
17 bedrs, 17 🚿/WC; TV tcf 🚭 P5
sB&B £16-£18 dB&B £32-£36; HB weekly £147-£161; D £5

Burlees *Highly Acclaimed* RAC
40 Knowle Avenue, North Shore, Blackpool FY2 9TQ 01253-354535 ♿
9 bedrs, 9 🚿/WC, 1 🛁; TV tcf 🚭
sB&B £20-£24 dB&B £40-£48; HB weekly £175-£195; [5%V]; cc Ac Vi

Claytons *Acclaimed* RAC
28 Northumberland Avenue, Blackpool FY2 9SA 01253-355397 Fax 01253-500142
6 bedrs, 6 🚿/WC; TV tcf 🐕 🚭
Child restrictions
sB&B £16-£18 dB&B £32-£36 Breakfast only [10%V]; cc Ac Amex DC Vi

Cliff Head *Highly Acclaimed* RAC
174 Queens Promenade, Bispham, Blackpool FY2 9JN 01253-591086

Denely　RAC
15 King Edward Avenue, Blackpool FY2 9TA
01253-52757

Derwent *Acclaimed*　RAC
8 Gynn Avenue, North Shore, Blackpool FY1
2LD 01253-355194
12 bedrs, 4 ®/WC, 2 ➡; tcf ✘ P5
sB&B £15.50-£20 dB&B £25-£72; cc Ac Vi

Hartshead Private *Highly Acclaimed*　RAC
17 King Edward Avenue, Blackpool FY2 9TA
01253-53133

Knowsley　RAC
68 Dean Street, Blackpool FY4 1BP
01253-43414
12 bedrs, 1 ➡/WC, 6 ®/WC, 1 ➡; TV tcf P14
sB&B £13-£15 dB&B £26-£41; HB weekly
£119-£133; D £6; cc Ac Vi

Langwood　RAC
250 Queens Promenade, Blackpool FY2 9HA
01253-51370
27 bedrs, 16 ®/WC, 1 ➡; tcf ✘ P12
sB&B £15 dB&B £30; HB weekly £140-£150;
D £8 [10%V]

Lynstead *Highly Acclaimed*　RAC
40 King Edward Avenue, Blackpool FY2 9TA
01253-351050
10 bedrs, 10 ®/WC; tcf ⅛
Child restrictions
sB&B £17.50 dB&B £35; HB weekly £128-
£130;

Lynwood *Highly Acclaimed*　RAC
38 Osborne Road, Blackpool FY4 1HQ
01253-344628
8 bedrs, 6 ®/WC, 1 ➡; TV tcf
dB&B £26-£45; HB weekly £108-£135; [5%V]

Mimosa *Acclaimed*　RAC
24a Lonsdale Road, Blackpool FY1 6EE
01253-341906　ბ
15 bedrs, 9 ➡/WC, 6 ®/WC; TV tcf ✘ P15
sB&B £16 dB&B £32-£35; HB weekly £112;
[10%V]; cc Ac Vi

New Esplanade　RAC
551 New South Promenade, Blackpool FY4
1NF 01253-41646

Old Coach House *Highly Acclaimed*　RAC
50 Dean Street, Blackpool FY4 1BP

01253-44330
5 bedrs, 5 ®/WC; TV tcf ⅛ P10
sB&B £19.50-£22.50 dB&B £39-£45; HB
weekly £178.15; D £6.95 [5%V]; cc Ac Vi

Sunny Cliff　RAC
98 Queens Promenade, Blackpool FY2 9NS
01253-351155
9 bedrs, 8 ®/WC, 1 ➡; TV tcf ✘ P6
D £5 [10%V]

Sunray *Highly Acclaimed*　RAC
42 Knowle Avenue, North Shore, Blackpool
FY2 9TQ 01253-351937
9 bedrs, 1 ➡/WC, 8 ®/WC, 1 ➡; TV tcf ✘ P6
sB&B £24-£28 dB&B £48-£56; HB weekly
£204-£228; D £10 [10%V]; cc Ac Vi

Surrey House *Acclaimed*　RAC
9 Northumberland Avenue, Blackpool FY2
9SB 01253-351743
11 bedrs, 2 ➡/WC, 8 ®/WC, 2 ➡; tcf ✘ ⅛ P6
sB&B £14-£15 dB&B £28-£30; HB weekly
£133-£140; D £5 [5%V]

Villa *Acclaimed*　RAC
9-11 Withnell Road, Blackpool FY4 1HF
01253-43314
18 bedrs, 14 ®/WC, 2 ➡; TV tcf ✘ ⅛ P10
sB&B £15-£18 dB&B £30-£36; [10%V]; cc Ac
Amex DC Vi

Windsor *Highly Acclaimed*　RAC
21, King Edward Avenue, Blackpool FY2 9TA
01253-53735
9 bedrs, 1 ➡/WC, 8 ®/WC; TV tcf ✘ ⅛ P4
Child restrictions
sB&B £18-£19.50 dB&B £36-£39; D £6 [10%V]

Woodleigh Villa *Acclaimed*　RAC
32 King Edward Avenue, North Shore,
Blackpool FY2 9TA 01253-593624
10 bedrs, 10 ®/WC; TV tcf ⅛
sB&B £15-£17.50 dB&B £30-£35; HB weekly
£115-£135;

BLYTH Nottinghamshire　8B1

Granada　RAC
Junction A1M/A614, Hilltop Roundabout,
Blyth S81 8HG 01909-591836

BOLTON Gtr Manchester (Lancashire) 10B4

★★★Egerton House RAC
Blackburn Rd, Bolton BL7 9PL
01204-307171 Fax 01204-59303
32 bedrs, 32 [bath]/WC; [dog] P150
Breakfast only; cc Ac Amex DC Vi

★★Friendly Stop Inn RAC
Hyde Road, West Gorton, Bolton M12 5NT
0161-2208700 Fax 0161-2208848 [wheelchair]
95 bedrs, 95 [bath]/WC; TV tcf [dog] [no smoking] P80
sB&B £34.75-£58.75 dB&B £42.50-£65.50 D £9.75; cc Ac Amex DC Vi

BRAMPTON Cumbria 10B1

Abbey Bridge Inn *Acclaimed* RAC
Lanercost, Brampton CA8 2HG 016977-2224

Hullerbank *Acclaimed* RAC
Talkin, Brampton CA8 1LB 01697-746668

Oakwood House *Highly Acclaimed* RAC
Longtown Road, Brampton CA8 2AP
016977-2436 [wheelchair]
5 bedrs, 2 [bath]/WC, 3 [shower]/WC, 1 [bath]; TV tcf [no smoking] P10
sB&B £26 dB&B £40 D £11; cc Ac Vi

★★Tarn End House RAC
Talkin Tarn, Brampton CA8 1LS 016977-2340
Fax 016977-2089 [wheelchair]
7 bedrs, 6 [bath]/WC, 1 [shower]/WC; tcf [dog] P40
sB&B £29.50-£39.50 dB&B £49-£62; HB weekly £180-£250; D £13.50 [10%V]; cc Ac Amex Vi

BROMBOROUGH Merseyside 7D1

Dresden RAC
866 New Chester Road, Bromborough L62 7HF 0151-3341331

Royal Oak RAC
High St, Bromborough L62 7H2
0151-334-2912 Fax 0151-346-1175

BROUGHTON-IN-FURNESS Cumbria 10A2

(Inn) Manor Arms RAC
The Square, Broughton-in-Furness LA20 6HY
01229-716286
3 bedrs, 3 [shower]/WC; TV tcf [no smoking]
sB&B £17 dB&B £28 Breakfast only [5%V]; cc Ac Amex Vi

BURNLEY Lancashire 10C3

★(Inn) Plane Tree RAC
Westgate, Burnley BB11 1RT 01282-35442 Fax 01282-21896
6 bedrs, 6 [bath]/WC; [dog] P8
cc Ac Vi

BUTTERMERE Cumbria 10A2

Pickett Howe *Highly Acclaimed* RAC
Buttermere Valley, Buttermere CA13 9UY
01900-85444
4 bedrs, 3 [bath]/WC, 1 [shower]/WC; TV tcf P6
Child restrictions
dB&B £35; HB weekly £357; D £20; cc Ac Vi

CARLISLE Cumbria 10B1

Abbey Court Guest 24 London Road, Carlisle CA3 0ED 01228-28696

(Inn) Angus *Acclaimed* RAC
14 Scotland Road, Carlisle CA3 9DG
01228-23546
12 bedrs, 7 [shower]/WC, 2 [bath]; TV tcf [dog] [no smoking] P6
sB&B £21-£25 D £9; cc Ac Amex Vi

Avondale *Acclaimed* RAC
3 St Aidans Road, Carlisle CA1 1LT
01228-23012

Bessiestown Farm *Highly Acclaimed* RAC
Nr Longtown, Carlisle CA6 5QP 01228-577219

Courtfield 169 Warwick Road, Carlisle CA1
1LP 01228-22767
3 bedrs;
Breakfast only

East View *Acclaimed* RAC
110 Warwick Road, Carlisle CA1 1JU
01228-22112

Granada Lodge RAC
Carlisle CA4 ONT 016974-73131

Howard House 27 Howard Place, Carlisle
CA1 1HR 01228-29159

4 bedrs, 2 ☞/WC, 2 ➡; TV tcf ✹
sB&B £14; HB weekly £150-£170; D £8

Royal *Acclaimed* RAC
9 Lowther Street, Carlisle CA3 8ES
01228-22103 Fax 01228-23904
23 bedrs, 1 ➡/WC, 14 ☞/WC, 3 ➡; TV tcf ✹
sB&B £16.90-£20.50 dB&B £33-£34 D £5.50
[5%V]; cc Ac Vi

The Warren RAC
368 Warwick Road, Carlisle CA1 2RU
01228-33663

Wallsend Guesthouse The Old Rectory,
Bowness on Solway, Carlisle CA5 5AF
016973-51055
*Large farmer Rectory, set in one acre grounds
on fringe of quiet family/ fishing village 25
minutes from Carlisle. Convenient for walking
Hadrians Wall, bird watching on Solway
Estuary, Cumbria Cycle and Coastal Way.*

3 bedrs, 1 ➡; tcf ✹ P4
Child restrictions under 12
sB&B £12 Breakfast only

CARNFORTH Lancashire   10B3

Marton Arms Thornton-In-Lonsdale,
Carnforth LA6 3PB 01524-241281   ♿
8 bedrs, 7 ➡/WC, 1 ➡; P60
sB&B £20; HB weekly £125;

CHESTER Cheshire   7D1

Ba Ba 65 Hoole Road, Hoole, Chester CH2
3NJ 01244-315047 Fax 01244-315046
5 bedrs, 3 ☞/WC, 1 ➡; TV tcf P5
sB&B £15 Breakfast only

Bawn Park RAC
10 Hoole Road, Hoole, Chester CH2 3NH
01244-324971 Fax 01244-310951
7 bedrs, 5 ➡/WC, 2 ☞/WC, 1 ➡; TV tcf P12
dB&B £28-£38 Breakfast only [5%V]; cc Ac
Amex Vi JCB

★★★★**Birches Hotel and Carden Park** RAC
Chester 01244-731000 Fax 01829-250539   ♿
83 bedrs, 83 ➡/WC; TV tcf ✹ P200
sB&B £85 dB&B £120 [10%V]; cc Ac Amex
DC Vi

★★**Brookside** RAC
Brook Lane, Chester CH2 2AN 01244-381943
Fax 01244-379701   ♿
26 bedrs, 26 ➡/WC, 2 ➡; TV tcf ✹ ✂
sB&B £30 dB&B £44 [10%V]; cc Ac Vi

Cavendish *Highly Acclaimed* RAC
42-44 Hough Green, Chester CH4 8JQ
01244-675100 Fax 01244-679942
18 bedrs, 18 ➡/WC; TV tcf ✂ P35
sB&B £39.50 dB&B £49.50; HB weekly
£276.50;; cc Ac Amex Vi

★★★★**Chester Moat
House International** RAC
Trinity Street, Chester CH1 2BD 01244-322330
Fax 01244-316118   ♿
152 bedrs, 152 ➡/WC; TV tcf ✹ ✂ P70
sB&B £55-£99 dB&B £113 D £18 [10%V]; cc
Ac Amex DC Vi

Commercial St Peters Churchyard, Chester
CH1 2HG 01244-320749

Devonia RAC
33-35 Hoole Road, Chester CH2 3NH
01244-322236
10 bedrs, 3 ;
Breakfast only [5%V]

Eaton RAC
29 City Road, Chester CH1 3AE 01244-320840
Fax 01244-320850
19 bedrs, 7 /WC, 7 /WC; TV tcf P10
sB&B £28 dB&B £35 D £8.95 [10%V]; cc Ac Amex DC Vi JCB

Egerton Lodge RAC
57 Hoole Road, Hoole, Chester CH2 3NJ
01244-320712
7 bedrs, 1 /WC, 4 /WC, 2 ; TV tcf P4
Child restrictions
sB&B £14-£16 dB&B £29-£32 Breakfast only [5%V]; cc Ac Amex Vi

Eversley RAC
9 Eversley Park, off Liverpool Road, Chester CH2 2AJ 01244-373744
11 bedrs, 8 /WC, 1 ; P17
Breakfast only; cc Ac Amex Vi

Gables RAC
5 Vicarage Road, Hoole, Chester CH2 3HZ
01244-323969
6 bedrs, 2 ; P6
Breakfast only [10%V]

Green Gables *Highly Acclaimed* RAC
11 Eversley Park, Chester CH2 2AJ
01244-372243 Fax 01244-376352
4 bedrs, 4 /WC; TV tcf P8
sB&B £20-£22 dB&B £33-£35 [5%V]

Hamilton Court RAC
5-7 Hamilton Street, Hoole, Chester CH2 3JG
01244-345387
12 bedrs, 1 /WC, 5 /WC, 2 ; TV tcf
sB&B £18-£20 dB&B £39; HB weekly £370; D £12.50; cc Ac Amex Vi

Leahurst Court 74 Hoole Road, Chester CH2 3NL 01244-327542

Limes 12 Hoole Road, Chester CH2 3NJ
01244-328239
8 bedrs, 8 /WC; P8
sB&B £28 Breakfast only

Malvern RAC
21 Victoria Road, Chester CH2 2AX
01244-380865
6 bedrs, 2 ;
Child restrictions
Breakfast only [10%V]

Redland *Highly Acclaimed* **64 Hough Green, Chester CH4 8JY 01244-671024** RAC
An old Victorian style house with authentic decor. Three four poster beds. Exquisite beds and rooms.
13 bedrs, 13 /WC; P15
sB&B £40 Breakfast only

Riverside Hotel & Recorder RAC
22 City Walls, off Lower Bridge Street, Chester CH1 1SB 01244-326580 Fax 01244-311567
22 bedrs, 22 /WC, 1 ;
Breakfast only [10%V]; cc Ac Amex Vi

Stafford City Road, Chester CH1 3AE
01244-326052

Stone Villa 3 Stone Place, Hoole, Chester
CH2 3NR 01244-345014

Vicarage Lodge RAC
11 Vicarage Road, Chester CH2 3HZ
01244-319533
4 bedrs, 2 ➡/WC, 1 ➡; P7
Breakfast only

Westminster City Road, Chester CH1 3AF
01244-317341 &
74 bedrs, 74 ➡/WC, 2 ➡; 🐕
sB&B £35; HB weekly £235-£305;

Weston *Acclaimed* RAC
82 Hoole Road, Chester CH2 3NT
01244-326735
8 bedrs, 3 ➡/WC, 1 ➡/WC, 2 ➡; TV tcf P30
sB&B £26 dB&B £36; HB weekly £210-£250;
D £8.50 [5%V]; cc Ac Amex Vi

CLAYTON-LE-WOODS Lancashire 10B4

Brook House *Highly Acclaimed* RAC
662 Preston Road, Clayton-le-Woods PR6 7EH
01772-36403 Fax 01772-36403
19 bedrs, 17 ➡/WC, 2 ➡;
sB&B £35 dB&B £42 [10%V]; cc Ac Vi

CLITHEROE Lancashire 10C3

Brooklyn *Highly Acclaimed* RAC
32 Pimlico Road, Clitheroe BB7 2AH
01200-28268
4 bedrs, 4 ➡/WC; ⊁
sB&B £23-£25 dB&B £32 [10%V]; cc Ac Vi

CONGLETON Cheshire 7E1

★★★(Inn) Lion & Swan RAC
Swan Bank, Congleton CW12 1JR
01260-273115 Fax 01260-299270
21 bedrs, 21 ➡/WC; P40
[10%V]; cc Ac Amex DC Vi

CONISTON Cumbria 10B2

Coniston Lodge *Highly Acclaimed* RAC
Sunny Brow, Coniston LA21 8HH
015394-41201
6 bedrs, 6 ➡/WC; TV tcf 🖈 P2
Child restrictions
sB&B £26-£34 dB&B £54-£68 [5%V]; cc Ac
Amex Vi

(Inn) Crown Inn RAC
Coniston LA21 8EA 015394-41243
A small family-run hotel, situated in the
centre of the picturesque village of Coniston.
8 bedrs, 1 ➡/WC, 2 ➡; P30
sB&B £20-£34 dB&B £36; HB weekly £180-
£240; D £8 [10%V]; cc Ac Amex DC Vi

CREWE Cheshire 7E1

Balterley Hall Balterley, Crewe CW2 5QG
01270-820206

Clayhanger Hall Farm *Highly Acclaimed* RAC
Maw Lane, Haslington, Crewe CW1 1SH
01270-583952
4 bedrs, 4 ➡/WC; ⊁
Breakfast only

FORTON (M6) Lancashire

Pavilion Lodge RAC
Forton (M6) LA2 9DY 01524-792227

GRANGE-OVER-SANDS Cumbria 10B3

Elton *Highly Acclaimed* RAC
Windermere Road, Grange-Over-Sands LA11
6EQ 01539-532838
7 bedrs;
Breakfast only

Somerset House Kents Bank Road,
Grange-Over-Sands LA11 7DJ
01539-532631

GRASMERE Cumbria 10B2

Ben Place RAC
2 Ben Place, Grasmere LA22 9RL
01539-435581
3 bedrs; P6
sB&B £22 dB&B £40 Breakfast only

Bridge House *Highly Acclaimed* RAC
Stock Lane, Grasmere LA22 9SN 015394-35425
12 bedrs, 10 ➖/WC, 2 ♠/WC; TV tcf ⌇ P20
Child restrictions
sB&B £30-£35 dB&B £60-£70; cc Ac Vi

Fairy Glen RAC
Swan Lane, Grasmere LA22 9RN
01539-435620
3 bedrs, 1 ➖; tcf ⌇ P3
Child restrictions
dB&B £34-£36 Breakfast only [10%V]

Titteringdales Pye Lane, Grasmere LA22
9RQ 01539-435439

HAWKSHEAD Cumbria 10B2

Greenbank Country House *Acclaimed* RAC
Ambleside, Hawkshead LA22 0NS
015394-36497
10 bedrs, 5 ➖/WC, 3 ➖; ⌇ ✕ P12
Breakfast only [5%V]

Ivy House *Acclaimed* RAC
Ambleside, Hawkshead LA22 0NS
015394-36204
6 bedrs, 4 ➖/WC, 2 ♠/WC; tcf ✕ P16
sB&B £36-£38 dB&B £72-£76; HB weekly
£220.50-£234.50; D £10.50 [10%V]

★★(Inn) Red Lion RAC
The Square, Hawkshead LA22 0NS
01539-436213
9 bedrs, 9 ➖/WC; P12 cc Ac Vi

HOLMROOK Cumbria 10A2

Stanley Ghyll House Boot, Holmrook CA19
1TF 01946-723327

HYDE Greater Manchester 10C4

Needhams Farm *Acclaimed* RAC
Uplands Road, Werneth Low, Hyde SK14
3AQ 0161-3684610 Fax 0161-3679106
7 bedrs, 5 ➖/WC, 1 ➖; ✕ P10
sB&B £17-£19 dB&B £30-£32 [5%V]; cc Ac
Amex Vi

KENDAL Cumbria 10B2

Borran's New Hutton, Kendal LA8 0AT
01539-722969

*Built in 1729, old ex- farmhouse, with central
heating and oak beams and real fire in the
countryside.*
5 bedrs, 2 ➖;
sB&B £14 Breakfast only

Brantholme 7 Sedberg Road, Kendal LA9
6AD 01539-722340

Da Francos 101 Highgate, Kendal LA9 4EN
01539-722430

Garnett House Farm *Acclaimed* RAC
Burneside, Kendal LA9 5SF 01539-724542

*A 15th century farmhouse combining period
features, oak beams, paneling and cupboards
with all modern facilities.*
4 bedrs, 3 ♠/WC, 2 ➖; TV tcf P6
dB&B £26 Breakfast only [5%V]

Gateside Farm *Acclaimed* RAC
Windermere Road, Kendal LA9 5SE
01539-722036

Highgate 128 Highgate, Kendal LA9 4HE
01539-724229

Jolly Anglers Inn Burneside, Kendal LA9 5QS 01539-732552

A village inn with log fires and beamed ceilings.
3 bedrs, 1 ⇥/WC, 1 ⇥; TV tcf ✖ P3
sB&B £12 Breakfast only

Lane Head House *Highly Acclaimed* RAC
Helsington, Kendal LA9 5RJ 01539-731283
17th Century Country House of character set in an elevated position enjoying magnificent panoramic views of surrounding hills. Most guest room overlooking Knot Garden.
7 bedrs, 4 ⇥/WC, 3 ⇥/WC; TV tcf P7
Child restrictions
sB&B £35-£40 dB&B £50-£60 [5%V]; cc Ac Amex DC Vi JCB

Martindales *Acclaimed* RAC
9-11 Sandes Avenue, Kendal LA9 4LL
01539-724028
8 bedrs, 8 ⇥/WC; P6
Child restrictions
Breakfast only

KESWICK Cumbria 10B2

Abacourt House *Highly Acclaimed* RAC
26 Stanger Street, Keswick CA12 5JU
017687-72967
4 bedrs, 4 ⇥/WC; ✗ P4
Breakfast only [5%V]

Acorn House *Highly Acclaimed* RAC
Ambleside Road, Keswick CA12 4DL
017687-72553
10 bedrs, 9 ⇥/WC, 1 ⇥; TV ✗ P10
Child restrictions
dB&B £22.50 Breakfast only; cc Ac Vi

Allerdale House *Highly Acclaimed* RAC
1 Eskin Street, Keswick CA12 4DH
01768-773891
6 bedrs, 6 ⇥/WC; ✖ P6
Child restrictions
sB&B £22 dB&B £44; HB weekly £227.50;

Applethwaite
Country House Hotel
Tel. (017687) 72413

Characterful family run Victorian country residence in idyllic and peaceful location. Stunning views over Derwentwater and Borrowdale. 2½ acres woodland gardens. Excellent home cooked food with vegetarian specialities always available. Charming period lounge with log fire. Keswick 1½ miles. Open all year. Resident proprietors: Tom & Gail Ryan.

Applethwaite Country House *Highly Acclaimed* RAC
Applethwaite, Keswick CA12 4PL
017687-72413
12 bedrs, 7 ➡/WC, 5 ☕/WC, 1 ➡; TV tcf ✂ P10
sB&B £26-£28 dB&B £52-£56; HB weekly £250-£265; D £14.50 [5%V]; cc Ac Vi

Avondale 20 Southey Street, Keswick CA12 4EF 01768-772735

Beckside *Highly Acclaimed* RAC
5 Wordsworth Street, Keswick CA12 4HU
017687-730933
3 bedrs, 3 ☕/WC; TV tcf
Child restrictions
dB&B £33-£35; HB weekly £180-£190; D £10 [5%V]

Charnwood *Acclaimed* RAC
6 Eskin Street, Keswick CA12 4DH
017687-74111
5 bedrs, 1 ➡;
Child restrictions under 5
Breakfast only [10%V]

Coledale Inn Braithwaite, Keswick CA12 5TN 01768-778272

Dalegarth House *Highly Acclaimed* RAC
Portinscale, Keswick CA12 5RQ 017687-72817
10 bedrs, 10 ➡/WC; TV tcf ✂
Child restrictions
sB&B £25-£26.50 dB&B £50-£53; cc Ac Vi

Derwent Cottage Portinscale, Keswick CA12 5RF 01768-774838

Edwardene 26 Southey Street, Keswick CA12 4EF 01768-773586

Fell House *Acclaimed* RAC
28 Stanger Street, Keswick CA12 5JU
01768-772669
6 bedrs, 2 ➡/WC, 1 ➡; P4
Breakfast only

Glamarama Seatoller, Keswick CA12 5XQ
01768-777222

Greystoke House *Acclaimed* RAC
Leonard Street, Keswick CA12 4EL
017687-72603
6 bedrs, 2 ☕/WC, 2 ➡; TV tcf ✖ ✂ P4
Child restrictions
sB&B £16 dB&B £32; HB weekly £164;

Greystones *Highly Acclaimed* RAC
Ambleside Road, Keswick CA12 4DP
017687-73108

A traditional, slate-built Lakeland house.
8 bedrs, 8 ➡/WC; ✂ P6
Child restrictions
sB&B £21.50 dB&B £43 D £12.50 [5%V]

Hazelgrove *Acclaimed* RAC
4 Ratcliffe Place, Keswick CA12 4DZ
01768-773391
4 bedrs, 2 ➡/WC, 1 ➡;
Breakfast only

Lake View Portinscale, Keswick CA12 5RD
017687-73249
A friendly guest house in a quiet village one mile from Keswick.
3 bedrs, 2 ➡/WC, 1 ☕/WC; TV tcf ✖ P3
sB&B £15 Breakfast only

Leonards Field RAC
3 Leonard's Street, Keswick CA12 4EJ
017687-741706
8 bedrs, 3 ☕/WC, 2 ➡; TV tcf ✖
Child restrictions
sB&B £14-£15.50 dB&B £28-£33 Breakfast only

Lonnin Garth Portinscale, Keswick CA12
5RS 01768-774095

Lynwood *Highly Acclaimed* RAC
12 Ambleside Road, Keswick CA12 4DL
017687-72081 Fax 017687-75021
7 bedrs, 6 ♠/WC, 1 ➡; TV tcf ✕
sB&B £17.50 dB&B £40 Breakfast only; cc Ac
Vi

Melbreak House RAC
29 Church Street, Keswick CA12 4DX
017687-73398
10 bedrs, 9 ➡/WC, 9 ♠/WC, 3 ➡; TV tcf ✕ ✕
Child restrictions under 3
sB&B £12.50-£14.50 dB&B £25-£31

Pennybrigg Grange-In-Borrowdale, Keswick
CA12 5UQ 01768-777616
6 bedrs, 1 ➡/WC, 1 ➡; P6
sB&B £19 Breakfast only

Ravensworth *Highly Acclaimed* RAC
29 Station Street, Keswick CA12 5HH
017687-72476
8 bedrs, 7 ➡/WC; TV tcf ✕ P5
Child restrictions
dB&B £26-£37; cc Ac Vi

Rickerby Grange *Acclaimed* RAC
Portinscale, Keswick CA12 5RH 017687-72344
13 bedrs, 1 ➡/WC, 10 ♠/WC, 1 ➡; TV tcf ✕ P15
Child restrictions
sB&B £21-£22 dB&B £48-£50

Rooking House *Highly Acclaimed*
Portinscale, Keswick CA12 5RD 017687-72506

Royal Oak Rosthwaite, Keswick CA12 5XB
01768-777214

Shemara *Highly Acclaimed* RAC
27 Bank Street, Keswick CA12 5JZ
017687-73936
7 bedrs, 7 ➡/WC; P5
Child restrictions
Breakfast only

Silverdale *Highly Acclaimed* RAC
Blencathra Street, Keswick CA12 4HT
017687-72294
12 bedrs, 1 ➡/WC, 8 ♠/WC, 1 ➡; TV tcf ✕ P5
Child restrictions
sB&B £17-£22 dB&B £34-£44; HB weekly
£164-£195; [10%V]; cc Ac Vi

Skiddaw Grove *Highly Acclaimed* RAC
Vicarage Hill, Keswick CA12 5QB
017687-73324
10 bedrs, 8 ➡/WC, 2 ♠/WC, 1 ➡; TV tcf P12
sB&B £23 dB&B £46 Breakfast only [5%V]

Stonegarth *Highly Acclaimed* RAC
2 Eskin Street, Keswick CA12 4DH
017687-72436
9 bedrs, 4 ➡/WC, 5 ♠/WC; TV tcf ✕ ✕ P9
Child restrictions
sB&B £17-£22 dB&B £34-£44; HB weekly
£185-£220;; cc Ac Vi

Stybeck Farm Thirlmere, Threlkeld, Keswick
CA12 4TN 017687-73232

*A beautiful Lakeland stone farmhouse, on a
working farm consisting of sheep, dairy cattle,
beef cattle and poultry.*
4 bedrs, 1 ♠/WC, 2 ➡;
sB&B £14 D £10-£12

Sunnyside RAC
25 Southey Street, Keswick CA12 4EF
017687-7244566
8 bedrs, 3 ➡; ✕ P8
Breakfast only; cc Ac

Swiss Court *Highly Acclaimed* RAC
25 Bank Street, Keswick CA12 5JZ
017687-72637
7 bedrs, 7 ➡/WC;
Breakfast only

The Cartwheel 5 Blencathra Street, Keswick
CA12 4HW 01768-773182 Fax 017687-73182
6 bedrs, 1 ➡; TV tcf
sB&B £14; HB weekly £145; D £8; cc Ac
Amex DC Vi

Thelmlea Country Braithwaite, Keswick
CA12 5TD 01768-778305

**Thirnbeck Portinscale, Keswick CA12
5RD 017687-72869 Fax 017687-72869** &
6 bedrs, 5 ☞/WC, 1 🚽; TV tcf 🐾 P6
sB&B £17.50 Breakfast only

Thornleigh *Highly Acclaimed*   🔷RAC
23 Bank Street, Keswick CA12 5JZ
017687-72863
6 bedrs, 6 ☞/WC; TV tcf ✂ P3
Child restrictions
sB&B £19-£22.50 Breakfast only [10%V]; cc Ac Vi

KIRKBY STEPHEN Cumbria   10C2

Augill House Farm *Highly Acclaimed*   🔷RAC
Brough, Kirkby Stephen CA17 4DX
017683-41305
3 bedrs, 2 🚽/WC, 1 ☞/WC; TV tcf P6
Child restrictions
dB&B £38-£40; HB weekly £165-£175; [5%V]

Thrang Country *Highly Acclaimed*   🔷RAC
Mallerstang, Kirkby Stephen CA17 4JX
017683-71889
6 bedrs, 5 🚽/WC, 1 🚽; 🐾 P8
Breakfast only [5%V]; cc Ac Vi

Town Head House *Highly Acclaimed*   🔷RAC
High Street, Kirkby Stephen CA17 4SH
017683-71044 Fax 017683-72128
6 bedrs, 6 🚽/WC; 🐾 ✂ P10
Child restrictions
Breakfast only [10%V]

KNUTSFORD Cheshire   7E1

**Pickmere House Park Lane, Pickmere,
Knutsford WA16 0JX 01565-733433 Fax
01565-733433**
*A listed three story Georgian House,
overlooking farmland, in a rural hamlet two
miles west of junction 19 (M6). Rural
Cheshire.*
7 bedrs, 6 🚽/WC, 1 🚽; TV tcf 🐾 P12
sB&B £29.50; HB weekly £135; D £9.50; cc
Ac Vi

(Inn) The Dog Inn   🔷RAC
Well Bank Lane, Over Peover, Knutsford
WA16 8UP 01625-861421 Fax 01625-861421 &
3 bedrs, 3 🚽/WC; TV tcf ✂ P100
sB&B £38 dB&B £48 Breakfast only; cc Ac Vi

LANCASTER Lancashire   10B3

Flying Horse Shoe Clapham, Lancaster LA2
8ES 01524-251229

Shakespeare *Acclaimed*   🔷RAC
96 St Leonardgate, Lancaster LA1 1NN
01524-841041

LIVERPOOL Merseyside   7D1

Aachen   🔷RAC
91 Mount Pleasant, Liverpool L3 5TB
0151-7093477 Fax 0151-7091126
17 bedrs, 1 🚽/WC, 9 ☞/WC, 2 🚽; TV tcf 🐾
✂ P4
sB&B £20-£30 dB&B £30-£38 D £5.75 [10%V];
cc Ac Amex DC Vi JCB

Blenheim
37 Aigburth Drive, Sefton Park, Liverpool L17 4JE 0151-7277380
17 bedrs, 3 🚿/WC, 4 🛁; TV tcf P17
sB&B £17.50 dB&B £29 [5%V]

Royal
Marine Terrace, Waterloo, Liverpool L22 5PS 0151-9283333 Fax 0151-9490330
25 bedrs, 14 🛁/WC, 11 🚿/WC; TV tcf 🚭 P25
sB&B £38 dB&B £57 D £9.95; cc Ac Amex DC Vi

LYTHAM ST ANNES Lancashire 10B4

Endsleigh *Acclaimed*
315 Clifton Drive South, Lytham-St-Annes FY8 1HN 01253-725622
15 bedrs, 2 🛁/WC, 13 🚿/WC, 1 🛁; TV tcf 🚭 P9
sB&B £19.75 dB&B £39-£39.50; HB weekly £159-£169; [5%V]

Strathmore *Acclaimed*
305 Clifton Drive South, Lytham-St-Annes FY8 1HN 01253-725478
10 bedrs, 5 🛁/WC, 1 🛁; 🚭 P10
Child restrictions
sB&B £19 dB&B £38; HB weekly £147; D £8

MACCLESFIELD Cheshire 7E1

Moorhayes House
27 Manchester Rd, Tytherington, Macclesfield SK10 2JJ 01625-433228

Oldhams Hollow Farm Manchester Road, Tytherington, Macclesfield SK10 2JW 01625-424128
4 bedrs; 🐕
sB&B £16 D £9

MANCHESTER Greater Manchester 10C4

Ebor
402 Wilbraham Road, Chorlton Cum Hardy, Manchester M21 0UH 0161-881-1911
16 bedrs, 8 🚿/WC, 3 🛁; TV tcf P20
Child restrictions
sB&B £22 dB&B £32 D £8 [5%V]; cc Ac Amex Vi

Highbury *Highly Acclaimed*
113 Monton Road, Eccles, Manchester M30 9HQ 0161-7878545 Fax 0161-7879023
8 bedrs, 5 🛁/WC, 3 🚿/WC; TV tcf P11
sB&B £21.50-£41 dB&B £38; HB weekly £280; D £10; cc Ac Amex Vi

Horizon 69 Palatine Road, West Didsbury, Manchester M20 9LJ 0161-445-4705

Imperial
157 Hathersage Road, Manchester M13 0HY 0161-225-6500 Fax 0161-225-6500 ♿
27 bedrs, 21 🛁/WC, 3 🛁; 🚭 P30
sB&B £30 dB&B £44 D £12.50 [10%V]; cc Ac Amex DC Vi

Kempton House
400 Wilbraham Road, Chorlton-cum-Hardy, Manchester M21 0UH 0161-8818766
14 bedrs, 3 🚿/WC, 2 🛁; TV tcf P9
sB&B £22-£27 dB&B £29.50-£36.50 Breakfast only [10%V]; cc Ac Vi

New Central
144-146 Heywood Street, Manchester M8 7PD 0161-205-2169 Fax 0161-205-2169
10 bedrs, 2 🛁; 🐕 P5
sB&B £20.50 dB&B £30 Breakfast only [10%V]

MARYPORT Cumbria 10A1

Royal Victoria John Street, Maryport CA15 6JT 01900-818495

MORECAMBE Lancashire 10B3

Ashley *Acclaimed*
371 Marine Road East, Morecambe LA4 5AH 01524-412034
13 bedrs, 3 🛁/WC, 8 🚿/WC, 1 🛁; TV tcf P5
sB&B £18-£21 dB&B £36-£38; HB weekly £136-£150;

Beach Mount *Highly Acclaimed*
395 Marine Road East, Morecambe LA4 5AN 01524-420753
26 bedrs, 22 🛁/WC, 2 🛁; 🐕 P6
sB&B £17.50-£20.75 dB&B £32-£38.50; HB weekly £140-£160; D £9.50 [10%V]; cc Ac Amex DC Vi

Carr Garth
18 Bailey Lane, Heysham Village, Morecambe LA3 2PS 01524-851175
8 bedrs, 2 🛁; tcf P8
sB&B £13-£14 dB&B £25 Breakfast only

Hotel Prospect *Highly Acclaimed* RAC
363 Marine Road, Morecambe LA4 5AQ
01524-417819
14 bedrs, 14 ➡/WC, 1 ➡; ✕ ✍ P30
sB&B £12-£17.50 dB&B £32-£35; HB weekly
£132-£151; [10%V]; cc Ac Amex DC Vi

New Hazelmere *Acclaimed* RAC
391 Promenade East, Morecambe LA4 5AN
01524-417876 Fax 01524-414488
18 bedrs, 18 ➡/WC; P3
Breakfast only

Wimslow *Acclaimed* RAC
374 Marine Road East, Morecambe LA4 5AH
01524-417804
13 bedrs, 13 ➡/WC, 1 ➡; TV tcf P11
sB&B £19-£20 dB&B £38; HB weekly £158-
£168; D £9 [10%V]; cc Ac Vi

NANTWICH Cheshire 7E1

Cedars 134-136 Crewe Road, Nantwich CW5
6NB 01270-626455

NORTHWICH Cheshire 7E1

Friendly Floatel RAC
London Road, Northwich CW9 5HD
01606-44443 Fax 01603-741500 ♿
60 bedrs, 7 ➡/WC, 53 ➡/WC; TV tcf ✕ P70
sB&B £32-£58.75 dB&B £53.25 D £13.50; cc
Ac Amex DC Vi JCB Awaiting inspection

PENRITH Cumbria 10B1

Brookfield Shap, Penrith CA10 3PZ
01931-716397

**Holmewood 5 Portland Place, Penrith
CA11 7QN 01768-63072**
5 bedrs, 1 ➡/WC, 1 ➡; TV tcf P1
sB&B £14.50 Breakfast only

Hornby Hall *Acclaimed* RAC
Brougham, Penrith CA10 2AR 01768-891114
Fax 01768-88248
7 bedrs, 2 ➡/WC, 3 ➡; tcf ✕ P7
Breakfast only [10%V]; cc Ac Vi

Limes Country RAC
Redhills, Stainton, Penrith CA11 0DT
01768-63343
6 bedrs, 1 ➡/WC, 4 ➡/WC, 1 ➡; TV tcf P7
sB&B £22-£24 dB&B £36-£40; HB weekly
£180-£240; [5%V]; cc Ac Vi

Town Head Farm Blencowe, Penrith CA11
0DB 01768-483263

Tymparon Hall *Acclaimed* RAC
Newbiggin, Stainton, Penrith CA11 0HS
017684-83236
4 bedrs, 2 ➡/WC, 1 ➡; tcf ✍
sB&B £17 dB&B £35; HB weekly £180; [5%V]

Woodland House *Acclaimed* RAC
Wordsworth Street, Penrith CA11 7QY
01768-64177 Fax 01768-890152
8 bedrs, 5 ➡/WC, 3 ➡/WC, 1 ➡; TV tcf P10
sB&B £23 dB&B £40 Breakfast only [5%V]

PRESTON Lancashire 10B4

Tulketh *Highly Acclaimed* RAC
209 Tulketh Road, Ashton, Preston PR2 1ES
01772-728096 Fax 01772-723743
12 bedrs, 4 ➡/WC, 8 ➡/WC, 1 ➡; TV tcf ✍
P12
sB&B £35 dB&B £42 Breakfast only; cc Ac
Amex DC Vi

PULFORD Cheshire 7D1

★★★(Inn) Grosvenor Arms RAC
Wrexham Road, Pulford CH4 9DG
01244-570560 Fax 01244-570809 ♿
42 bedrs, 42 ➡/WC; ✕ P160
cc Ac Amex DC Vi

RAVENGLASS Cumbria 10A2

Muncaster RAC
**Muncaster, Ravenglass CA18 1RD
01229-717693 Fax 01229-717693**
9 bedrs, 2 ➡/WC, 2 ➡; tcf ✕ P20
sB&B £14-£20 dB&B £36-£38 Breakfast only
[10%V]

Pennington Arms Main Street, Ravenglass
CA18 1SD 01229-717222

RUNCORN Cheshire 7D1

Hotel Campanile RAC
Lowlands Road, Runcorn WA7 5TP
01928-581771

SANDBACH Cheshire 7E1

Bears Head Brereton, Sandbach CW11 9RS
01477-535251

Poplar Mount *Acclaimed* ♛
2 Station Road, Elworth, Sandbach CW11 9JG
01270-761268
7 bedrs, 2 ➠/WC, 2 ☞/WC, 1 ➠; TV tcf P9
sB&B £18 dB&B £36 D £7.50 [10%V]; cc Vi

★★The Grove House ♛
Mill Lane, Wheelock, Sandbach CW11 0RD
01270-762582 Fax 01270-759465
10 bedrs, 1 ➠/WC, 9 ☞/WC; TV tcf ✘ P40
sB&B £25-£40 dB&B £40 D £9.95 [5%V]; cc
Ac Amex Vi

SAWREY Cumbria   10B2

Garth Country House *Highly Acclaimed* ♛
Hawkshead, Sawrey LA22 0JZ
015394-36373
8 bedrs, 2 ➠/WC, 8 ☞/WC, 1 ➠; TV tcf ✘ ✂
P12
Child restrictions
dB&B £50 Breakfast only [5%V]

High Green Gate *Acclaimed* ♛
nr Ambleside, Sawrey LA22 0LF 01539-436296
5 bedrs, 1 ➠/WC, 2 ☞/WC, 1 ➠; ✘ P7
sB&B £21-£24 dB&B £55-£61; HB weekly
£170-£190; D £11 [10%V]

Sawrey House *Acclaimed* ♛
Sawrey LA22 0LF 01539-436387 Fax
01539-436010
17 bedrs, 13 ➠/WC, 1 ➠; ✘ P30
Breakfast only

West Vale Country *Highly Acclaimed* ♛
Far Sawrey, Ambleside, Sawrey LA22 0LQ
01539-442817
8 bedrs, 8 ☞/WC; tcf ✂ P8
Child restrictions
sB&B £21.50 dB&B £43; HB weekly £206.50;

SOUTHPORT Lancashire   10B4

Ambassador ♛
13 Bath Street, Southport PR9 0DP
01704-543998 Fax 01704-536269
8 bedrs, 8 ➠/WC, 2 ➠; tcf ✘ ✂ P6
Child restrictions
sB&B £27-£29 dB&B £46; HB weekly £180; cc
Ac Vi

Edendale ♛
83 Avondale Road, Southport PR9 0NE
01704-530718
10 bedrs, 2 ➠/WC, 8 ☞/WC, 1 ➠; TV tcf ✂ P10
sB&B £18 dB&B £34; cc Ac Amex DC Vi

Fairways 106 Leyland Rd, Southport PR9
0DQ 01704-542069

Lake ♛
55-56 Promenade, Southport PR9 0DY
01704-530996
21 bedrs, 20 ➠/WC, 1 ➠; ✂ P14
Child restrictions
sB&B £25 dB&B £42; HB weekly £167-
£185.40; D £8 [10%V]; cc Ac Vi

Leicester ♛
24 Leicester Street, Southport PR9 0EZ
01704-530049
7 bedrs, 2 ☞/WC; TV tcf ✘ P6
Child restrictions
sB&B £15 dB&B £30 Breakfast only [10%V];
cc Ac DC Vi

Lyndhurst ♛
101 King Street, Southport PR8 1LQ
01704-537520
7 bedrs, 3 ➠; P3
Child restrictions
Breakfast only; cc Vi

Merlwood *Acclaimed* ♛
22 Portland Street, Southport PR8 1HU
01704-531247
6 bedrs, 3 ☞/WC, 2 ➠; TV tcf ✂ P8
Child restrictions
sB&B £15-£16 dB&B £30-£32; HB weekly
£140-£154; [10%V]

Oakwood ♛
7 Portland Street, Southport PR8 1LJ
01704-53185
6 bedrs, 4 ➠/WC, 1 ➠; P10
Child restrictions
Breakfast only

Location Maps
Hotel locations are shown on the maps at
the back of the guide. All towns and
villages containing a hotel listed in the
guide are shown in black.

Rosedale 🏰
Talbot Street, Southport PR8 1HP
01704-530604
Family hotel with car park, close to station,
shops and promenade. Hotel situated in quiet
residential road.
10 bedrs, 7 ⇆/WC, 2 ⇆; P8
sB&B £18-£21.50 dB&B £36-£43 Breakfast
only; cc Ac Amex Vi

★Sidbrook 🏰
14 Talbot Street, Southport PR8 1HP
01704-530608 Fax 01704-531198

A detached Edwardian building in a
secluded area of the town centre, close to the
shopping area.
9 bedrs, 5 ⇆/WC, 4 🐾/WC, 1 ⇆; TV tcf 🐕 ✂ P9
sB&B £20-£25 dB&B £35-£44; HB weekly
£165-£185; D £9.50 [5%V]; cc Ac DC Vi

White Lodge 🏰
12 Talbot Street, Southport PR8 1HP
01704-53632
8 bedrs, 1 ⇆/WC, 3 🐾/WC, 2 ⇆; TV ✂ P6
sB&B £17-£19 dB&B £34-£38; HB weekly
£120-£160; [5%V]

Whitworth Falls 16 Latham Rd, Southport
PR9 0JL 01704-530074

Windsor Lodge 🏰
37 Saunders Street, Southport PR9 0HJ
01704-53007 &
12 bedrs, 4 ⇆/WC, 2 ⇆; ✂ P9
Breakfast only [10%V]

ST BEES Cumbria 10A2

Crescent 4/5 Richmond Crescent, St Bees
CA27 0EP 01946-822748

Queens St Bees CA27 0EP 01946-822287
15 bedrs, 15 ⇆/WC; 🐕 P6
sB&B £25.50 Breakfast only

TEBAY Cumbria 10B2

Carmel House *Acclaimed* 🏰
Carmel House, Mount Pleasant, Tebay CA10
3TH 015396-24651
7 bedrs, 7 🐾/WC; TV tcf P6
Breakfast only; cc Amex Vi

THORNTON CLEVELEYS Lancashire 10B3

Victorian House *Highly Acclaimed* 🏰
Trunnan Road, Thornton Cleveleys FY5 4HF
01253-860619 Fax 01253-865350
3 bedrs, 3 ⇆/WC, 2 ⇆; TV tcf 🐕 P20
Child restrictions
sB&B £47.50 dB&B £75 Breakfast only; cc Ac
Vi

TYTHERINGTON Cheshire 7E1

Odhams Hollow Farm Manchester Road,
Tytherington SK10 2JW 01625-424128

ULVERSTON Cumbria 10B3

Rock House 1 Alexander Road, Ulverston
LA12 0DE 01229-586879

WALLASEY Merseyside 10B4

Clifton 🏰
293 Seabank Road, Wallasey L45 5AF
0151-6396505

Sea Level 🏰
126 Victoria Road, New Brighton, Wallasey
L45 9LD 0151-639-3408 Fax 0151-639-3408
15 bedrs, 1 ⇆/WC, 3 ⇆; TV tcf 🐕 P10
sB&B £16 dB&B £29; HB weekly £115;
[10%V]; cc Ac Vi

WARRINGTON Cheshire   7E1

Birchdale *Acclaimed*   RAC
Birchdale Road, Appleton, Warrington WA4
5AW 01925-263662 Fax 01925-860607
16 bedrs, 7 ➥/WC, 3 ➥; TV tcf P40
sB&B £35-£40 dB&B £45 [10%V]; cc Ac Vi

Kenilworth *Acclaimed*   RAC
2 Victoria Road, Warrington WA4 2EN
01925-262323
17 bedrs, 17 ➥/WC, 1 ➥; ✕ P18
sB&B £35 dB&B £32 [5%V]; cc Ac Amex Vi

The Hawthorns 110 Runcorn Road, Moore,
Warrington WA4 6UD 01925-740528

WIGAN Greater Manchester   10B4

Aalton Court   RAC
23 Upper Dicconson Street, Wigan WN1 2AG
01942-322220

Kenilworth Hotel

Excellent accommodation at very competitive rates

2 VICTORIA ROAD (A50 Knutsford Rd)
GRAPPENHALL, WARRINGTON
CHESHIRE WA4 2EN

Telephone: Reservations: (01925) 262323
Visitors: (01925) 268320

A comfortable family run hotel. Conveniently
situated for Warrington and the major North-
West business centres and Tourist attractions.
2½ miles from M6/M56/M62 motorway
network. 15 minutes Manchester Airport.
Especially noted for our hearty
traditional food. Licensed.
A warm welcome guaranteed.

Charles Dickens Inn   RAC
14 Upper Dicconson Street, Wigan WN1 2AD
01942-323263

WINDERMERE Cumbria   10B2

Aaron Slack *Acclaimed*   RAC
48 Ellerthwaite Road, Windermere LA23 2BS
015394-44649
3 bedrs, 1 ➥/WC, 2 🛏/WC; TV tcf
Child restrictions
sB&B £14-£22 Breakfast only [5%V]; cc Ac
Amex Vi

Beaumont *Highly Acclaimed*   RAC
Holly Road, Windermere LA23 2AF
015394-47075
10 bedrs, 3 ➥/WC, 7 🛏/WC; TV tcf P10
Child restrictions
sB&B £25-£35 Breakfast only; cc Ac Amex Vi

Blenheim Lodge *Highly Acclaimed*   RAC
Brantfell Road, Bowness on Windermere,
Windermere LA23 3AE 015394-43440
10 bedrs, 3 ➥/WC, 7 🛏/WC; TV tcf ✕ P14
Child restrictions
sB&B £24-£27 dB&B £42 D £16 [10%V]; cc Ac
Amex Vi

Boston House *Highly Acclaimed*   RAC
4 The Terrace, Windermere LA23 2BS
015394-43654 Fax 015394-43654
6 bedrs, 5 🛏/WC, 2 ➥; TV tcf ✕ P6
dB&B £32-£44; HB weekly £170-£210; D £10
[5%V]; cc Ac Vi

Brendan Chase *Acclaimed*   RAC
College Road, Windermere LA23 1BU
015394-45638   ♿
8 bedrs, 4 ➥/WC, 3 🛏/WC, 3 ➥; TV tcf ✕ ✕
P6
sB&B £12-£15 Breakfast only [5%V]

Broad Oak Country House *Highly
Acclaimed*   RAC
Bridge Lane, Troutbeck, Windermere LA23
1LA 015394-45566 Fax 015394-88766   ♿
10 bedrs, 8 ➥/WC, 2 🛏/WC; TV tcf ✕ P30
Child restrictions under 5
sB&B £35 dB&B £50-£80; HB weekly £265-
£350; D £21.95 [10%V]; cc Ac Vi

Brooklands Ferry View, Bowness,
Windermere LA23 3JB 01539-442344

Cambridge House 9 Oak Street, Windermere LA23 1EN 01539-443846

Cranleigh *Highly Acclaimed* ⚓RAC
Kendal Road, Windermere LA23 3EW
01539-443293
9 bedrs, 9 🛁/WC; TV tcf ⌦ P16
sB&B £18-£26 dB&B £36-£52 D £10 [10%V];
cc Ac Vi JCB

Eastbourne *Acclaimed* ⚓RAC
Biskey Howe Road, Windermere LA23 2JR
015394-43525

Traditionally built, Lakeland house, situated in a quiet area of Bowness. Located below Biskey Howe viewpoint and within easy walking distance to lake, amenities and restaurants.
8 bedrs, 5 🛁/WC, 1 🛁; TV tcf ⌦ P3
Child restrictions
sB&B £18-£25 dB&B £32-£37 Breakfast only;
cc Ac Vi

Elim Bank ⚓RAC
Lake Road, Windermere LA23 2JJ
01539-444810
9 bedrs, 4 🛁/WC, 1 🛁/WC, 1 🛁; TV tcf 🐾 ⌦ P9
sB&B £22.50-£25 dB&B £45-£48; HB weekly
£210-£230; D £10; cc Ac Amex Vi

Fairfield Country House *Highly Acclaimed* ⚓RAC
Brantfell Road, Windermere LA23 3AE
015394-46565 Fax 015394-46565
9 bedrs, 3 🛁/WC, 5 🛁/WC, 1 🛁; TV tcf P14
sB&B £19-£28 dB&B £48-£56; HB weekly
£255-£280; cc Ac Vi

Fayre Holme Country House Upper Storrs
Road, Bowness, Windermere LA23 3JP
01539-488195 &
14 bedrs, 11 🛁/WC, 3 🛁/WC; 🐾
sB&B £35; HB weekly £265-£375; cc Ac Amex Vi

Fir Trees *Highly Acclaimed* ⚓RAC
Lake Road, Windermere LA23 2EQ
015394-42272 Fax 015394-42272

Fir Trees is a well situated Victorian Guest House of considerable charm and character and is furnished with antiques and fine prints throughout.
7 bedrs, 1 🛁/WC, 6 🛁/WC; TV tcf ⌦ P9
sB&B £24.50-£30.50 dB&B £39-£51 Breakfast only [5%V]; cc Ac Amex Vi

★★★Gilpin Lodge ⚓RAC
Crook Road, Windermere LA29 3NE
015394-88818 Fax 015394-88058

Glencree *Highly Acclaimed*   RAC
Lake Road, Windermere LA23 2EQ
015394-45822
5 bedrs, 3 ⇒/WC, 2 ⬥/WC; TV tcf ⥢
Child restrictions
sB&B £39 dB&B £45 Breakfast only [5%V]; cc
Ac Vi

Glenville *Highly Acclaimed*   RAC
Lake Road, Windermere LA23 2EQ
01539-443371

*Set in its own grounds the Glenville is
perfectly positioned for access to all amenities
and within walking distance of the Lake. The
hotel retains original features which give
added character.*
9 bedrs, 1 ⇒/WC, 6 ⬥/WC, 2 ⇒; TV tcf ⚒
P10
sB&B £18-£24 Breakfast only [10%V]; cc Ac Vi

Green Gables *Acclaimed*   RAC
37 Broad Street, Windermere LA23 2AB
01539-443886

Haisthorpe *Acclaimed*   RAC
Holly Road, Windermere LA23 2AF
015394-43445

Hawksmoor *Highly Acclaimed*   RAC
Lake Road, Windermere LA23 2EQ
01539-442110   ♿
10 bedrs, 6 ⇒/WC, 4 ⬥/WC; TV tcf
Child restrictions
sB&B £20-£30 dB&B £40-£52 Breakfast only;
cc Ac Vi

Holly Lodge 6 College Road, Windermere
LA23 1BX 01539-443873 Fax 015394-43873
11 bedrs, 4 ⬥/WC, 2 ⇒; TV tcf P7
sB&B £16; HB weekly £182-£210; D £10

Holly Park *Highly Acclaimed*   RAC
1 Park Road, Windermere LA23 2AW
019662-42107
6 bedrs; ⥢
sB&B £20-£30 dB&B £32-£40 Breakfast only
[5%V]

Holly Wood *Acclaimed*   RAC
Holly Road, Windermere LA23 2AF
015394-42219
6 bedrs, 3 ⬥/WC, 2 ⇒; TV tcf ⥢ P3
sB&B £14-£16 dB&B £27-£30 Breakfast only
[10%V]

**Holmlea Kendal Road, Bowness,
Windermere LA23 3EW 015394-42597**
*Lakeland stone guest house. Friendly,
comfortable, quietly situated, parking.*
6 bedrs, 4 ⬥/WC; TV tcf P6
sB&B £16 Breakfast only

Location Maps
Hotel locations are shown on the maps at
the back of the guide. All towns and
villages containing a hotel listed in the
guide are shown in black.

Kirkwood *Highly Acclaimed* RAC
Princes Road, Windermere LA23 2DD
015394-43907

A large, stone-built Victorian house in a corner position in a garden setting with a flower covered arch leading to the entrance. Situated in a quiet area of Windermere, convenient for local transport and all amenities.
7 bedrs, 1 ♿/WC, 6 🛏/WC; TV tcf 🐾 ✕
dB&B £19 Breakfast only; cc Ac Vi JCB

Lynwood *Acclaimed* RAC
Broad Street, Windermere LA23 2AB
015394-42550
9 bedrs, 9 🛏/WC; TV tcf ✕
sB&B £13-£20 dB&B £26-£40 Breakfast only
[10%V]

Mylne Bridge *Acclaimed* RAC
Brookside Lake, Windermere LA23 2BY
015394-43314

New Hall Bank Fallbarrow Road, Bowness,
Windermere LA23 3DJ 01539-443558 ♿
14 bedrs, 2 ♿; TV tcf 🐾 P20
sB&B £15 Breakfast only

Newstead *Highly Acclaimed* RAC
New Road, Windermere LA23 2EE
015394-44485
7 bedrs, 7 🛏/WC; TV tcf P10
Child restrictions
dB&B £18-£22.50 Breakfast only

Oak Bank Helm Road, Bowness,
Windermere LA23 3BU 01539-443386
11 bedrs, 4 ♿/WC, 11 🛏/WC; 🐾 P11
sB&B £25; HB weekly £157.50-£327;

Oakthorpe *Acclaimed* RAC
High Street, Windermere LA23 1AF
015394-43547

Oldfield House *Acclaimed* RAC
Oldfield Road, Windermere LA23 2BY
015394-88445 Fax 015294-88445
7 bedrs, 1 ♿/WC, 6 🛏/WC; TV tcf ✕ P7
Child restrictions
sB&B £19-£27 dB&B £34-£50 Breakfast only
[5%V]; cc Ac Amex Vi JCB

Orrest Close *Acclaimed* RAC
3 The Terrace, Windermere LA23 1AJ
015394-43325
6 bedrs, 4 🛏/WC, 2 ♿; TV tcf 🐾 P6
dB&B £30-£46; HB weekly £100-£150; cc Vi

Rockside *Acclaimed* RAC
Ambleside Road, Windermere LA23 1AQ
01539-445343 Fax 01539-445533
15 bedrs, 10 🛏/WC, 2 ♿; TV tcf ✕ P12
sB&B £12.50-£15.50 dB&B £31-£42 Breakfast
only [10%V]; cc Ac Amex DC Vi JCB

Rosemount *Acclaimed* RAC
Lake Road, Windermere LA23 2EQ
015394-43739
8 bedrs, 8 🛏/WC; TV tcf P8
Child restrictions
sB&B £17.50-£24 dB&B £35-£48 Breakfast
only [5%V]; cc Ac Vi

Royal Lodge 🔱 RAC
Royal Square, Bowness, Windermere LA23
3DB 01539-443045

St John's Lodge *Highly Acclaimed* RAC
Lake Road, Windermere LA23 2EQ
01539-443078
14 bedrs, 1 ➥/WC; TV tcf ✗ ⅙ P10
Child restrictions
sB&B £18.50-£23 dB&B £37-£42; HB weekly
£189-£210; [5%V]; cc Vi

Thornleigh *Acclaimed* RAC
Thornbarrow Road, Windermere LA23 2EW
015394-44203

Westlake *Highly Acclaimed* RAC
Lake Road, Windermere LA23 2EQ
015394-43020

White Rose Broad Street, Windermere LA23
2AB 01539-445108

Winbrook House *Acclaimed* RAC
30 Ellerthwaite Road, Windermere LA23 2AH
015394-44932

Woodlands *Highly Acclaimed* RAC
New Road, Windermere LA23 2EE
015394-43915

Yew Grove Troutbeck, Windermere LA23
1PG 01539-433304

Yorkshire House 1 Upper Oak Street,
Windermere LA23 2LB 01539-444689

WORKINGTON Cumbria 10A1

Morven *Highly Acclaimed* RAC
Siddick Road, Workington CA14 1LE
01900-602118 ⅻ
6 bedrs, 4 ➥/WC, 2 ➥; TV tcf
sB&B £20-£29 dB&B £34-£44 Breakfast only

The Briery Stainburn Road, Stainburn,
Workington CA14 1ST 01900-603395 ⅻ
4 bedrs, 2 ➥; TV tcf ✗ P60
sB&B £15 D £4.79-£9.95; cc Ac DC Vi JCB

Scotland

There's something more than scenery, golf, fishing and the grouse moors which makes Scotland so special. Perhaps it has to do with national pride, enterprise and spirit in which no doubt the single malt plays its part! Now that so many aristocratic Scots have opened their estates, there's no lack of castle-homes to visit. For a breed reputed to be tight fisted, sporrans have shelled out liberally and world-wide for treasures which fill these magnificent fortifications. Some have incomparable gardens despite, or even because of the climate!. Let the pipes and drums set you feet a-tapping and be it pub, castle or modest B & B, enjoy the renowned warmth of Scottish hospitality.

A SELECTION OF ATTRACTIONS:

Unless otherwise stated, all can be visited at Easter then May to September – some longer. Telephone for days/hours of opening, except 'HS' [Historic Scotland, Tel: 0131-244 3101] properties which all open Apl – Sept Mon – Sat 9.30 – 6.30, Sun 2 – 4.30. Winter closing 4.30.

Aberdeen Amusement Park, Grmp: *Mega-size park. Wristband ticket to all attractions.* Tel: 01224-581909.

Aberdeen Fishmarket,Grmp: *Mon-Fri- 7 - 8a.m. Fishing boats unload – fish auction.* Tel: 01224-897744.

Abbotsford House, Melrose, Bord: *Built by Sir Walter Scott in 'Scottish Baronial' style. Personal relics:* Tel: 01896-2043.

Abbotsford House

Aigas Dam Fish Lift, nr. Beauly, High: *Viewing chamber shows salmon rising to upper reservoir to spawn in autumn.* Tel: 01463-782412.

Angus Folk Museum, Glamis, Tays: *Five 19th-c cottages showing social/domestic history. NTScot.* Tel: 01307-840288.

Arduaine Garden, Argyll, Stra: *18 acre garden on promontary, best in spring. NTScot.* 018522-287.

Batchelors' Club, nr. Ayr, Str: *17th-c thatched cottage where Rabbie Burns hung oot wi' his friends. Furnished in period. NTScot.* Tel: 01292-541940.

Bell's Cherrybank Gardens, Perth, Tays: *National Heather collection in 18 acres. Play area, waterfall.* Tel: 01738-27330.

Blair Atholl Distillery, Tays: *Tour of old distillery buildings. Bells from burn water to cask.* Tel: 01796-472234.

Blair Atholl Mill, Tays: *Water mill built 1613 producing oatmeal used in on site bakery. Tea Room:* Tel: 01796-483317.

Blair Castle, Blair Athol, Tays: *Superbly furnished, arms, armour, china costumes. Nature trails, deer.* Tel: 01796-481207.

Border Abbeys: *Melrose, Jedburgh, Kelso & Dryburgh, in Tweed valley. Latter is burial place of Scott.* Tel; 0131-244 3101.

Braemar Castle, Aberdeenshire, Grmp: *This attractive, lived in castle has tower, spiral stair, pit-prison.* Tel: 013397-41219.

Brass Rubbing Centre, Chambers Close, Edinburgh: *Pictish stones make an original rubbing. Brasses too.* Tel: 0131-556 4364.

Brodick Castle, Isle of Arran: *Home of Dukes of Hamilton. Paintings, objets d'art. Gardens:* NTScot. Tel: 01770-302202.

Cairngorm Chair Lift,nr. Aviemore, High: *To highest observation building in Britain at 3,600ft.* Tel: 01479-861 228.

Cashmere Woollen Mill & Museum [Peter Anderson], Galashield, Bord: *Yarn to tweed in 40 minute tour.* Tel: 01896-2091.

Castle Fraser, Sauchen, nr. Aberdeen, Grmp: *Arranged by NTScot as pre-classical era home. Built 16th-c.* Tel: 0133 03- 463.

Castle Kennedy Gardens, Stranraer, Dm & G: *Best in spring, rhododendrons, notable pinetum. Scenery.* Tel: 01776-2024.

Cawdor Castle, nr. Inverness, High: *Setting for Macbeth's murder of Duncan. Central tower of 1372. Notable gardens.* Tel: 01667-404615.

Clan Tantan Centre, Leith, Loth: *Computer research discovers your Scottish heritage.* Tel: 0131-553 5161.

Crathes Castle & Garden, nr. Banchory, Grmp: *Ancient castle with series of enclosed gardens. NTScot.* Tel: 0133 044-525.

Culzean Castle Garden & Country Park, Maybole, Stra: *Features Round Drawingroom. Farm buildings by Adam. Camelia House, Orangery, Adventure Playground. NTScot.* Tel:016556-274.

Dalmeny House, Queensferry, W. Loth: *Paintings, porcelain, French furniture in Gothic style home on Firth of Forth. May-Sept.* Tel: 0131-331 1888.

Deep Sea World, N. Queensferry, Loth: *Underwater safari, bigest aquarium in thre world. Educational, fun.* Tel: 01383-411411.

Doune Motor Museum, Perthshire, High: *Over 50 cars with second oldest Rolls Royce in the world.* 01786-841203.

Drum Castle, nr. Aberdeen, Grmp: *Massive 13th-c granite tower/17th-c mansion. Antiques, silver, roses. NTScot.* Tel: 01330-811204.

Drummond Castle Gardens, nr. Crieff, Tays: *Finest 17th-c formal gardens in Europe.* Tel: 01764-681257.

Dundee Discovery Point Tays: *Tour Captain Scott's 'Discovery'. Near Tay Bridge.*

Dunvegan Castle, Isle of Skye: *Still 13th-c stronghold home of the Clan MacLeod for 600 years set on sea loch. Historic treasures, bottle dungeon, water garden, seal colony trips.* Tel: 0147 022-206.

Eilean Donan Castle, Wester Ross, High: *Causeway approach to restored castle of 1220 on Loch Duich.* Tel: 0159 985-202.

Edinburgh Castle, Loth: *A must on any visit. Crown jewels of Scotland sited on a volcanic rock!* Tel: 0131-244 3101.

Falkland Palace & Garden, Fife, Loth: *Lovely early 16th-c palace. Royal tennis court, small attractive garden.*Tel: 01337-57397.

Floors Castle, Kelso, Bord: *First, view it from Rennie's bridge over the Tweed at Kelso. Superb furnishings.* Tel: 01573-223333.

The Georgian House, Charlotte Square, Edinburgh, Loth: *A Robert Adam masterpiece in city's finest 18th-c square.* Tel: 0131-225 2160.

Gladstone's Land, Edinburgh, Loth: *One of the Auld Toon's precipitous tenement buildings of 1620.* Tel: 0131-226 5856.

Glamis Castle

Glamis Castle, Tays: *Fine collections of china, tapestry & furniture in childhood home of Queen Mother.* Tel: 01307-840242.

Glenfiddich Distillery, Dufftown,Grmp: *Audio-visual presentation then tour and tasting.* Tel: 01340-820373.

Glenlivet Distillery Visitors Centre, nr. Tomintoul, Grmp: *Distillery Tour, wee dram and souvenirs.* Tel: 01807-590 427.

Hill House, Helensburgh, Stra: *House and furniture designed and built by Charles Rennie Mackintosh. NTScot.* Tel: 01436-73900.

Hill of Tarvet, nr. Cupar, Fife: *Edwardian mansion . Fine topiary, furniture, tapestries, paintings.* NTScot.Tel: 01334-53127.

Hopetown House, S. Queensferry, W. Loth: *Superb state apartments, nature trails, deer park.* Tel: 0131-331 2451.

Inveraray Castle, Argyllshire, Stra: *Chief seat of chiefs of Clan Campbell, Dukes of Argyll. Magnificent interior decor, paintings etc.* Tel: 01499-2203.

Inveraray Goal, Argyllshire, Stra: *Torture, Death & Damnation Exhibition, sounds and smells!* Tel: 01499-2381.

Inverewe Gardens, Wester Ross: *Rare subtropical plants thrive in famous, continuously colourful garden.* Tel: 0144 586-200.

Lady Victoria Colliery, Newtongrange, Loth: *Tours by ex-miners, exhibition, tea-room:* Tel: 0131-663 7519.

Lauriston Castle, Edinburgh, Loth: *16th-c tower house furnished as Edwardian home. Guided tours.* Tel: 0131-336 2060.

Linlithgow Palace, Loth: *Splendid ruins on the shores of its loch. Birthplace of Mary Q. of Scots.* Tel: 0131-244 3101.

Loch Ness Monster Exhibition, Drumnadrochit, High: *Audio-visual of equipment used to seek 'Nessie'. Life size model.* Tel:01465-450573.

Logan Botanic Garden, nr. Stranraer, Dm & G: *Temperate climate encourages the subtropical – cabbage palms, tree ferns.* Tel: 01776-860231.

Charles Rennie Macintosh Society, Glasgow, Stra: *In the architect's only church. Display plus information on his other buildings.* Tel: 0141-946-6600.

Manderston, Duns, Bord: *A silver staircase, a marble dairy, even 'downstairs' is up-market.* Tel: 01361-83450.

Mellerstain, Gordon, Bord: *Exceptional decor and plasterwork in Wm. & Robert Adam mansion.* Tel:01573-410225.

Museum of Lead Mining Industry, Wanlockhead, Dm & G: *Gold panning high*

in Lowther Hills, beam engine, but-&-ben cottages. Tel: 01659-74387.

National Gallery of Scotland & Royal Scottish Academy, The Mound, Edinburgh, Loth: *Both outstanding.* Tel: 0131-556 8921 & 225 6671.

Palace of Holyroodhouse, Edinburgh, Loth: *Queen's official residence in Scotland. Royal Apartments.* Tel: 0131-556 1096.

Paxton House, nr. Berwick-on-Tweed, N'mbd: *Palladian mansion. Chippendale furniture, paintings from N. Galleries.* Tel: 01289-386291.

Preston Mill & Phantassie Doocot, E. Loth: *Picturesque red pantilled smallest & oldest surviving mill. NTScot.* Tel: 01620-860426.

Provost Ross's House, Aberdeen, Grmp: *Built 1594, old kitchen, beam-&-board ceilings, maritime museum. NTScot.* Tel: 01224-572215.

Skara Brae, nr. Kirkwall, Orkney: *Neolithic village of 8 dwellings circa 3000BC.* Tel: 0131 244-3101.

Scone Palace, Perth, Tays: *Original location of Coronation Stone of Scone. Magnificent collections in medieval Palace, still family home.* Tel: 01738-52300.

Stirling Castle, Cent: *Awesome sight on top of 250ft. rock. Steeped in history from Wallace the Bruce onwards:* Tel: 0131 244 3101.

Teddy Melrose, Melrose, Bords: *Teddy bear museum, famous characters, Rupert, Paddington Winnie plus.* Tel: 0189 682-2464.

Thirstane Castle, Lauder, Berwick-on-Tweed, N'mbd: *Nursery toys and 'dressing-up' in one of the oldest castles.* Tel: 01578-722430.

Threave Garden, nr. Castle Douglas, Dm & G: *Gardens of NT for Scotland. Peat, rock & water gardens.* Tel: 01556-2575.

Traquair House, nr. Peebles, Stra: *Inhabited since 10th-c, has housed 27 monarchs . 18th-c brewery still going strong.* Tel: 01896-830323.

The Weather Centre, Laurieston, Dm & G: *See how forecasts are prepared using satellite equipment.* Tel: 01644 450 264.

SOME ANNUAL EVENTS:

Argyllshire Highland Gathering, Oban, Stra: *Major gathering with traditional events & solo piping competition. 24 Aug.* Tel: 01631-562671.

Blair Atholl Int'l Highland Games, Perthshire, Tays: *28 May.* Tel: 01796-481355.

Braemar Royal Highland Games, Grmp: *Includes traditional Scottish sports - toss the caber, put the shot. 2 Sept.* Tel: 01339-755377.

Glasgow Int'l Jazz Festival, Stra: *Established feature in the European jazz calendar. Masterclasses. 30 Jun – 9 July.* Tel: 0141-522 3572/227 5511.

Edinburgh Int'l Film Festival, Loth: *New British films; American independent cinema. Important event. 12 – 27 Aug.* Tel: 0131-228 4051.

Edinburgh Int'l Festival, Loth: *Theatre, music dance opera & visual arts of highest calibre. 13 Aug – 2 Sept.* Tel: 0131-226 4001

Edinburgh Military Tattoo, Loth: *Blend of music, ceremony & entertainment on esplanade of castle. 4 – 26 Aug.* Tel:0131-2251188.

Glenshee Snow Fun Week, Blairgowrie, Tays: *Races, childrens' events, apres ski entertainments. Early March.* Tel: 01250-873701.

Highland Traditional Music Festival, Dingwall, High: *Gathering in the best Celtic tradition. 30 Jun – 2 Jul.* Tel: 01349-883341.

Inverness Tattoo, High: *Pipes, drums, regimental bands, Highland/country dancing. 24 – 29 July.* Tel: 01463-234511.

Lammas Fair & Market, St. Andrews, Fife: *One of the country's oldest street fairs. 7 – 8 Aug.* Tel: 01334-53722.

Mayfest, Glasgow, Stra: *Int'l community event of the boldest in theatre, popular & classical music. 28 Apl – 20 May.* Tel: 0141-5528000/227 5511.

Open Golf Championship, St. Andrews, Fife: *Major event attracts world's top players, 50,000 spectators! 20 – 23 July.* Tel: 01334-72112.

Pitlochry Festival '95, Tays: *Up to 7 plays in 6 days, plus concerts, fringe events. 28 Apl – 7 Oct.* Tel: 01796-473054/472680.

R.A.F. Leuchars Battle of Britian Air Show, Fife: *Scotland's largest int'l air show plus Go-Karting, Bungee Jumping, funfair. 16 Sept.* Tel: 01334-839000.

RSAC Scottish Rally, Perth, *Int'l motor sport event. A round of the European championships. 2 – 4 Jun.* Tel: 0141-221 3850.

River Tweed Festival, *throughout the Borders: Celebrating riversports, cycling, theatre, hot-air balloons. 1 – 31 May.* Tel: 01750-20555.

Royal Highland Show, nr. Edinburgh, Loth: *Scotland's national agricultural show. 22 – 25June.* Tel: 0131-333 2444.

Rugby Int'l, Murrayfield, Edinburgh, Loth: *4 Mar.* Tel: 0131-3372346.

St. Andrews Highland Games, Fife: *Traditional games, piping, dancing, Heavyweights etc. 30 July.* Tel: 01334-476305.

The Scottish Alternative Games, Parton, Dm & G: *Gird 'n' Cleek, Hurlin' the Curlin' Stane, Spinning Peerie, Hop Scotch, Arm Wrestling until the 'Last Fling'. 6 Aug.* Tel: 016447-282.

Scottish Open Carriage Driving Championships, Newport on Tay, Fife: *Full supporting country fair, antiques.* Tel: 01334-85708.

Scottish Transport Extravaganza, Forfar, Tays: *Display/judging of 500 vehicles, auto jumble, antique & trade srands, main ring entertainment. 15 – 16 July.* Tel: 01307-462496.

Sheep & Wool Day, Traquair House, Innerleithen, Bords: *Sheepdog demos, weaving, dyeing, spinning & sheering. Rare breeds & llamas. 30 July.* Tel: 01896-830323.

Snow Fun Weekend, Tomintoul, Grmp: *Ski & sleigh rides, treasure hunts, torchlight skiing, dinner dance. Late Feb.* Tel: 019756-51440.

Three Mile Fun Run, Newtonmore, High: *For all the family, fancy dress optional. mid-May.* Tel: 01479-810363.

West Highland Yachting Week, *Centred around Crinan, Oban & Tobermory on W. coast. 28 Jul – 4 Aug.* Tel: 01631-63309.

World Pipe Band Championships, Glasgow, Stra: *12 Aug. World's main competitive gathering. Highland dancing, trade stands. 13 Aug.* Tel: 0141-221 5414.

ABERDEEN Grampian   15F4

Abbotswell 28 Abbotswell Crescent,
Kincorth, Aberdeen AB1 1AR 01224-871788
Fax 01224-891257

*Family run guest house with exellent off road
parking, snacks also available, restricted
license.*
12 bedrs, 2 ☛/WC, 3 ➡; TV tcf ✂ P12
Child restrictions
sB&B £15; HB weekly £163-£238; D £9

Abenjean 85 Constitution Street, Aberdeen
AB2 1ET 01224-640171

Aberdeen Springbank Guesthouse
6 Springbank Terrace, Aberdeen AB1 2LS
01224-592048

Allan 56 Polmuir Road, Aberdeen AB1 2RT
01224-584484

Beeches Private 193 Great Western Road,
Aberdeen AB1 6PS 01224-586413

Belhaven *Acclaimed*   RAC
152 Bon Accord Street, Aberdeen AB1 2TX
01224-588384 Fax 01224-588384
8 bedrs, 3 ☛/WC, 3 ➡; TV tcf 🐾 ✂
sB&B £20 dB&B £30-£40 Breakfast only

Bimini   RAC
69 Constitution Street, Aberdeen AB2 IET
01224-646912 Fax 01224-646912
7 bedrs, 2 ➡; TV tcf P7
sB&B £18-£22 dB&B £34-£38 Breakfast only
[5%V]; cc Ac Vi

Blackdog Heights Bridge of Don, Aberdeen
AB23 8BT 01224-704287

Cedars *Acclaimed*   RAC
339 Great Western Road, Aberdeen AB1 6NW

01224-583225 Fax 01224-585050
13 bedrs, 3 ➡/WC, 6 ☛/WC, 1 ➡; TV tcf ✂
P13
sB&B £38-£45 dB&B £52-£54 Breakfast only;
cc Ac Amex Vi

Colwyn 73-75 Dee Street, Aberdeen AB1 2EE
01224-582102

Corner House 385 Great Western Road,
Aberdeen AB1 6NY 01224-313063

Craiglynn *Highly Acclaimed*   RAC
36 Fonthill Road, Aberdeen AB1 2UJ
01224-584050 Fax 01224-584050
9 bedrs, 4 ➡/WC, 3 ☛/WC, 2 ➡; TV tcf ✂ P8
sB&B £34-£52.50 dB&B £50 D £14.95; cc Ac
Amex DC Vi

Crown Private 10 Springbank Terrace,
Aberdeen AB1 2LS 01224-586842

Dunavon House 60 Victoria Street, Dyce,
Aberdeen AB2 0EE 01224-722483

Dunnydeer 402 Great Western Road,
Aberdeen AB1 6NR 01224-312821

Fourways *Acclaimed*   RAC
435 Great Western Road, Aberdeen AB1 6NJ
01224-310218
7 bedrs, 1 ➡/WC, 5 ☛/WC, 1 ➡; TV tcf P5
sB&B £22 dB&B £36 Breakfast only;
cc Amex Vi

Gushetneuk 3 Belvedere Street, Aberdeen
AB2 4QS 01224-636435

Haven 62 Albergeldie Road, Aberdeen AB1
6EN 01224-585659

Jays   RAC
422 King Street, Aberdeen AB2 3BR
01224-638295
10 bedrs, 10 ☛/WC; TV tcf P80
Child restrictions
sB&B £20-£30 dB&B £40-£50 Breakfast only

Kilbreck   RAC
410 Great Western Rd, Aberdeen AB1 6NR
01224-316115
6 bedrs, 2 ➡; P3
sB&B £19 dB&B £29 Breakfast only

Mount Pleasant 28 Abbotswell Crescent, Kincorth, Aberdeen AB1 5AR 01224-871788

Nicolls 63 Springbank Terrace, Aberdeen AB1 2JZ 01224-572867
4 bedrs, 2 🛏; 🏲 P3
sB&B £18 Breakfast only

Roselodge 3 Springbank Terrace, Aberdeen AB1 2LS 01224-586794
5 bedrs, 2 🛏; TV tcf P3
sB&B £18 Breakfast only

Stewart Lodge 89 Bon Accord Street, Aberdeen AB1 2ED 01224-573823

Strathboyne ⚓RAC
26 Abergeldie Terrace, Aberdeen AB1 6EE 01224-593400
7 bedrs, 2 🕭/WC, 2 🛏; TV tcf 🏲 🍴
sB&B £18-£19 dB&B £29-£32 Breakfast only [10%V]

ABERFELDY Tayside 13D1

★★★Moness House ⚓RAC
Aberfeldy PH15 2DY 01887-820446 Fax 01887-820062

ABOYNE Grampian 15E4

Arbor Lodge Ballater Road, Aboyne AB34 5HY 01339-886951

Birkwood Lodge Gordon Crescent, Aboyne AB34 5HU 01339-886347

Gordon Arms North Deeside Road, Kincardine O'Neil, Aboyne AB34 5AA 013398-84236
7 bedrs, 1 🛏/WC, 4 🕭/WC, 2 🛏; TV tcf 🏲 P7
sB&B £16; HB weekly £160-£235; D £3.50-£15; cc Ac Amex Vi

Huntly Arms Aboyne AB34 5HS 01339-886101

Profeits Ballater Road, Dinnet, Aboyne AB34 5JY 01339-885229

Struan Hall Ballater Road, Aboyne AB34 5HY 013398-887241 Fax 013398-87241

Our elegant 19th century home is beautifully situated in a woodland garden within walking distance of Aboyne village centre. All bedrooms have en-suite shower rooms, tea making facilities and TV. Part of Scotland Deluxe Consortium.
3 bedrs, 3 🕭/WC; TV tcf P14
Child restrictions under 7
sB&B £22; HB weekly £140;; cc Vi

ACHNASHEEN Highland 14C3

Ocean View Sand, Laid, Achnasheen IV22 2ND 01445-731385

Oran Na Mara Drumchork, Achnasheen IV22 2HU 01445-731394

AIRDRIE Strathclyde 12C2

Easter Glentore Farm Greengairs, Airdrie ML6 7TJ 01236-830243
3 bedrs, 3 🕭/WC;
Breakfast only

ALFORD Grampian 15E3

The Smiddy House Glenkindie, Alford AB33 8RX 01975-641216

ANNAN Dumfries & Galloway 13D4

Stanfield Farm Eastriggs, Annan DG12 6TF 01431-40367

ANSTRUTHER Fife 13E1

Anchor Inn 42 Charles Street, Pittenweem, Anstruther KY10 2QJ 01333-311326
4 bedrs, 1 🛏; TV tcf P30
sB&B £18 Breakfast only; cc Ac Amex Vi

Hazelton 29 Marketgate, Anstruther KY10 3TH 01333-50250

Mayview O'the Lands & Barony O, Crail Road, Anstruther 01333-310677

Royal RAC
20 Rodger Street, Anstruther KY10 3DU
01333-310581 Fax 01333-310270

Spindrift *Highly Acclaimed* RAC
Pittenweem Road, Anstruther KY10 3DT
01333-310573
8 bedrs, 7 ⇋/WC, 1 ♠/WC; TV tcf P10
Child restrictions
sB&B £30-£40 dB&B £50-£60; HB weekly
£231-£350; cc Ac Vi

The Hermitage Ladywalk, Anstruther KY10 3EX 01333-310909

APPIN Strathclyde 12B1

Holly Tree RAC
Kentallen, Appin PA38 4BY 01631-74292 ⅋
10 bedrs, 10 ⇋/WC; TV tcf ✗ P40
sB&B £41.50 dB&B £75 D £23.50 [10%V]; cc
Ac Vi

ARBROATH Tayside 13E1

Kingsley House RAC
29/31 Market Gate, Arbroath DD11 1AU
01241-873933 Fax 01241-873933
14 bedrs, 4 ⇋; TV tcf ✗
sB&B £15 dB&B £23; HB weekly £115;
[10%V]

Scurdy *Acclaimed* RAC
33, Marketgate, Arbroath DD11 1AU
01241-872417 Fax 01241-872417 ⅋
10 bedrs, 3 ♠/WC, 3 ⇋; TV tcf ✗ ⅍
sB&B £16-£20 dB&B £29-£32; HB weekly
£147-£150; D £7.50 [5%V]; cc Ac

ARDGAY Highland 15D2

Ardgay House Ardgay IV24 3DH
01863-766345

Rowanlea 12 Airdens, Bonar Bridge, Ardgay
IV24 3AS 01863-766440

AUCHTERARDER Tayside 13D1

Cairn Lodge RAC
Orchil Road, Auchterarder PH3 1LX
01764-662634

AUCHTERMUCHTY Fife 13D1

Ardchoille Farmhouse *Highly Acclaimed* RAC
Dunshalt, Auchtermuchty KY14 7ER
01337-828414 Fax 01337-828414

AULTBEA Highland 15B2

Buena Vista Aultbea IV22 2HU 01445-731374

**Sandale 5 Pier Road, Aultbea IV22 2JQ
01445-731336**
*Looking over the loch, it is situated in a very
nice garden, guests have own sun lounge,
dinners can be included.*
3 bedrs, 1 ⇋/WC, 1 ♠/WC, 1 ⇋;
sB&B £14 D £10

The Croft Aultbea IV22 2JA 01445-731352

AVIEMORE Highland 15D3

Balavoulin RAC
Grampian Road, Aviemore PH22 1RL
01479-810672 Fax 01479-811575
5 bedrs, 5 ♠/WC; TV tcf ✗ P16
dB&B £36-£45 Breakfast only [10%V]; cc Ac
Amex Vi

Ravenscraig RAC
141 Grampian Road, Aviemore PH22 1RP
01479-810278

AYR Strathclyde	12C3

Brenalder Lodge *Highly Acclaimed* RAC
39 Dunure Road, Doonfoot, Ayr KA7 4HR
01292-443939   &
3 bedrs, 3 ☂/WC; TV tcf ✝
Child restrictions
sB&B £30-£38 dB&B £50 Breakfast only
[10%V]

Windsor *Highly Acclaimed* RAC
6 Alloway Place, Ayr KA7 2AA
01292-264689   &
10 bedrs, 5 ➡/WC, 3 ☂/WC, 1 ➡; TV tcf ✝ ✂
sB&B £20 dB&B £44; HB weekly £195; [5%V];
cc Ac Vi

BALLACHULISH Highland	14C4

Lyn-Leven *Acclaimed* RAC
West Laroch, Ballachulish PA39 4JP
01855-812392 Fax 01855-811600; cc Ac Vi

THE LYN LEVEN GUEST HOUSE

A very warm highland welcome awaits
you at Lyn Leven, only 1 mile from
Glencoe. The house is family run with
good home cooking. We are situated
with attractive well cared for gardens
overlooking Loch Leven in the heart of
Scotland's most spectacular scenery. All
rooms are en-suite. Private Car Parking.
RAC Acclaimed.

Ballachulish: Argyll
Tel: 01855 811392
Fax: 01855 811600

BALLATER Grampian	15E4

Auld Bank Hoose Braemar, Ballater AB35
5YP 01339-741336

Auld Kirk Braemar Road, Ballater AB35
5RQ 013397-55762 Fax 013397-55707 &

*A converted church of charm and character
with a family-run restaurant using local
produce. Well-equipped bedrooms.*
6 bedrs, 6 ☂/WC; TV tcf ✝ P10
sB&B £18 D £6-£17; cc Ac Vi

Ballater *Acclaimed* RAC
34 Victoria Road, Ballater AB3 5QX
013397-55346

Balnellan House Braemar, Ballater AB35
5YQ 01339-741474
3 bedrs, 1 ➡/WC, 2 ☂/WC; ✝ P4
sB&B £19.50 Breakfast only

Birchwood Chapel Brae, Braemar, Ballater
AB35 5YT 01339-741599

Craggan Bridge of Gairn, Ballater AB35 5TY
01339-755782

Craig Gowan 53 Golf Road, Ballater AB35
5RU 01339-755008

Cranford 15 Glenshee Road, Braemar,
Ballater AB35 5YT 01339-741675

Creag Meggan Bridge of Gairn, Ballater
AB35 5UD 01339-755767

Dee Valley 26 Viewfield Road, Ballater AB35
5RD 01339-755408

Deeside Braemar Road, Ballater AB35 5RQ
01339-755420

Gairnshiel Lodge Glengairn, Ballater AB35 5UQ 01339-755582

Highland Invercauld Road, Ballater AB35 5RP 01339-755468

Moorfield House Braemar, Ballater AB35 5YT 01339-741244

Moorside *Acclaimed*   RAC
Braemar Road, Ballater AB35 5RL
01339-755492 Fax 01339-755492
9 bedrs, 3 ➡/WC, 6 ⬥/WC; TV tcf ⅍ P10
sB&B £16-£20 dB&B £40 Breakfast only; cc Ac Vi

Netherley 2 Netherley Place, Ballater AB35 5QE 013397-55792
9 bedrs, 2 ➡/WC, 2 ⬥/WC, 1 ➡; TV tcf ✖
Child restrictions under 4
sB&B £15 Breakfast only

BANCHORY Grampian   15F4

Aldor 74 Station Road, Banchory AB31 3JY 01330-824026

Mains Of Drums North Deeside Road, Drumoak, Banchory AB31 3AE 01330-811335

Village 83 High Street, Banchory AB31 3TJ 01330-23307

BANFF Grampian   15F3

Banff Links Swordanes, Banff AB45 2JJ
01261-812414   &
9 bedrs, 9 ⬥/WC, 1 ➡; ✖ P30
sB&B £31; HB weekly £186;

Clayfolds Farm Kirktown of Alvah, Banff AB45 3UD 01261-6288

Montcoffer House Montcoffer, Banff AB45 3LJ 01261-812979

Royal Oak Bridge Street, Banff AB45 1HB 01261-812494
5 bedrs, 2 ⬥/WC, 1 ➡; P20
sB&B £16.50 Breakfast only

Whitehouse Of Park Castle of Park, Cornhill, Banff AB45 2AX 01466-6269 Fax 01466-6269
5 bedrs, 2 ➡/WC, 2 ⬥/WC; TV tcf
sB&B £18; HB weekly £194-£333; D £12-£15; cc Ac Amex Vi

BARRHEAD Strathclyde   12C2

East Uplaw Uplawmoor, Barrhead
01505-850383
4 bedrs, 1 ⬥/WC, 2 ➡; ✖ P20
sB&B £14 Breakfast only

BEAULY Highland   15D3

Chrialdon *Acclaimed*   RAC
Station Road, Beauly IV4 7EH 01463-782336
8 bedrs, 2 ➡/WC, 4 ⬥/WC, 1 ➡; P21
sB&B £23-£28 dB&B £44-£52 D £16.50; cc Ac Vi

Heathmount   RAC
Station Road, Beauly IV4 7EQ 01463-782411
5 bedrs, 1 ➡; ✖ P6
sB&B £15-£17 dB&B £30-£34 Breakfast only

BLAIRGOWRIE Tayside   13D1

Ivy Bank House   RAC
Boat Brae, Rattray, Blairgowrie PH10 7BH
01250-53056

Rosebank House *Highly Acclaimed*   RAC
Balmoral Road, Blairgowrie PH10 7AF
01250-872912
7 bedrs, 1 ➡/WC, 5 ⬥/WC, 1 ➡; tcf ⅍ P12
Child restrictions
sB&B £21-£23 dB&B £42-£46; HB weekly £199-£210;

BO'NESS Central   13D2

The Knowe Erngath Road, Bo'ness EH51 9EN 01506-828222 Fax 01506-828226

Detached Victorian mansion with many original features, Set in its own grounds in an elevated position overlooking the Firth of Forth and Ochin Hills.
3 bedrs, 1 ➡; ✖ P3
sB&B £16; HB weekly £150; D £5-£10

BOAT OF GARTEN Highland — 15D3

Moorfield House *Acclaimed* RÃC
Deshar Road, Boat Of Garten PH24 3BN
01479-831646

Large Victorian house.
4 bedrs, 1 ⇨/WC, 3 ℟/WC; TV tcf ✖ P8
Child restrictions
sB&B £21 dB&B £36; HB weekly £189;
[10%V]

BONAR BRIDGE Highland — 15D2

Kyle House Dornoch Road, Bonar Bridge
IV24 3EB 8632360

Old established Scottish house overlooking
Kyle of Sutherland to Ross-Shire Hills with
beautifully furnished and decorated rooms.
All bedrooms with tea/coffee making
facilities, electric blankets and heating.
Restricted hotel license.
6 bedrs, 1 ⇨/WC, 1 ℟/WC, 1 ⇨; tcf ✖ P6
Child restrictions under 3
sB&B £16 Breakfast only

BRAEMAR Grampian — 15E4

Schiehallion House Glenshee Road,
Braemar AB35 5YQ 01339-741679 ♿

Traditional Highland house with a
comfortable and welcoming atmosphere. Set
in a charming village amongst magnificent
scenery. Enjoy log fires in a relaxed congenial
atmosphere.
11 bedrs, 7 ℟/WC, 1 ⇨; tcf ✖ P11
sB&B £14.50; HB weekly £157-£169; D £10;
cc Ac Vi

BRODICK Isle of Arran — 12B3

★★★**Auchrannie** RÃC
Isle of Arran, Brodick KA27 8BZ
01770-302234 Fax 01770-302812

BRORA Highland — 15D2

Ard Beag Badnellan, Brora KW9 6NQ
01408-612398

★★★**Links** RÃC
Brora KW9 6QS 01408-621225 Fax
01408-621383 ♿
24 bedrs, 22 ⇨/WC, 2 ⇨; TV tcf ✖ P30
sB&B £45-£50 dB&B £72-£90 [10%V]; cc Ac
Amex DC Vi JCB

No Smoking/Dogs

✖ Indicates a hotel which either bans
smoking throughout the establishment or
does not allow smoking in some areas.

✖ Indicates a hotel which either does not
welcome dogs or restricts dogs to certain
areas of the hotel.
Please telephone the hotel
for further details.

Lynwood Golf Road, Brora KW9 6QS
01408-621226   &

Designer-decorated Georgian home, with charm, warmth and comfort.
4 bedrs, 1 ➨/WC, 2 ☞/WC, 1 ➨; TV tcf ✖ P4
sB&B £16; HB weekly £175-£195; D £5-£10;
cc Ac Vi

Non Smokers Haven Tigh Fada, Golf Road, Brora KW9 6QS 01408-621332

Sutherland Arms Brora KW9 6NX
01408-321209

BUCKIE Banffshire   15E3

Highlander 75 West Church Street, Buckie AB56 1BQ 01542-34008

Rosemount 62 East Church Street, Buckie AB56 1ER 01542-33434

Royal Oak Cullen, Buckie AB56 2SD
01542-40252

Waverley 12 Blantyre Street, Cullen, Buckie AB56 2RP 01542-40210
7 bedrs, 2 ➨; tcf P5
sB&B £14; HB weekly £130; D £5

Child restrictions
Most hotels and guest houses are happy to welcome children. A few prefer to welcome only adults and older children; these are shown by 'Child Restrictions' in the entry. If you are travelling with children, please telephone the establishment to check the age limit set by the management.

Elms 2 Seafield Place, Cullen AB56 2UU
01542-841271   &

Located in the main street of Cullen the hotel is a beautiful Victorian house with a large garden. Spacious and comfortably furnished bedrooms.
6 bedrs, 1 ➨/WC, 1 ☞/WC, 1 ➨; TV tcf ✖ P5
sB&B £12 Breakfast only; cc Vi

BURNTISLAND Fife   13D2

Aberdour 38 High Street, Aberdour, Burntisland KY3 0SW 01383-860325

Gleniffer 28 Kirkton Road, Burntisland KY3 0BY 01592-873320

Orcadia Lochies Road, Off Kinghorn Road, Burntisland KY3 9JX 01592-872230

CALLANDER Central   12C1

Annfield House   RAC
18 North Church Street, Callander FK17 8EG
01877-330204
8 bedrs, 2 ☞/WC, 2 ➨; tcf ✖ ⊁ P9
sB&B £15 dB&B £30 Breakfast only

Arden House *Highly Acclaimed*   RAC
Bracklinn Road, Callander FK17 8EQ
01877-330235
6 bedrs, 1 ➨/WC, 5 ☞/WC; tcf ✖ P12
sB&B £18-£20 dB&B £36; HB weekly £170-£185; [5%V]

Arran Lodge *Highly Acclaimed*   RAC
Leny Road, Callander FK17 8AJ
01877-330976   &
4 bedrs, 2 ➨/WC, 2 ☞/WC; TV tcf P5
Child restrictions
sB&B £38.40-£53.60 dB&B £48-£67; HB weekly £262.50-£287;

Bridgend House Bridgend, Callander FK17
8AH 01877-330130 Fax 01877-331512
*Family run 18th century hotel with well-
equipped bedrooms, bars, lounge, dining
room and gardens.*
6 bedrs, 3 ➥/WC, 2 ♋/WC, 1 ➥;
TV tcf ✖ P30
sB&B £14.50 D £9.50-£19.50;
cc Ac Amex DC Vi

Brook Linn Country House Callander FK17
8AU 01877-330103

**Campfield Cottage 138 Main Street,
Callander FK17 8BG 01877-330597**
3 bedrs, 1 ➥; tcf ✖ P4
sB&B £15; D £10-£11

Coire Buidhe Strathyre, Callander FK18 8NA
01877-384288
8 bedrs, 1 ➥/WC, 3 ➥; P6
sB&B £13.50 D £10

Cregan House Restaurant Strathyre, Cregan,
Callander FK18 8ND 01877-384638   ♿
5 bedrs, 2 ➥/WC, 1 ♋/WC, 1 ➥; ✖ P25
sB&B £34.25; HB weekly £216-£384.30;

Highland House *Highly Acclaimed*   ⚜RAC
South Church Street, Callander FK17 8BN
01877-330269
9 bedrs, 1 ➥/WC, 5 ♋/WC, 2 ➥; ✖ ✂
sB&B £18-£22.50 dB&B £36-£45; D £15
[10%V]; cc Ac Amex Vi

Kinnell House 24 Main Street, Callander
FK17 8BB 01877-30181

Linley   ⚜RAC
139 Main Street, Callander FK17 8BH
01877-330087
3 bedrs, 2 ♋/WC; P5
sB&B £14-£20 Breakfast only

Riverview House Leny Road, Callander FK17
8AL 01877-330635

Rock Villa *Acclaimed*   ⚜RAC
1 Bracklinn Road, Callander FK17 8EH
01877-330331

Roslin Cottage Lagrannoch, Callander FK17
8LE 01877-30638

Teithside House Bridgend, Callander FK17
8AF 01877-331333

The Inn At Strathyre Main Street, Strathyre,
Callander FK18 8NA 01877-384224   ♿
7 bedrs, 1 ♋/WC, 2 ➥; P15
sB&B £25 Breakfast only

White Shutters 6 South Church Street,
Callander FK17 8BN 01877-30442

CAMPBELTOWN Strathclyde	12B3

Westbank   ⚜RAC
Dell Road, Campbeltown PA26 6JG
01586-553660
9 bedrs, 2 ♋/WC, 2 ➥; TV ✂
Child restrictions
sB&B £20 dB&B £32 D £10 [10%V]; cc Ac Vi

CARDROSS Strathclyde	12C2

Kirkton House *Highly Acclaimed*   ⚜RAC
Darleith Road, Cardross G82 5EZ
01389-841951 Fax 01389-841-868
6 bedrs, 3 ➥/WC, 3 ♋/WC; ✖
sB&B £31-£36 dB&B £50-£55; HB weekly
£266-£283.50; D £15.50; cc Ac Amex Vi

CARRBRIDGE Highland	15D3

Carrmoor *Acclaimed*   ⚜RAC
**Carr Road, Carrbridge PH23 3AD
01479-84244**

A cosy guest house with friendly hospitality.
5 bedrs, 5 ♋/WC; ✖ ✂ P5
sB&B £19-£23.50 dB&B £33-£37; HB weekly
£175-£189; D £10.50 [10%V]; cc Ac Vi

Fairwinds *Highly Acclaimed* 🔱RAC
Carrbridge PH23 3AA 01479-841240
5 bedrs, 3 ➡/WC, 2 🏷/WC; 🎯 🍴 P8
Child restrictions
sB&B £23-£25 dB&B £44-£52; HB weekly
£215-£240; D £12 [5%V]; **cc** Ac Vi

CASTLE DOUGLAS
Dumfries & Galloway   12C4

**Craigadam Castle Douglas DG7 3HU
01556-650233 Fax 01556-650489**

*18th century farmhouse situated in the
Galloway Hills with log fires and Cordon-Bleu
cuisine.*
4 bedrs, 3 ➡/WC, 1 🏷/WC; **TV** tcf 🎯 P6
sB&B £16; HB weekly £182; D £10

Cross Keys High Street, Castle Douglas DG7
3RN 01644-2494

**Deeside 42 Main Street, Castle Douglas
DG7 3AU 01556-670239**

*A family house, includes home cooking. Rear
of premises overlooks the river. The house is
situated in a spacious garden.*
3 bedrs, 2 ➡/WC, 1 🏷/WC, 1 ➡; **TV** tcf 🎯 P2
sB&B £13.50; HB weekly £85-£91.45; D £6.75

Gatehouse Of Fleet 29 Fleet Street, Castle
Douglas DG7 2JT 01557-814647

Girthon Kirk Sandgreen Road, Gatehouse of
Fleet, Castle Douglas DG7 2DW 01557-814352

High Park Balmaclellan, Castle Douglas DG7
3PT 01644-2298   ♿

3 bedrs, 1 ➡; tcf 🎯 P3
HB weekly £140; D £7

Janefield 28 Main Street, Castle Douglas
DG7 3AU 01556-67321

Kenmure Port Road, Palnackie, Castle
Douglas DG7 1PQ 01556-60279

Leamington High Street, Castle Douglas
DG7 3RN 01644-2327

Market Inn Queen Street, Castle Douglas
DG7 1HX 01556-2105

Meiklewood Ringford, Castle Douglas DG7
2AL 01557-22226

Milton Park Farm Haugh Os Urr, Castle
Douglas DG7 3JJ 01556-0-66212

Rascarrel Cottage Castle Douglas DG7 1RJ
01556-64214

Rose Cottage Gelston, Castle Douglas DG7
1SH 01556-2513

**The Rossan Castle Douglas DG7 1QR
01556-640269**
*A bed & breakfast specialising in vegetarian,
vegan and gluten free diets using whole and
organic foods. Can cater for other special
dietary requirements.*
3 bedrs, 2 ⇓; ✗ P4
sB&B £12; HB weekly £140; D £20

Woodburn House Castle Douglas DG7 3YB
01556-66217

CHARLESTOWN OF ABERLOUR
Grampian   15E3

The Station Bar 7-8 Broomfield Square,
Charlestown Of Aberlour AB38 9QP
01340-871858
3 bedrs, 2 ⇓; ✗
sB&B £13.50 Breakfast only

83 High Street Charlestown Of Aberlour
AB38 9QB 01340-871319

CONNEL Strathclyde   12B1

Ards House *Acclaimed*   🔱RAC
Connel PA37 1PT 01631-71255

Ronebhal *Acclaimed*   🔱RAC
Connel PA37 1PJ 01631-71310   ♿

*Ronebhal is a large granite, traditional style
house set back from the road in its own
grounds, with spectacular views over Loch
Etive.. All our rooms are tastefully decorated
to a very high standard and have TV's.*
6 bedrs, 4 🛁/WC, 1 ⇓; P6
Child restrictions
sB&B £15-£21 dB&B £32-£50; HB weekly
£105-£154; [5%V]; cc Ac Vi

Loch Etive *Acclaimed*   🔱RAC
Connel, Oban PA37 1PH 01631-71400 Fax
01631-71400
6 bedrs, 2 ⇓/WC, 2 🛁/WC, 1 ⇓; ✗ ✗ P7
sB&B £25-£28 dB&B £40-£50; HB weekly
£227-£246; [5%V]; cc Ac Vi

CONTIN Highland   14C3

Coul House *Highly Acclaimed*   🔱RAC
Contin IV14 9EY 01997-421487 Fax
01997-421445   ♿
21 bedrs, 20 ⇓/WC, 1 🛁/WC; P40
sB&B £45-£56 dB&B £66-£90; HB weekly
£262.50-£413; D £25 [10%V]; cc Amex DC JCB

COWDENBEATH Fife   13D2

Struan Bank 74 Perth Road, Cowdenbeath
KY4 9BG 01383-1511057

CRAIL Fife   13E1

Caiplie House   🔱RAC
53 High Street, Crail KY10 3RA 01333-50564

Woodlands Balcomie Road, Crail KY10 3TN
01333-450147   ♿
3 bedrs, 2 ⇓; TV tcf ✗ P8
sB&B £16; HB weekly £150-£175; D £8-£10

CRAWFORD Strathclyde 13D3

Field End *Acclaimed* RAC
The Loaning (opposite Church), Crawford
ML12 6TN 018642-276
3 bedrs; **P**5
sB&B £16-£22 dB&B £32-£36; HB weekly
£140-£160; [5%V]; **cc** Ac Vi

CRIANLARICH Central 12C1

Glenardran RAC
Crianlarich FK20 8QS 01838-300236
6 bedrs, 1 ♠/WC, 1 ➡; ✖ **P**6
Child restrictions
sB&B £20 dB&B £36 D £10; **cc** Ac Vi

**Invervey Tyndrum, Crianlarich FK20 8RY
01838-400219 Fax 01838-400280** ♿

*A family-run hotel surrounded by the
beautiful Scottish hills.*
21 bedrs, 3 ➡/WC, 15 ♠/WC, 1 ➡;
TV tcf ✖ **P**50
sB&B £; HB weekly £183-£228; D £9; **cc** Ac
Amex Vi

CRIEFF Tayside 13D1

★**Gwydyr House** RAC
Comrie Road, Crieff PH7 4BP 01764-653277
10 bedrs, 3 ➡; ✖ **P**15
sB&B £15 dB&B £30; HB weekly £185.50; D
£11.50

Heatherville RAC
29-31 Burrell Street, Crieff PH7 4DT
01764-652825
4 bedrs, 1 ♠/WC, 2 ➡; ✖ ⅄ **P**5
sB&B £13-£14.50 dB&B £26-£33 Breakfast
only [10%V]

Leven House *Acclaimed* RAC
Comrie Road, Crieff PH7 4BA 01764-652529
12 bedrs, 6 ➡/WC, 2 ♠/WC, 2 ➡; TV tcf ✖
⅄ **P**14

sB&B £17-£20 dB&B £34-£40; HB weekly
£187-£190

Sydney Villa RAC
57 Burrell Street, Crieff PH7 4DG
01764-652757
4 bedrs;
Child restrictions
sB&B £14 dB&B £28-£30

CULLEN Grampian 15E2

Bayview *Highly Acclaimed* RAC
57 Seafield Street, Cullen AB5 2SU
01542-41031

CUPAR Fife 13E1

Easter Clunie Newburgh, Cupar KY14 6EJ
01337-840218
3 bedrs, 1 ♠/WC, 2 ➡; tcf **P**3
Child restrictions under 3
sB&B £14 Breakfast only

Forest Hills High Street, Auchtermuchty,
Cupar KY14 7OP 01337-828318

10 bedrs, 4 ➡/WC, 4 ♠/WC, 1 ➡; ✖ **P**6
sB&B £40 Breakfast only

Redlands Country Lodge *Highly Acclaimed* RAC
By Ladybank, Cupar KY7 7SH 01337-31091

Location Maps

Hotel locations are shown on the maps at
the back of the guide. All towns and
villages containing an hotel listed in the
guide are shown in black.

Todhall House Dairsie, Cupar KY15 4RQ
01334-656344 Fax 01334-656344

A traditional country house surrounded by superb scenery with all facilities and country comforts.
3 bedrs, 1 ➜/WC, 2 🛏/WC, 2 ➜; TV tcf P5
Child restrictions under 12
sB&B £18.50; HB weekly £186.55-£262.50; D £10-£15

4 South Road Cupar KY15 5JF 01334-52813

DALBEATTIE Dumfries & Galloway   13D4

Auchenskeoch Lodge Dalbeattie DG5 4PG
01387-780277

Burnside John Street, Dalbeattie DG5 4JJ
01556-610219

Cairngill House Sandyhills, Dalbeattie DG5
4NZ 01387-780681

Parkway 14 Mill Street, Dalbeattie DG5 4BE
01556-610142

Pheasant 1 Maxwell Street, Dalbeattie DD5
5AH 01556-610345
7 bedrs, 1 ➜/WC, 1 ➜; 🛏
sB&B £19 D £5

Rosemount Kippford, Dalbeattie DG5 4LN
01556-62214

DALRY Strathclyde   12C2

★★**Dalry Inn**   ṚÁC
Kilbirnie Road, Dalry KA24 5JS 01294-835135
Fax 01294-76651
6 bedrs, 6 ➜/WC; 🛏 P50
sB&B £20-£25 dB&B £40-£44 D £7.25 [10%V];
cc Ac Amex Vi

DENNY Central   12C2

Lochend Farm Denny FK6 5JJ 01324-822778
2 bedrs, 1 ➜; tcf
Child restrictions under 5
sB&B £16 Breakfast only

Topps *Highly Acclaimed*   ṚÁC
Topps Farm, Fintry Road, Denny FK6 5JF
01324-822471

DERVAIG Isle of Mull   14B4

Druimard Country *Highly Acclaimed*   ṚÁC
Druimard, Dervaig PA75 6QW 01688-4345

DORNOCH Highland   15D2

Achandean   ṚÁC
Meadows Road, Dornoch 1V25 3SF
01862-810413   ⅔
3 bedrs, 2 🛏/WC; 🛏 ✗ P4
dB&B £35-£40; HB weekly £180;

Burnside Shore Road, Dornoch IV25 3LS
01862-810919

Highfield *Highly Acclaimed*   ṚÁC
Evelix Road, Sutherland, Dornoch 1V25 3HR
01862-810909
3 bedrs, 1 ➜/WC, 2 🛏/WC; TV tcf 🛏 P8
sB&B £28 dB&B £42 Breakfast only [10%V]

**Mallin House Church Street, Dornoch
IV25 3LP 01862-810335**   ⅔
11 bedrs, 2 ➜/WC, 9 🛏/WC; TV tcf 🛏 P20
sB&B £25; D £6-£28; cc Ac Amex Vi

Parfour Rowan Crescent, Dornoch IV25 4SF
01862-810955

Rosslyn Villa Castle Street, Dornoch IV25
3SN 01862-810237

★★★**Royal Golf**   ṚÁC
Grange Road, Dornoch IV25 3LG
01862-810283 Fax 01862-810923

Trevose The Square, Dornoch IV25 3QF
01862-810269

DRYMEN Central   12C2

Ceardach Gartness Road, Drymen G63 0BH
01360-60596

DUFFTOWN Grampian   15E3

Morven The Square, Dufftown AB55 4AD
01340-820507

DUMFRIES Dumfries & Galloway   13D4

Cairndoon 14 Newall Terrace, Dumfries
DG1 1LW 01387-256991

Carsemannoch House Carsethorn,
Kirkbean, Dumfries DG2 8DS 01387-288275

Charter House 2 Troqueer Road, Dumfries
DG2 7RE 01387-252185

Druid's Park 45 Moffat Road, Dumfries DG1
1NN 01387-261949

Fulwood Private Lovers Walk, Dumfries
DG1 1LP 01387-252262

Galloway Arms Crocketford, Dumfries DG2
8RA 01556-690248

Inverallochy 15 Lockerbie Road, Dumfries
DG1 3AP 01387-267298

Kirkland Country House Ruthwell,
Dumfries DG1 4NP 01387-287284   &
5 bedrs, 5 🖍/WC; P20
sB&B £25 Breakfast only

Knock 1 Lockerbie Road, Dumfries DG1 3AP
01387-53487

Locharthur House Beeswing, Dumfries DG2
8JG 01387-276235

3 bedrs, 1 🖍/WC, 1 ➡; TV tcf ✶ P8
sB&B £14; HB weekly £135-£150; D £6.50-£7

Lochenlee 32 Ardwall Road, Dumfries DG1
3AQ 01387-265153

Lochrigghead Farmhouse Nethermill,
Parkgate, Dumfries DG1 3NG 01387-286381
3 bedrs, 1 ➡; ✶
sB&B £14; HB weekly £21;

Mabie House Mabie, Dumfries DG2 8HB
01387-263188

Mouswald Place Mouswald, Dumfries DG1
4JS 01387-283226

*A secluded family run Manor House with
comfortable rooms and adjoining licensed
bar. 6 miles south of Dumfries.*
4 bedrs, 2 ➡; TV tcf ✶ P12
Child restrictions
sB&B £14.30 D £3.20-£10

Smithy House Torthorwald, Dumfries DG1
3PT 01387-275518

4 Cassalands Dumfries DG2 7NS
01387-253701

DUNBAR Lothian   13E2

Marine   RAC
7 Marine Road, Dunbar EH42 1AR
01368-863315

Overcliffe   RAC
11 Bayswell Park, Dunbar EH42 1AE
01368-864004
6 bedrs, 3 ⁿ/WC, 2 🛁; 🐾 ⵜ P2
sB&B £16 dB&B £32 Breakfast only

Springfield   RAC
42 Belhaven Road, Dunbar EH42 1NH
01368-862502
5 bedrs, 2 🛁; 🐾 P7
sB&B £17.50 dB&B £33 Breakfast only
[10%V]; cc Ac Vi

St Beys   RAC
2 Bayswell Road, Dunbar EH42 1AB
01368-863571

DUNBLANE Central   12C1

Chimes Cathedral Square, Dunblane FK15
0AL 01786-822164

Dunblane Stirling Road, Dunblane FK15 9EP
01786-822178

Inveradoch Mains Farm Doune, Dunblane
FK15 9NZ 01786-841268

**Mossgiel Doune Road, Dunblane FK15
9ND 01786-824325**   &
*Modern countryside bungalow, ideally
situated for touring central Scotland and the
Trossachs.*
3 bedrs, 2 ⁿ/WC, 1 🛁; P6
sB&B £15.50 Breakfast only

Westlands Doune Road, Dunblane FK15 9HT
01786-822118

Westwood Doune Road, Dunblane FK15
9ND 01786-822579

*A guest house in a quiet country location,
with comfortable, well-equipped bedrooms.*
3 bedrs, 1 🛁/WC, 2 ⁿ/WC; tcf P6
sB&B £16.50 Breakfast only

DUNDEE Tayside   13E1

Beach House *Acclaimed*   RAC
22 Esplanade, Broughty Ferry, Dundee DD5
2EQ 01382-776614 Fax 01382-480241
5 bedrs, 3 🛁/WC, 2 ⁿ/WC; ⵜ
Child restrictions
dB&B £44-£45 D £10.50; cc Ac Vi

Kemback   RAC
8 Mcgill Street, Dundee DD4 6PH
01382-461273
9 bedrs, 2 ⁿ/WC, 2 🛁; P7
sB&B £16 dB&B £27 Breakfast only [10%V]

★★★Swallow   RAC
Kingsway West, Dundee DD2 5JT
01382-641122 Fax 01382-568340   &
110 bedrs, 110 🛁/WC; 🐾 ⵜ P200
sB&B £85 D £18.50; cc Ac Amex DC Vi

DUNFERMLINE Fife   13D2

Abbey Park 5 Abbeypark Place, Dunfermline
KY12 7PT 01383-739688

Bowleys Farm Roscobie, Dunfermline KY12
0SG 01383-721056

Garvock 82 Halbeath Road, Dunfermline
KY12 7RS 01383-734689

Hillview House 9 Aberdour Road,
Dunfermline KY11 4PB 01383-726278

Learig 2a Victoria Street, Dunfermline KY12
0LW 01383-729676

Pitreavie 3 Aberdour Road, Dunfermline
KY11 4PB 01383-724244

The Haven 82 Pilmuir Street, Dunfermline
KY12 0LN 01383-729039

3 bedrs, 2 ➧; ✖
sB&B £16; HB weekly £112;

59 Buffies Brae Dunfermline KY12 8ED
01383-733677

DUNKELD Tayside   13D1

★★**Atholl Arms**   RAC
Bridge Street, Dunkeld PH8 0AQ
01350-727219

DUNOON Strathclyde   12B2

Anchorage *Highly Acclaimed*   RAC
Shore Road, Ardnadam, Sandbank, Dunoon
PA23 8Q9 01369-705108 Fax 01369-705108
4 bedrs, 1 ➧/WC, 3 ❦/WC; P12
dB&B £17.50-£21.50; HB weekly £217-£238;
D £12.50 [5%V]; cc Ac Vi

Ardtully *Acclaimed*   RAC
297 Marine Parade, Hunters Quay, Dunoon
PA23 8HN 01369-702478
10 bedrs, 10 ❦/WC; ✖ ✕ P10
Child restrictions
sB&B £20-£30 dB&B £40-£50; HB weekly
£185-£195; D £12.50 [10%V]

Cedars *Highly Acclaimed*   RAC
51 Alexandra Parade, Dunoon PA23 8AF
01369-2425 Fax 01369-6964
10 bedrs, 3 ➧/WC, 7 ❦/WC, 1 ➧; ✕
Child restrictions
sB&B £17.50-£24.50 dB&B £30-£45 Breakfast
only [10%V]; cc Ac Amex DC Vi

Rosscairn *Acclaimed*   RAC
51 Hunter Street, Kirn, Dunoon PA23 8JR
01369-4344

DUNS Borders   13E2

Allanton Inn Allanton, Chirnside, Duns
TD11 3JZ 01890-818260
5 bedrs, 1 ➧; ✖ P20
sB&B £19 Breakfast only

Fogorig House Greenlaw, Duns TD11 3RB
01890-84535

Haggerston House Grantshouse, Duns TD11
3RW 01361-5229

EARLSTON Borders   13E2

Birkhill House *Acclaimed*   RAC
Earlston TD4 6AR 0189684-307

The Smithy Legerwood, Earlston TD4 6AS
01896-84518

EDINBURGH Lothian   13D2

A Haven in Edinburgh *Acclaimed*   RAC
180 Ferry Road, Edinburgh EH6 4NS
0131-554-6559
11 bedrs, 1 ➧/WC, 10 ❦/WC; ✕ P10
sB&B £25-£40 dB&B £45-£65 D £12.50; cc Ac
Vi

Allison House *Acclaimed*   RAC
15-17 Mayfield Gardens, Edinburgh EH9 2AX
0131-667-8049 Fax 0131-667-5001

Arthurs View *Acclaimed*   RAC
10 Mayfield Gardens, Edinburgh EH9 2BZ
0131-6673468

Ashdene House *Acclaimed*   RAC
23 Fountainhall Road, Edinburgh EH9 2LN
0131-6676026
5 bedrs, 5 ❦/WC; P3
dB&B £36-£50 Breakfast only

Ashgrove House *Highly Acclaimed*   RAC
12 Osborne Terrace, Edinburgh EH12 5HG
0131-3375014 Fax 0131-3135043
7 bedrs, 5 ➧/WC; P10
sB&B £22.50-£50 dB&B £20-£25 Breakfast
only

Ashlyn *Acclaimed*   RAC
42 Inverleith Row, Edinburgh EH3 5PY
0131-5522954

Boisdale *Acclaimed*   RAC
9 Coates Gardens, Edinburgh EH12 5LG
0131-3371134

Brunswick *Highly Acclaimed*   RAC
7 Brunswick Street, Edinburgh EH7 5JB
0131-556-1238 Fax 0131-556-1238
11 bedrs, 11 ♖/WC;
Child restrictions
sB&B £25-£45 dB&B £46-£90 Breakfast only
[10%V]; **cc** Ac Amex Vi

Buchan *Acclaimed*   RAC
3 Coates Gardens, Edinburgh EH12 5LG
0131-337-1045

Commodore   RAC
Cramond Foreshore, Edinburgh EH4 5EP
0131-336-1700 Fax 0131-3364934   &
87 bedrs, 87 ➡/WC; ✕ ✄ P100
sB&B £55-£61.75 dB&B £70 D £13.50; **cc** Ac
Amex DC Vi

Cumberland *Highly Acclaimed*   RAC
1 West Coates, Edinburgh EH12 5JQ
0131-337-1198

Dorstan *Highly Acclaimed*   RAC
7 Priestfield Road, Edinburgh EH16 5HJ
0131-667-5138 Fax 0131-6684644
14 bedrs, 5 ➡/WC, 4 ♖/WC, 2 ➡; P7
sB&B £22-£37 dB&B £50-£70 Breakfast only;
cc Ac Vi

Galloway *Acclaimed*   RAC
22 Dean Park Crescent, Edinburgh EH4 1PH
0131-3323672
10 bedrs, 5 ➡/WC, 1 ♖/WC, 2 ➡;
sB&B £22-£30 dB&B £34-£40 Breakfast only
[10%V]

Glenora *Acclaimed*   RAC
14 Rosebery Crescent, Edinburgh EH12 5JY
0131-337-1186

Granada Lodge   RAC
Old Craghall Junction, Edinburgh EH21 8RE
0131-6536070

Heriott Park *Acclaimed*   RAC
256 Ferry Road, Edinburgh EH5 3AN
0131-552-6628
6 bedrs, 2 ♖/WC, 2 ➡; ✕ ✄
sB&B £18-£20 dB&B £30-£40 Breakfast only

Ivy House *Acclaimed*   RAC
7 Mayfield Gardens, Edinburgh EH9 2AX
0131-6673411
8 bedrs, 4 ♖/WC, 2 ➡; ✕ ✄ P9
sB&B £15-£20 dB&B £30-£40 Breakfast only
[10%V]

Joppa Turrets Guesthouse   RAC
1 Lower Joppa, Edinburgh EH15 2ER
0131-6695806
5 bedrs, 1 ♖/WC, 2 ➡; ✄
Child restrictions
sB&B £15-£17 dB&B £28-£36 Breakfast only;
cc Ac Vi

Kariba   RAC
10 Granville Terrace, Edinburgh EH10 4PQ
0131-229-3773   &
9 bedrs, 3 ➡/WC, 3 ➡; ✄ P4
sB&B £20-£25 dB&B £36-£40 Breakfast only

Kew *Acclaimed* ⚜ RAC
1 Kew Terrace, Murrayfield, Edinburgh EH12
5JE 0131-3130700 &
5 bedrs, 2 ⚐/WC, 2 ➡; ✈ ✂ P6
sB&B £22-£25 dB&B £44-£50 Breakfast only
[10%V]; **cc** Ac Vi

Lindsay *Acclaimed* RAC
108 Polwarth Terrace, Edinburgh EH11 1NN
0131-337-1580

Lodge *Highly Acclaimed* RAC
6 Hampton Terrace, West Coates, Edinburgh
EH12 5JD 0131-337-3682
10 bedrs, 10 ⚐/WC, 1 ➡; ✂ P10
sB&B £40-£50 dB&B £50-£80 Breakfast only
[5%V]; **cc** Ac Vi

Lovat RAC
5 Inverleith Terrace, Edinburgh EH3 5NS
0131-5562745 Fax 0131-6581837

Marchhall *Acclaimed* RAC
14-16 Marchhall Crescent, Edinburgh EH16
5HL 0131-667-2743

Marvin *Acclaimed* RAC
46 Pilrig Street, Edinburgh EH6 5AL
0131-5546605

Newington *Acclaimed* RAC
18 Newington Road, Edinburgh EH9 1QS
0131-667-3356
8 bedrs, 5 ⚐/WC, 1 ➡; ✈ P3
sB&B £26-£30 dB&B £37-£57 Breakfast only

Roselea House *Highly Acclaimed* RAC
11 Mayfield Road, Edinburgh EH9 2NG
0131-6676115 Fax 0131-6673556
7 bedrs, 2 ⚐/WC, 2 ➡; ✈ ✂ P4
sB&B £30-£45 dB&B £50-£80 Breakfast only
[5%V]; **cc** Ac Vi

Salisbury *Acclaimed* RAC
45 Salisbury Road, Edinburgh EH16 5AA
0131-6671264 Fax 0131-6671264
12 bedrs, 2 ➡/WC, 9 ⚐/WC, 2 ➡; P12
sB&B £22-£25 dB&B £40-£48 Breakfast only
[5%V]

Shalimar RAC
20 Newington Road, Edinburgh EH9 1QS
0131-667-2827

Sherwood RAC
42 Minto Street, Edinburgh EH9 2BR
0131-6671200
6 bedrs, 2 ➡; ✈ P3
dB&B £24-£32 Breakfast only

Stra'ven *Acclaimed* RAC
3 Brunstane Road North, Edinburgh EH15
2DL 0131-6695580

Thrums *Highly Acclaimed* RAC
14 Minto Street, Edinburgh EH9 1RQ
0131-667-8545 Fax 0131-667-8707
6 bedrs, 3 ➡/WC, 3 ⚐/WC, 1 ➡; ✈ P10
sB&B £32-£40 dB&B £60-£67 D £6.50; **cc** Ac Vi

ELGIN Grampian   15E3

Ardent House 43 Forsyth Street, Hopeman,
Elgin IV30 2SY 01343-830694

Ardgye House Elgin IV30 3UP 01343-85618

Carronvale 18 South Guildry Street, Elgin
IV30 1QN 01343-546864
2 bedrs, 1 ➡; tcf P4
Child restrictions under 5
sB&B £13; HB weekly £150.50-£199.50; D
£8.50

Commercial 6 Young Street, Burghead, Elgin
IV30 2UB 01343-835628
6 bedrs, 3 ➡; ✈
sB&B £19 Breakfast only

Lahaina Kellas, Elgin IV30 3TW 01343-89209

ELLON Grampian   15F3

Gight House Sunnybrae, Methlick, Ellon AB41 0BP 01651-806389

GIGHT HOUSE HOTEL
SUNNYBRAE. METHLICK, ABERDEENSHIRE
TELEPHONE: 0651 806389
PROPRIETORS: LES & CAROLE ROSS

3 bedrs, 1 ➹/WC, 2 ☞/WC; TV tcf P30
sB&B £19.50 D £4.50-£10.95; cc Ac Vi

EYEMOUTH Borders   13F2

Greystoneless Farm House Burnmouth, Eyemouth TD14 5SZ 01890-781709
3 bedrs, 1 ➹/WC, 1 ☞/WC, 2 ➹; ✖
sB&B £12; HB weekly £135-£150;

Westwood House The Old Coaching Inn, Houndwood, Eyemouth TD14 5TB
01361-5232

Wheatsheaf Main Street, Reston, Eyemouth TD14 5JS 01890-761219

FALKIRK Central   13D2

Union Inn Lock 16, Portdownie, Camelon, Falkirk FK1 4QZ 01324-23578

Viewforth House Main Street, Airth, Falkirk FK2 8JJ 01324-831711

FALKLAND Fife   13D1

Covenanter *Acclaimed*   ⬥RAC
The Square, Falkland KY7 7BU 01337-57224
Fax 01337-57272

FOCHABERS Grampian   15E3

Spey Bay Spey Bay, Fochabers IV32 7PY
01343-820362

FORRES Grampian   15E3

Caranardh Sanquhar Road, Forres IV36 0DG
01309-672581

Carisbrooks Drumduan Road, Forres IV36 0QT 01309-672585 Fax 01309-672123

Crown & Anchor Inn Findhorn, Forres IV30 0YF 01309-690243 Fax 01309-690201   ⅙
6 bedrs, 6 ☞/WC, 1 ➹; TV tcf ✖ P30
sB&B £18.50 D £4.50-£14

Hazelbank Alexandra Terrace, Forres IV36 0DL 01309-673409

Heather Lodge Tytler Street, Forres IV36 0EL 01309-672377   ⅙
7 bedrs, 1 ➹/WC, 6 ☞/WC; ✖ P12
sB&B £15 Breakfast only

Morven Caroline Steet, Forres IV36 0AN 01309-673788
3 bedrs, 2 ➹; TV tcf ✖ P5
sB&B £15 Breakfast only

Scania Cathay, Forres IV36 0RE 01309-672583

Strathiolaire Findhorn Bridge, Findhorn, Forres IV13 7YA 01808-2359

Tormhor 11 High Street, Forres IV36 0BU
01309-673831

Victoria 1 Tytler Street, Forres IV36 0EL
01309-672744

FORT WILLIAM Highland   14C4

Ashburn House *Highly Acclaimed*   ⬥RAC
Achintore Road, Fort William PH33 6RQ
01397-706000 Fax 01397-706000
6 bedrs, 1 ➹/WC, 4 ☞/WC, 1 ➹; P7
sB&B £20-£30 dB&B £40-£60 Breakfast only;
cc Ac Vi

FRASERBURGH Grampian   15F2

78 Charlotte Street Fraserburgh AB34 5JH
01346-514432

GALASHIELS Borders   13E3

Clovenfords 1 Vine Street, Cloverfords, Galashiels TD1 3NG 01896-850203
5 bedrs, 3 ➹/WC, 2 ☞/WC; ✖ P30
sB&B £31.50 Breakfast only

Ettrickvale 33 Abbotsford Road, Galashiels
TD1 3HW 01896-755224 &
3 bedrs, 1 ♨; TV tcf ✹ P2
sB&B £13; HB weekly £126; D £5

Keranalt 3 Bridge Street, Galashiels TD1
1SW 01896-4859

Kings Galashiels TD1 3AN 01896-55497

Springfield 5 Abbotsview Court, Galashiels
TD1 3HY 01896-59423

**Wakefield Bank 9 Abbotsford Road,
Galashiels TD1 3DP 01896-752641**

Wheatlands House Galashiels TD1 1QR
01896-753068
3 bedrs, 1 ♨/WC, 1 ♨; ✹ P8
sB&B £15 Breakfast only

GARTOCHARN Strathclyde   12C2

Mardella Farmhouse ⛨
Old School Road, Gartocharn GS3 8SO
01389-830428
3 bedrs, 1 ♨/WC, 1 ♨; ✹ P4
sB&B £20-£26.50 dB&B £33-£40 Breakfast
only

GATEHOUSE OF FLEET
Dumfries & Galloway   12C4

Bank O'Fleet ⛨
47 High Street, Gatehouse-of-Fleet DG7 2HR
01557-814302 &
6 bedrs, 2 ♨/WC, 3 ♨/WC, 1 ♨; ✹
sB&B £16.50-£21.50 dB&B £39-£90 Breakfast
only [5%V]; cc Ac Amex Vi

GLASGOW Strathclyde   12C2

Albion *Acclaimed* ⛨
405 North Woodside Road, Glasgow G20 6NN
0141-339-8620

Ambassador *Acclaimed* ⛨
7 Kelvin Drive, Glasgow G20 8QS
0141-946-1018

Arrochoile Balmaha, Glasgow G63 0JG
01360-87231 &
3 bedrs, 2 ♨/WC, 1 ♨/WC; P4
sB&B £18 Breakfast only

Bay Cottage Balmaha, Glasgow G63 0BX
01360-87346

Granada Lodge ⛨
251 Paisley Road, Glasgow G5 8RA
0800-555-300

Marie Stuart ⛨
46-48 Queen Mary Avenue, Glasgow G42
8DT 0141-4243939 Fax 0141-4239070 &
28 bedrs, 28 ♨/WC; ✹ ✂ P40
sB&B £44.50 dB&B £55 D £9.50 [10%V]; cc Ac
Vi

Smith's ⛨
963 Sauchiehall Street, Glasgow G3 7TQ
0141-3396363
33 bedrs, 8 ♨;
sB&B £22 dB&B £34 Breakfast only [10%V]

GLENROTHES Fife   13D1

Briarmont 42 Church Street, Ladybank,
Glenrothes KY7 7LE 01337-30359

Firlands Ladybank, Monkstown, Glenrothes
Y7 7JX 01337-30845

Laurel Bank 1 Balbirnie Street, Markinch, Glenrothes KY7 6DB 01592-611205 Fax 01592-611104 &

Exellent food-wide choice of starters, main courses & sweets, home made dishes and a delicious range of steaks. Efficient and friendly staff to welcome you. Comfortable bedrooms all with TV, tea/coffee making facilities. Some en-suite , hairdrier.
11 bedrs, 1 ⇥/WC, 4 ☞/WC, 1 ⇥; TV tcf ✗
sB&B £25 D £3; cc Ac Vi

Tarry-A-While 11 Ardgartan Court, Balfarg, Glenrothes KY7 6XB 01592-745259

Wester Markinch Cottage Balbirnie Estate, Markinch, Glenrothes KY7 6JN 01592-756719

13 Laxford Road Glenrothes KY6 2EB 01592-75413

GOLSPIE Highland	15D2

Granite Villa Fountain Road, Golspie KW10 6TH 01408-633146

GORDON Lothian	13E2

Old School Gallery The Old School, Gordon TD3 6LS 01573-410582

GRANTOWN-ON-SPEY Highland	15E3

Culdearn House *Highly Acclaimed* ☂
Woodlands Terrace, Grantown-on-Spey PH26 3JU 01479-872106 Fax 01479-873641
9 bedrs, 2 ⇥/WC, 7 ☞/WC; ✞ P10
Child restrictions
sB&B £48 dB&B £96; HB weekly £270-£295; [10%V]; cc Ac DC Vi

Garden Park *Acclaimed* ☂
Woodside Avenue, Grantown-on-Spey PH26 3JN 01479-873235
5 bedrs, 3 ⇥/WC, 2 ☞/WC; P8
Child restrictions
sB&B £18.50-£21 dB&B £37-£42; HB weekly £180-£198;

Ravenscourt House *Highly Acclaimed* ☂
Seafield Avenue, Grantown-on-Spey PH26 3JG 01479-872286 Fax 01479-873260 &
9 bedrs, 8 ☞/WC, 1 ⇥; ✿ ✞ P9
sB&B £39-£45 dB&B £58-£75; HB weekly £413; D £18 [10%V]; cc Ac Vi

GRETNA Dumfries & Galloway	13D4

Gables 1 Annan Road, Gretna CA6 5DQ 01461-38300

Surrone House *Highly Acclaimed* ☂
Annan Road, Gretna DG16 5DL 01461-338341
7 bedrs, 6 ⇥/WC; P10
sB&B £32 dB&B £46 D £9 [5%V];
cc Ac Amex Vi

HADDINGTON Lothian	13E2

Brown's *Highly Acclaimed* ☂
1 West Road, Haddington EH41 3RD
01620-822254 Fax 01620-822254 &
5 bedrs, 3 ⇥/WC, 2 ☞/WC; ✞ P10
sB&B £60 dB&B £80 D £24.50 [5%V]; cc Ac Amex DC Vi

Eaglescairnie Mains Gifford, Haddington EH41 4HN 01620-810491 Fax 01620-810491

Beautifully furnished Georgian farmhouse on a 350 acre arable/sheep farm. Peaceful location with magnificent views.
3 bedrs, 2 ⇥/WC, 1 ⇥; ✿ ✗
sB&B £16 Breakfast only

HALKIRK Highland 15E1

Glenlivet Fairview, Halkirk KW12 6XF
01847-83302

HAMILTON Strathclyde 12C2

Road Chef Lodge
M74 Northbound, Hamilton ML3 6JW
01689-891904

HAWICK Borders 13E3

Dunira House Buccleuch Road, Hawick TD9 0EL 01450-78493

Ellistrin 6 Fenwick Park, Hawick TD9 9PA
01450-374216

Large comfortable villa with garden situated in a quiet and convenient location.
3 bedrs, 2 🚿/WC, 1 🛁; 🐕 P3
sB&B £15 Breakfast only

Hobsburn House Bonchester Bridge, Hawick TD9 8JW 0145-0860642 Fax 0145-0860330
6 bedrs, 3 🛁; 🐕 P20
sB&B £22; HB weekly £308;

Kirkton Farmhouse Hawick TD9 8QJ
01450-372421

Comfortable farmhouse accommodation with log fires and home cooking, set in the beautiful Border countryside.
3 bedrs, 1 🛁; tcf 🐕 P10
sB&B £13.50; HB weekly £120; D £6.50-£7

Oakwood House Buccleuch Road, Hawick TD9 0EH 01450-72896

HELENSBURGH Strathclyde 12C2

★★★Rosslea Hall
Ferry Road, Rhu, Helensburgh G84 8NF
01436-820684 Fax 01436-820897 ♿
30 bedrs, 27 🛁/WC, 3 🚿/WC; 🐕 P70
sB&B £58-£63 dB&B £77 D £17.50 [5%V]; cc Ac Amex DC Vi

HELMSDALE Highland 15E2

Broomhill House Navidale Road, Helmsdale KW8 6HH 01431-2259

Clovelly Dunrobin Street, Helmsdale KW8 6JS 01431-2226

Using RAC discount vouchers

Please tell the hotel when booking if you plan to use an RAC discount voucher in part payment of your bill. Only one voucher will be accepted per party per stay. Discount vouchers will only be accepted in payment for accommodation, not for food.

Child Restrictions

Most hotels and guest houses are happy to welcome children. A few prefer to welcome only adults and older children; these are shown by 'Child restrictions' in the entry. If you are travelling with children, please telephone the establishment to check the age limit set by the management.

**Fir Brae 189 Marrel, Helmsdale KW8 6HU
01431-821223**
*Traditional, stone-built, Croft house in a quiet
rural setting offering comfortable
accommodation and home cooking.*
3 bedrs, 1 ➡; tcf ✈ P5
sB&B £13; HB weekly £96-£126; D £3-£8

HUNTLY Grampian 15E3

Braeside Provost Street, Huntly AB54 5BB
01466-793825

Castle Huntly AB54 4SH 01466-792696

Glenburn 19 Castle Street, Huntly AB54 5BP
01466-792798

**Monedie Aberchirder, Huntly AB54 5PL
01466-708287** ♿
*A welcoming 18th century farm house on a
working farm, situated in a beautiful area.*
3 bedrs, 1 ➡; ✈ P4
sB&B £11 Breakfast only

New Inn 79 Main Street, Aberchirder, Huntly
AB54 5TB 01466-780534

Old Manse of Marnoch *Highly Acclaimed* 🅁🅐🅒
Bridge of Marnoch, Huntly AB54 5RS
01466-780873
5 bedrs, 4 ➡/WC, 1 ☎/WC; ✈ ⅄ P10
Child restrictions
sB&B £45 dB&B £60-£70; HB weekly £370; D
£20; cc Ac Vi

Southview Victoria Road, Huntly AB56 5AH
01466-792456

The Rose & Thistle Inn 46 Duke Street,
Huntly AB54 5DT 01466-792578

INNELLAN Strathclyde 12B2

Osborne 🅁🅐🅒
Shore Road, Dunoon PA23 7TJ 0136-983-445

INNERLEITHEN Borders 13D3

Caddon View 14 Pirn Road, Innerleithen
EH44 6HF 01896-830208

Tweedside Avalon, Leithen Crescent,
Innerleithen EH44 6HF 01896-830386

INVERGARRY Highland 14C4

Craigard House 🅁🅐🅒
Invergarry PH35 4HG 01809-501258

*Craigard is a large house in the country built
in 1865 standing in 3 acres of garden
screened from the road by trees and shrubs.
Situated one mile from the Great Glen,
Craigard House has a warm, relaxing
atmosphere.*
7 bedrs, 2 ➡/WC, 1 ☎/WC, 2 ➡; ⅄ P10
Child restrictions
sB&B £16-£20 dB&B £32-£40; HB weekly
£196-£224;

INVERKEITHING Fife 13D2

Borland Lodge Private 31-33 Boreland
Road, Inverkeithing KY11 1DA 01383-413792

**Forth Craig 90 Hope Street, Inverkeithing
KY11 1LL 01383-418440**
*A small, modern family-run hotel overlooking
the River Forth Estuary.*
5 bedrs, 5 ☎/WC; TV tcf ✈ P8
sB&B £18.50 D £7-£10; cc Ac Amex Vi

INVERNESS Highland · 15D3

Brae Ness *Acclaimed* · RAC
Ness Bank, Inverness IV2 4SF 01463-712266 · &
10 bedrs, 2 ⇒/WC, 7 ☾/WC, 1 ⇒; ⅍ P7
sB&B £30-£33 dB&B £44-£58; HB weekly
£220-£269; D £13.50; cc Ac Vi

Clach Mhuillin *Highly Acclaimed* · RAC
7 Harris Road, Inverness IV2 3LS
01463-237059
3 bedrs, 1 ☾/WC, 1 ⇒; P4
Child restrictions
sB&B £18-£21 dB&B £36-£42 Breakfast only
[5%V]; cc Vi

Culduthel Lodge *Highly Acclaimed* · RAC
14 Culduthel Road, Inverness IV2 4AG
01463-240089 Fax 01463-240089
12 bedrs, 6 ⇒/WC; ⋈ ⅍ P12
Child restrictions
sB&B £40 dB&B £64-£66; HB weekly £320-
£330; cc Ac Vi

Four Winds *Acclaimed* · RAC
42 Old Edinburgh Road, Inverness IV2 3PG
01463-230397

St Ann's House · RAC
37 Harrowden Road, Inverness IV3 5QN
01463-236157

Sunnyholm *Acclaimed* · RAC
12 Mayfield Road, Inverness IV2 4AE
01463-231336

Tower *Acclaimed* · RAC
4 Ardross Terrace, Inverness IV3 5NQ
01463-232765
12 bedrs, 6 ⇒/WC, 6 ☾/WC, 1 ⇒;
sB&B £26-£30 dB&B £40-£44 Breakfast only;
cc Ac Vi

White Lodge *Acclaimed* · RAC
15 Bishops Road, Inverness IV3 5SB
01463-230693 Fax 01463-230693
7 bedrs, 5 ⇒/WC, 2 ⇒; ⅍ P7
Breakfast only; cc Ac Amex Vi

INVERURIE Grampian · 15F3

Banks Of Ury 20 High Street, Inverurie AB51
3XQ 01467-620409

Breaslann Old Chapel Road, Inverurie AB51
9QN 01467-621608

Cromlet Hill South Road, Oldmeldrum,
Inverurie AB51 0AB 01561-872315

Market Place Guest 50 Market Place,
Inverurie AB51 9XN 01467-623424

Strathburn · RAC
Burghmuir Drive, Inverurie AB5 9GY
01467-24422 Fax 01467-25133

JEDBURGH Borders · 13E3

Akaso-Uram 7 Queen Street, Jedburgh TD8
6EP 01835-862482
3 bedrs, 1 ⇒; TV tcf ⋈ P1
sB&B £12.50 Breakfast only

Craigowen 30 High Street, Jedburgh TD8
6AG 01835-862604

Ferniehurst Mill Lodge *Acclaimed* · RAC
Jedburgh TD8 6PQ 01835-863279
10 bedrs, 5 ⇒/WC, 3 ☾/WC, 2 ⇒; ⋈ P10
sB&B £21; HB weekly £224; cc Ac Vi

Fernlea Allerton Place, Jedburgh TD8 6LG
01835-862318

Brae Ness Hotel

*Ness Bank,
Inverness IV2 4SF*
Telephone:
(01463) 712266

Ideally situated beside the river, 5
minutes' walk from the town centre.
We offer excellent home cooking and
baking in our no-smoking dining room with
table licence. Rooms have private bathroom
(some with bath), TV, tea facilities, and some
are reserved for non-smokers only.

Personally run by John and Margaret Hill.
Brochure on request.
Bed & Breakfast per person per night
sharing from **£20 to £29**. Dinner **£14.50**

Hundalee House Jedburgh TD8 6PA 01835-863011

An historic, early 17th century, country house, set in 10 acres of secluded gardens and woodlands.
5 bedrs, 1 ⬒/WC, 2 🛉/WC, 1 ⬒; TV tcf P10
sB&B £16.50 Breakfast only

Kenmore Bank Oxnam Road, Jedburgh TD8 6JJ 01835-862369

A charming, family-run hotel, overlooking the River and Abbey, 5 minutes walk from the town centre. Well-equipped bedrooms.
6 bedrs, 1 ⬒/WC, 5 🛉/WC; TV tcf ✗ P6
sB&B £18.50; D £14; cc Ac Vi

Maple Bank 3 Smiths Wynd, Jedburgh TD8 6DH 01835-862051

Royal Canongate, Jedburgh TD8 6AJ 01835-863152

The Spinney Langlee, Jedburgh TD8 6PB 01835-863525

Willow Court The Friars, Jedburgh TD8 6BN 01835-863702 &
4 bedrs, 1 ⬒/WC, 3 🛉/WC; TV tcf ✗ P6
sB&B £15; HB weekly £182-£203; D £11-£16

JOHN O'GROATS Highland   15E1

Shorelands Huna, John O'Groats KW1 4YL 01955-81376

KEITH Grampian   15E3

Ar Dachaidh Wood Lane, Off Conval Lane, Dufftown, Keith AB55 4AH 01340-20697

Craighurst Seafield Avenue, Keith AB55 3BS 01542-886063

Errolbank 134 Fife Street, Dufftown, Keith AB55 4DP 01340-20229

Fife Arms 2 The Square, Dufftown, Keith AB55 4AD 01340-20220

KELSO Borders   13E3

Black Swan Horsemarket, Kelso TD5 7HE 01573-224563

Craignethan House Jedburgh Road, Kelso TD5 8AZ 01573-224818 &
3 bedrs, 2 ⬒; tcf ✗ P10
sB&B £16.50 Breakfast only

Duncan House Chalkheugh Terrace, Kelso TD5 7DX 01573-225682 &

6 bedrs, 2 ⬒/WC, 1 🛉/WC, 2 ⬒; ✗ P7
sB&B £14 Breakfast only

Eccles House Eccles, Kelso TD5 7QS 01890-840205

Greenhill Hownam, Kelso TD5 8AW 01573-440505

Lochside Yetholm, Kelso TD5 8PD 01573-420349

Morebattle Tofts Kelso TD5 8AD
01573-440364 Fax 01573-420227
An elegant, 18th century farmhouse in an
idyllic location beside the Kale River.
3 bedrs, 2 ➡/WC, 1 ➚/WC, 3 ➡; tcf ✖ P6
sB&B £14; HB weekly £168-£182; D £10-£11

★★★**Sunlaws**   RÃC
Kelso TD5 8JZ 01573-450331 Fax
01573-450611

Temple Hall Inn Main Street, Morebattle,
Kelso TD5 8QQ 01573-440249

Wester House 155 Roxburgh Street, Kelso
TD5 7DU 01573-225479

KENMORE Tayside   12C1

★★★**Kenmore**   RÃC
Village Square, Kenmore PH15 2NA
01887-830205 Fax 01887-830262

KILLIECRANKIE Tayside   15D4

Dalnasgadh House   RÃC
Pitlochry, Killiecrankie PH16 5LN
01796-473237
5 bedrs, 2 ➡; P10
Child restrictions
sB&B £18-£19 dB&B £17-£18

KILLIN Tayside   12C1

Clachaig Falls Of Dochart, Killin FK21 8SL
01567-820270

Craigbuie Main Street, Killin FK21 8UH
01567-820439

Fernbank Main Street, Killin FK21 8UW
01567-820511

Killin Killin FK21 8TP 01567-820296

Rowancroft Main Street, Killin FK21 8UT
01567-820219

KINGHORN Fife   13D2

Craigo-Er 45 Pettycur Road, Kinghorn KY3
9RN 01592-890527

Longboat Inn 107 Pettycur Road, Kinghorn
KY3 9RU 01592-890625

KINGUSSIE Highland   15D4

Craig An Darach   RÃC
Kingussie PH21 1JE 01540-661235 Fax
01540-661235

KINROSS Tayside   13D1

Granada Lodge   RÃC
Kincardine Road, Kinross KY13 7HQ
01577-64646

★★**Kirklands**   RÃC
20 High Street, Kinross KY13 7AN
01557-863313

KIRKCALDY Fife   13D2

Bennochy Bank 26a Carlyle Road, Kirkcaldy
KY1 1DB 01592-200733
5 bedrs, 1 ➚/WC, 2 ➡; ✖ P8
sB&B £15 Breakfast only

Cherrydene 44 Bennochy Road, Kirkcaldy
KY2 5RB 01592-202147
3 bedrs, 2 ➚/WC, 2 ➡; ✖ P4
sB&B £18 Breakfast only

Crown 7 Main Street, Kirkcaldy KY1 4AF
01592-774416

Main Street Kirkcaldy KY1 4NN
01592-654938

Rowan Cottage 5 Melrose Crescent,
Kirkcaldy KY2 5BN 01592-267305

Royal Townhead, Dysart, Kirkcaldy KY1 2XQ
01592-654112

Wemysshof 69 Lady Nairn Avenue, Kirkcaldy
KY1 2AR 01592-65806

143 Victoria Road Kirkcaldy KY1 1DQ
01592-268864

Discount vouchers
Hotels with a (V) at the end of the price
information will accept RAC discount
vouchers in part payment for
accommodation bills on the full,
standard rate, not against bargain breaks
or any other special offer.

KIRKCUDBRIGHT
Dumfries & Galloway   12C4

Gladstone House 48 High Street, Kirkcudbright DG6 4JX 01554-331734

An 18th century house in a picturesque harbour town. Elegant drawing room, secluded gardens and well-appointed bedrooms. Non smoking.
3 bedrs, 2 ⇥/WC, 1 ☞/WC, 1 ⇥; TV tcf ✂
Child restrictions under 12
sB&B £24 Breakfast only; cc Ac Vi

Glencroft Twynholm, Kirkcudbright DG6 4NT 01557-6252

Gordon House 116 High Street, Kirkcudbright DG6 4JQ 01557-30670

Millburn House Millburn Street, Kirkcudbright DG6 4ED 01557-30926

LAIRG Highland   15D2

Carnbren Lairg IV27 4AY 01549-2259

Cruachan Stoer, Lochinver, Lairg IV27 4JE 01571-5303

Invershin Farm Invershin, Lairg IV27 4ET 01549-82206

Kylesku Kylesku, Lairg IV27 4HW
01971-502231   &
7 bedrs, 5 ⇥/WC, 1 ☞/WC, 1 ⇥; ✖ 🐾
sB&B £20; HB weekly £160-£250;

Morven Lerin, Durness, Lairg IV27 4QB 01971-511252

Newton Lodge Kylesku, Lairg IV27 4HW 01971-502070

Old School Restaurant Inshegra, Kinlochbervie, Lairg IV27 4RH 01971-521383

Port Na Con House Laid, Loch Eriboll, via Altnaharra, Lairg IV27 4UN 01971-511367

Rangoon Scourie, Lairg IV27 4TE 01971-502011

Stoer Villa Stoer, Lairg IV27 4JE 01571-5305

The Albannach Baddidarach, Lochinver, Lairg IV27 4LP 01571-4407

216 Clashmore Stoer, Lochinver, Lairg IV27 4JQ 01571-295

LATHERON Highland   15E1

Tatcher Latheron KW5 6DX 01594-313

LAUDER Borders   13E2

The Grange 6 Edinburgh Road, Lauder TD2 6TW 01578-722649
A large, detached house in its own grounds.
3 bedrs, 1 ⇥; tcf P5
sB&B £14 Breakfast only

LAURENCEKIRK Grampian   15F4

Royal Conveth Place, Laurencekirk AB30 1AD 01561-377487

LEVEN Fife   13E1

Forth Bay Promenade, Leven KY8 4HZ
01333-423009
5 bedrs, 2 ☞/WC, 1 ⇥; ✖ P3
sB&B £12.50; HB weekly £75-£120;

Milford House 19 High Street, Elie, Leven KY9 1BY 01333-330567

LOCHEARNHEAD Central   12C1

Bencloich Kendrum Road, Lochearnhead
FK19 8PX 01567-830307

Monachachyle Mhor Balquhidder,
Lochearnhead FK19 8PQ 01877-384622

LOCHGELLY Fife

**Navitie House Ballingry, Lochgelly KY5
8LR 01592-860295**

LOCHMADDY Highland   14A2

★★**Lochmaddy**   RAC
North Uist, Lochmaddy PA22 5AA 01876-3331

LOCKERBIE Dumfries & Galloway   13D4

Carik Cottage Waterbeck, Lockerbie DG11
3EU 01461-600652

Carlyle House Ecclefechan, Lockerbie DG11
3DG 01576-300322

★★★**Lockerbie Manor**   RAC
Borkland Road, Lockerbie DG11 2RJ
01576-202610 Fax 01576-203046
28 bedrs, 26 ➡/WC, 2 ☛/WC; ✖ P80
sB&B £52.50-£63 dB&B £76.50-£80; HB
weekly £262.50-£275; D £16.50 [10%V]; cc Ac
Amex DC Vi

Ravenshill House Dumfries Road, Lockerbie
DG11 2EF 01576-202882 Fax 01576-202882
*A family owned hotel set in 2 1/2 acres of
garden, enjoying a reputation for good food,
comfortable accommodation and friendly
service. Weekend and short breaks.*
8 bedrs, 2 ➡/WC, 2 ☛/WC, 1 ➡; TV tcf ✖
P35
Child restrictions
sB&B £34 D £9-£15; cc Ac Amex Vi

★★**Somerton House**   RAC
Carlisle Road, Lockerbie DG11 2DR
01576-202583 Fax 01576-505384

LOSSIEMOUTH Grampian   15E2

Lossiemouth House 33 Clifton Road,
Lossiemouth IV31 6DP 01343-813397
4 bedrs, 2 ➡; TV tcf P4
sB&B £15; HB weekly £140; D £6

Mormond Prospect Terrace, Lossiemouth
IV31 6JS 01343-813143

**Skerryhill 63 Dunbar Street, Lossiemouth
IV31 6AN 01343-813035**   &
3 bedrs, 1 ➡; TV tcf ✖
sB&B £13 Breakfast only

LYBSTER Highland   15E1

★★★**Portland Arms**   RAC
Lybster KW3 6BS 01593-2208 Fax 01593-2208

MACDUFF Grampian   15F3

Monica & Martin B & B 21 Gellymill Street,
Macduff AB44 1TN 01261-32336
3 bedrs, 2 ☛/WC, 1 ➡; TV tcf ✖
sB&B £11 D £6

Location Maps

Hotel locations are shown on the
maps at the back of the guide.
All towns and villages containing
an hotel listed in the guide
are shown in black.

New Telephone Numbers

All UK telephone codes are being
changed. The number 1 is being
inserted after the first 0. For example,
081 is changing to 0181. The new
codes were available in August 1994
and the two codes will run in parallel
until 16 April 1995, when the new
code will take over. The new codes
are given throughout the guide, as
they will be in use in November when
the guide is published The old codes
can be used up to 16 April 1995.
Five cities will have a complete change of
code and an additional digit to the
number.

	old	new
Bristol	0272-xxxxx	0117-9xxxxxx
Leeds	0532-xxxxx	0113-2xxxxxx
Leicester	0533-xxxxx	0116-2xxxxxx
Nottingham	0602-xxxxx	0115-9xxxxxx
Sheffield	0742-xxxxx	0114-2xxxxxx

MELROSE Borders 13E3

Clachan Main Street, St Boswells, Melrose
TD6 0BG 01835-822266

*Large family home, warm welcome, good
food, on edge of beautiful village. 2 minutes
from golf course and River Tweed.*
4 bedrs, 2 ⇥; tcf ✖ P3
sB&B £12 D £6

Collingwood Waverley Road, Melrose TD6
9AA 01896-822670

Dunfermline House Buccleuch Street,
Melrose TD6 9LB 01896-822148
5 bedrs, 4 ☎/WC, 1 ⇥; ✖
sB&B £20; HB weekly £130-£135;

Kings Arms High Street, Melrose TD6 9PB
01896-822143

North Lodge Drygrange, Melrose TD6 9DJ
01896-848174

Plough Inn Lilliesleaf, Melrose TD6 9SD
01835-7271
*An old coaching inn set in a picturesque
village in the heart of the Scottish Borders.*
3 bedrs, 3 ☎/WC, 1 ⇥; tcf P20
Child restrictions under 10
sB&B £25; HB weekly £245; D £10

Whitehouse Farmhouse St Boswells,
Melrose TD6 0ED 01573-460343 Fax
01573-460361

*Large comfortable farmhouse with log fires,
home cooking and warm welcome. Fabulous
views from all rooms, situated in central
borders. STB 2 crowns commended.*
3 bedrs, 1 ☎/WC, 2 ⇥; tcf P10
sB&B £15; HB weekly £160-£210; D £8-£12

MOFFAT Dumfries & Galloway 13D3

Arden House *Acclaimed* RAC
High Street, Moffat DG10 9HG
01683-20220 ♿
8 bedrs, 4 ☎/WC, 2 ⇥; ✖ P10
sB&B £18.50 dB&B £30; HB weekly £231; D
£7.50

Belmont House Sidmount Avenue, Moffat
DG10 9BS 01683-20057

Black Bull Churchgate, Moffat DG10 9EG
01683-20206

Craigie Lodge Ballplay Road, Moffat DG10 9JU 01683-21037

Gilbert House *Acclaimed*   RAC
Beechgrove, Old Edinburgh Road, Moffat DG10 9RS 01683-20050

Long Bed Holm Farm Beattock, Moffat DG10 9SN

Ramlodge High Street, Moffat DG10 9RU 01683-20594
5 bedrs, 1 ➡; ✗
sB&B £14.50 Breakfast only

Red House Newton Wamphray, Moffat DG10 9NF 01576-470470
3 bedrs, 1 ☞/WC, 1 ➡; P20
sB&B £20; HB weekly £200-£250; D £10-£15; cc Ac Vi

Waterside Moffat DG10 9LF 01683-20092

Well View *Highly Acclaimed*   RAC
Ballplay Road, Moffat DG1O 9JU 01683-20184
6 bedrs, 3 ➡/WC, 3 ☞/WC; ✗
sB&B £33-£42 dB&B £50-£70; HB weekly £330-£400; D £22 [10%V]; cc Ac Amex Vi

---

MONTROSE Tayside   15F4

Linksgate   RAC
11 Dorward Road, Montrose DD10 8SB 01674-72273

NEW ABBEY Dumfries & Galloway   13D4

Cavens *Highly Acclaimed*   RAC
Kirkbean, New Abbey DG2 8AA
0138-788234   ♿
6 bedrs, 4 ➡/WC, 2 ☞/WC; ✗ ✗ P10
sB&B £27-£35 dB&B £44-£52; HB weekly £200-£245; [5%V]; cc Ac Vi

---

NEWTON STEWART
Dumfries & Galloway   12C4

Abercree House Corsbie Road, Newton Stewart DG8 6JD 01671-403489

Baltier Farm Whithorn, Newton Stewart DG8 8HA 01988-406241

Belle Isle Country House Garlieston, Newton Stewart DG8 8AF 01988-600214

A hotel with all home comforts and a peaceful, tranquil atmosphere ideal for convalescence and relaxation. Situated a mile from the sea. Non- smoking.
3 bedrs, 2 ➡/WC, 1 ☞/WC; tcf ✗ P5
sB&B £58 D £15

Belmont St John Street, Whithorn, Newton Stewart DG8 8PG 01988-500890
3 bedrs, 1 ➡/WC, 1 ☞/WC, 1 ➡; TV tcf ✗ P6
sB&B £12; HB weekly £126-£154; D £6-£7

Churchend 6 Main Street, Kirkcowan, Newton Stewart DG8 0HG 01671-830246 ♿
3 bedrs, 1 ➡/WC, 2 ☞/WC; TV tcf ✗ P3
sB&B £14; HB weekly £147; D £7-£9; cc Ac

Clugston Farm Newton Stewart DG8 9BH 01671-83338

Flowerbank Minnigaff, Newton Stewart DG8 6PJ 01671-402629

Jubilee Cottage Brahead, Kirkinner, Newton Stewart DG8 9AH 01988-84604

Lynwood Corvisel Road, Newton Stewart DG8 6LN 01671-402074

Marclaysean 51 St John Street, Creetown, Newton Stewart DG8 7JB 01671-82319

Oakbank Corsbie Road, Newton Stewart DG8 6JB 01671-402822

Palakona 30 Queen Street, Newton Stewart DG8 6JL 01671-402323

Rowantree 38 Main Street, Newton Stewart
DG8 0PS 01581-300244   ♿
5 bedrs, 1 🛏; ✗ P8
sB&B £15 Breakfast only

OBAN Strathclyde   12B1

Ardblair *Acclaimed*   RAC
Dalriach Road, Oban PA34 5JB 01631-62668

Briar Bank *Acclaimed*   RAC
Glencruitten Road, Oban 01631-66549
4 bedrs, 2 🛏/WC, 2 🛁/WC, 1 🛏; ✗ P4
Child restrictions
sB&B £15-£18 dB&B £38-£40 Breakfast only

Craigvarren House   RAC
Ardconnel Road, Oban PA34 5DJ 01631-62686

Drumriggend, *Acclaimed*   RAC
Drummore Road, Oban PA34 4JL 01631-63330

Foxholes *Highly Acclaimed*   RAC
Cologin, Lerags, Oban PA34 4SE 01631-64982
7 bedrs, 3 🛏/WC, 4 🛁/WC; P8
Child restrictions
HB weekly £245-£252;

Glenburnie *Acclaimed*   RAC
Esplanade, Oban PA34 5AQ 01631-62089
15 bedrs, 15 🛁/WC, 1 🛏; ✗ ⚓ P10
sB&B £20-£25 dB&B £40-£60 Breakfast only
[5%V]; cc Ac Vi

Roseneath   RAC
Dalriach Road, Oban PA34 5EQ 01631-62929
10 bedrs, 5 🛁/WC, 2 🛏; P8
sB&B £14-£17 dB&B £30-£38 Breakfast only

Sgeir-mhaol *Acclaimed*   RAC
Soroba Road, Oban PA34 4JF 01631-62650
7 bedrs, 5 🛁/WC, 1 🛏; P10
Breakfast only [10%V]

ONICH Highland   14C4

Tigh-a-righ   RAC
Onich PH33 6SE 01855-3255   ♿
5 bedrs; ✗ ⚓ P20
sB&B £14 dB&B £23.50 D £10

PAISLEY Strathclyde   12C2

Ashburn   RAC
Milliken Park Road, Kilbarchan, Paisley PA10
2DB 01505-705477 Fax 01505-705477
6 bedrs, 2 🛁/WC, 2 🛏;
sB&B £20-£22 dB&B £34-£38 D £10 [10%V];
cc Ac Vi

PEEBLES Borders   13D2

Brookside Eshiels, Peebles EH45
01721-721178

Robingarth 46 Edinburgh Road, Peebles
EH45 8EB 01721-720226

12 Dukehaugh Peebles EH45 9DN
01721-720118

PERTH Tayside   13D1

Achnacarry *Acclaimed*   RAC
3 Pitcullen Crescent, Perth PH2 7HT
01738-621421

Ardfern House   RAC
15 Pitcullen Crescent, Perth PH2 7HT
01738-622259

Clunie *Acclaimed*   RAC
12 Pitcullen Crescent, Perth PH2 7HT
01738-623625

Iona *Acclaimed*   RAC
2 Pitcullen Crescent, Perth PH2 7HT
01738-627261
5 bedrs, 2 🛁/WC, 2 🛏; ✗ ⚓ P6
sB&B £14-£18 dB&B £28-£36; HB weekly
£150-£175; [10%V]; cc Ac Vi

Ninewells Farm Woodriffe Road, Newburgh,
Cupar, Perth KY14 6EY 01337-840307

Pitcullen *Acclaimed*   RAC
17 Pitcullen Crescent, Perth PH2 7HT
01738-626506

PETERHEAD Grampian   15F3

Aden Arms Russel Street, Old Deer,
Peterhead AB42 8LN 01771-22573

> ### Symbols
> For an explanation of the symbols used in
> hotel entries, please see inside the front cover.

Carrick 16 Merchant Street, Peterhead AB42
6BU 01779-470610 Fax 01779-470610
7 bedrs, 7 **f**/WC; TV tcf **⊀** P3
sB&B £16 Breakfast only

Clifton 96 Queen Street, Peterhead AB42
6TT 01779-77649

Country Park Inn Station Road, Mintlaw,
Peterhead AB42 8EB 01771-22622

Palace Prince Street, Peterhead AB42 6PL
01779-74821

PITLOCHRY Tayside   15D4

Knockendarroch House *Highly Acclaimed* **RAC**
Higher Oakfield, Pitlochry PH16 5HT
01796-473473 Fax 01796-474068
12 bedrs, 7 **➡**/WC, 5 **f**/WC; **⊀** P15
dB&B £70-£80; HB weekly £250-£300; D £14
[10%V]; **cc** Ac Amex DC Vi

Well House *Acclaimed*   **RAC**
11 Toberargan Road, Pitlochry PH16 5HG
01796-472239

PORTREE Isle of Skye   14B3

★Isles   **RAC**
Somerled Square, Portree IV51 9EH
01478-612129

*A traditional highland building, tastefully
restored in a quiet corner of Portree's main
square.*
9 bedrs, 7 **➡**/WC, 1 **➡**; **⊀**
sB&B £21-£23 dB&B £24-£30; **cc** Ac Vi

PORTSOY Grampian   15F3

Academy House School Road, Fordyce,
Portsy AB45 2SJ 01261-42743

Boyne Portsy AB4 2PA 01261-42242

PRESTWICK Strathclyde   12C3

Braemar   **RAC**
113 Ayr Road, Prestwick KA9 1TN
01292-75820

Fernbank *Acclaimed*   **RAC**
213 Main Street, Prestwick KA9 1SU
01292-75027
7 bedrs, 4 **f**/WC, 2 **➡**; **⊀** P7
Child restrictions
sB&B £15-£17 dB&B £34-£38 Breakfast only

Kincraig *Acclaimed*   **RAC**
39 Ayr Road, Prestwick KA9 1SY 01292-79480

ROGART Highland   15D2

Benview Morness, Rogart IV28 3XG
01408-641222

ROSYTH Fife   13D2

★★Gladyer Inn   **RAC**
10 Heath Road, Rosyth KY11 2BT
01383-419977   **&**
21 bedrs, 21 **➡**/WC; **⊀** P97
sB&B £32 dB&B £50 D £13.50 [10%V]; **cc** Ac
Amex Vi

ROTHESAY Isle of Bute   12B2

Ardyne *Highly Acclaimed*   **RAC**
38 Mountstuart Road, Rothesay PA20 9EB
01700-502052 Fax 01700-505129
10 bedrs, 3 **➡**/WC, 7 **f**/WC; **⊁**
sB&B £24 dB&B £34-£44 D £10.50 [5%V]; **cc**
Ac Amex Vi

SANQUHAR Dumfries & Galloway   13D3

Drumbringan 53 Castle Street, Sanquhar
DG4 6AB 01659-50409

Nithsdale Glasgow Road, Sanquhar DG4
6BZ 01659-50288

Penhurst Townhead Street, Sanquhar DG4
6DA 01659-50751

SELKIRK Borders   13E3

County 35 High Street, Selkirk TD7 4BZ
01750-21233

Hillholm 36 Hillside Terrace, Selkirk TD7
4ND 01750-21293

Oakwood Farm Ettrickbridge, Selkirk TD7 5HJ 01750-52245

ST ANDREWS Fife   13E1

Albany *Acclaimed*   RAC
56 North Street, St Andrews KY16 9AH
01334-477737 Fax 01334-477737
10 bedrs, 5 ⁂/WC, 2 ➧; ⌇
sB&B £25-£28 dB&B £58 D £15; cc Ac Vi

Amberside *Acclaimed*   RAC
4 Murray Park, St Andrews KY16 9AW
01334-474644
6 bedrs, 5 ⁂/WC, 1 ➧; ✗ ⌇
sB&B £18-£27 dB&B £36-£52 Breakfast only
[10%V]; cc Amex

Argyle *Acclaimed*   RAC
127 North Street, St Andrews KY16 9AG
01334-473387

Arran House *Acclaimed*   RAC
5 Murray Park, St Andrews KY16 9AW
01334-474724 Fax 01334-472072
4 bedrs, 3 ⁂/WC, 1 ➧; TV tcf ⌇
sB&B £20-£30 dB&B £46-£50 Breakfast only
[10%V]; cc Ac Amex Vi

Aslar House 120 North Street, St Andrews
KY16 9AF 01334-73460

Beachway House *Acclaimed*   RAC
4-8 Murray Park, St Andrews KY16 9AW
01334-473319

Bell Craig *Acclaimed*   RAC
8 Murray Park, St Andrews KY16 9HS
01334-472962 Fax 01334-472962
5 bedrs, 3 ⁂/WC, 2 ➧; TV tcf ✗
sB&B £20-£25 dB&B £36-£46 Breakfast only
[10%V]

**Brownlees 7 Murray Place, St Andrews
KY16 9AP 01334-473868**
*Victorian Town House centrally located to all
local amenities.*
6 bedrs, 1 ➧/WC, 4 ⁂/WC, 1 ➧; TV tcf
sB&B £16 Breakfast only

Cadzow *Acclaimed*   RAC
58 North Street, St Andrews KY16 9AH
01334-476933
8 bedrs, 6 ⁂/WC, 2 ➧; TV tcf ✗ ⌇
sB&B £20-£27 dB&B £28-£44 Breakfast only

Cleveden House *Acclaimed*   RAC
3 Murray Place, St Andrews KY16 9AP
01334-474212
6 bedrs, 4 ⁂/WC, 1 ➧; ⌇
sB&B £15-£19 dB&B £32-£44 Breakfast only
[5%V]

Craigmore *Acclaimed*   RAC
3 Murray Park, St Andrews KY16 9AW
01334-472142 Fax 01334-477963
6 bedrs, 1 ➧/WC, 5 ⁂/WC;
dB&B £17-£25 Breakfast only [5%V]; cc Ac Vi

Drumskaith 8 Doldson Gardens, St Andrews
KY16 9UL 01334-73265

Edenside House Edenside, St Andrews KY16
9SQ 01334-838108 Fax 01334-838493

*St Andrews five minutes by car. Superb
waterfront setting on bird sanctuary.
Tastefully modernised former farmhouse
predating 1775. Guaranteed parking spaces.
Golf information. S.T.B. 2 Crown
Commended.*
9 bedrs, 9 ⁂/WC; TV tcf ✗ P10
Child restrictions under 10
sB&B £20 Breakfast only; cc Ac Vi

Glenderran 9 Murray Park, St Andrews
KY16 9AW 01334-77951

Hazelbank *Acclaimed*   RAC
28 The Scores, St Andrews KY16 9HS
01334-472466 Fax 01334-472466
10 bedrs, 3 ➧/WC, 7 ⁂/WC; ✗
sB&B £25-£50 dB&B £45-£75 D £10 [10%V];
cc Ac Vi

Links 1 Golf Place, St Andrews KY16 9JA
01334-72059

Linton 16 Hepburn Gardens, St Andrews
KY16 9DD 01334-74673

Lorimer House *Acclaimed* ⚜️RAC
19 Murray Park, St Andrews KY16 9AW
01334-476599

Michael & Inky Frodsham Parkmill,
Boarhills, St Andrews KY16 8PS 01334-88254

Milton Farm Leuchar, St Andrews KY16 0AB
01334-839281

**Number Ten 10 Hope Street, St Andrews
KY16 9HJ 01334-74601 Fax 01334-74601** ♿
10 bedrs, 2 ➖/WC, 8 🛁/WC; TV tcf
sB&B £20 Breakfast only; cc Ac Vi

Peover House 22 Murray Park, St Andrews
KY16 9AW 01334-75787

Riverview *Acclaimed* ⚜️RAC
Edenside, St Andrews KY16 9ST
01334-838009 Fax 01334-838808

Shorecrest 23 Murray Park, St Andrews
KY16 9AW 01334-75310

Spinkstown Farmhouse St Andrews KY16
8PN 01334-473475
3 bedrs, 3 ➖/WC,
sB&B £17 D £10-£12

Sporting Laird *Acclaimed* ⚜️RAC
5 Playfair Terrace, St Andrews KY16 9HX
01334-475906 Fax 01334-473881

**The Larches 7 River Terrace,
Guardbridge, St Andrews KY16 0XA
01334-838008**

West Park House *Acclaimed* ⚜️RAC
5 St Mary's Place, St Andrews FY16 9UY
01334-475933
4 bedrs, 3 ➖/WC, 2 ➖; TV tcf
sB&B £20-£25 dB&B £40-£44 Breakfast only

Yorkston House *Acclaimed* ⚜️RAC
68-70 Argyle Street, St Andrews KY16 9BV
01334-472019

5 Dempster Terrace St Andrews KY16 9QQ
01334-76827

151 South Street St Andrews KY16 9UN
01334-75913

ST MONANS Fife   13E1

Inverforth 20 Braehead, St Monans KY10
2AN 01333-730205

Mayview 40 Station Road, St Monans KY10
2BN 01333-730564

STIRLING Central   12C2

Corshill Cottage Thornhill, Stirling FK8 3DQ
01786-850270
3 bedrs, 3 🛁/WC; tcf 🦮 P6
sB&B £18 D £12

Creag Ard House B & B Milton, Stirling FK8
3TQ 01877-382297

East Lodge Leckie, Gargunnock, Stirling FK8
3BN 01786-860605

Granada Lodge   ⚜️RAC
Pirnall Roundabout, Snabhead, Bannockburn,
Stirling FK7 6EU 01786-813614

**Inverard Lochard Road, Stirling FK8 3DT
01877-382229 Fax 01877-382396**

*Set overlooking the river Forth surrounded by
the spectacular scenery of the Trossachs. The
Inverard Hotel offers a relaxed, cosy &
informal atmosphere .*
16 bedrs, 13 ➖/WC, 2 ➖; TV tcf 🦮 P35
sB&B £20 D £3.85-£15; cc Ac Amex DC Vi

Liang Garston 114 Bannockburn Road,
Stirling FK7 0DQ 01786-813   ♿
2 bedrs, 1 ➖; 🦮 P3
sB&B £14 Breakfast only

Mia Roo 37 Snowdon Place, Stirling FK8 2JP
01786-47379

Shaw Of Touch Farm Stirling FK8 3AE
01786-471147

St Ninians 114 Bannockburn Road, Stirling
FK7 0DQ 01786-813214
2 bedrs, 1 ➡; TV tcf P3
sB&B £14 Breakfast only

Walmer 90 Henderson Street, Bridge Of
Allan, Stirling FK9 4HD 01786-832967
10 bedrs, 7 ➡/WC, 10 ➡/WC; ✖ P20
sB&B £32.50 Breakfast only

**Whitegables 112 Causewayhead Road,
Stirling FK9 5HT 01786-479838**   &
*Tudor style detached villa. Guests will enjoy
the happy astmosphere, personal attention
and a hearty well cooked breakfast.*
3 bedrs, 2 ➡/WC, 1 ➡; TV tcf P6
sB&B £16 Breakfast only

**Woodside 4 Back Walk, Stirling FK8 2QA
01786-475470**

*Beautifully situated on the old historical wall,
lovely view. Warm welcome assured, 5
minutes walk from rail & bus stations.*
6 bedrs, 3 ➡/WC; TV tcf ✖
sB&B £15 Breakfast only

1 Ochill Road Causewayhead, Stirling FK9
5JF 01786-473690

7 Mayne Avenue Bridge Of Allan, Stirling
FK9 4UQ 01786-832178

11 Victoria Square Stirling FK8 2RA
01786-75545

19 Barnsdale Road St Ninians, Stirling FK7
0PT 01786-461729

32 Queen Street Stirling FK8 1HN
01786-63716

STONEHAVEN Grampian   15F4

Car-Lyn-Vale Rickarton, Stonehaven AB3
2TD 01569-762406

STRANRAER Dumfries & Galloway   12B3

Auld Ayre 4 Park Lane, Stranraer DG9 0DS
01776-704500
3 bedrs, 3 ➡/WC; tcf P3
sB&B £17 D £7

Bendochy Heugh Road, Portpatrick,
Stranraer DG9 8TD 01776-81318

Blinkbonnie Portpatrick, Stranraer DG9 8LG
01776-81282

Braefield House Portpatrick, Stranraer DG9
8TA 01776-81255

Fernlea Lewis Street, Stranraer DG9 7AQ
01776-703037

Jan Da Mar 1 Ivy Place, London Road,
Stranraer DG9 8ER 01776-6194

Kildrochet House Kildrochet, Stranraer DG9
9BB 01776-820216
3 bedrs, 3 ➡/WC; tcf P8
sB&B £22; HB weekly £238-£280; D £12-£14

Melvin Lodge South Crescent, Stranraer DG9
8LE 01776-81238

Southcliffe House Portpatrick, Stranraer
DG9 8LE 01776-81411
7 bedrs, 4 ➡/WC, 4 ➡/WC, 2 ➡; ✖ P7
sB&B £17 Breakfast only

Thornton Clenoch Street, Stranraer DG9
7HB 01776-4217

2 Birnam Place Station Street, Stranraer DG9
7HN 01776-703935

STRATHCARRON Highland   14C3

An Dail Kirshorn, Strathcarron IV54 8XB
01520-3455

**Ocean View Kishorn, Strathcarron IV54
2LG 01445-731558**

The Creagan Lochcarron, Strathcarron IV54
8HY 01520-2430

Uist Cottage Lochcarron, Strathcarron IV54 8YH 01502-306

TAIN Highland   15D2

Balintore Balintore, Tain IV20 1UA 01862-832219

Caledonian Portmahomack, Tain IV20 1YS 01862-87345

THORNHILL Dumfries & Galloway   13D3

Thornhill Gallery 47-48 Drumlanrig Street, Thornhill DG3 5LJ 01848-330566
3 bedrs, 3 ➡/WC, 2 ☞/WC; ✖
sB&B £15 Breakfast only

THURSO Highland   15E1

Celtic Firs Whitebridge, Scarfskerry, Thurso KW14 8XW 01848-5616

Glenearn East Mey, Thurso KW14 8XL 01847-85608

Shinval Glengolly, Thurso KW14 7XN 01847-64306   &
3 bedrs, 2 ➡; ✖ P2
sB&B £13; HB weekly £70;

St Johns House Dunnet, Thurso KW1 8YE 01847-85792

TILLICOULTRY Central   13D1

Westbourne 10 Dollar Road, Tillicoultry FK13 6PA 01259-750314

TOBERMORY Isle of Mull   14B4

Strongarbh House *Highly Acclaimed*   ⛫
Strongarbh, Tobermory PA75 6PR
01688-2328 Fax 01688-2238
4 bedrs, 4 ➡/WC; TV tcf ✖ P8
dB&B £57-£67; HB weekly £260-£319; D £20
[10%V]; cc Ac Vi

TOMINTOUL Grampian   15E4

Findron Farm Braemar Road, Tomintoul, Tomintoul AB37 9ER 01807-580382

Glenavon The Square, Tomintoul AB37 9ET 01807-580218

Milton Farm Tomintoul AB37 9EN
01807-580288
6 bedrs, 1 ➡/WC, 3 ☞/WC, 1 ➡; ✖ P20
sB&B £16 Breakfast only

TROON Strathclyde   12C3

★★★South Beach   ⛫
73 South Beach, Troon KA10 6EG
01292-312033 Fax 01292-318438

UIG Isle of Skye   14B3

Corran View   ⛫
22A Breasclete, Uig 01851-621-300
3 bedrs, 3 ☞/WC, 2 ➡; ✖ ⚸ P12
sB&B £23 dB&B £46 Breakfast only; cc Ac Vi

ULLAPOOL Highland   14C2

Tigh na Mara The Shore, Ardindrean, Loch Broom, Ullapool IV23 2SE 01854-655282 Fax 01854-655282

Highly acclaimed / gourmet scottish vegetarian cooking in idyllic secluded lochside location.
3 bedrs, 1 ➡/WC, 1 ➡; TV tcf ✖ P5
HB weekly £179-£237; D £28.50-£32

Torran Loggie, Lochbroom, Ullapool IV23 2SG 01854-85227
3 bedrs, 1 ➡; tcf P3
sB&B £13 Breakfast only

VIRKIE Shetlands Mainland   13F2

Meadowvale *Acclaimed*   ⛫
Virkie ZE3 9JS 01950-60240

WALKERBURN Borders   13D2

**George Galashiels Road, Walkerburn
EH43 6AF 01896-870336**

*Family run hotel overlooking the river Tweed.
Reputation for good food and comfort. Ideal
for fishing, walking, golfing, touring etc..*
8 bedrs, 1 ➡/WC, 4 🐾/WC; TV tcf 🍴 P30
sB&B £20; HB weekly £175-£196; D £4.50-
£12.95; cc Ac Vi

WEST LINTON Borders   13D2

**Lynehurst Carlops Road, West Linton
EH46 7DS 01968-660795 Fax
01968-660993**
3 bedrs, 3 ➡/WC, 3 🐾/WC; TV tcf 🍴 P6
sB&B £27; HB weekly £284-£347; D £18-£22

Rowallan Mountain Cross, West Linton EH46
7DF 01968-660329

WHITING BAY Isle of Arran   12B3

Invermay *Acclaimed*   🛡RAC
Shore Road, Whiting Bay KA27 8PZ
017707-700431

WICK Highland   15E1

Haven Gore Huna, Wick KW1 4YL
01955-611314
*Modernised bungalow, ground floor rooms
with wash hands basins . Central heating
throughout. TV lounge and tea/coffee on
request.*
3 bedrs, 1 ➡; 🍴 P6
sB&B £12.50 Breakfast only

Upper Thrumster Farm Thrumster, Wick
KW1 5TR 01955-82217

WIGTOWN Dumfries & Galloway   12C4

Glaisnock House 20 South Main Street,
Wigtown DG8 9EH 01988-402249
4 bedrs, 1 ➡/WC, 1 🐾/WC, 1 ➡; tcf 🍴
Child restrictions
sB&B £14.50; HB weekly £22; D £7.50

Wigtown House 19 Bank Street, Wigtown
DG8 9HR 01988-42391

Wales

Some aspects of Wales are changing fast. As mining declined, the proud Welsh people created more incentives to woo visitors to their country. Mines can now be visited. More sophisticated cuisine accompanies traditional Welsh fare, and en suite bathrooms have mushroomed like leeks! The beauty of the landscape, dramatic one moment, gentle the next, remains, still accessible via uncrowded roads.

SOME PRINCIPAL ATTRACTIONS

Unless otherwise stated, all can be visited between April and October – some longer. Telephone for days/times of opening.

Air Caernarfon Ltd, Caernarfon Airport, Gwynedd: *Hands-on experience in various cockpits. Model aircraft, engines, adventure playground:* Tel: 01286-830800.

Beaumaris Castle, Anglesey, Gwynedd: *Sophisticated example of military medieval archetecture. Built Ed I.* Tel: 01248-810361.

Bishop's Palace, St. Davids, Dyfed: *Extensive, battlemented medieval ruins by St. Davids Cathedral.* Tel: 01437-720517.

Bodelwyddan Castle, St. Asaph, Clwyd: *Fascinating collection of Victoriana – parlour games, puzzles, inventions, participation. Also eminent 19th -c portraits.* Tel: 01745-583539.

Bodnant Garden, Tal-y-Cafn, Gwynedd: *Important garden features Pin Mill. Photographic delight. NT.* Tel: 01492- 650460.

Bro-Meigan Gardens, Boncath, Dyfed: *Series of enclosed gardens, wild to formal. Unusual trees, shrubs, perennials.* Tel: 01239-841232.

Caernarfon Castle, Gwynedd: *One of Europe's great medieval fortresses. P. of Wales investiture in 1969. Exhibitions, regimental museum of Royal Welsh Fusiliers.* Tel: 01286-677617.

Carew Castle & Tidal Mill, Carew, Dyfed: *Two attractions in beautiful river-bank setting.* Tel: 01646-651782.

Castel Coch, Tongwynlais, nr. Cardiff: *Fairy tale exterior, ornate Gothic extravaganza within.* Tel: 01222-810101.

Castel Henllys Iron Age Hill Fort, Felindre Farog, Pembs: *Original hill fort with reconstructed houses.* Tel: 01239-79319.

Erdigg, nr. Wrexham, Clwyd: *Furnishings and garden stock both appropriate to 17th and 18th -c house. NT.* Tel: 01978-313333.

Ffestiniog Railway, Porthmadog, Gwynedd: *13 steam-driven scenic miles.* Tel: 01766-512340.

Graham Sutherland Gallery, Picton Castle, nr. Haverfordwest, Dyfed: *Gallery closes Sept.30.* Tel: 01437- 751296.

Great Wedlock Dinosaur Experience, nr. Tenby: *New woodland based activity playground with life size dinosaurs:* Tel: 01834-845272.

Harlech Castle, Gwynedd: *Climb 143 gatehouse steps for all round view from this World Heritage listed site. Open daily.*

Llancaiach Fawr, Treharris, Mid-Glam: *Living history award winner. Participate in costume in Civil War house.* Tel: 01443-412248.

Llechwedd Slate Caverns, Blaenau Ffestiniog, Gwynedd: *Slate Mill in Victorian village with working smithy.* Tel: 01766- 830306.

Museum of Childhood, Beaumaris, Anglesey: *2,000 nostalgic childhood memories.* Tel: 01248-712498.

Caernarfon Castle

Museum of the Welsh Woollen Industry, Dre-fach Felindre, Dyfed. *Working mill and craft workshops.* Tel: 01559-370929.

National Museum of Wales, Cardiff: *Contains everything one could expect of a National Museum, expertly presented.* Tel: 010222-397951.

Pembrokeshire Coastal Path: *181 miles from St. Dogmaels to Tenby of superb scenic walking.*

Plas Brondanw Gardens, nr. Penrhyndeudraeth, Gwynedd: *Italianate gardens of Wm. Clough-Ellis' home.* Tel: 01766-771136.

Plas Newydd, Anglesey, Gwynedd: *Interesting mixture of styles last comfortably refurbished 1930s. Rex Whistler mural. NT.* Tel: 01248-714795.

Plas Newydd, Llangollen, Clwyd: *Historic house, former home of the 'Ladies of Llangollen'.* Tel: 01978-861514.

Portmeirion, Gwynedd: *Wm. Clough Ellis fantasy village now a hotel – set in botanically interesting sub-tropical garden.* Tel: 01766-770228.

Powis Castle, Welshpool, Powys: *Furnished medieval stronghold. Magnificent terraced garden, views. NT.* Tel: 01938-554336.

Rhondda Heritage Park, Trehafod, Mid-Glam: *Recent simulated mine re-creates mining for 'black gold'. Play area.* Tel: 01443-862036.

Ruthin Craft Centre, Ruthin, Clwyd: *Craft Council gallery of top talent plus studio work shops.* Tel: 01824-704774.

South Wales Police Museum, Bridgend, Mid. Glam: *Policing Glamorgan through the ages. 19th-c cell, hands-on opportunity.* Tel: 01656-655555 ext. 427.

Sygun Copper Mine, Beddgelert, Gwynedd: *Families enjoy going down under this 19th-c mine.* Tel: 0176-86595.

Techniquest, Cardiff Inner Harbour: *Look, touch and play in Britain's largest science centre.* Tel: 01222-460211.

Tintern Abbey, Gwent: *Impressive ruins of Cistercian abbey set against woodland valley of River Wye.* Tel: 01291-689251.

Tredegar House, nr. Newport, Gwent: *Something for everyone on 90-acre park of 16/17th-c ancestral home.* Tel: 01633-815880.

Ffestiniog Railway, Porthmadog

Welsh Folk Museum, St. Fagans, S. Glam:
*Re-assembled buildings create past lifestyles.
Real craftsfolk demonstrate.*
Tel: 01222-569441.

Welsh Industrial & Maritime Museum,
*Cardiff: History of industrial and maritime
laid out in docklands.* Tel: 010222-481919.

Weobley Castel, Llanrhidian, W. Glam:
*Borrow key from farm to explore fun ruins
with fabulous views of salt flats of Gower.*

SOME ANNUAL EVENTS.

Barmouth Arts Festival, Gwynedd: *A
National Trust Centenary commemorative
event, opera, ballet, drama, childrens'
entertainment. 7-15 Sep.* Tel: 01341-280845.

Beyond the Border, St. Donats, S. Glam:
*International festical of storytelling at Wm.
Randolf Hearst's castle! 30 Jun-2 Jul.*
Tel: 01446-792151.

Brecon Jazz Festival, Powys: *Some of the
best names in Jazz here. Increasingly popular!
11-13 Aug.* Tel: 01874-625557.

Conwy Festival, Gwynedd: *Street
entertainment, arts & crafts within 13th-c
walled town. 24-30 July.* Tel: 01492-592650.

Cricceth Festival, Gwynedd: *An Arts
Festival, mainly classical. Walks, art, crafts,
gardens. 21-26 Jun.* Tel: 01766-810584.

Landsker Walking Festival, Pembs: *Guided
walks exploring heritage & culture of South
Pembs. 29 Apr-6 May.* Tel: 01834-860965.

Llangollen Musical Eisteddfod, Clwyd: *49th
international festival of song and dance.
4th-9th Jul.*Tel: 01978-860236.

Mid Wales Festival of Transport,
Welshpool: *Transport rally. Trade stands.
8-9 Jul.* Tel: 01938-553680.

Musicfest, Aberystwyth, Dyfed: *Music festival
combined with summer school. 22 Jul-4 Aug.*
Tel: 01970-622889.

Potters Festival, Aberystwyth, Dyfed:
*Britian's largest potters festival held every two
years. 14-16 Jul.* Tel: 01970-622889.

Royal National Eisteddfod of Wales,
Abergele, Clwyd: *Wales' greatest cultural
event. 5-12 Aug.* Tel: 01222-763777.

**Swansea: Hosts the Year of Literature &
Writing – 1995**. Tel: 01792-480211.

Tenby Arts Festival, Dyfed: *'Under Milk
Wood' features this year with many other arts
events. 16-23 Sep.* Tel: 01834-843774.

United Counties Show, Carmarthen, Dyfed:
*Agriculture plus dog and fashion shows etc.
10-11 Aug.* Tel: 01267-232141.

Usk Show, Gwernesney, nr. Usk, Gwent:
*Full agricultural show with all the trimmings.
9 Sept.* Tel: 01291-672379.

Vale of Glamorgan Festival, S. Glam:
*Celebration of living composers. Various local
venues. 21-27 Aug.* Tel: 01446-792151.

Welsh Proms '95, St. David's Hall Cardiff:
13-31 Jul. Tel: 01222-342611.

ABERAVON Dyfed 2C1

Arosfa 8 Cadwgan Place, Aberavon SA46
0BU 01545-570120 &
6 bedrs, 1 🛏/WC, 2 📷/WC, 2 🛏; P50
sB&B £20; HB weekly £160

Moldavia 7/8 Bell Vue Terrace, Aberavon
SA46 0BB 01545-570107

ABERCRAF Powys 6C4

Maes y Gwernen *Acclaimed* 🏅
School Road, Abercrave SA9 1XD
01639-730218 Fax 01639-730765 &
5 bedrs, 3 🛏/WC, 2 📷/WC, 1 🛏; TV tcf 🎯 ✂ P8
[10%V]; cc Ac Vi

Maes-Y-Gwernen

Guest House

**School Road, Abercraf, Swansea Valley,
South Wales SA9 1XD.
Tel: 01639 730218, Fax: 01639 730765**

A well furnished country house in it's own grounds,
with well kept gardens and ample private parking
facilities, situated in the lovely upper Swansea Valley
close to Dan-Yr-Ogof Show Caves, Henrhyd
Waterfalls and Craig-Y-Nos Castle.

Acclaimed by the RAC and Welsh Tourist Board
for offering excellent accommodation and home
cooking at competitive rates.

All rooms are well appointed, with colour
television, coffee & tea making facilities.

Guests have exclusive use of the bar, television
lounge, conservatory lounge, patio area and gardens.

**Bed & Breakfast is from £14.00 per
person, and a home cooked three course
evening meal is offered at £7.00. Reduced
rates for children under 12 years, and
stays of 3 days or more are also available.**

ABERDARE Mid Glam 6C4

Green Meadow Riding Centre Dare Valley
Country Park, Aberdare CF44 7PT
01685-874961

ABERDYFI (ABERDOVY) 6B3

Bodfor 🏅
Sea Front, Aberdyfi LL35 0EA 01654-767475
Fax 01654-767679

Brodawel *Highly Acclaimed* 🏅
Tywyn Road, Aberdyfi LL35 OSA
01654-767347

Cartref *Acclaimed* 🏅
Aberdyfi LL35 0NR 01654-767273
7 bedrs, 4 📷/WC, 1 🛏; TV tcf 🎯 P8
sB&B £17 dB&B £18.50 D £8.50 [10%V]

ABERGAVENNY Gwent 7D4

Rock & Fountain Main Road, Clydach,
Abergavenny NP7 0LL 01873-8303393
8 bedrs, 8 🛏/WC, 8 📷/WC;
Breakfast only

ABERGELE Clwyd 6C1

Dolhyfryd Lodge Rhuddlan Rd, Abergele
LL22 7HL 01745-826505 Fax 01745-827402 &
10 bedrs, 10 🛏/WC; P24
sB&B £31.50 Breakfast only; cc Ac Vi

Haven Towyn Rd, Belgrano, Abergele LL22
9AB 01745-823534

The Wheatsheaf Inn Betws-Yn-Rhos,
Abergele LL22 8AW 01492-60218

ABERGYNOLWYN Gwynedd 6C2

Dolgoch Falls *Acclaimed* 🏅
Tywyn, Abergynolwyn LL36 9UW
01654-782258
6 bedrs, 1 🛏/WC, 2 📷/WC, 1 🛏; tcf 🎯 ✂ P50
Child restrictions
sB&B £19.50 dB&B £39; HB weekly £182; D
£11.50; cc Vi

ABERYSTWYTH Dyfed 6B3

Brendan 19 Marine Terrace, Aberystwyth
SY23 2AZ 01970-612252

Cambrian Alexandra Rd, Aberystwyth SY23 1LG 01970-612446

Erwbarfe Farmhouse Devil's Bridge, Aberystwyth SY23 3JR 01970-890251

400 acre mixed hill farm. Spectacular views. Old stone farmhouse, fresh home cooking, warm & friendly welcome.
2 bedrs, 1 🛏;
sB&B £16; HB weekly £150-£200; D £6-£8

Garreg Lwyd Bow Street, Aberystwyth SY24 5BE 01970-828830
3 bedrs, 1 🛏; tcf ✖ P6
sB&B £13.50 Breakfast only

Glyn Garth *Acclaimed*   RAC
South Road, Aberystwyth SY23 1JS
01970-615050
10 bedrs, 3 🛏/WC, 3 ☕/WC, 1 🛏; TV tcf ✄
P1
sB&B £16-£17 dB&B £32-£34 Breakfast only
[5%V]

Glynwern Llanilar, Aberystwyth SY23 4NY 01974-7203

Helmsman 43 Marine Terrace, Aberystwyth SY23 2BX 01970-624132

Pen-Y-Castell Farm Llanrhystud, Aberystwyth SY23 5BZ 01974-272622

Southgate Anatron Avenue, Penparcau, Aberystwyth SY23 1SF 01970-611550

The Barn House Llanon, Aberystwyth SY23 5LS 01974-202581

Yr Hafod 1 South Marine Terrace, Aberystwyth SY23 1JX 01970-617579

AMMANFORD Dyfed   6C4

Hall Street 2 Hall Street, Ammanford SA18 3BW 01269-592734

Mount Pleasant Pontardulais Road, Garnswllt, Ammanford SA18 2RT 01269-591722

BALA Gwynedd   6C2

Rhyd Y Defaid Farm Frongoch, Bala LL23 7NT 01678-520456
3 bedrs, 1 🛏/WC, 1 ☕/WC, 1 🛏; ✖ P4
sB&B £15 Breakfast only

Talybont Isa Rhyduchaf, Bala LL23 7SD
01678-520234   ♿
3 bedrs, 1 ☕/WC, 2 🛏; ✖ P5
sB&B £15; HB weekly £125-£140; D £6-£7

BANGOR Gwynedd   7F2

Country Bumpkin *Acclaimed*   RAC
Cefn Coed, Llandegai, Bangor LL57 4BG
01248-370477 Fax 01248-354166
3 bedrs, 3 🛏/WC; TV tcf ✖ ✄ P10
Child restrictions
sB&B £30-£33 dB&B £40-£45 D £16; cc Ac Vi

Goetre Isaf Farmhouse Caernarfon Road, Bangor LL57 4DB 01248-364541 Fax 01248-364541

BARMOUTH Gwynedd   6C2

Marwyn *Acclaimed*   RAC
21 Marine Parade, Barmouth LL42 1NA
01341-280228

Child Restrictions
Most hotels and guest houses are happy to welcome children. A few prefer to welcome only adults and older children; these are shown by 'Child restrictions' in the entry. If you are travelling with children, please telephone the establishment to check the age limit set by the management.

BEAUMARIS Gwynedd

**Plas Cichle Beaumaris LL58 8PS
01248-810488**
3 bedrs, 1 ⇒/WC, 3 ↟/WC; ✖ P15
Child restrictions under 6
sB&B £19 Breakfast only

BEDDGELERT Gwynedd   6B1

Sygun Fawr Country House *Acclaimed*   RAC
Beddgelert LL55 4NE 01766-890258
7 bedrs, 3 ⇒/WC, 4 ↟/WC, 1 ⇒; tcf ✖
sB&B £25-£30 dB&B £50; HB weekly £242; D
£15 [10%V]

BETWS-Y-COED Gwynned   6C1

Bryn Llewelyn   RAC
Holyhead Road, Betws-Y-Coed LL24 OBN
01690-710601
7 bedrs, 2 ↟/WC, 2 ⇒; TV tcf ✖ P11
sB&B £15-£17 dB&B £28-£36 Breakfast only

Ferns *Acclaimed*   RAC
Holyhead Road, Betws-Y-Coed LL24 0AN
01690-710587

**Giler Arms Pentrefoelas, Betws-Y-Coed
LL24 0LL 01690-5612**

*Set in 7 acres of gardens which include a
fishing lake.*
7 bedrs, 5 ↟/WC; tcf ✖ P40
sB&B £16 D £5-£12; cc Ac Vi

★★Gwydyr   RAC
**Betws-Y-Coed LL24 0AB 01690-710777
Fax 01690-710777**

*Family-run hotel in Victorian building set in
delightful surroundings.*
20 bedrs, 20 ⇒/WC; ✖ P20
sB&B £26 dB&B £49; HB weekly £190-£240;
D £12.50 [10%V]; cc Ac Vi

Henllys *Acclaimed*   RAC
Old Church Road, Betws-Y-Coed LL24 OAL
01690-710-534   රු
10 bedrs, 8 ⇒/WC, 10 ⇒; tcf P10
sB&B £21.50-£27 dB&B £23-£27; HB weekly
£240-£255; [10%V]; cc Ac Vi

Summer Hill   RAC
Coedcynhelier Road, Betws-Y-Coed LL24 0BL
01690-710306
7 bedrs, 3 ↟/WC, 2 ⇒; tcf P6
sB&B £15 dB&B £27 Breakfast only

Tan-y-Foel Country House *Highly
Acclaimed*   RAC
Capel Garmon, Betws-Y-Coed LL26 ORE
01690-710507
9 bedrs, 3 ⇒/WC, 6 ↟/WC; TV tcf P14
Child restrictions
dB&B £92-£99.50; HB weekly £294-£378; D
£19.50 [5%V]; cc Ac Amex DC Vi

Ty'n-y-Celyn *Acclaimed* RAC
Llanrwst Road, Betws-Y-Coed LL24 0HD
01690-710202 Fax 01690-710800

Victorian style with modernised exterior, incorporating large picture windows.
8 bedrs, 2 🛁/WC, 6 🚿/WC; TV tcf 🐕 🚭 P10
dB&B £40 Breakfast only [5%V]

BONCATH Dyfed 6B4

Awel-Y-Grug Boncath SA37 0JP
01239-814260

A detached, Victorian, slate-built house in the centre of the village. Set in landscaped gardens.
3 bedrs, 2 🚿/WC, 2 🛁; TV tcf 🐕 P5
sB&B £16; HB weekly £180.25-£225; D £9.75-£12.50; cc Ac Vi

BONTDDU Gwynedd 6C2

Borthwnog Hall *Highly Acclaimed* RAC
Dolgellau, Bontddu LL40 2TT 01341-430271
Fax 01341-430682
3 bedrs, 2 🛁/WC, 1 🚿/WC; TV tcf 🐕 🚭 P8
sB&B £25-£45 dB&B £50-£100; HB weekly £260-£365; D £16.50 [5%V]; cc Ac Vi

BORTH Dyfed 6C3

Glanmor RAC
Borth SY24 5JP 01970-871689
7 bedrs, 2 🚿/WC, 2 🛁; TV tcf 🐕 P8
sB&B £15-£18.50 dB&B £37; HB weekly £189; D £8.50 [10%V]

BRECON Powys 7D4

Beacons *Acclaimed* RAC
16 Bridge Street, Brecon LD3 8AH
01874-623339
10 bedrs, 2 🛁/WC, 5 🚿/WC, 2 🛁; TV tcf 🐕 🚭 P10
sB&B £16 dB&B £32; HB weekly £147; D £10; cc Ac Amex Vi

Coach *Highly Acclaimed* RAC
Orchard Street, Llanfaes, Brecon LD3 8AN
01874-623803

Lower Rhydness Bungalow Llyswen, Brecon LD3 0AZ 01874-754264

★(Inn) Tai'r Bull Inn RAC
Libanus, Brecon LD3 8EL 01874-625849
5 bedrs, 1 🛁/WC, 4 🚿/WC; TV tcf 🚭 P12
sB&B £20 dB&B £34 Breakfast only

The Old Rectory *Acclaimed* RAC
Llanddew, Brecon LD3 9SS 01874-622058
3 bedrs, 2 🚿/WC, 1 🛁; TV tcf P6
sB&B £22 dB&B £32-£36 Breakfast only

BRIDGEND Mid Glamorgan 3D1

Chatterton Arms 2 Hendre Road, Pencoed, Bridgend CF35 5NW 01656-860293

BROAD HAVEN Dyfed 6A4

Broad Haven *Acclaimed* RAC ♿
Broad Haven SA62 3JN 01437-781366
40 bedrs, 40 🛁/WC; 🐕 P200

BUILTH WELLS Powys 6C3

Cedars *Acclaimed* RAC
Hay Road, Builth Wells LD2 3AR
01982-553356

★★Lion RAC
2 Broad Street, Builth Wells LD2 3DT
01982-553226 Fax 01982-552347

Ty-isaf Farm Erwood, Builth Wells LD2 2SZ 01982-560607

This mixed working farm of 340 acres lies just off the A470, south of Builth Wells/ The farmhouse is comfortably furnished throughout. Good home cooking served. Cot and high chair available.
3 bedrs, 1 ⇥; ✖
sB&B £13; HB weekly £84;

CAERNARFON Gwynedd   6B1

Menai View   ᴿᴬᶜ
North Road, Caernarfon LL55 1BD
01286-674602
8 bedrs, 3 ⬔/WC, 2 ⇥; TV tcf ✖
sB&B £16-£18 dB&B £25-£28 Breakfast only
[5%V]

Pengwern Farm Llangrug, Saron, Llanwnda, Caernarfon LL54 5UH 01286-830717

This charming spacious farmhouse is beautifully situated between the mountains and the sea, with unobstructed views of Snowdonia. The farm covers over 130-acres, which covers Foryd Bay, noted for its birdlife. Meals prepared to a professional standard.
9 bedrs, 9 ⇥/WC,
sB&B £19; HB weekly £196-£22; D £10-£12

CAERPHILLY Mid Glamorgan   3D1

Parc Cardiff Road, Bargoed, Caerphilly CF8
8SP 01443-837599

Springfield Bungalow Rudry Road,
Caerphilly CF8 3DT 01222-866607

Y- Fron Pwll-Y-Pant, Caerphilly CF8 3DT
01222-882896

CAPEL CURIG Gwynedd   6C1

★★Tyn-y-Coed   ᴿᴬᶜ
Capel Curig LL24 0EE 01690-4331 Fax 01690-710777
14 bedrs, 14 ⇥/WC, 2 ⇥; ✖ P80
sB&B £27-£30 dB&B £40-£50 D £10 [10%V];
cc Ac Amex DC Vi

CARDIFF South Glamorgan   3D1

Albany *Acclaimed*   ᴿᴬᶜ
191/193 Albany Road, Roath, Cardiff CF2 3NU
01222-494121
12 bedrs, 1 ⇥/WC, 4 ⬔/WC, 3 ⇥; TV tcf
sB&B £17 dB&B £35 Breakfast only [10%V]

Austins 11 Coldstream Terrace, Cardiff CF1
8LJ 01222-377148

Balkan   ᴿᴬᶜ
144 Newport Road, Cardiff CF2 1DT
01222-463673

Bon Maison 39 Plasturton Gardens,
Pontcanna, Cardiff CF1 9HG 01222-383660

Clare Court *Acclaimed*   ᴿᴬᶜ
46-48 Clare Road, Grangetown, Cardiff CF1
7QP 01222-344839 Fax 01222-665856
8 bedrs, 2 ⇥/WC, 6 ⬔/WC; TV tcf
sB&B £26 dB&B £34.20 [5%V]; cc Ac Amex Vi

Clayton   ᴿᴬᶜ
65 Stacey Road, Cardiff CF2 1DS
01222-492345

Domus   ᴿᴬᶜ
201 Newport Road, Cardiff CF2 1AJ
01222-473311
10 bedrs, 2 ⬔/WC, 2 ⇥; TV tcf P10
sB&B £20 dB&B £33 Breakfast only

**Grays Culverhouse Cross, Cardiff CF5 5TF
01222-591050 Fax 01222-591050**

*A family run guest house, with a small,
private lounge bar.*
9 bedrs, 2 ☛/WC, 2 ➡; TV tcf ✗ P30
sB&B £13 D £7-£9; cc Amex Vi

Lincoln   RAC
118 Cathedral Road, Cardiff CF1 9LQ
01222-395558 Fax 01222-230537

Maxines 150 Cathedral Road, Pontcanna,
Cardiff CF1 9JB 01222-220288

Pavilion Lodge   RAC
Pontclun, Cardiff CF7 8SB 01222-892253 Fax
01222-892497   ♿
50 bedrs, 50 ➡/WC; TV tcf
sB&B £33.50-£37.45 dB&B £45.50 D £9
[10%V]; cc Ac Amex DC Vi

**Preste Garden 181 Cathedral Road,
Pontcanna, Cardiff CF1 9PN 01222-228607**

*A restored Norwegian consulate, this homely
Victorian town house offers modern facilities
and a warm welcome.*
10 bedrs, 2 ➡/WC, 6 ☛/WC, 2 ➡; TV tcf ✗ P2
sB&B £15 Breakfast only; cc Amex

Ramla Court 188 Cathedral Road,
Pontcanna, Cardiff CF1 9JE 01222-221187

Tane's   RAC
148 Newport Road, Roath, Cardiff CF2 1DJ
01222-491755 Fax 01222-491755   ♿
10 bedrs, 1 ➡/WC, 2 ☛/WC, 2 ➡; TV tcf P10
Child restrictions
sB&B £17 dB&B £28 D £6 [10%V]

The Willows *Acclaimed*   RAC
128 Cathedral Road, Pontcanna, Cardiff CF1
9LQ 01222-240881

Wynford Clare Street, Cardiff CF1 8SD
01222-371983

CARDIGAN Dyfed   6B4

Bingham House Pendre, Cardigan SA43 1JU
01239-615190

Brynhyfryd *Acclaimed*   RAC
Gwbert Road, Cardigan SA43 1AE
01239-612861
7 bedrs, 3 ☛/WC, 2 ➡; TV tcf
sB&B £15 dB&B £29-£34; HB weekly £140-
£160

Ffynonwen Country Aberporth, Cardigan
SA43 2HT 01239-810312

Maes-y-Mor   RAC
Gwbert Road, Cardigan SA43 1AE
01239-614929

Penralt Ceibwr Farm Guesthouse
Moylgrove, Cardigan SA43 3BX 01239-86217

Trellacca Tremain, Cardigan SA43 1SJ
01239-810730

3 bedrs, 2 ☛/WC, 1 ➡; TV tcf P4
sB&B £15 D £7

CARMARTHEN Dyfed   6B4

Boars Head Lammas Street, Carmarthen SA31
3AZ 01267-222789
12 bedrs, 12 ➡/WC; **TV tcf P**15
sB&B £20; HB weekly £133-£196; D £4-£8; **cc**
Amex DC

**Brig-Y-Don The Green, Llanstephan,
Carmarthen SA33 5LW 01267-241349**

*Seafront accommodation on estuary, home
baked bread, central heating.*
3 bedrs, 3 ➡; **P**10
sB&B £14 Breakfast only

**Cothi Bridge Pontargothi, Carmarthen
SA32 7NG 01267-290251**   ⅃
10 bedrs, 3 ➡/WC, 7 ✿/WC, 1 ➡;
TV tcf ✕ **P**60
sB&B £22.50; HB weekly £192.50-£265; D £5-
£20; **cc** Ac Amex DC Vi

Cwmtwrch Nantgaredig, Carmarthen SA32
7NY 01267-290238   ⅃
6 bedrs, 6 ➡/WC, 6 ✿/WC; ✕
sB&B £34 Breakfast only

Glog Llangain, Carmarthen SA33 5AY
01267-83271

Golden Grove Arms Llanarthney,
Carmarthen SA32 8JU 01558-668551
4 bedrs, 3 ➡/WC, 1 ✿/WC; ✕ **P**40
sB&B £25 Breakfast only

New Park Lammas Street, Carmarthen SA31
3AZ 01267-221429

Pantgwyn Farm Whitemill, Carmarthen SA32
7ES 01267-290247   ⅃
3 bedrs, 2 ➡/WC, 1 ✿/WC; **TV tcf P**10
sB&B £19; HB weekly £212-£268; D £14.50

Plas Farm Llangynog, Carmarthen SA33 4JU
01267-211492

The Wern Inn LLangynog, Carmarthen SA33
5HS 01267-83678

Troedyrhiw Llanfynydd, Carmarthen SA32
7TQ 01558-668792

Ty Mawr *Highly Acclaimed*   RAC
Brechfa, Carmarthen SA32 7RA 01267-202332
Fax 01267-202437
5 bedrs, 4 ➡/WC, 4 ✿/WC; **tcf** ✕ ⅄ **P**20
sB&B £39-£48 dB&B £76; HB weekly £425; D
£16 [5%V]; **cc** Ac Amex Vi

CARMEL Gwynedd   6B1

**Clydfan Nr Caernarfon, Carmel LL54 7SA
01286-881104 Fax 01286-880600**

*A typical Welsh cottage on the edge of Carmel
offering homely accommodation. Convenient
for Snowdonia, Castles, and beaches.*
2 bedrs, 1 ✿/WC, 1 ➡; **tcf**
sB&B £14.50 Breakfast only

CLYNDERWEN Dyfed   6B4

Dolau Isaf Farm Mynachlog-Ddu,
Clynderwen SA66 7SB 01994-419327

Yethen Isaf Mynachlogddu, Clynderwen
SA66 7SN 01437-532256

COLWYN BAY Clwyd   6C1

Cabin Hill *Acclaimed*   RAC
College Avenue, Rhos-on-Sea, Colwyn Bay
LL28 4NT 01492-544568
10 bedrs, 7 ✿/WC, 2 ➡; **TV tcf**
Child restrictions
sB&B £18-£19 dB&B £40-£42; HB weekly
£150-£152

Cedar Tree 27 Whitehall Rd, Colwyn Bay
LL28 4HW 01492-545867

Claverdon 22 Colwyn Crescent, Rhos-on-Sea,
Colwyn Bay LL28 4RG 01492-545630
6 bedrs, 2 ➡/WC, 2 ☞/WC, 1 ➡;
sB&B £13 Breakfast only

Clevedon 20 Hawarden Rd, Colwyn Bay
LL29 8NA 01492-532194
16 bedrs, 5 ➡; ✗ P7
sB&B £11; HB weekly £108;

Crossroads Guest 15 Coed Pella Road,
Colwyn Bay LL29 7AT 01492-530736
5 bedrs, 2 ☞/WC, 2 ➡; TV tcf ✗
sB&B £12 Breakfast only

Glyndwr 11 Marine Rd, Colwyn Bay LL29
8PH 01492-533254
10 bedrs, 7 ☞/WC, 1 ➡; P10
sB&B £20 Breakfast only

Grosvenor   RAC
106-108 Abergele Road, Colwyn Bay LL29 7PS
01492-531586

Marine West Promenade, Colwyn Bay LL28
4BP 01492-530295
14 bedrs, 10 ☞/WC, 3 ➡; TV tcf ✗ P10
sB&B £16.25; HB weekly £157-£176.50; D
£7.50; cc Amex

Meadowcroft Llannerch Rd East, Colwyn
Bay LL28 4DF 01492-548375

Monksweir 66 Colwyn Avenue, Rhos-on-Sea,
Colwyn Bay LL28 4NN 01492-549420
5 bedrs, 1 ➡/WC, 2 ☞/WC, 1 ➡; P4
sB&B £17 Breakfast only

Norbury 22 Hawarden Road, Colwyn Bay
LL29 8NA 531520

Northwood   RAC
47 Rhos Road, Rhos-on-Sea, Colwyn Bay
LL28 4RS 01492-549931   &
12 bedrs, 1 ➡/WC, 10 ☞/WC, 1 ➡; TV tcf ✗
✗ P12
sB&B £18 dB&B £36; HB weekly £138-£149;
D £9 [10%V]; cc Ac Vi

St Enochs West Promenade, Colwyn Bay
LL28 4BL 01492-532031

Sunny Downs   RAC
66 Abbey Road, Rhos-on-Sea, Colwyn Bay
LL28 4NU 01492-544256

A family-run hotel situated between Colwyn
Bay and Llandudno, close to both the beach
and shops.
15 bedrs, 8 ➡/WC; ✗ P15
HB weekly £150

Westwood 51 Princes Drive, Colwyn Bay
LL29 8PL 01492-532078

Child Restrictions
Most hotels and guest houses are happy
to welcome children. A few prefer to
welcome only adults and older children;
these are shown by 'Child restrictions' in
the entry. If you are travelling with children,
please telephone the establishment to check
the age limit set by the management.

CONWY Gwynedd   6C1

★★Castle Bank
Mount Pleasant, Conwy LL32 8NY
01492-593888
RAC

*Stone built house set in own pretty grounds
close to Conwy Town Walls.*
9 bedrs, 8 ☞/WC, 2 ➡; TV tcf P12
sB&B £23.50-£25 dB&B £53 D £14; cc Ac Vi

CORWEN Clwyd   7D1

Corwen Court Private London Rd,
Corwen LL21 0DP 01490-412854

*Converted old police station and courthouse
with a comfortable lounge and dining room.*
10 bedrs, 4 ➡/WC, 4 ☞/WC, 2 ➡; ✗
sB&B £14; HB weekly £141-£146; D £7

Fron Goch Farmhouse Cynwyd, Corwen
LL21 0NA 01490-440418   ♿

*Warm and comfortable farm house, four
miles south of Corwen. Set in superb gardens
overlooking the countryside. Delicious home
cooking and log fires.*
6 bedrs, 2 ☞/WC, 2 ➡; TV tcf ✗ P10
sB&B £17; HB weekly £185-£210; D £13

Llawr Betws Farm Glanyrafon, Corwen LL21
0HD 01490-460224
2 bedrs, 1 ➡; ✗ P8
sB&B £12.50; HB weekly £105;

Tyddyn Farm Guest House Restaurant
Cefn Brith, Cerrigydrudion, Corwen LL21 9TS
01490-420680   ♿
4 bedrs, 1 ➡/WC, 2 ➡; ✗ P15
sB&B £12.50; HB weekly £140

COWBRIDGE South Glamorgan   3D1

★★★Bear
High Street, Cowbridge CF7 2AF
01446-774814
RAC
21 bedrs, 20 ➡/WC, 1 ☞/WC; TV tcf ✗ P60
sB&B £45 dB&B £50 D £12.95 [10%V]; cc Ac
Amex Vi

Plas Llanmihangel Llanmihangel,
Cowbridge CF7 7LQ 01446-774610

CRICCIETH Gwynedd   6C2

Glyn-y-Coed *Acclaimed*   RAC
Portmadoc Road, Criccieth LL52 OHL
01766-522870
10 bedrs, 4 ➡/WC, 3 ➡/WC; TV tcf ✗ P14
sB&B £16-£20 dB&B £32-£40; HB weekly
£175-£195; D £7.50 [10%V]; cc Ac Vi

Min-y-Gaer *Acclaimed*   RAC
Porthmadog Road, Criccieth LL52 0HP
01766-522151 Fax 01766-522151

A substantial Victorian building in a convenient position overlooking Criccieth castle and the Cardigan Bay coastline. 200 yards from the beach. An ideal base for touring Snowdonia and the Lleyn Peninsula.
10 bedrs, 9 ➡/WC, 1 ➡; TV tcf ✗ P12
sB&B £17-£20 dB&B £34-£40; HB weekly
£175-£182; [5%V]; cc Ac Amex Vi

Neptune & Mor Heli   RAC
Marine Terrace, Criccieth LL52 0EF
01766-522794
8 bedrs, 6 ➡/WC, 2 ➡/WC, 5 ➡; TV tcf ✗ ⅍
sB&B £15 dB&B £30 Breakfast only [5%V]

CRICKHOWELL Powys   7D4

Dragon House *Acclaimed*   RAC
High Street, Crickhowell NP8 1BE
01873-810362 Fax 01873-811868
13 bedrs, 7 ➡/WC, 1 ➡/WC, 2 ➡; TV tcf ✗
⅍ P1
sB&B £23 dB&B £38-£48 D £10 [10%V]; cc Ac
Amex Vi

Stables *Acclaimed*   RAC
Llangattock, Crickhowell NP8 1LE
01873-810244
14 bedrs, 8 ➡/WC, 6 ➡/WC; TV tcf ✗ P35
sB&B £30-£35 dB&B £40-£45; HB weekly
£210-£227.50; D £15 [5%V]; cc Ac Amex Vi

CROESGOCH Dyfed   6A4

Torbant Farm   RAC
Croesgoch SA62 5JN 01348-831276

DENBIGH Clwyd   6C1

Cayo 74 Vale Street, Denbigh LL16 3BW
01745-812686

Fron-Haul Bodfari, Denbigh LL16 4DY
01745-710301

DOLGELLAU Gwynedd   6C2

Fronoleu Farm   RAC
Tabor, Dolgellau LL40 2PS 01341-422361 &
10 bedrs, 6 ➡/WC, 2 ➡; TV tcf ✗ ⅍ P38
sB&B £17.50-£23.50 dB&B £29-£40 Breakfast only

Glyn Farm Dolgellau LL40 17A 01341-422286
4 bedrs, 1 ➡/WC, 1 ➡; ✗ P10
sB&B £14 Breakfast only

Tanyfron Arran Road, Dolgellau LL40 2AA
01341-422638
3 bedrs, 1 ➡/WC, 2 ➡/WC; P6
sB&B £36 Breakfast only

DYFFRYN ARDUDWY Gwynedd   6B2

Bryntirion Country House *Acclaimed*   RAC
Dyffryn Ardudwy LL44 2HX 013416-770

FFESTINIOG Gwent   7D4

Tyddyn Du Farm Gellilydan, Ffestiniog LL41
4RB 01766-590281 Fax 01766-590281
4 bedrs, 4 ➡/WC, 1 ➡; ✗
sB&B £16; HB weekly £150-£175; D £8.50-£9

FISHGUARD Dyfed   6A4

Cri'r Wylan Pen Wallis, Fishguard SA65 9HR
01348-873398

Hamilton 21-23 Hamilton Street, Fishguard
SA65 9HL 01348-873834

Manor House *Acclaimed*   RAC
Main Street, Fishguard SA65 9HJ
01348-873260
6 bedrs, 1 ➡/WC, 3 ➡/WC, 1 ➡; TV tcf ✗
sB&B £18 dB&B £44 D £14; cc Ac Vi

Rhos Felen Scleddau, Fishguard SA65 9RD
01348-873711

Seaview Seafront, Fishguard SA65 9RD
01348-874282

Stanley House Quay Rd, Goodwick,
Fishguard SA64 0BS 01348-873024
3 bedrs, 2 ⇨; P3
Breakfast only

Tregynon Country Farmhouse *Highly
Acclaimed* ⏣
Tregynon, Gwaun Valley, Fishguard SA65
9TU 01239-820531 Fax 01239-820808
8 bedrs, 5 ⇨/WC, 3 ⏺/WC; TV tcf ⤢
dB&B £46-£64; HB weekly £248.75-£310.50;
D £15.50; cc Ac Vi

HANMER Clwyd   7D2

Buck Farm Hanmer, S414 7LX 01922-418762

HARLECH Gwynedd   6B2

Byrdir ⏣
High Street, Harlech LL46 2YA 01766-780316

Castle Cottage *Highly Acclaimed* ⏣
Harlech LL46 2YL 01766-780479
6 bedrs, 4 ⇨/WC, 1 ⇨; tcf ⤢ ⤢
sB&B £23 dB&B £50 D £15 [5%V]; cc Ac
Amex Vi

St David's *Acclaimed* ⏣
Harlech LL46 2UB 01766-780366 Fax
01766-780820
60 bedrs, 45 ⇨/WC, 15 ⏺/WC; TV tcf P60
sB&B £22-£32 dB&B £44-£64 D £13.50
[10%V]; cc Ac Amex DC Vi

HAVERFORDWEST Dyfed   6A4

Bryngarw Abercastle Road, Trefin, Trevine,
Haverfordwest SA62 5AR 01348-831211

College 93 Hill Street, Haverfordwest SA1
1QX 01437-763710
10 bedrs, 5 ⏺/WC, 2 ⇨; TV tcf ⤢ P300
sB&B £15 Breakfast only

Cuckoo Mill St. Davids Road, Pelcomb
Bridge, Haverfordwest SA62 6EA
01437-762139
3 bedrs, 1 ⇨/WC, 2 ⇨; ⤢
sB&B £14; HB weekly £130-£140; D £7.50

**Foxdale Glebe Lane, Marloes,
Haverfordwest SA62 3AX 01646-636243**

*A large, comfortable, detached house in the
heart of the Pembrokeshire Coast National
Park.*
3 bedrs, 1 ⏺/WC, 1 ⇨; tcf ⤢ P7
Child restrictions under 10
sB&B £16 Breakfast only

Greenacre Marloes, Haverfordwest SA62 3BE
01646-636400

Greenways Shoals Hook Lane,
Haverfordwest SA61 2XN 01437-762345

High Roost Mathry, Haverfordwest SA62
5HD 01348-831695

Lower Haythog Spittal, Haverfordwest
SA62 5QL 01437-731279   ⚹
12 bedrs, 8 ⇨/WC, 5 ⏺/WC, 1 ⇨; ⤢ P20
sB&B £17.50; HB weekly £185-£200; D £9.50-
£11

Penrhiwllan Old Rectory Well Lane,
Prendergast, Haverfordwest SA61 2PL
01437-769049
3 bedrs, 1 ⇨/WC, 2 ⇨;
sB&B £15 Breakfast only

Ringstone Haroldston Hill, Broad Haven,
Haverfordwest SA62 3JP 01437-781051

Rising Sun Inn St Davids Road, Pelcomb
Bridge, Haverfordwest SA62 6EA
01437-765171

Skerryback Farmhouse Sandy Haven, St
Ishmaels, Haverfordwest SA623DN
01646-636598

**The Bower Farm Little Haven,
Haverfordwest SA62 3TY 01437-781554**
5 bedrs, 3 ➡/WC, 2 🛁/WC; TV tcf 🐾 P20
sB&B £18; HB weekly £195-£250; D £12.50-
£15

The Foxes Inn Marloes, Haverfordwest SA62
3AY 01646-636527

Wilton House *Highly Acclaimed* 🔶RAC
6 Quay Street, Haverfordwest SA61 1BG
01437-760033

HAY-ON-WYE Powys   7D4

York House *Acclaimed* 🔶RAC
Hardwicke Road, Cusop, Hay-on-Wye HR3
5QX 01497-820705
5 bedrs, 1 ➡/WC, 2 🛁/WC, 1 ➡; TV tcf 🐾 P6
Child restrictions
sB&B £17.50 dB&B £35; HB weekly £182.70

HOLYWELL Clwyd   7D1

Greenhill Farm 🔶RAC
Holywell CH8 7QF 01352-713270
3 bedrs, 1 ➡/WC, 2 ➡; tcf P6
dB&B £32 Breakfast only [10%V]

The Hall Lygan Y Wern, Pentre Halkyn,
Holywell CH8 8BD 01352-780215 Fax
01352-780187
5 bedrs, 1 ➡/WC, 2 ➡; tcf P5
sB&B £14 Breakfast only; cc Ac Vi

KIDWELLY Dyfed   6B4

Castle Farm Castle Rd, Kidwelly SA17 5BQ
01554-890321

Mountain Lodge Four Roads, Kidwelly
SA17 4SW 01554-890680 Fax 01554-890680 ♿
3 bedrs, 2 ➡; TV tcf P10
sB&B £15 Breakfast only

LAUGHARNE Dyfed   6B4

Hall Down Farm Laugharne SA33 4QS
01994-427452

LLANBERIS Gwynedd   6B1

Lake View *Acclaimed* 🔶RAC
Tan-y-Pant, Llanberis LL55 4EL 01286-870422
cc Ac DC Vi

LLANDEILO Dyfed   6C4

Brynawel *Acclaimed* 🔶RAC
19 New Road, Llandeilo SA19 6DD
01558-822925

Large brick building fronting main A40.
5 bedrs, 2 ➡/WC, 1 🛁/WC, 1 ➡; TV tcf P5
sB&B £19 dB&B £29 Breakfast only; cc Ac Vi

Glanrannell Park Crugybar, Llandeilo SA19
8SA 01558-685230

LLANDELOY Dyfed   6A4

Upper Vanley Farm 🔶RAC
Nr Solva, Llandeloy SA62 6LJ 01348-831418

LLANDOGO Gwent   7D4

Browns 🔶RAC
Llandogo NP5 4TW 01594-530262

Sloop Inn 🔶RAC
Llandogo NP5 4TN 01594-530291 Fax
01594-530935
4 bedrs, 3 ➡/WC, 1 🛁/WC; TV tcf 🐾
Child restrictions
sB&B £25.50 dB&B £39 D £8 [10%V]; cc Ac
Amex Vi

LLANDOVERY Dyfed   6C4

Ashgrove Llangadog Rd, Llandovery SA20
0DJ 01550-20136

Bwlch-Y-Ffin Rhandirmwyn, Llandovery
SA20 0PG 01550-6311
3 bedrs, 1 ➡; 🐾 P8
Child restrictions under 12
sB&B £13.50 D £8

Kings Head Inn Market Square, Llandovery
SA20 0AB 01550-20393

Llanerchindda Farm Cynghordy, Llandovery SA20 0NB 01550-5274

Llwyncelyn RAC
Chain Bridge, Llandovery SA20 0EP
01550-720566
6 bedrs, 2 ➾; tcf ✂ P12
sB&B £18-£22 dB&B £32-£34; HB weekly £171.85-£211; [5%V]

Y Neuadd Guesthouse Pentre Ty Gwyn, Llandovery SA20 0RN 01550-20603

LLANDRINDOD WELLS Powys   6C3

Griffin Lodge *Acclaimed* RAC
Temple Street, Llandrindod Wells LD1 5HF
01597-822432
8 bedrs, 5 ☏/WC, 2 ➾; TV tcf ✖ ✂ P8
sB&B £13-£23 dB&B £38-£42; HB weekly £175-£198; D £11 [10%V]; cc Ac Amex Vi

Kincoed RAC
Temple Street, Llandrindod Wells LD1 5HF
01597-822656 Fax 01597-824660
10 bedrs, 1 ➾/WC, 4 ☏/WC, 2 ➾; TV tcf ✖ P6
Child restrictions
sB&B £15-£16.50 dB&B £30-£40; HB weekly £171.50-£180; D £13.50 [10%V]; cc Ac Vi

Three Wells Farm *Highly Acclaimed* RAC
Chapel Road, Howey, Llandrindod Wells LD1 5PB 01597-822484
15 bedrs, 11 ➾/WC, 4 ☏/WC, 1 ➾; TV tcf ✖ ✂ P20
Child restrictions
sB&B £17-£22 dB&B £34-£44; HB weekly £165-£200

LLANDUDNO Gwynedd   6C1

Beach Cove RAC
8 Church Walks, Llandudno LL30 2HD
01492-879638
7 bedrs, 5 ☏/WC, 1 ➾; TV tcf ✂
sB&B £13 dB&B £32 Breakfast only [5%V]

Bedford RAC
Graig-y-Don Par, Llandudno LL30 1BN
01492-876647 Fax 01492-860185

Brannock RAC
36 St David's Road, Llandudno LL30 2UH
01492-877483

Brigstock *Acclaimed* RAC
1 St Davids Place, Llandudno LL30 2UG
01492-876416
10 bedrs, 3 ➾/WC, 3 ☏/WC, 1 ➾; TV tcf P5
Child restrictions
sB&B £20 dB&B £40; HB weekly £176; D £8 [10%V]

Britannia *Acclaimed* RAC
15 Craig-y-Don Parade, Promenade, Llandudno LL30 1BG 01492-877185

Buile Hill *Acclaimed* RAC
46 St Marys Road, Llandudno LL30 2UE
01492-876972

Carmel RAC
17 Craig-y-Don Parade, Llandudno LL30 1BG
01492-877643
9 bedrs, 6 ☏/WC, 2 ➾; TV tcf ✖ ✂ P6
Child restrictions
sB&B £14 dB&B £28; HB weekly £133-£140;

Concord *Acclaimed* RAC
35 Abbey Road, Llandudno LL30 2EH
01492-875504

Cornerways *Acclaimed* RAC
2 St Davids Place, Llandudno LL30 2UG
01492-877334

Cranberry House 12 Abbey Road, Llandudno LL30 2EA 01492-879760
5 bedrs, 1 ☏/WC, 2 ➾; Breakfast only

★Hilbre Court RAC
Great Ormes Road, Llandudno LL30 2AR
01492-876632

Detached black and white painted house under a red tiled roof. Well appointed and nicely furnished rooms. Near West Shore.
9 bedrs, 7 ➾/WC, 1 ➾; ✖ P4
Breakfast only [10%V]

Karden 🔱 RAC
16 Charlton Street, Llandudno LL30 2AN
01492-879347

Kinmel *Acclaimed* 🔱 RAC
Central Promenade, Llandudno LL30 1AR
01492-876171

Mayfield 🔱 RAC
19 Curzon Road, Craig-y-Don, Llandudno
LL30 1TB 01492-877427

Minion 🔱 RAC
21-23 Carmen Sylva, Llandudno LL30 1EQ
01492-877740
12 bedrs, 4 ➡/WC, 8 ♘/WC; tcf 🗙 ⚖
sB&B £14-£15 dB&B £28-£30; HB weekly
£140-£154; [10%V]

Montclare 🔱 RAC
4 North Parade, Llandudno LL30 2LP
01492-877061
15 bedrs, 1 ➡/WC, 12 ♘/WC; TV tcf ⚖
sB&B £18 dB&B £36 Breakfast only

Orotava *Acclaimed* 🔱 RAC
105 Glen-y-Mor Road, Llandudno LL30 3PH
01492-549780

Rosaire 🔱 RAC
2 St Seiriols Road, Llandudno LL30 2YY
01492-877677

Seaclyffe 🔱 RAC
11 Church Walks, Llandudno LL30 2HG
01492-876803

Spindrift *Acclaimed* 🔱 RAC
24 St Davids Road, Llandudno LL30 2UL
01492-876490

St Hilary *Acclaimed* 🔱 RAC
16 Craig-y-don Parade, Promenade,
Llandudno LL30 1BG 01492-875551
11 bedrs, 8 ♘/WC, 2 ➡; TV tcf
sB&B £13.50-£30 dB&B £27-£33; HB weekly
£129-£149; D £5.75 [10%V]; cc Ac Vi

Tilstone 🔱 RAC
Carmen Sylva Road, Craig-y-Don, Llandudno
LL30 1EQ 01492-875588
7 bedrs; 2➡
Child restrictions
sB&B £13.50 dB&B £27; HB weekly £129.50;

Warwick *Acclaimed* 🔱 RAC
56 Church Walks, Llandudno LL30 2HL
01492-876823

Westbourne 🔱 RAC
8 Arvon Avenue, Llandudno LL30 2DY
01492-877450

Westdale 🔱 RAC
37 Abbey Road, Llandudno LL30 2EH
01492-877996
12 bedrs, 1 ➡/WC, 2 ♘/WC, 2 ➡; tcf 🗙 P5
sB&B £12.50-£15.50 dB&B £29-£31; HB
weekly £136.50-£143.50; [5%V]

White Lodge *Acclaimed* 🔱 RAC
Central Promenade, Llandudno LL30 1AT
01492-877713

★★Wilton 🔱 RAC
South Parade, Llandudno LL30 2LN
01492-876086 Fax 01492-876086
14 bedrs, 9 ➡/WC, 5 ♘/WC; TV tcf 🗙 ⚖
sB&B £22-£24 dB&B £44-£48; HB weekly
£182-£192; D £8 [10%V]

LLANDYSUL Dyfed — 6B4

★Pellorwel RAC
Bwlch Y Groes, Llandysul SA44 5JU
01239-851226

LLANELLI Dyfed — 2C1

The George Stepney Road, Burry Port,
Llanelli SA16 0BH 01554-832211
5 bedrs, 1 ⇨;
Child restrictions under 3
Breakfast only

LLANERCH-Y-MEDD Gwynedd — 6B1

Drws y Coed Llanerch-Y-Medd LL71 8AD
01248-470473

*This beautifully appointed award-winning
farmhouse is set on a 550 acre working farm
of beef, sheep, and arable produce. The farm
is surrounded by peaceful wooded
countryside, with panoramic views of
Snowdonia.*
3 bedrs, 3 ⇨/WC; ✈ P5
sB&B £19; HB weekly £179

LLANFYRNACH Powys — 7D4

Bron-Y-Gaer Llanfyrnach SA35 0DA
01239-831265

LLANGADOG Dyfed — 6C4

Cefn Cilgwyn Llangadog SA19 9LF
01550-777493

LLANGOLLEN Clwyd — 7D2

Cefn Y Fedw Farm Panorama Walk, Garth,
Trevor, Llangollen LL14 1UA 01978-823403
2 bedrs, 1 🛁/WC, 2 ⇨; TV tcf P6
Child restrictions under 14
sB&B £20 Breakfast only

Dinbren Hall Llangollen LL20 8EB
01978-860640

Dinbren House Dinbren Rd, Llangollen LL20
8TF 01978-860593

Glanafon Abbey Rd, Llangollen LL20 8SS
01978-860725

Hendy Isa Horseshoe Pass, Llangollen LL20
8DE 01978-861232 ♿

*A quiet, country house in a picturesque valley
with abundant wildlife. Spacious, tastefully
furnished rooms.*
4 bedrs, 4 ⇨/WC; TV tcf P10
sB&B £15 Breakfast only

Hillcrest Hill Street, Llangollen LL20 8EU
01978-860208

*This owner-run hotel is a large Victorian
house that has been tastefully converted and
modernised. In a quiet location within a few
minutes walk of the town centre.*
7 bedrs, 7 🛁/WC; TV tcf ✗ P10
sB&B £19; HB weekly £164.50-£199.50; D
£4.50-£8.50

Oaklands Trevor, Llangollen LL20 7TG
01978-820152

Old Vicarage Guest Bryn Howel Lane, Llangollen LL20 7YR 01978-823018 Fax 01978-823018 &

A Georgian country house set in private grounds with spacious quality accommodation.
4 bedrs, 1 ⇥/WC, 3 ↾/WC, 1 ⇥; TV tcf ✘ P8
sB&B £15 Breakfast only

Tower Farm Llangollen LL20 8TE
01978-860252

LLANON Dyfed   6B3

Plas Morfa Heol Y Mor, Llanon, Aberystwyth SY23 5LX 01974-202415

LLANRHAEDR   7D2

Wynnstay Arms Llanrhaeadr SY10 0JL
01691-780210

LLANRWST Gwynedd   6C1

★★Eagles   RAC
**Ancaster Square, Llanrwst LL26 0LG
01492-640454**

Imposing building in the Market Place. A privately-owned and run hotel.
12 bedrs, 12 ⇥/WC; ✘ P50
Breakfast only; cc Ac Vi

LLANWRDA Dyfed   6C4

Myrtle Hill Llansadwrn, Llanwrda SA19 8HL
01550-777530

LLANWRTYD WELLS Powys   6C4

Carlton House *Acclaimed*   RAC
Dolycoed Road, Llanwrtyd Wells LD5 4SN
01591-610248

Lasswade House *Highly Acclaimed*   RAC
Station Road, Llanwrtyd Wells LD5 4RW
015913-515 Fax 019513-611
8 bedrs, 4 ⇥/WC, 4 ↾/WC; TV tcf ✘ ✚ P8
Child restrictions
sB&B £27.50 dB&B £55; HB weekly £252; D
£14.95 [10%V]; cc Ac Vi

★Neuadd Arms   RAC
Llanwrtyd Wells LD5 4RB 015913-236

A Georgian and Victorian hotel standing in the square of the smallest town in Britain.
18 bedrs, 5 ⇥/WC, 4 ⇥; ✘ ✚ P10
sB&B £19-£20 dB&B £33-£38; HB weekly
£200-£220; D £10; cc Ac Vi

No Smoking/Dogs

✚ Indicates a hotel which either bans smoking throughout the establishment or does not allow smoking in some areas.

✘ Indicates a hotel which either does not welcome dogs or restricts dogs to certain areas of the hotel.
Please telephone the hotel
for further details.

LOGIN Dyfed   6B4

Maencochyrwyn Farm Login, Whitland
SA34 0TN 01994-419283
*An 80 acre dairy farm situated just over 2
miles from the village of Llanboidy near
Whitland.*
3 bedrs, 2 🛁; 🐕
Breakfast only

MACHYNLLETH Powys   6C2

Bryncelyn Farm Dinas Mawddwy,
Machynlleth 01650-531289

*The Edwards family offer a comfortable
holiday in a peaceful valley of Cywarch at the
foot of Aran Fawddwy. Spacious bedrooms
with colour TV and tea/ coffee making
facilities.*
2 bedrs, 1 🛁/WC, 1 🚿/WC; TV tcf 🐕 P4
Child restrictions under 9
sB&B £18 Breakfast only

MERTHYR TYDFIL Mid Glamorgan   6C4

★★★Baverstock   RAC
Heads of the Valley Road, Merthyr Tydfil
CF44 0LX 01685-386221 Fax 01685-723670

Brynawel Queens Road, Merthyr Tydfil CF47
0HD 01685-722573

Little Diner Dowlais Top, Merthyr Tydfil
CF48 2YF 01685-723362   ♿
6 bedrs, 1 🛁/WC, 5 🚿/WC; P30
sB&B £27.50 Breakfast only

Llwyn-On Cwntaf, Merthyr Tydfil CF48 2HS
01685-384384

Tredegar Arms 66 High Street, Dowlais Top,
Merthyr Tydfil CF48 2YE 01685-377467
5 bedrs, 2 🛁/WC, 3 🚿/WC;
Breakfast only

MILFORD HAVEN Dyfed   2B1

Belhaven House   RAC
**inc. Tallships Restaurant, 29 Hamilton
Terrace, Milford Haven SA73 3JJ
01646-695983 Fax 01646-690787**
11 bedrs, 2 🚿/WC, 4 🛁; TV tcf 🐕 P8
sB&B £25-£27 dB&B £34-£37 D £4.25-£20
[10%V]; cc Ac Amex DC Vi

Church Lakes 88 Church Road, Llanstadwell,
Neyland, Milford Haven SA73 1EA
01646-600840

Y Ftynnon 45 Honeyborough Road,
Neyland, Milford Haven SA73 1RF
01646-601369

MOLD Clwyd   7D1

Maes Garmon Farm Gwernaffield, Mold
CH7 5DB 01352-759887

*A 17th century farmhouse, with exposed
beams, furnished in oak and pine. Set in
beautiful gardens with a summerhouse, pond
and stream.*
3 bedrs, 3 🚿/WC; TV tcf P12
Child restrictions under 7
sB&B £15 D £8.50-£10

Old Mill *Acclaimed* ♠RAC
Melin y Wern, Denbigh Road, Nannerch,
Mold CH7 5RH 01352-741542 Fax
01352-740254
6 bedrs, 6 ⚑/WC; **TV** tcf ✖ P12
sB&B £37 dB&B £55 Breakfast only [10%V];
cc Ac Amex DC Vi JCB

Plas Penucha Caerwys, Mold CH7 5BH
01352-720210
4 bedrs, 2 ⚑/WC, 1 ➡; ✖
sB&B £16.50; HB weekly £150; D £10

MONMOUTH Gwent   7D4

Lower Pen-y-Clawdd Farm Dingestow,
Monmouth NP5 4BG 0160083-223/677
3 bedrs, 2 ➡; ✖
sB&B £15 Breakfast only

NARBERTH Dyfed   6B4

Canton House Robeston Wathen, Narberth
SA67 8EP 01834-8606020

Pen Y Bont Amroth Road, Llanteg, Narberth
SA67 8QL 01834-83648

**Robeston House Robeston Wathen,
Narberth SA67 01834-860392**
8 bedrs; P24
sB&B £32; HB weekly £130;

Timberlands Princes Gate, Narberth SA67
8TF 01834-860688

NEATH West Glamorgan   2C1

Cwmbach Cottages Cumbach Road,
Cadoxton, Neath SA10 8AH 01639-639825

Europa 32/34 Victoria Gardens, Neath SA11
3BH 01639-635094

Victoria 10 Victoria Gardens, Neath SA11
3BE 01639-63233

NEW QUAY Dyfed   6B3

Brynafor *Acclaimed* ♠RAC
New Road, New Quay SA45 9SB
01545-560358   ♿
5 bedrs, 2 ➡/WC; **TV** tcf ⚹ P10
sB&B £25-£30 dB&B £42-£60; HB weekly
£160-£195; [5%V]; **cc** Ac Vi

Cambrian New Road, New Quay SA45 9SE
01545-560295

Park Hall *Highly Acclaimed* ♠RAC
Cwmtydu, New Quay SA44 6LG 01545-560306

Ty Hen Farm *Acclaimed* ♠RAC
Llwyndafydd, New Quay SA44 6BZ
01545-560346   ♿
2 bedrs, 2 ⚑/WC; **TV** tcf ✖ P20
sB&B £20-£29 dB&B £40-£58 D £10 [10%V];
cc Ac Vi

NEW RADNOR Powys   7D3

The Fforest Inn ♠RAC
Llanfihangel-nant-Melan, New Radnor LD8
2TN 01544-21246

NEWCASTLE EMLYN Dyfed   6B4

Maes Y Derw Newcastle Emlyn SA38 9RD
01239-710860 Fax 01239-710860
6 bedrs, 3 ➡; **TV** tcf ✖ P12
sB&B £16; HB weekly £168-£196; D £12.50;
cc Ac Vi

NEWPORT Gwent   16A3

Granada Lodge ♠RAC
Junc 23 (M4), Magor, Newport NP6 3YL
01633-88011

**Grove Park Pen Y Bont, Newport SA42
0LT 01239-820122**
4 bedrs, 2 ⚑/WC, 1 ➡; **TV** tcf ✖ P4
sB&B £18; HB weekly £199.50-£226.10; D
£12-£14

**Guesthouse 2 Springhill, Parrog Road,
Newport SA42 0RH 01239-820626**
3 bedrs, 2 ➡; **TV** tcf ✖ P2
sB&B £14; HB weekly £168-£175; D £10

Llysmeddyg East Street, Newport SA42 0SY
01239-820008

Springhill 2 Springhill, Parrog Road,
Newport SA42 0RH 01239-820626

★★★Westgate   ᴿᴬᴄ
Commercial Street, Newport NP9 1TT
01633-244444 Fax 01633-246616   ♿
69 bedrs, 59 ➡/WC; ✖ ⚹ P500
sB&B £27.50-£64 dB&B £68 D £13.95 [5%V];
cc Ac Amex DC Vi

NOLTON HAVEN Dyfed   6A4

Nolton Haven Farmhouse Nolton Haven
SA62 21NH 01437-710263

NORTHOP Clwyd   7D1

Auto Lodge Northop Hall, West Bound A55,
Northop CH5 6HB 01244-550011   ♿
38 bedrs, 38 ➡/WC, 38 ⬥/WC; ✖ P50
sB&B £15 Breakfast only

OXWICH BAY West Glamorgan   2C1

Woodside Oxwich SA3 1LS 01792-390791

*200 year old converted cottage. En- suite
ground floor accommodation all available
with easy access from our car park. Beamed
dining room and bar.*
5 bedrs, 4 ➡/WC, 4 ⬥/WC, 1 ➡; TV tcf P12
sB&B £18; HB weekly £353-£429; D £9.50

Discount vouchers
Hotels with a (V) at the end of the price
information will accept RAC discount
vouchers in part payment for
accommodation bills on the full,
standard rate, not against bargain breaks
or any other special offer.

★★Oxwich Bay   ᴿᴬᴄ
Oxwich Bay, Gower, Swansea SA3 1LS
01792-390329 Fax 01792-391254

*Comfortable family hotel situated at the edge
of a beautiful 2 mile sandy beach in totally
unspoiled countryside of the Gower
Peninsula.*
13 bedrs, 13 ➡/WC; TV tcf ✖ P250
HB weekly £196-£284; D £12; cc Ac Vi

PEMBROKE Dyfed   2B1

Chapel Farm Castlemartin, Pembroke SA71
5HW 01646-661312

**The Old Rectory Cosheston, Pembroke
SA72 4UJ 01646-684968**
3 bedrs, 2 ➡; tcf ✖ P6
sB&B £15; HB weekly £170-£190; D £10

PENARTH South Glamorgan   3D1

Anglesea 9 Romilly Road, Penarth CF6 6AZ
01446-749660

Kenilworth House Station Road, Llantwit
Manor, Penarth CF6 9ST 01446-796900

Raisdale House Raisdale Road, Penarth CF6
2BN 01222-707317

★Walton House   ᴿᴬᴄ
37 Victoria Road, Penarth CF6 2HY
01222-707782 Fax 01222-711012
12 bedrs, 5 ➡/WC, 1 ➡; P16
cc Ac Vi

Westbourne 8 Victoria Road, Penarth CF64
3EF 01222-707268

PENMACHNO Gwynedd   6C1

Penmachno Hall *Acclaimed*   ᴿᴬᴄ
Penmachno LL24 0PU 016903-207

PONTYPRIDD Mid Glamorgan   3D1

Market Tavern Market Street, Pontypridd CF37 2ST
01443-485331 Fax 01443-402806   &
11 bedrs, 6 ➡/WC, 5 ☎/WC; TV tcf
sB&B £24.50 D £2.95-£4.50; cc Ac Vi

PORT EYNON West Glamorgan   2C1

Culver House Port Eynon SA3 1NN
01792-390755

PORTH Mid Glamorgan   3D1

G & T's 64-66 Pontypridd Road, Porth CF39
9PL 01443-6857775

PORTHCAWL Mid Glamorgan   3D1

Collingwood   RAC
40 Mary Street, Porthcawl CF36 3YA
01656-782899

Haven 50 New Road, Porthcawl CF36 5DN
01656-788706
5 bedrs, 4 ☎/WC, 1 ➡; TV tcf
sB&B £16; HB weekly £140-£155; D £7; cc Ac Vi

Ocean View *Acclaimed*   RAC
46 Mary Street, Porthcawl CF36 3YA
01656-713643

Penoyre *Acclaimed*   RAC
29 Mary Street, Porthcawl CF36 3YN
01656-784550
6 bedrs, 2 ➡/WC, 2 ☎/WC, 1 ➡; ✈
sB&B £15 dB&B £30; HB weekly £140; D £7

Picton Villa 14 Picton Avenue, Porthcawl
CF36 3AJ 01656-716386

Rockybank Guest 15 De Breos Drive,
Porthcawl CF36 3JP 01656-785823 Fax
01656-771744
2 bedrs, 2 ➡/WC; TV tcf P6
sB&B £18 Breakfast only

The Pines 15 Beach Road, Newton,
Porthcawl CF365NH 01656-771759

Tre-Mor 46 Esplanade Avenue, Porthcawl
CF36 3YU 01656-771839

PRESTATYN Clwyd   6C1

Roughsedge House 26/28 Marine Road,
Prestatyn LL19 7HG 01745-887359 Fax
01745-887359
10 bedrs, 2 ➡/WC, 1 ☎/WC, 2 ➡; TV tcf P4
sB&B £13 D £6.50-£7.50; cc Ac Amex DC Vi

Traeth Ganol 41 Beach Road West, Prestatyn
LL19 7LL 01745-853594

RHYL Clwyd   6C1

Carlton House 25 Palace Avenue, Rhyl LL18
1HS 01745-350257

Gwynfa 6 Beechwood Rd, Rhyl LL18 3EU
01745-353848

Links 20 Beechwood Rd, Rhyl LL18 3EU
01745-344381

Pier   RAC
23 East Parade, Rhyl LL18 3AL 01745-350280
8 bedrs, 3 ➡/WC, 6 ☎/WC, 1 ➡; TV tcf P2
sB&B £16-£17 dB&B £32-£34; HB weekly
£130-£150; cc Ac Vi

Westcliffe 88 West Parade, Rhyl LL18 1HW
01745-353705

RUTHIN Clwyd   7D1

Eyarth Station Llanfair, Dyffryn, Ruthin
LL15 2EE 01824-703643 Fax 0184-707464   &
*A beautifully converted old railway station, set
in its own grounds in the heart of lovely Vale of
Clwyd and surrounded by spectacular scenery.*
6 bedrs, 1 ➡/WC, 5 ☎/WC, 1 ➡; tcf ✈ P10
sB&B £20 D £6.50-£12; cc Ac Vi

SAUNDERSFOOT Dyfed   6B4

Bay View *Acclaimed*   RAC
Pleasant Valley, Stepaside, Saundersfoot
SA67 8LR 01834-813417
11 bedrs, 8 ☎/WC, 3 ➡; P15
sB&B £16-£20 dB&B £32-£40; HB weekly
£140-£170

Dalwood The Ridgeway, Saundersfoot SA69
9LD 01834-813342

Gower *Acclaimed* ꭇᴀᴄ
Milford Terrace, Saundersfoot SA69 9EL
01834-813452
23 bedrs, 10 ➡/WC, 4 ➡; TV tcf ✕ ⊱ P20
sB&B £17.50-£19.50 dB&B £35-£40; HB
weekly £172-£189; D £9 [10%V]; cc Ac Amex
DC Vi

Jalna *Acclaimed* ꭇᴀᴄ
Stammers Road, Saundersfoot SA69 9HH
01834-812282 ᵴ
*A modern, licensed hotel situated two
hundred yards from the harbour and shops.*
14 bedrs, 8 ➡/WC, 6 ➡/WC, 1 ➡; TV tcf ✕
sB&B £21-£23 dB&B £36-£40 Breakfast only
[5%V]; cc Ac Vi

★★Rhodewood House ꭇᴀᴄ
St Brides Hill, Saundersfoot SA69 9NU
01834-812200 Fax 01834-811863 ᵴ
34 bedrs, 25 ➡/WC; ✕ ⊱ P70
sB&B £23-£30 dB&B £36-£68; HB weekly
£167-£209; D £9.50; cc Ac Amex DC Vi

Sandy Hill *Acclaimed* ꭇᴀᴄ
Tenby Road, Saundersfoot SA69 9DR
01834-813165
5 bedrs, 3 ➡/WC, 1 ➡; TV tcf ✕ P7
Child restrictions
sB&B £13-£17 dB&B £26-£34; HB weekly
£140-£168;

Stammers Rock Stammers Road,
Saundersfoot SA69 9HZ 01834-813766

The Harbour Light 2 High Street,
Saundersfoot SA69 9EJ 01834-813496

Vine Farm *Acclaimed* ꭇᴀᴄ
The Ridgeway, Saundersfoot SA69 9LA
01834-813543 ᵴ
5 bedrs, 2 ➡/WC, 3 ➡/WC; TV tcf ✕ P12
sB&B £20 dB&B £40; HB weekly £180

Woodlands *Acclaimed* ꭇᴀᴄ
St Brides Hill, Saundersfoot SA69 9NP
01834-813338
10 bedrs, 5 ➡/WC, 1 ➡; TV tcf P10
sB&B £18-£20 dB&B £32-£36; cc DC Vi

SOLVA Dyfed   6A4

Lochmeyler Farm *Highly Acclaimed* ꭇᴀᴄ
Pen-y-Cwm, Llandeloy, Solva, Haverfordwest
SA62 6LL 01348-837724 Fax 01348-837724 ᵴ
10 bedrs, 10 ➡/WC, 1 ➡; TV tcf ✕ ⊱ P10
Child restrictions
sB&B £20; HB weekly £200; cc Ac Vi

Harbour House Lower Solva, Solva SA62
6UT 01437-721267

Pendinas St Brides View, Solva SA62 6TB
01437-721283

Riverview Cottage 6 River Street, Solva SA62
6UX 01437-720959
3 bedrs, 1 ➡; ✕ P3
sB&B £14 Breakfast only

Whitehouse Pencwm, Solva SA62 6LA
01437-720959

ST ASAPH Clwyd   6C1

Bach-y-Graig *Acclaimed* ꭇᴀᴄ
Tremeirchion, St Asaph LL17 0UH
01745-730627

★★★Talardy Park ꭇᴀᴄ
The Roe, St Asaph 01745-584957
Fax 01745-584385 ᵴ
18 bedrs, 5 ➡/WC, 3 ➡/WC; TV tcf ✕ P200
sB&B £41.50 dB&B £55 D £8.50 [10%V]; cc Ac
Vi

White House Rhuallt, St Asaph LL17 0AW
01745-582155

ST DAVID'S Dyfed   6A4

Grove High Street, St David's SA62 6SB
01437-720341
18 bedrs, 18 ➡/WC, 12 ➡/WC; ✕ P60
sB&B £25; HB weekly £175

Ramsey House *Acclaimed*
Lower Moor, St David's SA62 6RP
01437-720321
7 bedrs, 2 ⇨/WC, 5 🐾/WC; tcf ✖ ⚹ P10
Child restrictions
sB&B £25-£30 dB&B £44-£48; HB weekly
£199.50-£219; [10%V]

Swn-Y-Don 18 Cross Square, St David's SA62
6SE 01437-720744

Y Glennydd *Acclaimed*
51 Nun Street, St David's SA62 6NU
01437-720576
10 bedrs, 2 ⇨/WC, 5 🐾/WC, 2 ⇨; TV tcf
sB&B £17.50-£25 dB&B £36 D £12.50 [5%V];
cc Ac Vi

Y-Gorlan
77 Nun Street, St David's SA62 6NU
01473-720837 Fax 01437-720837

*Friendly family run licensed guest house close
to beaches, golf course, fishing, horse riding.
Comfortable guest lounge with panoramic
views.*
5 bedrs, 2 🐾/WC, 1 ⇨; TV tcf
sB&B £14.50; HB weekly £140-£154; D £7.95

SWANSEA West Glamorgan   2C1

Alexander *Acclaimed*
3 Sketty Road, Uplands, Swansea SA2 0EU
01792-470045 Fax 01792-476012
7 bedrs, 4 ⇨/WC, 2 🐾/WC, 1 ⇨; TV tcf ⚹
Child restrictions
sB&B £25-£30 dB&B £36; HB weekly £175;
[10%V]; cc Ac Amex DC Vi

**Arches 280-282 Oystermouth Road,
Swansea SA1 3UL 01792-641913 Fax
0114-2644936**   ♿

*Family-run hotel on sea front. Good facilties
including licensed bar and Satellite TV.*
20 bedrs, 6 ⇨/WC, 3 🐾/WC, 1 ⇨; TV tcf ✖
sB&B £16; HB weekly £96-£176; D £4-£7; cc
Ac Amex DC Vi

Brittania Inn Llanmadoc, Gower, Swansea
SA3 1DB 01792-386624

Coynant & Ganol Farm
Felindre, Swansea SA5 7PU 01269-595640
5 bedrs, 1 ⇨/WC, 2 🐾/WC; TV tcf ⚹ P10
sB&B £18 [10%V]

Crescent *Acclaimed*
132 Eaton Crescent, Uplands, Swansea SA1
4QR 01792-466814
6 bedrs, 1 ⇨/WC, 5 🐾/WC; TV tcf ✖ ⚹ P6
sB&B £23-£25 dB&B £38-£40

Cwmdulais House Cwmdulais, Swansea,
Swansea SA4 1NP 01792-885008

Greenways Hills Farm, Reynoldston,
Swansea SA3 1AE 01792-390125

Harlton 89 King Edward Road, Brynmill,
Swansea SA1 4LU 01792-466938

Hathaway 87/89 Swansea Road, Pontlliw, Swansea SA4 1EF 01792-891777

Langrove Lodge Parkmill, Gower, Swansea SA3 2EB 01792-232410

Pavilion Lodge   RAC
Swansea West Services, M4 Junction 47,
Swansea 01792-894894 Fax 01792-898860   &
50 bedrs, 50 ➡/WC; TV tcf ✖ ✕ P300
sB&B £34.95 D £10 [10%V]; cc Ac Amex DC
Vi JCB

Rock Villa 1 George Bank, Mumbles, Swansea SA3 4EQ 01792-366744

St Annes Western Lane, Mumbles, Swansea SA3 4EY 01792-369147   &

28 bedrs, 19 ➡/WC, 19 ✖/WC, 3 ➡; ✖ P45
sB&B £29 Breakfast only

St James *Highly Acclaimed*   RAC
76b Walter Road, Swansea SA1 4QA
01792-649984

Stoney Forge Knelston, Reynoldston, Swansea SA3 1AR 01792-390920

Tallizmand Llanmadoc, Gower, Swansea SA3 1DE 01792-386373

The "Guest House" *Acclaimed*   RAC
Y Bryn Road, Brynmill, Swansea SA2 0AR
01792-466947
14 bedrs, 7 ✖/WC, 2 ➡; TV tcf ✖ ✕
Child restrictions
sB&B £12-£14 dB&B £28 Breakfast only; cc
Ac Amex Vi

The Coast House 708 Mumbles Road,
Mumbles, Swansea SA3 4EH 01792-368702
6 bedrs, 4 ✖/WC, 1 ➡; TV tcf ✖
sB&B £14 Breakfast only

Tides Reach 388 Mumbles Road, Mumbles,
Swansea SA3 5TN 01792-404877   &
*Elegant Victorian town house on the sea front
in the village of Mumbles. Beautifully
furnished with antiques, comfortable en-suite
rooms.*
8 bedrs, 4 ✖/WC, 1 ➡; TV tcf ✖
Child restrictions under 5
sB&B £15.50 Breakfast only

Tredilion House *Highly Acclaimed*   RAC
26 Uplands Crescent, Swansea SA2 OPB
01792-470766 Fax 01792-456064
7 bedrs, 2 ➡/WC, 5 ✖/WC; TV tcf ✖ P8
sB&B £34-£38 dB&B £41-£48; HB weekly
£220-£315; D £12 [10%V]; cc Ac Amex DC Vi

Uplands Court   RAC
134 Eaton Crescent, Uplands, Swansea SA1
4QS 01792-473046
8 bedrs, 1 ➡/WC, 2 ✖/WC, 3 ➡; TV tcf ✕
sB&B £18 dB&B £36 Breakfast only [10%V];
cc Ac Amex Vi

Winston *Acclaimed*   RAC
11 Church Lane, Bishopston, Swansea SA3
3JT 01792-232074

Wittemberg *Acclaimed*   RAC
2 Rotherslade Road, Langland, Swansea SA3
4QN 01792-369696 Fax 01792-366995
11 bedrs, 10 ✖/WC, 2 ➡; ✕ P10
sB&B £26-£32 dB&B £40-£52; HB weekly
£150-£195; D £9.50 [10%V]; cc Ac Amex Vi

Location Maps
Hotel locations are shown on the maps at
the back of the guide. All towns and
villages containing a hotel listed in the
guide are shown in black.

TENBY Dyfed　2B1

Ashby House *Acclaimed*　RAC
24 Victoria Street, Tenby SA70 7DY
01834-842867
9 bedrs, 8 ⁊/WC, 1 ⇥; TV tcf
Child restrictions
sB&B £17-£22 dB&B £26-£30 Breakfast only
[10%V]; cc Ac Vi

Ashford Villa Picton Road, Tenby SA70 7DP
01834-843519

Belgrave The Esplanade, Tenby SA70 7DU
01834-842377
45 bedrs, 30 ⇥/WC, 1 ⁊/WC, 8 ⇥; ✗ P10
sB&B £15; HB weekly £185

Broadmead Heywood Lane, Tenby SA70
8DA 01834-842641
20 bedrs, 12 ⁊/WC;
Breakfast only

Bryn Y Mor Narberth Road, Tenby SA70 8HT
01834-843145

Buckingham *Acclaimed*　RAC
The Esplanade, Tenby SA70 6DU
01834-842622
8 bedrs, 5 ⇥/WC; TV tcf ✗ ✰
Child restrictions
sB&B £20-£24 dB&B £32-£38; HB weekly
£150-£190; D £9; cc Ac Vi

Castle View　RAC
The Norton, Tenby SA70 8AA 01834-842666

Clarence House Esplanade, Tenby SA70 7DL
01834-844371 Fax 01834-844372　&
68 bedrs, 68 ⇥/WC, 68 ⁊/WC, 5 ⇥; ✗
Child restrictions under 3
sB&B £10; HB weekly £126-£301; D £9-£43;
cc Ac Vi

Clement Dale Southcliff Gardens, Tenby
SA70 7DS 01834-843165

Connaught House Guest House, Warren
Street, Tenby SA70 7JY 01834-843544

Croyland 10 Deer Park, Tenby SA70 7LE
01834-843880

Elm Grove Country House St Florence,
Tenby SA70 8LS 01834-871255

Flemish Court St Florence, Tenby SA70 8LS
01834-871413

Glenholme Picton Terrace, Tenby SA70 7DR
01834-843909

Green Hills　RAC
St Florence, Tenby 01834-871291 Fax
01834-871948　&
26 bedrs, 9 ⇥/WC, 13 ⁊/WC, 2 ⇥; TV tcf ✰
P20
sB&B £22-£25 dB&B £44-£50; HB weekly
£195-£215; D £12

Hallsville Victoria Street, Tenby SA70 7DY
01834-842410

Harbour Heights *Highly Acclaimed*　RAC
The Croft, Tenby SA70 8AP 01834-842132

Hildebrand *Acclaimed*　RAC
29 Victoria Street, Tenby SA70 7DY
01834-842403
8 bedrs, 3 ⇥/WC, 5 ⁊/WC; TV tcf ✗ ✰
Child restrictions
sB&B £13.50-£19 dB&B £28-£37; HB weekly
£145-£175; D £9.50 [5%V]; cc Ac Amex DC Vi

Kingsbridge House Warren Street, Tenby
SA70 7JT 01834-844148
6 bedrs, 3 ⇥/WC, 1 ⇥; P4
sB&B £15; HB weekly £135

Kinloch Court *Highly Acclaimed*　RAC
Queens Parade, Tenby SA70 7EG
01834-842777
12 bedrs, 7 ⇥/WC, 5 ⁊/WC, 1 ⇥; TV tcf P25
Child restrictions
sB&B £23-£28 dB&B £46-£56; HB weekly
£210-£230; [10%V]; cc Ac Vi

Lyndale Warren Street, Tenby SA70 7JX
01834-842836

Marlborough House　RAC
South Cliff Street, Tenby SA70 7EA
01834-542961
10 bedrs; ✰
Child restrictions
sB&B £12.50-£14.50 dB&B £25-£29; HB
weekly £84-£98; cc Ac Amex Vi

Merryfield Church Park, Tenby SA70 7EE
01834-842741

Parsonage Farm Inn St Florence, Tenby
SA70 8LR 01834-871436

Pen Mar New Hedges, Tenby SA70 8TL
01834-842435
10 bedrs, 2 ➦/WC, 4 ➦/WC, 2 ➦; TV tcf P10
sB&B £15; HB weekly £150-£175; D £8; cc Ac
Amex DC Vi JCB

Ripley St Mary's *Acclaimed*   RAC
St Mary's Street, Tenby SA70 7HN
01834-842837

Highly recommended hotel. Personally run by
proprietors, in a quiet floral street within the
walled town.
14 bedrs, 6 ➦/WC, 2 ➦/WC, 3 ➦; TV tcf ✖
sB&B £17-£20 dB&B £34-£40; HB weekly
£165-£190; D £4-£7.50 [10%V]; cc Ac Vi

Sea Breezes   RAC
18 The Norton, Tenby SA70 8AA
01834-842753

Somerville Warren Street, Tenby SA70 &JU
01834-843158

Tall Ships *Acclaimed*   RAC
34 Victoria Street, Tenby SA70 7DY
01834-842055
8 bedrs, 5 ➦/WC, 1 ➦; TV tcf
sB&B £16-£19 dB&B £28-£34; HB weekly
£135-£160; [5%V]; cc Ac Vi

The Grove Farmhouse St Florence, Tenby
SA70 8LZ 01834-871730

Waterwynch House *Highly Acclaimed*   RAC
Waterwynch Bay, Tenby SA70 8TJ
01834-842464 Fax 01834-845076   &
17 bedrs, 14 ➦/WC, 3 ➦/WC; TV tcf ✖ ✂ P25

Child restrictions
sB&B £30-£38 dB&B £60-£76; HB weekly
£260-£310; [10%V]

Weybourne 14 Warren Street, Tenby SA70
7JU 01834-843641

TINTERN Gwent   3E1

Parva Farmhouse *Highly Acclaimed*   RAC
Nr Chepstow, Tintern NP6 6SQ 01291-689411
Fax 01291-689557
9 bedrs, 7 ➦/WC, 2 ➦/WC, 1 ➦; TV tcf ✖ P15
sB&B £39-£42 dB&B £54-£60; HB weekly
£225-£250; D £16.50 [10%V]; cc Ac Vi

Valley House *Acclaimed*   RAC
Raglan Road, Tintern NP6 6TH 01291-689652
3 bedrs, 2 ➦/WC, 1 ➦/WC; TV tcf ✖ P7
Child restrictions
sB&B £25-£30 dB&B £35-£36 Breakfast only
[5%V]; cc Amex

Wye Valley   RAC
Tintern NP6 6SQ 01291-689441 Fax
01291-689440

TREARDDUR BAY Gwynedd   6B1

Moranedd   RAC
Trearddur Road, Trearddur Bay LL65 2UE
01407-860324
6 bedrs, 2 ➦; tcf P10
sB&B £14 dB&B £28 Breakfast only

TREGARON Dyfed   6C3

Neuaddlas Tregaron SY25 6LJ
01974-298905   &
6 bedrs, 2 ➦/WC; ✖
sB&B £16.50; HB weekly £171.50-£192.50; D
£8

TREHARRIS Mid Glamorgan   3D1

Wern Ganol Farm Nelson, Treharris CF46
6PS 01443-450413

TRESAITH Dyfed   6B3

Bryn Berwyn *Highly Acclaimed*   RAC
Nr. Aberporth, Tresaith CA43 2JG
01239-811126

TYWYN Gwynedd 6B2	**WOLFSCASTLE** Dyfed 6A4

TYWYN Gwynedd 6B2

**Dolffanog Fach Talyllyn, Tywyn LL36 9AJ
01654-761235**

*The farm is stone built and set at the foot of
Cader Idris in the Snowdonia National Park,
with fantastic views of Talyllyn Lake from the
garden. The farm has 1000 acres on the
mountain with sheep and suckler cows.*
3 bedrs, 1 ⇥/WC, 1 ⇥;
sB&B £15; HB weekly £150-£165; D £8-£9

USK Gwent 3E1

Tygwyn Farm Gwehelog, Usk NP5 1RT
01672-878

WELSHPOOL Powys 7D2

Trefnant Hall Farm *Acclaimed* RAC
Berriew, Welshpool SY21 8AS 01686-640262
3 bedrs, 2 ⇥/WC, 1 ⇫/WC; TV tcf P6
sB&B £20 dB&B £32 Breakfast only [5%V]

Tynllwyn Farm RAC
Welshpool SY21 9BW 01938-553175
6 bedrs, 2 ⇥; TV tcf ✖
sB&B £14.50 dB&B £29; HB weekly £140;
[5%V]

WOLFSCASTLE Dyfed 6A4

Stone Hall *Acclaimed* RAC
Welsh Hook, Wolfscastle SA62 5NS
01348-840212 Fax 01348-840815
5 bedrs, 4 ⇥/WC, 1 ⇥; TV tcf P50
sB&B £46 dB&B £63; HB weekly £280; D £15
[10%V]; cc Ac Amex Vi

WREXHAM Clwyd 7D1

**Brackenwood 67 Wynnstay Lane,
Marford, Wrexham LL12 8LH
01978-852866 Fax 01978-852065**

*Secluded family residence. Landscaped
gardens, conservatory, dining room, SKY TV,
lounge, evening meals. Mid way Wrexham
and Chester.*
7 bedrs, 1 ⇥/WC, 1 ⇫/WC, 2 ⇥; TV tcf P10
sB&B £14; HB weekly £157.50-£190; D £4-
£10.50

Lyndhurst 3 Gerald Street, Wrexham LL11
1EH 01978-290802

Plas Eyton Wrexham LL13 0YD
01978-820642

Raven Farm LLandegla, Wrexham LL11 3AW
01978-88224

Child Restrictions

Most hotels and guest houses are happy
to welcome children. A few prefer to
welcome only adults and older children;
these are shown by 'Child restrictions' in
the entry. If you are travelling with children,
please telephone the establishment to check
the age limit set by the management.

The Isle of Man

DOUGLAS Isle of Man — 10A4

Edelweiss ⚓RAC
Queen's Promenade, Douglas 01624-621218
&
20 bedrs, 20 ➡/WC; ✻
Breakfast only [10%V]; cc Ac DC Vi

Hydro ⚓RAC
Queens Promenade, Douglas 01624-676870
Fax 01624-663883
58 bedrs, 19 ➡/WC, 20 🐾/WC; TV tcf ✻
sB&B £25.50 dB&B £51; HB weekly £227.50;
D £7.50; cc Ac Vi

Modwena *Acclaimed* ⚓RAC
39-40 Loch Promenade, Douglas
01624-833811

Rio ⚓RAC
Loch Promenade, Douglas IM1 2LY
01624-623491 Fax 01624-670966
15 bedrs, 4 ➡/WC, 7 🐾/WC, 1 ➡; TV tcf ⚬
Child restrictions
D £7 [10%V]; cc Ac Vi

Seabank ⚓RAC
21 Loch Promenade, Douglas 01624-674815
Fax 01624-674815
12 bedrs, 1 ➡/WC, 4 🐾/WC, 3 ➡;
TV tcf 🐾 P10
sB&B £10-£14 dB&B £28 Breakfast only
[10%V]

PORT ERIN Isle of Man — 10A4

Regent House *Highly Acclaimed* ⚓RAC
Promenade, Port Erin 01624-833454 Fax
01624-833454
6 bedrs, 5 ➡/WC, 1 🐾/WC; TV tcf
Child restrictions
sB&B £21-£23 dB&B £42-£46
Breakfast only [5%V]

SULBY Isle of Man — 10A4

Sulby Glen ⚓RAC
Sulby 01624-897240

The Channel Islands

ALDERNEY — 2A1

Bibette House Newtown, Alderney GY9 3XP
01481-822536

Chez Nous Les Venelles, Alderney
01481-823633

Farm Court Les Mouriaux, Alderney GY9
3UX 01481-822075 Fax 01481-822075
7 bedrs, 2 ➡/WC, 5 🐾/WC; TV tcf
sB&B £20 Breakfast only; cc Ac Amex Vi

Les Quest Allee Es Fees, Alderney
01481-822809

Saye Farm Alderney 01481-822196

Simerock Les Velles, Alderney 01481-823645

St Annes Alderney 01481-823145

CASTEL Guernsey — 2A2

Le Galaad *Highly Acclaimed* ⚓RAC
Rue Des Francais, Castel 01481-57233 Fax
01481-53028
12 bedrs, 2 ➡/WC, 10 🐾/WC; TV tcf ⚬ P12
sB&B £17.50-£25.50 dB&B £17.50-£25.50
Breakfast only

L'ANCRESSE Guernsey — 2A2

Lynton Park *Highly Acclaimed* ⚓RAC
Hacse Lane, L'ancresse 01481-45418
13 bedrs, 3 ➡/WC, 2 ➡; TV tcf P25
Child restrictions
sB&B £20-£31 dB&B £50-£62 D £11 [10%V];
cc Ac Vi

L'ISLET Guernsey — 2A2

Manresa Sandy Lane, L'islet 01481-46074

ST MARTINS Guernsey   2A2

Rosewood La Grande Rue, St Martin,
Guernsey GY4 6RU 01481-38329

La Michele *Highly Acclaimed*   RAC
Les Hubits De Bas, St Martins 01481-38065
Fax 01481-39492   &
13 bedrs, 9 ⇻/WC, 4 🛁/WC; TV tcf ⅍ P15
Child restrictions
sB&B £20-£29 dB&B £40-£58; HB weekly
£175-£238; [5%V]; cc Ac Amex Vi

**Oneida Clos Des Caches, St Martins GY4
6PL 01481-37751**

*Small, friendly guest house offering Guernsey
hospitality in a comfortable, modern house.
In a quiet location near the shops.*
5 bedrs, 2 🛁/WC, 2 ⇻; tcf 🐾 P5
sB&B £12.50; HB weekly £140-£175; D £7.50;
cc Ac Vi

Tudor Lodge Deer Farm Forest Road, St
Martins GY8 0A8 01481-37849

Wellesley Sausmarez Road, St Martins
01481-38028

Woodlands Route Des Blanches, St Martins
01481-37481

ST PETER PORT Guernsey   2A2

Ashbourne Brock Road, St Peter Port GY1
1RS 01481-720568

Foresters Arms St Georges Esplanade, St
Peter Port 01481-723583
Guest house near the beach.
2 bedrs, 1 ⇻; TV tcf
Child restrictions under 16
sB&B £14 Breakfast only

Friends Vegetarian 20 Hauteville, St Peter
Port 01481-721146

Gainsborough 95 Mount Durand, St Peter
Port GY1 1DY 01481-721612

Hotel Trinico Collings Road, St Peter Port
GY1 1FS 01481-722949   &
13 bedrs, 13 ⇻/WC, 13 🛁/WC; 🐾 P18
sB&B £17; HB weekly £181.50;

Kings Ville Au Roi, St Peter Port GY 1NZ
01481-38672

Lindale Elm Grove, St Peter Port
01481-722136

Marine *Highly Acclaimed*   RAC
Well Road, St Peter Port 01481-724978
11 bedrs, 11 🛁/WC; tcf ⅍
sB&B £14.75 dB&B £29.50-£44 Breakfast
only; cc Ac Vi

Midhurst House *Highly Acclaimed*   RAC
Candie Road, St Peter Port 01481-24391

St Clare Court Brock Road, St Peter Port
01481-723240

ST SAMPSONS Guernsey   2A2

Ann-Dawn *Highly Acclaimed*   RAC
Route Des Capelles, St Sampsons
01481-725606

VALE Guernsey   2A2

Bordeaux Bordeaux Bay, Vale GY3 5LX
01481-47461

Fleur De Lys Houmtel Lane, Vale
01481-45030

L'Ancresse View La Garenne, Vale
01481-43963
5 bedrs, 2 ⇻; tcf 🐾 P2
sB&B £10 Breakfast only

ROZEL BAY Jersey   2B2

Malta House Farm Route Du Mont Mado,
Rozel Bay JE2 4DN 01534-861678

ST AUBIN'S BAY Jersey   2B2

Bryn-y-Mor   RAC
Route de la Haule, St Aubin's Bay JE3 8BA

01534-20295 Fax 01534-24262
14 bedrs, 2 🛁/WC, 10 🚿/WC, 2 🛁;
TV tcf ✹ ⍭ P6
sB&B £15-£27 dB&B £30-£54 D £9.50 [10%V];
cc Ac Amex DC Vi

ST BRELADE Jersey   2A2

Armada Route De La Haule, St Brelade JE3
8BA 01534-877191

Au Caprice Route De La Haule, St Brelade
JE3 8BA 01534-871746

Pebbles Market Hill, St Aubin Harbour, St
Brelade JE3 8AE 01534-43547

Peterborough House Rue du Croquet, High
Street, St Brelade JE3 8BR 01534-41568

ST CLEMENT Jersey   2B2

Brookland Blanc Mondin, St Clement JE2
6PR 01534-24705

Eden Country House St Clements Inner
Road, St Clement JE2 6QQ 01534-85216

Les Grandes Vagues Pontac, St Clement JE2
6SE 01534-851198

Picardy Plat Douet Road, St Clement JE2
6PN 01534-33708

**Rocqueberg View Rue De Samares, St
Clement JE2 6LS 01534-852642 Fax
01534-851694**

*A charming guest house with its own
swimming pool, in pleasant surroundings.
Large, bright rooms.*
9 bedrs, 1 🛁/WC, 8 🚿/WC, 1 🛁; TV tcf P9
sB&B £14 Breakfast only

ST HELIER Jersey   2B2

Alhambra Roseville Street, St Helier JE2 4PL
01534-32128

Andorra 30 Rouge Bouillon, St Helier JE2
3ZA 01534-39393

Atlas 1 Raleigh Avenue, St Helier JE2 3ZG
01534-35015

Avoca Villa 92 Great Union Road, St Helier
JE2 3YB 01534-31171

Boa Ventura 8 Royal Crescent, St Helier JE2
4QG 01534-33008

**Bromlet 7 Winchester Street, St Helier JE2
4TH 01534-25045**

Colesberg Rouge Bouillon, St Helier JE2 3ZA
01534-25918

De L'Etang 33 Havre Des Pas, St Helier JE2
4UQ 01534-21996

Domino   🆁🅰🅲
6 Vauxhall Street, St Helier 01534-30360 Fax
0153-431546

Dunraven 39 Saviours Road, St Helier JE2
4LA 01534-876047

Glen Vallee Des Vaux, St Helier JE2 3GB
01534-21212

Kaieteur 4 Raleigh Avenue, St Helier JE2
3ZG 01534-37004

La Bonne Vie Roseville Street, St Helier JE2
4PL 01534-35955

La Plata 24 Midvale Road, St Helier JE2 3YR
01534-33530

La Sirene 23 Clarendon Road, St Helier JE2
3YS 01534-23364

Linga Longa 24 Great Union Road, St Helier
JE2 3YA 01534-31926 Fax 01534-33978
7 bedrs, 4 🚿/WC, 1 🛁; TV tcf ✹
sB&B £14 Breakfast only; cc Ac Vi

Lion D'Or Havre Des Pas, St Helier JE2 4UQ
01534-30018

Millbrook House *Acclaimed*   RAC
Rue De Trachy, Millbrook, St Helier
01534-33036 Fax 01534-24317
27 bedrs, 20 ⇥/WC, 7 ☏/WC, 1 ⇥; TV tcf ⚬
P20
sB&B £24-£28.50 dB&B £48-£57; HB weekly
£210-£241.50; D £7.50; cc Amex

Palm's Sea Front Guesty House Havre Des
Pas, St Helier JE2 4UQ 01534-34001

**Panama Green Street, St Helier JE2 4UG
01534-21979**

Roselynne 16 Roseville Street, St Helier JE2
4PJ 01534-873223

Runnymede Court   RAC
46-52 Roseville Street, St Helier 01534-20044
Fax 01534-27880

**Shandene St Aubins Road, St Helier JE2
3LL 01534-20386**

Sunny Lodge 20 Belmont Road, St Helier JE2
4SA 01534-34834

Telford 17 Gloucester Street, St Helier JE2
3QR 01534-25618

Woodford 43 Stopford Road, St Helier JE2
4LB 01534-21372

ST LAWRENCE Jersey	2B2

Mont Felard House Millbrook, St Lawrence
JE3 1LL 01534-21804

Villa D'Oro Grande Route De St Laurent, St
Lawrence JE3 1FA 01534-862262

White Heather P/H *Acclaimed*   RAC
Rue de Haut, Millbrook, St Lawrence JE3 1JQ
01534-20978

ST OUEN Jersey	2B2

Hotel Des Pierres *Highly Acclaimed*   RAC
Greve De Lecq Bay, St Ouen 01534-481858
Fax 01534-485273
16 bedrs, 9 ⇥/WC, 7 ☏/WC; TV tcf P15
HB weekly £189-£196;; cc Ac Amex Vi

Lecq Farm Leoville, St Ouen JE3 2BU
01534-481745

ST PETER'S Jersey	2A2

Firman Villa Beaumont, St Peter's JE3 7BA
0153-422037

ST SAVIOUR'S Jersey	2B2

Anchor House Beach Road, St Saviour's JE2
7PE 01534-21476 Fax 01534-21476
8 bedrs, 2 ⇥; TV tcf ✖
sB&B £14 Breakfast only

Dudley House Bagot Road, St Saviour's JE2
7RG 0153-432104

Harthover Beach House, St Saviour's JE2
7PE 0153-422183

La Bonne Georgetown Road, St Saviour's JE2
7PH 0153-432747

SARK	2A2

Les Quatres Vents Les Quatres Vents, Sark
01481-832247

Northern Ireland

The Mountains of Mourne, the Giant's Causeway, the Glens of Antrim, Fermanagh Lakeland, the Sperrin Mountains and the desolate moors of western Ulster, are all features of Northern Ireland which can be encompassed within a mere five hundred miles of traffic-free motoring. Myths, legends, giants and castles galore merge past and present in a haze of Irish hospitality.

A SELECTION OF ATTRACTIONS

Unless otherwise stated, all can be visited between April and September – some longer. Telephone for days/hours of opening.

Ardress House, Co. Armagh: *17th-c house, garden plus woodland play area and agricultural displays.* NT. Tel 01762-851236.

The Argory, Co. Armagh: *four generations of family treasures lurk in time encapsulated 19th -c house in 315 riverside acres.* NT *Closes end Aug.* Tel: 018687-84753.

Belleek China, Co. Fermanagh: *Tour of factory of famous translucent porcelain.* Tel: 013656-58501.

Bread Making: Victoria Bakery, Newry, Co. Down: *Hot-plate baking of traditional Ulster breads.* Tel: 01693-62076

Castle Coole, Enniskillen, Co. Fermanagh: *Designed by James Wyatt, state rooms are remarkably fine.* NT. Tel: 01365-322690.

Castle Ward, Strangford, Co. Down: *A bizarre mixture of classical and whimsical Gothic style. Plus Strangford Lough Wildlife Centre.* NT. Tel: 01396-881204.

Crom Estate, Newtownbutler, Co. Fermanagh: *1,350 acres of nature conservation area by Upper Lough Erne:* NT. Tel: 013657-38174.

Crown Liquor Saloon, Gt. Victoria Street, Belfast: *A magnificent Victorian public house.* NT. Tel: 01232-325368.

Down County Museum, Downpatrick, Co. Down: *Housed in 18th-c county gaol. Archaeology, natural history.* Tel: 01396-615218.
Downhill Castle, Londonderry: *Panoramic views of north coast from landscaped grounds surrounding ruined palatial home.* NT. *Grounds/Glen open all year.* Tel: 01238-510721.

Dunluce Centre, Portrush, Co. Londonderry: *All weather centre – white-knuckle ride, multi-media show of myths & legends. View tower.* Tel: 01265-824444.

Enniskillen Castle, Co. Fermanagh: *New Heritage centre & museum complex beside River Erne.* Tel: 01365-325000.

Florence Court, Enniskillen, Co. Fermanagh: *Restored 18th-c house having fine plasterwork set in pleasure grounds; views of Benaughlin Mountain.* NT Tel: 01365-348249.

Giant's Causeway, Bushmills, Co. Antrim: *Unusual basalt & volcanic rock formation. Site of Armada wreck. Visitor Centre:* NT. Tel: 012657-31582.

Grays Printing Press, Strabane, Co. Tyrone: *18th-c press shop and stationers. Hand printing machines.* NT. Tel: 01504-884094.

Hezlett House, Liffock, Co. Londonderry: *17th-c thatched house of cruck-truss roof construction.* NT. Tel: 01265-848567.

Inch Abbey, nr Downpatrick, Co. Down: *Beautiful stonework in ruins of 12th-c Cistercian foundation reached by causeway.*

Mount Stewart, Newtownards, Co. Down: *A series of unrivalled gardens enhance spectacular art and furnishings.* NT. Tel: 012477-88387.

Old Bushmills Distillery, Co. Antrim: *One hour tour and tasting in the world's oldest whiskey distillery.* Tel: 012657-31521.

Palm House Botanic Gardens, Belfast City: *Temperate and tropical plants thrive in early curvilinear and cast iron glass house.* Tel: 01232-324902.

Physick Garden, Grey Abbey, Co. Down: *Delightful herbal garden by ruins of Norman Abbey.* Tel: 01232-235000.

Pickie Family Fun Park, Bangor: *A boating lagoon with swan pedal boats forms part of this resort's £18 million seafront development.* Tel: 01247-270069.

Rowallane Garden, Saintfield, Co. Down: *Fifty-two acres of natural plantsman's garden. NT.* Tel: 01238-510131.

St. Patrick's Trian, Armagh: *Land of Lilliput interprets Jonathan Swift's association with Armagh.* Tel: 01861-527808.

Seaforde Gardens, Co. Down: *Kitchen garden containing a tropical butterfly house. Also formal garden.* Tel: 0139-811225.

Shanes Castle, Co. Antrim: *Substantial ruins. Estate shelters fallow deer & wintering wildfowl. Antique Steam Locomotives.* Tel: 018494-28216.

Springhill, Moneymore, Co. Londonderry: *Haunted home of the Coyningham family for 300 years. Costume Museum. NT.* Tel: 01648-748210.

Tower Museum, Derry City: *Award winning new museum. 9 audio visual displays. Even tackles explaining 'the troubles' which began in Derry in the '60s.* Tel: 01504-372411.

Tyrone Crystal, Dungannon, Co. Tyrone: *Factory tours.* Tel: 01868-725335.

Ulster Museum, Belfast: *Irish archaeology, local history. Dinosaur Show. Irish & European art.* Tel: 01232-381251.

Ulster-American Folk Park, Camphill, Co. Tyrone: *Tells story of migration to the USA. Shows re-created buildings.* Tel: 01662-243292.

Ulster Way: *560 miles of waymarked walking trail.* For information – NITB London: 0171-493 0601; Belfast: 01232-246609.

Walls of Derry, Co. Londonderry: *Ramparts of massive 17th-c walls offer historic one mile walk.*

Wellbrook Beetling Mill, Cookstown, Co. Tyrone: *A water-powered hammer mill used for linen making. NT.* Tel: 016487-51735.

Zoological Gardens, Newtownabbey, Belfast: Tel: 01232-776277.

SOME ANNUAL EVENTS

Apple Blossom Festival, Armagh: *Featuring the cultural traditions of the county. 2nd/3rd weeks May.* Tel: 01861-527808.

Belfast Civic Festival, *Concerts, competitions, showjumping, tours, Lord Mayor's Show. 3 weeks May.* Tel: 01232-320202.

Belfast Marathon: *Epic race and fun starts and finishes at Maysfield, Belfast. May 8.* Tel: 01232-320202.

Classic Carrickfergus, Carrickfergus Marina: *Tall ships, traction engines, classic cars on display. Early Jun.* Tel: 01960-366666.

Dromore Horse Fair, Co Down: *Clydesdales, Shire horses and cavalcades of horse-drawn vehicles. 23 Sep.* Tel: 01846-692436.

Golf. N. of I. Amateur Open Championship, Royal Portrush Causeway Coast, Co. Antrim: *10-14 Jul.* Tel: 01265-822311.

Irish National Horse Trials, Rademon, Crossgar: *2 days late Apr.* Tel: 01247-872540.

Lough Melvin Open Trout Championship, Garrison, Fermanagh Lakeland: *Two 'heats' days & final. Late Aug.* Tel: 01365-323110.

Northern Lights Festival, Ballycastle, Co. Antrim: *Concerts, workshops, exhibitions. Late May.* Tel: 012657-62225.

Oul Lammas Fair, Ballycastle, Co. Antrim: *Oldest of Ireland's horsetrading fairs. 28-29 Aug.* Tel: 01265-762024.

P & O European Ferries Classic Fishing Festival, *Lough Erne, Co. Fermanagh. 8-13 May.* Tel: 01365-323110.

Portrush Raft Race, Co. Anrtim: *Home-made rafts, intrepid crews cross the resort's harbour. Part of 3-day carnival. 26-28 May.* Tel: 01265-823333.

RAC British Championship Autotests, Carnfunnock County Park, Larne. Tel: 01574-274875.

Royal Ulster Agricultural Society Show, Balmoral, Belfast: *International sheep-sheering, showjumping, fashion shows, bands. 10-12 May.* Tel: 01232-665225.

Sham Fight, Scarva, Co. Down: *Pageant re-lives battle of 300 years ago. 13 Jul.* Tel: 01762-831839.

Shell Motoring Spectacular, Kilbroney Park, Rostrevor, Co. Down: *Over 700 vehicles on display. Mid-Jun.* Tel: 016937-73347.

Steam & Jazz, Belfast *Yorkgate & Whitehead stations: Steam train excursion enlivened with jazz. Mid-June.* Tel: 01960-353567.

Ulster Story-Telling Festival, *Ulster Folk & Transport Museum, Cultra. Mid-June.* Tel: 01232-428428.

BANBRIDGE Co Down	17E3

Bella Vista 107 Scarva Road, Banbridge BT32 3QD 01820-627066

BANGOR Co. Down	17F2

O'Hara's Royal   🏅RAC
26 Quay Street, Bangor BT20 5ED
01247-271866 Fax 01247-467810
34 bedrs, 34 ➡/WC, 34 ➡/WC; TV tcf ✈
sB&B £61.50 dB&B £46.50 D £12.50 [10%V];
cc Ac Amex DC Vi

BELFAST Co. Down	17F2

Novotel Belfast International Airport   🏅RAC
Aldergrove, Belfast BT29 4AB 01849-422033
Fax 01849-432500   ♿
108 bedrs, 108 ➡/WC; TV tcf ✈ ✂ P100
sB&B £59.50-£67 dB&B £54 D £12 [10%V]; cc
Ac Amex DC Vi

DUNMURRY Co. Antrim	17F2

Forte Crest Belfast   🏅RAC
Dunmurry BT17 9ES 01232-612101 Fax
01232-626546

ENNISKILLEN Co. Fermanagh	17D3

Riverside Farm Guesthouse Gortadrehid,
Culkey P.O., Enniskillen 01365-322725   ♿
cc Vi

LARNE Co. Antrim	17F2

Hillview 30 Middle Road, Island-Magee,
Larne BT40 3SL 01960-372581

NEWCASTLE Co. Down	17F3

Brook Cottage *Acclaimed*   🏅RAC
58 Bryansford Road, Newcastle BT33 0LD
013967-22204 Fax 013967-22193
8 bedrs, 5 ➡/WC, 2 ➡; P50
sB&B £35-£40 dB&B £55-£60 D £12.50
[10%V]; cc Ac Amex Vi

NEWTOWNABBEY Co. Antrim	17F2

★★★Chimney Corner Motel   🏅RAC
630 Antrim Road, Newtownabbey BT36 8RH
01232-844925 Fax 01232-844352   ♿
63 bedrs, 63 ➡/WC; P300
sB&B £69.50 dB&B £37.50-£50 D £14.95; cc
Ac Amex DC Vi

Republic of Ireland

W hy Ireland? It's a different world over there, one in which time seems to stand still allowing people plenty of it to stop and talk. Fish enjoy sparkling clean rivers. World famous race horses thrive on the verdant turf. Celtic monuments and the round fortified towers of ancient holy places add mystery and magic to a landscape already enchanted.

A SELECTION OF ATTRACTIONS

Unless otherwise stated, all can be visited between April and October – some longer. Telephone for days/times of opening.

Annes Grove Gardens, Castletownroche, Co. Cork: *Naturalistic 'secret' garden on banks of River Awbeg.* Tel: 022-26145.

Bantry House, Co. Cork: *Occupied mansion of 1740 on Bantry Bay. Art collection, includes Aubusson & Gobelin tapestries.* Tel: 027-50047

Bir Castle Demesne, Co. Offaly: *An important 100 acre garden for all seasons. Periodic concerts, events.* Tel: 0509-20056.

Blarney Castle, Co. Cork: *Purse your lips for a visit to the famous stone.* Tel: 0 21-385252.

Bunratty Castle & Folk Park, Co. Clare: *Shows life-style of 15th and 16th-c.* Tel: 061 361511.

Butterstream Garden, Trim, Co. Meath: *A most imaginitive plantsman's garden begun early '70's.* Tel: 046-36017.

Castle Leslie, Glaslough, Co. Monaghan: *Only open Jun-Aug, but such variety.* Tel: 047 88109.

Chareville Forest Castle, Tullamore, Co. Offaly. *Complete living home plus unrestored areas in fairy tale 19th-c castle.* Tel: 0506-21279.

Connemara National Park, Letterfrack: *Untamed, robust landscape typical of the West of Ireland.*

Craggaunowen Project, Quin, Co. Clare: *6th-c life including a 'cooking place', a castle*

and the Atlantic-worthy 'St Bredan'. Tel: 061 367178.

Creagh Gardens, Skibbereen, Co. Cork: *Regency walled garden also woodlands down to sea estuary. Walks.* Tel: 028-22121..

Dunkathel, Glanmire, Co. Cork: *Wealth merchants house of 18th-c. Still private home with interesting content.* Tel: 021-821014.

Guinness Museum, Dublin: *Audio visual presentation and sample bar.* Tel: 01-536700.

Hugh Lane Municipal Gallery of Modern Art, Dublin: *Modern European painting & sculpture.* Tel: 01-8741903.

James Joyce Tower, Sandycove, Co. Dublin: *A Martello Tower given over to Joycian museum:* Tel: 01-2809265/2808571.

Japanese Gardens/Irish National Stud, Tully, Co. Kildare: *Symbolically traces life from cradle to eternity.* Tel: 045-21617.

Kilmore Quay Maritime Museum, Kilmore Quay: *History of the Irish Navy displayed on fitted light ship.* Tel: 00353 29655.

Knappogue Castle, Quin, Co. Clare: *Typical of many 15th-c tower houses of this county, much restored:* Tel: 061-361511.

Kylemore Abbey, Connemara, Co. Galway: *19th-c castle, now an abbey school – part open. Idyllic lakeside setting, crafts, pottery.* Tel: 095-41146.

Lough Gur Interpretive Centre, Co. Limerick: *Modelled on 5,000 year old dwellings and lifestyle of pre-Celts. Mid May-mid Sep.* Tel: 061-85186.

Malahide Castle, Co. Dublin: *Inhabited by the Talbot family 1185-1976.* Tel: 01-8452655/8452337.

Monaghan County Museum, Co. Monaghan: *Heritage & contemporary arts, folk craft, lace.* Tel: 053-42888.

Mount Usher Gardens, Ashford, Co. Wicklow: *Splendid example of the romantic Robinsonian garden.* Tel: 0404-40116.

Muckross House & Gardens, *Located in Killarney National Park, Co. Kerry: Period furnishing plus displays of folklore of Kerry.* Tel: 064-31440.

National Gallery of Ireland, Dublin: *Old Masters, Drawings of Irish, European & British Schools.* Tel: 0615133.

National Museum of Ireland, Dublin: *Contains major national collections across the board.* Tel: 01-6618811.

Newbridge House, Donabate, Co. Dublin: *Built 1737 for Archbishop of Dublin. Museum of Curiosities.* Tel: 01-8436534/5.

Powerscourt Town House, Dublin 2: *This palazzo with fine rococo plasterwork is also an award winning shopping centre.* Tel: 01-6794144.

Powerscourt Gardens & Waterfall, Enniskerry, Co. Wicklow: *Glorious formal gardens, pond, fountain, statuary.* Tel: 01-2867676.

Riverstown House, Glanmire, Co. Cork: *Early work of Italian stuccodores La Francici. Now attractively furnished private home. May-Aug.* Tel: 021-821205.

Twenty Nine Lower Fitzwilliam Street, Dublin 2: *Fully furnished middle-class merchant family home.* Tel: 01-7026165.

SOME ANNUAL EVENTS

Abbyshrule International Fly-In Festival, Co. Longford: *Air-show, sky-diving, vintage cars, music. Early Aug.* Tel: 044-57424.

Ballinasloe International October Fair, Co. Galway: *One of Europe's oldest horse fairs. Early Oct.* Tel: 0905-43453.

Ballyshannon International Folk Festival, Co. Donegal: *Cream of Irish Folk and traditional music. 4-7Aug.* Tel: 072-51049.

Clarenbridge Oyster Festival, Co. Galway: *Tasting, music, dance plus ladies International Oyster Opening Competition. Sep.* Tel: 091-96342.

Cork International Choral Festival, Cork City: *International choirs in premier choral event. Late Apr/early May.* Tel: 021-308308.

Cork Film Festival, *40th year of this world cinema showcase. Early Oct.* Tel: 021-271711.

Cork Jazz Festival: *One of Ireland's most popular events with international performers. Late Oct.* Tel: 021-270463.

The Curragh, nr. Dublin: *Five classic horse races: 2,000 Guineas – 21 May: Irish Derby – 2 Jul: Irish Oaks – 16 Jul: Irish St. Leger – 16 Sep.* Tel: 045-41205.

Dublin Theatre Festival: *Promoting best of international theatre and new Irish writing. Early Oct.* Tel: 01-6778439/6712860.

Galway Arts Festival: *One of Ireland's biggest – parades, music, theatre, childrens' events. 11-23 Jul.* Tel: 091-63800.

Galway Races: *Summer Meeting. Late Jul.* Tel: Racing Board: 01-2892888.

Hurling, Croke Park, Dublin: *All Ireland Final. early Sep.* Tel: 01-363222.

International Motor Rally of the Lakes, Killarney, Co. Kerry: *Run through South Kerry and West Cork. Late Apr/early May.* Tel: 064-32026.

Kerrygold Dublin Horse Show, Dublin: *International equestrian event. Early Aug.* Tel: 01-6680866,

Letterkenny International Folk Festival, Co. Donegal: *28th annual event with top artists. 11-13 Aug.* Tel: 074 21754.

Monalty Steam Threshing, Kells, Co. Meath: *Blacksmith, spinning, buttermaking plus steam, horse & flail threshing. mid-Aug.* Tel: 046-44390.

Wicklow Gardens Festival: *At various locations throughout Co. Wicklow. mid-May.* Information Tel: 049-31501.

Wexford Opera Festival: *International event, opera and classical music. Late Oct/early Nov.* Tel: 053-22400.

ARDMORE Co. Waterford   19D3

Newton View Farmhouse Grange, Ardmore
024-94143 Fax 024-94143
6 bedrs, 6 🐾/WC; TV tcf 🗡 P10
sB&B £15; HB weekly £165-£180;; cc Ac Vi

ARKLOW Co. Wicklow   19F2

★★Lawless's   ᴿᴬᴄ
Aughrim, Arklow 0402-36146 Fax 0402-36384
&
10 bedrs, 1 🛏/WC, 7 🐾/WC, 2 🛏; TV P30
sB&B £37-£41 dB&B £55-£61.50; HB weekly
£295-£315; [10%V]; cc Ac Amex DC Vi

BALLINAMORE Co. Leitrim   17D3

Commercial & Tourist   ᴿᴬᴄ
Ballinamore 078-44675

Riversdale Farm House *Acclaimed*   ᴿᴬᴄ
Ballinamore 078-44122

BALLYBUNION Co. Kerry

Marine Links   ᴿᴬᴄ
Sandhill Road, Ballybunion 068-27139 Fax
068-27666
12 bedrs, 12 🛏/WC; TV tcf 🗡 P100
sB&B £33-£40 dB&B £50-£66; HB weekly
£225-£285; D £19.50 [10%V];
cc Ac Amex DC Vi

BALLYMACARBRY Co. Waterford   19D3

Clonanav Farm Guesthouse *Acclaimed*   ᴿᴬᴄ
Nire Valley, Ballymacarbry 052-36141 Fax
052-36141
10 bedrs, 10 🐾/WC; P20
sB&B £25 dB&B £40; HB weekly £210; D £12
[10%V]; cc Ac Amex Vi

BALLYVAUGHAN Co. Clare   18C1

Rusheen Lodge *Highly Acclaimed*   ᴿᴬᴄ
Knocknagrough, Ballyvaughan 065-77092 Fax
065-77152
6 bedrs, 6 🛏/WC; TV tcf ⅄ P12
sB&B £25 dB&B £36-£40 Breakfast only; cc
Ac Amex Vi

BANSHA Co. Tipperary   19D2

Bansha Castle *Acclaimed*   ᴿᴬᴄ
Bansha 053-6254187

BANTRY Co. Cork   18B4

Dunmahon Country House   ᴿᴬᴄ
Kilcrohane, Bantry 027-67092

BUNRATTY Co. Clare   18C2

Bunratty View *Highly Acclaimed*   ᴿᴬᴄ
Cratloe, Bunratty 061-357352   &
7 bedrs, 2 🛏/WC, 5 🐾/WC, 1 🛏; TV tcf P20
sB&B £18 dB&B £30; HB weekly £170; D £10
[10%V]; cc Ac Vi

CAPPOQUIN Co. Waterford   19D3

Aglish House Aglish, Cappoquin 024-9619 ᴿᴬᴄ
Fax 024-96191
4 bedrs;
Breakfast only

CARAGH LAKE Co. Kerry   18A3

Caragh Lodge *Highly Acclaimed*   ᴿᴬᴄ
Caragh Lake 066-69115 Fax 066-69316
3 bedrs, 3 🛏/WC; P10
Child restrictions
sB&B £66 dB&B £82.50 D £26.20; cc Vi

CARLOW Co. Carlow   19E2

Barrowville Town House *Highly Acclaimed*
ᴿᴬᴄ
Kilkenny Road, Carlow 0503-43324 Fax
0503-41953
7 bedrs, 5 🛏/WC, 2 🐾/WC; TV tcf P11
Child restrictions
sB&B £16.50-£18.50 dB&B £34-£38 Breakfast
only [10%V]

CARRIGBYRNE Co. Wexford   19E3

Woodlands House *Acclaimed*   ᴿᴬᴄ
Carrigbyrne 051-28287
4 bedrs, 3 🐾/WC, 1 🛏; ⅄ P7
sB&B £18 dB&B £28 Breakfast only [10%V];
cc Ac Vi

CASTLEISLAND Co. Kerry   18B3

Beech Grove Farm   ᴿᴬᴄ
Camp Road, Castleisland 066-41217

CELBRIDGE Co. Kildare   19F1

Green Acres   ᴿᴬᴄ
Dublin Road, Celbridge 016-271163

CLIFDEN Co. Galway 16A4

Ben View House RAC
Bridge Street, Clifden 095-21256
8 bedrs, 7 ſ/WC; ✕
sB&B £13-£26 dB&B £26-£32.50 Breakfast
only [10%V]

Maldua *Highly Acclaimed* RAC
**Galway Road, Clifden 095-21171 Fax
095-21739**

9 bedrs, 9 ſ/WC; ✗ P40
sB&B £18-£21 Breakfast only; cc Vi

Mallmore House RAC
Ballyconneely Road, Clifden 095-21460
6 bedrs, 6 ſ/WC, 1 ➡; ✗ P15
Breakfast only [5%V]

CLONDALKIN Co. Dublin 19F1

Kingswood RAC
Kingswood, Naas Road, Clondalkin
01-4592207 Fax 01-4592207
7 bedrs, 7 ſ/WC, 2 ➡; TV ✕ P70
sB&B £33.20-£50.63 dB&B £61.88 D £18.95;
cc Ac Amex DC Vi

CLONMEL Co. Tipperary 19D3

Amberville RAC
Glenconnor Road, (off Western Road),
Clonmel 052-21470

CORK Co. Cork 18C3

Killarney *Acclaimed* RAC
Western Road, Cork 021-270290 Fax
021-271010
18 bedrs, 1 ➡/WC, 17 ſ/WC; TV tcf ✗ P20
sB&B £18-£30 dB&B £30 Breakfast only; cc
Ac Amex Vi

Roserie Villa RAC
Mardyke Walk, Off Western Road, Cork
021-272958 Fax 021-274087
16 bedrs, 16 ſ/WC, 1 ➡; ✗
Child restrictions
sB&B £27.50 dB&B £40-£45 Breakfast only;
cc Ac Amex DC Vi

CRUSHEEN Co. Clare 18C1

Lahardan House *Acclaimed* RAC
Crusheen 065-27128 Fax 065-27319

DINGLE Co. Kerry 18A3

Alpine House *Acclaimed* RAC
Mail Road, Dingle 066-51250 Fax 066-51966
13 bedrs, 1 ➡/WC, 12 ſ/WC; P20
sB&B £15-£17.50 dB&B £30-£35 Breakfast
only; cc Ac Vi

Ard-na-greine *Acclaimed* RAC
Spa Road, Dingle 066-51113
4 bedrs, 4 ſ/WC; P4
Child restrictions
dB&B £30-£34 Breakfast only [5%V];
cc Ac Amex Vi

Bamburys Guesthouse RAC
Mail Road, Dingle 066-51244 Fax 066-51786 &
12 bedrs, 12 ſ/WC, 1 ➡; ✕ P12
dB&B £30 Breakfast only [5%V]; cc Ac Vi

Cleevaun House *Highly Acclaimed* RAC
Ladys Cross, Milltown, Dingle 066-51108

Doyle's Seafood Bar & Restaurant
Highly Acclaimed RAC
John Street, Dingle 066-51174 Fax 066-51816
&
8 bedrs, 8 ➡/WC; TV tcf
sB&B £39 dB&B £62 D £13.50; cc Ac DC Vi

Greenmount House *Highly Acclaimed* RAC
Upper John Street, Dingle 066-51414
8 bedrs, 1 ➡/WC, 7 ſ/WC; ✗ P8
Child restrictions
sB&B £20-£35 dB&B £32-£40 Breakfast only
[5%V]; cc Ac Vi

Milltown House *Highly Acclaimed* RAC
Dingle 066-51095 Fax 066-51095
7 bedrs, 7 ſ/WC; TV tcf P20
sB&B £23-£36 dB&B £32-£36 Breakfast only;
cc Ac Vi

DONEGAL Co. Donegal   16C2

Ardeevin *Acclaimed*   RAC
Lough Eske, Barnesmore, Donegal 073-21790
Fax 073-21790
5 bedrs, 5 ➡/WC, ✖ P12
sB&B £18 dB&B £29 Breakfast only [5%V]

DOOLIN Co. Clare   18B1

Churchfield   RAC
Doolin 065-74209

Doolin House *Acclaimed*   RAC
Doolin 065-74259

Doonmacfelim House *Acclaimed*   RAC
Doolin 065-74503

DROGHEDA Co. Louth   17E4

Tullyesker House *Highly Acclaimed*   RAC
Monasterboice, Drogheda 041-30430
5 bedrs, 5 ☞/WC, 1 ➡; TV tcf P10
sB&B £27 dB&B £36 Breakfast only

DUBLIN Co. Dublin   19F1

Aberdeen Lodge *Highly Acclaimed*   RAC
53-55 Park Avenue, Dublin 01-2838155

Ariel House *Highly Acclaimed*   RAC
50-52 Lansdowne Road, Ballsbridge, Dublin
01-6685512 Fax 01-6685845   ♿
28 bedrs, 25 ➡/WC, 3 ☞/WC; TV P30
Child restrictions
sB&B £39.50-£52.50 dB&B £75-£85.80
Breakfast only; cc Ac Vi

Egans House   RAC
7-9 Iona Park, Glasnevin, Dublin 01-8303611
Fax 01-8303312
25 bedrs, 2 ➡/WC, 23 ☞/WC; TV tcf ✖ ✄ P7
sB&B £23.50-£34.50 dB&B £50.60-£59.40; HB
weekly £230.40-£265; D £12.50 [10%V];
cc Ac Vi

Fitzwilliam *Acclaimed*   RAC
41 Upper Fitzwilliam Street, Dublin 2
01-6600199 Fax 01-6767488
12 bedrs, 2 ➡/WC, 10 ☞/WC; TV tcf ✖
sB&B £31.90-£39.60 dB&B £48.40-£70 D
£22.95; cc Ac Amex DC Vi

Glenogra House *Highly Acclaimed*   RAC
64 Merrion Street, Ballsbridge, Dublin
01-6683661 Fax 01-6683661

9 bedrs, 7 ➡/WC, 2 ☞/WC; TV tcf P9
sB&B £40-£50 dB&B £50-£70 Breakfast only
[10%V]; cc Ac Amex Vi

Merrion Hall *Highly Acclaimed*   RAC
54/56 Merrion Road, Ballsbridge, Dublin
01-6681426 Fax 01-6684250
15 bedrs, 13 ➡/WC, 2 ☞/WC; TV tcf P20
sB&B £32.50-£40 dB&B £50-£70 [10%V];
cc Ac Vi

Othello House *Acclaimed*   RAC
74 Lower Gardiner Street, Dublin 01-8786098
Fax 01-8743460
14 bedrs, 12 ☞/WC, 2 ➡; TV tcf ✖ P20
sB&B £20-£29 dB&B £36-£48 Breakfast only
[10%V]; cc Ac Amex DC Vi JCB

Raglan Lodge *Highly Acclaimed*   RAC
10 Raglan Road, Ballsbridge, Dublin
01-6606697 Fax 01-6606781
7 bedrs, 4 ➡/WC, 3 ☞/WC; tcf ✖ P20
sB&B £33.50-£42.50 dB&B £67-£77 Breakfast
only [10%V]; cc Ac Amex Vi

★★★Royal Dublin   RAC
O'Connell Street, Dublin 01-8733666 Fax
01-8733-120
107 bedrs, 107 ➡/WC; ✖ P40
sB&B £62-£80 dB&B £80-£99 D £16.95
[10%V]; cc Ac Amex DC Vi

★★★Temple Bar   RAC
Dublin 01-6773333 Fax 01-6773088   ♿
108 bedrs, 98 ➡/WC, 10 ☞/WC; TV tcf ✄
sB&B £72.50-£82.50 dB&B £100-£105 D
£11.50; cc Ac Amex DC Vi

Uppercross House *Acclaimed*   RAC
26-30 Upper Rathmines Road, Dublin
01-4975486
14 bedrs, 14 ➡/WC; TV tcf ✖ ✄
sB&B £30-£35 dB&B £45-£55 D £15; cc Ac
Amex Vi

DUN LAOGHAIRE Co. Dublin   19F1

Ferry House   RAC
15, Clarinda Park North, Dun Laoghaire
01-2808301 Fax 01-2846530
6 bedrs, 3 ☞/WC, 2 ➡; TV
sB&B £18.50-£20 dB&B £32-£35 Breakfast
only; cc Vi

★★★★Fitzpatrick Castle   🔒RAC
Killiney Bay, Dun Laoghaire 01-2840700 Fax
01-2850207
90 bedrs, 90 ➡/WC; TV tcf ⚓ P250
sB&B £80.50-£89.15 dB&B £115.05; HB
weekly £413; D £21.25 [5%V]; cc Ac Amex DC
Vi JCB

DUNDALK Co. Lough   17E3

★★★Ballymascanlon House   🔒RAC
Dundalk 042-71124 Fax 042-71598
35 bedrs, 32 ➡/WC, 3 🐾/WC; ⚓ ⚓ P300
sB&B £46-£50 dB&B £70-£78; HB weekly
£310-£325; D £17.50 [5%V]; cc Ac Amex DC Vi

DUNFANAGHY Co. Donegal   16C1

★★Arnolds   🔒RAC
Dunfanaghy 074-36208 Fax 074-36352
34 bedrs, 34 ➡/WC; ⚓ P50
sB&B £32-£45 dB&B £54-£70; HB weekly
£322-£378; D £20 [5%V]; cc Ac Amex DC Vi

ENNISKERRY Co. Wicklow   19F1

★★Enniscree Lodge   🔒RAC
Glencree Valley, Enniskerry 01-2863542 Fax
01-2866037
10 bedrs, 9 ➡/WC, 1 🐾/WC; tcf ⚓ ⚓ P20
sB&B £47-£57 dB&B £67-£77 [10%V]; cc Ac
Amex DC Vi

ENNISTYMON Co. Clare   18B1

Grovemount House *Highly Acclaimed*   🔒RAC
Lahinch Road, Ennistymon 065-71431
8 bedrs, 8 🐾/WC; ⚓ ⚓ P20
sB&B £20-£25 dB&B £30-£40 Breakfast only;
cc Ac Vi

GLENBEIGH Co. Kerry   18A3

Village House   🔒RAC
Glenbeigh 066-68486 Fax 066-68486
7 bedrs, 7 ➡/WC; TV ⚓ P9
Breakfast only [10%V]; cc Ac DC Vi

GLENDALOUGH Co. Wicklow   19F1

Carmel's *Acclaimed*   🔒RAC
Annamoe, Glendalough 0404-45297

Prices are shown in punts (IR£)

GLENGARRIFF Co. Cork   18C4

Casey's   🔒RAC
Glengarriff 027-63072 Fax 027-63010   ♿
19 bedrs, 3 ➡/WC, 16 🐾/WC; ⚓ P15
sB&B £20-£30 dB&B £50-£55; HB weekly
£350-£385; D £14 [5%V]; cc Ac Amex DC Vi

GRAIGUENAMANAGH Co. Kilkenny   19E2

Stablecroft *Acclaimed*   🔒RAC
Mooneen, Graiguenamanagh 0503-24714
4 bedrs, 1 ➡/WC, 2 🐾/WC; ⚓ P10
sB&B £13.50 dB&B £31; HB weekly £165; D
£12.50 [10%V]

INNISHANNON Co. Cork   18C4

★★Innishannon House   🔒RAC
Innishannon 021-775121 Fax 021-775609   ♿
14 bedrs, 14 ➡/WC; TV ⚓ ⚓ P100
sB&B £50-£65 dB&B £75-£95; HB weekly
£400-£470; D £19.50 [10%V]; cc Ac Amex DC Vi

KENMARE Co.Kerry   18B3

Ardmore House *Acclaimed*   🔒RAC
Killarney Road, Kenmare 064-41406
6 bedrs, 6 🐾/WC, 1 ➡; ⚓ P6
sB&B £20 dB&B £30 Breakfast only; cc Ac Vi

★★Lansdowne Arms   🔒RAC
Kenmare 064-41365 Fax 064-41114
25 bedrs, 22 ➡/WC, 3 🐾/WC; ⚓ P30
sB&B £30-£40 dB&B £48-£60; HB weekly
£235-£290; D £14.95 [10%V]; cc Ac Amex Vi

Muxnaw Lodge *Acclaimed*   🔒RAC
Castletownbere Road, Kenmare 064-41252

KILKEE Co. Clare   18B2

Halpins *Highly Acclaimed*   🔒RAC
Kilkee 065-56032

KILKENNY Co. Kilkenny   19F2

Shillogher House *Acclaimed*   🔒RAC
Callan Road, Kilkenny 056-63249

KILLARNEY Co. Kerry   18B3

★★Arbutus   🔒RAC
Killarney 064-31037 Fax 064-34033
34 bedrs, 28 ➡/WC, 6 🐾/WC; tcf
sB&B £25-£47 dB&B £50-£74; HB weekly
£195-£285; D £9 [10%V]; cc Ac DC Vi

Cedar Lodge *Acclaimed*　RÃC
Lissivigeen, Cork Road, Killarney 064-34754
6 bedrs, 1 ➡/WC, 5 ↟/WC; TV tcf ✂
sB&B £15-£22 dB&B £28-£32 Breakfast only
[10%V]; cc Ac Amex Vi

Foley's Townhouse *Highly Acclaimed*　RÃC
23 High Street, Killarney 064-34683 Fax
064-34683
12 bedrs, 4 ➡/WC, 8 ↟/WC; TV tcf ✂ P25
Child restrictions
sB&B £38 dB&B £70 Breakfast only [5%V];
cc Ac Amex Vi

Gleann Fia *Acclaimed*　RÃC
Deer Park, Killarney 064-35000 Fax 064-35000
8 bedrs, 8 ↟/WC, 1 ➡; TV ✂ P12
sB&B £18-£23 dB&B £34-£38 Breakfast only
[10%V]; cc Ac Vi

Glena House　RÃC
Muckross Road, Killarney 064-35611 Fax
064-35611　 ⌖
26 bedrs, 12 ➡/WC, 14 ↟/WC; TV tcf ✕ P30
sB&B £22-£24 dB&B £35-£38 D £11 [10%V];
cc Ac Amex DC Vi

Kathleens Country House *Highly
Acclaimed*　RÃC
Tralee Road, Killarney 064-32810
17 bedrs, 17 ➡/WC; TV tcf
Child restrictions
sB&B £30-£50 dB&B £50-£63 Breakfast only
[10%V]; cc Ac Amex Vi

Victoria House *Highly Acclaimed*　RÃC
Muckross Road, Killarney 064-35430
Fax 064-35439

KINSALE Co.Cork　　　　　　　　18C4

Moorings *Highly Acclaimed*　RÃC
Scilly, Kinsale 021-772675 Fax 021-772675　⌖
8 bedrs, 8 ➡/WC, 2 ➡; TV tcf ✕ ✂ P8
Child restrictions
sB&B £35-£50 dB&B £60-£90 Breakfast only
[5%V]; cc Ac Vi

Old Bank House *Highly Acclaimed*　RÃC
11 Pearse Street, Kinsale 021-774296 Fax
021-774296
9 bedrs, 9 ➡/WC; TV ✕ ✂
Child restrictions
sB&B £35-£50 dB&B £70-£100;
cc Ac Amex Vi

LETTERKENNY Co. Donegal　　　17D1

Hillcrest House *Highly Acclaimed*　RÃC
Lurgybrack, Letterkenny 074-22300 Fax
074-25137

LISDOONVARNA Co. Clare　　　18B1

★★**Sheedy's Spa View & Orchid
Restaurant**　RÃC
Lisdoonvarna 065-74026 Fax 065-74555
11 bedrs, 1 ➡/WC, 10 ↟/WC; P22
sB&B £35 dB&B £50 [5%V];
cc Ac Amex DC Vi

MACROOM Co. Cork　　　　　　18C3

Mills Inn *Highly Acclaimed*　RÃC
Ballyvourney, Macroom N22 026-45237 Fax
026-45454　　　　　　　　　　　　　⌖

NAAS Co. Kildare　　　　　　　19F1

★★**Curryhills House**　RÃC
Prosperous, Naas 045-68150 Fax 045-68805
10 bedrs, 10 ➡/WC; TV tcf ✕ P40
sB&B £22.50-£37.50 dB&B £40-£60; HB
weekly £200; cc Ac Amex DC Vi

NEWCASTLE WEST Co. Limerick　18B2

The Ranch House　RÃC
Cork Road, Newcastle West 069-62313

OGONNELLOE Co. Clare　　　　18C2

Lantern House *Acclaimed*　RÃC
Ogonnelloe 061-923034 Fax 061-923139
6 bedrs, 6 ↟/WC; tcf P20
sB&B £20-£24 dB&B £36; HB weekly £210; D
£14; cc Ac Amex DC Vi

OMEATH Co. Louth　　　　　　17E3

Granvue House *Acclaimed*　RÃC
Omeath 042-75415
9 bedrs, 2 ➡/WC, 7 ↟/WC, 1 ➡; TV ✂ P1
sB&B £20-£25 dB&B £44 D £12; cc Vi

ORANMORE Co.Galway　　　　18C1

Hazlewood House *Acclaimed*　RÃC
Cregganna, Oranmore 091-94275 Fax
091-94608
6 bedrs, 3 ↟/WC, 1 ➡; tcf ✕ ✂ P10
sB&B £23-£25 dB&B £26-£30; HB weekly
£196-£210; D £15 [10%V]; cc Ac Amex DC Vi

Moorings *Acclaimed*　　　　　　RAC
Main Street, Oranmore 091-90462　　⚹
6 bedrs, 6 ➡/WC; TV tcf P30
sB&B £20-£25 dB&B £20-£22.50 D £16.50
[10%V]; cc Ac Amex DC Vi

OUGHTERARD Co. Galway　　　16B4

Currarevagh House *Highly Acclaimed*　RAC
Oughterard 091-82312

PORT LAOISE Co. Laois　　　19E1

Chez Nous *Highly Acclaimed*　　RAC
Kilminchy, Port Laois 0502-21251
3 bedrs, 3 ➡/WC; ✂ P8
Breakfast only

PORTMARNOCK Co.Dublin　　19F1

Pine Lodge　　　　　　　RAC
Coast Road, Portmarnock 01-846-0097

RIVERSTOWN Co.Sligo　　　16C3

Coopershill House *Highly Acclaimed*　RAC
Riverstown 071-65108 Fax 071-65466

ROSCOMMON Co. Roscommon　16C4

★★★Abbey　　　　　　RAC
Roscommon 0242-51605 Fax 0242-51303　⚹
20 bedrs, 20 ➡/WC; P40
sB&B £40-£50 dB&B £60-£70 Breakfast only;
cc Ac Amex DC Vi

ROSSLARE HARBOUR Co. Wexford　19F3

Elmwood *Acclaimed* Station Rd, Rosslare
053-33321

SNEEM Co. Kerry　　　　　18A4

Tahilla Cove Country House *Highly
Acclaimed*　　　　　　　RAC
Tahilla, Sneem 064-45204　　　⚹
3 bedrs, 3 ➡/WC, 1 ➡; ✗ P12
sB&B £40-£45 dB&B £60-£70; HB weekly
£285-£295; D £16; cc Ac Amex DC Vi

TRAMORE Co.Waterford　　　19E3

Cliff House *Acclaimed*　　　RAC
Cliff Road, Tramore 051-81497

TULLAMORE Co.Offaly　　　19E1

Shepherds Wood *Acclaimed*　　RAC
Screggan, Tullamore 0506-21499
4 bedrs, 4 ➡/WC; TV tcf ✗ P10
Child restrictions
sB&B £22.50 dB&B £35 D £18 [5%V]; cc Ac Vi

WATERVILLE Co. Kerry　　　18A3

Klondyke House *Acclaimed*　　RAC
Waterville 066-74119 Fax 066-74666
6 bedrs, 6 🛁/WC; tcf ✗ ✂ P10
sB&B £18-£20 dB&B £26-£30 Breakfast only
[5%V]; cc Ac Vi

YOUGHAL Co. Antrim　　　19D3

Ahernes Seafood Restaurant　　RAC
163 Main Street, Youghal 024-92424 Fax
024-93633　　　　　　　　⚹
10 bedrs, 10 ➡/WC; TV P10
sB&B £35-£60 dB&B £70-£90 D £23 [10%V];
cc Ac Amex DC Vi

Telephoning to the Republic of Ireland

To telephone to the Republic of
Ireland from Britain, dial **00 353**
followed by the county code,
omitting the initial 0.
For example, to call Adare Manor,
dial **00 353 61 396566.**

KEY TO MAPS

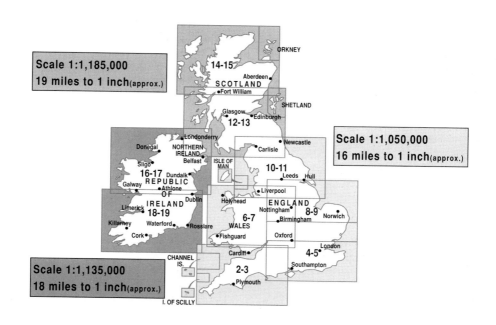

Scale 1:1,185,000
19 miles to 1 inch(approx.)

14-15

ORKNEY

Aberdeen
SCOTLAND
•Fort William

SHETLAND

Glasgow• •Edinburgh
12-13

Londonderry•

Scale 1:1,050,000
16 miles to 1 inch(approx.)

•Newcastle

Donegal• NORTHERN
IRELAND•
Sligo• Belfast
16-17 Dundalk•
Galway• Athlone•
REPUBLIC
OF
IRELAND
18-19
Limerick•
Killarney• Waterford•
Cork• Rosslare•

Carlisle•

ISLE OF
MAN

10-11
Leeds• Hull
•Liverpool

Holyhead•

Nottingham•
•Birmingham

ENGLAND
8-9
Norwich•

Dublin•

6-7
WALES
•Fishguard

Oxford•

London•
4-5•

CHANNEL
IS.

Cardiff•

Scale 1:1,135,000
18 miles to 1 inch(approx.)

2-3
•Plymouth

Southampton•

I. OF SCILLY

LEGEND

═══ M5 ═══ **Motorway**	┄┄┄┄┄┄ **Ferry Route**
═══ S ═══ Service Station	⊕ **Airport**
═══ 5 ═══ Junction	
── A361 ── **Primary Route** **Dual Carriageway**	EXMOOR **National Park**
── A385 ── **Primary Route**	◉**Guildford** **Bed & Breakfast Location**
A697 ── A38 **'A' Road** **(Dual Carriageway)**	•••••••••••••••••• **National Boundary**
B3165 **'B' Road**	·················· **County Boundary**

© RAC Enterprises Limited 1994.

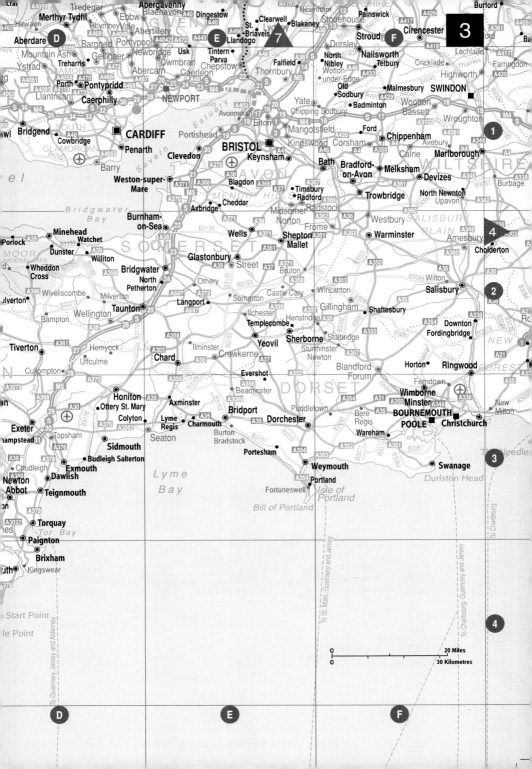

England

RAC BED & BREAKFAST

Index

Scotland